MICROSOFT®

Office 97

User Manual

MICROSOFT®

Office

97

User Manual

Rick Winter
Patty Winter

A Division of Macmillan Computer Publishing, USA
201 West 103rd St.
Indianapolis, IN 46290

Microsoft® Office 97 User Manual

Copyright© 1998 by Que® Corporation.

Library of Congress Catalog Card Number: 98-85049

International Standard Book Number: 0-7897-1706-9

00 99 98   4   3   2   1

Interpretation of the printing code: The rightmost double-digit number is the year of the book's printing; the rightmost single-digit, the number of the book's printing. For example, a printing code of 98-1 shows that the first printing of the book occurred in 1998.

Composed in Century Old Style by Macmillan Computer Publishing.

Printed in the United States of America.

Trademarks

EXECUTIVE EDITOR
Jim Minatel

ACQUISITIONS EDITOR
Jill Byus

DEVELOPMENT EDITOR
Rick Kughen

MANAGING EDITOR
Thomas F. Hayes

PROJECT EDITORS
Heather E. Butler
Damon Jordan

COPY EDITORS
Sydney Jones
June Waldman
Tom Stevens

INDEXER
Johnna VanHoose

TECHNICAL EDITOR
Doug Klippert

PRODUCTION
Cyndi Davis-Hubler
Terri L. Edwards
Donna Martin

COVER DESIGNERS
Nathan Clement
Ruth C. Lewis

BOOK DESIGNER
Nathan Clement

Contents at a Glance

Table of Contents

4 PowerPoint   453

5 Outlook 98   537

Dedication

To Joan Vieweg, who has consistently supported the children of our county through her hard work, consideration, compassion, and time. She has been an inspiration to us of what an involved community member should be.

—Rick Winter and Patty Winter

About the Authors

Patty Winter is a Senior Partner at PRW Computer Training and Services. She shares her home with Molly, her daughter, many local teens who need a safe haven, two dogs, a cat, and the wildlife that comes visiting. She has worked with computers since 1982, training adults, testing programs, developing course material, and creating solutions for user productivity. She has trained thousands of adults on the use of personal computers. Her emphasis has been on peopleware. She is the author of *Microsoft Word 97 Quick Reference* and *Excel 5 for Windows Essentials;* lead author of *Using Microsoft Office 95, Special Edition Using Microsoft Office 97,* and *Special Edition Using Microsoft Office Professional for Windows 95*; contributing author of *Special Edition Using Microsoft Office,* and coauthor of *Excel for Windows Sure Steps, Look Your Best with Excel,* and *Q&A QueCards.*

Rick Winter is a Senior Partner at PRW Computer Training and Services. He shares his home with Karen, his wife, Danny and Jimmy, Honey Bear (a dog), and the wildlife that doesn't want to go to Patty's house. He is a Microsoft Certified Trainer and has trained thousands of adults on personal computers. He is the author of *Microsoft Access 97 Quick Reference*; lead author of *Special Edition Using Microsoft Office 97 Small Business Edition, Special Edition Using Microsoft Office 97,* and *Special Edition Using Microsoft Office Professional for Windows 95*; coauthor of *Using Microsoft Office 95, Excel for Windows SureSteps, Look Your Best with Excel, Q&A QueCards,* and many other books for Que. Rick has a B.A. from Colorado College and an M.A. from the University of Colorado at Denver. In conjunction with Ideas Unlimited Inc., Rick also travels throughout the U.S. doing computer-aided group facilitation and strategic planning.

PRW Computer Training and Services, nested in Idaho Springs in the mountains of Colorado, is a recognized leader in training, training materials, and consulting. PRW provides classes in the Denver area on Microsoft Office, as well as on-site training, programming, and consulting across the country. PRW won the prestigious Rocky Mountain Chapter of the Society for Technical Communication's Distinguished Award for its work on Que's *Excel for Windows SureSteps* in 1994.

For information on course content, on-site corporate classes, or consulting, contact PRW at the following address:

PRW Computer Training and Services
491 Highway 103
Idaho Springs, Colorado 80452

prwtrain@compuserve.com

Gordon Padwick is a senior programmer analyst who develops applications based on Microsoft's Office suite. He has worked with computers for more years than he cares to remember, and has experience as an engineer and a manager in many hardware and software design projects. He has worked with Windows and Windows applications since Microsoft introduced the first version of Windows in 1987.

Previously, Padwick was an independent consultant who specialized in Windows applications. He has authored and contributed to many books about such subjects as word processing, spreadsheets, datbases, graphics, desktop publishing, and presentation software; his most recent publications are Que's *Building Integrated Office Applications, Special Edition Using Microsoft Office 97 Professional*, and *Special Edition Using Microsoft Outlook 97*.

Rebecca Tapley has been an author, software tester, project develper, and Web site designer since 1992. Her recent publishing credits include *The Web Authoring Desk Reference* from Hayden Books, and *How to Use Netscape Communicator* from Ziff-Davis Press.

Acknowledgments

We would especially like to thank Gordon Padwick, who came in at the last minute and created the Outlook section. Yes, this is the same Gordon Padwick who wrote the excellent *Using Microsoft Outlook 98*. Thanks also to Rebecca Tapley for her assistance with some of the PowerPoint sections.

We would also like to thank Rick Kughen, Development Editor, and Jim Minatel, Executive Editor, for being available to discuss ideas, make suggestions, and help us complete this project.

Thanks additionally to our agent, Chris Van Buren, and Jill Byus, Acquisitions Editor, for handling all the administrative work that goes into this type of project.

We also appreciate all the hard work of the editing team headed by Heather Butler and Damon Jordan, Production Editors. Thanks to the production team of Cyndi Davis-Hubler, Terri L. Edwards, and Donna Martin for the attention to details and many changes you had to endure at the last minute, and to our technical editor, Doug Klippert, for your valuable knowledge.

We appreciate everyone's willingness to give up time with family, miss weekends, and work long nights to help get this book, *Microsoft Office 97 User Manual,* to you.

—*Rick Winter and Patty Winter*

Who Should Use This Book?

If you need a reference of what Office 97 and Outlook 98 can do, you came to the right place. Whether you're just starting out and need a quick explanation of a feature you haven't used, or you need to refresh your memory because you haven't used a function in a while, this book is for you.

Although this book is not a tutorial, one of the ways people learn the software is to methodically go through each button, menu item, and option to figure out what it does. If you are in software support and training (as we are), we think this book is valuable for you.

About This Book

Because the type of manual we were looking for didn't exist, we decided to write one for you. We wanted something that was quick, not too big, yet still went into what every feature does. We also wanted to create a manual that was organized logically. We hope you find this user manual useful.

In order to set this book apart from others, we've focused on giving you extreme breadth in describing features of Microsoft Word, Excel, PowerPoint, and Outlook. We've included nearly every menu, toolbar, and dialog box option that you would see in a Typical installation of Microsoft Office.

We still cover the same features as four books that are each twice the size of this one, just not in-depth. If you want an explanation that is thorough, see the *Special Editions of Using Microsoft Word 97*, *Using Microsoft Excel 97*, *Using Microsoft PowerPoint 97*, and *Using Microsoft Outlook 98*.

We also had to make a few choices about what not to include: Visual Basic, Microsoft Query, and additional options installed in Custom setup that are not installed in Typical installation. For most of what you do, however, you should find a reference here.

How This Book Is Organized

This book is substantially different from most other Microsoft Office books (including our own). The other books put features and grab menu items from different places to address in one section. This book mirrors the software exactly. After a quick introduction on how to get started, we have four parts: Word, Excel, PowerPoint, and Outlook. Each section within a part is a menu (**File**, **Edit**, **View**, and so on). Each subsection is a menu item. We continue this organization down to options in the dialog box. Therefore, if you need to find a menu item, you can use this book to browse to the point you need.

This is a quick but thorough reference. We generally do not repeat what is in the text and what is on a diagram. Because it is often easier to see what is on a picture of the screen to visualize the options, we've included many screen shots with callouts to explain what is in dialog boxes.

Also, we've included a lot of cross-references. Think of Word as the base application. When there is little difference between a Word feature and the same feature in Excel, PowerPoint, or Outlook, we give you a cross-reference to the Word section and tell you what's different. This is another way that may help you learn the software. First learn what is similar, and then focus on the differences.

Conventions Used in This Book

We've tried to make the format as simple and as uncluttered as possible. The following are some issues to keep in mind:

- Whenever several quick ways to do the same thing are available—such as using a toolbar button, choosing a menu command, or using a shortcut key—we've grouped them under one heading, using bullets for each method.

- Whenever we talk about using the mouse, we're assuming the normal right-handed mouse operation. The left-button click is for selecting items, and the right-button click is for the shortcut menus. We say click or drag when we mean use the left mouse button. When we want you to use the right mouse button we say right-click.

- Menus and menu items, dialog box items, and keyboard shortcuts appear in bold.

- For section headers and cross-references, we've included the return character to let you know that the second item is a submenu. For example, **File - Open...** indicates choose the File menu and then the Open menu item. We've also included the hotkeys (marked with an underline) on menu and dialog box items. For example, when you see **File**, we're simply telling that you can press **Alt+F** to open the **File** menu. Notice also the ellipses after **Open....** This is to let you know that a dialog box opens when you choose this menu item.

- If you are instructed to click a button, you will often see it in the text. For example, "click the **Save** button 🖫 often to ensure that your work is not lost."

- *QuickChoices* give you the fast and easy way to get something done. For example, if you want to know how to save a documnet in Word, the following QuickChoice will tell you how to get that done in the shortest amount of time and without a long explanation.

Quick **Choices**   *USE ANY OF THESE OPTIONS TO SAVE YOUR DOCUMENTS*

- Click the **Save** button 🖫 on the Standard toolbar.
- Choose **File, Save**.
- Press **Ctrl+S** or **Shift+F12**.
- To save multiple documents at once, hold down Shift and choose **File, Save All**.
- Close the file (see **File - Close**, page xx) and click **Yes** to save.

- To help you know where each diagram came from, in almost every case we've included the steps on how to get to the diagram in the figure caption.

We'd Like to Hear from You!

Que Corporation has a long-standing reputation for high-quality books and products. To ensure your continued satisfaction, we also understand the importance of customer service and support.

Tech Support

If you need assistance with the information in this book or with a CD or disk accompanying the book, please access Macmillan Computer Publishing's online Knowledge Base at **www.superlibrary.com/general/support**.

Also be sure to visit Que's Web resource center for all the latest information, enhancements, errata, downloads, and more. It's located at **www.quecorp.com/**.

Orders, Catalogs, and Customer Service

To order other Que or Macmillan Computer Publishing books, catalogs, or products, please contact our Customer Service Department at 800-428-5331 or fax us at 800-882-8583 (International Fax: 317-228-4400). Or visit our online bookstore at **www.mcp.com/**.

Comments and Suggestions

We want you to let us know what you like or dislike most about this book or other Que products. Your comments will help us to continue publishing the best books available on computer topics in today's market.

Que Corporation
201 West 103rd Street, 4B
Indianapolis, Indiana 46290 USA
Fax: 317-581-4663

Please be sure to include the book's title and author as well as your name and phone or fax number. We will carefully review your comments and share them with the author. Please note that due to the high volume of mail we receive, we might not be able to reply to every message.

Thank you for choosing Que!

Getting Started

This section is a quick introduction to getting started with producing a Word, Excel, or PowerPoint document.

Starting a Document

To begin working, you first have to launch the application. If you've already saved a document, you need to open the file as well. Depending on the method you choose, you can start the application and then open the document or do both at the same time.

Open Application

Windows applications are designed to accommodate users coming from different platforms and possessing different skills. For example, you can launch an application in several different ways. You can use the keyboard, the mouse, or both devices together. You can use the Windows taskbar, the Office Shortcut Bar 97, or Windows Explorer.

Starting a Program from the Taskbar

To start a program in Windows 95 or NT, you begin by clicking the Start button on the bottom-left corner of the screen (see Figure 1.1).

❸ Choose subfolder, if necessary.   **❹** Choose a program name such as Microsoft Word.

Figure 1.1
Windows 95 Start button, Programs, application name launches a program.

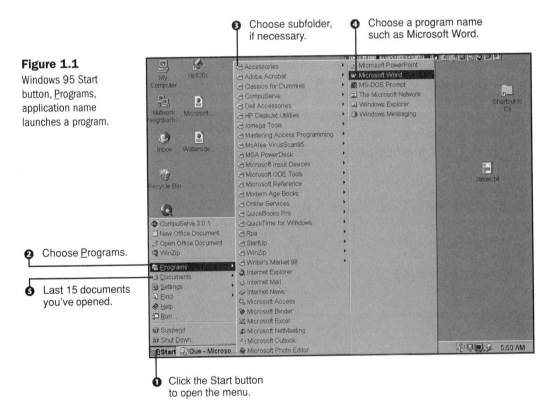

❷ Choose Programs.

❺ Last 15 documents you've opened.

❶ Click the Start button to open the menu.

If your setup of Office included the installation of the Microsoft Office Shortcut Bar (the small row of buttons at the top or side of the screen), you can click a button to launch an Office application. You can also customize this bar by clicking the first button and selecting **Customize**. Click the Buttons tab and then click the applications that you want to add or remove from the Shortcut Bar.

Opening a Document from the Taskbar

Opening a document from the desktop using the taskbar is as easy as starting a program from the taskbar—maybe even easier. You perform the same actions as you do when you launch programs. Click the **Start** button, point to the **Documents** folder, and click the document that you want to open. The **Documents** folder stores the names of the last 15 files that you opened, regardless of what program you used to create them. This technique makes it easy to find documents that you use over and over again.

Opening a Document from Windows Explorer

If you prefer using a tree structure to access your files, you can use Windows Explorer to open specific documents from folders. When you double-click a file in Explorer, Windows first launches the application and then opens the file (if the application is registered with Windows).

Quick Choices   *LAUNCH WINDOWS EXPLORER*

- Right-click the **Start** button and choose **Explore**.
- Click **Start**, point to **Programs**, and click Windows Explorer at the bottom of the Programs submenu.

After you have opened Windows Explorer, you can use the tree to move to the folder that stores the document file that you want to open (see Figure 1.2).

Opening a Document Within an Application

If you are already in an application and need to open a different document, do one of the following:

Quick Choices   *OPEN A DOCUMENT*

- If the document is one of the last few on which you've worked, click **File** and choose one of the documents from the bottom of the menu.
- Click the **Open** button 🗁 on the Standard toolbar, press **Ctrl+O**, or choose **File**, **Open** to display the Open dialog box. Navigate to the file that you want and double-click the file (see Word's **File - Open...**, page 21).

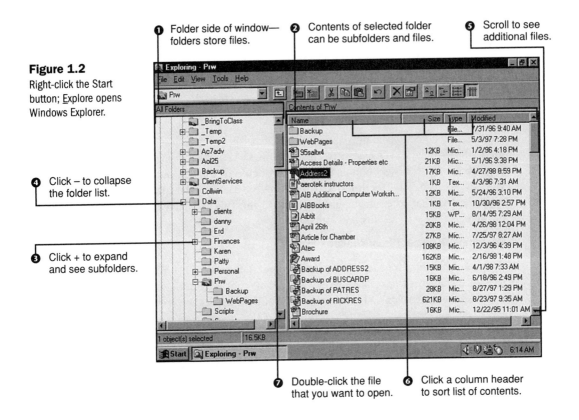

❶ Folder side of window—folders store files.

❷ Contents of selected folder can be subfolders and files.

❺ Scroll to see additional files.

Figure 1.2
Right-click the Start button; Explore opens Windows Explorer.

❹ Click – to collapse the folder list.

❸ Click + to expand and see subfolders.

❼ Double-click the file that you want to open.

❻ Click a column header to sort list of contents.

Starting a New Document

When you open an application, a blank document appears (in PowerPoint, you may need to choose **Blank presentation** on the opening screen). If you want to start a new document and there is not a blank document with which to begin, click the **New** ⬜ button on the Standard toolbar. In Word and Excel, you go to a new document or workbook (see Word's **File ▸ New...**, page 20). In PowerPoint, double click a slide layout you want in the New Slide dialog box (see Starting PowerPoint, page 456).

Typing

To begin your document, you may need to place the cursor where you are going to start. In Word, the insertion point (vertical blinking line) is at the beginning of the document. You just start typing characters. In Excel and PowerPoint, you click where you want to start, and then start typing characters. If you notice that you type an incorrect character, press **Backspace** to remove the typo.

In Word, when you get to the end of the screen, the insertion point automatically wraps to the next line. When you want to end a paragraph or type a short line, press **Enter** to create a carriage return (see Typing in Word, page 16).

In Excel, when you press **Enter**, you go down to the cell in the next row. Instead of pressing **Enter**, you can also press the tab key or an arrow key to move to the next cell right, left, up, or down (see Typing in an Excel Worksheet, page 255).

In PowerPoint, most of what you type is short lines. After you type in the title area, you can click the text area of the slide. Type the first bullet and press **Enter**. PowerPoint automatically enters another bullet (see Typing in PowerPoint, page 457).

Editing

Editing generally consists of three steps. The first step is to locate the text that you want to change. The second step is to select the text. The third step is to make the editing change.

Navigate in the Document

Although each of the applications has ways of moving around the document, the following are some quick generalities.

Quick Choices   *MOVING AROUND THE DOCUMENT*

- Press **Ctrl+Home** to move to the beginning of the document.
- Press **Ctrl+End** to move to the end of the document.
- Press **Left** or **Right** arrows to move a character to the left or right (or in Excel a cell to the right or left). In Excel, double-click the cell and then press **Left** or **Right** to move one character at a time.
- Press **Home** to move to the beginning of a line.
- Click the **Up** or **Down** arrow on the vertical scrollbar on the right side of the screen to move a line up or down at a time.
- Drag the vertical scrollbar box up or down. You see a ScreenTip indicating where you are. Release the mouse button where you want to begin.

Make Corrections

After you move to where you want to edit, click the mouse pointer in the text (in Excel, double-click a cell or click the cell that you want to edit and then click the formula bar). The insertion point indicates where your edits start.

Quick Choices   *MAKE EDITS*

- Type additional text to insert characters at the insertion point. Text after the insertion point is pushed to the right.
- Press **Backspace** to remove characters before the insertion point.
- Press **Delete** to remove characters after the insertion point.
- Drag the mouse pointer across text to select it and press **Delete** to remove the text.

- Drag the mouse pointer to select text and then click one of the formatting buttons to change the way text looks.

  B **Bold**

  I **Italicize**

  U **Underline**

  Times New Roman ▾ **Change the font face**

  44 ▾ **Change the font size**

Saving

After you're done with the document, you want to save it from the screen to a file on disk so that you can edit it again. You should also save before doing things to the document when you're not sure of the results. Additionally, save when you're doing work that could affect the document substantially (such as printing, sorting, spelling, searching and replacing, mail merges, and other advanced features). We live in the mountains and power problems are common (especially during spring thunderstorms), so we need to save often. Save your document also when you get up from your work.

Quick **Choices**   *SAVE A DOCUMENT*

1. Click the **Save** button 💾 on the Standard toolbar or press **Ctrl+S**.

2. If you haven't saved this document before, the Save As dialog box opens. Type the name of the document in the **File name** text box and press **Enter**. If you have already saved, the application does not ask for the name again.

For more options on saving (such as determining a location for saving your file), see Word's **File ▸ Save**, page 29.

Printing

Word, Excel, and PowerPoint generally show your document on your screen the way it will look when it is printed. In Word and Excel, you can click the **Print Preview** button 🔍 on the Standard toolbar to see what the margins and headers and footers look like (see **File ▸ Print Preview**, page 40 in Word, and page 268 in Excel). Click **Close** to get out of Print Preview.

Quick **Choices**   *TO PRINT A DOCUMENT*

- Click the Print button 🖨 on the Standard toolbar.

Printing has many options (pages, choosing the printer, and more). See the print section in each application for more detail (**File ▸ Print...**, page 42 in Word, page 268 in Excel, and page 464 in PowerPoint).

Ending

When you want to get out of the document, you can exit the document or the entire application.

Close the Document

If you want to work on another document in the same application, close the one on which you are working and then click the **New** button 🗋.

Quick **Choices**   *CLOSING A DOCUMENT*

- Click the **Close** button in the upper-right corner of the screen (or window). If your document is maximized, the Close button appears in the same row as your menu.
- Choose **File**, **Close**.
- Press **Ctrl+W** or **Ctrl+F4**.

If you have not saved your latest changes, your application prompts you. Click **Yes** to save the changes. If you have not given the document a name, type the name in the **File name** text box and click **Save**.

Exit the Application

If you don't want to create any more documents in this application for a while, exit your application.

Quick **Choices**   *CLOSING A DOCUMENT*

- Click the **Exit** button (the larger of the two Xs) in the upper-right corner of the screen (or window). This is the X that is on the title bar of the application.
- Choose **File**, **Exit**.
- Press **Alt+F4**.

If you have not saved your latest changes in any of your open documents, your application prompts you. Choose whether you want to save each document or not.

Screen Elements

One of the best parts of learning Windows and Microsoft Office 97 is the similarity between different applications. After you learn one program, the next and subsequent programs are easier to learn, especially because parts of the window are similar.

Common Window Elements

Figure 1.3 shows a review of the elements on a screen. Each application usually displays the application window itself and at least one document window. The following table describes the common elements on the application window and the document window.

Figure 1.3
The screen provides many choices that you can manipulate with the mouse.

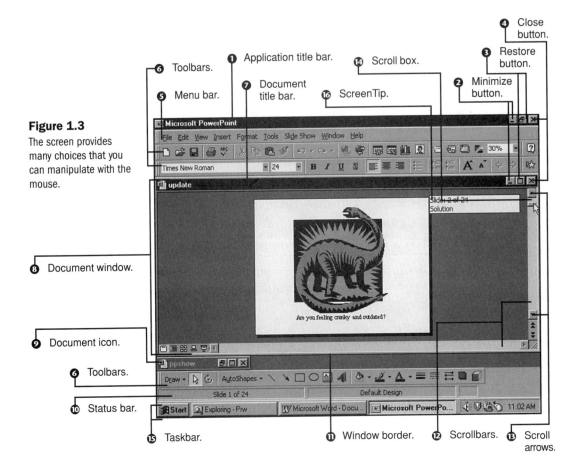

④ Close button.

③ Restore button.

② Minimize button.

⑥ Toolbars.

① Application title bar.

⑭ Scroll box.

⑤ Menu bar.

⑦ Document title bar.

⑯ ScreenTip.

⑧ Document window.

⑨ Document icon.

⑥ Toolbars.

⑩ Status bar.

⑮ Taskbar.

⑪ Window border.

⑫ Scrollbars.

⑬ Scroll arrows.

Window features common to application and document windows

Feature	Description/Use
Control-menu icon	Microsoft Program icon in upper-left corner of window. Double-click to close.
Title bar	Title bar is dark if window is active, grayed if other window is active. (The color may be different if you have changed colors in the Display Properties of the Control Panel.) If not maximized, drag to move window; double-click to maximize or restore.
Minimize button	Click to shrink window to icon.
Maximize button	Click button to change window to largest possible size.
Restore button	Click this button to change window to less than full screen.

Feature	Description/Use
Close button	An X appears on this button. Click this button to close the window.
Menu bar	Click one of the words to select a menu or press **Alt** and then type underlined letter on menus.
Window border	Thin gray line surrounding a window that is not maximized.
Window corner	Textured box in bottom-right corner of window. Drag to change size of window.

Toolbars

Toolbar buttons generally provide the quickest way for accomplishing a task such as printing, saving, and formatting. To turn a toolbar on or off:

1. Click the right mouse button on an active toolbar. A pop-up menu shows a list of the potential toolbars. Microsoft displays those toolbars with a check mark to the left of the name. (See **View ▾ Toolbars**—Word, page 66; Excel, page 289; PowerPoint, 484—in each application for a description of the toolbars.)

2. Click the toolbar that you want to turn on or off. If the toolbar is floating, you can also click the toolbar's Control-menu icon to close the toolbar.

If the program doesn't presently show any toolbars, choose **View**, **Toolbars** and select the toolbar(s) that you want to display.

Some toolbars display automatically or display other buttons when you change the view. For example, Word adds an Outline toolbar when you change to Outline view. Excel adds a Charting toolbar when you use the Chart Wizard.

If a toolbar button is dimmed, that means that the button is not currently available. If you want to see what a toolbar button does, simply point to it with the mouse until a yellow ScreenTip describing it appears.

Using Menus

Although toolbars give you the quickest way to accomplish a task, menus generally provide the most options for completing a task. For example, the **Print** button ▤ on the Standard toolbar simply prints a document, while **File**, **Print** enables you to choose which printer to use, what part of the document you want printed, and how many copies you want.

Directly below the title bar in all applications is the *menu bar*. In most Microsoft Office and Windows applications, the menu bar begins with the **File**, **Edit**, and **View** menus and ends with the **Window** and **Help** menus. When the mouse pointer is on a menu, the pointer changes to a white arrow. To pull down a menu, click the menu name. If you want to use the keyboard, press **Alt** and the underlined letter on the menu. When you open a menu, a list of commands appears. Click the command or type the letter of the underlined character.

If you accidentally go into the wrong menu, you can take one of these steps:

- Point to another menu.
- Click the document to turn off the menu.
- Press **Alt** or click the menu name again to get out of the menu.

In some cases, you can hold down the **Shift** key before you choose a menu and the menu items change. For example in Word, the **File**, **Save** changes to **File**, **Save All** and **File**, **Close** changes to **File**, **Close All**.

Common Menu Symbols

Menus throughout Windows applications have common symbols that help you know what happens when you select the command. The symbols include ellipses, arrows, check marks, option bullets, toolbar buttons, and shortcut keys.

Each menu is divided into sections by horizontal lines. The sections generally group similar commands together (such as **Save**, **Save As**, and **Save As HTML**) or group commands that are mutually exclusive. The following list describes common menu symbols:

- Three dots, an *ellipsis*, after a command indicates that a dialog box appears after you choose the command. For example, the command **File**, **Print** occurs in all Office applications, and an ellipsis indicates that the Print dialog box follows the selection of this command. (For more information on dialog boxes, see "Using Dialog Boxes" later in this chapter.)
- Microsoft Office applications have arrows on the right side of some menus indicating that another drop-down menu appears. After you point to the command with an arrow, you choose another command on the resulting menu. Click **File**, **Send To** for an example.
- Another character on some menus is a *check mark* to the left of the menu choice. A check mark indicates that the choice is selected and that the choice can be on or off. For example, the **Window** menu of all Microsoft Office 97 applications shows a list of open documents at the bottom. The active open document is indicated by a check mark.
- To the right of some commands are *keyboard shortcuts*. Instead of using the menu, you can press the shortcut key or key combination to choose the command. Most shortcuts begin by holding the **Ctrl** key down in combination with a letter. For example, to undo your latest action, press **Ctrl+Z** in all applications. Shortcut keys also include function keys (for example, **F7** for Spelling) and editing keys (for example, **Delete** to erase the selection).
- On the left of some commands are toolbar buttons. This is a reminder that you can also do this command by clicking a button on a toolbar. For example, see the **File** menu and note the buttons for **New**, **Open**, **Save** and **Print**.
- Finally, some submenus are actually floating menus that you can drag to any location and leave onscreen. If you see a title bar at the top of a submenu, you can tear off that

submenu and drag it to any location that you prefer onscreen so that its choices remain available. For an example, see PowerPoint's **Slide Show**, **Action Buttons**.

Shortcut Menus

Office also has shortcut menus for each application. To access a shortcut menu, select the item that you want to change and click the *right* mouse button in the selected area. The menu that appears gives you options for only the selection. You don't have to wade through the menu bar to figure out what menu items go with what you are doing.

In addition to shortcut menus for toolbars, Microsoft has shortcut menus for selected text, drawing and graphic objects, rows, columns, and others depending on your application.

Using Dialog Boxes

When you choose a command with an ellipsis, a dialog box appears. The dialog box can be very simple with only one button (such as **OK**), or the dialog box can have many choices. Just as the menus have common symbols, so do the dialog boxes. (Figures 1.4 and 1.5 show examples of two dialog boxes.)

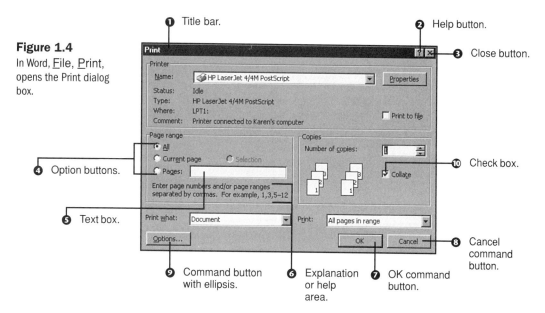

Figure 1.4
In Word, File, Print, opens the Print dialog box.

❶ Title bar.
❷ Help button.
❸ Close button.
❹ Option buttons.
❺ Text box.
❻ Explanation or help area.
❼ OK command button.
❽ Cancel command button.
❾ Command button with ellipsis.
❿ Check box.

Figure 1.5

In Excel, Format, Cells, Font tab opens to the Font page of the Format Cells dialog box.

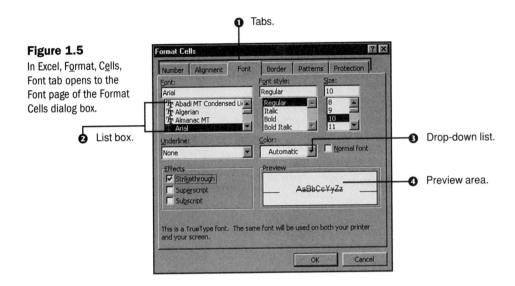

❶ Tabs.

❷ List box.

❸ Drop-down list.

❹ Preview area.

Dialog boxes enable you to see all the current settings for a command as well as change them. As features have become richer in options, Microsoft has added tabs (for example, the Font tab is selected and displayed in the Format Cells dialog box shown in Figure 1.5). Click a tab to go to that area of the dialog box. Sometimes, you may need to see your underlying document to make a choice in the dialog box. Drag the title bar of the dialog box to move the dialog box out of the way. Within a dialog box, you click an object to select or change the value. For example, in the **Font Style** list box, click Italic to select the font as italic. Within a dialog box, you generally click an object, type a value, or select from a list.

Microsoft includes the **?** button on the top-right corner of almost every dialog box window. If you need help on a specific part of the dialog box, you can click the **?** button and point to the part of the dialog box where you need help and click again. Microsoft displays a pop-up help window for that area of the dialog box. This method is called *context-sensitive help*.

In addition to using the mouse to make selections in a dialog box, you also can use several keyboard methods:

- Press **Tab** to move to each section of a dialog box.
- Press **Shift+Tab** to move backward through the dialog box.
- Press **Alt+** any underlined letter on a choice in the dialog box to move to that choice.
- Press the **Up** or **Down** arrow to make a selection in a list.
- Press the **Spacebar** to select or deselect a choice in a check box.

To get out of a dialog box without selecting any settings, choose **Cancel** or press **Esc**. To use the settings, choose **OK**. In some cases, click the **Close** button to finish your selections. Notice that some command buttons have ellipses (for example, the **Options** button in Figure 1.4). An ellipsis indicates that another dialog box appears when you choose this button.

Word

In this chapter

Using the Keyboard and Mouse

Typing

Use the keyboard to type characters. First click the mouse or use the arrow keys to position the insertion point (a vertical blinking line). When you type, any characters after the insertion point are pushed to the right.

If you double-click the OVR box on the Status bar, OVR appears (it's no longer dimmed). When you type with overwrite activated, Word types over and replaces the characters after the insertion point. The following table shows additional keys you can use to insert characters.

Insert special characters	
Press	**To**
Enter	Insert the end of a paragraph, blank line, or end of a short line. Enter also activates an AutoText entry when the ScreenTip appears (see **Insert ₋AutoText**, page 101).
Shift+Enter	Insert a line break (keeps paragraph formatting).
Ctrl+Enter	Force the page to break to the next page.
Ctrl+Shift+Enter	Insert a column break.
Ctrl+Hyphen	Insert an optional hyphen.
Ctrl+Shift+Hyphen	Insert a hyphen that doesn't break at the end of a line.
Ctrl+Shift+Spacebar	Insert a space that doesn't break at the end of a line.
Alt+Ctrl+C	Insert ©.
Alt+Ctrl+R	Insert ®.
Alt+Ctrl+T	Insert ™.
Alt+Ctrl+Period	Insert an ellipsis (…).

Editing Text

To correct your document, you use the following keys.

Delete text	
Press	**To**
Backspace	Delete one character to the left of insertion point.
Delete	Delete one character to the right of insertion point or selected text or object.
Ctrl+Backspace	Delete one word to the left.

Press	To
Ctrl+Delete	Delete one word to the right.
Ctrl+Z	Undo the last action.

Navigating

To type in the document, you need to be able to position the insertion point and to view different parts of the document. Click the mouse pointer to move the insertion point or use the keyboard.

Use the keyboard to move the insertion point

Press	To Move
Left Arrow←	A character to the left
Right Arrow→	A character to the right
Up Arrow↑	Up a line
Down Arrow↓	Down a line
Ctrl+Left Arrow←	A word to the left
Ctrl+Right Arrow→	A word to the right
Ctrl+Up Arrow↑	A paragraph up
Ctrl+Down Arrow↓	A paragraph down
Shift+Tab	A cell to the left (in a table)
Tab	A cell to the right (in a table)
End	To end of a line
Home	To beginning of a line
Alt+Ctrl+Page Up	To top of the window
Alt+Ctrl+Page Down	To end of the window
Page Up	Up one screen
Page Down	Down one screen
Ctrl+End	To end of a document
Ctrl+Home	To beginning of a document
Shift+F5	To the last place you edited or searched. Also, do this immediately after you open a document to go to the location of the insertion point when you closed the document.

After you use the mouse to scroll, make sure that you click to move the insertion point to where you want to start editing.

Use the mouse to scroll on the screen

Click	To
Up scroll arrow	Scroll up one line
Down scroll arrow	Scroll down one line
Above the scroll box	Scroll up one screen
Below the scroll box	Scroll down one screen
And drag the scroll box	A screen tip shows the page number and, optionally, text formatted with a Heading style while you scroll to a specific page.
Left scroll arrow	Scroll left
Right scroll arrow	Scroll right
Press Shift+left scroll arrow	Scroll left, beyond the margin, in normal view
Select Browse Object ⊙ and choose Browse by Page ▢ Then click Previous Page ⬆ or Next Page ⬇ .	Move a page at a time

Use Microsoft IntelliMouse

Do This	To
Rotate the wheel toward you.	Scroll down a few lines
Rotate the wheel away from you.	Scroll up a few lines
Hold down the wheel button and drag up or down (the further from the starting mark, the faster you pan).	Pan up or down
Click the wheel button. Move mouse pointer above or below the starting point in the vertical scrollbar for direction. Word starts scrolling down (the further from the starting mark, the faster you scroll). Click the mouse to stop scrolling.	Automatically scroll up or down
Hold **Ctrl** as you rotate the wheel toward you.	Zoom so that the view is smaller
Hold **Ctrl** as you rotate the wheel away from you.	Zoom so that the view is magnified

Selecting Text

Before you do major editing or formatting, you first need to select text. After you select text you can press Delete to remove the text. (See also the **Format**, page 160, and **Edit**, page 49, sections for many of the features you can use with selected text.)

See the navigation keys with the preceding keyboard. Select text by holding down the **Shift** key and using the movement keys (see Navigating, page 17). For example, if you hold **Shift** and press **Ctrl+Right arrow**, you select one word at a time. The following are some additional keys with which to select text in the document.

Press	To Select
Ctrl+A	To include the entire document
Ctrl+Shift+F8. Use arrow keys. Press **Esc** to cancel selection mode.	Vertical block
F8+ any navigation keys. Press **Esc** to cancel the selection mode.	From the point you pressed **F8** to wherever you end up

Select with the mouse

Do This	To Select
Drag over the text	Any text
Double-click	A word
Click the graphic	A graphic
Click with the mouse pointer in the left margin (white right-facing arrow) or drag	One or more lines
Ctrl+click a sentence	A sentence
Double-click with the mouse pointer in the left margin (white right-facing arrow) and then drag	A paragraph (drag selects multiple paragraphs)
Triple-click a paragraph	A paragraph
Click at the start of the selection. Move to the end of the selection with mouse. Hold down **Shift** and click again.	A block of text (Use this method when the screen scrolls too fast to effectively select a large block of text.)
Triple-click with the mouse pointer in left margin (white right-facing arrow)	An entire document
Hold down **Alt** and drag the mouse	A vertical block

File

The **File** menu helps you manage the document as a whole—where it is stored, the size and formatting, where you want to print or email it, and summary information.

File ➜ New...

The first item on the **File** menu, **New**, is your first step to creating a document or a template that contains formatting features for other new documents. From the File New dialog box you choose formulated documents such as letters, faxes, envelopes, or memos that speed up the work of completing documents. When you first start Word or use the **New** button 🗋 on the Standard toolbar, the default document is based on the Normal.dot template (shown as Blank Document in the dialog box).

Quick Choices   *START A DOCUMENT*

- Click **New** 🗋 on the Standard toolbar or press **Ctrl+N**. A new, blank document opens. The title bar displays a generic name such as Document2 until you save the document.
- Choose the Windows Start button and click New Office Document or click the New Office Document button on the Office Shortcut bar. Then double-click the Blank Document icon on the General tab or choose a different kind of document.

To start a document or create a new template:

1. Choose **File**, **New**. The New dialog box opens (see Figure 2.1).

❶ Click a tab for the type of document.

❸ Click one of these buttons to change the way the files are displayed.

Figure 2.1

File, New opens the New dialog box.

❷ Double-click to open the template or launch a wizard.

❻ The Wizard icon indicates that Word asks a number of questions to create the document.

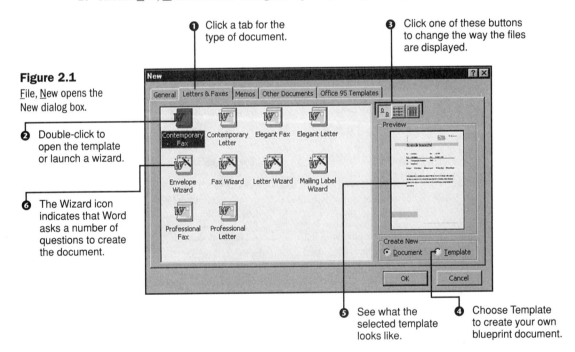

❺ See what the selected template looks like.

❹ Choose Template to create your own blueprint document.

2. In the Create New section do one of the following:

   To create a new document, click **Document**.

   To create a new template based on the selected template, click **Template**. When you save your file later, Word automatically defaults to a template (DOT) document type and displays the templates directory (giving you an option of folders that correspond to the tabs of this dialog box).

3. You have three options for viewing the list of templates on each tab. Click one of the following buttons:

Button	Name	Purpose
	Large Icons	Shows template names with a large file type icon only.
	List	Shows template names with a small file type icon only.
	Details	Shows template names, file type icon, size of file, file type, and modified date and time. Click the column header at the top of the list to toggle the sort order between ascending and descending.

4. Choose a template file on any tab and, if an overview of the formatting is available, it appears in the Preview area. Templates that lead you step-by-step through the building of a document have a wand icon and say Wizard.

5. After you choose the file on which you want to base your new document or new template, click **OK.**

If the file you chose was a wizard, Word will lead you through the steps to create the document.

File ➡ Open...

File, Open enables you to load a file stored on a disk. You then display and edit the file on your screen. When you get to the Open dialog box, you have many options with which to narrow or expand your search. These options in the Open dialog box replace the Find File feature from Windows 3.1 versions of Microsoft Office.

Quick Choices   *USE EITHER OF THE FOLLOWING OPTIONS TO QUICKLY OPEN A DOCUMENT*

1. Click **Open** on the standard toolbar or press Ctrl+O.
2. Double-click the file that you want to open.

To use the **Open** command on the **File** menu, do the following:

1. Choose **File, Open.** The Open dialog box displays (see Figure 2.2).
2. In the **Look in** drop-down box, select a drive or folder to display the files from which to choose. You can change the Look-in startup location (see **Tools ➡ Options... File locations,** page 223).
3. Maneuver through the list until you find the file that you want to open. (If necessary, use the procedure outlined in **File ➡ Open... Find a File,** page 21).
4. Click the file that you want to open to select it. If you want to open more than one file, press **Ctrl** and click additional files.
5. Click **Open.**

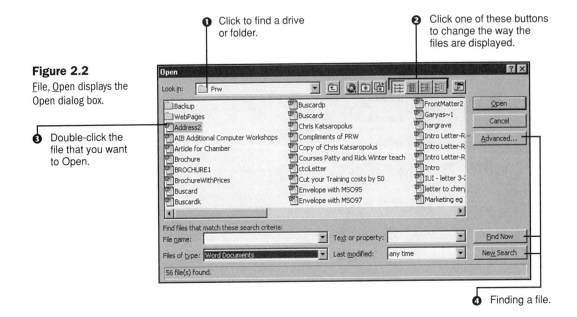

Click to find a drive
or folder.

Click one of these buttons
to change the way the
files are displayed.

Figure 2.2
File, Open displays the
Open dialog box.

Double-click the
file that you want
to Open.

Finding a file.

File ⇥ Open... Toolbar Buttons

To help you navigate to other areas where your file may be located, use one of the following buttons:

Button	Name	Purpose
	Up One Level	Moves the **Look in** and file list to a higher level in hierarchy of folders.
	Search the Web	Launches your Web browser and goes to Microsoft's default search page.
	Look in Favorites	Changes the file list to display the Favorites folder (usually located as a subfolder of the Windows folder).
	Add to Favorites	Gives two menu options. **Add filename to Favorites** stores the active document to the Favorites folder. **Add Selected Item(s) to Favorites** stores the item or items selected in the file list to the Favorites folder. (Select contiguous files by holding down the Shift key as you click. Select noncontiguous files by holding down the Ctrl key as you click.)

You have four options for viewing the Open dialog box file list. Click one of the following buttons:

Button	Name	Purpose
	List	Shows filenames with a file type icon only.
	Details	Shows filenames, file type icon, size of file, file type, and modified date and time. Click the column header at the top of the list to toggle the sort order between ascending and descending.
	Properties	Shows user-added summary information such as title, author, keywords, and others. Use the scrollbar to see additional properties such as the number of words, size, or date modified. To add properties, see the **File - Properties** section on page 46.
	Preview	Shows what the first part of the file looks like.

The last button on the Open dialog box toolbar is Commands and Settings . This button opens a menu that enables you to do a number of file operations.

Menu Item	Purpose
Open Read-Only	Opens the selected file(s) without changing the file(s). If you want to save any changes, you must give the file a new name.
Open as Copy	Creates a duplicate of the file named "Copy of filename." If you want to change the name after you close the document, see **Rename** in **File - Open... Shortcut Menu**, on page 28 for more details.
Print	Send selected file(s) to the default printer without opening them up for editing.
Properties	Goes to the Properties (title, author, statistics, and so on) of the selected file (see **File - Properties**, page 46 for more details). You can read or edit the properties here. If you select multiple files before this choice, you are given the total size of the files and the ability to view and change file attributes such as Read-only, Hidden, and Archive.
Sorting	Opens a dialog box that enables you to sort (either ascending or descending) the folder by name, size of file, type of file, and last modified date. You can also accomplish this by choosing the Details button and clicking the column headers in the file list.
Search Subfolders	This shows a tree view of all files within each subfolder that match the criteria section of the Open dialog box.
Group files by folder	Normally this is checked when you use **Search Subfolders**. When you uncheck the menu item, subfolders do not appear, and only a list of files displays.

continues

Menu Item	Purpose
Map **N**etwork Drive	Enables you to use a drive letter instead a long path name to a network computer folder. This choice opens the Map Network Drive dialog box, which enables you to assign a letter to a network computer's folder. Choose the **D**rive letter and type a **P**ath name in the following format: \\computername\ SharedFolder. If you want to use the drive letter the next time you start Windows, check the **Reconnect at logon** check box.
Add/Modify **F**TP Locations	At the bottom of the **Look in** list, you find a section for Internet Locations (FTP). FTP (File Transfer Protocol) sites contain special Internet sites that enable you to download files. To change the list of locations, choose this option (or double-click Add/ Modify FTP Locations at the bottom of the **Look in** list) to open the Add/Modify FTP Locations dialog box. Type the address in the **Name of FTP site** text box (such as **ftp.microsoft.com/**). Choose whether you log on as **Anonymous** or as a **U**ser, and if necessary, type a **P**assword and click the **Add** button. To modify an existing site, click it in the **FTP sites** list box and then click **Modify**. To remove a site, click it and choose **Remove**.
Saved Searches	Lists searches saved (criteria to find files) on the Advance Find dialog box with the Save Search button. On the Advance Find dialog box you can also choose Open Search (see **File - Open... - Find a File** on page 24).

File ➥ **O**pen... ➥ Find a File

If your list is long or you don't remember where you placed your file, you can use several options in the Open dialog box to locate your file.

Quick Choices USE ANY OF THESE QUICK OPTIONS TO FIND FILES

■ Click **O**pen 🖻 to display the Open dialog box.

■ Choose a location (drive or folder) from the **Look in** drop-down list where the file is located.

■ Type a filename or portion of a filename in the **File name** text box and click **Find Now**.

To use the Open dialog box to find a file:

1. Click **O**pen 🖻 to display the Open dialog box.

2. Choose a location (drive or folder) from the **Look in** drop-down list where the file is located.

3. Do one or more of the following options:

   • To find a file by name, type the name of the file in the **File name** text box. Use wild cards if you don't know the whole name. Asterisks replace multiple letters, and question marks replace individual letters. To find Customer Orders 1999 you could type Cust*Ord*99 or Customer Orders 19??.

- To narrow the search for files or look for a file created in a different program (or saved as a different type), click the **Files of type** drop-down list and choose a different file format. This list includes All Files, Word Documents (Word 97 version), other versions of Word, Document Templates (preformatted documents that you base new documents on), different kinds of text files, other word processing formats (Write, Rich Text Format, WordStar, Works, WordPerfect), and other HTML (Internet) documents. You can also translate Schedule+, Outlook address information, and Excel worksheets into tabbed information or a table.

- To look for text within a file (or in any property), type the phrase in quotes in the **Text or property** text box.

- To narrow the search for files during a specified time period, choose a time period (for example, last week or last month) in the **Last modified** drop-down box.

4. If you want more high-powered searching options, click the **Advanced** button and choose any of the following options mentioned in or following Figure 2.3.

Figure 2.3

File, Open, Advanced opens the Advanced Find dialog box.

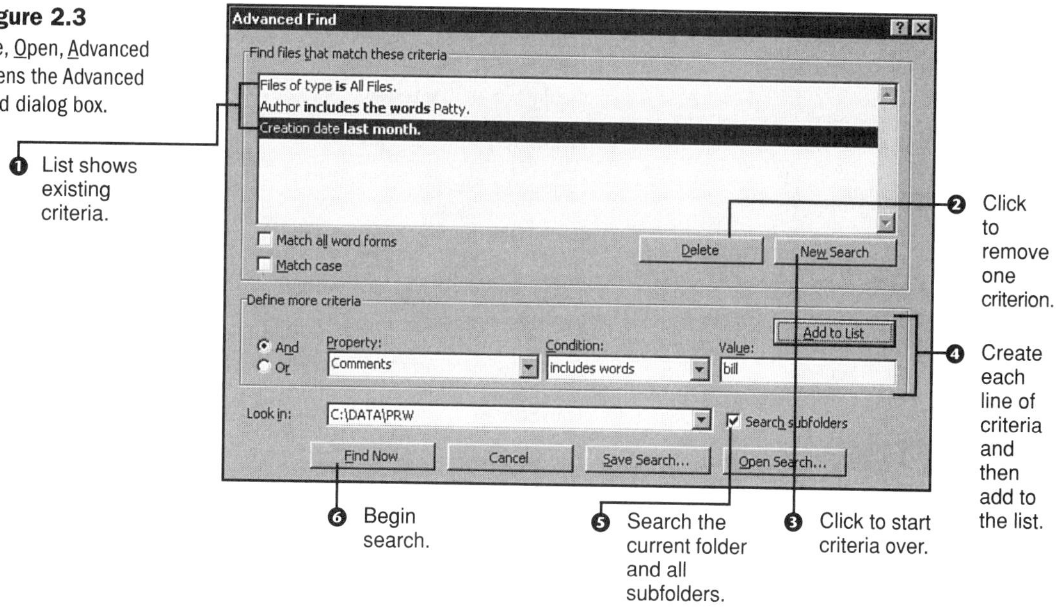

❶ List shows existing criteria.

❷ Click to remove one criterion.

❹ Create each line of criteria and then add to the list.

❻ Begin search.

❺ Search the current folder and all subfolders.

❸ Click to start criteria over.

- To search based on a property (such as Author or Company Name) associated with the file, choose the **Property** from the drop-down list, select a **Condition** (such as includes words or last month, depending on the property), and type a **Value** such as **IBM** or **4/8/99**. Choose **And** to require that all conditions are met, or choose **Or** to have any of the conditions met. Click **Add to List** to add this criterion to the **Find files that match these criteria** list box. Repeat this step as necessary to add new conditions (see the following table for properties and conditions). Most of the properties you can search on are those you see on the Properties dialog box (see **File ⁃ Properties**, page 46), but any custom property you've created is also included.

- To find different forms of the word (for example, if you type **be** and you want to find **is** or **are**), check the **Match all word forms** check box.
- To duplicate the upper- and lowercase of all criteria, check **Match case**.
- To display files within all subfolders of the folder in the **Look in** text box, check the **Search subfolders**.
- To save all the criteria with a name to be able to select again, choose **Save Search**, type in the **Name for this Search**, and click **OK**.
- To open a list of saved criteria, click the **Open Search** button and double-click the search.

5. When ready to apply the criteria, click the **Find Now** button on either the Advanced Find or Open dialog box.

Properties you can search for

Property	Where You Set or View Properties	Conditions (see below)
Application name	Determined by the file type the document is saved as	1
Author	Properties, Summary tab	1
Category	Properties, Summary tab	1
Comments	Properties, Summary tab	1
Company	Properties, Summary tab	1
Contents	The text in the file	2
Creation Date	Properties, Statistics tab (read)	3
Filename	File, Save As	4
Files of type	File, Save As	5
Hyperlink base	Properties, Summary tab	1
Keywords	Properties, Summary tab	1
Last modified	Properties, Statistics tab (read)	3
Last printed	Properties, Statistics tab (read)	3
Last saved by	Properties, Statistics tab (read)	1
Manager	Properties, Summary tab	1
Number of characters	Properties, Statistics tab (read)	6
Number of characters + spaces	Properties, Statistics tab (read)	6
Number of hidden slides	PowerPoint Properties, Statistics tab (read)	6
Number of lines	Properties, Statistics tab (read)	6

Property	Where You Set or View Properties	Conditions (see below)
Number of multimedia clips	PowerPoint Properties, Statistics tab (read)	6
Number of notes	PowerPoint Properties, Statistics tab (read)	6
Number of pages	Properties, Statistics tab (read)	6
Number of paragraphs	Properties, Statistics tab (read)	6
Number of slides	PowerPoint Properties, Statistics tab (read)	6
Number of words	Properties, Statistics tab (read)	6
Revision	Properties, Statistics tab (read)	1
Size	Properties, Size tab (read)	6
Subject	Properties, Summary tab	1
Template	Properties, Summary tab (set through Tools, Templates and Add-Ins)	1
Text or property	This is a combination of any text in the document or a property that you've set	1
Title	Properties, Summary tab	1
Total editing time	Properties, Statistics tab (read)	6

Conditions to use to search for properties

Sample Property and Number for Preceding Table	Conditions
Application name (1)	Includes words, includes phrase, begins with phrase, ends with phrase, includes near each other, is (exactly), is not
Contents (2)	Includes words, includes phrase, includes near each other
Creation date (3)	Yesterday, today, last week, last month, this month, any time, anytime between, on, on or after, on or before, in the last
Filename (4)	Includes, begins with, ends with
Files of type (5)—Note: no Value text box	All Files, Word Documents, Document Templates, Rich Text Format (all file format options listed in the **Files of type** drop-down box in file dialog boxes)
Number of characters (6)	Equals, does not equal, any number between (in **Value** text box type word **and**—for example **5 and 10**) at most, at least, more than, less than

File ➥ Open... Shortcut Menu

The Open dialog box enables you to use the right-mouse button to display a shortcut menu. If you right-click a filename, you get some of the same options you do when clicking the Commands and Settings buttons mentioned in the preceding section (see **File ‑ Open... Toolbar Buttons**). The duplicated options include **Open Read Only, Open as Copy, Print**, and **Properties**. Additional options are listed in the following table.

Right-click file options

Menu Item	Purpose
Open	Opens the selected file enabling you to save changes with the selected name.
Send To	Displays a submenu enabling you to copy the file to a **Floppy**, put the file on the **Desktop as Shortcut**, launch a wizard that takes you through the steps of sending to a **Fax Recipient**, open a blank email message with the file as an attachment and send to a **Mail Recipient Using Microsoft Outlook**, and copy the file to **My Briefcase** enabling you to synchronize two files and choose which of two updated files you want on your network and laptop. Double-click on **My Briefcase** on the Windows Desktop to use this briefcase feature. To add another drive or folder to this menu, in Windows Explorer, right-drag into the SentTo subfolder of the Windows directory and choose **Create Shortcut(s) Here** from the shortcut menu.
Cut	Places the file in the Clipboard and deletes the file from the list (after pasting).
Copy	Copies the file to the Clipboard.
Create Shortcut	Creates an icon to launch the file. From the Explorer, drag this icon where you want it to go.
Delete	Removes the file from the folder.
Rename	Changes the name of a file (type the new name in the highlight and press **Enter**). You can also click the filename and click again to highlight the filename (not a double-click).

Right-click folder options (additional items)

Menu Item	Purpose
Explore	Launch Windows Explorer to display contents of the folder.
Paste	Paste a file copied to the Clipboard with **Cut** or **Copy**.
Sharing	Share files with others on the network. This opens the Properties dialog box to the Share tab. Click **Shared As** and type the **Share Name** for users to see on the network (and type a **Comment** if desired). **Read-Only** allows a user only to copy or view a file. **Full** allows users to edit and delete your file. **Depends on Password** enables you to assign a **Read-Only Password** or a **Full Access Password**. The **Web Sharing** button enables you to set options if the folder is on a Web server or FTP server.

File ↦ Close

To remove the current document from the screen, use **File**, **Close**. If you haven't saved the file since your last change, Word prompts you to save (see Figure 2.4).

Quick **Choices** *USE ANY OF THE FOLLOWING METHODS TO QUICKLY CLOSE A DOCUMENT*

▪ Choose **File**, **Close**.

▪ Click the **Close** button (x) in upper-right corner of document window.

▪ Press **Ctrl+F4** or **Ctrl W**.

▪ To close all open documents, hold down **Shift** and choose **File**, **Close All**.

Figure 2.4
If you haven't saved, File, Close opens this dialog box.

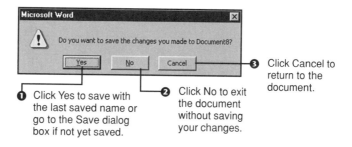

❶ Click Yes to save with the last saved name or go to the Save dialog box if not yet saved.

❷ Click No to exit the document without saving your changes.

❸ Click Cancel to return to the document.

File ↦ Save

If you already have given a document a name, **File**, **Save** saves the file changes to that document name on your disk. If you haven't given the document a name, **File**, **Save** opens the Save As dialog box (see the next section, **File ↦ Save As...**, page 29).

Quick **Choices** *USE ANY OF THESE OPTIONS TO SAVE YOUR DOCUMENTS*

▪ Click the **Save** button 💾 on the Standard toolbar.

▪ Choose **File**, **Save**.

▪ Press **Ctrl+S** or **Shift+F12**.

▪ To save multiple documents at once, hold down **Shift** and choose **File**, **Save All**.

▪ Close the file (see **File ↦ Close**, page 29) and click **Yes** to save.

File ↦ Save As...

Saving a file places a copy of what is on the screen to a location on a disk. The first time you save a file with **File**, **Save** or the **Save** button 💾, you enter the Save As dialog box (see Figure 2.5). If you use the Save icon or **File**, **Save** again, the dialog box does not open, but you overwrite the file on the disk with changes you made. After the first save, if you want to save the document with another name, you choose **File**, **Save As** to open the Save As dialog box.

Figure 2.5

File, Save (on the first save) opens the Save dialog box.

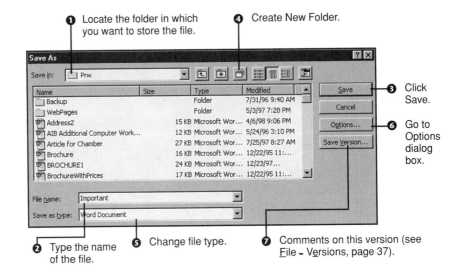

❶ Locate the folder in which you want to store the file.

❹ Create New Folder.

❸ Click Save.

❻ Go to Options dialog box.

❷ Type the name of the file.

❺ Change file type.

❼ Comments on this version (see File – Versions, page 37).

To use the **Save As** command, follow these steps:

1. Choose **File**, **Save As** or press **F12**. The Save As dialog box displays.

   Most of the buttons on the toolbar are the same as the Open dialog box (see **File – Open... Toolbar Buttons**, page 21). The Create New Folder button is not in the Open dialog box.

2. To change the location of where you store the file, click the **Save in** drop-down and choose a drive and a folder.

   If you have permissions to save to an FTP site, you can choose the site under the Internet Locations (FTP) in the **Save in** drop-down. To add a new FTP site see the **Add/ Modify FTP Locations** under the Commands and Setting button in the **File – Open... Toolbar Buttons** on page 21.

3. If you need to create a location to store your file, click the **Create New Folder** button 🗀. In the New Folder dialog box, type the name of the Folder in the **Name** text box and click **OK**. The new folder appears in the file list. Double-click it to enter that folder.

4. If you want to save the document as a different file format, click the **Save as type** drop-down and select another word processing format (such as text, Rich Text Format, Windows Write, previous versions of Word, Word for the Macintosh, WordStar, Works, or WordPerfect versions).

5. Type the **File name** in the text box. Word suggests the first few words within the text of the document. Type over these words or edit them as desired.

6. If you want to keep a record of a snapshot of the document at this point in time, click the **Save Version** button, type **Comments on version** in the text box, and click **OK** (see **File - Versions...**, page 37, to view different versions).

7. To save the file with a password, click the **Options** button and type either a **Password to open** or a **Password to modify** and click **OK**. You are asked to verify the password. Type it again and click **OK**.

8. If you want a dialog box to appear that prompts you to choose to open the file read-only or allow you to save changes when you open the file, click the **Options** button, check **Read-only recommended**, and click **OK**.

9. Click **Save**.

File - Save As... Options

In addition to the Password and Read-only options on the Save Options dialog box mentioned in the preceding section, Word enables you to set a number of options for saving all documents. You can enter the Options Save dialog box through the Options button on the Save dialog box or through **Tools, Options** and clicking the Save tab. (Figure 2.6 shows this dialog box and the following table summarizes the options.)

Figure 2.6

File, Save, Options opens this Save tab of the Options dialog box.

❷ These options are for all documents.

❶ These options are for the current file.

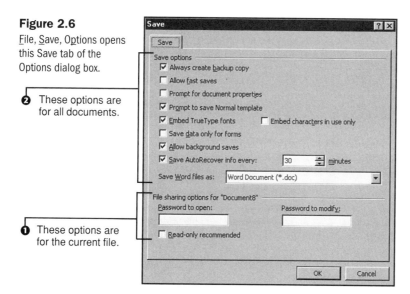

Save options for all files

Dialog Box Item	Purpose
Always create **b**ackup copy	When you save a file the second time, Word stores your first file as **Backup of *filename*.wbk**. (*Filename* stands for your actual filename.)
Allow **f**ast saves	Speeds file saving by only saving what is new to the disk. You cannot use this option with **Always create backup copy**. The general consensus, however, is not to use fast save; it tends to corrupt documents.
Prompt for document properti**e**s	After you save the document, Word displays the Properties dialog box (see **File ‑ Properties** on page 46).
Pr**o**mpt to save Normal template	When you exit Word, a message appears asking whether you want to save changes that you made to default settings, such as default margins. When not checked, Word automatically saves changes to the Normal template.
Embed TrueType fonts	Enables users who do not have your TrueType fonts installed on their computer to read and print the document if the font has been designed to be embedded.
Embed chara**c**ters in use only	If you select **Embed TrueType fonts**, you can choose to only store the font styles that you used rather than all styles for the TrueType font. This may save disk space.
Save **d**ata only for forms	When you use forms (check boxes, text boxes, and so on), this only saves the items entered as part of the form (not the form itself) as a tab-delimited record in Text Only file format.
Allow background saves	Enables you to continue working while Word saves the document. See the pulsing disk icon on the Status bar when saving.
Save AutoRecover info every...	If the computer crashes, the AutoRecover file automatically opens the next time you start Word and displays documents you had open when the last AutoRecover save event happened. Enter a number in the **minutes** spinner box for this save frequency.
Save **W**ord files as	Changes the default **Save as type** option in the Save As dialog box (see **File ‑ Save As...**, page 29) when you first save a file. If you use a type different from Word Document, Word prompts you to choose to save as this type, not this type (use Word Document), or open a help file to see what you might lose with the new file type.

File ▸ Save as HTML...

One of the new features of Office 97 is the capability to save documents in HTML file format. After the file is in this format, you can load it on a Web server, and others can view the document with a Web browser (either through an intranet or the Internet).

To save a Word document as an HTML file, follow these steps:

1. Choose **File**, **Save as HTML**. The Save As dialog opens with HTML Document automatically selected in the **Save As type** drop-down box.

   This is the same Save As dialog box seen in the preceding section (**File ▸ Save As...**, see page 29). Choose any of the other options desired.

2. Type the **File name** in the text box and press **Enter**.

3. If you have styles or other formatting, a dialog box may appear warning that you may lose some of your formatting when the document is converted to an HTML file. Click **Yes** to save as an HTML file. (If you choose No, you return to the Save As dialog box with Word Document as the **Save as type**).

When you save a document as HTML, a number of additions are made to toolbars and menus.

Additions to toolbars and menus

Button	Description or Menu Item	How to Use
New buttons on the Standard toolbar		
	Web Page Preview	Click to launch your Web browser and load the current document to see what it looks like on screen. This is the same as **File**, **Web Page Preview**.
	Insert Picture	Click to open the Insert Picture dialog box to insert a graphic on the document (see **Insert ▸ Picture**, page 149). This button is also added to the Drawing toolbar. After you insert the picture, the new Picture toolbar displays.
	Form Design Mode	Click to display the Control Toolbox and the Exit Design Mode button (see **View ▸ Toolbars ▸ Control Toolbox**, page 70). This enables you to place check boxes, option buttons, and other controls on the document (and see below).

continues

Continued

Button	Description or Menu Item	How to Use
New buttons on the Control Toolbox		
	Text Area	Position the insertion point and click to create a text box with both vertical and horizontal scrollbars available.
	Submit	For a fill-in form, click to create a button with which the user sends the information.
	Image Submit	Click to create an image with which the user submits the data.
	Reset	Click to create a button the user presses to remove entered data and reset elements to default settings.
	Hidden Text	Click to insert a control that is used to pass information to the Web server when the user submits a form.
	Password	Position the insertion point and click to create a text box that displays asterisks (*) as the user types.
New buttons on the Formatting toolbar		
	Increase Font Size	Select text and click to increase the font to the next available font size.
	Decrease Font Size	Select text and click to decrease the font to the next available font size.
	Horizontal Line	Position the insertion point and click to add a line across the page. This adds the last line style created with **Insert**, **Horizontal Line**. This button is also added to the Drawing toolbar.
	Background	Click and choose a color for the page, or choose patterns and fill effects (see **Format - Background**, page 180). This button is also added to the Drawing toolbar.
New buttons on Drawing toolbar		
	Video	Click to open the Video Clip dialog box enabling you to add a video to the document. This is the same as **Insert**, **Video**. In the dialog box, type the **Video** filename, choose

Button	Description or Menu Item	How to Use
New buttons on the Formatting toolbar		
		from the previous names in the drop-down, or click **Browse** to find the file. If the video can't be played, choose an Alternate **I**mage or type **Alternate** **T**ext. In the **S**tart drop-down choose whether you want the video to start when the file is opened, when the mouse moves to the image, or both. After the video starts, choose whether you want it to **Loop** 1-5 times or play infinitely. Check **Display Video** **C**ontrols if you want the user to be able to replay the video. Check **U**se **Relative Path** to identify the file in the same directory as the HTML document. Check **Copy to** **D**ocument **Folder** to copy the sound file to the location where the HTML document is stored.
	Format Picture	Select a picture and click to open the Picture dialog box. On the Settings tab, choose **Text** and type something to display in the event that the picture is not available or the user cannot or does not want to see graphics. Check **U**se **absolute path** to indicate the complete path name to the file. This box may be dimmed if the picture is stored with the document. On the Table Properties tab, choose **Text wrapping (None)** if you don't want text wrapped or choose text to wrap on the left or right. Type or click the spinner buttons to determine the **H**orizontal or **V**ertical distance the picture is to be from the text.
New buttons on the Picture toolbar		
	No Wrapping	Click the picture and this button to not wrap text around the picture.
	Left Wrapping	Click the picture and this button to wrap text to the left side (and not the right side) of the picture.
	Right Wrapping	Click the picture and this button to wrap text to the right side (and not the left side) of the picture.

continues

Continued		
Button	**Description or Menu Item**	**How to Use**
New menu items (in addition to the preceding new toolbar button features)		
	File, Save as Word Document	Choose to convert the HTML document back to a Word document. In the Save As dialog box , type the **File name** (see **File - Save As**, page 29).
	View, HTML **S**ource	Click to change the screen to show the HTML codes for the document. Click the **Exit HTML Source** button to return to Online layout mode.
	Insert, **H**orizontal Line	Position the insertion point and click to open the Insert Line dialog box. Double-click one of the line styles, or choose **More**, and choose a graphic file.
	Insert, Background Soun**d**	Click to display a submenu. If a sound is playing, choose **Stop** to terminate the sound. Choose **Play** to start the sound again. Choose **Properties** to open the Insert Sound dialog box and add a sound. In the dialog box, type the name of the **Sound** file or use the **Browse** button to find the file. Click the **Loop** drop-down and choose to play the song 1-5 times or in an infinite loop. Check **Use Relative Path** to identify file in the same directory as the HTML document. Check **Copy to Document Folder** to copy the sound file to the location where the HTML document is stored.
	Insert, **F**orms	Click to display a submenu with all the items from the Control Toolbox mentioned in conjunction with the Form Design Mode button.
	Insert, Sc**r**olling Text	Click to open the Scrolling Text dialog box to enable you to add animated text on your screen. **Type the Scrolling Text Here** and drag the **Speed** handle to adjust the speed. In the **Behavior** drop-down, choose whether you want the text to Scroll, Slide (to one side of the box), or Alternate (back and forth in the box). If you chose Scroll or Slide, choose

Button	Description or Menu Item	How to Use
New menu items (in addition to the preceding new toolbar button features)		
		the **Direction** (left or right). If desired, change the **Background Color**. If you chose Scroll or Alternate, choose the number of times you want the text to move in the **Loop** drop-down (or choose Infinite to keep the text moving).
	Format, Text Colors	Click to open the Text Colors dialog box and change the color of **Body text color** (all text in the document), **Hyperlink**, and **Followed** (hyperlinks those which the user clicked).
	Tools, AutoUpdate	Click to go to the Microsoft Web site for updating the Web authoring tools on your computer. Follow the instructions on your screen.

Additionally some of the dialog boxes have fewer or additional options (such as the Font dialog box).

File ➥ Versions...

With Word 97, you can save multiple versions of a document. Imagine that each version is a snapshot of the document in time. After saving a document with versions, you can return to any version. Versions are an alternative to track changes (see **Tools ➥ Track Changes**, page 196). When you choose **File**, **Versions**, the Versions dialog box opens (see Figure 2.7).

❶ Click Save Now and add comments to create a new version.

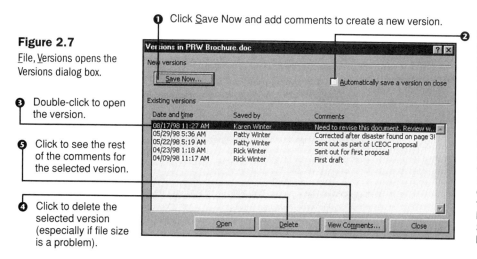

Figure 2.7
File, Versions opens the Versions dialog box.

❸ Double-click to open the version.

❺ Click to see the rest of the comments for the selected version.

❹ Click to delete the selected version (especially if file size is a problem).

❷ Check to create a new version when you close the document. This increases file size, but keeps a copy of each set of changes you make. Clear to save versions only when you use this command or click the Save Version button on the Save As dialog box.

File ➥ Page Setup...

The Page Setup dialog box has four tabs that control the formatting of the page as a whole including margins, size of the paper and orientation, trays for paper, and layout. Choose **File**, **Page Setup** and the Page Setup dialog box appears (see Figure 2.8). The table below describes the options on the dialog box.

Figure 2.8

File, Page Setup opens the Page Setup dialog box.

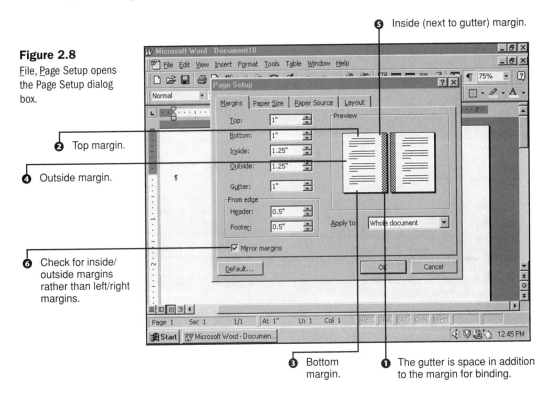

❺ Inside (next to gutter) margin.

❷ Top margin.

❹ Outside margin.

❻ Check for inside/outside margins rather than left/right margins.

❸ Bottom margin.

❶ The gutter is space in addition to the margin for binding.

Page Setup options

Dialog Box Item	Purpose
All tabs	
Apply to	Apply settings for margins, paper size, paper source, and layout to This Section of the document, from the cursor to This point forward, or to the Whole document.
Default	Change the Normal template (used when you create new documents) to include the settings on this dialog box. When you choose this option, Word prompts you to confirm this choice.

Dialog Box Item	Purpose
Margins tab	
Top	Set the space between the top edge of the page and where print starts.
Bottom	Set the space between the bottom edge of the page and the print area.
Le**f**t or **I**nside	Set the space on left side of the page or, if **Mirror margins** is selected, on the interior margins of facing pages.
Ri**g**ht or **O**utside	Set the space on the right side of page or, if **Mirror margins** is selected, on the exterior margins of facing pages.
G**u**tter	Area in addition to the left or inside margins for binding.
H**e**ader	Space between the edge of the page and where the header starts. If larger than the **T**op margin, text starts below the header.
Foote**r**	Space between the edge of a page and where the footer starts. If it is larger than **B**ottom margin, the text starts above the footer.
M**i**rror margins	Creates facing pages by making the right margin of the left page equal to the left margin of the right page.
Paper Size tab	
Pape**r** size	Change the paper size from Letter to Legal, A4, or envelopes.
Width	Change the page size across.
H**ei**ght	Change the page size up and down.
Portrai**t**	Printing runs across the width of the paper.
Lands**c**ape	Printing runs across the length of the paper.
Paper Source tab	
First page	These options depend on the printer. Choose which tray the first page of a document comes from. Sometimes letterhead is stored in one tray, while other paper is stored in another tray. Choose options such as upper or lower tray, paper cassette, envelope feeder, or manual feed.
Other pages	Choose which tray the second and subsequent pages print from.
Layout tab	
Section sta**r**t	For multiple sections, where to start the current section (on a new page, even or odd page, in a new column, or at the cursor— continuous).
Different **o**dd and even	Print one header and footer on odd pages and a different one on even pages. To add a header or footer, choose **V**iew, **H**eader and Footer (see page 93).

continues

Continued

Dialog Box Item	Purpose
Layout tab	
Different first page	Print different headers and footers on the first page versus other pages of the document.
Vertical alignment	Place the text at the top or center of page. The third option, justified, spreads multiple paragraphs so they are evenly spaced on an entire page.
Line Numbers	Add numbers in the margin for each line printed on the page. When you choose this option, the Line Numbers dialog box opens enabling you to choose the number to **Start at**, the space from the left edge of the text (**From text**) to the numbers, and the increment to **Count by**. You can also have numbering restart on each page, each section, or continue through the whole document.
Suppress endnotes	Print endnotes at the end of each section (see **Insert - Footnote**, page 131).

File ➥ Print Preview

Print Preview enables you to see a bird's-eye view of what your document will look like when printed. You can graphically change margins or see more than one page at a time. (Figure 2.9 shows a document in print preview mode. The following table the available toolbar buttons.)

Click the **Print Preview** icon or choose **File**, **Print Preview** to display a document in preview mode.

Buttons in Print Preview

Button	Name	Purpose
	Print	Prints document.
	Magnifier	Changes between magnify mode (mouse zooms in/out on document) and edit mode. In edit mode, you can type or format text. This is especially useful when inserting and moving pictures, changing columns, and working with page setup.
	One Page	Displays one page on the screen.
	Multiple Pages	Displays a drop-down box that enables you to choose how many documents to show on the screen at a time. Drag to display a number of pages down and across.
44%	**Zoom**	Changes the percentage to shrink or blow up the view of the document relative to its original size (100% approxi-

Button	Name	Purpose
		mates the size of a printed page). You can choose the drop-down arrow or type a number in the text box.
	View Ruler	Hides or displays the vertical and horizontal rulers.
	Shrink to Fit	Changes the margins and font size to try to fit slightly long documents onto one page.
	Full Screen	Displays the document without menus, toolbars, or the Status bar to see more on the screen. Click the **Close Full Screen** button or Press Esc to return to Print Preview.
Close	**Close Preview**	Returns to document. You can also choose **File, Print Preview** to deselect preview mode and get back to the document.
	Context Sensitive Help	Click this button and then any button or portion of the screen to get a pop-up help window explaining what you clicked.

From print preview you can also choose **File**, **Page Setup** (see page 38), make changes, and when you finish, you can see the effect on the page.

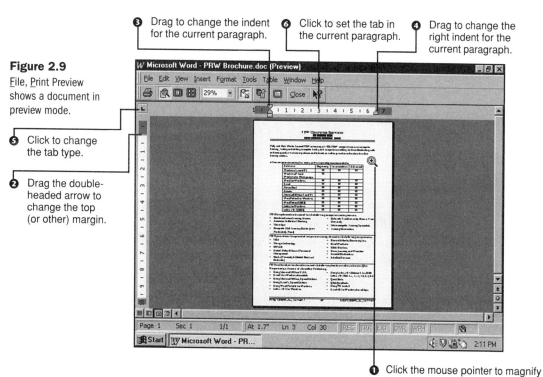

❸ Drag to change the indent for the current paragraph.

❻ Click to set the tab in the current paragraph.

❹ Drag to change the right indent for the current paragraph.

Figure 2.9
File, Print Preview shows a document in preview mode.

❺ Click to change the tab type.

❷ Drag the double-headed arrow to change the top (or other) margin.

❶ Click the mouse pointer to magnify the screen at that point.

File ➥ Print...

Quick Choices   PRINT

■ Click the **Print** button 🖨 on the Standard toolbar. The document prints to the default printer.

Follow these steps to send your document to a printer:

1. Choose **File**, **Print** or press **Ctrl+P**. The Print dialog box displays (see Figure 2.10).

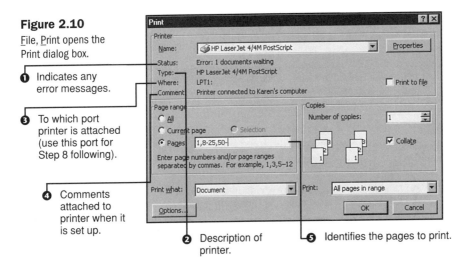

Figure 2.10
File, Print opens the
Print dialog box.

❶ Indicates any error messages.

❸ To which port printer is attached (use this port for Step 8 following).

❹ Comments attached to printer when it is set up.

❷ Description of printer.

❺ Identifies the pages to print.

2. To change the printer, or print to a fax, select from the **Name** drop-down box.

3. If you want to change Windows options for your printing, click the **Properties** button and change such things as paper size, paper orientation, where to get paper, and printer resolution. You want to change many of these options for the document through **File**, **Page Setup** instead (see page 38).

4. To print a portion of or the entire document, choose one of the following:

   ● Click **All** to print the entire document.

   ● Click the option button for the **Current page**.

   ● Click **Selection** to print if you have selected text.

   ● Type a range of page numbers in the **Pages** box. A dash (–) indicates print pages in the range between the two numbers. A dash following the last number indicates print all pages from the numbered page to the end of the document. Commas can separate pages and other ranges. An example of a print range is 1–3, 5, 21–. For sections, type a p for page and an s for the section number. An example of a print range with section numbers is p3s1–p5s2.

   ● Click the drop-down **Print what** to choose to print the document, the document properties, comments, a list of styles, AutoText entries, or key assignments.

5. Click the **Print** drop-down arrow to choose to print all the pages in the range or to print odd or even pages.

6. To print more than one copy, use the spinner buttons or text box to reset the **Number of copies**.

7. If you are printing more than one copy and you want them in sets, check **Collate**. With this option unchecked, you print multiple copies of page 1, page 2, and so on.

8. If you don't have the selected printer connected to your computer, choose to **Print to file** on your disk. When you choose **OK**, Word opens the Print to file dialog box. Give the file a name and location and click **OK** again. Word automatically gives the file a PRN extension.

   When you want to print the file, click the Windows **Start** button, choose **Programs**, **MS-DOS Prompt**. From the DOS window, type **COPY /B** *filename port*. A specific example would be **COPY /B c:\docs\print.prn lpt1**. (When using Print to file, you need to have the print driver for the destination printer installed, even if you are not attached to it.)

9. When finished setting dialog options, click **OK**.

File ▸ Print... Options

If you want to set options for printing all documents, you can choose **File**, **Print** and click the **Options** button on the Print dialog box. The Print options dialog box opens (see Figure 2.11). You can also choose **Tools**, **Options**, and click the **Print** tab.

Figure 2.11
File, Print, Options opens the Print option dialog box.

❶ You have only one tab when you enter through the Print dialog box; however, through Tools, Options, you have many tabs.

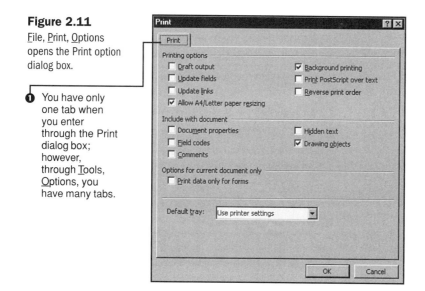

Print options

Dialog Box Item	Purpose
Print options section	
Draft output	This option is not supported by all printers. If it is supported, it prints with little formatting, which may help the document print faster.
Update fields	Updates the data in any fields (such as dates and calculations). Fields are generally entered through the **Insert**, **F**ield menu (see page 106).
Update **l**inks	If you have links to other documents (Word or other applications), this option updates the information in the link before printing. You can create a link through **Insert**, **Fi**le (see page 158) or **Insert**, **O**bject.
Allow A4/Letter paper r**e**sizing	Check this option to have Word automatically adjust the document to print on your country's standard paper size.
Background printing	Enables you to work while the document prints. To speed up printing, clear this check box.
Pri**n**t PostScript over text	Used for PRINT fields in converted Macintosh documents.
Reverse print order	Prints the last page first. Don't use this for envelopes.
Include with document section	
Docu**m**ent properties	Also print properties associated with the document. To enter properties choose **F**ile, **Proper**ties (see page 46).
Field codes	To print codes instead of the result of the code. To see codes onscreen press **Alt+F9**. Enter codes with **Insert**, **F**ield (see page 106).
Comments	Prints comments with the document. Enter comments with **Insert**, **Co**mment (see page 129).
H**i**dden text	Prints hidden text with the document. Hide selected text with **Format**, **F**ont... (see page 160).
Drawing **o**bjects	Prints circles, squares, text boxes, and other drawing objects. Draw objects with the Drawing toolbar.
Options for current document section	
Print data only for forms	If using forms, prints only the data from fields. To create a form, use the Forms toolbar and save the document as a template.
Other	
Default **t**ray	Choose the paper tray to use for documents. You can use the Windows printer settings or select a tray, manual feed, or an envelope feeder depending on the printer.

File ➟ Send To

The **File**, **Send To** menu enables you to transmit your document electronically to one or more recipients.

File ➟ Send To ➟ Mail Recipient...

To create an email message with the current document as an attachment, choose **File**, **Send To**, **Mail Recipient**. Your MAPI compliant email program opens. The default Subject is the first lines of your document (which you can edit). Complete the email by addressing whom the document is to, changing any other options you want, and sending the message.

File ➟ Send To ➟ Routing Recipient...

If you want to send the document to a list of people (all at once or one at a time), choose **File**, **Send To**, **Routing Recipient**. The Routing Slip dialog box opens (shown in Figure 2.12).

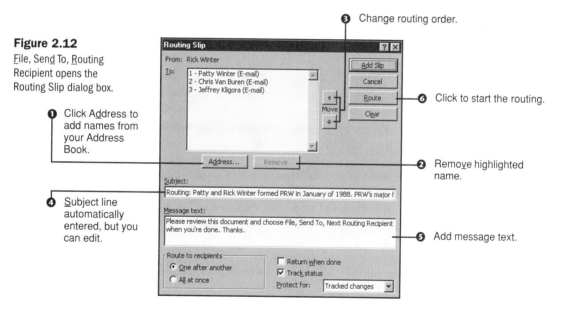

❸ Change routing order.

Figure 2.12
File, Send To, Routing Recipient opens the Routing Slip dialog box.

❶ Click Address to add names from your Address Book.

❹ Subject line automatically entered, but you can edit.

❻ Click to start the routing.

❷ Remove highlighted name.

❺ Add message text.

After you click **Route**, the message may be sent or it may go to your Outbox. If it is in your Outbox, start your email program and send messages (in Outlook press **F5**) to start the routing.

Additional options on the Routing Slip dialog box not described in Figure 2.12 can be found below:

Dialog Box Item	Purpose
Add Slip	Adds the routing slip to the document but does not send it. To send, choose **File**, **Send To**, **Next Routing Recipient** (the menu changes from the original **Send To** menu). You can choose from two options to route the document or send a copy of the document without the routing slip.

continues

Dialog Box Item	Purpose
Cl**e**ar	Removes all recipients from the **To** list and **Message text**. Also restores the **Subject** box.
One after another	Routes the document to the first person in the To box. When they are done, they choose **File**, **Send To**, **Next Routing Recipient** (Word automatically adds instructions in the email message).
A**ll** at once	Everybody gets the message at once with tracked changes. To merge the returned documents, choose **Tools**, **Merge Documents** (see page 199).
Return **w**hen done	When the last person closes the document, it is automatically sent back to you by email.
Trac**k** status	You get an email when each person forwards to the next person.
Protect for	Choose Comments for reviewers to add notes but not change contents of the document. Choose Tracked Changes to turn on revision marking. Choose Forms if the document is a form that you want filled out. None does not allow any changes to be tracked.

File ➥ Sen**d** To ➥ **E**xchange Folder...

You may have a storage place in Outlook for documents that you would like to save. To place the document in a Folder in Exchange or Outlook, choose **File**, **Send To**, **Exchange Folder** to open the Send to Exchange Folder dialog box. Navigate to the folder you want, and click **OK**.

File ➥ Sen**d** To ➥ **F**ax Recipient...

You can create a cover sheet and fax to one or more people as long as you have a fax modem. When you choose **File**, **Send To**, **Fax Recipient**, the Fax Wizard dialog box opens. Click **Next** to go to each step of the wizard to choose a cover sheet, recipients, and information about yourself. On the recipient list you can choose from people you've already faxed to or go into your address book. If you chose a cover sheet, you return to Word where you can edit the cover sheet. When finished, click the **Send Fax Now** button. You can also fax a document by choosing **File**, **Print** and selecting the Fax from the **Name** drop-down list.

File ➥ Sen**d** To ➥ Microsoft **P**owerPoint

If you create an outline, (see **View ➥ Outline**, page 63) you can create PowerPoint slides. Choose **File**, **Send To**, **Microsoft PowerPoint**. PowerPoint launches. Each Heading 1 style becomes the title of the slide. Heading 2 (and lower level) styles become the bullets on the slides.

File ➥ Propert**i**es

File properties enable you to identify and categorize your file in more detail than you can with just a name. You can add notes in many different fields (such as **Subject** and **Comments**). File properties also enable you to see more information about your file, such as the number of words, the creation date, and the MS-DOS name.

Quick Choices USE ANY OF THE FOLLOWING OPTIONS TO WORK WITH FILE PROPERTIES

- Choose **File**, **Properties** to view the Properties dialog box (see Figure 2.13).

- In a file dialog box (**File**, **Open**, page 21, or **File**, **Save As**, page 29), right-click a file and choose **Properties**.

- To print the properties with the current document, choose **File**, **Print**, and in the **Print what** drop-down choose Document properties.

- To print properties with all documents, choose **File**, **Print**, click the **Options** button, and check **Document properties**.

- To change DOS file attributes, right-click the Windows **Start** button, choose **Explore**, right-click the file, and choose **Properties**.

- To search on any of the file Properties, from a file dialog box (see **File** – **Open**, page 21), click the **Advanced** button, click the **Property** drop-down, select the property, and fill out the **Condition** and **Value** boxes (see **File** – **Open... – Find a File**, p. 24).

Figure 2.13 shows the options on the General tab.

Figure 2.13
File, Properties opens the Properties dialog box.

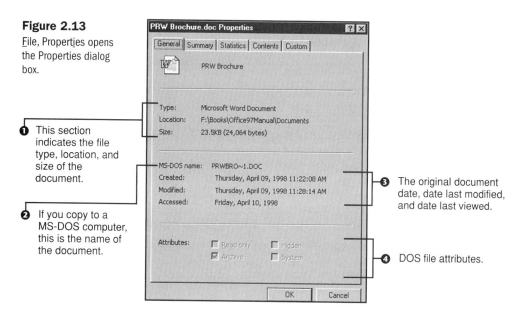

❶ This section indicates the file type, location, and size of the document.

❷ If you copy to a MS-DOS computer, this is the name of the document.

❸ The original document date, date last modified, and date last viewed.

❹ DOS file attributes.

File ↪ Properties Summary Tab

The Summary tab enables you to categorize the file with a number of fields including **Title**, **Subject**, **Author**, **Manager**, **Company**, **Category**, **Keywords**, and **Comments**. The Summary tab also has the **Hyperlink base** text box. If you insert hyperlinks (see **Insert** – **Hyperlink**, page 159), type a path in **Hyperlink Base** where the hyperlinks in the document start. Check the **Save preview picture** box to save a picture of the first page of the file for viewing in the Open dialog box.

File ➧ Properties Statistics Tab

This tab shows the dates mentioned on the General tab and includes the last date printed, by whom the file was last saved, how many times the file has been open and edited (**Revision number**), and the total time the file has been opened while edited (**Total editing time**). The **Statistics** box also shows the number of pages, paragraphs, lines, words, and characters.

File ➧ Properties Contents Tab

The Contents tab shows the first line of the document.

File ➧ Properties Custom Tab

In addition to the fields on the Summary tab, you can input many more properties and even add your own in the Custom tab. Do the following:

1. Click a property in the **Name** list or type a new property.
2. If desired, change the **Type** of information that the field contains (Text, Date, Number, Yes or no).
3. Type a **Value** in the text box, or if bookmarks are defined, you can check **Link to content** and choose the bookmark from the **Source** drop-down.
4. Click the **Add** button (or **Modify**, if you're changing a property already filled out). The property displays in the **Properties** section.
5. If you want to remove a property, click it in the **Properties** section and click the **Delete** button.

File ➧ Recent Used File List

To open one of the last documents you saved, choose **File** and select one of the files at the bottom of the file menu. The hot keys are numbered for each of the files (1, 2, 3, and so on) with the last file saved indicated with a number 1. If the names do not display at the bottom of the **File** menu, do the following:

1. Choose **Tools, Options**. The Options dialog box displays.
2. Click the **General** tab.
3. Type or use the **entries** spinner button to change the number of files you want to see in the **Recently used file list**.
4. Click **OK**.

Word displays the number of files you chose in step 3.

If you want to remove a filename from the recently used file list, press **Ctrl+Alt+–** (minus), click the **File** menu and then the filename.

File ➧ Exit

To get out of Word, do one of the following:

Quick Choices — *EXIT WORD*

- Press **Alt+F4**.
- Click the application close button (the X in the upper-right corner of the screen).
- Choose **File**, **Exit**.

Word asks whether you want to save each document changed since your last save. If you choose **Yes** and have not given the document a name, you enter the Save As dialog box (see **File – Save As...**, page 29).

Edit

The Edit menu enables you to make changes to the document as a whole: undo and repeat commands; cut, copy, and paste information; select the entire document; delete selected information; find specific information in a document; replace information that has been found; create links; and edit objects.

Edit ➧ Undo...

The first item on the Edit menu enables you to Undo specific actions.

Quick Choices — *USE ANY OF THE FOLLOWING METHODS TO UNDO AN ACTION*

- Click **Undo** on the Standard toolbar.
- Choose **Edit**, **Undo Action**. The bracketed action is the last action you performed—for instance, Typing, Formatting, Insert Cells, and so on.
- Press **Ctrl+Z**. The last action you performed is undone.

Quick Choices — *UNDO MULTIPLE ACTIONS*

- Click the drop-down arrow on the **Undo** button, and select the actions you want to undo. All the actions up to the one you select are undone.

Redo

Redo does not appear on the Edit menu, but it is a valuable tool to use with Undo. Click **Redo** on the Standard toolbar to redo what you have undone. You can also click the drop-down arrow on the Redo button to select multiple items to redo.

Edit ➥ Repeat

Choose **Edit**, **Repeat** or press **F4** or **Ctrl+Y** to repeat the last action or command.

Edit ➥ Cut

The **Cut** command enables you to remove selected text and place it on the Windows Clipboard to **Paste** somewhere else.

Quick Choices *CHOOSE ANY OF THE FOLLOWING METHODS TO CUT A SELECTION*

- Click **Cut** 🔳 on the Standard toolbar.
- Press **Ctrl+X**.
- Choose **Edit**, **Cut**.
- Right-click the selection and choose **Cut**.
- Drag and drop—Point to the selected text. When the mouse pointer changes to a white arrow, click and drag the selection to the new location.
- Right-click and drag the selection to the new location, and then select **Move Here**, **Copy Here**, **Create Hyperlink Here**, or **Cancel**.

Spike

The Spike command does not appear on any menu but is a valuable tool to move text and graphics from nonadjacent locations. To use the Spike, you remove or cut two or more items from nonadjacent locations, which appends each item to the Spike's contents. Then you insert the items as a group in a new location or document. The items remain in the Spike so that you can insert them repeatedly or add additional items. If you want to add a different set of items to the Spike, you must first empty the Spike's contents.

To move selected items to the Spike, do the following:

1. Select the text or graphic you want, and press **Ctrl+F3**. Repeat this step for each additional item you want to move to the Spike.
2. Move the insertion point where you want to insert the Spike's contents.

Do the following to insert the Spike's contents:

- To insert the Spike's contents without emptying the Spike, type spike and press **F3**.
- To insert the Spike's contents and empty the Spike, press **Ctrl+Shift+F3**.

To view the contents of the Spike, follow these steps:

1. Choose **Insert**, **AutoText**, **AutoText**.
2. In the **Enter AutoText entries here** list box, scroll to Spike or begin typing spike in the text box. When you see spike in the list, click on it and look in the **Preview** box to see the Spike's contents.

You can also insert or delete the contents of the Spike from the AutoText dialog box. (See **Insert ▸ AutoText ▸ AutoText...** on page 101 for more information.)

Edit ▸ Copy

The **Copy** command enables you to copy selected text and place it on the Windows Clipboard to paste somewhere else.

Quick Choices **CHOOSE ANY OF THE FOLLOWING OPTIONS TO COPY A SELECTION**

- Click **Copy** 🖹 on the Standard toolbar.
- Press **Ctrl+C**.
- Choose **Edit**, **Copy**.
- Right-click the selection and choose **Copy**.
- Drag and drop—Point to the selection. When the mouse pointer changes to a white arrow, hold down the **Ctrl** key, and click and drag the selection to the new location.
- Right-click and drag the selection to the new location, and then select **Move Here**, **Copy Here**, **Create Hyperlink Here**, or **Cancel**.

Edit ▸ Paste

The **Paste** command enables you to paste what is on the Windows Clipboard at the location of the insertion point. Used with **Edit**, **Cut**, you move the original text. Used with **Edit**, **Copy**, you create a copy of the original text.

Quick Choices **CHOOSE ANY OF THE FOLLOWING METHODS TO QUICKLY PASTE A SELECTION**

- Click **Paste** 🖹 on the Standard toolbar.
- Press **Ctrl+V**.
- Choose **Edit**, **Paste**.
- Right-click where you want to insert the copied information and choose **Paste**.

Move Text or Graphics

Although you can move text or graphics by cutting and pasting, it's sometimes easier to press **F2**. If you prefer using the mouse you can also use the drag-and-drop procedure.

To move a selection using the **F2** shortcut:

1. Select the text or graphics to move.
2. Press **F2**.
3. Move the insertion point to the new location and press **Enter.**

Do the following to move a selection using Drag-and-Drop:

1. Select the text or graphics to move.

2. Point to the selected item; the mouse pointer changes to a white arrow pointing to the left.

3. Click and drag the selected item to the new location.

Alternatively, you can right-click and drag the item to the new location. If you choose this method, a shortcut menu is displayed when you release the mouse button. You can then choose to **Move**, **Copy**, **Link**, or **Create a Hyperlink** with the selected item. (See the **Edit ▸ Paste as Hyperlink** section on page 54 for more information on Hyperlinks.)

Edit ▸ Paste Special...

The **Paste Special** command enables you to paste, link, or embed what is on the Windows Clipboard (at the location of the insertion point) with the formatting you specify. To use the Paste Special command Choose **Edit**, **Paste Special**. The Paste Special dialog box displays. (see Figure 2.14).

Figure 2.14
Choose Edit, Paste Special to open the Paste Special dialog box.

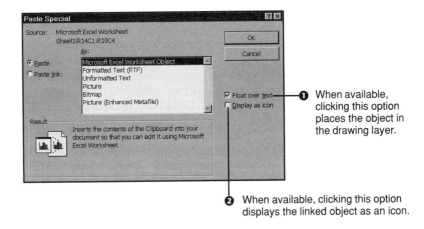

① When available, clicking this option places the object in the drawing layer.

② When available, clicking this option displays the linked object as an icon.

Depending on the source application, when you choose the **Paste Special** option the following formats, **as well as Float over text**, and **Display as icon** options may be available.

The **Float over text** option places the object in the drawing layer, where you can position it in front of or behind text and other objects using commands on the Drawing toolbar. If you clear this check box to place the object inline, in the current paragraph, it behaves like regular text.

The **Display as icon** displays the linked or embedded object as an icon so that you can open or edit the object by double-clicking the icon.

Option	Format	Float Over Text—Active	Display as Icon—Active
Application Object	Inserts the object so you can edit it with the source application.	Yes	Yes

Option	Format	Float Over Text—Active	Display as Icon—Active
Formatted Text (RTF)	Inserts the contents of the Clipboard as text with table and font formatting.	No	No
Unformatted Text	Inserts the contents of the Clipboard with no formatting.	No	No
Picture	Inserts the contents of the Clipboard as a picture. This option takes the least amount of space to store and displays the quickest.	No	Yes
Bitmap	Inserts the contents of the Clipboard as a bitmap. This format is exactly what you see on screen, but takes a lot of memory and disk space and is slower than picture to display.	Yes	No
Picture (Enhanced Metafile)	Inserts the contents of the Clipboard as an enhanced metafile.	No	No

When you choose the **Paste link** option any changes in the source document are reflected in the active document. Depending on the source application, the following formats, **Float over text**, and **Display as icon** options may be available:

Option	Format	Float Over Text—Active	Display as Icon—Active
Application Object	Inserts the contents of the Clipboard as a picture and creates a shortcut to the source file.	Yes	Yes
Formatted Text (RTF)	Inserts the contents of the Clipboard as text with table and font formatting and creates a shortcut to the source file.	No	Yes
Unformatted Text	Inserts the contents of the Clipboard with no formatting and creates a shortcut to the source file.	No	Yes

continues

Option	Format	Float Over Text—Active	Display as Icon—Active
Picture	Inserts the contents of the Clipboard as a picture and creates a shortcut to the source file.	Yes	Yes
Bitmap	Inserts the contents of the Clipboard as a bitmap and creates a shortcut to the source file.	Yes	Yes
Word Hyperlink	Inserts the contents of the Clipboard as text with table and font formatting. Creates a hyperlink to the source document. Click the hyperlink to jump to the source document	No	No

1. Choose **Paste** or **Paste link**.
2. In the **As** list box, choose one of the available formats.
3. If necessary, select the **Float over text** option to turn it on or off.
4. If necessary, select the **Display as icon** option to turn it on or off.
5. Choose **OK** to paste your selection in the active document.

Edit ➥ Paste as Hyperlink

The **Paste as Hyperlink** command enables you to paste Clipboard contents as a hyperlink. A hyperlink creates a shortcut to the source document. Click the hyperlink to jump to the source document. If the application that created the hyperlink is not open, both the application and the document open.

Quick **Choices** *ADD A HYPERLINK*

■ After you have cut or copied text to the Clipboard, move the insertion point to the location where you want to paste and click the **Add Hyperlink** button 📷 on the Standard toolbar.

or

■ Select the text to be moved, right-click and drag it to the new location, and choose Create Hyperlink Here.

Edit ➥ Clear

Choose **Edit**, **Clear** or press Delete to delete the selected text or object without placing it on the Clipboard.

Other Delete options

To	Press
Delete one character to the left	**Backspace**
Delete one word to the left	**Ctrl+Backspace**
Delete one character to the right	**Delete**
Delete one word to the right	**Ctrl+Delete**

Edit ➥ Select All

Choose **Edit, Select All** or press Ctrl+A to select the whole document.

Other Select options

To Extend a Selection	Press
One character to the right	**Shift+→**
One character to the left	**Shift+←**
To the end of a word	**Ctrl+Shift+→**
To the beginning of a word	**Ctrl+Shift+←**
To the end of a line	**Shift+End**
To the beginning of a line	**Shift+Home**
One line down	**Shift+↓**
One line up	**Shift+↑**
To the end of a paragraph	**Ctrl+Shift+↓**
To the beginning of a paragraph	**Ctrl+Shift+↑**
One screen down	**Shift+Page Down**
One screen up	**Shift+Page Up**
To the beginning of the document	**Ctrl+Shift+Home**
To the end of the document	**Ctrl+Shift+End**

Edit ➥ Find...

The **Edit, Find** command enables you to search for text, symbols, comments, endnotes, foot-notes and formatting commands. To use the Find command, do the following:

1. Press **Ctrl+F**.

2. Type what you are looking for in the **Find what** text box, and choose the **Find Next** button or press **Enter**.

You may find that it is easier to press **Shift+F4** without the Find and Replace dialog box open, to repeat the last Find action. Using this shortcut enables you to see the document without the dialog box in the way.

Setting the Find and Replace Tabs Options

To set options for using either the Find or Replace tabs in the Find and Replace dialog box:

1. Choose **Edit, Find** to display the Find and Replace dialog box (see Figure 2.15).

Figure 2.15
Choose Edit, Find to display the Find and Replace dialog box.

Click this button to expand the dialog box to show additional search options.

2. If necessary, type what you want to search for in the Find what text box.
3. Select any additional options (see Figure 2.16 and the following table for a description of all the options).

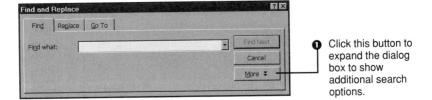

Figure 2.16
The More button changes to Less to shrink the dialog box.

❶ Click this pull-down arrow to choose the direction of the search.

❷ Choose one of these options to enhance the search.

❸ Choose this button to select formatting options to include in the search.

❹ Choose this button to include special characters in the search.

Find and Replace dialog box options

Option	Description
Search	Searches forward (Down), backward (Up), or through the entire document (All).
Match case	Matches capitalization (uppercase, lowercase, initial caps) when searching for text.

Option	Description
Find whole words only	Finds a match that is an entire word only (if you are looking for **the**, Word doesn't find other or their).
Use wildcards	Use with special characters. A question mark (?) is a wild card for any one character. An asterisk (*) is a wild card for any number of characters. **S?t** finds Sat, Sit, Set. **S*t** finds all the preceding items as well as Soot, Sachet, Saddest, and others.
Sounds like	Searches for different spellings of words that sound the same. If you're looking for **there**, Word finds their, there, and they're.
Find all word forms	Searches for all the different grammatical forms of a word. If you type **is** in the Find what text box, Word finds is, are, be, am.
No Formatting	Removes formatting from the search criteria if any formatting is added with the Format button.
Format	Searches for an item that includes Font, Paragraph, Tabs, Language, Frame, Styles, and Highlight formatting commands.
Special	Searches for special characters such as Paragraph Mark (^p), Tab Character (^t), Manual Line Break (^l), Field (^d), Section Breaks (^b), and many others.

4. Choose the **Find Next** button.

5. When you get to the first occurrence of the item, you can choose **Find Next** again, **Cancel**, or click the **Replace** tab. (For more information about Replace, see the next section, **Edit - Replace....**)

Edit ➡ Replace...

The **Edit**, **Replace** command enables you to search for and replace text, symbols, comments, endnotes, footnotes and formatting commands.

To use the Replace command, take these steps:

1. Press **Ctrl+H** or choose **Edit**, **Find**.

2. Type what you are looking for in the **Find what** text box.

3. Type what you want to replace in the **Replace with** text box.

4. Select any additional options (use the Find and Replace table in the preceding **Edit - Find...** section, page 55 for a description of all the options).

5. Choose the **Find Next** button.

6. To replace the found text with the new text, choose the **Replace** button. To replace all occurrences of the found text with the new text, choose **Replace All.** To skip this occurrence of the found text and continue the search, choose the **Find Next** button. To end this session, choose the **Cancel** button.

7. When there are no more occurrences of the **Find what** text, Word displays the message "Word has finished searching the document." Choose **OK**, and then **Cancel**.

<u>E</u>dit ➥ <u>G</u>o To...

The **Edit**, **Go To** command moves the insertion point to the item you want to go to. You can choose to go to a page number, comment, bookmark, footnote, or other location.

To use the <u>G</u>o To command, follow these steps:

1. Press **Ctrl+G** to open the Go To dialog box.

2. Enter the Page number you want to go to and choose the **Go <u>T</u>o** button or press **Enter**.

3. Click the **Next** ▼ or **Previous** ▲ buttons on the vertical scrollbar to go to the next or previous item of the same type.

With the Go To dialog box closed, press **Shift+F4** or **F5** to repeat the last Go To action.

Another method for using the Go To function is to click the **Select Browse Object** ⊙ button on the vertical scrollbar, or press **Ctrl+Alt+Home**, and then click the item you want from the pop-up menu that appears (see Figure 2.17). (See the table below for a description of your choices.)

Figure 2.17
Click the Select Browse Object button to see your choices.

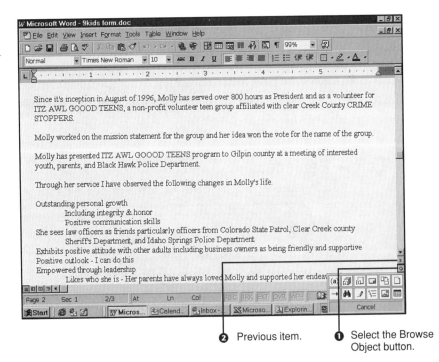

❷ Previous item. ❶ Select the Browse Object button.

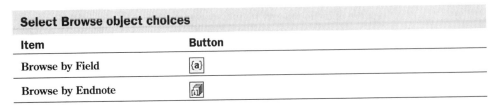

Select Browse object choices

Item	Button
Browse by Field	{a}
Browse by Endnote	🔢

Item	Button
Browse by Footnote	
Browse by Comment	
Browse by Section	
Browse by Page	
Go To	
Find	
Browse by Edits	
Browse by Heading	
Browse by Graphic	
Browse by Table	

Setting the G<u>o</u> To Tab Options

To set the G<u>o</u> To tab options:

1. Choose **<u>E</u>dit**, **<u>G</u>o To** to display the G<u>o</u> To dialog box (see Figure 2.18).

Figure 2.18
Choose <u>E</u>dit, <u>G</u>o To to display the Go To tab on the Find and Replace dialog box.

❶ Choose the element you want to go to.

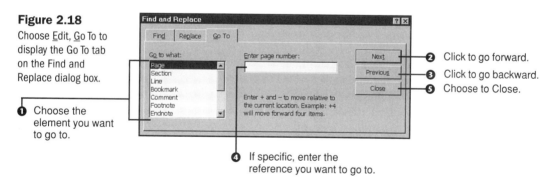

❷ Click to go forward.
❸ Click to go backward.
❺ Choose to Close.

❹ If specific, enter the reference you want to go to.

G<u>o</u> To options

G<u>o</u> To What	What You <u>E</u>nter
Page	Page number
Section	Section number
Line	Line number
Bookmark	Bookmark name
Comment	Reviewer's name

continues

Continued

Go To What	What You Enter
Footnote	Footnote number
Endnote	Endnote number
Field	Field name
Table	Table number
Graphic	Graphic number
Equation	Equation number
Object	Any object, or by application name, i.e. Calendar Control, Microsoft Clip Gallery, and so on
Heading	Heading number

2. Optionally, in the Enter page number text box, enter + or – and a number to move relative to the current location for every item except bookmark. For example, in the Go to what list box, select Page and in the Enter page number text box, type **-2**. You can even enter a percentage to move to that area of the document. For example, enter 50% to move to the middle of the document.

3. Choose the **Go To** button.

4. Choose **Close** or press **Esc** when you are finished using Go To.

Edit ➡ Links...

Edit, **Links** remains dimmed until you have linked objects. After you have linked objects you may need to edit the information related to the object. If you move the source document or change the name of the document, the link is broken and you get an error in the target document.

To use the Links function, take the following steps:

1. Choose **Edit**, **Links** to display the Links dialog box (see Figure 2.19).

Figure 2.19
Edit, Links opens the Links dialog box.

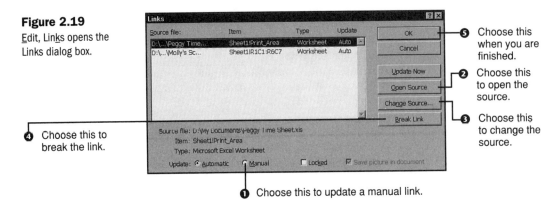

Choose this to break the link.

Choose this when you are finished.

Choose this to open the source.

Choose this to change the source.

Choose this to update a manual link.

2. In the **Source file** list box, select the file or files you want to work with.

3. In the Update options section, select one of the following:

- **Automatic** to have the link updated every time the data is available.
- **Manual** to require updating through the **Update Now** choice or by selecting the link and pressing **F9**.
- **Locked** to prevent updates to the link. This choice dims the **Automatic** and **Manual** choices.
- **Save picture in document** to clear this check box and store a link to a graphic in your document, instead of storing the graphic itself. When you store only the link you reduce the size of your document. To edit the graphic in your document, you must first select the **Save picture in document** check box.

Change the Source

If you choose the **Change Source** button on the Links dialog box, the Change Source dialog box is displayed (see Figure 2.20). Notice that it looks very similar to the Open and Save As dialog boxes. (For more information about using these dialog boxes, see **File ▪ Open...** on page 21, and **File ▪ Save As...** on page 29.)

❶ Navigate to the location   ❷ Select the file.
for the source file.

Figure 2.20
Choose Edit, Links and then choose Change Source to display this dialog box.

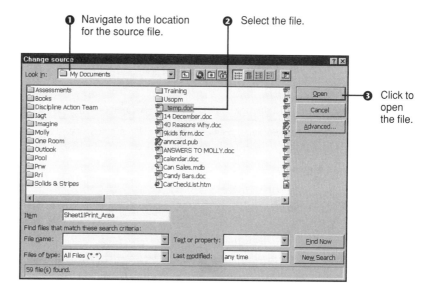

❸ Click to open the file.

Edit ➥ Object

Edit, Object is available if you have an object selected. The menu name and additional choices change to reflect the type of object that is selected. These menu commands may relate to the **Edit, Paste Special** choices and the **Edit, Links** choices. (For more information see the **Edit ▪ Paste Special...** section on page 52, and the **Edit ▪ Links...** section on page 60.)

Some of the Edit, Object choices

Command	Description
Edit	Opens the source application and enables you to edit the object in place.
Open	Opens the source application and enables you to edit the object in a separate window.
Replace	Opens the source application so that you can replace the object.
Convert	Converts an OLE object from one type to another.

Use the shortcut menu to edit an object. Right-click an object and select one of the commands in the following table.

Edit commands on the shortcut menu

Command	Description
Add Text	Places the insertion point in the object so that you can type text.
Edit Text	Selects the added text for you to edit. **Add Text** and **Edit Text** replace each other on the shortcut menu.
Grouping	If you have more than one object selected, this gives you the grouping submenu options: **Group**, **Ungroup**, and **Regroup**.
Order	Displays the submenu options: **Bring to Front**, **Send to Back**, **Bring Forward**, **Send Backward**, **Bring in Front of Text**, **Send Behind Text**.
Create Text Box Link	Links text boxes (see **Insert - Text Box** on page 156).
Set AutoShape Defaults	Sets formatting for all the AutoShapes that you insert to these settings (see **Format - Object...** on page 183).
Format AutoShape	Opens the Format AutoShape dialog box (see **Format - Object...** on page 183).

View

The View menu changes the way your screen looks. You can change the view to see rulers and headers and footers and make the view larger or smaller.

View ➡ Normal

The normal view is the default view for most typing and editing. Headers, footers, and margins do not show.

Quick Choices   *GO TO NORMAL VIEW*

- Click the **Normal** button ▤ on the bottom left of the horizontal scrollbar.
- Press **Ctrl+Alt+N**.
- Choose **View**, **Normal.**

View ➥ Online Layout

Online Layout view enables you to see how a document will look as a Web page. To get back to Normal view, choose **View**, **Normal** or press **Ctrl+Alt+N**.

View ➥ Page Layout

Page Layout view shows how the entire page will look including headers and footers, page numbers, and margins.

Quick Choices   *CHANGE TO PAGE LAYOUT*

- Click the **Page Layout View** button ▣ on the bottom left of the horizontal scrollbar.
- Press **Ctrl+Alt+P**.
- Choose **View**, **Page Layout**.

While in Page Layout view, it is easier to change and view the margins of the document, edit the header or footer, and change tabs and indents.

Quick Choices   *FORMATTING PAGE AND PARAGRAPHS IN PAGE LAYOUT*

- Drag the double-headed arrow mouse pointer on the vertical or horizontal ruler (between the white and dark gray rectangles) to change margins (see also **File ➥ Page Setup**, page 38).
- Use the horizontal ruler to change tabs (click to set a tab) and indents (drag to change the indent) for the selected paragraphs (see **View ➥ Ruler**, page 92, for more detailed description).
- Double-click a header or footer to edit it (see **View ➥ Header and Footer**, page 93).

View ➥ Outline

Outline view enables you to create and organize your work by heading styles. Each progressive Heading level (1, 2, 3, and so on) is displayed.

Quick Choices   *CHANGE TO OUTLINE VIEW*

- Click the **Outline View** button ▤ on the bottom left of the horizontal scrollbar.
- Press **Ctrl+Alt+O**.
- Choose **View**, **Outline.**

Outline view displays a toolbar, which functions as follows:

Outlining toolbar buttons

Button	Name	Purpose
⬅	**Promote**	Move a heading one level higher (Heading 2 becomes Heading 1). You can also press Shift+Tab or drag the plus or minus to the left.
➡	**Demote**	Move a heading one level lower. You can also press Tab or drag the plus or minus to the right.
⮕	**Demote to Body Text**	Change from any Heading style to Normal text style.
⬆ ⬇	**Move Up or Move Down**	Move the selected paragraph(s) to precede the previous paragraph or to follow the next paragraph. If you have subordinate paragraphs collapsed under the selected paragraph, they are also moved together with the selected paragraph. You can also drag the open plus or minus symbol.
✚	**Expand**	Show collapsed paragraph(s) one level at a time. To expand an entire section, double-click the plus sign to the left of the paragraph.
▬	**Collapse**	Hide subordinated paragraph(s) one level at a time. To collapse an entire section, double-click the plus sign to the left of the paragraph. A thin gray line indicates collapsed paragraphs.
1 2 3 4 5 6 7	**Show Heading 1-7**	Show all paragraph headings leading up to the given level. If you click Show Heading 3, Word displays all paragraphs for Heading 1, 2, and 3 styles.
All	**Show Navigating All Headings**	Display everything (headings and body text).
▬	**Show First Line Only**	Hide all but the first line of every Body Text paragraph. An ellipsis (...) indicates that other lines are hidden.
ᴬ/A	**Show Formatting**	Display paragraphs with their fonts and other formatting. If not selected, all heading levels look the same.
▤	**Master Document View**	Turn on the Master Document toolbar and show subdocument icons (see **View - Master Document** in the next section).

To add numbering to your outline, select the entire outline and choose **Format**, **Bullets and Numbering**, click the **Outline Numbered** tab, click one of the styles, and click **OK**. (For more information, see **Format - Bullets and Numbering**, page 166.)

View ⇒ Master Document

Master Document view enables you to show, insert, and manage subdocuments which are separate files that you can work on together or individually. Subdocuments enable you to work together in teams or to manage complex, large documents. When you choose **View**, **Master Document** or click the **Master Document** button 🗐 on the Outlining toolbar, the Master Document toolbar appears.

Master Document toolbar buttons

Button	Name	Purpose
🔁	**Collapse Subdocuments**	Click to toggle between showing the text in subdocuments and only one, hyperlinked line for the subdocument. When the subdocuments are collapsed, you can click the hyperlink to go to the subdocument. Close the subdocument to return to the master document.
📄	**Create Subdocument**	Click after selecting part or all of an outline. The first Heading style selected and all of the same level become subdocuments.
📄	**Remove Subdocument**	Click a subdocument to convert the selected subdocuments to text.
📄	**Insert Subdocument**	Click to display the Insert Subdocument dialog box. Find the file you want and double-click to add the file as a subdocument (see **File - Open...**, page 21, for notes on how to use the file dialog box).
📄	**Merge Subdocument**	Select two or more subdocuments that are directly adjacent to each other (no text or spaces between the subdocuments). Then click this button to convert two or more subdocuments into one subdocument.
📄	**Split Subdocument**	Select any line except the first line in a subdocument and click to split the original subdocument into two subdocuments.
📄	**Lock Subdocument**	Click while in a subdocument to prevent editing, adding and deleting text, merging, and splitting the subdocument. You can still click the **Delete Subdocument** button. Click the **Lock Subdocument** button again to unlock.

While in a master document you can double-click the subdocument icon on the upper-left edge to open the subdocument. If you want to change the name of the document, do it here while the master document is open (see **File ‑ Save As...**, page 29). If you rename a subdocument without the master document open, the link breaks between the subdocument and the master document.

After working in Master Document view, switch to **Normal Document View** ☰ to print the document 🖨 and add headers and footers (see **View ‑ Header and Footer**, page 93), a table of contents and index (see **Insert ‑ Index and Tables**, page 137), and cross-references (see **Insert ‑ Cross-reference**, page 136). You can also use the features of Outline view while in master documents (see **View ‑ Outline**, page 63).

View ➥ Toolbars

To get many of your tasks done quickly, use a toolbar button rather than a menu item. The toolbar button (or a keyboard shortcut) usually is the quickest way to accomplish a task, while the corresponding menu item gives you more details.

Quick Choices   TOOLBARS

- ■ To display most toolbars, right-click any toolbar and choose the toolbar from the shortcut menu.
- ■ To see what a tool does, hover over the tool to display the screen tip.
- ■ If screen tips don't show, choose **Tools**, **Options**, **View Tab**, and check the **Screen Tips** check box.
- ■ To see a longer description of a tool, press **Shift+F1** and click the tool.
- ■ To use the keyboard with a toolbar, press **F10** to get to the menu bar and press **Ctrl+Tab** or **Ctrl+Shift+Tab** to get to the next or previous toolbar. Press **Tab** or **Shift+Tab** when the toolbar is active to go to the buttons. Use **Up** and **Down** arrow keys to move through a list on a button with a drop-down arrow. Press **Enter** when you want to activate the button.

View ‑ Toolbars ‑ Standard

The Standard toolbar is one of the two default toolbars that appear on your screen unless you turn them off. Some of the features you use the most (such as opening a file, saving, and printing) are on this toolbar.

Standard toolbar buttons		
Button	**Name**	**How to Use**
🗋	New	Click to create a new document based on the Normal.dot template.

Button	Name	How to Use
	Open	Click to display the Open dialog box. Double-click the file you want to open (see **File – Open...**page 21).
	Save	Click to save the document with the existing name or to display the Save As dialog box if no name is yet given. Type a filename in the **File name** text box (see **File – Save As...**, page 29).
	Print	Click to print the document. For additional options, see **File – Print...**, page 42.
	Print Preview	Click to see what the document will look like when printed (see **File – Print Preview**, page 40).
	Spelling and Grammar	Click to open the Spelling and Grammar dialog box. Click the **Change** button to make a suggested change or Ignore to skip the word or phrase (see **Tools – Spelling and Grammar...**, page 188).
	Cut	Click to place the cut selection onto the Clipboard (see **Edit – Cut**, page 50).
	Copy	Click to place a copy of selection onto the Clipboard (see **Edit – Copy**, page 51).
	Paste	Click to paste what you cut or copied into the document (see **Edit – Paste**, page 51).
	Format Painter	Click the text whose format you want to pick up. Then click the button and click the text to format it. If you want to format multiple sections, double-click the button, then paint the sections you want to format. Click the **Format Painter** button again to turn it off.
	Undo	Click to cancel the last thing you did. You can cancel the last series of items you did by choosing them from the drop-down arrow (see **Edit – Undo**, page 49).
	Redo	Click to cancel the Undo for the last item, or click the drop-down arrow for the last series of items.
	Insert Hyperlink	Click to open the Insert Hyperlink dialog box. Type the hyperlink in the **Link to File or URL** text box (see **Insert – Hyperlink...**, page 159).

continues

Continued

Button	Name	How to Use
	Web Toolbar	Click to show or hide the Web toolbar (see **View - Toolbars - Web**, page 85).
	Tables and Borders	Click to begin drawing a table. Drag the pencil mouse pointer to form a rectangle. Then drag the pencil horizontally and vertically to create rows and columns. This also activates the Tables and Borders toolbar (see **View - Toolbars - Tables and Borders**, page 82).
	Insert Table	Click and drag in a grid to insert a table with a number of rows and columns. If a row or column is selected, this button changes to insert a row or a column. For more details on working with tables, see **Table**, page 230.
	Insert Microsoft Excel Worksheet	Click and drag in a grid to insert a worksheet with a number of rows and columns. For details on working with Excel, see the Excel chapter, page 251.
	Columns	Click and drag to convert the selected text or document into the number of columns. For formatting columns, see **Format - Columns...**, page 173.
	Drawing	Click to show or hide the Drawing toolbar (see **View - Toolbars - Drawing**, page 73).
	Document Map	Click to split the window into two vertical panes. The left pane shows all the Heading styles in the document. Click a Heading style to navigate to that location in the document. Click a minus sign (–) in the left pane to collapse the section. Click a plus sign (+) to expand a section.
	Show/Hide	Click to show or hide nonprinting characters, such as carriage returns, tabs, spaces, and hidden text. For more control, see **Tools - Options...View Tab**, page 223.
90%	Zoom	Click the drop-down arrow or type in the box to change the magnification of what you see on the screen (does not affect printing). For more details, see **View - Zoom...**, page 95.
	Office Assistant	Click and type a question for help. If you are in the middle of trying to do a task, choose from one of the bullet items (see **Help - Microsoft Word Help**, page 240).

View - Toolbars - Formatting

Like the Standard toolbar, the Formatting toolbar also appears by default unless you've turned it off. Most items are on the Format menu.

Formatting toolbar buttons

Button	Name	How to Use
Normal	Style	Place the insertion point within a paragraph, or select text, and click the drop-down to change the style of the selected text. You can also create a style by selecting the text with the format and typing in the name of the style in the Style text box (see **Format - Style...**, page 178). To see a list of all styles, hold down Shift when you click this drop-down.
Times New Roman	Font	Select text and click the drop-down arrow to change the font. (For this button and the next four buttons, see more details at **Format - Font...**, page 160.)
12	Font Size	Select text and click the drop-down arrow to change the size of the text.
B	Bold	Click to make selected text bold.
I	Italic	Click to make selected text italic.
U	Underline	Click to make selected text underlined.
≣	Align Left	Click to line up selected paragraphs on the left margin (and not the right margin). (For this button and the next three, see **Format - Paragraph...**, page 164.)
≣	Center	Click to center selected paragraphs between the margins.
≣	Align Right	Click to line up selected paragraphs on the right margin (and not the left margin).
≣	Justify	Click to line up selected paragraphs on both the left and right margins.
≣	Numbering	Click to number or remove numbering from selected paragraphs. If no paragraphs are selected, it begins numbering. Type an item and press Enter. Numbering continues in sequence. Press Enter a second time to remove the number (see **Format - Bullets and Numbering...**, page 166).
≣	Bullets	Click to add or remove bullets to the selected paragraphs. If paragraphs aren't selected, it begins bulleting. Type an item and press Enter. Bullets continue. Press Enter a second time to remove a bullet (see **Format - Bullets and Numbering...**, page 166).

continues

Continued

Button	Name	How to Use
	Decrease Indent and **Increase Indent**	Click to move the left margin of the paragraph to the previous and next tab stop (see **Format - Paragraph...** and go to Indentation section, page 164).
	Borders	Select paragraphs or parts of a table and click this button to apply the last border style. Click the drop-down arrow to select borders for different sides. If you use the borders often, after you click the drop-down arrow, drag the top of the palette to create a new toolbar.
	Highlight	Select text and click this button to apply the last highlight. Click the drop-down arrow to apply a different color.
	Font Color	Click to apply the last font color to selected text or the current word. Click the drop-down to apply a different color. If you use the font colors often, after you click on the drop-down arrow, drag the top of the palette to create a new toolbar.

View - Toolbars - AutoText

The AutoText toolbar facilitates adding text or graphics that you use over and over. The items you add are given a name, and you then use that name to add the item to the document. (For more details, see **Insert - AutoText**, page 101.) To expand an AutoText entry, type it and press F3.

AutoText toolbar buttons

Button	Name	How to Use
	AutoText	Opens the AutoText tab of the AutoCorrect dialog box. Double-click on the entry to add to the document.
All Entries	**All Entries**	Click the drop-down, and then one of the menus. If you are in a style that you used to define AutoText entries, only those items show when you click this button (to override this, hold down Shift as you click this button).
New...	**New**	Select the text with which you want to create a new AutoText entry, click the button, and type in an abbreviation for the entry.

View - Toolbars - Control Toolbox

ActiveX controls are available by using the Control toolbox. You can place controls on a UserForm or directly on a document. ActiveX controls enable the user to make choices. You can create macros and Visual Basic code to respond to user actions. To place a control on your document, move to that place in the document and click the control button. To place a control on a form, press **Alt+F11** to go to the Visual Basic window and choose **I_nsert**, **U_serForm**.

Control toolbox buttons

Button	Name	How to Use
	Design Mode	Toggle between designing the controls (and changing properties) and using the controls. When you click this button, another toolbar with only this same button displays.
	Properties	Click the control or other item and this button to see or change the properties such as name, color, style, and caption.
	View Code	Enables you to go to the Visual Basic module behind the control. This enables you to create or edit the statements associated with an action such as clicking the control. Choose the close (X) button to return to Word.
	Check Box	The check box enables the user to choose an on or off state.
	Text Box	The text box enables the user to type text (see **Insert – Te_xt Box**, page 156).
	Command Button	Click to create a button on the document. Right-click and choose **V_iew Code** to program the button.
	Option Button	Option buttons are usually part of a group that enable you to pick one of the choices.
	List Box	A list box displays a box that enables you to choose from a list of options.
	Combo Box	A combo box enables you to type text in a box or choose from a drop-down arrow.
	Toggle Button	A toggle button is similar to a check box because it enables you to choose on or off. When the button is on, it appears pressed.
	Spin Button	The spin button is usually associated with a text box. Clicking the up or down arrow causes numbers to increase or decrease.
	Scrollbar	The scrollbar usually indicates up or down movement in a document or dialog box.

continues

Continued

Button	Name	How to Use
A	Label	A label is usually text that provides instructions for the user or is associated with another control describing what the control does.
	Image	The image control enables you to insert graphics on a document or dialog box.
	More Controls	Click to see a list of additional registered controls. These controls may be automatically registered when you load Office or any other program that supports ActiveX controls.

View ► Toolbars ► Database

In addition to displaying through th **View**, **Toolbars** menu, the Database toolbar appears when you work with the data file of a mail merge or when you click **View Source** from the Data Form dialog box (see **Tools ► Mail Merge...**, page 200).

Database toolbar buttons

Button	Name	How to Use
	Data Form	Click while in any table (especially one with headings in the first row) to open the Data Form dialog box. This enables you to see one record (row) at a time. You can use the Data Form to find, delete, edit, and add new rows to your table.
	Manage Fields	Click while in a table to open the Manage Fields dialog box. You can add, rename, or delete columns.
	Add New Record	Click while in a table to add a new row at the bottom.
	Delete Record	Click while in a table to delete the current row.
	Sort Ascending	Click while in a table to sort the table by the selected column in ascending order.
	Sort Descending	Click to sort a column in descending order.
	Insert Database	Click to display the Database dialog box (see Figure 2.21). Click the **Get Data** button and double-click the database file.
	Update Field	If you chose the **Insert Data as Field** check box on the Insert Data dialog box, click this toolbar button to display any changes in the underlying database (see Figure 2.21).

Button	Name	How to Use
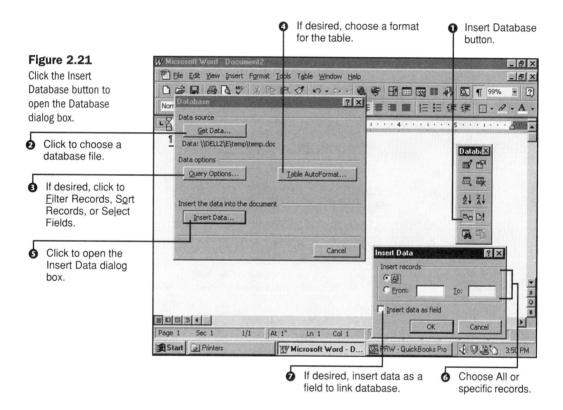	**Find Record**	In a database, click this button to bring up the Find in Field dialog box. Type text in the **Find what** text box and choose the column from the **In field** drop-down list.
	Mail Merge Main Document	In a mail merge data source, click to return to the main document.

Figure 2.21
Click the Insert Database button to open the Database dialog box.

④ If desired, choose a format for the table.

① Insert Database button.

② Click to choose a database file.

③ If desired, click to Filter Records, Sort Records, or Select Fields.

⑤ Click to open the Insert Data dialog box.

⑦ If desired, insert data as a field to link database.

⑥ Choose All or specific records.

View ⇨ Toolbars ⇨ Drawing

When you use the Drawing toolbar, you add a layer of graphic objects on top of your Word document (the text on the document is on a different layer).

Quick Choices *DRAW AN OBJECT*

1. Click a drawing object button on the Drawing toolbar.
2. Drag the mouse pointer in the document.
3. If desired, press **Delete** to remove the object.

Drawing toolbar buttons

Button	Name	How to Use
Draw ▾	**Draw**	Use this button to display a menu that edits the object. (See the following table.)
�	**Select Objects**	Click to select a drawing object. Hold down Shift and click to select multiple objects.
Ꮕ	**Free Rotate**	Select an object and click this button. Small circles appear around the edge of the object. Drag circles to rotate the object.
AutoShapes ▾	**AutoShapes**	Click to show the menu and select an item from one of submenus (**Callouts**, **Stars and Banners**, **Flowchart**, **Block Arrows**, **Basic Shapes**, **Lines**). Click start point, drag, and click end point. For a Curve and Freeform shapes, click or drag multiple points and double-click when done. For a Scribble shape drag the mouse. If you use the AutoShapes often, after you click the drop-down arrow, drag the top of the palette to create a new toolbar.
╲	**Line**	Click the start and stop points to create a line.
◤	**Arrow**	Click the start and stop points to create an arrow.
▢	**Rectangle**	Click the diagonal start and stop points to create a rectangle. Hold down Shift to create a square.
◯	**Oval**	Click diagonal start and stop points to create an oval. Hold down to create a circle.
▣	**Text Box**	Click the diagonal start and stop points to create a box. Type text within the box (see **Insert ‑ Text Box**, page 156).
◢	**Insert WordArt**	Click to display the WordArt Gallery dialog box. Double-click choice and enter text in Enter WordArt Text dialog box (see **View ‑ Toolbars ‑ WordArt**, page 86).
◔ ▾	**Fill Color**	Click an object and choose a color for the inside of the object. If you use the fill colors often, after you click the drop-down arrow, drag the top of the palette to create a new toolbar.
✎ ▾	**Line Color**	Click an object and choose a color for the line around the object. If you use the line colors often, after you click the drop-down arrow, drag the top of the palette to create a new toolbar.
A ▾	**Font Color**	Click an object and choose a color for the text associated with the object. If you use the font colors often, after you click the drop-down arrow, drag the top of the palette to create a new toolbar.
≡	**Line Style**	Click an object and choose a line thickness or style.

Button	Name	How to Use
	Dash Style	Click an object and choose a line dash pattern.
	Arrow Style	Click a line or arrow and choose an arrow head style.
	Shadow	Click an object and choose shadow direction and style. On the Shadow menu choose **Shadow Settings** to open the toolbar.
	3-D	Click an object and choose 3D direction and style. On the menu choose **3-D Settings** to open the toolbar.

After you draw and select a shape, use the four-headed arrow mouse pointer to move the object. You use the double-headed arrow on the small boxes to change the size. Some shapes have a yellow diamond adjustment handle when the object is selected. Drag the diamond to change the most prominent feature of the shape. Other menu options for editing the shape are provided when you click the Draw button.

Draw button menu options

Menu Item	How to Use
Group	Hold down **Shift** and click multiple objects. Then choose this option to create one object from these selected objects.
Ungroup	Click to return a grouped object to its individual objects.
Regroup	Click one of the objects in a former group and then choose this item to return these items to their group.
Order	With one item in a stack of items, choose this menu to move the item in front, in back, or between other drawing objects or the text on the document.
Grid	Choose to display the Snap to Grid dialog box which enables you to define the spacing of the drawing objects' invisible grid. When you check **Snap to grid**, objects move to these grid points when you drag an object. To override the grid, hold down **Alt** as you drag an object. Check **Snap to shapes** to draw ovals and rectangles to the size of the grid.
Nudge	If either of the Snap options is checked in the Snap to Grid dialog box, it moves the selected object to the next point on the grid in the direction selected. If both options are unchecked, it moves the object a small increment.
Align or Distribute	When two or more objects are selected, it aligns the objects to their lefts, centers, rights, tops, or middles. If three or more objects are selected you can also evenly distribute them horizontally or vertically. If **Relative to Page** is checked, it aligns or distributes the objects throughout the page rather than in relationship with each other.

Continued

Menu Item	How to Use
Rotate or Flip	Choose menu items off this menu to spin the object on its axis or flip 180 degrees horizontally or vertically.
Edit Points	If the shape is a Curve, Freeform, or Scribble, this displays many points. Drag any of the points to change the shape of the object.
Change AutoShape	Change the selected object(s) to the AutoShape chosen.
Set AutoShape Defaults	Choose a sample object with fill, line, shadow, and 3D formatting. When you create another object, the object take on the first object's formatting.

You can also right-click the object to edit it. In addition to the grouping, order, and set AutoShape defaults options mentioned, you have the following shortcut menu (right-click) options:

Draw button shortcut menu options

Menu Item	How to Use
Cut	Copies the shape to the Clipboard (and removes it from the original location after pasted).
Copy	Copies the shape to the Clipboard.
Paste	Places the Clipboard shape onto the document.
Add Text	Places text within the shape.
Format AutoShape	Enables you to change the shape's colors, size, position, and text wrapping around the shape. Many of these options are on the Drawing toolbar but this dialog box gives you more options.
Format AutoShape – Colors and Lines tab	Choose the color for the inside and outside line of the shape as well as dashed pattern and line thickness. If the selected object is an arrow or line, you can change the arrow size and shape of either end. If you have no wrapping, check **Semitransparent** to see a shadow of the text behind the shape.

Menu Item	How to Use
Format AutoShape - Size tab	In addition to using the sizing handles and rotate options, you can change the **Height** and **Width** of the object as well as rotate the object a degree at a time. You can also increase or decrease the size by a percentage with the Scale options.
Format AutoShape - Position tab	Use the Position tab to change the location of the object relative to the Margin, Page, Column, and Paragraph. Check **Move object with text** if you want the object to move when the surrounding text moves. Check **Lock anchor** to keep the object on the same page.
Format AutoShape - Wrapping tab	Use the Wrapping tab to change how text surrounds (or goes through) the object.

View ⇒ Toolbars ⇒ Forms

Forms enable the user to fill in a text box, toggle a check box on or off, or select from a drop-down list. Generally, most forms are created in a template file (see **File - New...**, page 20) so that the user doesn't change the original file, just a copy of it. Tables are often used with forms to make formatting easier (see **Table**, page 230).

Quick Choices *CREATING A FORM*

1. Create the text or tables you want on the form.
2. Position the insertion point where you want a form field and click the **Text Form Field** ⓐ, **Check Box Form Field** ☑, or **Drop-Down Form Field** ⊞ buttons.
3. If desired, click the **Form Field Options** button ⓐ and fill out the options for the field.
4. Click the **Protect Form** button ⓐ.
5. Choose **File**, **Save As**, type the name in the **File name** text box, change the **Save as type** to Document Template (*.dot), and click **Save**.

When users create new documents based on the template, they only can fill in the form fields. Press **Tab** or **Shift+Tab** to move between the fields.

Quick Choices *ADDITIONAL OPTIONS WITH FORMS*

■ To save the data only on the form, choose **Tools**, **Options**, click the **Save** tab, and check **Save data only for forms**.

■ To print only the data on the form, choose **Tools**, **Options**, click the **Print** tab, and check **Print data only for forms**.

Forms toolbar buttons

Button	Name	How to Use
abl	**Text Form Field**	Places a text field at the insertion point (see Figure 2.22).
☑	**Check Box Form Field**	Places a box that you can check on or off at the insertion point (see Figure 2.23).
	Drop-Down Form Field	Places a box you can type in or choose from a list at the insertion point (see Figure 2.24).
	Form Field Options	Allows you to set default options.
	Draw Table	Enables you to draw a table on the document (see **Table - Draw Table**, page 230).
	Insert Table	Create a table with your choice of rows and columns (see **Table - Insert Table...**, page 230). If you have a row or column selected, this button changes to Insert Rows or Insert Columns.
	Insert Frame	Inserts a frame around selected text and objects, enabling you to move to a position on the page. To change the format, choose **Format, Frame**.
	Form Field Shading	Toggles field shading on and off for quicker identification.
	Protect Form	Toggles on or off to allow editing of the document or allow only input in the form fields.

View - Toolbars - Picture

After you insert a picture in your document (see **Insert - Picture**, page 149), the Picture toolbar appears, unless you turned it off when working with another picture. If necessary, show the toolbar by choosing **View**, **Toolbars**, **Picture**.

❸ Choose Type of information in the field (Current Date or Current Time automatically enters without user input).

❺ What appears before the user starts typing.

Figure 2.22
On Forms toolbar, click Text Form Field and then Form Field Options buttons to open the Text Form Field Options dialog box.

❹ The user cannot type more characters.

❻ A macro can run as a user gets into a field or after the user leaves.

❶ Text Form field.

❷ Form Field Options.

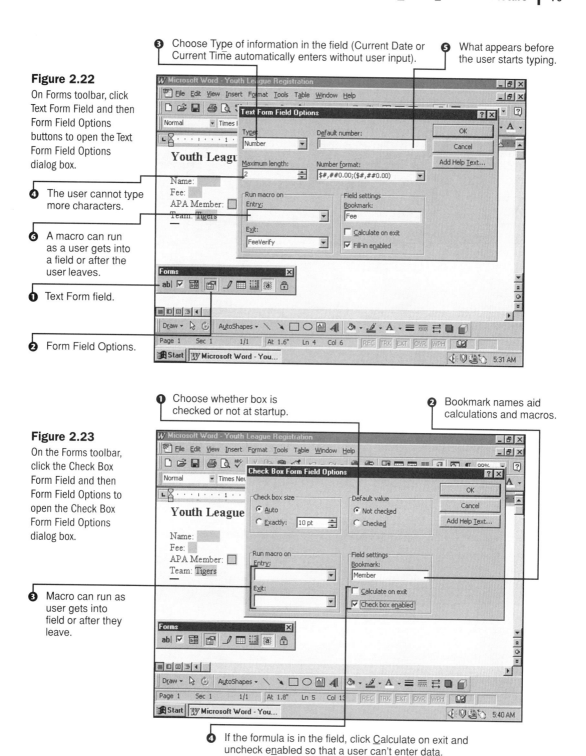

❶ Choose whether box is checked or not at startup.

❷ Bookmark names aid calculations and macros.

Figure 2.23
On the Forms toolbar, click the Check Box Form Field and then Form Field Options to open the Check Box Form Field Options dialog box.

❸ Macro can run as user gets into field or after they leave.

❹ If the formula is in the field, click Calculate on exit and uncheck enabled so that a user can't enter data.

Figure 2.24

On the Forms toolbar, click the Drop-Down Form Field and then Form Field Options to open the Drop-Down Form Field Options dialog box.

❸ Click Add.

❹ Remove item from list.

❶ Drop-Down Form Field.

❷ Type new item.

❺ Change order in list.

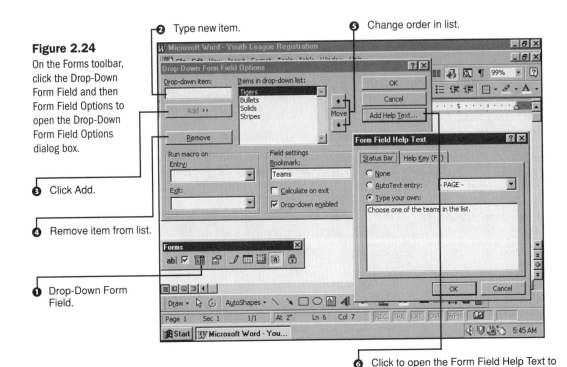

❻ Click to open the Form Field Help Text to set text that appears in the status bar and text that appears when you press F1.

Picture toolbar buttons

Button	Name	How to Use
	Insert Picture	Click to bring up the Insert Picture dialog box. Double-click a filename to insert a picture in addition to the one on the document.
	Image Control	Click to display a menu. **Automatic** enables the program to choose the format. **Grayscale** means each color converts to a shade of gray. **Black and White** is also known as line art. **Watermark** is visible behind the text and has less contrast (**Draw, Order, Send Behind Text**).
	More Contrast	Click to increase the intensity of colors (less gray).

Button	Name	How to Use
	Less Contrast	Click to decrease the intensity of colors (more gray).
	More Brightness	Click to add white to brighten the colors.
	Less Brightness	Click to add black to darken the colors.
	Crop	Click to change to an angle mouse pointer. Drag a small white box surrounding the figure toward the center to remove a portion of the figure.
	Line Style	Click to open line widths and multiple line menu. Choose one to add a border around a picture. **More Lines** opens up the Format dialog box to change the pattern and color of a line.
	Text Wrapping	Click to bring up a menu indicating how you want text to wrap around the picture (**Square**, **Tight**, **Through**, **None**, **Top and Bottom**). Also, a new feature found only on this button is **Edit Wrap Points**. Click this button and then drag the small boxes around the figure to choose where text wraps.
	Format Object	Click to open the Format Picture dialog box. On the Picture tab, you can set cropping, color, brightness, and contrast options (see the buttons in this table). Choose **Reset** to return the picture to its original settings.
	Set Transparent Color	Click to change mouse pointer to a pen(only on bitmap images). Then click a color in the picture to make that color white or the same color as the background of the document (see **Format – Background…**, page 180).
	Reset Picture	Click to return the picture to its original settings.

View – Toolbars – Reviewing

You can use the Reviewing toolbar to navigate and edit comments you added (see **Insert – Comment**, page 129) and additions and deletions marked with the track changes feature (see **Tools – Track Changes**, page 196). You can also view a comment by hovering over the highlight in the text. Track Changes appear when you edit the document; added and deleted text appears in a different color. Added text is underlined and deleted text shows with strikethrough.

Reviewing toolbar buttons

Button	Name	How to Use
	Insert Comment	Click to add a comment. The window splits into two panes. Your initials appear with a number in the lower pane. Type the comment and click the **Close** button.
	Edit Comment	Click to open the Comment pane and edit the next comment.
	Previous Comment	Click to move to and display the previous comment.
	Next Comment	Click to move to and display the next comment.
	Delete Comment	Use one of the previous two buttons to move to the comment and click this button to remove the comment.
	Track Changes	Click to activate the Track Changes feature where additions and deletions are indicated on screen.
	Previous Change	Click to move to and highlight the previous addition or deletion.
	Next Change	Click to move to and highlight the next addition or deletion.
	Accept Change	Click to agree to the highlighted change.
	Reject Change	Click to remove the addition or restore deleted text.
	Highlight	Select text and click to apply background color to the selection.
	Create Microsoft Outlook Task	Click to open Microsoft Outlook and create a task. The subject becomes the name of the document. The task area shows a shortcut to the document and enters the lines of text around the current paragraph.
	Save Version	Click to open the Save Version dialog box. Add your comment about the version and click **OK** (see **File - Versions...**, page 37).
	Send to Mail Recipient	Click to open up your email program with the current document as an attachment.

<u>V</u>iew ‑ <u>T</u>oolbars ‑ Tables and Borders

When you click the **Tables and Borders** button on the Standard toolbar, the Tables and Borders toolbar opens. Many of the options on the toolbar have equivalents on the Tables menu (see **Table**, page 230).

Tables and Borders toolbar buttons

Button	Name	How to Use
	Draw Table	Click and drag opposite corners to draw the outside of a table. Then drag vertical or horizontal lines to draw columns and rows. Click again to turn off the button so that you can select text and cells in the table.
	Eraser	Click and drag across lines of a table to delete rows and columns.
	Line Style	Before using the Draw Table tool, click the drop-down arrow to choose a different line pattern.
½ pt	**Line Weight**	Before using the Draw Table tool, click the drop-down arrow to choose a different line thickness.
	Border Color	Before using the Draw Table tool, click the drop-down arrow to choose a color for the surrounding border.
	Borders	Select a portion of the table, click the drop-down arrow, and choose which side(s) of the cells on which to apply the current Line Style, Line Weight, and Border Color.
	Shading Color	Select a portion of the table and click the drop-down arrow to choose a color, or click the button to choose the last color.
	Merge Cells	Select multiple cells and click this button to create one larger cell.
	Split Cells	Click this button to bring up the Split Cells dialog box and indicate the number of columns and rows. If multiple cells are selected, check the **Merge cells before split** to change the selection to the total number of columns and rows. With this box unchecked, each selected cell multiplies into the number of columns and rows indicated.
	Align Top	Click to position text in selected cells along the top of the cells.
	Center Vertically	Click to center text in the selected cells in the vertical middle of the cells.
	Align Bottom	Click to position text in selected cells along the bottom of the cells.

continues

Continued

Button	Name	How to Use
	Distribute Rows Evenly	Select one or more cells in multiple rows. Click this button so that the row height of all cells becomes equal.
	Distribute Columns Evenly	Select one or more cells in multiple columns. Click this button so that the column width of all cells becomes equal.
	Table AutoFormat	Click this button to bring up the Table AutoFormat dialog box to enable you to apply borders, shading, colors, and fonts to the table (see **Table - Table AutoFormat...**, page 233).
	Change Text Direction	Select a portion of the table and click this button to make text one of three options—normal, going down the cell, or going up the cell (see **Format - Text Direction...**, page 175).
	Sort Ascending	Click this button to sort the table A–Z and 1–9 by the current column.
	Sort Descending	Click this button to sort the table Z–A and 9–1 by the current column.
	AutoSum	Select a cell or row below numbers or cell or row to the right of numbers. Click this button to create a total of the numbers. This creates a function field in the cell (see **Table - Formula...**, page 237).

View - Toolbars - Visual Basic

The Visual Basic toolbar enables you to create, edit, and run macros. Macros are Visual Basic procedures of recorded keystrokes and programming (see **Tools - Macro**, page 220).

Visual Basic toolbar buttons

Button	Name	How to Use
	Run Macro	Click this button to open the Macros dialog box. Double-click the macro you want to run (see **Tools - Macro - Macros...**, page 220).
	Record Macro	Click this button to open the Record Macro dialog box. Type a macro name and click **OK** to start recording. Complete your actions and click the **Stop Recording** button (see **Tools - Macro - Record New Macro...**, page 221).
	Visual Basic Editor	Click this button to go to the Visual Basic Editor to edit your macro statements.

Button	Name	How to Use
⚒	**Control Toolbox**	Click this button to display the Control toolbox (see **View – Toolbars – Control Toolbox**, page 70) to add controls to your document.
☑	**Design Mode**	Click this button to toggle between editing the document controls and user input mode (clicking controls triggers the programming associated with the control).

View – Toolbars – Web

When you click the Web Toolbar button 🌐 on the Standard toolbar, the Web Toolbar displays or hides. This toolbar enables you to browse the Web and move to hyperlinks.

Web toolbar buttons

Button	Name	How to Use
⇐	**Back**	After you've clicked a hyperlink, click to return to the Web page or document that displayed the hyperlink.
⇒	**Forward**	After you click **Back**, click this button to display the next document in the hyperlink history list.
⊗	**Stop Current Jump**	Click to stop the current Web page or document from loading.
↻	**Refresh Current Page**	Click to reload the current Web page or document.
⌂	**Start Page**	Click to display the startup Web page or document. Set this page by clicking the **Go** button and choosing **Set Start Page.**
↻	**Search the Web**	Click to display the Web page or document that acts as your search page. Set this page by clicking the **Go** button and choosing **Set Search Page.**
Favorites ▾	Favorites	Click the button to open a menu you can use to go to a previously saved favorite Web page or document. To add the displayed Web page or document to this list, choose **Add to Favorites**, navigate to a subfolder if desired, and click **Add**.
Go ▾	Go	Click this button to display a menu that enables you to open a Web page or document or to do other items already mentioned in this table.
⬆	**Show Only Web Toolbar**	Click to hide any other toolbars. Click this button again to redisplay the toolbars.

continues

Continued

Button	Name	How to Use
	Address	
C:\DATA\temp3.doc		Type the address of a Web page (such as **ameriteach. com/**), network document (such as **\\Finance\Budget\ Bud99.doc**), or a document on your computer (such as **C:\Data\Marketing\Brochure.doc**). Press Enter to load the Web page or document.

View ▸ Toolbars ▸ WordArt

After you create a WordArt object, the WordArt toolbar displays (see **Insert ▸ Picture ▸ WordArt...**, page 155). You can also insert WordArt by clicking the **WordArt** button [4] on the Drawing toolbar. When you double-click an existing WordArt object, the WordArt toolbar also displays.

WordArt toolbar buttons

Button	Name	How to Use
[4]	**Insert WordArt**	Click to display the WordArt Gallery dialog box. Double-click your choice and enter text in the Enter WordArt Text dialog box (see **View ▸ Toolbars ▸ WordArt**, page 86).
Edit Text...	**Edit Text**	Click to open the Edit WordArt Text dialog box. You can change the **Font**, font **Size**, make the text bold or italic, and edit the **Text**.
[icon]	**WordArt Gallery**	Click to display the WordArt Gallery, enabling you to change the color and shape of the WordArt object.
[icon]	**Format Object**	Click to open the Format WordArt dialog box. You can change the color and change the pattern and thickness of the lines on the Colors and Lines tab. Change the size, rotation, and scaling on the Size tab. On the Position tab change the location of the WordArt on the page and whether you want to **Move the object with text** or **Lock anchor** to keep the WordArt on the page. On the Wrapping tab change how you want other text on the page to wrap around the WordArt. (See **Format, Object...** page 183.)
Abc	**WordArt Shape**	Click to choose from a palette of possible shapes for the WordArt.
[icon]	**Free Rotate**	Click to display small circles around the edge of your WordArt object. Drag the circles to rotate.

Button	Name	How to Use
Aa	**WordArt Same Letter Heights**	Click to make upper- and lower case letters the same height. Click again to return the letters to normal heights.
Ab bJ	**WordArt Vertical Text**	Click to stack the letters on top of each other. Click again to return the letters to left-to-right orientation.
☰	**WordArt Alignment**	If there are multiple lines of text in the WordArt object, click this button to bring up a menu to align the lines left, centered, or right. You can also justify (both left and right edges line up) by spaces between words, by spaces between each letter, or by stretching the letters.
AV ↔	**WordArt Character Spacing**	Click to display a menu to change the spacing between characters (from Tight to Very Loose). You can use the Custom choice option and type a number (the lower the number, the tighter the spacing). Choose **Kern Character Pairs** to adjust the space between certain letters so that the letters look more evenly spaced.

View – Toolbars – Customize...

In addition to displaying toolbars, you can create a new toolbar, and add and remove buttons or menu items on toolbars or menus.

Quick Choices *CREATE A TOOLBAR*

1. Right-click a toolbar and choose **Customize** to open the Customize dialog box.
2. Click **New** on the **Toolbars** tab to open the New Toolbar box. Type in the **Toolbar name** and click **OK**. The blank toolbar appears on the screen (you may have to move the Customize dialog box to work with the toolbar).
3. Click the **Commands** tab, choose an item from the **Categories** list, and drag an item from the **Commands** list to the new toolbar.
4. Repeat step 3 for each button and click **Close** when done.

Choose **View**, **Toolbars**, **Customize** or right-click a toolbar and choose **Customize** to open the Customize dialog box. The following sections describe each of the tabs.

View – Toolbars – Customize... Toolbars Tab

Customize toolbars

Dialog Box Item	How to Use
Toolbars	Check the box next to the toolbar name to display the toolbar for use or for editing. This list includes Shortcut Menus with three menus (Text, Table, and

continues

Continued

Dialog Box Item	How to Use
	Draw). These are the menus that appear when you right-click the document or an object.
New	Click to open the New Toolbar dialog box. Type the name in the **Toolbar name** text box. You can **Make toolbar available to** the current document or to the Normal template (documents that you create when you choose the New button on the Standard toolbar). Click **OK** to create the new toolbar.
Rename	Select a custom toolbar and then click this button to open the Rename Toolbar dialog box. Type the new name and click **OK**.
Delete	Select a custom toolbar and then click to delete the toolbar. Click **OK** to verify the deletion.
Reset	Select a toolbar native to Word. If you added or deleted buttons or changed the button properties, click this button to return the toolbar to the original settings. The Reset Toolbar dialog box displays. Choose whether you want to reset the changes for the Normal template or for this document.

View ➥ Toolbars ➥ Customize... Commands Tab

When you click the **Command** tab of the Customize dialog box, the screen displays (shown in Figure 2.25).

❶ Choose from Categories to change the Commands list.

Figure 2.25
View, Toolbars, Customize opens the Customize dialog box.

❸ To remove a button, drag from the toolbar to the document.

❷ Drag an item from the Commands list to the toolbar.

❹ See help on the button.

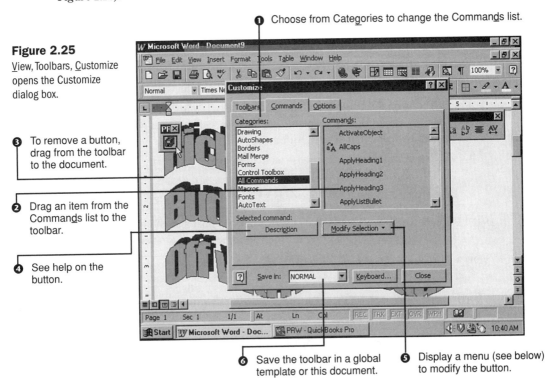

❻ Save the toolbar in a global template or this document.

❺ Display a menu (see below) to modify the button.

In the **Categories** list box, you can see commands associated with most menus and some toolbars (File, Edit, View, Insert, Format, Tools, Table, Web, Window and Help, Drawing, AutoShapes, Borders, Mail Merge, Forms, and Control Toolbox). You drag any item from the Commands list to a toolbar or menu to create a new item. The following table shows the additional items found in the **Categories** list:

Category	Description
All Commands	This displays all commands available on all menus (and items that are not on menus) in one convenient location.
Macros	This displays your macros so that you can drag a macro to create a button. The Commands column shows the name of your macro in the following format: Template or Document name, a period, the name of the macro Module, another period, and then the name of the macro procedure (see **Tools ▸ Macro**, page 220). When you drag your macro to a toolbar or menu, you get the icon and name. See the next section **View ▸ Toolbars ▸ Customize... Right-click Options** to display just the icon.
Fonts	Drag the font name to the toolbar or menu to create a button or menu item (the font name appears by default).
AutoText	Drag to create a button or menu item for a specific AutoText entry (see **Insert ▸ AutoText**, page 101).
Styles	Drag to add a button or menu item for a specific Style. Only styles that you've used in your document display in the **Commands** list (see **Format ▸ Style...**, page 178).
Built-in Menus	You can drag an entire menu (File, Edit, Insert, and so on.) and add it to a toolbar. The Font menu shows a list of all fonts (like the Font drop-down on the Formatting toolbar). Use the special **Work** menu for managing your most used documents. After you create the toolbar or menu, open the document you want to reference, choose the **Work** menu and choose **Add to Work Menu**. That document is now stored on the **Work** menu. To remove an item from the menu, press **Ctrl+Alt+−** (minus) and click the filename.
New Menu	Only one command is stored under this option. Drag the New Menu item to a toolbar or other menu. Drag items for the menu first to the menu and then down to the area that you want on the menu. Right-click the menu and change the **Name**.

The **Save in** option enables you to save the toolbar globally (in the Normal template) or only for this document.

View ▸ Toolbars ▸ Customize... Right-click Options

While you still have the Customize dialog box open, you can modify a button on a toolbar (or menu) by right-clicking the button. You can also modify the button by selecting it and then clicking the **Modify Selection** button on the **Commands** tab. This menu has the following items:

Menu Item	How to Use
Reset	Choose to return the item to its original settings.
Delete	Choose to delete the button or menu item.
Name	Type a name that appears if a text option is selected below. Type an & before the letter that you want as a hot key (for example, see Save &As on the &File menu).
Copy Button Image	Choose this to copy onto another button (or paste the image into the document).
Paste Button Image	Choose to paste a copied image onto the current button.
Reset Button Image	Choose to change the image back to the original image for this button.
Edit Button Image	Click to open the Button Editor dialog box (see Figure 2.26).

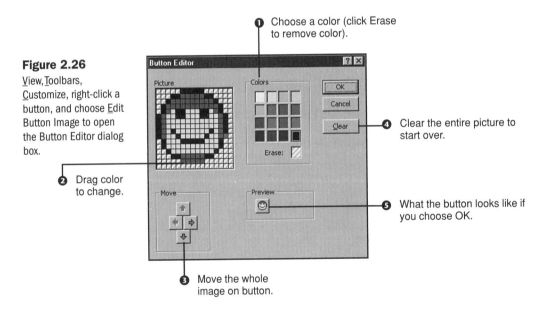

Figure 2.26

View, Toolbars, Customize, right-click a button, and choose Edit Button Image to open the Button Editor dialog box.

❶ Choose a color (click Erase to remove color).

❷ Drag color to change.

❸ Move the whole image on button.

❹ Clear the entire picture to start over.

❺ What the button looks like if you choose OK.

Menu Item	How to Use
Change Button Image	Choose to display a different image for the button.
Default Style	If on the menu, display the **Name**. If on a toolbar, display the **Name** and image.
Text Only (Always)	Choose to just display the **Name**.
Text Only (In Menus)	Choose to display only text on menus, but an image on toolbars.
Image and Text	Choose to display both the **Name** and the image, whether it is a toolbar or menu.
Begin a Group	Choose to place a dividing line to the left or above the selected item.

View ▪ Toolbars ▪ Customize... Options Tab

Dialog Box Item	How to Use
Large Icons	Check to show larger icons. Depending on your monitor settings, the icons may appear on more than one line.
Show ScreenTips on Toolbars	Check to enable you to hover over a button on a toolbar to get the name.
Show shortcut keys in ScreenTips	Check to see the keyboard shortcut associated with the command attached to the button (if available).
Menu animations	Choose an item (Random, Unfold, or Slide) to have the menu appear to move as you click it.

View ▪ Toolbars ▪ Customize... Keyboard Button

If you want to change or create a shortcut associated with any command, you can click the **Keyboard** button on the Custom dialog box. The Customize Keyboard dialog box opens (shown in Figure 2.27).

When you choose the Categories list, the same choices appear as did on the Command tab of the Customize dialog box (see **View ▪ Toolbars ▪ Customize... Commands Tab**, page 88). You have an additional category, Common Symbols, which enables you to assign keyboard shortcuts to a symbol.

Figure 2.27
View, Toolbars, Customize, Keyboard button opens the Customize Keyboard dialog box.

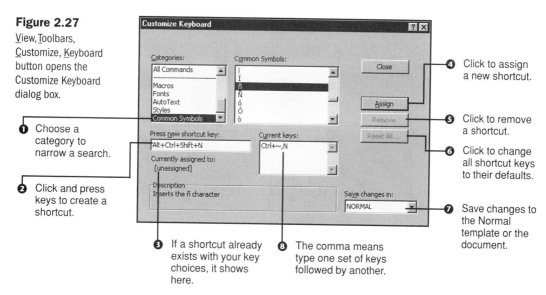

❶ Choose a category to narrow a search.

❷ Click and press keys to create a shortcut.

❸ If a shortcut already exists with your key choices, it shows here.

❹ Click to assign a new shortcut.

❺ Click to remove a shortcut.

❻ Click to change all shortcut keys to their defaults.

❼ Save changes to the Normal template or the document.

❽ The comma means type one set of keys followed by another.

View ➥ Ruler

The ruler enables you to set tabs (see **Format – Tabs...**, page 174) and indents for the current paragraph (or selected paragraphs). You can also set the indents with the **Increase Indent** ⮕ and **Decrease Indent** ⬅ buttons on the Formatting toolbar.

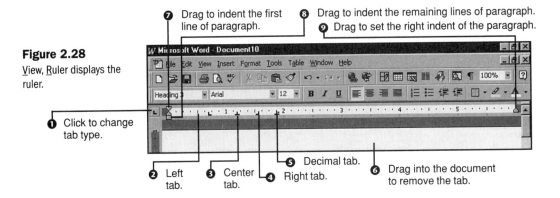

❼ Drag to indent the first line of paragraph.
❽ Drag to indent the remaining lines of paragraph.
❾ Drag to set the right indent of the paragraph.

Figure 2.28
View, Ruler displays the ruler.

❶ Click to change tab type.

❷ Left tab.
❸ Center tab.
❹ Right tab.
❺ Decimal tab.
❻ Drag into the document to remove the tab.

View ➥ Document Map

The document map splits the window into two vertical panes. Click the **Document Map** button 🔲 on the Standard toolbar or choose View, Document Map. The left panes show the text formatted in paragraph styles different from Normal text (see Figure 2.29).

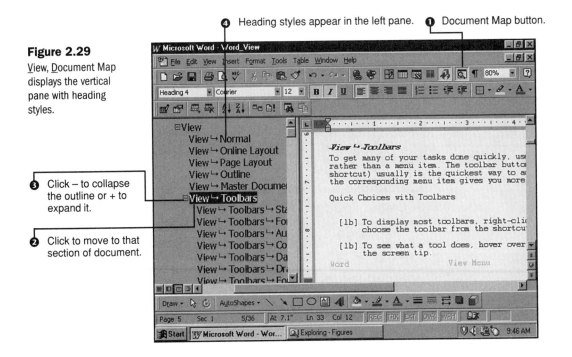

❹ Heading styles appear in the left pane.   ❶ Document Map button.

Figure 2.29
View, Document Map displays the vertical pane with heading styles.

❸ Click – to collapse the outline or + to expand it.

❷ Click to move to that section of document.

View → Header and Footer

Headers and footers print at the tops and bottoms of the pages of your document. You can choose to print different headers just on the first page or following pages, even or odd pages, or print different headers in different sections.

Quick **Choices** **CREATE HEADER OR FOOTER**

1. Choose **View**, **Header and Footer** or double-click an existing header or footer in Page Layout view (see **View – Page Layout**, page 63). The header section opens, and the Header and Footer toolbar displays.

2. Type in the header text, pressing tab to go to the center or tab again to go to the right edge of the header.

3. If desired, click the **Insert Page Number** 🔢 button.

4. Click the **Switch Between Header and Footer** 🔁 button to go to the footer and repeat steps 2 and 3.

5. Click Close when done.

Header and Footer toolbar

Button	Name	How to Use
Insert AutoText ▾	**AutoText**	Click to display a list of AutoText entries created while in a header or footer (see **Insert – AutoText**, page 101). To display all AutoText categories, hold down Shift when you click this button.
🔢	**Page Number**	Click to place a code for the page number.
📄	**Insert Number of Pages**	Click to place a code for the total number of pages.
🔧	**Format Page Number**	Click to open the Page Number Format dialog box. Choose the **Number format** to be letters or numbers, whether to **Include chapter number**, and what number to **Start at** (see **Insert – Page Numbers...**, page 97).
📅	**Insert Date**	Click to insert a code for the date that prints the date when the document is printed. To change the default date format, click **Default** on the Date and Time dialog box (see **Insert – Date and Time...**, page 99).

continues

Continued

Button	Name	How to Use
	Insert Time	Click to insert a code to print the current time when printed.
	Page Setup	Click to open the Page Setup dialog box. You can choose to print **Different odd and even** (page 3 would be different than page 4), and **Different first page** headers and footers. If you have multiple sections (to create, see **Insert - Break...**, page 96), you can also choose whether to **Apply to** This section, This point forward, or the Whole document (see **File - Page Setup...**, page 38).
	Show/Hide Document Text	Click this button to toggle between showing or hiding the body of your document.
	Same as Previous	When you have multiple sections and are on the second or later section, click this button to copy the header or footer from the previous section.
	Switch Between Header and Footer	Click to toggle between the header and footer for the current section.
	Show Previous	Show header or footer for the previous section (if you have multiple sections).
	Show Next	Show the header or footer for the following section (if you have multiple sections).
Close	Close Header and Footer	Close the header and footer section and toolbar, and return to the document.

View ➥ Footnotes

Word combines footnotes and endnotes together for viewing and creating. Footnotes appear at the bottom of a page. Endnotes appear at the end of your document. After you create a footnote or endnote with **Insert - Footnote** (see page 131), you can later view or edit them by selecting **View, Footnotes**. When you choose this menu option, Word splits the screen into two panes. One includes your document, the other includes the footnote pane. You can do the following:

■ Click the **Footnotes/Endnotes** drop-down arrow and choose either All Footnotes or All Endnotes.

■ Edit a footnote or endnote.

- Click the **Close** button to close the footnote pane and return to the document.
- Move the mouse pointer to the top edge of the footnote pane until it is a double-headed arrow and change the height of the pane.

You can also move to each footnote or endnote in your document by clicking the **Select Browse Object** button ⊙ on the bottom right of the vertical scrollbar and clicking the **Browse by Footnote** or **Browse by Endnote** buttons. Use the **Previous** or **Next** button to continue moving to Footnotes and Endnotes.

View ➥ Comments

Comments enable you to add a note directly within the text. When you hover your mouse pointer over a comment (shown by a highlight) in the text, the note appears as a ScreenTip (see **Insert ⁃ Comment**, page 129, to add a comment). **View**, **Comments** also splits the window into two panes to enable you to edit comments. If more than one person is working on this document, select the **Comments From** drop-down list to see comments from each individual.

To move to each comment, click the **Select Browse Object** button ⊙ on the lower-right of the vertical scrollbar and then click the **Browse by Comment** button. Use the **Previous** or **Next** button to continue moving to the comments.

View ➥ Full Screen

Full screen hides most of the elements on the screen, such as menu bars, toolbars, and the status bar, so that you can see more of your screen. Click the **Close Full Screen** button or press **Esc** to close the Full Screen view.

View ➥ Zoom...

Zoom enables you to see more or less of your document at one time. The magnification of the document changes on the screen but does not affect printing.

Click the **Zoom** button `90%` on the Standard toolbar and choose a magnification from the drop-down list or type a value in the box. The Page Width option shows the entire width of the page. Alternatively, you can choose **View**, **Zoom** to make changes on the Zoom dialog box (see Figure 2.30).

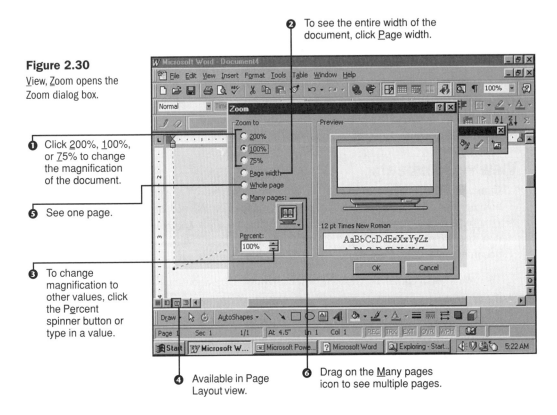

Figure 2.30

View, Zoom opens the Zoom dialog box.

❷ To see the entire width of the document, click Page width.

❶ Click 200%, 100%, or 75% to change the magnification of the document.

❺ See one page.

❸ To change magnification to other values, click the Percent spinner button or type in a value.

❹ Available in Page Layout view.

❻ Drag on the Many pages icon to see multiple pages.

Insert

The insert menu gives you options to insert document and field codes as well as objects from other programs such as clip art pictures, Excel spreadsheets or charts, PowerPoint slides, organization charts and many others, depending on what you have installed on your computer.

Insert ➥ Break...

The **Insert**, **Break** command gives you options to insert page breaks, column breaks, and section breaks. Use section breaks if you want to change page numbering (see **Insert ‑ Page Numbers...**, page 97), headers and footers (see **View ‑ Header and Footer**, page 93), the number and formatting of columns (see **Format ‑ Columns...**, page 173), page margins, orientation (see **File ‑ Page Setup...**, page 38), and footnotes (see **Insert ‑ Footnote...**, page 131) in the middle of a document.

A section break stores the section formatting elements, such as the margins, the page orientation, headers and footers, and sequence of page numbers. Each section can have different formatting elements. One of the best uses for section breaks is to create different headers and footers in a document.

Quick **Choices**   *INSERT BREAKS*

1. Press **Ctrl+Enter** to insert a Page Break.

2. Press **Ctrl+Shift+Enter** to insert a Column Break.

3. Press **Shift+Enter** to insert a Manual Line Break.

1. Choose **Insert, Break** to display the Break dialog box (see Figure 2.31).

Figure 2.31

Insert, Break opens the Break dialog box.

❶ Choose to insert a manual page break.

❷ Choose to insert a manual column break.

2. In the Section breaks area of the dialog box, select one of the following:

Type of Break	Inserts a Section Break
Next page	Breaks the page and starts a new section at the top of the next page.
Continuous	Starts the new section immediately, without inserting a new page.
Even page	Starts the next section on the next even-numbered page. If the section break falls on an even-numbered page, Word leaves the next odd-numbered page blank.
Odd page	Starts the next section on the next odd-numbered page. If the section break falls on an odd-numbered page, Word leaves the next even-numbered page blank.

3. Choose **OK** to insert the break.

To remove a section break, go to normal view (see **View – Normal**, page 62), click the double-dotted line that says break, and press **Delete**.

Insert ➥ Page Numbers...

The **Insert, Page Numbers** command inserts page numbers that automatically update when you add or remove pages.

Quick **Choices**   *INSERT PAGE NUMBERS*

1. Choose **Insert, Page Numbers** to display the Page Numbers dialog box.

2. Choose **OK** to insert page numbers in the Header aligned on the right margin.

1. Choose **Insert, Page Numbers** to display the Page Numbers dialog box (see Figure 2.32).

❶ Click the drop-down arrow to select the Top of the page (Header) or the Bottom of the page (Footer).

Figure 2.32

Insert, Page Numbers opens the Page Numbers dialog box.

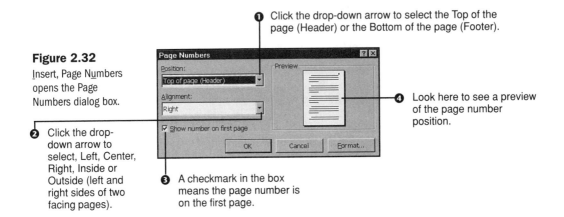

❹ Look here to see a preview of the page number position.

❷ Click the drop-down arrow to select, Left, Center, Right, Inside or Outside (left and right sides of two facing pages).

❸ A checkmark in the box means the page number is on the first page.

2. Choose the **Format** button to make changes to the page number format (see Figure 2.33).

Figure 2.33

Choose the Format button from the Page Numbers dialog box to open the Page Number Format dialog box.

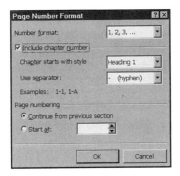

3. Select the **Number format** drop-down arrow to choose a different format. The available formats are

- 1, 2, 3…
- a, b, c…
- A, B, C…
- i, ii, iii…
- I, II, III…

4. Check **Include chapter number** to include the chapter number in the page number format. This makes the two options in that section of the dialog box available.

5. Select one of the Heading styles in the list for the **Chapter starts with style** list box. If you checked **Include chapter number**, this will include the next chapter number and then restart page numbering each time Word comes to this style.

6. In the **Use separator list** box, click the drop-down arrow and select one of the following separators to go between the chapter number and page number:

   - - (hyphen)
   - . (period)
   - : (colon)
   - — (em dash)
   - – (en dash)

7. In the Page numbering section, click the **Continue from previous section** option to keep the page numbering consecutive. Alternatively, deselect **Continue from previous section** if you want each section's page numbers to be independent.

8. Click the **Start at** option and type a number in the text box to the beginning page number.

9. Choose **OK** when you are finished.

10. Choose **OK** on the Page Numbers dialog box.

Insert ▾ Date and Time...

Insert, **Date and Time** enables you to pick a format for the date or time and insert it into your document.

Quick Choices   *TO INSERT THE DATE*

- Press **Alt+Shift+D** to insert the current date in the MM/DD/YY format (for example, 05/13/99).

- Begin typing the date (for example, April), and when you see the Screen Tip for the current date, press **Enter** (for example, April 12, 1998).

Quick Choices   *TO INSERT THE TIME*

- Press **Alt+Shift+T** to insert the current time in the HH:MM PM format (for example, 8:31 AM).

Choose **Insert, Date and Time** to display the Date and Time dialog box (see Figure 2.34).

Figure 2. 34

Choose Insert, Date and Time to display the Date and Time dialog box.

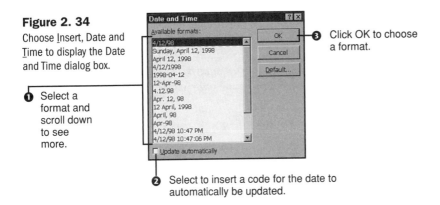

❶ Select a format and scroll down to see more.

❸ Click OK to choose a format.

❷ Select to insert a code for the date to automatically be updated.

Change the Default Date and Time Format

If you use the keyboard shortcut to insert the current date or time, you may find that you want to change the default format.

To change the default date or time format, follow these steps:

1. Choose **Insert**, **Date and Time** to display the Date and Time dialog box.

2. Select the format you prefer to use in the **Available formats** list box.

3. Click the **Default** button. A message from Word is displayed (see Figure 2.35).

Figure 2.35

Choose Insert, Date and Time, and click the Default button to display the message dialog box.

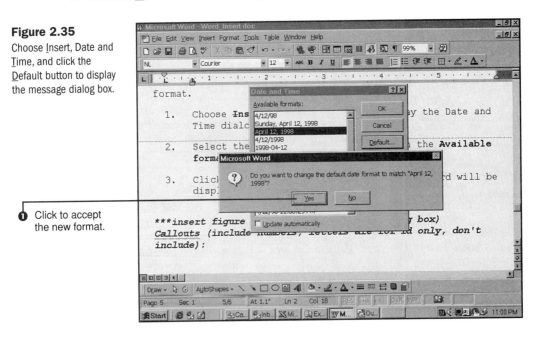

❶ Click to accept the new format.

4. Choose **OK** to close the Date and Time dialog box.

Insert ➥ AutoText

The **Insert**, **AutoText** feature is comparable to word processing shorthand. You have the option of using predefined AutoText entries or creating your own. AutoText entries can contain text, graphics, pictures, or symbols. For instance, if you have a digitized signature or even your company logo with the address, either can be made an AutoText item.

Quick Choices   *INSERTING AUTOTEXT ENTRIES*

1. Type the name of the AutoText entry. In cases where the AutoText entries don't start with the same characters, you can type the first four characters to show the ScreenTip.

2. If you see a ScreenTip for the AutoText entry, press **Enter**, or **Tab** to insert the item. If you don't see a ScreenTip, press **F3** to insert the item.

Quick Choices   *CREATING AUTOTEXT ENTRIES*

1. Select the text or graphics you want to use for an AutoText entry.

2. Press **Alt+F3** to display the Create AutoText dialog box.

3. Type a name (the shorter the better) for the AutoText entry, or accept the name suggested, and choose **OK**.

Insert ➥ AutoText ➥ AutoText...

To manage AutoText entries choose **Insert**, **AutoText**, 🖳 **AutoText**. This displays the AutoText tab of the AutoCorrect dialog box (see Figure 2.36).

Figure 2.36
Choose Insert, AutoText, 🖳 AutoText to display the AutoCorrect dialog box open to the AutoText tab.

❷ Accept this name or type a short name for the AutoText entry.

❸ Look here to see what the AutoText entry is for.

❶ Leave this checked to see the AutoComplete ScreenTip as you type.

❹ Click this button to Add the new AutoText entry to your list.

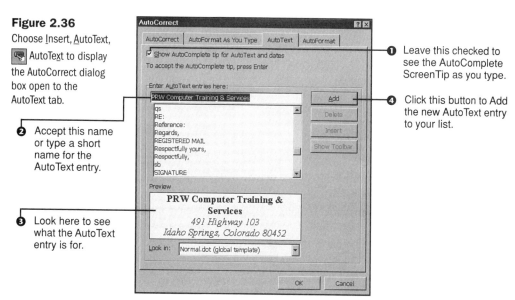

To manage AutoText entries, follow these steps:

1. Choose **Insert**, **AutoText**, 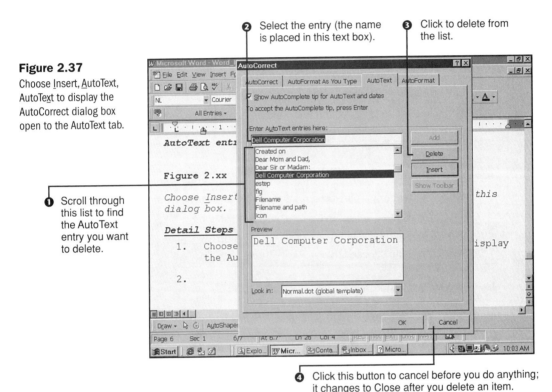 **AutoText** to display the AutoText tab of the AutoCorrect dialog box (see Figure 2.37).

Figure 2.37

Choose Insert, AutoText, AutoText to display the AutoCorrect dialog box open to the AutoText tab.

❷ Select the entry (the name is placed in this text box).

❸ Click to delete from the list.

❶ Scroll through this list to find the AutoText entry you want to delete.

❹ Click this button to cancel before you do anything; it changes to Close after you delete an item.

2. Repeat the steps on the figure to delete as many entries as you need.

3. If you click the **Insert** button, place the AutoText entry in your document and close the dialog box.

4. Click the **Show Toolbar** button to activate the AutoText toolbar and close the dialog box.

5. Use the **Look in** list box to change where the AutoText entry is stored.

   - Normal.dot (global template) and All active templates makes the AutoText entry available all the time.

   - If you have any other templates available, choosing one limits the use of a specific AutoText entry. This is useful if you want to separate your AutoText entries by types of documents. For instance, if you need specific AutoText items when you are typing Memos, you would attach those entries to the memo template that you create. (See the **File ▪ New...** section, specifically Detail Options—To start document or create new template, page 20.)

6. Choose **OK** or **Close** when you are finished managing the AutoText entries.

Insert ▾ AutoText ▾ New...

To create a new AutoText entry, select the text or graphics. Choose **Insert**, **AutoText**, **New** to display the Create AutoText dialog box. Type a short name for the AutoText item, or accept the one suggested. Choose **OK** to create the item.

Insert ▾ AutoText ▾ (List of AutoText Entries)

There are more than 40 predefined AutoText entries that come with Word. On the **Insert**, **AutoText** menu these entries are listed on submenus (groups) along with any of the AutoText entries you create. Your menu looks similar to the one shown in Figure 2.38.

❸ Click to see all your AutoText entries.

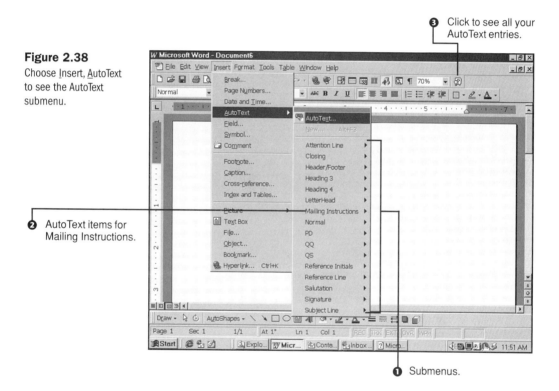

Figure 2.38
Choose Insert, AutoText to see the AutoText submenu.

❷ AutoText items for Mailing Instructions.

❶ Submenus.

The submenus are created depending on where you are when you create the AutoText entry. If you created text and applied a style to the text, then you select that text and create a new AutoText entry. The style name becomes the name of the submenu. Because the Header and Footer panes are styles, this includes creating AutoText entries when you are in the Header or Footer (the submenu is called Header/Footer).

Quick Choices   *TO USE AUTOTEXT ENTRIES FROM SUBMENUS*

■ Choose **I**nsert, **A**utoText (see Figure 2.39).

Figure 2.39

Choose Insert, AutoText, and point to the submenu.

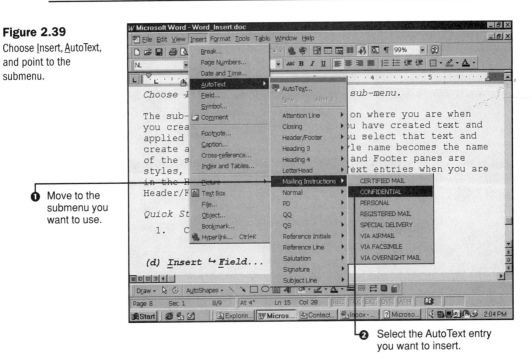

❶ Move to the submenu you want to use.

❷ Select the AutoText entry you want to insert.

To create an AutoText entry on a submenu, do the following:

1. Type the text and insert any graphics or symbols needed.
2. Assign a style to the new text. (See **Format ▪ Style…** on page 178 for more information about styles.)
3. Format the text however you want to. (See the **Format** section on page 160 for more information about formatting.)
4. Select the text or graphics.
5. Press **Alt+F3** to display the Create AutoText dialog box (see Figure 2.40).

The new AutoText entry is displayed on a submenu with the name of the style (see Figure 2.41).

Display All AutoText Entry Groups

When the insertion point is located on a line that has a style other than normal, and you choose the **I**nsert, **A**utoText command, you see AutoText entries specific to the style associated with the line you are on.

Figure 2.40

Choose Insert, AutoText, New to display the Create AutoText dialog box.

❷ Style assigned to the selected text.

❶ Selected text for the new AutoText entry.

❸ Type a name for the AutoText entry.

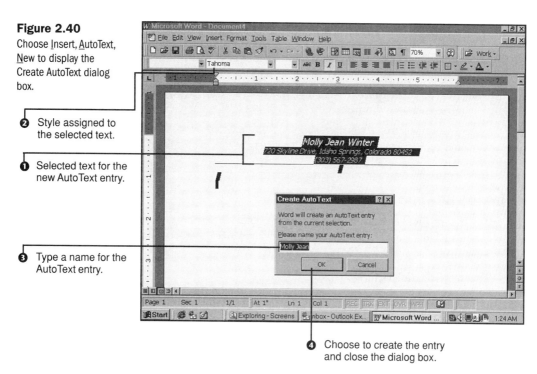

❹ Choose to create the entry and close the dialog box.

Figure 2.41

Choose Insert, AutoText, LetterHead to display the Letterhead AutoText entries.

❶ Submenu.

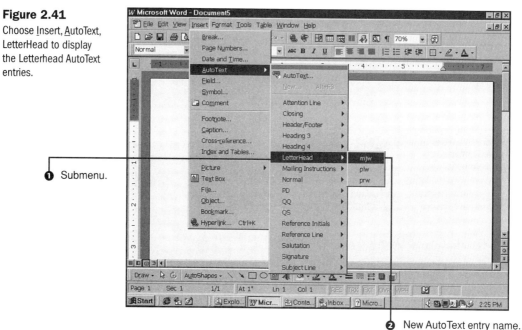

❷ New AutoText entry name.

Quick **Choices**   *VIEW ALL AUTOTEXT ENTRY GROUPS*

1. Move the mouse pointer up or down the insert menu to move off of the **AutoText** command.

2. Hold down the **Shift** key and then move back to the **AutoText** command. The submenu now shows you the groups.

   The same is true if you are using the AutoText toolbar. If the middle button on the toolbar has any other text than All Entries, hold down the **Shift** key and click the middle button.

Insert ➥ Field...

The **Insert, Field** command gives you the flexibility to use any of the fields available in Word. Fields are hidden codes that perform tasks related to word processing, similar to functions in worksheets.

To insert fields, follow these steps:

1. Position the insertion point where you want the field result to appear.

2. Choose **Insert, Field** to display the Field dialog box (see Figure 2.42).

Figure 2.42

Choose Insert, Field to display the Field dialog box.

❶ Select the type of field you want from this list.

❸ View this area for a description of the field code.

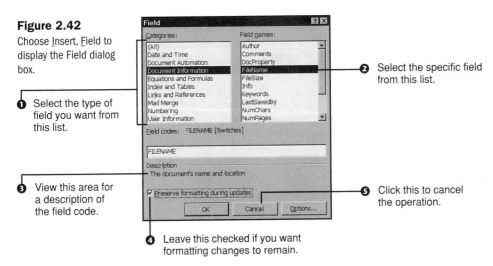

❷ Select the specific field from this list.

❺ Click this to cancel the operation.

❹ Leave this checked if you want formatting changes to remain.

3. Choose **OK** when you have made all your selections.

The field codes are broken into categories to make finding the fields easier for you. On the Field dialog box (refer to Figure 2.42), click a category in the **Categories** list box to see the related fields in the **Field names** list box. A description of the field is also displayed.

The following is an alphabetic list of all the field codes with a description of what the code is for. In some cases, the description is very detailed, including available switches and what they mean. Because of space limitations, not all the fields are explained in as much detail.

When you look at the syntax for each field code, brackets [ ] mean the instruction or argument is optional, and you do not type the bracket [ ].

In most cases it is easiest to use the **Insert, Field** command to insert the field codes. If you prefer to type the code yourself, press **Ctrl+F9** to insert the curly brackets for the field code, leaving the insertion point in the middle of the brackets ready for you to type.

After you manually type a field code instruction, update the field code. Move the insertion point into the field, and press **F9**. Then see whether the code worked.

Alt+F9 changes the view of the field code to the result of the field code and back again.

(f)= (Formula)

{= Formula [Bookmark][\# Numeric Picture]}

Calculates a number by using a mathematical formula. You can use the Formula command on the Table menu to insert an = (Formula) field in a table or in regular text. (See **Table ‑ Formula...**, page 237.)

You can reference *bookmarks* or table *cell references* in the formula. (See **Insert ‑ Bookmark...**, page 159.) Cell references are the same in Excel without the column and row headings. (See Excel's **Creating Formulas**, page 255.)

Formulas can include any of the following functions:

Functions that are available to use with the Formula field

Function	Description
ABS(x)	The positive value of a number or formula, regardless of its actual positive or negative value.
AND(x,y)	The value 1 if the logical expressions x and y are both true, or the value 0 (zero) if either expression is false.
AVERAGE( )	The average of a list of values.
COUNT( )	The number of items in a list.
DEFINED(x)	The value 1 (true) if the expression x is valid, or the value 0 (false) if the expression cannot be computed.
FALSE	0 (zero).
IF(x,y,z)	The result y if the conditional expression x is true, or the result z if the conditional expression is false. Note that y and z (usually 1 and 0, zero) can be either any numeric value or the words true and false.
INT(x)	The numbers to the left of the decimal place in the value or formula x.
MAX( )	The largest value in a list.
MIN( )	The smallest value in a list.

continues

Continued

Function	Description
MOD(x,y)	The remainder that results from dividing the value x by the value y a whole number of times.
NOT(x)	The value 0 (false) if the logical expression x is true, or the value 1 (true) if the expression is false.
OR(x,y)	The value 1 (true) if either or both logical expressions x and y are true, or the value 0 (false) if both expressions are false.
PRODUCT()	The result of multiplying a list of values. For example, the function {= PRODUCT (1,3,7,9)} returns the value 189.
ROUND(x,y)	The value of x rounded to the specified number of decimal places y; x can be either a number or the result of a formula.
SIGN(x)	The value 1 if x is a positive value, or the value –1 if x is a negative value.
SUM()	The sum of a list of values or formulas.
TRUE	1.

Example using *bookmarks*: {= *GrossSales-Expenses* \# "$#,##0.00"}

Example using *cell references*: {=average(*d1:d8*)}

Note: The following functions can accept references to table cells as arguments: AVERAGE(), COUNT(), MAX(), MIN(), PRODUCT(), and SUM().

Advance

{ADVANCE [Switches]}

Offsets the starting point of text that follows the ADVANCE field to the right or left, up or down, or to a specific horizontal or vertical position.

ADVANCE field switches

Switch	Result
\d	Down
\u	Up
\l	Left
\r	Right
\x	Specified distance in points from the left margin of the text column or frame
\y	Specified vertical position relative to the current line position (the entire line moves)

Example: {ADVANCE \d 5}—moves the text that follows this code down 5 points.

Ask

{ASK Bookmark "Prompt " [Switches]}

Prompts you to enter information and assigns a bookmark to represent your response. You must insert a **REF** or **BOOKMARK** field after the **ASK** field where you want Word to print the response in the document. You can use the information entered in other fields such as an = (Formula field) by inserting the bookmark name in the other field's instructions.

Switch	Result
\d "Default"	Defines the default text for the dialog box. If no default text is defined, the last entry is repeated. If you want nothing as the default, use \d" ".
\o	Requests a response to the dialog box only at the beginning of the first document during a mail merge.

Example: {ASK IntRate "Enter the current interest rate:" \d}

Author

{AUTHOR ["NewName"]}

Inserts the author name from the Summary tab in the Properties dialog box (see **File - Properties** on page 46). The author name for a new document or template is initially the name specified on the User Information tab in the Options dialog box (see **Tools - Options...**, page 223).

When you enter a "NewName" for the author, it is used in the document and also changed on the Properties dialog box. The example uses the FILLIN field to find the new author name.

Example: Created by: {AUTHOR "{FILLIN "Author name?"}"}

AutoNum

{AUTONUM}

Creates sequential Arabic numbers (1, 2, 3, and so on) and updates automatically when other AUTONUM codes are added. When used at the beginning of paragraphs, the numbering format is easier (see **Format - Bullets and Numbering...**, page 166).

The AUTONUM field is provided for compatibility with previous versions of Word. The LISTNUM field can be used in place of the AUTONUM field.

Example: Figure 3.{AUTONUM}

AutoNumLgl

{AUTONUMLGL [Switches]}

Automatically numbers paragraphs for legal and technical publications. It is easier to number paragraphs by using **F̲ormat ▪ Bullets and N̲umbering...** (see page 166).

Switch: **\e** = displays the number in legal format without the period.

The AUTONUMLGL field is provided for compatibility with previous versions of Word. The LISTNUM field can be used in place of the AUTONUMLGL field.

Example: {AUTONUMLGL} (at the beginning of a paragraph).

AutoNumOut

{AUTONUMOUT}

Automatically numbers paragraphs in outline style. It is easier to number paragraphs by using **F̲ormat ▪ Bullets and N̲umbering...** (see page 166).

The AUTONUMOUT field is provided for compatibility with previous versions of Word. The LISTNUM field can be used in place of the AUTONUMOUT field.

Example: {AUTONUMOUT} (at the beginning of a paragraph).

AutoText

{**AUTOTEXT** AutoTextEntry}

Inserts the specified AutoText entry. When you use an AUTOTEXT field instead of inserting an AutoText entry, Word can automatically update all instances of an AutoText entry in your documents if you later redefine the entry. First define the AutoText entry, and then insert an AUTOTEXT field wherever you want to insert the entry. If you change the AutoText entry, update the AUTOTEXT fields in the document to reflect the change.

When you update the example, {AUTOTEXT Disclaimer}, Word replaces Disclaimer with the current text defined for the AutoText entry "Disclaimer."

Example: {AUTOTEXT Disclaimer}

Auto TextList

{AUTOTEXTLIST "LiteralText" \s [StyleName] \t [TipText]}

Creates an AutoText drop-down list that is displayed in the document based on AutoText entries in the active template. To activate the list, the user right-clicks the "LiteralText". The list can vary based on the styles applied to the AutoText entries.

Instructions	
Field Parameter	**Description**
LiteralText	Text you want displayed in the document to begin with, for the user to right-click to display the drop-down list. If this text contains spaces, enclose it in quotation marks.

Field Parameter	Description
\s StyleName	Name of the style for the AutoText entries you want to appear in the list. If there are no AutoText entries defined for this style, all the entries are displayed. If the StyleName contains spaces, enclose it in quotation marks.
\t TipText	The text you want displayed in the ScreenTip when the user hovers the mouse over the field result (Literal Text). If the TipText contains spaces, enclose it in quotation marks.

Example: {AUTOTEXTLIST "Right-click for Letter Head options" \s LetterHead \t "PRW Letter Head Options"}

Barcode

{BARCODE \u "LiteralText" or Bookmark \b [Switches]}

Inserts a postal barcode. The BARCODE field can insert either a POSTNET delivery-point barcode or a Facing Identification Mark, or FIM. It may be easier to insert postal barcodes with the **Tools - Envelopes and Labels...** command (see page 213).

Switch	Result
\b	Specifies that a bookmark contains the address and Zip code information.
\f	Designates that one of two Facing Identification marks (FIM) should be inserted: "A" inserts a courtesy reply mark; "C" inserts a business reply mark.
\u	Recognizes the bar code as a United States postal address.

Comments

{COMMENTS ["NewComments"]}

Inserts or replaces comments from the Comments box on the Summary tab in the Properties dialog box for the active document or template. (For more information, see **File - Properties Summary Tab**, page 47.)

Compare

{COMPARE Expression1 Operator Expression2}

Compares two values and displays either "1" if the comparison is true, or "0" (zero) if the comparison is false. You can use this field to create compound logical comparisons with AND and OR functions in an = (Formula) field, and then you can use the result of the = (Formula) field in an IF field.

Use Expression1 and Expression2 as the values to compare. Expressions can be strings of text, numbers, bookmark names, nested fields that return a value, or a mathematical formula. If the expression contains spaces, enclose it in quotation marks.

Insert a space before and after the operator. You can use the following operators:

Operator	What It Means
=	Equal to
<>	Not equal to
>	Greater than
<	Less than
>=	Greater than or equal to
<=	Less than or equal to

If you use the = or <> operators, the second expression can use the question mark(?) to represent any single character or the asterisk (*) to represent a string of characters. The expression must be enclosed in quotation marks so that it is compared as a character string. If you use an asterisk in the second expression, the portion of the first expression that relates to the asterisk and any remaining characters in the second expression cannot exceed 128 characters.

Example: {COMPARE "{MERGEFIELD PostalCode}" = "802*"}

CreateDate

{CREATEDATE [\@ "Date-Time Picture"]}

Inserts the date and time the document was created (first saved).

Adding the \@ *"Date-Time Picture"* instruction enables you to define the format to display for the date or time. If you leave this instruction off, the default format is used (see **Insert ▪ Date and Time...**, page 99).

Switch: \@ "Date-Time Picture"

Designates the display of a date or time. This switch is called a "picture" switch because you use symbols to represent the format of the field result. For example, the switch \@ "dddd, MMMM d, yyyy" in the field {CREATEDATE \@ "dddd, MMMM d, yyyy" } displays "Friday, May 26, 2000." Combine date and time instructions—day, month (M), and year (y); hours (h) and minutes (m)—to build a date-time picture. You can also include text, punctuation, and spaces.

Date and time symbols	
Picture Item	**Displays the Date Element As**
Month (M)	Must be an uppercase M to distinguish from minutes.
M	A number without a leading 0 (zero) for single-digit months. For example, July is "7".

Picture Item	Displays the Date Element As
MM	A number with a leading 0 (zero) for single-digit months. For example, July is "07".
MMM	A three-letter abbreviation. For example, July is "Jul".
MMMM	The full name of the month. Day can be upper- or lowercase.
d	A number without a leading 0 (zero) for single-digit days. For example, the sixth day of the month is displayed as "6".
dd	A number with a leading 0 (zero) for single-digit days. For example, the sixth day of the month is displayed as "06".
ddd	A three-letter abbreviation. For example, Tuesday is displayed as "Tue".
dddd	The full name of the day of the week.
Year (y)	Can be upper or lowercase.
yy	Two digits with a leading 0 (zero) for years 01 through 09. For example, 1995 is displayed as "95", and 2006 is displayed as "06".
yyyy	Four digits.
Hours (h)	A lowercase "h" bases time on the 12-hour clock. An uppercase "H" bases time on the 24-hour, or military, clock; for example, 5 P.M. is displayed as "17".
h or H	Without a leading 0 (zero) for single-digit hours. For example, the hour of 9 A.M. is displayed as "9".
hh or HH	With a leading 0 (zero) for single-digit hours. For example, the hour of 9 A.M. is displayed as "09".
Minutes (m)	The letter "m" must be lowercase to distinguish minutes from months.
m	Without a leading 0 (zero) for single-digit minutes. For example, {TIME \@ "m"} displays "2".
mm	With a leading 0 (zero) for single-digit minutes. For example, {TIME \@ "mm"} displays "02".
AM/PM	Uppercase. For example, {TIME \@ "h AM/PM"} displays "9 AM" or "5 PM".
am/pm	Lowercase. For example, {TIME \@ "h am/pm"} displays "9 am" or "5 pm".
A/P	Abbreviated uppercase. For example, {TIME \@ "h A/P"} displays "9 A" or "5 P".
a/p	Abbreviated lowercase. For example, {DATE \@ "h a/p"} displays "9 a" or "5 p".

continues

Continued

Picture Item	Displays the Date Element As
'text'	Any specified text. Enclose the text in single quotation marks. For example, {TIME \@ "HH:mm 'Mountain Standard time' "} displays "12:45 Mountain Standard time".
character	The specified character, such as a : (colon), - (hyphen), * (asterisk), or space. For example, {DATE \@ "HH:mm MMM-d, "yy"} displays "11:15 Nov-6, '95".
'numbereditem'	The number of the preceding item that you numbered by using the Caption command on the Insert menu, or by inserting a SEQ field. Enclose the item identifier, such as "table" or "figure," in single primes ('). Word displays the sequential number in Arabic numerals. For example,{CREATEDATE \@ "'Table' 'table' 'was Created on' M/d/yy"} displays "Table 2 was Created on 5/22/99".

Database

{DATABASE [Switches]}

Inserts the results of a database query from an external database in a Word table. If the number of columns is 32 or greater, the DATABASE field inserts the results of a query in columns separated by tabs. The DATABASE field contains all the information needed to connect to a database and perform a Structured Query Language (SQL) query. You update the field to query the database again.

A DATABASE field can also be inserted by using the **Database button** 🔲 on the Database toolbar (see **View ‑ Toolbars ‑ Database**, page 72).

Switch	Explanation
\b "Sum"	Designates which attributes of the format set by the \l switch to apply to the table. If the \l switch is blank, the \b switch value must be 16 (AutoFit). Include the sum of any combination of the following values to specify the value for the switch.
This value	Specifies
	0 None
	1 Borders
	2 Shading
	4 Font
	8 Color
	16 AutoFit

Switch	Explanation
	32 Heading Rows
	64 Last Row
	128 First Column
	256 Last Column
	For example, the switches \l "3" \b "11" apply only the borders, shading, and color attributes of the table format set by the \l switch.
\c "ConnectInfo"	Defines a connection to the data. For example, a query to a range of cells in Microsoft Excel might have the connection instructions \c "DSN=MS Access Databases; DBQ=C:\\Data\\Sales99.mdb; FIL=RedISAM;".
\d "Location"	The path and filename of the database. Used for all database queries except a query to an SQL database table using ODBC. Use double backslashes in the path—for example, "C:\\Data\\Sales99.mdb".
\f "StartNumber"	Specifies the record number of the first data record to insert—for example, \f "1652".
\h	Inserts field names from the database as column headings in the resulting table.
\l "Format#"	Applies a format from the Table AutoFormat dialog box (see **Table - Table AutoFormat...**, page 233) to the result of the database query. The number Format# is resolved by the table format you select in the dialog box. If this switch is used and the \b switch doesn't define the table attributes, Word inserts an unformatted table.
\s "SQL"	SQL instructions. You must insert a backslash (\) before each quotation mark in the instructions. For example, instructions for a Microsoft Access database might be as follows: "select * from \"Customer List\"".
\t "EndNumber"	Ascertain the record number of the last data record to insert—for example: \t "2486".

Date

{DATE [\@ "Date-Time Picture"] [Switches]}

Inserts the current date or time. Select the field and press F9 to manually update. It is also updated when you print. (See **CREATEDATE** on page 112 for information related to [\@ "Date-Time Picture"] instructions.)

DocProperty

{DOCPROPERTY "Name"}

Inserts the selected document information that is currently entered in the Properties dialog box (see **File - Properties**, page 46). "Name" represents the property you want to display. Choose **Insert**, **Field** and on the Field dialog box, use the **Options** button to define the "Name".

DocVariable

{DOCVARIABLE "Name"}

Inserts the string assigned to a document variable. Each document has a series of variables, which can be added and referenced by the Visual Basic for Applications programming language. This field furnishes a way to display the contents of the document variables in the document. For more information about document variables, see "Document Variables" in the Visual Basic for Applications Help.

EditTime

{EDITTIME}

Inserts the number of minutes the document has been edited since its creation. Word gets the time from the Statistics tab on the Properties dialog box (see **File ▪ Properties ▪ Statistics Tab**, page 46).

Eq (equation)

{EQ Switches}

Yields a mathematical equation. It is easier to use the Equation Editor for creating equations. However, you can use the EQ field if you have not installed Equation Editor or if you want to formulate inline equations. An EQ field cannot be unlinked. If you double-click an EQ field, Word converts the field to an embedded Equation Editor object.

FileName

{FILENAME [Switches]}

Inserts the filename of the document, as recorded on the Properties dialog box (see **File ▪ Properties**, page 46).

FileSize

{FILESIZE [Switches]}

Inserts the size of the document, in bytes, using information from the Statistics tab on the Properties dialog box (see **File ▪ Properties ▪ Statistics Tab**, page 46).

Fillin

{FILLIN ["Prompt"] [Switches]}

Produces a dialog box that prompts you to enter text. Your response is printed in place of the field. To use your response in more than one location, use an ASK field.

The prompt is displayed each time the FILLIN field is updated (with the insertion point in the field, press F9). If the FILLIN field is in a mail merge main document, the prompt is displayed each time a new data record is merged unless you use the \o switch.

GoToButton

{GOTOBUTTON Destination DisplayText }

Inserts a button in the document at the field's location that is a jump command, which helps you move in long online documents. When you double-click the results of a GOTOBUTTON field, Word moves the insertion point to the Destination in the document. Hyperlinks, which are represented by the HYPERLINK field, are often a better alternative to the GOTOBUTTON field. (For more information about creating hyperlinks, see **Insert ▪ Hyperlink...** on page 159 and **Edit ▪ Paste as Hyperlink** on page 54.)

Hyperlink

{ HYPERLINK "FileName" [Switches]}

Inserts a hyperlink that enables you to jump to another location. The location can be another file on your hard disk or your company's network (such as a Microsoft Word document or a Microsoft Excel worksheet), an Internet address (such as **www.microsoft.com**), or a location such as a bookmark or slide. The field includes display text, which is often blue and underlined, that the user clicks to jump to the specified location. You can insert hyperlinks by clicking the **Hyperlink** command on the **Insert** menu (see **Insert ▪ Hyperlink...**, page 159).

If

{IF Expression1 Operator Expression2 TrueText FalseText}

Use this to compare two values and then insert the text appropriate to the result of the comparison. If used in a mail merge main document, the IF field can examine information in the merged data records, such as postal codes or account numbers. For example, you can send letters to only those clients located in a particular city. (See **Tools ▪ Mail Merge... Merge the data with the document section** on page 211 for more information.)

IncludePicture

{INCLUDEPICTURE "FileName" [Switches]}

Inserts the contents of "FileName" in the document. To insert an INCLUDEPICTURE field, choose **Insert, Picture, From File**, and then select the **Link to File** check box on the Insert Picture dialog box.

IncludeText

{INCLUDETEXT "FileName" [Bookmark] [Switches]}

Inserts the contents of "FileName" at the location of the Bookmark. You can insert the entire document, or if it's a Word document, you can insert only the portion referred to by a bookmark.

Index

{INDEX [Switches]}

Collects all the text and page numbers from the {XE} (index entry) fields or from outline headings and assembles an index. The INDEX field is inserted by the Index and Tables command on the Insert menu (see **Insert - Index and Tables...**, page 137).

Info

{[INFO] InfoType ["NewValue"]}

Inserts information about the active document or template as stored on the Properties dialog box (see **File - Properties - Summary Tab**, page 46).

The available types of information are author, comments, createdate, edittime, filename, filesize, keywords, lastsavedby, numchars, numpages, numwords, printdate, revnum, savedate, subject, template, and title.

Keywords

{KEYWORDS ["NewKeywords"]}

Inserts or replaces the key words on the Summary tab in the Properties dialog box for the active document or template (see **File - Properties - Summary Tab**, page 46).

LastSavedBy

{LASTSAVEDBY}

Inserts the name of the last person who modified and saved the document as displayed on the Statistics tab in the Properties dialog box (see **File - Properties - Summary Tab**, page 46).

Link

{LINK ClassName "FileName" [PlaceReference] [Switches]}

Links the contents of a file into the Word document. This link is created when you copy information from another application and use the **Paste Special** command on the **Edit** menu. (See **Edit - Paste Special...**, page 52.)

ListNum

{LISTNUM "Name" [Switches]}

Inserts a set of numbers anywhere in a paragraph. LISTNUM fields can be incorporated into numbering from a simple or outline-numbered list. The LISTNUM field can be used in place of the AUTONUM, AUTONUMLGL, and AUTONUMOUT fields.

Field specific switches

Switch	Result
\l	Specifies the level in the list. In the example, \l **7** shows the lowercase roman numerals.
\s	Defines the start-at value for this list. In the example, \s **1** makes this second list start at number 1.

List name switches

Switch	Result
LegalDefault	Emulates the AUTONUMLGL field
NumberDefault	Emulates the AUTONUM field
OutlineDefault	Emulates the AUTONUMOUT field

Example: Please bring the following with you to make your application (i) employment history, (ii) credit history information, and (iii) your driver's license. Sections 5.1, 5.2, and 5.3 explain the details further.

The codes look like this: Please bring the following with you to make your application **{ LISTNUM \l 7 OutlineDefault }** employment history, **{ LISTNUM OutlineDefault }** credit history information, and **{ LISTNUM OutlineDefault }** your driver's license. Sections 5.**{ LISTNUM NumberDefault\s 1 }**, 5.**{ LISTNUM NumberDefault }**, and 5.**{ LISTNUM NumberDefault }** explain the details further.

MacroButton

{MACROBUTTON MacroName DisplayText}

Inserts a macro command by displaying the DisplayText. The macro defined by MacroName runs by double-clicking the results of a MACROBUTTON field (DisplayText). You can also select the MACROBUTTON field and then press Alt+Shift+F9 to run the macro.

MergeField

{MERGEFIELD FieldName}

Shows the name of a data field within the "chevron" merge characters (guillemets) in a mail merge main document—for example, «FirstName». When the main document is merged with the data source, information from the specified data field is inserted in place of the merge field.

You must select the data source for the main document before you insert merge fields. To insert a merge field, click Insert Merge Field on the Mail Merge toolbar (see **Tools – Mail Merge...**, page 200).

MergeRec

{MERGEREC}

Inserts the number of the current print-merge record. (See **Tools ▪ Mail Merge...**, page 200 for more information.)

MergeSeq

{MERGESEQ}

Computes the number of data records that were successfully merged with the main document. Word starts numbering merged records from 1, each time you merge documents. The number may be different from the value inserted by the MERGEREC field.

For example, suppose that you merge only the range of records 10 through 25. The MERGESEQ number corresponding to the first data record merged is 1, even though the MERGEREC number for that data record is 10.

Next

{ NEXT }

No result is displayed, and this field instructs Word to use the next record in the selected data file. Word uses this field when you set up mailing label and envelope main documents by using the Mail Merge command (see **Tools ▪ Mail Merge...**, page 200).

To list information from many data records in the same document, such as a membership directory or a price list, select the Catalog main document type in the Mail Merge Helper dialog box (see **Tools ▪ Mail Merge...**, page 200).

NextIf

{ NEXTIF Expression1 Operator Expression2 }

Compares two expressions and if the comparison is true, Word merges the next data record into the current merge document. No result is displayed.

You can select data records more easily by clicking the **Query Options** button in the Mail Merge Helper dialog box (see **Tools ▪ Mail Merge...**, **Query Options...**, page 212).

NoteRef

{ NOTEREF Bookmark [Switches] }

Inserts a footnote or endnote reference mark that you've marked with a bookmark. This permits you to make multiple references to the same note or to cross-reference footnotes or endnotes. If you modify the sequence of footnotes or endnotes, the new result of the NOTEREF field reflects the new numbering.

Bookmark is the name of the bookmark that refers to the footnote or endnote reference mark. Bookmark must refer to the reference mark in the document text, not in the footnote or endnote pane. If the Bookmark does not exist, you must create it.

Switches	
Switch	**Result**
\f	Inserts the reference mark with the same character formatting as the Footnote or Endnote Reference style.
\h	Inserts a hyperlink to the footnote.
\p	Inserts the relative position of the footnote or endnote. If the NOTEREF field appears before the bookmark in the document, the NOTEREF field evaluates to "below". If the NOTEREF field appears after the bookmark, the field evaluates to "above". If the NOTEREF field appears in the bookmark, Word returns an error.

NumChars

{NUMCHARS}

Inserts the number of characters in the document, using information from the Statistics tab in the Properties dialog box (see **File ‑ Properties ‑ Statistics Tab**, page 46).

Example:

The = (Formula) field {= {NUMCHARS} / {NUMWORDS}} determines the average word length by dividing the number of characters by the number of words.

NumPages

{NUMPAGES}

Inserts the number of pages the document contained the last time it was printed or updated. The number comes from the Statistics tab in the Properties dialog box (see **File ‑ Properties ‑ Statistics Tab**, page 48).

Examples:

To print page numbers such as "Page 16 of 122" on each page of a document, insert the following text and fields in a header or footer. To insert the PAGE field, click the **Page Number** button ⊞ on the Header and Footer toolbar.

Page {PAGE} of {NUMPAGES}

If the page numbering starts on a page number other than 1, use an = (Formula) field to compute the total page number count. To determine the starting page number for the active document (StartingNumber), choose **Insert, Page Numbers**, and then choose **Format**. In the Page numbering section of the dialog box, use the **Start at** number for the (StartingNumber).

Page {PAGE} of {= (StartingNumber - 1) + {NUMPAGES}}

NumWords

{NUMWORDS}

Inserts the number of words in the document as of the last update, using information from the Statistics tab in the Properties dialog box (see **File ‑ Properties ‑ Statistics Tab**, page 48).

Page

{PAGE [* Format Switch]}

Inserts the page number for the page on which the PAGE field is located. Word inserts the PAGE field when you choose **Insert**, **Page Numbers** or when you click the **Page Number** button #️ on the Header and Footer toolbar.

PageRef

{PAGEREF Bookmark [* Format Switch]}

Inserts the page number of a Bookmark for a cross-reference. To cross-reference items in a document, use the **Insert**, **Cross-reference** command.

Print

{PRINT "PrinterInstructions"}

Sends printer-control code characters to the selected printer. A result is only displayed when the document is printed. For appropriate printer codes, consult your printer manual.

Note: The PRINT field works well with a PostScript printer or a Hewlett-Packard LaserJet Series II or Series III printer. It may not work properly with other types of laser printers. The PRINT field works with a dot-matrix printer only if the printer supports the PassThrough command.

PrintDate

{PRINTDATE \@ "Date-Time Picture"}

Inserts the date and time that a document was last printed, as included on the Statistics tab in the Properties dialog box (see **File ▪ Properties ▪ Statistics Tab**, page 48).

The default date and time are displayed in the format selected on the Date and Time tabs in the Regional Settings Properties dialog box in the Windows Control Panel. (See **CREATEDATE** on page 112 for information related to [\@ "Date-Time Picture"] instructions.)

Private

{PRIVATE}

Word inserts a PRIVATE field when converting file formats to store data for documents converted from other file formats. The PRIVATE field holds data needed for converting a document back to its original file format.

A PRIVATE field is formatted as hidden text and doesn't affect the document layout in Word. To hide a PRIVATE field, choose **Tools**, **Options**, and on the View tab, clear the **Hidden text** check box.

Quote

{QUOTE "LiteralText"}

Inserts the "LiteralText" into a document. Enclose the LiteralText in quotation marks.

RD (Referenced Document)

{RD "FileName"}

Identifies a file to include when you create a table of contents, a table of authorities, or an index with the TOC, TOA, or INDEX field. You must manually set the starting page numbers and sequence values in files named in RD fields before updating the TOC, TOA, or INDEX field. The RD field doesn't display a result in the document. You cannot unlink an RD field.

RD fields that reference a group of files must be in the same order as the files in the final document. For example, files Chap1 and Chap2 both have an index entry for "apple" on the first page. The first page number in Chap1 is 1, and the first page number in Chap2 is 120.

Ref

{[ref] Bookmark [Switches]}

Inserts the contents of the Bookmark, which specifies a selection of text. The formatting of the Bookmark displays as the original bookmark text.

RevNum

{REVNUM}

Inserts the number of document revisions, using information from the Statistics tab on the Properties dialog box (see **File ▸ Properties ▸ Statistics Tab**, page 48).

SaveDate

{SAVEDATE [\@ "Date-Time Picture"]}

Inserts the date and time a document was last saved, using information ("Modified") on the Statistics tab in the Properties dialog box (see **File ▸ Properties ▸ Statistics Tab**, page 48).

See **CREATEDATE** on page 112 for information related to [\@ "Date-Time Picture"] instructions.

Section

{SECTION}

Inserts the number of the current section.

SectionPages

{SECTIONPAGES}

Inserts the total number of pages in a section. When using this field, you should restart page numbering from 1 in each section after the first section. For example, to print page number references using the format "Page 6 of 55" on each page of a document you've divided into sections, insert the following fields and text in the header or footer:

Page {PAGE} of {SECTIONPAGES}

Seq (Sequence)

{SEQ Identifier [Bookmark] [Switches]}

Inserts sequential numbers for items. Use this for numbering tables, figures, chapters, and other items in a document. If you add, delete, or move an item and its corresponding SEQ field, you can update remaining SEQ fields in the document to reflect the new sequence. The LISTNUM field also produces automatic numbering and may be a better alternative if you are creating a complex numbered list. (For more information about the LISTNUM field, see **Insert**, **Field**, **LISTNUM**, page 118.)

The easiest way to insert SEQ fields to number tables, figures, and other items in a document is to use **Insert**, **Caption**. (For more information, see **Insert** ‑ **Caption...**, page 133.)

SET

{SET Bookmark "Text"}

Assigns new text to a bookmark. You can then refer to the bookmark in multiple locations to repeat the text. No result appears when you use the SET field. To print the information, you must insert a REF or BOOKMARK field in the document.

SkipIf

{SKIPIF Expression1 Operator Expression2}

Compares two expressions. If the comparison is true, SKIPIF aborts the current merge document, moves to the next data record in the data source, and starts a new merge document. If the comparison is false, Word continues the current merge document.

You can select data records more easily by clicking the **Query Options** button in the Mail Merge Helper dialog box (see **Tools** ‑ **Mail Merge... Query Options...**, page 212).

StyleRef

{STYLEREF StyleIdentifier [Switches]}

Inserts text that is formatted with the specified StyleIdentifier. If inserted in a header or footer, the STYLEREF field prints the first or last text formatted with the specified StyleIdentifier on the current page, permitting you to print dictionary-style headers or footers.

Subject

{SUBJECT ["NewSubject"]}

Inserts or replaces the contents of the Subject box from the Summary tab in the Properties dialog box (see **File** ‑ **Properties** ‑ **Summary Tab**, page 48).

Symbol

{SYMBOL CharNum [Switches]}

Inserts a symbol character. Using **Insert**, **Symbol** is an easier way to insert symbols or special characters. See **Insert - Symbol...**, page 127.

TA (Table of Authorities Entry)

{TA [Switches]}

Defines the text and page number for a table of authorities entry. The TA field is formatted as hidden text and displays no result in the document. To view this field, click the **Show/Hide** button ¶ on the Standard toolbar. For more information, see **Insert - Index and Tables... Table of Authorities Tab**, page 147.

TC (Table of Contents Entry)

{TC "Text " [Switches]}

Marks the text and page numbers for entries in a table of contents and in lists of tables, figures, and similar contents. No result is displayed. (For more information, see **Table of Contents Entry Fields**, page 144. To generate a table of contents, see **Insert - Index and Tables... Table of Contents Tab**, page 142.)

Template

{TEMPLATE [Switches]}

Inserts the name of the document's template, using information from the Summary tab on the Properties dialog box (see **File - Properties - Summary Tab**, page 48).

Time

{TIME [\@ "Date-Time Picture"]}

Inserts the current time. Word inserts a TIME field when you click the **Time** button on the Header and Footer toolbar. (See **Insert - Field... CreateDate** on page 112 for information related to [\@ "Date-Time Picture"] instructions.)

Title

{TITLE ["NewTitle"]}

Inserts or replaces the contents of the Title box from the Summary tab in the Properties dialog box (see **File - Properties - Summary Tab**, page 48).

TOA (Table of Authorities)

{TOA [Switches]}

Builds and inserts a table of authorities. The TOA field collects entries marked by TA (Table of Authorities Entry) fields. (To insert a TOA field, see **Insert - Index and Tables... Table of Authorities Tab**, page 147.)

TOC (Table of contents)

{TOC [Switches]}

Builds a table of contents. The TOC field collects entries for a table of contents using heading levels, specified styles, or entries specified by TC (Table of Contents Entry) fields. (To insert the TOC, see **Insert ▸ Index and Tables... Table of Contents Tab**, page 142.)

UserAddress

{USERADDRESS ["NewAddress"]}

Inserts the user name and address from the **Mailing Address** box on the User Information tab in the Options dialog box (see **Tools ▸ Options... User Information Tab**, page 227).

UserInitials

{USERINITIALS ["NewInitials"]}

Inserts the user initials from the **Initials** box on the User Information tab in the Options dialog box (see **Tools ▸ Options... User Information Tab**, page 227).

UserName

{USERNAME ["NewName"]}

Inserts the user name from the **Name** box on the User Information tab in the Options dialog box (see **Tools ▸ Options... User Information Tab**, page 227).

XE (Index Entry)

{XE "Text" [Switches]}

Defines the text and page number for an index entry. No result is displayed. You insert an XE field to define an item to include in the index. (For more information, see **Insert ▸ Index and Tables... Index Tab**, page 140.)

Insert ▸ Field, Options...

Some fields have mandatory or optional switches. Some also require a bookmark (see **Insert ▸ Bookmark...**, page 159, for more information). You add switches and bookmarks from the Options button on the Field dialog box.

To Define Field Options, do the following:

1. Choose **Insert, Field** to display the Field dialog box.
2. Choose the **Options** button to display the Field Options dialog box (see Figure 2.43).
3. Select one of the switches in the list of switches shown.
4. Choose the **Add to Field** button.
5. Repeat steps 3 and 4 for optional and multiple switches you can add.
6. Choose **OK** when you are done.
7. Choose **OK** on the Field dialog box to insert the field code with the switches.

Figure 2.43

Choose Insert, Field and click the Options button to display the Field Options dialog box.

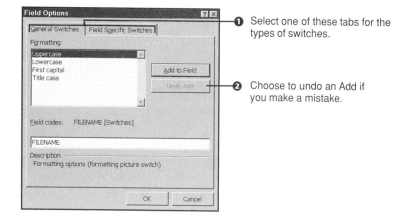

❶ Select one of these tabs for the types of switches.

❷ Choose to undo an Add if you make a mistake.

The field is inserted in your document with the result displayed. If you want to see the field codes instead of the result, choose **Tools**, **Options**, click the **View** tab, and select **Field Codes**. Make sure you don't type in the brackets of a code or you more than likely mess the code up.

Insert ➥ Symbol...

The **Insert**, **Symbol** command enables you to insert symbols and special characters in your text based on the fonts you have installed on your computer. You can insert foreign language characters, decorative characters, scientific characters or even special characters such as ™, ©, ®, nonbreaking spaces, and many more.

To Insert Symbols, do the following:

1. Move the insertion point to the place you need the symbol.

2. Choose **Insert**, **Symbol** to display the Symbol dialog box (see Figure 2.44).

Figure 2.44

Choose Insert, Symbol to display the Symbol dialog box.

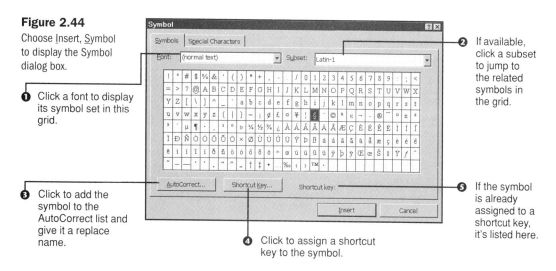

❶ Click a font to display its symbol set in this grid.

❷ If available, click a subset to jump to the related symbols in the grid.

❸ Click to add the symbol to the AutoCorrect list and give it a replace name.

❹ Click to assign a shortcut key to the symbol.

❺ If the symbol is already assigned to a shortcut key, it's listed here.

3. Select a symbol in the grid provided and choose the **Insert** button. Repeat for as many symbols as you need.

   - Double-clicking a symbol is the same as selecting the symbol and choosing the **Insert** button.
   - Click and drag the Title bar to move the Symbol dialog box out of your way.

4. Choose the **Close** button when you are finished.

Inserting Special Characters

You may need to insert special characters such as the Trademark, Copyright, or Section symbols. Some of these symbols may be included in the font character set, but it is easier to use the Special Characters tab on the Symbol dialog box.

To Insert Special Characters, follow these steps:

1. Move the insertion point to the place you need the special character.

2. Choose **Insert**, **Symbol** to display the Symbol dialog box.

3. Click the **Special Characters** tab (see Figure 2.45).

Figure 2.45

Choose Insert, Symbol and click the Special Characters tab to display the Symbol dialog box open to the Special Characters tab.

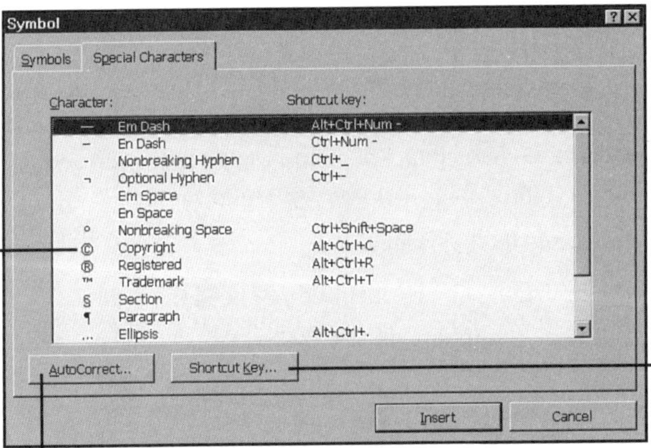

❶ Select the special character you need to insert.

❷ Click to add the symbol to the AutoCorrect list and give it a replace name.

❸ Click to assign a shortcut key to the symbol.

4. Choose the **Insert** button to insert the symbol.

5. Choose **Close** when you are finished.

Insert Special Characters Using ANSI Character Numbers

If you know the ANSI character numbers for the symbols you want to insert, you can use the keyboard to insert the symbols.

To Insert Special Characters with the Keyboard, do the following:

1. Move the insertion point to the place you need the ANSI character.
2. Press Num Lock on the numeric keypad (so that numbers appear when you type).
3. While you hold down the **Alt** key, type **0** (zero) followed by the **ANSI code** for the symbol you want. To insert the Copyright symbol, press and hold **Alt** and type 0169 on the numeric keypad.

   - **0167** is the Section symbol (§)
   - **0174** is the Registered symbol (®)
   - **0162** is the cent symbol (¢)

Most printer manuals have a list of ANSI codes. You can find a substantial list of ANSI codes on the Internet at "The ANSI Code Page," **bau2.uibk.ac.at/schuste2/english/ansi.html**. There are also symbols you can use from the IBM Extended Symbol Set. These characters are formed with the **Alt** key and a number. For example, **Alt+21** equals §.

You can also use the Character Map application that comes with Windows to see the codes for characters. Choose the Windows **Start** button and **Run**. Type CHARMAP and press **Enter**. The Character map dialog box is displayed with the ANSI code for a selected symbol in the lower right corner.

Insert ➡ Comment

The Insert, Comment command gives you the ability to write comments to yourself or someone else. You can write the comment directly where you want it, and choose to print it or not.

Quick Choices   *TO INSERT A COMMENT*

1. Move the insertion point to the place in the text you want the comment, or select the word or phrase you want to comment on.
2. Press **Alt+Ctrl+M** to mark the location of the comment and open the Comments pane.
3. Type your comment and choose the **Close** button to get back to the document.

To insert comments using the Menu command, take these steps:

1. Position the insertion point where you want the comment.
2. Choose **Insert, Comment** to open the Comments pane (see Figure 2.46).
3. If you choose to add an audible comment, the Sound Object dialog box is displayed (see Figure 2.47).

Figure 2.46

Choose Insert, Comment to open the comments area of the document.

❶ Type comments here—they are automatically numbered.

❷ Click this to insert a sound comment (object).

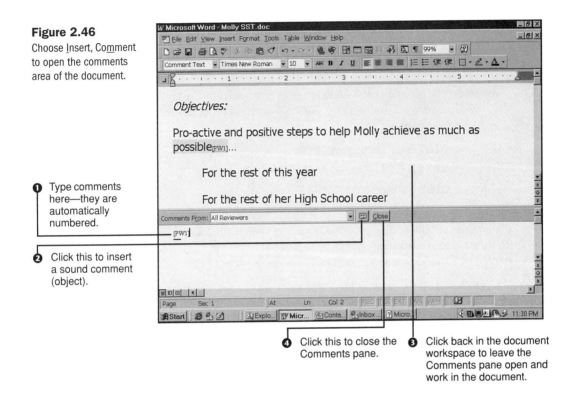

❹ Click this to close the Comments pane.

❸ Click back in the document workspace to leave the Comments pane open and work in the document.

4. After you have recorded the audible comment, click the **Close** button on the Comments pane or double-click any comment mark in the pane.

5. Comments are marked with yellow highlight and contain the reviewer's initials and a sequential number.

Finding and Viewing Comments

After you have inserted comments, you may want to review them one at a time. (For more information, see the sections **View ▪ Toolbars ▪ Reviewing** on page 81 and **View ▪ Comments** on page 95.)

Quick **Choices**   *TO FIND COMMENTS*

1. Click the **Select Browse Object** ⊙ button on the vertical scrollbar or press Alt+Ctrl+Home.

2. Click the **Browse by Comment** ▭ button on the Select Browse Object toolbar to browse by comment.

3. Click the **Next** ▾ button to go to the next comment.

4. Point to the comment to see the ScreenTip for the comment.

Figure 2.47
Choose Insert, Comment and click the Insert Sound object button to display the Sound Object in [document name] dialog box.

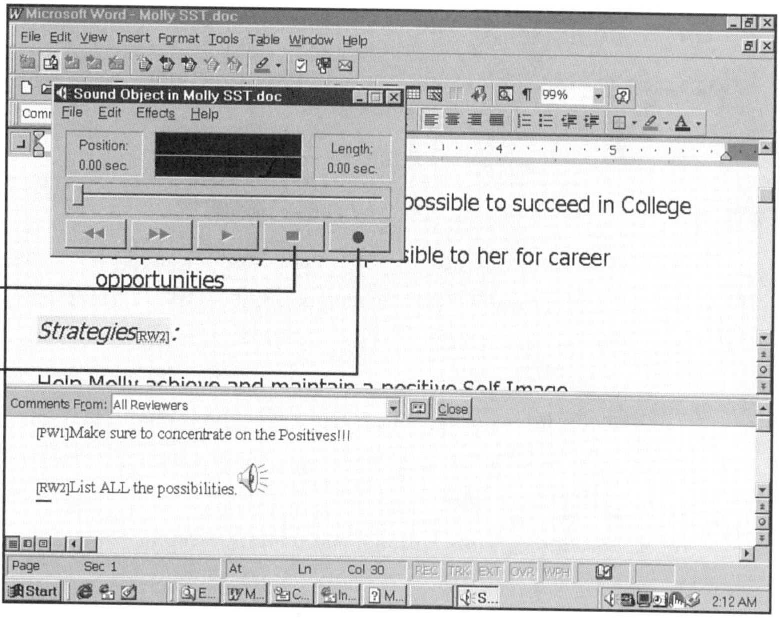

❷ Click to stop recording.

❶ Click to begin recording.

To Edit Comments

1. Right-click a comment to display the shortcut menu.
2. Choose **Edit Comment** to open the Comments pane and display the Reviewing toolbar.
3. Make any changes to the comment in the Comments pane.
4. To go to the next comment, click anywhere in the document.
5. Click the **Next Comment** ⊡ button on the Reviewing toolbar to go to the next comment.
6. After making all your changes, click the **Close** button to close the comments pane.

Insert ➥ Footnote...

The **Insert, Footnote** command gives you the choice to insert footnotes or endnotes to provide additional information about a topic or to reference information. Footnotes appear on the bottom of the page for which the reference is made. Endnotes appear at the end of a section (or chapter).

Quick Choices *TO INSERT A FOOTNOTE*

1. Press **Alt+Ctrl+F** to open the **Footnotes** pane.
2. Type the footnote text.
3. Choose **Close** on the **Footnotes** pane.

1. Press **Alt+Ctrl+E** to open the **Endnotes** pane.
2. Type the endnote text.
3. Choose **Close** on the **Endnotes** pane.

To insert footnotes and endnotes, take these steps:

1. Choose **Insert, Footnote** to open the Footnote and Endnote dialog box.
2. In the Insert section of the dialog box, choose either **Footnote** or **Endnote**.
3. In the Numbering section of the dialog box, choose one of the following:
   - **AutoNumber** numbers sequentially by text, numbers or section symbols.
   - **Custom mark** enables you to type the symbol you want in the text box.
   - **Symbol** button enables you to choose a symbol to use from the font character sets for the footnote or endnote.
4. Choose the **Options** button if you want to select more detailed options for the Footnote or Endnote.
5. Select either the All Footnotes or All Endnotes tab.
6. Select any of the following options:

Footnote and endnote options

Tab	Option	Choices
All Footnotes	**Place at**	Bottom of Page
		Beneath Text
All Endnotes	**Place at**	End of Document
		End of Section
Both	**Number format**	1, 2, 3…
		a, b, c…
		A, B, C…
		i, ii, iii…
		I, II, III…
		*, †, ‡, §
Both	**Start at**	Type number or use spinner buttons to increase or decrease.
Both	**Numbering**	Continuous
		Restart each section
All Footnotes		Restart each page

7. Choose **OK** to close the Note Options dialog box.

8. Choose **OK** to close the Footnote and Endnote dialog box.

Finding and Viewing Footnotes or Endnotes

After you have inserted Footnotes or Endnotes, you may want to review them one at a time. (For more information, see the section **View - Footnotes**, page 94.)

Quick Choices *FINDING FOOTNOTES OR ENDNOTES*

1. Click the **Select Browse Object** button on the vertical scrollbar or press **Alt+Ctrl+Home**.

2. Click the **Browse by Footnote** button or the **Browse by Endnote** button on the Select Browse Object toolbar to browse by Footnote or Endnote.

3. Click the **Next** button to go to the next footnote or endnote.

4. Point to the note mark to see the ScreenTip for the note.

Edit Footnotes or Endnotes

1. Double-click the note mark to open the Footnotes or Endnotes pane.

2. Make any changes to the note in the Footnotes or Endnotes pane.

3. To go to the next note, click or move in the Footnotes or Endnotes pane (the document part of the window moves with you).

4. After making all your changes, click the **Close** button to close the Footnotes or Endnotes pane.

Insert ➥ Caption...

The **Insert**, **Caption** command gives you choices to insert captions for figures, tables, objects, and even text. If you insert captions manually, you can create consistent labeling for varying types of illustrations.

To Insert Captions, take these steps:

1. Select the object to which you want to add a caption.

2. Choose **Insert**, **Caption** to display the Caption dialog box (see Figure 2.48).

Figure 2.48
Choose Insert, Caption to display the Caption dialog box.

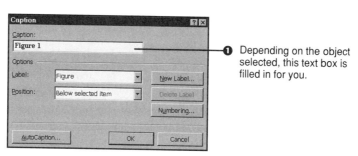

❶ Depending on the object selected, this text box is filled in for you.

3. If the default label is acceptable, in the **Caption** text box, type any additional text you want to include in the caption.

4. If you want to define a unique label, choose the **Label** drop-down arrow, select Table or Equation, and then type any additional text you want to include in the caption.

5. Choose the drop-down arrow for the **Position** list box to change the location of the caption:

   - Below selected item
   - Above selected item

6. Click the **Numbering** button to make changes to the numbering format. Select any of the following options to format the number and chapter number (see **Insert** ▸ **Page Numbers...**, page 97).

Caption numbering options

Option	Description
Format	1, 2, 3...
	a, b, c...
	A, B, C...
	i, ii, iii...
	I, II, III...
Include chapter number	Checkbox; ☑ Yes
Chapter starts with style	List of Heading 1 to Heading 9
Use separator	- (hyphen)
	. (period)
	: (colon)
	— (em dash)
	– (en dash)

7. Choose **OK** when you are finished.

8. Choose **OK** to close the Caption dialog box.

Create New Caption Labels

You may decide that the predefined labels don't have what you want for your caption. You can create a new caption label that is available any time you insert captions.

To create new caption labels, take the following steps:

1. Select the object for a new caption or to edit the existing caption.

2. Choose **Insert, Caption** to display the Caption dialog box.

3. Choose the **New Label** button, the New label dialog box is displayed.

4. In the **Label** text box, type the text for the label.

5. Choose **OK** to close the New Label dialog box.

6. Choose **OK** to close the Caption dialog box.

Delete Labels

When you create new caption labels, they are added to the list of labels. You can delete the labels you create, but not the three built-in labels—Equation, Figure, and Table.

To delete caption labels, do the following:

1. Choose **Insert**, **Caption** to display the Caption dialog box.

2. Select the label from the **Label** list.

3. Choose **Delete Label**.

4. Choose **Close**.

Insert ➧ Caption... AutoCaption...

If you are going to insert many figures, tables, pictures, or illustrations, you find that using the AutoCaption command saves an incredible amount of time.

Take these steps to use AutoCaption:

1. Choose **Insert**, **Caption** to display the Caption dialog box.

2. Click the **AutoCaption** button to display the AutoCaption dialog box.

3. In the **Add caption when inserting** list box, select the type of document to which you want Word to add automatic captions. You can select several different elements if you want them all to have the same label and numbering sequence.

4. Select Options for the type of caption (see Figure 2.49).

Figure 2.49

Choose Insert, Caption, and click AutoCaption to display the AutoCaption dialog box.

❶ Click to select the type of label.

❷ Click to select above item or below item.

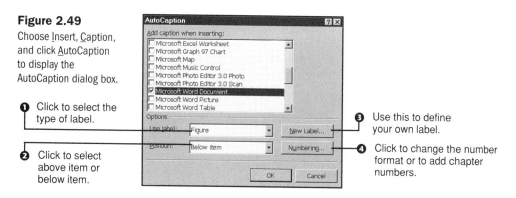

❸ Use this to define your own label.

❹ Click to change the number format or to add chapter numbers.

5. Repeat steps 3 and 4 for additional captions for other document types. This creates a unique label and numbering sequence for each type of document element.

6. Choose **OK**.

Insert ➙ Cross-reference...

The **Insert**, **Cross-reference** command enables you to refer to other sections in your document. Before you can insert cross-references, you need to mark the text you want to reference. You can mark the text with a heading style, a bookmark, a footnote or endnote, or a caption. (See **Format – Style...** on page 178, **Insert – Bookmark...** on page 159, **Insert – Footnote...** on page 131, and **Insert – Caption...** on page 133.)

To insert cross-references, do the following:

1. Type the introductory text that will precede the cross-reference. For example, type see `Insert Bookmark on page.` Leave the insertion point where you want the cross-reference to appear.

2. Choose **Insert**, **Cross-reference** to display the Cross-reference dialog box (see Figure 2.50). The following table describes the type of cross-references you can have and what you need to do first.

Creating a specific type of cross-reference

Cross-Reference to	You Need to Have...
Numbered Item	Numbered items in the document.
Heading	Heading level 1 through 9 styles applied to sections of the document (see **View ➙ Outline**, page 63, and **Format ➙ Style...**, page 178).
Bookmark	Text marked with bookmarks (see **Insert ➙ Bookmark...**, page 159).
Footnotes	Footnotes entered in the document (see **Insert ➙ Footnote...**, page 131).
Endnotes	Endnotes entered in the document (see **Insert ➙ Footnote...**, page 131).
Equation	Equation references in the document (**Insert ➙ Caption...**, page 133).
Figure	Figure captions in the document (see **Insert ➙ Caption...**, page 133).
Table	Table references in the document (see **Insert ➙ Caption...**, page 133).

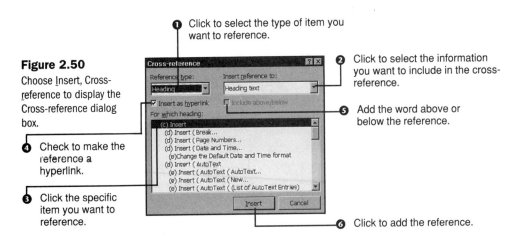

❶ Click to select the type of item you want to reference.

❷ Click to select the information you want to include in the cross-reference.

❺ Add the word above or below the reference.

Figure 2.50

Choose Insert, Cross-reference to display the Cross-reference dialog box.

❹ Check to make the reference a hyperlink.

❸ Click the specific item you want to reference.

❻ Click to add the reference.

3. If you want to type more information in the document, click the document and type the text. You can also move to the next location for which you want to create a cross-reference.

4. Repeat the process to add additional cross-references.

5. Choose **Close** when you are finished.

Cross-reference Another Document

Both documents must be part of a Master document to cross-reference another document. (For more information about Master Documents, see **View** – **Master Document** on page 65.)

All the bookmarks, headings, and so on in all of the documents linked by a master document will be available in the Cross-reference dialog box.

Follow the procedure to insert cross-references in **Insert** – **Cross-reference...** on page 136.

Update Cross-references

Quick Choices   *CHOOSE ONE OF THE FOLLOWING TO UPDATE CROSS-REFERENCES:*

- Print the document.
- Select the cross-reference to update and press **F9**.
- Select the whole document (press **Ctrl+A**) and press **F9**.

Insert ➥ Index and Tables...

The **Insert, Index and Tables** command provides a quick way to create lists—an Index (back of the book), a table of figures (anywhere in the book), a table of contents (front of the book), and a table of authorities (list of cases, statutes, rules, and such for legal documents). There are two primary steps to creating an index or table: marking the entries, and generating the list or table.

Insert – Index and Tables... Index Tab

An index is created by marking the index entries and then generating the Index.

To mark index entries, take these steps:

1. Select the word or words to be included in the Index.

2. Choose **Insert, Index and Tables**; the Index and Tables dialog box is displayed. Optionally, press **Alt+Shift+X** to display the Mark Index Entry dialog box (see Figure 2.51).

3. Choose the **Mark Entry** button to display the Mark Index Entry dialog box (see Figure 2.51).

Figure 2.51

Choose Insert, Index and
Tables and click the
Mark Entry button to
display the Mark Index
Entry dialog box.

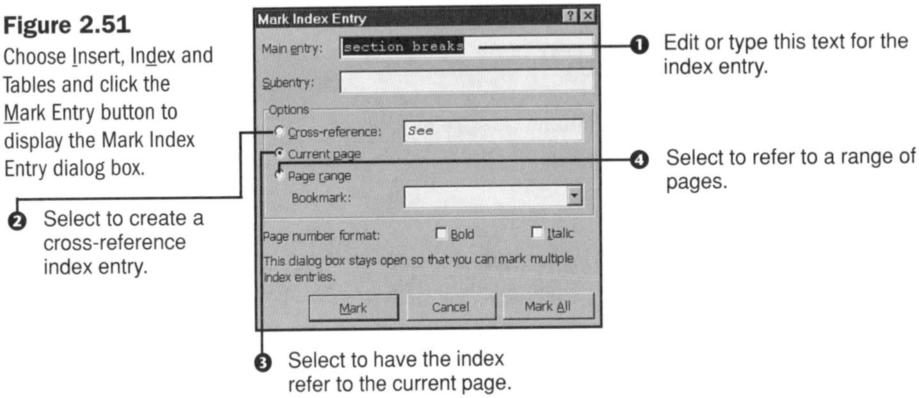

❶ Edit or type this text for the
index entry.

❷ Select to create a
cross-reference
index entry.

❹ Select to refer to a range of
pages.

❸ Select to have the index
refer to the current page.

4. Select either or both of the Page number formats, **Bold** or **Italic**.

5. Choose **Mark** to mark only this entry or choose **Mark All** to have Word search the entire document and mark all the entries that match the text in the **Main entry** text box. **Mark All** is only available if you selected the text in the document for the Main entry and have the **Current page** option selected.

6. This dialog box stays open so you can continue to mark additional index entries. Scroll in the document to the next text that you want to select for an entry and repeat the process.

7. Choose **Close** when you are finished.

To generate an index, follow these steps:

1. Position the insertion point in the document where you want the index to appear. If you are creating an index for a master document, first choose **View**, **Master Document**.

2. Choose **Insert**, **Index and Tables** to display the Index and Tables dialog box.

3. Select the **Index** tab if it is not displayed.

4. In the Type section, select **Indented** or **Run-in**:

Type of index	
Choice	**Example**
Indented	Section breaks Continuous, 63
Run-in	Section breaks: Continuous, 63

5. In the **Formats** list box, select one of the following seven formats. Look at the Preview box to see an example of what the format will look like:

   - *From Template.* If you choose Template, the **Modify** button becomes active. Select **Modify** to change the style of the text used in the index.

- *Classic.* Letter header centered in column or page, indented items and page numbers after a comma.
- *Fancy.* Same as Classic, but letter header in double border and shadow box.
- *Modern.* Letter header with line and left aligned; page numbers after a dot.
- *Bulleted.* Same as classic, except that the letter header is indented.
- *Formal.* Letter header left justified; dot leader tab to right edge of column or margin and page number.
- *Simple.* Same as Classic, except no letter header.

6. Select **Headings for accented letters** if you would like headings beginning with accented letters separated under their own heading. For instance, words beginning with A and with À would be sorted separately.

7. In the **Co**l**umns** box, select the number of columns you want for the index.

8. Select **R**i**ght align page numbers** to line up page numbers on the right margin. If this is selected, the **Ta**b **leader** list box becomes active.

9. In the **Tab leader** list box, select a leader style from the following options.

Leader options

Type	Example
None	
Dots	. . . .
Dashes	- - - - -
Solid line	_____

10. Choose **OK**. Word repaginates the document, compiles the index, and inserts it at the location of the insertion point.

Insert ➥ In*d*ex and Tables... Modify

If you choose the From template in Forma*t*s when you create an index, the **Modify** button is activated. You can change any of the Index styles associated with the template.

To modify styles for the index, do the following:

1. Choose **Insert, In**d**ex and Tables** to display the Index and Tables dialog box.

2. In the Forma*t*s list, choose **From template**.

3. Click the **M**odify button to display the Style dialog box (see Figure 2.52).

Figure 2.52
Choose Insert, Index and Tables, and click the Modify button to display the Style dialog box.

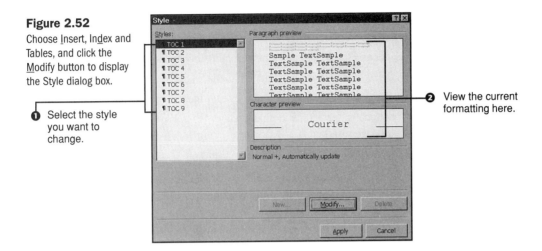

❶ Select the style you want to change.

❷ View the current formatting here.

4. Choose the **Modify** button to make format changes. (See **Format ▾ Style...**, page 178, for detailed information on changing styles.)

5. Choose **Apply** to apply the changes, or **Cancel** to close the dialog box without making any changes and return to the Index tab.

Add Heading Separators to an Index

If you choose the From template in the Formats list when you create an index, you will not have alphabetic headers. You can edit the field code for the index and add the switch to include alphabetic separators.

To add alphabetic separators to an index, do this:

1. Place the insertion point in the index.

2. Press **Shift+F9** to display the field code for the index.

3. Edit the field code to include the **\h "A"** switch—similar to the following example:
   {INDEX \h "A" \c "2"}

4. Press **Shift+F9** to see the index, and press **F9** to update the index.

For more information about editing field codes, see **Insert ▾ Field...**, **Edit Field Codes**, page 106.

Insert ▾ Index and Tables... Index tab, AutoMark button

If you have a large number of items to index or you want to standardize the capitalization of your index entries, you can use the **AutoMark** button to have Word index the entries for you. First you need to create a concordance file containing the words or phrases you want to index and their corresponding main entries and subentries. You can then select the **AutoMark** button to automatically mark the index entries.

To create a concordance file, do the following:

1. Start a new document, click the **New Document** ▯ button on the Standard toolbar.

2. Create a two-column table, click the Insert Table ▦ button on the Standard toolbar, and drag to select a 1 × 2 table. (For more information about creating tables, see **View ‑ Toolbars ‑ Standard**, page 66, and **Table ‑ Insert Table…**, page 230.)

3. In the first column, type the text you want Word to search for and mark it as an index entry. Make sure to enter the text exactly as it appears; the concordance file is case-sensitive. You need to include both upper- and lowercase entries if you want them to be included in the index.

4. Press **Tab** to move to the second column of the table.

5. In the second column, type the index main entry for the text you are searching for. If you want to create a subentry, type the main entry followed by a colon and the subentry.

6. Repeat steps 3, 4, and 5 for each index reference and entry.

7. Save the concordance file and press **Ctrl+S** or click the **Save** ▧ button on the Standard toolbar. (For more information about saving files, see **File ‑ Save As…**, page 29.)

To make sure Word marks all the text you want to index, list all forms of the text you want to search for on separate rows in the table. For an example, see the following table.

Example of a concordance file

Ctrl+C	Keyboard Shortcuts
Ctrl+V	Keyboard Shortcuts
Ctrl+X	Keyboard Shortcuts
Left Align	Paragraph Formatting
Align Left	Paragraph Formatting
Ctrl+L	Paragraph Formatting

To speed up the creation of a concordance file, open both documents and choose **Window, Arrange All** to see both documents at the same time. Copy the text you want to index from the document and paste it in the first column of the concordance file. Then go back and add the Main entry and subentry references in the second column.

To use AutoMark, follow these steps:

1. Position the insertion point where you want the index to appear.

2. Choose **Insert, Index and Tables** to display the Index and Tables dialog box.

3. Click the **Index** tab if it is not displayed.

4. Choose the **AutoMark** button. The Open Index AutoMark File dialog box is displayed.

5. Select the concordance file you want to use and choose **Open**. (For more information about opening files, see **File ‑ Open…**, page 21.)

Word searches through your document and inserts an index entry at every location where a word or phrase matches a word or phrase in the first column of your concordance file.

After using the **A<u>u</u>toMark** button to insert index entries in the document, you need to insert the index. (See the detail steps for generate indexes earlier in this section on page 137.)

Insert ➥ Index and Tables... Table of Contents Tab

A table of contents is generally used in the front of a document to show selected items and their page numbers. A table of contents may be created in two ways: use heading styles, or use special table of contents entry fields. The easiest way is to use the heading styles.

If you use Word's predefined heading styles 1 through 9, it is even easier to create the table of contents. You can also use other heading styles as entries for the table of contents.

Quick **Choices**   *TO APPLY HEADING STYLES*

▪ Place the insertion point in the text to apply a style and do one of the following:

- Select the Style (Heading 1 through Heading 9) from the [Normal ▼] button on the Standard toolbar.
- Use **<u>V</u>iew**, **<u>O</u>utline** to create your document and use the built-in Heading 1 through Heading 9 styles. For more information about creating a document in Outline view, see **<u>V</u>iew ➥ <u>O</u>utline** on page 63.
- Press **Alt+Shift+Left Arrow** or **Alt+Shift+Right Arrow** to change the paragraph into a heading style and move it to a higher (left arrow) or lower (right arrow) style.
- Choose **F<u>o</u>rmat**, **<u>S</u>tyle**, select the style from the **<u>S</u>tyles** list box and choose **Apply**. For more information about Styles, see **F<u>o</u>rmat ➥ <u>S</u>tyle...** on page 178.
- Press **Ctrl+Alt+1**, **Ctrl+Alt+2**, or **Ctrl+Alt+3** to apply the Heading 1, Heading 2, or Heading 3 style.

To generate the table of contents, do the following:

1. Place the insertion point where you want the table to appear.

   If you are creating a table of contents for a master document, switch to **Master Document** View first.

2. Choose **<u>I</u>nsert**, **In<u>d</u>ex and Tables** to display the Index and Tables dialog box (see Figure 2.53).

3. Choose **OK**. Word repaginates the document and inserts the table of contents.

Insert ➥ Index and Tables... Table of Contents Tab, Options Button

When you are inserting a table of contents and use heading styles other than Heading 1 through Heading 9 or table entry fields, you need to use the options button to tell Word which styles to include in your table.

Figure 2.53

Choose Insert, Index and Tables to display the Index and Tables dialog box.

❷ See what they look like here.

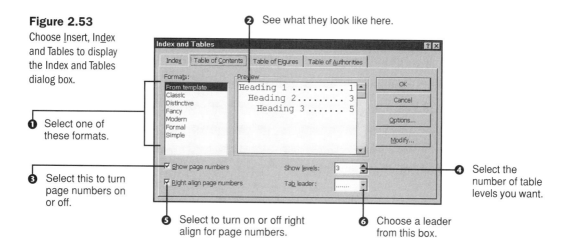

❶ Select one of these formats.

❸ Select this to turn page numbers on or off.

❹ Select the number of table levels you want.

❺ Select to turn on or off right align for page numbers.

❻ Choose a leader from this box.

To use table of contents options, do the following:

1. Choose **Insert, Index and Tables** to display the Index and Tables dialog box.

2. Choose the **Options** button to display the Table of Contents Options dialog box (see Figure 2.54).

Figure 2.54

Choose Insert, Index and Tables, and click the Options button to display the Table of Contents Options dialog box.

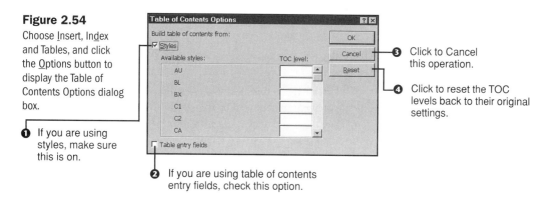

❸ Click to Cancel this operation.

❹ Click to reset the TOC levels back to their original settings.

❶ If you are using styles, make sure this is on.

❷ If you are using table of contents entry fields, check this option.

3. For every style in the Available styles list that you want to include in the table of contents, type a number (between 1 and 9) in the TOC level text boxes. The number represents what level you want that style to have in the table of contents.

   If you don't want a style to be included in the table of contents, make sure the TOC level text box is empty.

4. Choose **OK** to go back to the Table of Contents tab.

If you want to generate a table of contents using just table entry fields, clear the **Styles** option on the Table of Contents Options dialog box to turn it off. See **Table of Contents Entry Fields** on page 144.

Insert ▾ Index and Tables... Table of Contents Tab, Modify Button

When you create a table of contents and choose the From template format, the **Modify** button is activated. You can change any of the TOC styles associated with the template.

To modify styles for the table of contents, do the following:

1. Choose **Insert, Index and Tables** to display the Index and Tables dialog box.
2. Choose the **Modify** button to display the Style dialog box.
3. Choose the **Modify** button to make format changes. See **Format ▾ Style...** on page 178 for detailed information on changing styles.
4. Choose **Apply** to apply the changes, or **Cancel** to close the dialog box without making any changes and return to the Table of Contents tab.

Table of Contents Entry Fields

You may want to refer to items in a table of contents (or a table of figures) that don't have a heading, caption, or other style to use as a reference. In these cases you can insert a table of contents entry field to mark the location. You include switches to tell Word where this information should go.

To use the table of contents entry fields, do the following:

1. Position the insertion point in the text you want to mark.
2. Press **Alt+Shift+O** to open the Mark Table of Contents Entry dialog box, or press **Ctrl+F9** to insert the brackets for the field code.
3. On the dialog box in the Entry text box, type the text for the table of contents item. Select a Table identifier and the Level at which the item should appear in the table of contents.

   Optionally, if you pressed **Ctrl+F9**, you type all the information for the field code. Type TC for the table of contents entry field, followed by the text for the table entry, and then the appropriate switches. See the following table for examples.
4. Repeat these steps for each table entry code you want to insert.

Table of Contents entry field

"text"	Switches	Definition of Switch	Additional Information
Text you want to appear in the table, include the quotes	\l	Indicates this is for the outline level of the TOC	A number between 1 and 9 to identify the level you want this to take in the finished TOC
	\f	Identifies the entry for use in multiple tables	A letter to associate this entry with others with the same table indentifier
	\n	Suppress page number	

"text"	Switches	Definition of Switch	Additional Information

Example for table of contents entry:

{TC "Keyboard Shortcuts" \l 2}

Example for special table entry:

{TC "Photo of North Office" \f p}

You can also select the text to mark before you use a keyboard shortcut. When you press **Alt+Shift+O,** the selected text is displayed in the **Entry** text box of the Mark Table of Contents Entry dialog box. When you press **Ctrl+F9,** the selected text is marked and the TC field code is inserted at the end of the selected text.

Insert Index ⁃ and Tables... Table of Figures Tab

A table of figures is generally in the front of a document after the table of contents. The Table of Figures dialog box can be used to create special-purpose tables such as a table of photos, charts, tables, or equations. Any table for which you created captions can be generated. For more information about captions, see **Insert ⁃ Caption...** on page 133 earlier in this section.

You can create a table of figures in two ways: Use caption styles, or use special table of figures entry fields. The easiest way is to use the caption styles: Equation, Figure, and Table.

To generate the table of figures:

1. Place the insertion point where you want the table to appear.
2. If you are creating a table of figures for a master document, choose **View, Master Document** first.
3. Choose **Insert, Index and Tables** to display the Index and Tables dialog box.
4. Click the **Table of Figures** tab (see Figure 2.55).
5. Choose **OK.** Word repaginates the document and inserts the table of figures.

Insert ⁃ Index and Tables... Table of Figures Tab, Options Button

Use the **Options** button if you want to change the style on which the table of figures is based, or create a table compiled from the selected style and from table entry fields.

To change options for the table of figures, do the following:

1. Choose **Insert, Index and Tables** to display the Index and Tables dialog box.
2. Click the **Table of Figures** tab if it is not displayed.
3. Choose the **Options** button to display the Table of Figures Options dialog box (see Figure 2.56).

Figure 2.55

Choose Insert, Index and Tables, and click the Table of Figures tab to display the Index and Tables dialog box open to the Table of Figures tab.

❶ Select the caption for the table.

❸ Preview the selections here.

❷ Select the format.

❹ Select this to turn page numbers on or off.

❺ Check to right align page numbers.

❻ Check to include Caption label and sequential number.

❼ Choose a leader from this box.

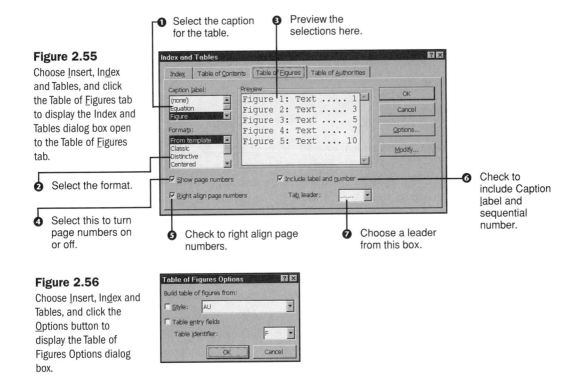

Figure 2.56

Choose Insert, Index and Tables, and click the Options button to display the Table of Figures Options dialog box.

4. If you are using styles, choose Style and select the text style in the list box.

5. Click the **Table entry fields** check box if you are using table entry fields.

6. Choose the Table indentifier from the list box. This is the letter associated with the table entry field.

7. Choose **OK** to go back to the **Table of Figures** tab.

If you want to generate a table of figures using just table entry fields, clear the **Style** option on the Table of Figures Options dialog box.

Insert ▪ Index and Tables... Table of Figures Tab, Modify

When you create a table of figures and choose the From template format, the **Modify** button is activated. You can change any of the styles associated with the template.

To modify styles for the table of figures, do the following:

1. Choose **Insert, Index and Tables** to display the Index and Tables dialog box.

2. Choose the **Modify** button to display the Style dialog box.

3. Choose the **Modify** button to make format changes. See **Format ▪ Style...** on page 178 for detailed information on changing styles.

4. Choose **Apply** to apply the changes, or **Cancel** to close the dialog box without making any changes and return to the Table of Figures tab.

Insert ~ Field... Codes for Special Tables

You can mark any place in your document for inclusion in a special table by entering a TC field code. You can type the field codes directly in your document or choose **Insert**, **Field** to insert them. For more information about TC fields see **Table of Contents Entry Fields** earlier in this chapter on page 144. For more information about fields in general, see **Insert ~ Field...** on page 106.

Insert ~ Index and Tables... Table of Authorities Tab

The Table of Authorities tab helps you create a table listing where citations appear in a legal brief. A table of authorities is created in two steps: mark the citations, and generate the table.

To mark citation entries, do the following:

1. Select the word or words to be included in the table.

2. Choose **Insert**, **Index and Tables**, and the Index and Tables dialog box is displayed.

3. Click the **Table of Authorities** tab.

4. Choose the Mark Citation button to display the Mark Citation dialog box (see Figure 2.57).

Figure 2.57

Choose Insert, Index and Tables and click the Mark Entry button to display the Mark Citation dialog box.

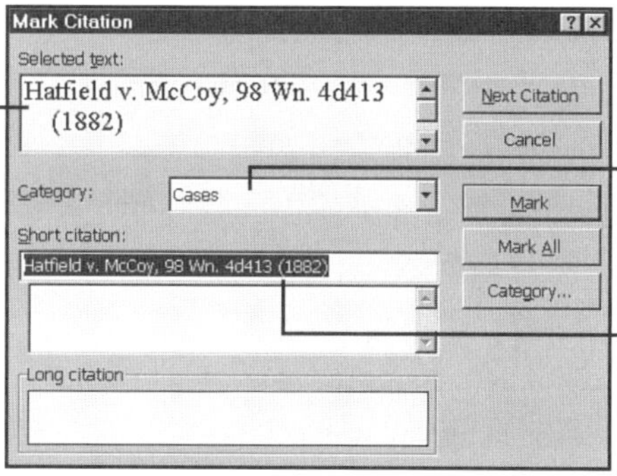

❶ Edit this text for the long form of the citation entry.

❷ Select the citation category.

❸ Edit this text so it is the way you want it to appear.

5. Choose **Mark** to mark only this entry or choose **Mark All** to have Word search the entire document and mark all the entries that match the text in this dialog box.

6. This dialog box stays open so you can continue to mark additional index entries. Scroll in the document to the next text you want to select for an entry and repeat the process.

7. Choose the Next Citation button to have Word search your document for common legal citations ("in re," "v.," "Ibid.," and so forth) and then repeat the steps.

8. Choose **Close** when you are finished.

If you mark a citation and want to mark additional citations later, you can select the original long citation, press **Alt+Shift+I** to display the Mark Citation dialog box, and then choose **Mark All**.

Insert - Index and Tables... Table of Authorities Tab, Category

The **Category** button enables you to change or add categories:

1. Choose **Insert, Index and Tables**.
2. If necessary, click the **Table of Authorities** tab.
3. Choose **Mark Citation** to display the Mark Citation dialog box.
4. Choose **Category** to display the Edit Category dialog box (see Figure 2.58).

Figure 2.58

Choose Insert, Index and Tables, click the Table of Authorities tab, choose the Mark Citation button, and choose Category to display the Edit Category dialog box.

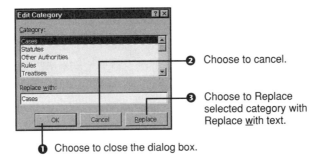

❷ Choose to cancel.

❸ Choose to Replace selected category with Replace with text.

❶ Choose to close the dialog box.

5. In the Category list box, select the category you want to change.

   Word allows up to 16 categories, and predefines the first seven. The remaining categories are numbered 8 through 16.

6. In the Replace with text box, type the new category name.
7. Choose **Replace** to change the category name.
8. Repeat steps 5 through 7 for each category name you want to change.
9. Choose **OK** when you are finished.

Generate the Table of Authorities

After you have marked the citations in your brief, you need to insert the table of authorities.

To insert the table of authorities, do the following:

1. Place the insertion point where you want the table to appear.

   If you are creating a table of authorities for a master document, choose **View, Master Document** first.

2. Choose **Insert, Index and Tables** to display the Index and Tables dialog box.
3. Click the **Table of Authorities** tab (see Figure 2.59).
4. Select the Use passim check box to substitute the word "passim" whenever a citation has five or more different page numbers.
5. Select Keep original formatting to preserve the character formatting of the long citations when inserting the table.
6. In the Category drop-down list, select the category for this table.
7. Choose **OK**. Word repaginates the document and inserts the table of authorities.

Figure 2.59

Choose Insert, Index and Tables, and click the Tables of Authorities tab to display the Index and Tables dialog box open to the Table of Authorities tab.

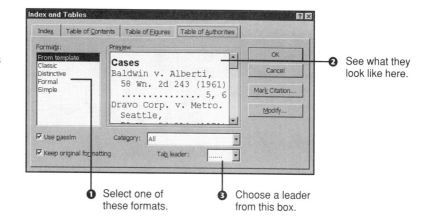

❷ See what they look like here.

❶ Select one of these formats.

❸ Choose a leader from this box.

Insert ➥ Index and Tables... Table of Authorities Tab, Modify Button

When you create a table of authorities and choose the From template format, the **Modify** button is activated. You can change any of the styles associated with the template.

To modify styles for the table of authorities, do the following:

1. Choose **Insert, Index and Tables** to display the Index and Tables dialog box.
2. Choose the **Modify** button to display the Style dialog box.
3. In the Styles list select the style you want to change.
4. Choose the **Modify** button to make format changes. See **Format ➥ Style...** on page 178 for detailed information on changing styles.
5. Choose **Apply** to apply the changes, or **Cancel** to close the dialog box without making any changes and return to the Table of Contents tab.

Insert ➥ Picture

The **Insert, Picture** command enables you to insert pictures from many outside sources, such as drawing programs, scanners, and clip art collections. You can also insert pictures using Word's built-in drawing tools: AutoShapes, WordArt, Chart, and the drawing toolbar.

Insert ➥ Picture ➥ Clip Art...

The **Insert, Picture, Clip Art** command connects you to unlimited pictures.

Quick **Choices**   *TO INSERT CLIP ART*

1. Put your Microsoft Office CD in the CD player (or any other CD or disk that has clip art pictures you want to access).
2. Position the insertion point where you want the picture to appear.
3. Choose **Insert, Picture, Clip Art** to display the Microsoft Clip Gallery 3.0 dialog box and switch to Page Layout View (see Figure 2.60).

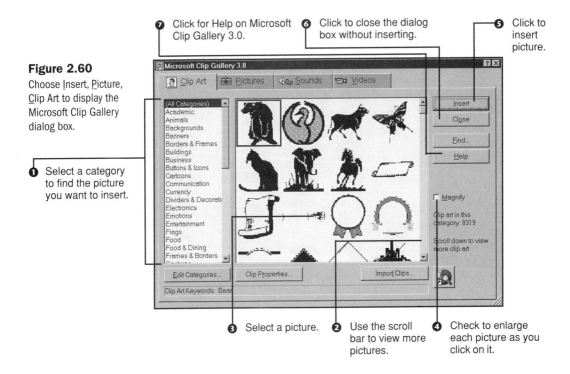

Figure 2.60

Choose Insert, Picture, Clip Art to display the Microsoft Clip Gallery dialog box.

❼ Click for Help on Microsoft Clip Gallery 3.0.

❻ Click to close the dialog box without inserting.

❺ Click to insert picture.

❶ Select a category to find the picture you want to insert.

❸ Select a picture.

❷ Use the scroll bar to view more pictures.

❹ Check to enlarge each picture as you click on it.

Insert → Picture → Clip Art... Find Button

When looking for a clip art picture you are presented with many pictures. To make it easier to find what you want, use the Find command to narrow your search.

To use the find command, do the following:

1. Choose **Insert**, **Picture**, **Clip Art** to display the Microsoft Clip Gallery 3.0 dialog box.

2. Choose the **Find** button to display the Find Clip dialog box (see Figure 2.61).

Figure 2.61

Choose Insert, Picture, Clip Art and click the Find button to display the Find Clip dialog box.

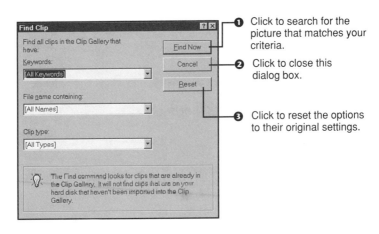

❶ Click to search for the picture that matches your criteria.

❷ Click to close this dialog box.

❸ Click to reset the options to their original settings.

3. In the Keywords list box, type a word associated with the picture you want. To repeat a previous search, click the drop-down arrow and select one of the keywords you used before.

4. In the File name containing list box, type part of the filename for the picture you want. To repeat a previous search, click the drop-down arrow and select one of the files for which you searched before.

5. If you know the file type of the clip art you want, click the drop-down arrow for the Clip type and select from the list.

6. Choose **Find Now** when you are ready to perform the search.

Insert ▾ Picture ▾ Clip Art... Edit Categories...

The list of categories on the Microsoft Clip Gallery dialog box may not reflect the groups the way you need to see them.

Quick Choices   *TO EDIT THE CATEGORY LIST*

1. Choose **Insert, Picture, Clip Art** to display the Microsoft Clip Gallery 3.0 dialog box.

2. Right-click a category name in the list.

3. Select one of the following commands from the shortcut list:

   • Delete Category

   • Rename Category

   • New Category

   • Edit Category List

   • Cancel

To edit the category list, do the following:

1. Choose **Insert, Picture, Clip Art** to display the Microsoft Clip Gallery 3.0 dialog box.

2. Choose the **Edit Categories** button to display the Edit Category dialog box (see Figure 2.62).

Figure 2.62

Choose Insert, Picture, Clip Art, and choose the Edit Categories button to display the Edit Category List dialog box.

❸ Click a category in this list to rename or delete.

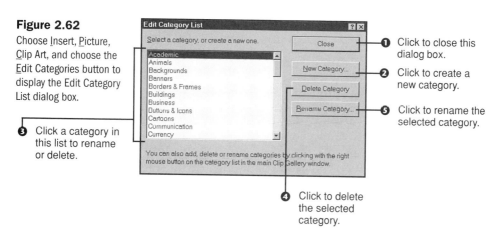

❶ Click to close this dialog box.

❷ Click to create a new category.

❺ Click to rename the selected category.

❹ Click to delete the selected category.

3. If you choose the **New Category** button or the **Rename Category** button, a dialog box is displayed in which you can type the category name. Type the name and choose **OK**.

4. Choose **Close** when you are finished.

Insert ► Picture ► Clip Art... Clip Properties...

You can view information about the clip art such as the name of the file, the type of file, where it is stored, and keywords assigned.

To view ClipArt properties, do the following:

1. Choose **Insert, Picture, Clip Art** to display the Microsoft Clip Gallery 3.0 dialog box.

2. Choose the **Clip Properties** button to display the Clip Properties dialog box.

3. If the file is read-only, this is for information purposes only. Otherwise, you can change information related to the file.

Insert ► Picture ► Clip Art... Import Clips Button

To add clip art to the Gallery, do the following:

1. Choose **Insert, Picture, Clip Art** to display the Microsoft Clip Gallery 3.0 dialog box.

2. Choose the **Import Clips** button to display the Add Clip Art to Clip Gallery dialog box.

3. Navigate to the location for the files you want to add and select the file or files. For more information on how to open files, see **File ► Open...** on page 21.

4. Choose **Open** to add the images to your Clip Art Gallery.

Insert ► Picture ► Clip Art... Connect to the Web

To connect to the World Wide Web to find additional clip art, do the following:

1. Choose **Insert, Picture, Clip Art** to display the Microsoft Clip Gallery 3.0 dialog box.

2. Choose the **Connect to the Web** button. The first time you do this you get a message about connecting to the Web.

3. If you don't want to see the message the next time you connect to the Web, click on the **Don't show this message again** check box.

4. Choose **OK**. You then connect to the Web and are on a Microsoft license agreement page. If you want to continue, click on the **Agree** button to accept the terms of the license agreement. The Microsoft Clip Gallery page is displayed (see Figure 2.63).

5. Click on the **Close** button (top right corner of the window) to disconnect from the Web.

Insert ► Picture ► From File...

You can use **Insert, Picture, From File** to insert pictures that are not in the Clip Gallery:

1. Position the insertion point where you want the picture to appear.

2. Choose **Insert, Picture, From File** to display the Insert Picture dialog box.

❶ Use this toolbar to navigate to more pictures.

Figure 2.63
Choose Insert, Picture, Clip Art and click on the Connect to the Web button to connect to the Microsoft Clip Gallery Live Web site.

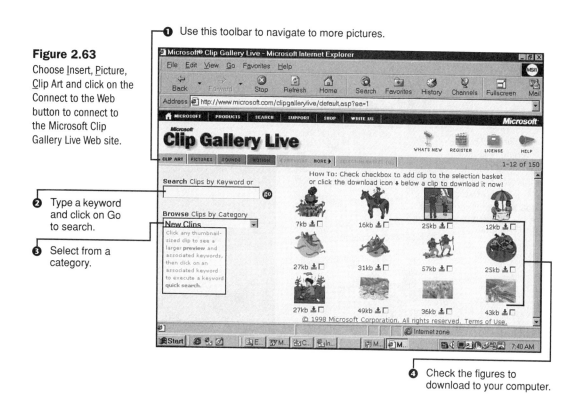

❷ Type a keyword and click on Go to search.

❸ Select from a category.

❹ Check the figures to download to your computer.

3. Navigate to the drive and folder that contains the file you want to insert. See **File ►
Open...** on page 21 for more information on navigating in this dialog box.

4. Check **Link to file** if you want a pointer to the picture and not the actual picture inserted
in your document. Choose this option if you're going to edit the picture or want the same
picture in many documents. When you edit the picture it is automatically updated in all
the documents that contain links to it.

5. Check **Float over text** to place the picture in a drawing layer that you can place over or
behind text. Clear this box to place within the current paragraph where you can move it
like regular text.

6. Select the file to insert and choose **Insert** (or double-click on the file to skip clicking on
the **Insert** button).

Insert ► Picture ► AutoShapes

The **Insert**, **Picture**, **AutoShapes** command offers another way to display the **AutoShapes**
toolbar (see Figure 2.64). For more information about the shapes available, see **View ►
Toolbars ► Drawing**, page 73.

Figure 2.64

Insert, Picture, AutoShapes displays the AutoShapes toolbar.

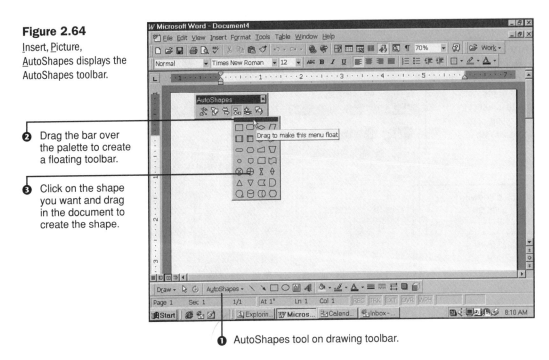

❷ Drag the bar over the palette to create a floating toolbar.

❸ Click on the shape you want and drag in the document to create the shape.

❶ AutoShapes tool on drawing toolbar.

After you have drawn an AutoShape you may want to change something about the shape. Click on the shape and use the sizing and adjustment handles to change the size and appearance (see Figure 2.65).

Figure 2.65

Click on a shape to see the adjustment and sizing handles.

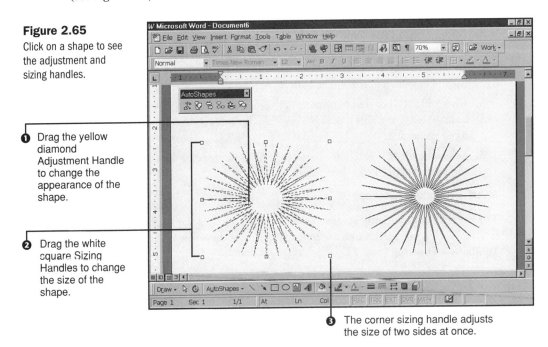

❶ Drag the yellow diamond Adjustment Handle to change the appearance of the shape.

❷ Drag the white square Sizing Handles to change the size of the shape.

❸ The corner sizing handle adjusts the size of two sides at once.

To change the line styles, color, and other formatting of AutoShapes, use the formatting tools on the Drawing toolbar or the **Format**, **Object [AutoShape]** command. See **View ‑ Toolbars ‑ Drawing** on page 73, and **Format ‑ Object...** on page 183 for more information.

Insert ‑ Picture ‑ WordArt...

WordArt enables you to bend text in many different shapes and colors.

Quick **Choices**   *TO INSERT WORDART PICTURES*

1. Choose **Insert**, **Picture**, **WordArt** to display the WordArt Gallery dialog box.
2. Select a WordArt style and choose **OK** to open the Edit WordArt Text dialog box (see Figure 2.66).

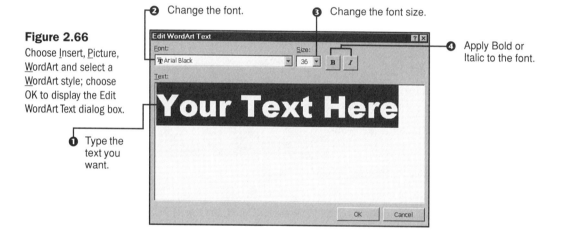

❷ Change the font.   **❸** Change the font size.

Figure 2.66
Choose Insert, Picture, WordArt and select a WordArt style; choose OK to display the Edit WordArt Text dialog box.

❹ Apply Bold or Italic to the font.

❶ Type the text you want.

3. When you are finished editing the WordArt object, choose **OK**.

Edit and Format WordArt

To make changes to the WordArt object, use the WordArt toolbar (see **View ‑ Toolbars ‑ WordArt** on page 86 for more information).

Quick **Choices**   *TO EDIT AND FORMAT WORDART*

1. You can use the shortcut menu by right-clicking on the object and selecting a command from the menu.
2. Use the **Format**, **Object [WordArt]** command (see **Format ‑ Object...** on page 183 for more information).

Insert ➥ Picture ➥ From Scanner

With the **Insert**, **Picture**, **From Scanner** command, you open the Microsoft Photo Editor program and your scanner software. This is the quickest way to insert scanned objects.

To insert scanned objects, do the following:

1. Choose **Insert**, **Picture**, **From Scanner** to open Microsoft Photo Editor and start the scanner software.
2. Use the scanner software to complete the scan. Your scanned image appears in the Microsoft Photo Editor window.
3. Use Microsoft Photo Editor to edit the scanned image, if necessary.
4. Choose **File**, **Exit and Return** to Document to close Photo Editor and return to your document.

After you have a scanned image in your document, you may need to edit it. Double-click the scanned image to open Microsoft Photo Editor and use the editing tools available.

Insert ➥ Picture ➥ Chart

The **Insert**, **Picture**, **Chart** command opens the Microsoft Graph 97 Chart applet. This is a quick way to create a simple chart.

To insert a chart, do the following:

1. Position the insertion point where you want the chart to appear.
2. Choose **Insert**, **Picture**, **Chart** to display the datasheet for your chart.
3. Enter the text and numbers in the cells on the datasheet for the chart data.
4. When you are finished, click the **Close** button on the top right corner of the datasheet window.
5. To get back to your document, click anywhere outside the chart.

When you close the datasheet, the Standard toolbar changes to display charting tools. See the Excel section **View ➥ Toolbars ➥ Chart** on page 292 for more information on charting.

Double-click the chart to open the datasheet and change information on the sheet.

Insert ➥ Text Box

The **Insert**, **Text Box** command enables you to insert a text box object. Position the document so you can point to where you want the text box to appear and choose **Insert**, **Text Box**, or click 🔳 on the Drawing toolbar. The mouse pointer changes to a black plus; click and drag to draw the rectangle for the text box.

When you release the mouse button, the insertion point is in the top left corner of the text box, with a hashed outline defining the borders of the text box. You can now type in the text box, use one of the buttons on the Text Box toolbar, click outside the text box to continue typing in the document, or draw another object. If the Text Box toolbar did not automatically open, right-click on any visible toolbar and select Text Box to display the toolbar.

You can apply formatting to text inside a text box just as you do in the document (see **Format ▸ Font...** on page 160, **Format ▸ Paragraph...** on page 164, **Format ▸ Bullets and Numbering...** on page 166, and **Format ▸ Borders and Shading...** on page 170).

If you insert multiple text boxes, you can connect them with the Create Text Box Link button 🔗 on the Text Box toolbar. The text boxes to which you link must be empty to create the link.

To link text boxes, do the following:

1. Click the first text box in the link.
2. Click 🔗 on the Text Box toolbar.
3. Click the text box to which you want to link.
4. Repeat steps 2 and 3 to link additional text boxes.

After you link text boxes, the text you type wraps to the next linked text box when it reaches the end of the first text box.

Buttons on the Text Box toolbar

Button	Description
🔗	Click to create a link to another text box.
🔗	Click to break the link to the next text box.
🔳	Click to move to the preceding text box.
🔳	Click to move to the next text box.
‖	Click to change the direction of the text.

Insert ▸ File...

The **Insert, File** command enables you to insert all or part of a file in the active document.

To insert a file, do the following:

1. Position the insertion point where you want the inserted file to appear.
2. Choose **Insert, File** to display the Insert File dialog box.
3. Navigate to and select the file you want to insert. See **File ▸ Open...** on page 21 for more information.

4. Check **Link to file** if you want a pointer to the file. Choose this option if you're going to edit the file and you want changes in the file to appear in the document as well. This is useful when you use the file in multiple documents or have another person responsible for editing the file.

5. Choose **OK**.

Insert ➟ Object...

The **Insert**, **Object** command gives you a choice of inserting many types of objects in your document. The choices are related to the software you have installed on your computer.

To insert an object, do the following:

1. Choose **Insert**, **Object** to display the Insert Object dialog box.

2. On the **Create New** tab, select an object to insert from the **Object type** list (see Figure 2.67).

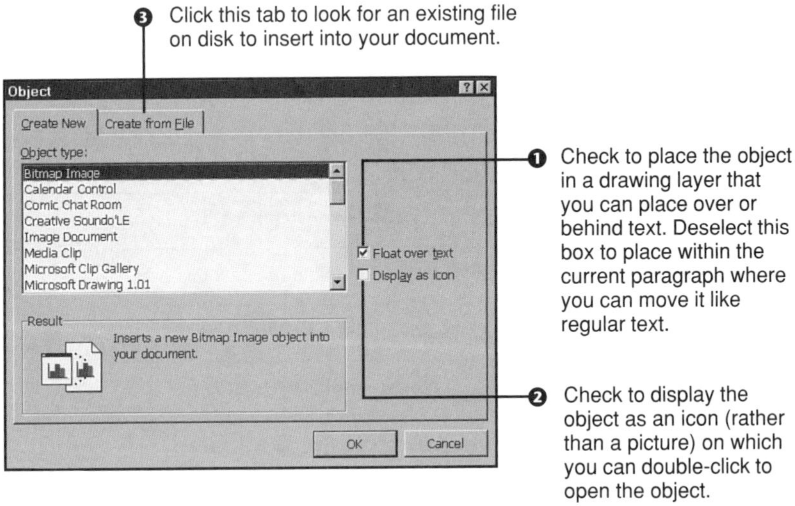

❸ Click this tab to look for an existing file on disk to insert into your document.

Figure 2.67
Insert, Object opens the Object dialog box.

❶ Check to place the object in a drawing layer that you can place over or behind text. Deselect this box to place within the current paragraph where you can move it like regular text.

❷ Check to display the object as an icon (rather than a picture) on which you can double-click to open the object.

3. Choose **OK** to insert the object.

4. Use any of the formatting and editing options built into the applet or program.

5. Click outside the object to return to the document.

To edit objects, double-click the object to return to the applet or program commands.

To format objects, use the **Format**, **Object** command; see **Format ➟ Object...** on page 183 for more information.

Insert ➟ Bookmark...

The **Insert**, **Bookmark** command enables you to mark specific text, tables, or graphics with a named item that can be referenced later.

To insert bookmarks, do the following:

1. Select the text, table, or graphic, or position the insertion point where you want your bookmark to be located.

2. Choose **Insert**, **Bookmark**, or press **Shift+Ctrl+F5** to display the Bookmark dialog box (see Figure 2.68).

Figure 2.68

Choose Insert, Bookmark to display the Bookmark dialog box.

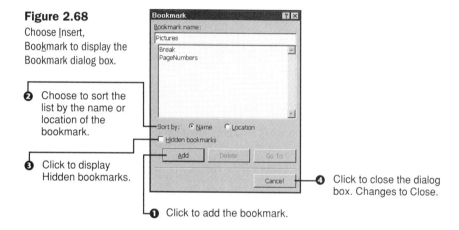

❷ Choose to sort the list by the name or location of the bookmark.

❸ Click to display Hidden bookmarks.

❹ Click to close the dialog box. Changes to Close.

❶ Click to add the bookmark.

3. In the Bookmark name text box, type a name for the bookmark (do not use spaces), or select an existing bookmark in the list to Delete or Go To.

4. Choose the **Add** button to add the bookmark.

5. Choose **Delete** to delete the bookmark.

6. Choose **Go To** to go to the location of the bookmark (see also **Edit** ➟ **Go To...**, page 58).

Insert ➟ Hyperlink...

The **Insert**, **Hyperlink** command enables you to create or edit a link to a document on your computer, a network, or the Internet. Position the insertion point in your document where you want the link to appear or select text you want to change to a hyperlink. Choose **Insert**, **Hyperlink** or click ▨ on the Standard toolbar to display the Insert Hyperlink dialog box (see Figure 2.69).

Figure 2.69

Choose Insert, Hyperlink to display the Insert Hyperlink dialog box.

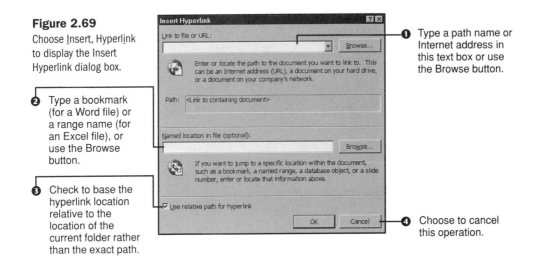

❶ Type a path name or Internet address in this text box or use the Browse button.

❷ Type a bookmark (for a Word file) or a range name (for an Excel file), or use the Browse button.

❸ Check to base the hyperlink location relative to the location of the current folder rather than the exact path.

❹ Choose to cancel this operation.

Format

Formatting enables you to change the text and how figures look on the page.

Format ➥ Font...

Font is the way characters are printed on the page or how they appear on the screen. Font includes the type style, size, and effects such as strikethrough or underline. To change the font, first select the text you want to change and then do any of the following:

Quick Choices — *CHANGE THE FORMAT OF SELECTED TEXT*

Do What	Button on Formatting Toolbar	Keyboard Shortcut
Bold	**B**	Ctrl+B
Italicize	*I*	Ctrl+I
Underline	U	Ctrl+U
Underline words but not spaces		Ctrl+Shift+W
Double underline		Ctrl+Shift+D
Change font face	Times New Roman ▼	Ctrl+Shift+F then use Up or Down arrow

Do What	Button on Formatting Toolbar	Keyboard Shortcut
Symbol font		Ctrl+Shift+Q
Font color		
Highlight (background color)		
Change font size	 12	Ctrl+Shift+P then use Up or Down arrow
Increase font size		Ctrl+Shift+>
Decrease font size		Ctrl+Shift+<
Increase font size by 1 point		Ctrl+]
Decrease font size by 1 point		Ctrl+[
Subscript		Ctrl+=
Superscript		Ctrl+Shift+=
Cycle through uppercase, title case, and lowercase		Shift+F3
All uppercase		Ctrl+Shift+A
Small capitals (lowercase letters look like capitals)		Ctrl+Shift+K
Hide text		Ctrl+Shift+H

To change multiple font characteristics at once, first select the text you want to change and then do one of the following:

Quick Choices   BRING UP THE FONT DIALOG BOX

- Press **Ctrl+D**.
- Choose **Format**, **Font**.
- Click the right mouse button on the selection and choose **Font**.

The Font dialog box appears (see Figure 2.70).

Figure 2.70

Format, Font opens the
Font dialog box.

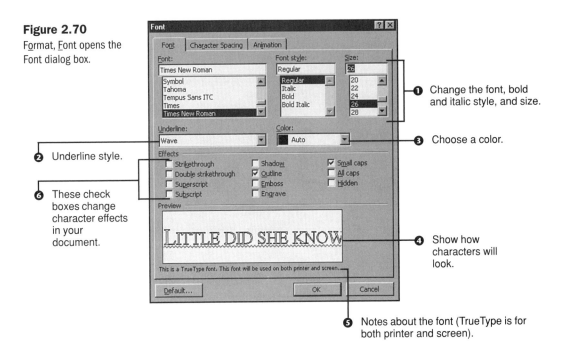

① Change the font, bold
   and italic style, and size.

② Underline style.

⑥ These check
   boxes change
   character effects
   in your
   document.

③ Choose a color.

④ Show how
   characters will
   look.

⑤ Notes about the font (TrueType is for
   both printer and screen).

The following table includes additional notes about the Font dialog box not shown in the figure.

Dialog Box Item	What It Looks Like and Notes
Font tab	
Underline	Different underline types include: Single, words only, double, dotted, thick, dash, dot dash, dot dot dash, wave
Strikethrough	Strikethrough
Double strikethrough	Double strikethrough
Superscript	Superscript
Subscript	Subscript
Shadow	Shadow
Outline	Outline
Emboss	Emboss
Engrave	Engrave
Small caps	Small caps
All caps	All caps

Dialog Box Item	What It Looks Like and Notes
Hidden	Does not display or print text. Click the Show/Hide button ¶ to show text on screen with dotted underline.
Character Spacing tab	
Scale	Type or use down-arrow to magnify or shrink the size of the text by a percentage.
Spacing By	Choose Normal, Expanded, or Condensed to spread out the letters by the size in the By box.
Position By	Choose Normal, Raised, or Lowered to move the text up or down relative to the baseline.
Kerning for fonts Points and above	Check the box and choose which size font you want to start with to adjust the space between pairs of letters (only works with TrueType and Adobe fonts).
Animation tab	
Animations	Choose none or one of the animations to create a blinking or moving effect on the screen. The effect does not print.

Note: Not all attributes are available for every font.

You can also do the following with fonts:

- To display nonprinting characters, click the **Show/Hide** button ¶ on the Standard toolbar or press **Ctrl+Shift+*** (asterisk).

- To see a description of text (and paragraph formatting), press **Shift+F1** and click on the text. Press **Esc** to turn off review.

- To copy text formatting, select the text with formatting you want to copy and do one of the following:

  - Click the **Format painter** button on the Standard toolbar. The mouse pointer changes to a paint brush with an I-beam. Select the text you want to change.

  - Double-click the **Format painter** button and apply the format to multiple areas. Click the **Format painter** button again to turn off the copy.

  - Press **Ctrl+Shift+C** to copy the format. Select the text to accept the format and press **Ctrl+Shift+V**.

- To remove manual formatting, press **Ctrl+Spacebar**.

Format ➡ Paragraph...

Paragraph formatting changes the spacing between lines, how text is aligned, and other formats to the paragraph as a unit. Paragraph formatting takes place for the current paragraphs or if you have any part of multiple paragraphs selected.

Quick Choices — *CHANGE THE FORMAT OF SELECTED PARAGRAPHS*

Do What	Button on Formatting Toolbar	Keyboard Shortcut
Single-space lines		Ctrl+1
Double-space lines		Ctrl+2
1.5-line spacing		Ctrl+5
Add or remove one line space before current paragraph		Ctrl+0
Left align	▤	Ctrl+L
Center	▤	Ctrl+E
Right align	▤	Ctrl+R
Justify (both left and right align)	▤	Ctrl+J
Increase left indent (all lines of paragraph moved in)	▤	Ctrl+M
Decrease left indent	▤	Ctrl+Shift+M
Hanging indent (all but first line of paragraph indented)		Ctrl+T
Reduce hanging indent		Ctrl+Shift+T
Create "old-fashioned" indent with the first line indented		Ctrl+M then Ctrl+Shift+T

To remove paragraph formatting, press **Ctrl+Q**.

To change multiple formats for one paragraph at one time, first select the paragraphs you want to change and then choose **Format**, **Paragraph** or right-click on the selection and choose **Paragraph**. The Paragraph dialog box appears (see Figure 2.71).

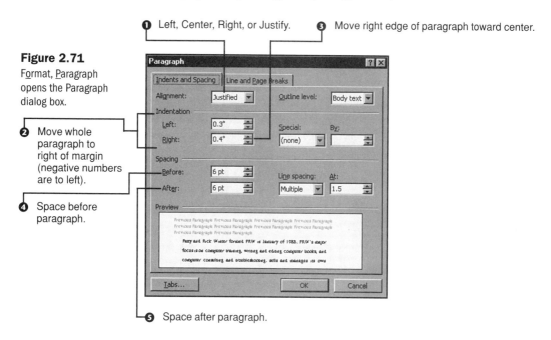

① Left, Center, Right, or Justify.   **③ Move right edge of paragraph toward center.**

Figure 2.71
Format, Paragraph opens the Paragraph dialog box.

② Move whole paragraph to right of margin (negative numbers are to left).

④ Space before paragraph.

⑤ Space after paragraph.

The following table includes additional notes about the Paragraph dialog box not shown in the figure.

Dialog Box Item	How to Use
Indents and Spacing tab	
Outline level	If you don't want to use the formatting associated with Heading 1, Heading 2 (and other) styles, but still want to use the outline toolbar (see **View - Outline**, page 63).
Special	Choose First line if you want to indent the first line of the paragraph, or Hanging if you want to indent the rest of the paragraph.
By	Type or use spinner button to say how much to indent your choice in **Special**.
Line spacing	To space lines, choose Single, 1.5 lines, Double. To set a minimum line height (larger fonts can take more room), choose At least. To set the height regardless of font size, choose Exactly. To set the number of rows, choose Multiple.

continues

Dialog Box Item	How to Use
A̲t	If Line spacing is At least or Exactly, type or use spinner button to choose point size. For Multiple, type decimal number (for example, .9) or use spinner button to increment in half-line heights.
T̲abs	Click to open the tab dialog box (see **Format – T̲abs...**, page 174).

Line and P̲age Breaks tab

W̲idow/Orphan control	Check to prevent one line of a multiline paragraph from appearing on a page by itself. You're prohibiting widows (lines alone at the top of a page) and orphans (lines alone at the bottom of the page).
K̲eep lines together	Check to prevent a page break in the middle of a paragraph (unless paragraph is more than one page).
Keep with nex̲t	Check to prevent page break between current paragraph and next one.
Page b̲reak before	Check to insert a page break before current paragraph.
S̲uppress line numbers	Check to hide numbers for current paragraph when line numbers have been set (see **File – Page Set̲up...**, page 38).
D̲on't hyphenate	Check to turn off hyphenation for selected paragraphs (see **Tools – Language – Hyphenation...**, page 193).

Fo̲rmat ➥ Bullets and N̲umbering...

If you want to add bullets or numbers to your paragraphs, you can use the bullets and numbering features. You can also use AutoFormatting options to create bullets and numbering (see **Format – A̲utoFormat...**, page 175 and look at the **O̲ptions** button choices).

Quick Choices   *ADD BULLETS OR NUMBERS*

■ Select the paragraphs (or start with no paragraphs selected) and click the Numbering button ▦ on the Formatting toolbar.

■ Select the paragraphs (or start with no paragraphs selected) and click the Bullets button ▦ on the Formatting toolbar.

■ Turn on AutoFormat options with **Fo̲rmat, A̲utoFormat, O̲ptions**, click the AutoFormat As You Type tab, and check **A̲utomatic bulleted lists** and **Automatic n̲umbered lists**. Then begin typing a bulleted list with * (asterisk) or a 1 for a numbered list. When you press **Enter** after your first entry, Word creates the bullets or numbers for you.

■ Move to the last number or bullet and press Enter to add another number or bullet. Press **Enter** again or **Esc** to remove the number or bullet.

For more options when working with bullets and numbering, see each of the following sections.

F**o**rmat - Bullets and **N**umbering..., **B**ulleted Tab

You can customize your bullets beyond the standard bullet that appears when you use the Bullets button ⊞ on the Formatting toolbar.

1. Select the paragraph(s) you want to bullet.

2. Choose **F**o**rmat**, **Bullets and **N**umbering** and click the **Bulleted** tab or right-click the selection and click **Bullets and **N**umbering**.

3. Choose one of the types of bullets in the gallery.

4. If you want to change the bullet, click the **Cus**t**omize** button. The Customize Bulleted List dialog box opens (see Figure 2.72). Choose the options displayed in the figure.

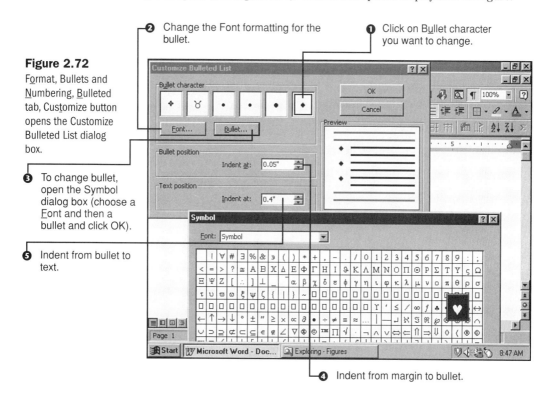

Figure 2.72
F**o**rmat, Bullets and **N**umbering, **B**ulleted tab, Cus**t**omize button opens the Customize Bulleted List dialog box.

❷ Change the Font formatting for the bullet.

❶ Click on B**u**llet character you want to change.

❸ To change bullet, open the Symbol dialog box (choose a **F**ont and then a bullet and click OK).

❺ Indent from bullet to text.

❹ Indent from margin to bullet.

5. If you want to reset the gallery of bullets to Word's original bullets, click **Reset**.

6. Choose **OK** when finished.

F̲ormat ⇒ Bullets and N̲umbering..., N̲umbered Tab

You can customize your numbers beyond the standard numbering that appears when you use
the Numbering button 📊 on the Formatting toolbar. Select the paragraphs you want to number and choose F̲ormat, Bullets and N̲umbering or right-click the selection and click Bul̲-
lets and N̲umbering and click the N̲umbered tab (see Figure 2.73).

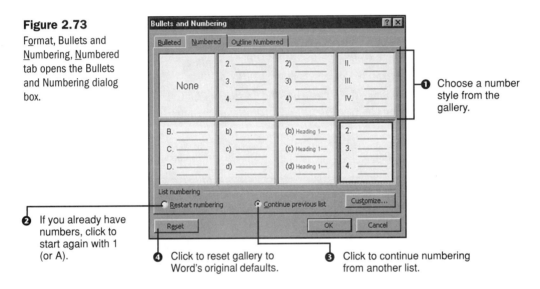

Figure 2.73
F̲ormat, Bullets and N̲umbering, N̲umbered tab opens the Bullets and Numbering dialog box.

① Choose a number style from the gallery.

② If you already have numbers, click to start again with 1 (or A).

④ Click to reset gallery to Word's original defaults.

③ Click to continue numbering from another list.

Click the **Cus̲tomize** button for additional options (see Figure 2.74).

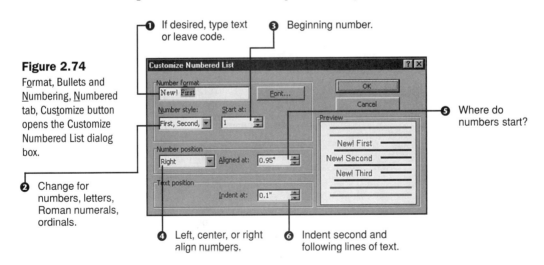

Figure 2.74
F̲ormat, Bullets and N̲umbering, N̲umbered tab, Cus̲tomize button opens the Customize Numbered List dialog box.

① If desired, type text or leave code.

③ Beginning number.

⑤ Where do numbers start?

② Change for numbers, letters, Roman numerals, ordinals.

④ Left, center, or right align numbers.

⑥ Indent second and following lines of text.

Format ~ Bullets and Numbering..., Outline Numbered Tab

If you're working with an outline (see **View ~ Outline**, page 63), you can create and customize outline numbering. Select the paragraphs you want to number and choose **Format, Bullets and Numbering** and click the **Outline Numbered** tab (see Figure 2.75).

Figure 2.75
Format, Bullets and Numbering, Outline Numbered tab opens the Bullets and Numbering dialog box.

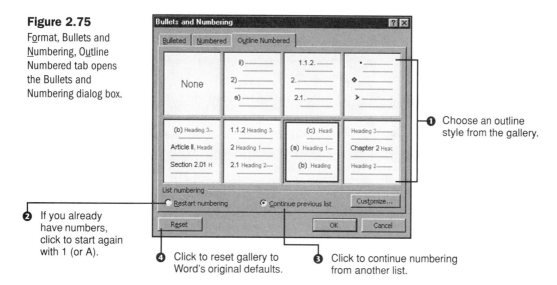

❶ Choose an outline style from the gallery.

❷ If you already have numbers, click to start again with 1 (or A).

❹ Click to reset gallery to Word's original defaults.

❸ Click to continue numbering from another list.

Click the **Customize** button for additional options (see Figure 2.76).

❷ If desired, type text or leave code.

❸ Change for numbers, letters, Roman numerals, ordinals.

Figure 2.76
Format, Bullets and Numbering, Outline Numbered tab, Customize button opens the Customize Outline Numbered List dialog box.

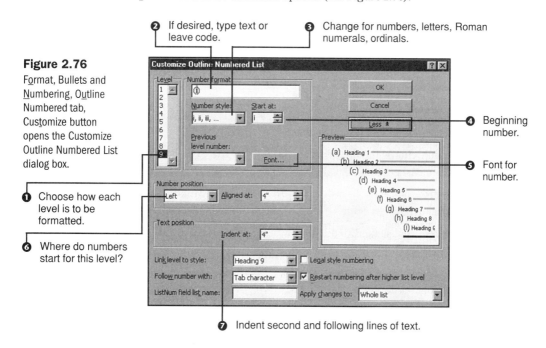

❹ Beginning number.

❺ Font for number.

❶ Choose how each level is to be formatted.

❻ Where do numbers start for this level?

❼ Indent second and following lines of text.

The following table shows additional options for the Customize Outline Numbered List dialog box not explained in the figure.

Dialog Box Item	How to Use
Previous level number	Add code to **Number format** text box that displays preceding level's number.
More	Click to open bottom of dialog box (changes to Less as shown on figure). Click **Less** to return dialog box to opening choices.
Link level to style	Choose a style (or no style) to attach with the outline numbering **Level**.
Follow number with	Choose to follow number with a Tab character, Space, or Nothing.
ListNum field list name	Type a label to include for lists you create with the ListNum field code. Use ListNum to include multiple outline numbers on a single line (see **Insert ‑ Field…**, page 106).
Legal style numbering	Check to change current Level's numbers to Arabic numbers (IV becomes 4).
Restart numbering after higher level list	Uncheck to continue numbering for each level. Check to restart numbering for each new higher level.
Apply changes to	Choose whether you want to have these changes apply to the Whole list, Selected text, or This point forward.

Format ➧ Borders and Shading...

The Borders option enables you to add lines around a paragraph or around cells of a table. You can also add shading to a paragraph or a table and add a border around a page.

Quick Choices   *ADD LINES*

Use the Tables and Borders toolbar buttons for the following steps:

1. Select paragraphs or cells in a table.
2. If desired, choose the drop-down arrow on the **Line Style** button [─────── ▼] and choose a dashed, solid, double, or other line style.
3. If desired, choose the drop-down arrow on the **Line Weight** button [½ pt‑ ▼] and choose the thickness of the line.
4. If desired, choose the **Border Color** button 🖊 and select a color.
5. Click the **Borders** button ⊞ ▼ to apply these formats to the selected border. If you want to change which border to apply, click on the drop-down arrow on this button and choose a different border.

Quick Choices *OTHER BORDER AND SHADING OPTIONS*

You can also do the following to selected paragraphs or cells in a table:

- Click the **Shading Color** button to choose the last shading or click on the arrow to choose a different shading.

- Click the **Borders** button and drag the top of the palette (thick bar above the drop-down) if you're going to use the different border buttons often. You can also do this with the **Shading Color** button.

Format - Borders and Shading... Borders Tab

For more detail options, choose **Format**, **Borders and Shading** and click the **Borders** tab to open the Borders and Shading dialog box (see Figure 2.77). Within a table, you can also right-click the mouse button and choose **Borders and Shading**.

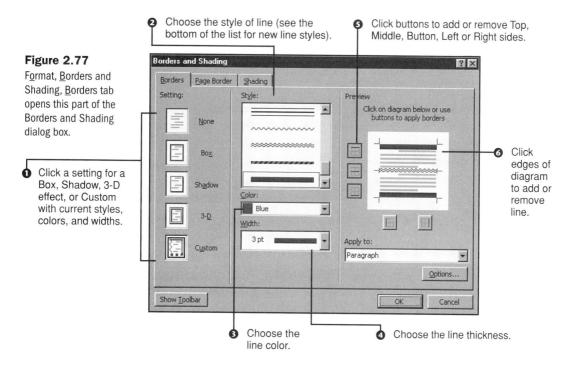

Figure 2.77
Format, Borders and Shading, Borders tab opens this part of the Borders and Shading dialog box.

❷ Choose the style of line (see the bottom of the list for new line styles).

❺ Click buttons to add or remove Top, Middle, Button, Left or Right sides.

❶ Click a setting for a Box, Shadow, 3-D effect, or Custom with current styles, colors, and widths.

❻ Click edges of diagram to add or remove line.

❸ Choose the line color.

❹ Choose the line thickness.

The following table shows additional options on this dialog box.

Dialog Box Item	How to Use
Apply to	If text is selected, choose Text to put an outline around the text or Paragraph to outline the entire paragraph. If the selection is within a table, you can also choose to apply this to just the selected Cell(s) or to the entire Table.

continues

Dialog Box Item	How to Use
Show Toolbar	If the Tables and Borders toolbar is not displayed, click to display the toolbar.
Options	If the Apply to option is Paragraph, click to bring up the Border and Shading Options dialog box. Type or use the spinner button to choose the distance you want from the border to the text on the Top, Bottom, Left, and Right edges.

Format ⇥ Borders and Shading... Page Border Tab

Most of the options on the Page Border tab of the Borders and Shading dialog box are the same as on the Borders tab. Rather than change the paragraph or table, these options change the border around the page. The differences between the Page Border tab and the Borders tab are shown in the table below:

Dialog Box Item	How to Use
Art	Choose figures (such as apples, cake, firecrackers, butterflies, geometric designs, and many others) to repeat around the border of the page.
Apply to	Choose to apply the page border to every page of the Whole document, just **This section, This section—First page only**, or **This section—All except first page**.

When you click the **Options** button, the Border and Shading Options dialog box opens (see Figure 2.78).

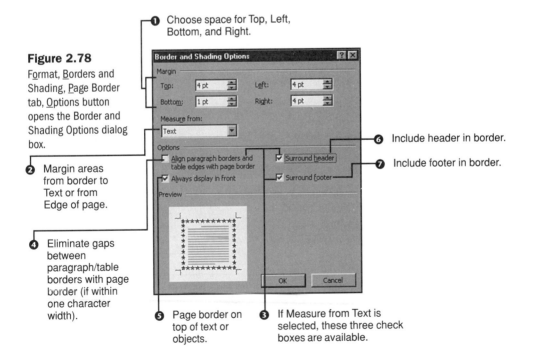

Figure 2.78
Format, Borders and Shading, Page Border tab, Options button opens the Border and Shading Options dialog box.

❶ Choose space for Top, Left, Bottom, and Right.

❷ Margin areas from border to Text or from Edge of page.

❹ Eliminate gaps between paragraph/table borders with page border (if within one character width).

❺ Page border on top of text or objects.

❸ If Measure from Text is selected, these three check boxes are available.

❻ Include header in border.

❼ Include footer in border.

Format → Borders and Shading... Shading Tab

In addition to adding borders to the paragraph, page, or table, you can also add colors or shading. Choose **Format**, **Borders and Shading**, and click the **Shading** tab. Then do any of the following:

- Click on a color (or percent gray) box in the **Fill** section. Click None for no shading.
- Click the **Style** drop-down to choose a proportion of gray, lined, or other pattern.
- Click the **Color** drop-down to choose a color for the lines or dots in the pattern.
- Choose **Apply to** for the changes to affect the entire Table, Cell, Paragraph, or selected Text.

Format → Columns...

If you want to create newspaper or "snaking columns," where you read the text in one column all the way to the bottom of the page (or section) and continue in the second column, choose the columns feature.

Quick Choices   CREATE COLUMNS

1. Select paragraphs that you want to convert into columns or don't select any text if you want to create columns for the whole document (or section).
2. Click the **Columns** button on the Standard toolbar.
3. In **Page Layout** view, move the mouse pointer to the ruler (the pointer is a double-arrow) and drag to increase or decrease the space between the columns.
4. If the columns are not of equal width, you can drag the center dotted pattern in the space between columns to change an individual column width.

If you want more options to set columns, choose **Format**, **Columns**. The Columns dialog box opens (see Figure 2.79).

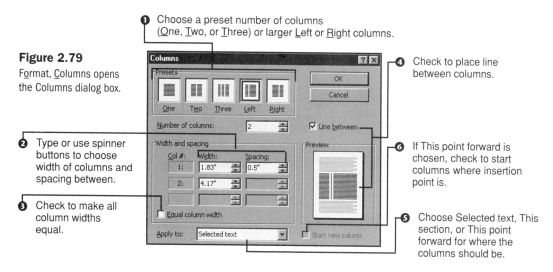

❶ Choose a preset number of columns (One, Two, or Three) or larger Left or Right columns.

❹ Check to place line between columns.

Figure 2.79
Format, Columns opens the Columns dialog box.

❷ Type or use spinner buttons to choose width of columns and spacing between.

❸ Check to make all column widths equal.

❻ If This point forward is chosen, check to start columns where insertion point is.

❺ Choose Selected text, This section, or This point forward for where the columns should be.

Format ➥ Tabs...

An alternative to tables is to use tabs. When you set tab stops, the insertion point stops at these locations each time you press **Tab**.

Quick Choices   SET TABS

1. Select paragraphs for which you want to set tabs.

2. Click the **Tab type** button to the left of the horizontal ruler until the tab is the type you want (Left, Center, Right, or Decimal Aligned).

3. Click in the ruler (see **View** ▪ **Ruler**, page 92) where you want the tab stop.

4. To remove a tab, drag it into the document.

5. To move a tab, drag it to another spot on the ruler.

If you want more options to set tabs, choose **Format, Tabs**. The Tabs dialog box opens (see Figure 2.80).

Figure 2.80
Format, Tabs opens the Tabs dialog box.

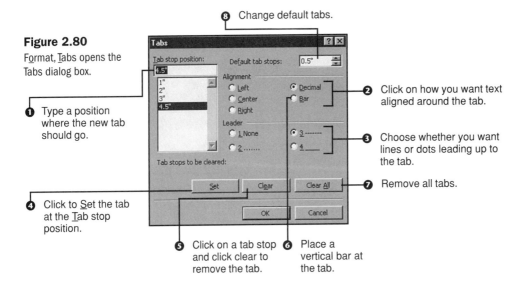

❽ Change default tabs.

❶ Type a position where the new tab should go.

❷ Click on how you want text aligned around the tab.

❸ Choose whether you want lines or dots leading up to the tab.

❼ Remove all tabs.

❹ Click to Set the tab at the Tab stop position.

❺ Click on a tab stop and click clear to remove the tab.

❻ Place a vertical bar at the tab.

Format ➥ Drop Cap...

The drop cap feature makes the first letter of the paragraph larger than the rest. To use this feature, click in a paragraph and choose **Format, Drop Cap**. The Drop Cap dialog box opens (see Figure 2.81).

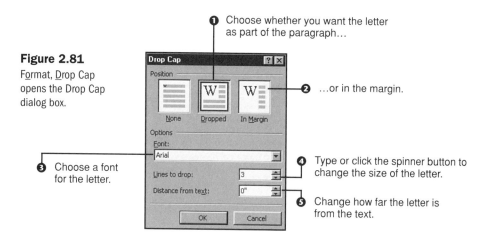

① Choose whether you want the letter as part of the paragraph...

② ...or in the margin.

Figure 2.81
Format, Drop Cap opens the Drop Cap dialog box.

③ Choose a font for the letter.

④ Type or click the spinner button to change the size of the letter.

⑤ Change how far the letter is from the text.

Word places the letter in a frame within the document (see **Format ▪ Frame**, page 187). Choose **Format, Drop Cap, None** to remove the Drop Cap.

Format ➥ Text Direction...

You can change the text direction within a frame, table cell, or text box so text is facing up or down or the familiar left and right.

Quick Choices   *CHANGE TEXT DIRECTION*

1. Select the frame, table cells (see **Table ▪ Draw Table**, page 230), or text box (see **View ▪ Toolbars ▪ Drawing**, page 73).

2. Click the **Change Text Direction** button ▥ on the Tables and Borders toolbar or choose **Format, Text Direction** and double-click on the **Orientation** you want.

Format ➥ Change Case...

To change the capitalization of selected text, press **Shift+F3** until it is the case you want or choose **Format, Change Case**, and choose whether you want the text **Sentence case**, **lowercase**, **UPPERCASE**, **Title Case**, or **tOGGLE cASE** (change all uppercase to lowercase and vice versa).

Format ➥ AutoFormat...

You can have Word analyze your document and automatically decide the formatting to apply. If you want to AutoFormat and accept the default choices without going into the dialog box, press **Alt+Ctrl+K**. Otherwise, choose **Format, AutoFormat**. The AutoFormat dialog box opens with the following options:

Options on AutoFormat dialog box

Dialog Box Option	How to Use
AutoFormat now	Click this option to have Word apply all formatting without prompting.
AutoFormat and review	Click this option to have Word format each change the document but prompt you for each change.
Please select a document type to help improve the formatting process	Choose General document, Letter, or Email to help Word decide on the formatting.

Choose **OK** to format the document. You can also click the **Options** button to tell Word how you want to format the document. The AutoCorrect dialog box opens to the AutoFormat tab.

Options on AutoCorrect dialog box—AutoFormat tab

Dialog Box Option	How to Use
Apply section	
Headings	Check this box to automatically apply headings 1 through 9 to headings (determined by short phrases on one line).
Lists	Check this box to apply list styles and bullet styles to numbered, bulleted, multilevel, and other lists. Word then removes any manually inserted numbers or bullets.
Automatic bulleted lists	Check this box to automatically convert to bulleted items lists typed with asterisks (*), lowercase O, >, or hyphen followed by a space or tab at the beginning of a paragraph.
Other paragraphs	Check this box to convert other paragraphs (not mentioned above) to styles such as Body Text and Closing.
Replace section	
"Straight quotes" with "smart quotes"	Check this box to replace straight-up-and-down quotes with curly quotes.
Ordinals (1st) with superscript	Check this box to replace ordinal numbers (1st, 2nd, 3rd with superscript—1st, 2nd, 3rd).

Dialog Box Option	How to Use
Fractions ($\frac{1}{2}$) with fraction character ($\frac{1}{2}$)	Check this box to show fraction characters for $\frac{1}{2}$, $\frac{1}{4}$, and $\frac{3}{4}$.
Symbol characters (—) with symbols (—)	Check this box to replace two dashes with an en dash (–) and three dashes with an em dash (—).
Bold and _underline_ with real formatting	Check this box to replace text between asterisks with bold text and text between underscores with underlined text.
Internet and network paths with hyperlinks	Check this box to replace Web addresses (for example, **www.microsoft.com**) and network paths to hyperlink fields. You can click on the hyperlink to go to the item if you have an Internet connection or a network.
Preserve section	
Styles	Check this box to keep the styles you've already applied.
Always AutoFormat section	
Plain text WordMail documents	Check this box to AutoFormat WordMail messages in Outlook when you open them.

Word can also format text as you type. Only three options are on the AutoFormat as You Type tab of the AutoCorrect dialog box and not the AutoFormat tab. The following table shows these options.

Additional Options on AutoCorrect dialog box—AutoFormat as You Type tab	
Dialog Box Option	**How to Use**
AutoFormat as You Type tab—The options below are not covered on the AutoFormat tab.	
Borders	Type three or more hyphens, underscore characters, or equal signs, to create a thin, thick, or double border.
Tables	Type a series of hyphens and plus signs (+ - - -+ - - -+) to create a column for each plus sign.
Automatic numbered lists	Type a letter or number (1, A, I, a) followed by a period and a space or tab and then the item. Word automatically inserts the next number. To stop numbering, press Enter twice (see **Format - Bullets and Numbering...**, page 166).

Format ↦ Style Gallery...

In addition to AutoFormat, you can use another option to automatically change the format of a document based on the templates you have loaded (see **File ‑ New...**, page 20). Choose **Format**, **Style Gallery**. The Style Gallery dialog box opens (see Figure 2.82).

Figure 2.82

Format, Style Gallery opens the Style Gallery dialog box.

❶ Choose a Template (these are the same as on File, New tabs).

❷ Preview your underlying document.

❸ Preview an example file.

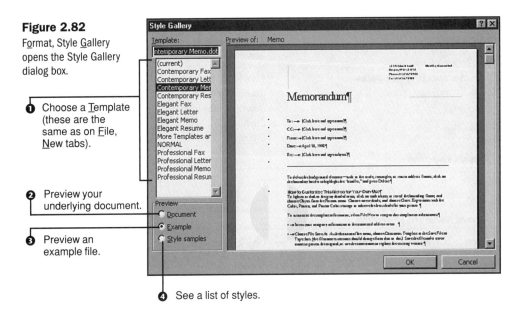

❹ See a list of styles.

Format ↦ Style...

Styles enable you to save and reapply multiple formatting to paragraphs or text.

Quick Choices   APPLY OR CREATE STYLES

■ To apply a style to selected text, click on the drop-down arrow of the **Styles** button `Normal ▼` on the Formatting toolbar and choose a style from the list.

■ To show all styles (and not just current and standard styles in the document), hold down Shift and click on the drop-down arrow of the **Styles** `Normal ▼`.

■ To create a style, format a paragraph the way you want. Click in the Styles text box part of the **Styles** button `Normal ▼`, type a new style name, and press **Enter**.

■ To apply a predefined format to the selected paragraph(s), do one of the following:

  • To apply the Normal style, press **Ctrl+Shift+N**.

  • To apply the Heading 1 style, press **Alt+Ctrl+1**.

  • To apply the Heading 2 style, press **Alt+Ctrl+2**.

  • To apply the Heading 3 style, press **Alt+Ctrl+3**.

  • To apply the List Bullet style, press **Ctrl+Shift+L**.

For more options when working with styles, choose **Format**, **Style**. The Style dialog box opens (see Figure 2.83).

Figure 2.83

Format, Style opens the Style dialog box.

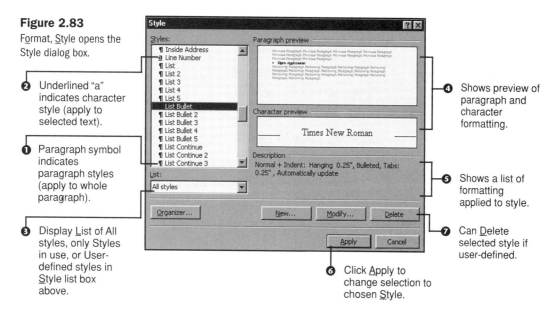

❷ Underlined "a" indicates character style (apply to selected text).

❶ Paragraph symbol indicates paragraph styles (apply to whole paragraph).

❸ Display List of All styles, only Styles in use, or User-defined styles in Style list box above.

❹ Shows preview of paragraph and character formatting.

❺ Shows a list of formatting applied to style.

❼ Can Delete selected style if user-defined.

❻ Click Apply to change selection to chosen Style.

The other buttons on the Style dialog box (**Organizer**, **New**, and **Modify**) are described in the following steps.

The dialog box for New and Modify are identical except for the title bar. When you click the **New** button on the Style dialog box, the New Style dialog box opens (see Figure 2.84).

Figure 2.84

Format, Style, New button opens the New Style dialog box.

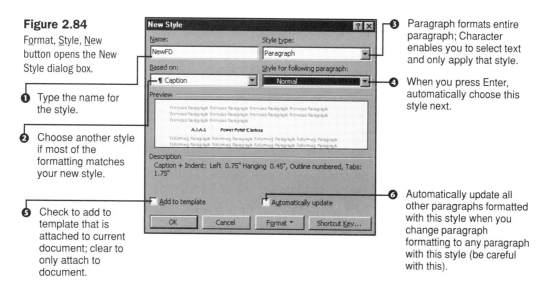

❶ Type the name for the style.

❷ Choose another style if most of the formatting matches your new style.

❺ Check to add to template that is attached to current document; clear to only attach to document.

❸ Paragraph formats entire paragraph; Character enables you to select text and only apply that style.

❹ When you press Enter, automatically choose this style next.

❻ Automatically update all other paragraphs formatted with this style when you change paragraph formatting to any paragraph with this style (be careful with this).

The **Format** button on the New Style (and Modify Style) dialog box shows a menu with choices that correspond to manual formatting. The following table shows each menu item and where you see instructions for using the dialog boxes.

Menu Item	See
Font	**Format - Font...**, page 160
Paragraph	**Format - Paragraph...**, page 164
Tabs	**Format - Tabs...**, page 174
Border	**Format - Borders and Shading...**, **Borders Tab**, page 170
Language	**Tools - Language - Set Language...**, page 192
Frame	**Format - Frame...**, page 187
Numbering	**Format - Bullets and Numbering...**, **Outline Numbered Tab**, page 166

To assign a shortcut key to the style, do the following:

1. From the New Style (or Modify Style) dialog box (**Format**, **Style**, **New** or **Modify** button), click the **Shortcut Key** button. The Customize Keyboard dialog box opens.
2. Click in the **Press new shortcut key** text box and press your desired key. If the key is assigned to another command, you see it below this text box.
3. In the **Save changes in** drop-down list, choose to save the shortcut key with the NORMAL template (available to all documents) or your current document.
4. When you have the correct shortcut key, click **Assign** and **Close**. You then return to the New Style dialog box. Click **OK** when you are finished with this box.

To copy styles from one document or template to another, from the Style dialog box, click the **Organizer** button (see Figure 2.85).

Format ➥ Background...

Background is a new feature for Word 97. This enables you to change the background color or pattern for online viewing or for use when converting as an HTML file (see **File - Save as HTML...**, page 29) for use as a Web page. Choose **Format**, **Background**. A palette of colors appears. Do one of the following:

- Click one of the colors.
- If the color is not in the palette, click **More Colors**. The Colors dialog box opens. Choose colors by using one of the tabs:
  - On the Standard tab, choose one of the **Colors**.
  - On the Custom tab, click on a color or choose the color by dragging the crosshair in the **Colors** box. When you drag left to right, you change the color. When you drag up or down, you change the amount of gray in the color (more gray toward the bottom of the box). The long rectangle to the right has a triangle. Drag the

triangle up or down to add more white or black to the color. You also can manually change the color by typing or clicking the spinner buttons to change any of the six items that make up the color:

Figure 2.85

Format, Style, Organizer button opens the Organizer dialog box to the Styles tab.

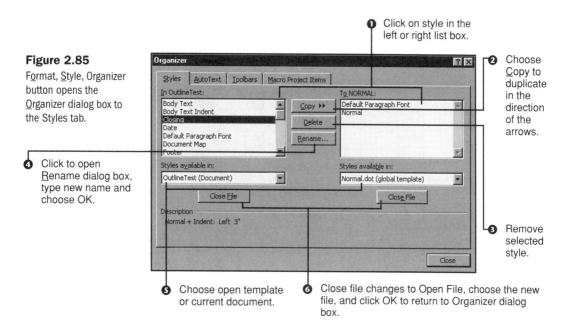

1 Click on style in the left or right list box.

2 Choose Copy to duplicate in the direction of the arrows.

4 Click to open Rename dialog box, type new name and choose OK.

3 Remove selected style.

5 Choose open template or current document.

6 Close file changes to Open File, choose the new file, and click OK to return to Organizer dialog box.

Colors dialog box options

Dialog Box Item	Description
Hue	Enter 0-255 for a color. You can also drag the crosshair horizontally in the **Color** box.
Sat	Enter 0-255 for the intensity of the color. The higher the number, the more intense the color. You can also drag the crosshair vertically in the **Color** box.
Lum	Enter 0-255 for the brightness of the color. The higher the number, the brighter the color. You can also drag the slider on the vertical color bar.
Red	Enter 0-255 for the amount of red. The higher the number, the more red in the color.
Green	0-255 for the amount of green.
Blue	0-255 for the amount of blue.

■ Rather than use a color, you can use a pattern, texture, or picture for your background. Click **Fill Effects**. The Fill Effects dialog box opens (see Figure 2.86).

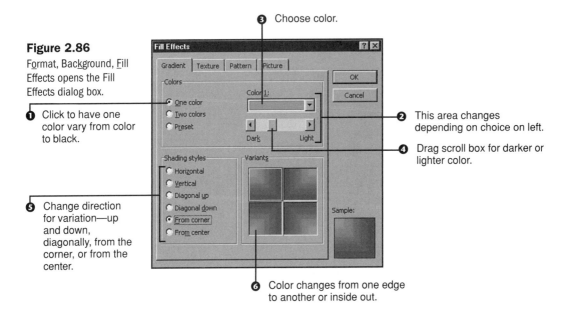

Figure 2.86

Format, Background, Fill Effects opens the Fill Effects dialog box.

❶ Click to have one color vary from color to black.

❸ Choose color.

❷ This area changes depending on choice on left.

❹ Drag scroll box for darker or lighter color.

❺ Change direction for variation—up and down, diagonally, from the corner, or from the center.

❻ Color changes from one edge to another or inside out.

Fill Effects dialog box

Dialog Box Item	How to Use
Gradient tab	
Two colors	When you choose **One color**, the second color is black. When you choose this option (**Two colors**), you can choose both **Color 1** and **Color 2**. The pattern is a gradient between the two colors.
Preset	When you choose **Preset**, a **Preset colors** drop-down appears to the right. Choose a name such as Early Sunset, Desert, and so forth. The Sample box shows what the color scheme looks like.
Texture tab	
Texture	Click one of the colored patterns that look like stone, sand, cloth, or wood.
Other Texture	Click to open the Select Text dialog box to find a file on disk. This is an open file dialog box (see **File - Open...**, page 21). Choose the file folder and name.
Pattern tab	
Pattern	Choose a dotted, lined, or other pattern.

Dialog Box Item	How to Use
Foreground	The **Pattern** has two colors. Choose the **Foreground** drop-down list to change the color of the dots or lines.
Background	Choose the **Background** drop-down list to change the color of the area behind the foreground. This is not the same as a watermark. (The background does not print.)
Picture tab	
Select Picture	Click on the button to open the Select Picture dialog box. Find a picture file and double-click. The picture displays in the Picture box.

Format ➡ Object...

The last item on the **Format** menu item is only active when you have an object selected. The object could be a text box, picture, organization chart, AutoShape, or other item. The actual name of the menu may change depending on the object (**Format, Object**; **Format, Picture**; **Format, AutoShape**; **Format, Text Box**; **Format, WordArt**). Generally, this is something you've added by pasting from the Clipboard or through the **Insert** menu (see **Insert – Object...**, page 158, **Insert – Picture**, page 149, and **Insert – Text Box**, page 156).

When you have an item selected and choose **Format, Object** (or another item on the bottom of the menu), or right-click on the object and choose the format item, the Format Object dialog box appears. The following table shows a list of all tabs and options. However, depending on the object, not every tab or option is enabled. For many of these options, you can also use the Drawing toolbar to change an object (see **View – Toolbars – Drawing**, page 73), or the Picture toolbar to modify a picture (see **View – Toolbars – Picture**, page 78). The dialog box is different for a frame (see **Format, Frame**, page 187).

Format Object dialog box

Dialog Box Item	How to Use
Colors and Lines Tab, Fill section	
Color	Click the drop-down and choose the fill color for the object. The same palette appears when you work with the document background (see **Format – Background...**, page 180).
Semitransparent	If you select a **Color**, this box becomes enabled. Check the box to make the solid color (not fill effect) partially transparent so text from the document can show through.
Colors and Lines Tab, Line section	
Color	Click the drop-down arrow to choose a color for the line. Choose **More Colors** to open the Colors dialog box (see

continues

Continued

Dialog Box Item	How to Use
	Format - Background..., page 180). Choose **Patterned Lines** to open the Patterned Lines dialog box. This is equivalent to the Patterned tab of the Fill Effects dialog box (see **Format - Background...**, page 180).
Dashed	Click the drop-down arrow to choose the pattern of dots and lines for your line.
Style	Click the drop-down to choose the thickness and multiple-line style you want for the line.
Weight	Type or click the spinner buttons to choose how thick you want the line to be.
Colors and Lines Tab, Arrows section	
Begin style	Click the drop-down arrow to choose one of the arrowheads (or no arrowhead) for the start of the line.
Begin size	If you choose an arrowhead for the **Begin style**, click this drop-down to choose the size of the arrowhead.
End style	Click the drop-down to choose one of the arrowheads (or no arrowhead) for the end of the line.
End size	If you choose an arrowhead for the **End style**, click this drop-down arrow to choose the size of the arrowhead.
Size Tab, Size and rotate section	
Height	Type or click spinner buttons to change how tall the object is.
Rotation	For objects that can rotate, type or click the spinner buttons to indicate how many degrees you want to rotate the object.
Width	Type or click spinner buttons to change how wide the object is.
Size Tab, Scale section	
Height	Type or click spinner buttons to change height as a percent of the original.
Width	Type or click spinner buttons to change width as a percent of the original.
Lock aspect ratio	Check this box to keep the height and width proportional to each other. When you change the height, the width automatically changes.

Dialog Box Item	How to Use
Relative to original picture size	For pictures, check this box to keep the **Height** and **Width** proportional to the dimensions the picture had when you first added it to the document.
Re**s**et	For pictures, click this button to return the picture to its original size.
Position Tab	
Horizontal	Type or click the spinner button to change the distance to the right from the item in the **From** box.
From	Choose whether you want the **Horizontal** distance measured from the Margin, Page, or Column.
Vertical	Type or click the spinner button to change the distance down from the item in the **From** box.
F**r**om	Choose whether you want the **Vertical** distance measured from the Margin, Page, or Paragraph.
Move object with text	Check this box to move the selected object with the text on the page.
Lock anchor	Check this box to keep the object on the same page as the text to which you anchor it.
Float over **t**ext	For pictures, check this box to place the picture in the drawing layer. You can then position it in front of or behind text and other objects (see **View - Toolbars - Drawing**, page 73). Clear this box to place the picture on the document where it behaves as text.
Wrapping Tab	
Wrapping style	Click on **S**quare, **Tight**, **Th**rough, **N**one, or **Top and bottom** to indicate how you want text to wrap around the object. If you select **None**, text appears behind or on top of the object.
Wrap to	If you choose the first three choices in Wrapping style, choose which sides you want to wrap around: **Both sides**, **Left**, **Right**, or **Largest side**. For an additional option only available on the Picture toolbar (see **View - Toolbars - Picture**, page 78), click the Text Wrapping button and choose Edit Wrap Points. Then drag the small boxes to choose where you want to wrap text.
Distance from text	Depending on the Wrapping style, the text boxes in this area are enabled or not. Type or click the spinner buttons to determine how far text should be from the object on the **Top**, **Bottom**, **Left**, and **Right**.

continues

Continued

Dialog Box Item	How to Use
Picture Tab	
Crop from	Type or click spinner buttons in **L**eft, **R**ight, **T**op, and **B**ottom to cut off portions of the picture.
Picture Tab, Image control section	
Color	Click the drop-down to display a list. **A**utomatic enables the program to choose the format. **G**rayscale means each color converts to a shade of gray. **B**lack and White is also known as line art. **W**atermark is visible behind text and has less contrast.
Brightness	Drag the scroll bar or change the text box to vary the brightness. Increased brightness has more white to brighten the colors and decreased brightness has more black to darken the colors.
Co**n**trast	Drag the scroll bar or change the text box to vary the intensity of colors. When you increase contrast, you decrease the amount of gray in the picture.
Re**s**et	Click to return the picture to its original colors and without cropping.
Picture Tab, Text Box Tab	
Internal margin	Type or use the **L**eft, **R**ight, **T**op, and **B**ottom spinner boxes to indicate the amount of space between text and the box.
Format **C**allout	If the object is a callout and you want to change the line to the callout, click this button to open the Format Callout dialog box (see Figure 2.87).
Convert to **F**rame	If you want to convert the drawing object to a frame, click this button. You are prompted to verify this choice because some formatting may be lost. To format the frame, see **F**ormat – **F**rame..., page 187.

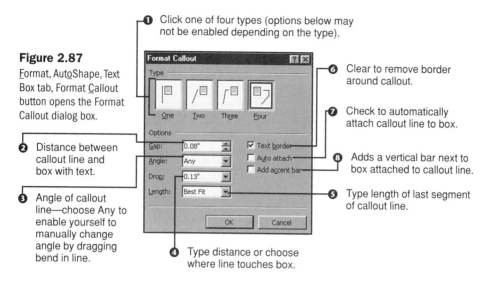

Figure 2.87
Format, AutoShape, Text Box tab, Format Callout button opens the Format Callout dialog box.

❶ Click one of four types (options below may not be enabled depending on the type).

❷ Distance between callout line and box with text.

❸ Angle of callout line—choose Any to enable yourself to manually change angle by dragging bend in line.

❹ Type distance or choose where line touches box.

❻ Clear to remove border around callout.

❼ Check to automatically attach callout line to box.

❽ Adds a vertical bar next to box attached to callout line.

❺ Type length of last segment of callout line.

Format ➧ Frame...

Most of the objects you format have the same menu choices regardless of the object. One exception is if the object is a frame. Choose **Format, Frame** or right-click on a frame and choose **Format Frame** to open the Frame dialog box (see Figure 2.88).

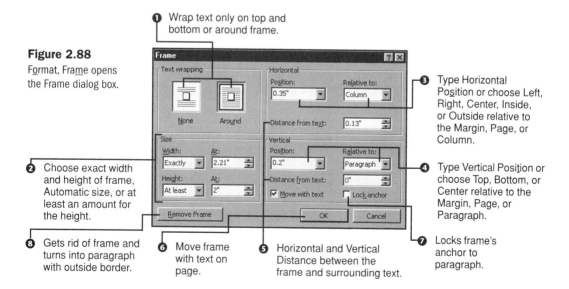

Figure 2.88
Format, Frame opens the Frame dialog box.

❶ Wrap text only on top and bottom or around frame.

❷ Choose exact width and height of frame, Automatic size, or at least an amount for the height.

❸ Gets rid of frame and turns into paragraph with outside border.

❻ Move frame with text on page.

❺ Horizontal and Vertical Distance between the frame and surrounding text.

❸ Type Horizontal Position or choose Left, Right, Center, Inside, or Outside relative to the Margin, Page, or Column.

❹ Type Vertical Position or choose Top, Bottom, or Center relative to the Margin, Page, or Paragraph.

❼ Locks frame's anchor to paragraph.

Tools

The **Tools** menu is a smorgasbord of options including working with words, managing revisions, mass mailings, macros, and setting the environment in which Word works.

Tools ➥ Spelling and Grammar...

The Spelling and Grammar dialog box checks the spelling of each word in your document and looks for common grammatical and style mistakes.

Quick Choices   *SPELLING*

1. A misspelled word appears as a red wavy line. Right click on the word or press **Alt+F7**.
2. Do one of the following:
   - Choose the correct word in the top of the shortcut menu.
   - Choose **Ignore All** to ignore this word through the whole document.
   - Choose **Add** to permanently add the word to the dictionary.
   - Choose **AutoCorrect**. From the menu, choose a word to correct the word. The same misspelling will be corrected automatically in the future as you type.
   - Choose **Spelling** to open the Spelling dialog box.

---

1. Open the Spelling and Grammar dialog box in one of these ways:
   - Click the **Spelling and Grammar** button ![abc] on the Standard toolbar.
   - Press **F7**.
   - Press **Alt+F7** and choose **Spelling**.
   - Choose **Tools**, **Spelling and Grammar**.
2. If you want to check both spelling and grammar for all documents, check the **Check grammar** box. Otherwise, only spelling is verified.
3. Questionable spelling or potential grammar problems display in the top half of dialog box, highlighted in red. The question appears as the label attached to the first text box (and changes with each item). Do one of the following:
   - Click **Ignore** to skip the misspelled word or grammar problem.
   - Click **Ignore All** to skip this word or grammar problem throughout the document. Word adds the word to the internal list of words for each document and does not check again it when you run the spell and grammar checker.
   - Click **Add** to add the word to the dictionary (and not check it for other documents).
   - Choose from the **Suggestions** and click **Change** to correct your document, **Change All** to change every occurrence in your document, or **AutoCorrect** to correct this mistake every time you type the word this way.
   - If the problem is grammatical, click **Next Sentence** to skip this sentence and move to the next.
4. If you accidentally made a correction, click **Undo** to go back to the last change.
5. Continue checking the document and click **Close** when finished.

Tools – Spelling and Grammar...Options

On the Spelling and Grammar dialog box, click the **Options** button to open the Spelling and Grammar tab of the Options dialog box (you can also choose **Tools**, **Options** or right-click the Spelling book icon on the status bar and choose **Options**).

Spelling and grammar options

Dialog Box Item	How to Use
Spelling section	
Check spelling as you type	With the following option unchecked, check this box to enable Word to show you a spelling error as soon as you press **Spacebar** or **Enter** after the word.
Hide spelling errors in this document	Check to hide the (nonprinting) red wavy underline on words you spell wrong as you type. If not hidden, right-click to display suggested words. To change this check box, you can also right-click on the Spelling icon on the status bar and choose **Hide Spelling Errors**.
Always suggest corrections	Check to always display a list of suggestions in the Spelling and grammar dialog box (even if you really messed up the word). If the spell checker can't find a close word, the **Suggestions** text box displays "no spelling suggestions" rather than appears blank.
Suggest from main dictionary only	Check to ignore words in custom dictionaries.
Ignore words in UPPERCASE	Check to skip words in uppercase.
Ignore words with numbers	Check to skip words that have a number.
Ignore Internet and file addresses	Check to skip Internet addresses, filenames, and email addresses.
Custom dictionary	Choose the additional dictionary where you want to store words (when you choose **Add** on the Spelling and Grammar dialog box) that are not in the main dictionary.
Dictionaries	Click to Open the Custom Dictionaries box. Choose all the custom dictionaries you want to check for spelling. Choose **Language** to associate the highlighted dictionary when checking text formatted for that language (see **Tools – Language – Set Language...**, page 192). Choose **New** and name a new file for a custom dictionary. Choose **Edit** to edit the highlighted dictionary. Choose **Add** to find a

continues

Continued

Dialog Box Item	How to Use
	custom dictionary. Choose **Remove** to delete the selected dictionary.
Grammar section	
Check grammar as you type	With the following option unchecked, check this box to enable Word to show you a grammar error as soon as you type it.
Hide grammatical errors in this document	Check to hide the (nonprinting) green wavy underline on phrases that have potential grammar errors. If not hidden, right-click the green wavy underline to display suggested corrections. To change this check box, you can also right-click on the Spelling icon on the status bar and choose **Hide Grammatical Errors**.
Check grammar with spelling	This is the same option as on the Spelling and Grammar dialog box. Uncheck to verify spelling only.
Show readability statistics	Check this box to show the reading level of your document after the spelling check is completed (see **Tools ▸ Spelling and Grammar... Options, Readability Statistics**, page 190).
Writing style	Choose one of the five styles to determine which grammar rules you want to check.
Settings	Click this button to open the Grammar Settings dialog box. See **Tools ▸ Spelling** and **Grammar... Options, Settings** (page 191) for a list of rules.
Recheck Document	This button's label is **Check Document** if you haven't run spelling and grammar yet. Click this button to run spelling and grammar and ignore the internal list of words and phrases you created by choosing **Ignore** or **Ignore All**.

Tools ▸ Spelling and Grammar... Options, Readability Statistics

If you mark the **Show readability statistics** check box on the Spelling & Grammar tab of the Options dialog box (see **Tools ▸ Spelling and Grammar... Options**, page 189), you see statistics that give you an idea of how easy your document is to read after the spelling check is completed (see Figure 2.89).

Figure 2.89

Tools, Options, Spelling & Grammar tab, check Show readability statistics. After the spelling check is completed, the Readability Statistics dialog box opens.

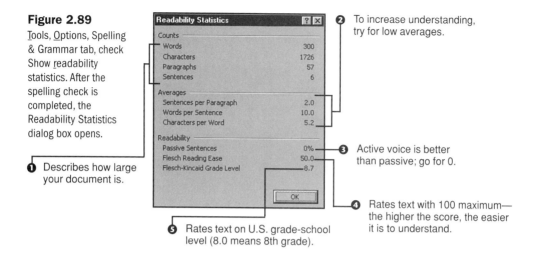

❶ Describes how large your document is.

❷ To increase understanding, try for low averages.

❸ Active voice is better than passive; go for 0.

❹ Rates text with 100 maximum— the higher the score, the easier it is to understand.

❺ Rates text on U.S. grade-school level (8.0 means 8th grade).

Tools – Spelling and Grammar... Options, Settings

On the Spelling and Grammar tab of the Options dialog box, choose **Settings** to bring up the Grammar Settings dialog box.

Dialog Box Option	Description
Writing style	The checked items in the Grammar and style options change depending on the style you choose. Casual style follows the least rules. Formal or Technical apply the strictest rules. If you want to create your own style, choose Custom.
Grammar and writing style options	Check the box next to any of these items you want to review when grammar check is turned on: Capitalization Commonly confused words Hyphenated and split words Misused words Negation Numbers Passive sentences Phrases Possessives and plurals Punctuation Relative clauses Sentence structure Subject-verb agreement Style—Clichés Style—Colloquialisms Style—Contractions

continues

Dialog Box Option	Description
	Style—Gender-specific words
	Style—Jargon
	Style—Sentences beginning with And, But, and Hopefully
	Style—Unclear phrasing
	Style—Wordiness
Comma before last list item	Choose whether you always want a comma before the last item in a list, never want a comma, or you don't want to check.
Punctuation with quotes	If there are quotes in a sentence, choose whether you want the punctuation inside or outside the quotes (or not to check).
Spaces between sentences	Choose whether you want one or two spaces between words (or not to check).
Reset All	Click to restore all the settings in the dialog box to the **Writing style** selected.

Tools ➥ Language

Choose **Tools**, **Language** to bring up a submenu to identify the language of selection of your document, to replace a word with a same or similar meaning, or to hyphenate your document.

Tools ➥ Language ➥ Set Language...

If you want spelling and grammar to skip a selection of text, choose **Tools**, **Language**, **Set Language**. In the Language dialog box, choose (no proofing). You can also use this dialog box to change the language dictionary to use (if you have it installed) for a section of text. Click the **Default** button to change the dictionary for all documents. You may need to contact Alki Software (800-669-9673 or **www.alki.com**) for another language dictionary. If you set the language of a selection, you can tell which custom dictionary you want to use for that language by clicking the **Dictionaries** button on the Spelling and Grammar dialog box (see **Tools ➥ Spelling and Grammar...**, page 188).

Tools ➥ Language ➥ Thesaurus...

When you repeat the same word continuously in your document, you might want to look for another word that means the same thing. Use the Thesaurus.

Press **Shift+F7** to open the Thesaurus dialog box (as shown in Figure 2.90).

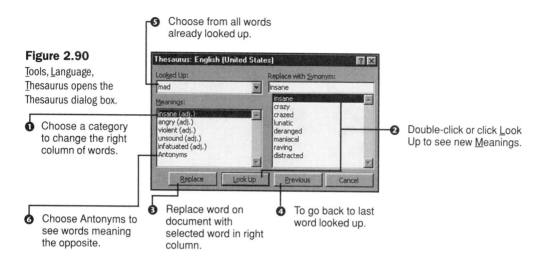

Figure 2.90

Tools, Language, Thesaurus opens the Thesaurus dialog box.

⑤ Choose from all words already looked up.

① Choose a category to change the right column of words.

② Double-click or click Look Up to see new Meanings.

⑥ Choose Antonyms to see words meaning the opposite.

③ Replace word on document with selected word in right column.

④ To go back to last word looked up.

Tools ~ Language ~ Hyphenation...

Hyphenation adds hyphens to long words at the right margin of your document. This avoids a deeply jagged right margin if you choose **Align Left** ▤ or significant differences in spacing between words if your document is **Justified** ▤.

Quick Choices *INSERT HYPHENS*

- ▣ To insert an optional hyphen (one that breaks at the end of a line if necessary), press **Ctrl+ –** (minus).
- ▣ To insert a nonbreaking hyphen (a dash that does not break at the end of a line), press **Ctrl+Shift+ –** (minus).

1. Choose **Tools, Language, Hyphenation** to open the Hyphenation dialog box.

2. Check **Automatically hyphenate document** to hyphenate the document as you type.

3. Type or use the spinner buttons in **Hyphenation zone** if you want to change the width of the area on the right margin where words need to be hyphenated. A smaller number reduces the raggedness of the right margin, but gives the document more hyphens.

4. If desired, enter the maximum number of consecutive lines that can have hyphenation in the **Limit consecutive hyphens to** text box, or choose **No limit**.

5. If you want to verify each location of a hyphen, click the **Manual** button to open the Manual Hyphenation box. If you don't like where the suggested hyphenation is, click in a new location and choose **Yes**.

6. If you didn't choose Manual, choose **OK** to begin automatic hyphenation.

Tools ➥ Word Count...

Use **Tools**, **Word Count** to open the Word Count dialog box shown in Figure 2.91. If you have Readability Statistics turned on, Word also displays some of these counts after you spell check the document (see **Tools - Spelling and Grammar...**, page 188).

Figure 2.91
Tools, Word Count opens the Word Count dialog box.

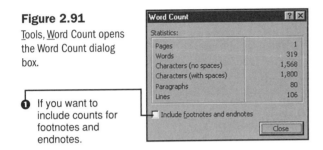

① If you want to include counts for footnotes and endnotes.

Tools ➥ AutoSummarize...

Use AutoSummarize to pull out key sentences. Choose **Tools**, **AutoSummarize** to bring up the AutoSummarize dialog box shown in Figure 2.92.

① Accent key points.   **②** Summarize at top of document.

Figure 2.92
Tools, AutoSummarize opens the AutoSummarize dialog box.

④ Summarize in new document.

③ Summarize at top and hide rest.

⑤ Make summary longer or shorter.

⑥ Change property sheet.

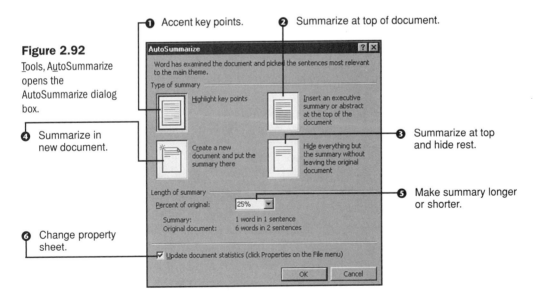

If you check **Update document statistics**, Word updates the properties sheet (see **File - Properties**, page 46). The top five keywords go into the **Keywords** box and summary text goes into the **Document contents** box.

If you choose **Highlight key points**, Word opens the document, highlights summary information, and displays the AutoSummarize toolbar.

AutoSummarize toolbar buttons

Button	Name	How to Use
¾	Highlight/Show Only Summary	Click to hide the rest of the document and show the summary. Click again to show document.
◄ 25% ►	Percent of Original	Click right or left arrow or drag bar in middle to change the length of the summary.
Close	Close	Click to turn off AutoSummarize and hide the toolbar.

Tools ↪ AutoCorrect...

The AutoCorrect dialog box tells Word to fix mistakes as you type, automatically format text, and expand abbreviations for words. The dialog box has four tabs. For an explanation of the AutoText tab, see **Insert ‑ AutoText**, page 101. For a description of the AutoFormat and AutoFormat as You Type tabs, see **Format ‑ AutoFormat...**, page 175.

Options on the AutoCorrect dialog box

Dialog Box Option	How to Use
AutoCorrect Tab	
Correct TWo INitial CApitals	If you often type letters in uppercase at the beginning of a word, check to automatically change the second letter to lowercase.
Capitalize first letter of sentences	Check to have Word convert a lowercase letter to uppercase for the first letter of a sentence.
Exceptions	Click on this button to open the AutoCorrect Exceptions dialog box. To ignore a word for uppercase, click the **First Letter** tab, type the word, and click **Add**. To ignore words in initial caps, click the **INitial CAps** tab, type the word, and click **Add**. If you want to automatically add words to these two types of exceptions when you **Backspace** over the correction and retype the word, check **Automatically add words to list**.
Capitalize names of days	Check to capitalize the days of the week (Monday), even if you type them in lowercase.

continues

Continued

Dialog Box Option	How to Use
Correct accidental usage of cAPS LOCK key	Check to turn off Caps Lock and correct your typing if you type the first letter of a word lowercase and the rest of the letters uppercase.
Replace text as you type	Check to have all the abbreviations in the **Replace** column automatically convert to whatever is in the **With** column.
Replace	To add automatic completions for characters you type, place an entry in the text box below **Replace** and an entry in the text box below **With** and click on the **Add** button.
Formatted text	If you selected text before you entered this dialog box, click the **Formatted text** option button to include formatting in the AutoCorrect entry. Otherwise, choose **Plain text** to not include omit formatting with the entry when you use it.
Delete	To remove an item from the AutoCorrect list, choose the item you want to delete from the list and click **Delete.**

Tools ➥ Look Up Reference...

Microsoft Office comes with a collection of reference tools called Bookshelf Basics; it includes a dictionary, thesaurus, and book of quotations as well as previews of an encyclopedia, almanac, atlas, Internet directory, chronology, and an address builder that finds zip codes.

Select a word on your document and choose **Tools, Look Up Reference** to open the Look Up Reference dialog box. Depending on the options you have installed, choose the title you want to view; then click **Keyword** to search only article titles, **Full Text** to check all the references, or **None** to open up the reference without searching.

Tools ➥ Track Changes

The Track Changes feature enables you to keep track of your edits, additions, and deletions. This feature is especially helpful if you send your document out to other people for review. You can use this feature with the Reviewing toolbar (see **View ➥ Toolbars ➥ Reviewing**, page 81).

Tools ➥ Track Changes ➥ Highlight Changes...

Highlight Changes enables you to see editing on your document.

Quick Choices   *HIGHLIGHT CHANGES*

1. Choose **Tools**, **Track Changes**, **Highlight Changes**. The Highlight Changes dialog box opens.

2. To turn on highlighting, check **Track changes while editing** (uncheck to turn off highlighting).

3. To see the changes on your monitor while you edit, check **Highlight changes on screen**.

4. If you want to see the changes in the printed document, check **Highlight changes in printed document**.

5. Choose **OK** and edit your document as normal.

To change the way edits are indicated, click the **Options** button on the Highlight Changes dialog box. The Track Changes dialog box opens (see Figure 2.93). You can also choose **Tools**, **Options** and click the Track Changes tab to get to this dialog box.

After you turn on Track Changes and edit the document, you can see a ScreenTip for each change if you hover the mouse pointer over the change. The ScreenTip includes the name of the editor, the date and time of the changes, and what kind of change the editor made.

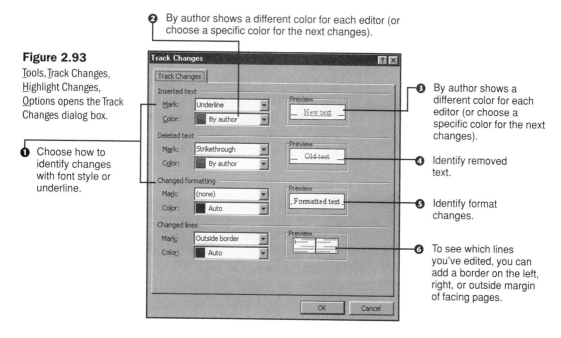

❷ By author shows a different color for each editor (or choose a specific color for the next changes).

Figure 2.93
Tools, Track Changes, Highlight Changes, Options opens the Track Changes dialog box.

❶ Choose how to identify changes with font style or underline.

❸ By author shows a different color for each editor (or choose a specific color for the next changes).

❹ Identify removed text.

❺ Identify format changes.

❻ To see which lines you've edited, you can add a border on the left, right, or outside margin of facing pages.

Tools – Track Changes – Accept or Reject Changes...

After you've tracked changes (see **Tools – Track Changes**, page 196), you can choose to keep or remove the changes. You can use these steps or the Reviewing toolbar (see **View –**

Toolbars ▪ Reviewing, page 81). Instead of Track Changes, you could use Versions to keep track of your different documents as they go through editing (see **File ▪ Versions...**, page 37).

To review changes in your document, do the following:

1. Press **Ctrl+Home** to move to the top of the document.

2. Choose **Tools**, **Track Changes**, **Accept or Reject Changes**. The Accept or Reject Changes dialog box opens.

3. In the View section, choose one of the following options:

   - **Changes with highlighting** shows the document with the options you marked on the Track Changes dialog box.

   - **Changes without highlighting** shows how the document would look if you accept all changes.

   - **Original** shows what the document looked like before you turned on Track Changes.

4. Click **Find** to go to the first change. If you just want to look at each change, you can click either Find button to move forward or backward. As you move to each change, the Changes section shows the editor, what kind of change was made, and the date and time. The name of the editor is on the User Information tab of the Options dialog box (see **Tools ▪ Options... User Information**, page 227).

5. To keep the change, click **Accept**; to disregard the change, click **Reject**. Word automatically goes to the next or previous change (the direction depends on which Find button you last chose).

6. To cancel your last choice, click **Undo**.

7. You can also deal with all changes at once. Click **Accept All** to keep all corrections or **Reject All** to turn the document back the way it was before changes.

8. When finished, click **Close**.

Tools ▪ Track Changes ▪ Compare Documents...

To see the differences between two similar documents, choose **Tools**, **Track Changes**, **Compare Documents**. A dialog box with the title Select File to Compare with Current Document appears. Choose the file to compare with the document on screen and click **Open**. The on-screen document displays the differences set in the Track Changes dialog box. Just like any other Track Changes document, you can accept or reject the differences (see **Tools ▪ Track Changes ▪ Accept or Reject Changes...**, page 197).

If you use the Versions feature (see **File ▪ Versions...**, page 37) and want to compare two different versions of your document, you need to first save (see **File ▪ Save As...**, page 29) the earlier version with a different name.

Tools ➥ Merge Documents...

If multiple reviewers are editing their own copies of the same document, you can merge the edited documents into one document that shows all the edits.

Quick **Choices**   *MERGE DOCUMENTS*

1. Open the document you sent with Track Changes on.
2. Choose **Tools**, **Merge Documents**. A dialog box with the title Select File to Merge into Current Document appears.
3. Locate that file and choose **Open**.
4. Repeat steps 2 and 3 for each edited document.

The resulting document shows text added and deleted depending on your settings in the Track Changes dialog box. You can accept or reject the changes (see **Tools ▪ Track Changes ▪ Accept or Reject Changes...**, page 197).

Tools ➥ Protect Document...

The Protect Document feature enables you to prevent certain changes from happening to your document.

1. Choose **Tools**, **Protect Document**. The Protect Document dialog box opens.
2. Choose one of the following three options:
   - Click **Tracked changes** to enable reviewers to make edits to your document, but not to turn off change tracking or accept or reject changes (see **Tools ▪ Track Changes**, page 196).
   - Click **Comments** to allow users to add comments, but not to edit the document itself (see **Insert ▪ Comment**, page 129).
   - Click **Forms** to allow users to make changes in form fields, but not in the rest of the document (see **View ▪ Toolbars ▪ Forms**, page 77).
3. If you choose **Forms** above, you can choose which sections of the document you want to protect. Click the **Sections** button. The Section Protection dialog box opens. Uncheck any sections where you want the user to be able to edit and click **OK**.
4. If you want to assign a password to the protection, type in a **Password**. Unless a user has the password, he or she will not be able to turn off protection.
5. Click **OK**. If you assigned a password in step 4, type the password again and click **OK**.

After you've turned on Protect Document, choose **Tools**, **Unprotect Document** to turn off protection. If you assigned a password, type the password when asked.

<u>T</u>ools ➡ Mail Me<u>r</u>ge...

Mail Merge enables you to combine a data source (of names and addresses, for example) with a word processing document (called a main document) such as a letter or envelope. When you choose **<u>T</u>ools, Mail Me<u>r</u>ge**, the Mail Merge Helper dialog box appears with three sections: **Main document, Data source**, and **Merge the data with the document**. Each section has two buttons. Figure 2.94 shows you where to find information about Mail Merge in this chapter.

Figure 2.94

<u>T</u>ools, Mail Me<u>r</u>ge opens the Mail Merge Helper.

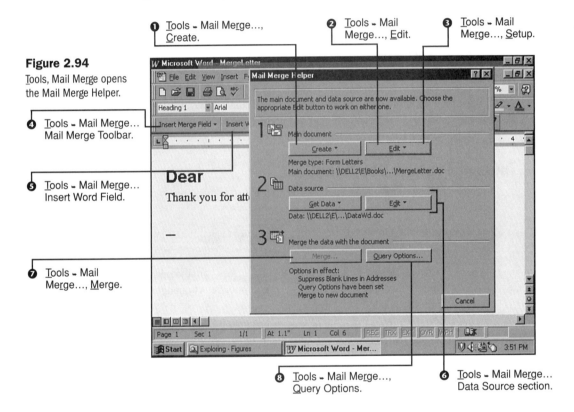

❶ <u>T</u>ools - Mail Me<u>r</u>ge..., Create.

❷ <u>T</u>ools - Mail Merge..., <u>E</u>dit.

❸ <u>T</u>ools - Mail Merge..., <u>S</u>etup.

❹ <u>T</u>ools - Mail Me<u>r</u>ge... Mail Merge Toolbar.

❺ <u>T</u>ools - Mail Me<u>r</u>ge... Insert Word Field.

❼ <u>T</u>ools - Mail Merge..., <u>M</u>erge.

❽ <u>T</u>ools - Mail Me<u>r</u>ge..., Query Options.

❻ <u>T</u>ools - Mail Me<u>r</u>ge... Data Source section.

<u>T</u>ools ➡ Mail Me<u>r</u>ge... Main Document Section

The Main document section of the Mail Merge Helper dialog box enables you to create and edit a document. You have to **<u>C</u>reate** before you can do any other steps.

<u>T</u>ools ➡ Mail Me<u>r</u>ge... <u>C</u>reate

The first step in merging a document and a database is to identify the document. You can also use **<u>C</u>reate** to change the type of merge document after you've selected other merge settings.

1. On the Mail Merge Helper dialog box, click the **<u>C</u>reate** button.

2. On the drop-down menu, choose one of the following options:

- **Form Letters**   This option is a normal document that fills in text for each field from your database. After each record merges, a section break occurs. If your main document is one page, the total pages in your merged document will be the total number of records merged.

- **Mailing Labels**   Each record of your database prints on one mailing label.

- **Envelopes**   Each record of your database prints on one envelope. For nonmerged documents, see **Tools ‑ Envelopes and Labels**, page 213.

- **Catalog**   Instead of a new page for each document, the merge continues at the end of main document. For example, if you want to create a table of the database records, create a table with one row and place merge fields in each cell of the row. Do not include a table header (add that after the merge is finished).

- **Restore to Normal Word Document**   Use this option to unattach the database from a merge document and hide the Mail Merge toolbar. After you choose this option, click **Yes** to confirm your choice; then click **Close** to finish the Mail Merge Helper.

3. If you chose one of the first four options, the dialog box that appears has two buttons for your document source:

    - Click **Active Window** to use the open document.

    - Click **New Main Document** to create a new document.

4. Continue with the **Tools ‑ Mail Merge…** Data source section.

Tools ‑ Mail Merge… Edit

You can edit the main document from different entry points:

- From the Mail Merge Helper dialog box, click **Edit** and then click the document type.

  After you **Create** a Form Letter or Catalog, the **Edit** button appears. For Mailing Labels and Envelopes, you have to **Create** them and then choose one of the options under **Get Data** before the **Setup** button appears. The **Edit** button appear after you finish the setup.

- After you create or choose a data source, choose **Edit Main Document**.

- After the main document has been closed, open it again (see **File ‑ Open…**, page21).

After you choose to edit the main document, the Mail Merge Helper dialog box disappears and Word displays the Mail Merge toolbar (see **Tools ‑ Mail Merge… Mail Merge Toolbar**, page 200). Edit the document as you would any other with the exception of adding merge fields. Move to the position on your document where you want the placeholder to appear for the field, click **Insert Merge Field** on the Mail Merge toolbar, and choose the field from the drop-down list.

Tools ➤ Mail Merge... Setup...

Depending on the type of document you originally chose on the **Create** button of the Mail Merge Helper, the second button on the Main document says either **Edit** or **Setup**. If your document is Mailing Labels or Envelopes, the button says **Setup**. The screen setup depends on the type of document you chose. Click the **Setup** button, and see one of the following sections for Mailing Labels or Envelopes.

Tools ➤ Mail Merge..., Setup... (Mailing Labels)

When you choose **Setup** on the Mail Merge Helper dialog box and your main document is a mailing label, the Label Options dialog box opens (see Figure 2.95).

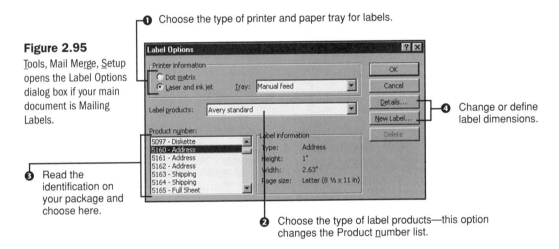

❶ Choose the type of printer and paper tray for labels.

Figure 2.95
Tools, Mail Merge, Setup opens the Label Options dialog box if your main document is Mailing Labels.

❸ Read the identification on your package and choose here.

❹ Change or define label dimensions.

❷ Choose the type of label products—this option changes the Product number list.

If you choose the **Details** or **New Label** button on the Label Option dialog box, you can change the size of the label (see also **Tools ➤ Envelopes and Labels... Labels**, page 215).

After you identify the type of label, the Create Labels dialog box opens (see Figure 2.96). Use this dialog box to enter the field placeholders that will pick up information from your database.

Tools ➤ Mail Merge..., Setup... (Envelopes)

When you choose **Setup** on the Mail Merge Helper dialog box and your main document is an envelope, the Envelope Options dialog box opens (see also **Tools ➤ Envelopes and Labels...**, page 213).

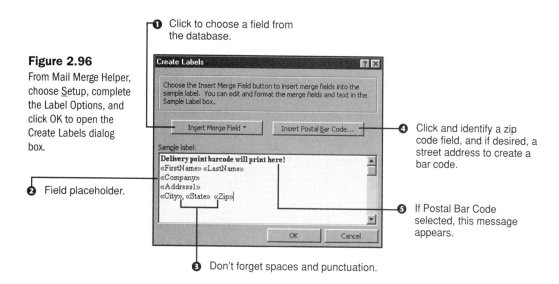

Figure 2.96
From Mail Merge Helper, choose Setup, complete the Label Options, and click OK to open the Create Labels dialog box.

❶ Click to choose a field from the database.

❷ Field placeholder.

❸ Don't forget spaces and punctuation.

❹ Click and identify a zip code field, and if desired, a street address to create a bar code.

❺ If Postal Bar Code selected, this message appears.

1. In the Envelope Options dialog box, do any of the following:

   Envelope Options tab

   - Choose the Envelope size.
   - Choose the Delivery address **Font** for Return address **Font** and make changes on the Font dialog box (see **Format – Font…**, page 160).

   Printing Options tab

   - Change the direction the envelope goes in the printer in the Feed method section.
   - Click whether you want the envelope to be **Face up** or **Face down**.
   - Choose whether you need to rotate the envelope 180 degrees by checking **Clockwise rotation**.
   - Choose the paper tray in the **Feed from** drop-down list.

2. Click **OK** to open the Envelope address dialog box. It is nearly identical to the Create Label dialog box in Figure 2.96.

3. Click **Insert Merge Field** and choose a field. Add spacing or punctuation and repeat this step for each field on your envelope.

4. To put a bar code on your envelope, click insert **Postal Bar Code**. The Insert Postal Bar Code dialog box opens. Choose from the following options:

   - From the drop-down arrow, choose **Merge field with ZIP code**.
   - If you want your bar code to include the street address, choose **Merge field with street address**.
   - If you want a facing identification mark (FIM) for courtesy reply envelopes (this feature speeds sorting), check **FIM-A courtesy reply mail**.

5. Click **OK**.

<u>T</u>ools ▪ Mail Mer<u>g</u>e... Mail Merge Toolbar

After you choose to edit any kind of main document, the Mail Merge toolbar displays.

Mail Merge toolbar buttons		
Button	**Name**	**How to Use**
Insert Merge Field ▾	Insert Merge Field	Position your insertion point where the field placeholder will go, click this button, and choose one of the fields from the database.
Insert Word Field ▾	Insert Word Field	To make prompts or have the result depend on what the user selects, click this button and choose one of the menu items. Each menu item is described in the following section (see **<u>T</u>ools ▪ Mail Mer<u>g</u>... Insert Word Field**, page 205).
«»	View Merged Data	Click this button to see the results of your merge for the first record (instead of the field name placeholders). Click again to display the placeholders.
⏮	First Record	While View Merged Data is selected, click to see the results for the first record in the database.
◀	Previous Record	While View Merged Data is selected and any record except the first is showing, click to see the results for the previous record.
1	Record	While View Merged Data is selected, type a record number in this box and press Enter.
▶	Next Record	While View Merged Data is selected, click to see the results for the next record.
⏭	Last Record	While View Merged Data is selected, click to see the results for the last record.
▦	Mail Merge Helper	Click to return the Mail Merge Helper dialog box.
▣	Check for Errors	Click to simulate the merge and report whether Word can find potential errors.
▣	Merge to New Document	Click to create a new document on-screen. After you create the document you can print one page, selected pages, or all pages (see **File ▪ <u>P</u>rint...**, page 42) with each page section corresponding to a record in the database (which is often a person).

Button	Name	How to Use
🖨	Merge to Printer	Click to print the merged information directly to the printer.
📧	Mail Merge	Click to open the Merge dialog box.
🔍	Find Record	While View Merged Data is selected, click to open the Find in Field dialog box. Type the text you're looking for in the **Find what** text box and choose **In field**. Click **Find Next** to find each record that meets the criteria.
📝	Edit Data Source	Click this button to open the Data Form dialog box (see **Tools - Mail Merge...**, **Edit**, page 210) when the data source is a Word document.

Tools - Mail Merge... Insert Word Field

When you click the **Insert Word Field** button of the Mail Merge toolbar, you have more complex options for merging documents. For example, you can prompt the user during the merge or decide whether you want to print specific fields under certain circumstances. The following sections describe each item on the **Insert Word Field** drop-down list. These codes are a subset of Word's field codes (see **Insert - Field...**, page 106).

To see the field codes, rather than the result of the field codes, in the main document, press **Alt+F9**. Press **Alt+F9** again to turn off field codes view.

Tools - Mail Merge... Insert Word Field, Ask...

When you run the merge, the **Ask** word field prompts you for text. After the user types the prompt, the value is stored where the bookmark exists (see Figure 2.97). You can insert the bookmark in multiple locations and use the bookmark field in other fields such as If...Then...Else.

Figure 2.97
On the Mail Merge toolbar's Insert Word Field, Ask opens the Ask dialog box.

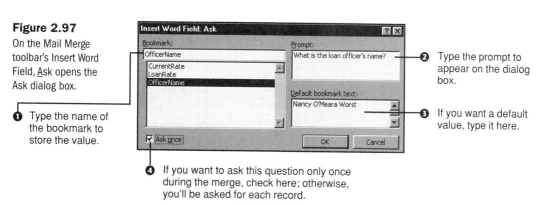

❶ Type the name of the bookmark to store the value.

❷ Type the prompt to appear on the dialog box.

❸ If you want a default value, type it here.

❹ If you want to ask this question only once during the merge, check here; otherwise, you'll be asked for each record.

To print the value of the bookmark, use the word field {REF *bookmarkname*}. This field is not on the Insert Word Field button, so you'll have to choose **Insert**, **Field** and choose Ref from the **Field names** column (in Links and References category). Click the **Options** button, click the **Bookmarks** tab, and choose the bookmark you want to place in the document.

Tools ► *Mail Merge... Insert Word Field, Fill-in...*

When you run the merge, the **Fill-in** word field prompts you for text and places the text you type in the document at the location of this field code (see Figure 2.98).

Figure 2.98
On the Mail Merge toolbar's Insert Word Field, Fill-in opens the Fill-in dialog box.

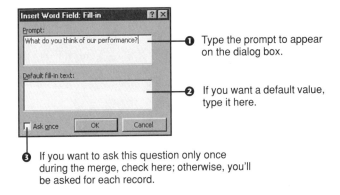

❶ Type the prompt to appear on the dialog box.

❷ If you want a default value, type it here.

❸ If you want to ask this question only once during the merge, check here; otherwise, you'll be asked for each record.

Tools ► *Mail Merge... Insert Word Field, If...Then...Else...*

When you run the merge, the **If...Then...Else** word field looks at the value of a merge field. If the field meets a criterion, Word inserts one set of text. If not, Word inserts other text or leaves the field blank (see Figure 2.99).

❶ Choose the field.

Figure 2.99
On the Mail Merge toolbar's Insert Word Field, If...Then...Else opens the IF dialog box.

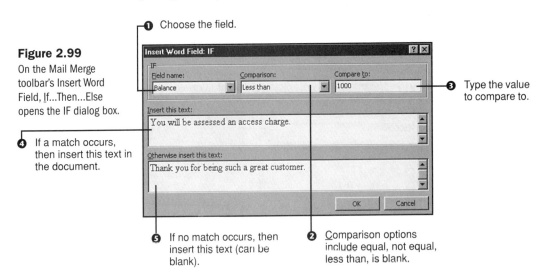

❸ Type the value to compare to.

❹ If a match occurs, then insert this text in the document.

❺ If no match occurs, then insert this text (can be blank).

❷ Comparison options include equal, not equal, less than, is blank.

Tools → Mail Merge... Insert Word Field, Merge Record

When you run the merge, the **Merge Record #** places the record number from the (filtered) data source into the merged document.

Tools → Mail Merge... Insert Word Field, Merge Sequence

When you run the merge, the **Merge Sequence #** places a 1 for the first record actually merged. Then even if a record is skipped, the next number inserted would be 2 and so forth.

Tools → Mail Merge... Insert Word Field, Next Record

When you run the merge, choose **Next Record** if you don't want to have a section break after the current record. If you insert this code and add a merge field, that field for the next record will print on the current page.

Tools → Mail Merge... Insert Word Field, Next Record If...

When you run the merge, choose **Next Record If** to omit a page break after the current record when a field name matches a criteria (see Figure 2.100).

Figure 2.100
On the Mail Merge toolbar's Insert Word Field, Next Record If opens the Next Record If dialog box.

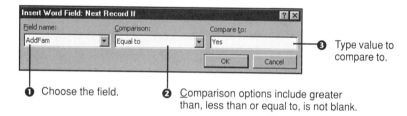

❸ Type value to compare to.

❶ Choose the field.

❷ Comparison options include greater than, less than or equal to, is not blank.

Tools → Mail Merge... Insert Word Field, Set Bookmark...

Choose **Set Bookmark** to set or change the value of a bookmark, generally so that you can use the value later in a formula (see Figure 2.101).

Figure 2.101
You can change or set values on the Insert Word Field. Set dialog box.

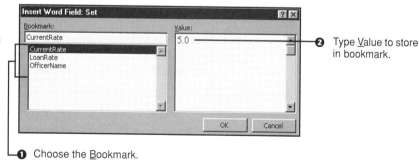

❷ Type Value to store in bookmark.

❶ Choose the Bookmark.

Tools → Mail Merge... Insert Word Field, Skip Record If...

When you run the merge, choose **Skip Record If** to omit a section break after the current record when a field name matches a criteria. The Skip Record If dialog box looks the same as the Next Record If dialog box (refer to Figure 2.100). However, Help says not to use the SKIPIF field in the current version of Word. Instead, it is easier to use the Query Options button in the Mail Merge Helper dialog box (see **T̲ools ▪ Mail Me̲rge... Query Options...**, page 212).

T̲ools ▪ Mail Merge... Data Source Section

The data source is a database that has the information that is different for each letter, envelope, label, or catalog. On the Mail Merge Helper dialog box, click the **G̲et Data** button to bring up a menu with four choices: **C̲reate Data Source**, **O̲pen Data Source**, **Use A̲ddress Book**, and **H̲eader Options**. These choices are discussed in the following sections.

T̲ools ▪ Mail Me̲rge... G̲et Data, C̲reate Data Source

Use the Create Data Source option if you still need to create a database. On the Mail Merge Helper dialog box, click the **G̲et Data** button and choose **C̲reate Data Source**. The Create Data Source dialog box opens as shown in Figure 2.102.

Figure 2.102
T̲ools, Mail Me̲rge, G̲et Data, C̲reate Data Source opens the Create Data Source dialog box.

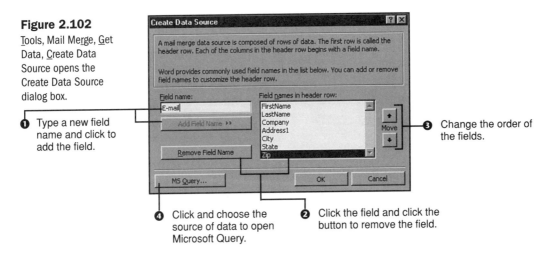

❶ Type a new field name and click to add the field.

❸ Change the order of the fields.

❹ Click and choose the source of data to open Microsoft Query.

❷ Click the field and click the button to remove the field.

After you choose your fields and click **OK**, the Save As dialog box opens (see **File ▪ Save A̲s...**, page 29). Choose a location and name for your file and click **S̲ave**. After the file is saved, a new dialog box opens (the buttons depend on the type of the main document).

- Choose **Edit the D̲ata Source** to open the Data Form and add or edit existing records (see **T̲ools ▪ Mail Merge... Data source section, E̲dit**, page 210).

- If your main document is a Form Letter or Catalog, click **Edit the Main Document** to go to the document (see **T̲ools ▪ Mail Merge... Main document section—E̲dit**, page 201).

- If your document is a Mailing Label or Envelope, click **Setup the Main Document** to select or change the dimensions and add the merge fields (see **T̲ools ▪ Mail Me̲rge... Main document section—S̲etup**, page 202).

Tools ▪ Mail Merge..., Get Data, Open Data Source

If you already have a database in another Word document, Excel spreadsheet, Access table or query, or other source, you can use this data source for merge fields in Word. If your data source is a text file, you may need to attach a header file first (see **Tools ▪ Mail Merge... Get Data, Header Options**, page 210).

1. From the Mail Merge Helper dialog box, choose **Get Data, Open Data Source**. The Open Data Source dialog box opens.

2. If necessary, choose your file type from the **Files of type** drop-down list.

3. Go to the location and name of the file as you would in any file open dialog box (see **File ▪ Open...**, page 21) and double-click the file.

4. If your file is one of these types, you may have an intermediate step to choose the portion of your file you want to use as the database:

   - If your data source is an Access database, a Microsoft Access dialog box opens with two tabs. Pick an object from the **Tables** or **Queries** tab. If you choose from the Queries tab, you can check **Link to Query** to always retrieve the most up-to-date version (criteria and fields) during a merge. Click the **View SQL** button to open a window and see the Structured Query Language statement for the table or query. When finished, click **OK**.

   - If your source is an Excel spreadsheet, a Microsoft Excel dialog box opens. Select either **Keep Entire Spreadsheet** or type the name of your range (for example, Budget) or range address (for example, B2:F100) for the database; then click **OK**.

   - If your data source is dBase, FoxPro, or another non-Microsoft Office file type, you may get a message box asking your to confirm your data source. Double-click the driver.

5. When you are finished, you may go either to the Mail Merge Helper or to a dialog box with option buttons.

   - If you return to the Mail Merge Helper, choose another option on that dialog box.

   - Click **Setup Main Document** to create a Mailing Label or Envelope (see **Tools ▪ Mail Merge... Main document section—Setup**, page 202).

   - Click **Edit Main Document** to go to the Word document (see **Tools ▪ Mail Merge... Main document section—Edit**, page 210).

Tools ▪ Mail Merge... Get Data, Use Address Book

To use addresses that you created in Outlook, Schedule+, or Microsoft Exchange, choose Address Book as a data source.

1. From the Mail Merge Helper, choose **Get Data** and **Use Address Book**. The User Address Book dialog box opens.

2. Choose one of the data sources such as Outlook Address Book, Personal Address Book, or Schedule+ Contacts.

3. If prompted, choose a folder or profile and click **OK**.

4. When finished you may go either to the Mail Merge Helper or to a dialog box with setup or edit option buttons.

    - If you return to the Mail Merge Helper, choose another option on that dialog box.

    - Click **Setup Main Document** to create a Mailing Label or Envelope (see **Tools - Mail Merge... Main document section—Setup**, page 202).

    - Click **Edit Main Document** to go to the Word document (see **Tools - Mail Merge... Main document section—Edit**, page 201).

Tools - Mail Merge... Get Data, Header Options

In some cases, you have to use a header for your data file because there are no field names. This situation includes text files. You may also want to use header files if you have multiple data sources and don't want to change the names of the fields in the main document.

1. From the Mail Merge Helper, choose **Get Data, Header Options**.

2. If you already have a header source file, choose **Open** and double-click the filename (see **File - Open...**, page 21).

3. To create a header source, do the following:

    - Choose **Create**. The Create Header Source dialog box opens.

    - Type any **Field name** you want and click **Add Field Name**.

    - You can also **Remove Field Name** and use the **Move** arrows to change the order of the fields.

    - When you click **OK,** a Save As dialog box opens (see **File - Save As...**, page 29). Give the file a name and click **OK**.

If you haven't identified the data source, use the **Get Data** button and choose **Open Data Source** (see **Tools - Mail Merge... Get Data, Open Data Source**, page 209).

Tools - Mail Merge... Edit

Editing your data source depends on the type of data file attached to your main document.

- If your data source is an Excel or Access document, these programs open as soon as you identify the data source. When you click the **Edit** button on the Mail Merge Helper, the program is already open but minimized. Click the minimized application icon on the Windows taskbar or press Alt+Tab to go to these programs.

- If your data source is a different file type, you may get a dialog box that asks whether you want to use Microsoft Query to edit the data.

- If your data source is another Word document, when you choose **Edit** from the Mail Merge Helper in the Data source section, the Data Form opens (see Figure 2.103).

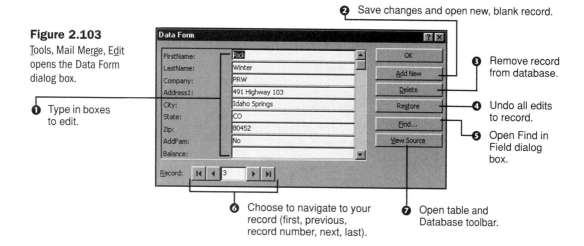

Figure 2.103

Tools, Mail Merge, Edit opens the Data Form dialog box.

❶ Type in boxes to edit.

❷ Save changes and open new, blank record.

❸ Remove record from database.

❹ Undo all edits to record.

❺ Open Find in Field dialog box.

❻ Choose to navigate to your record (first, previous, record number, next, last).

❼ Open table and Database toolbar.

If you click the Find button, the Find in Field dialog box opens (see Figure 2.104).

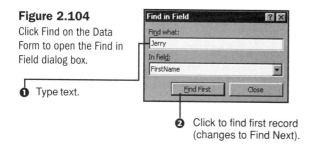

Figure 2.104

Click Find on the Data Form to open the Find in Field dialog box.

❶ Type text.

❷ Click to find first record (changes to Find Next).

If you click View Source on the Data Form dialog box, Word opens the database in a table format. You can edit the table (see **Table**, page 230) and use the Database toolbar (see **View – Toolbars – Database**, page 72).

Tools – Mail Merge... Merge the Data with the Document Section

After you create your main document and the data source, you are ready to go to the third section of the Mail Merge Helper dialog box. There are two buttons in this section, **Merge** and **Query Options**. These options are discussed in the following sections.

Tools – Mail Merge... Merge

The **Merge** button on the Mail Merge Helper dialog box enables you to merge to a document or a printer or to check for errors. When you choose **Merge**, the Merge dialog box opens and you have the following options:

- ■ Choose one of the options in the Merge to drop-down list:
  - New document
  - Printer
  - Electronic mail
  - Electronic fax
- ■ If you chose Electronic mail or Electronic fax in the Merge to drop-down list, click the **Setup** button. The Merge To Setup dialog box opens. Choose from the following options:
  - Choose an email address or fax phone field in the **Data field with Mail/Fax address**.
  - Type a **Mail message subject line**.
  - Check to **Send document as an attachment** for your email. If you clear this box, the document is copied to the message part of the email and some of the formatting in your document may be lost.
- ■ Choose **All** records or type the starting and stopping record numbers in the **From** and **To** text boxes.
- ■ For blank lines, choose one of these two options:
  - **Don't print blank lines when data fields are empty.**
  - **Print blank lines when data fields are empty.**
- ■ If you want to check for potential problems, click the **Check Errors** button and choose one of the three options to specify whether you really want to perform the merge and when to report the errors (click **OK** when finished):
  - **Simulate the merge and report errors in a new document.**
  - **Complete the merge, pausing to report each error as it occurs.**
  - **Complete the merge without pausing. Report errors in a new document.**
- ■ Click the **Query Options** button if you want to choose specific records or sort how the merge will run. This option opens the dialog box shown in the following section.
- ■ If you want to save the settings for a later merge, click **Close**.
- ■ When you are finished with the settings in the Merge dialog box, click **Merge** to begin the merge.

Tools ⮡ Mail Merge... Query Options...

From the Mail Merge Helper dialog box, click **Query Options** to display the two tabs on the Query Options dialog box. Filter Records (see Figure 2.105) enables you to choose which records you want in the merge. Use Sort Records (see Figure 2.106) to order the merged records.

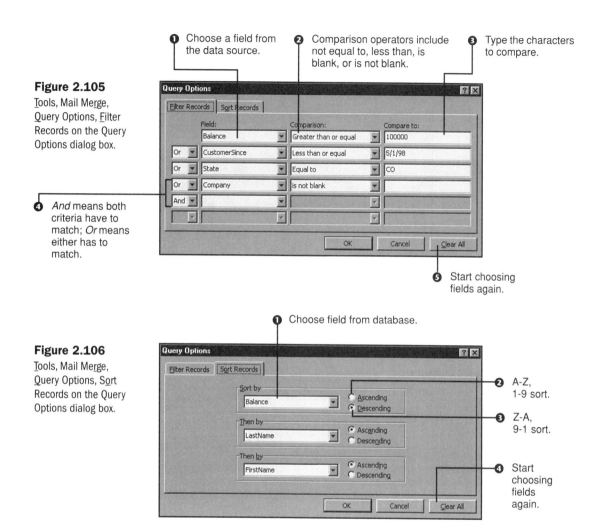

❶ Choose a field from the data source.

❷ Comparison operators include not equal to, less than, is blank, or is not blank.

❸ Type the characters to compare.

Figure 2.105
Tools, Mail Merge, Query Options, Filter Records on the Query Options dialog box.

❹ *And* means both criteria have to match; *Or* means either has to match.

❺ Start choosing fields again.

❶ Choose field from database.

Figure 2.106
Tools, Mail Merge, Query Options, Sort Records on the Query Options dialog box.

❷ A-Z, 1-9 sort.

❸ Z-A, 9-1 sort.

❹ Start choosing fields again.

Tools ➥ Envelopes and Labels...

When you type a letter, place your insertion point in the middle of the address and choose **Tools, Envelopes and Labels.** This step tells Word to place one recipient's address on an envelope or label. You can also merge multiple names and addresses to envelopes and labels (see **Tools – Mail Merge... Setup**, page 202).

Tools ➥ Envelopes and Labels... Envelopes

Click the **Envelopes** tab of the Envelopes and Labels dialog box to create an envelope (see Figure 2.107).

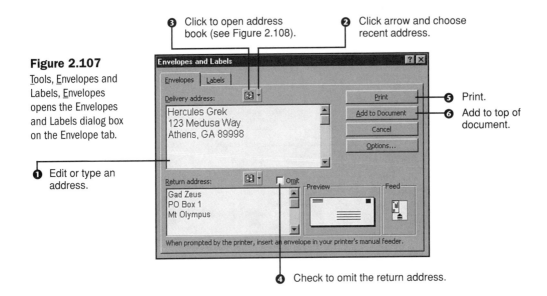

Figure 2.107

Tools, Envelopes and Labels, Envelopes opens the Envelopes and Labels dialog box on the Envelope tab.

❸ Click to open address book (see Figure 2.108).

❷ Click arrow and choose recent address.

❺ Print.

❻ Add to top of document.

❶ Edit or type an address.

❹ Check to omit the return address.

If you click the **Options** button on the Envelopes tab, you can change the settings for the Envelope as follows:

Dialog Box Item	How to Use
Envelope Options Tab	
Envelope size	Choose an option from the drop-down list. If you choose Custom size, the Envelope Size dialog box displays. Enter a **Width** and **Height**.
Delivery address Font and **Return address Font**	Click one of the Font buttons to open the Font dialog box. Make any changes in Font, Font style, Size, Underline, Color, or Effects (see **Format - Font...**, page 160).
Delivery and Return address From left and From top	Click the spinner buttons or type a number in the text box to change the position of the delivery or return address on the envelope.
Delivery point barcode	Check the box to add a machine-readable representation of the zip code and delivery address.
FIM-A courtesy reply mail	Check to add a Facing Identification Mark (FIM) on courtesy reply mail to identify the front of the envelope during presorting.

Printing Options Tab

Feed method	Click on one of the envelopes to change the direction the envelope goes in the printer.
Face up or Face down	Click whether you want the envelope to be **Face up** or **Face down**.
Clockwise rotation	Check to rotate the envelope 180 degrees from the picture shown under Feed method.
Feed from	Click to choose the paper tray for your printer.
Reset	Click to return the printer options to the defaults for Word.

Tools – Envelopes and Labels... Address Book

To use your address book from Outlook or Microsoft Exchange, click the **Address book** button 📇 ▾ above any of the addresses on the Envelopes or Labels tabs of the Envelopes and Labels dialog box. Clicking the button opens the Select Name dialog box (see Figure 2.108).

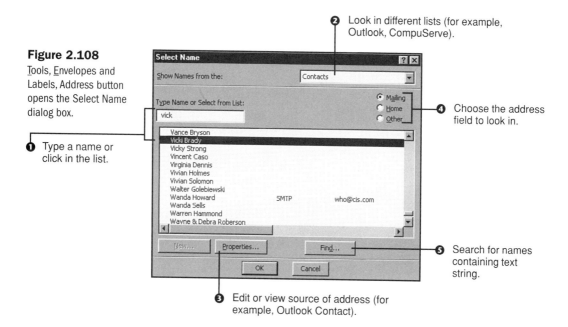

❷ Look in different lists (for example, Outlook, CompuServe).

Figure 2.108
Tools, Envelopes and Labels, Address button opens the Select Name dialog box.

❶ Type a name or click in the list.

❹ Choose the address field to look in.

❺ Search for names containing text string.

❸ Edit or view source of address (for example, Outlook Contact).

Tools – Envelopes and Labels... Labels

Click the **Labels** tab of the Envelopes and Labels dialog box to create a label (see Figure 2.109).

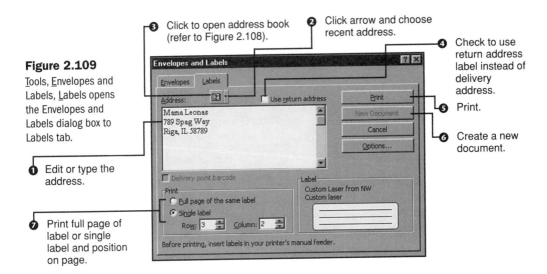

Figure 2.109

Tools, Envelopes and Labels, Labels opens the Envelopes and Labels dialog box to Labels tab.

➌ Click to open address book (refer to Figure 2.108).

➋ Click arrow and choose recent address.

➍ Check to use return address label instead of delivery address.

➎ Print.

➏ Create a new document.

➊ Edit or type the address.

➐ Print full page of label or single label and position on page.

If you click the **Options** button on the Labels tab, you can change the settings for the labels as follows:

Dialog Box Item	How to Use
Dot **m**atrix or **L**aser and ink jet	Click to choose category of printer.
Tray	If Laser and ink jet, click and choose a paper tray from the drop-down list.
Label p**r**oducts	Choose manufacturer and category of labels from the drop-down list.
Product n**u**mber	Look on your label package and choose the product ID from this list.
Details	Click this button to go to the information dialog box for this label (see Figure 2.110).
New Label	Click to open the New Custom Label dialog box. The screen is the same as Details, but you can type a **L**abel name in the text box.

If you choose the **Details** or **New Label** button on the Label Option dialog box, you can change the size of the label (see Figure 2.110). The choices in the dialog box depend on your printer and the label product you chose. If your label is a standard label, you should not have to edit its size.

Figure 2.110
Choose <u>N</u>ew Label or
<u>D</u>etails to open a
customize label dialog
box.

2 Set margins on
page before
labels start.

4 Set measurement
between start of
one label and
start of another.

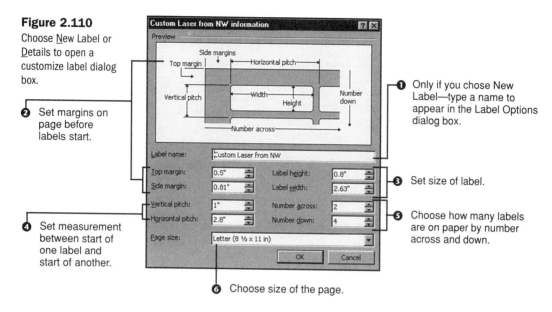

1 Only if you chose New
Label—type a name to
appear in the Label Options
dialog box.

3 Set size of label.

5 Choose how many labels
are on paper by number
across and down.

6 Choose size of the page.

Tools ➡ Letter Wizard...

The Letter Wizard takes you through the steps of creating a letter. To start the Letter Wizard, do one of the following:

Quick Choices   *DRAW BORDERS*

- Choose <u>T</u>ools, **Letter Wizard.**

- Choose <u>F</u>ile, <u>N</u>ew and double-click on Letter Wizard on the Letters & Faxes tab (see **File – <u>N</u>ew...**, page 20).

- Begin typing a letter. For example, type **Dear** and the person's name and a colon or comma and then press **Enter**. The Office Assistant says that it looks like you're writing a letter. Click **Get help with writing the letter**.

The following table shows the options on the four tabs of the Letter Wizard dialog box.

Dialog Box Item	How to Use
Letter Format Tab	
<u>D</u>ate line	Check the box and click on the drop-down arrow to choose the format for today's date.
Include <u>h</u>eader and footer with page design	Check to include a header and footer. This check box may not be enabled if you choose the current page design.

continues

Dialog Box Item	How to Use
Choose a page design	Choose a template from the drop-down list. See the preview area to see what the template looks like.
Choose a letter style	Choose Full block, Modified block, or Semi-block to indicate how your paragraphs, date, and closing line up. See the preview area to see what the style looks like.
Pre-printed letterhead	Check if you have letterhead paper and to enable the following two options.
Where on the page is the letterhead?	Choose whether the letterhead is on the top, bottom, left, or right side of the page.
How much space does the letterhead need?	Click the spinner buttons or type the size of the letterhead from the edge of the paper to the margin.

Recipient Info tab

Click here to use Address Book	Click the down arrow next to the Address book button to choose from a list of previously used names. Click the Address book button itself to choose a name from Outlook or Microsoft Exchange (see **Tools - Mail Merge... Get Data, Use Address Book**, page 209). When you choose either, the **Recipient's name** and **Delivery address** are entered.
Recipient's name	Use Address Book, type a name, or click the drop-down arrow and choose from previously entered names.
Delivery address	Use Address Book or type an address.
Informal, Formal, Business, or Other	Click one of options to narrow the **Example** drop-down list.
Example	Choose one of the examples for the opening of the letter (for example, Dear Sir or Madam).

Other Elements tab

Reference line	Check the box and click the drop-down arrow and choose from previously entered entries, or type a new entry. The reference line describes what the contents of the letter is about and appears on the line below the date.
Mailing instructions	Check the box and click the drop-down arrow and choose from previously entered entries, or type a new entry. Mailing instructions include certified mail, confidential, personal, or registered mail and appears on the line below the Reference line.

Dialog Box Item	How to Use
Attention	Check the box and click the drop-down arrow and choose from previously entered entries, or type a new entry. This item includes the word *Attention*, an abbreviation, or anything else you type and appears below the recipient's address.
Subject	Check box and click drop-down arrow and choose from previously entered entries, or type new entry. This includes the word subject or anything else you type and appears below the salutation.
Courtesy copies	Click the down arrow next to the address book to choose an previous existing entry or click the Address book button to choose a person in Outlook. You can add your first entry this way, but all additional CCs need to be typed.

Sender Info tab

Click here to use Address Book	Click the down arrow next to the Address book button to choose from a list of previously used names. Click the Address book button itself to choose a name from Outlook. When you choose either, the **Sender's name** and **Return address** are entered.
Sender's name	Use the Address Book, type a name, or click the drop-down arrow and choose from previously entered names.
Return address	Use the Address Book or type an address.
Omit	Check this box to leave off omit a return address.
Complimentary closing	Type or choose from a standard list of closings (e.g., Sincerely or Best wishes).
Job title	Type or choose from a previous list of entries for the job position.
Company	Type or choose from a previous list of company entries.
Writer/typist initials	Type or choose from a previous list of initials.
Enclosures	Check the box and use the spinner button to increase or decrease the number of enclosures.

After you click **OK** to finish the Letter Wizard, Word creates the letter for you in the style you chose with the names and addresses and other items. Type the text of your letter. The gray highlighted items on your letter are AutoTextList field codes (see **Insert ▸ Field...**, page 106). You can right-click the AutoTextList field code and choose a different option that was on the Letter Wizard dialog box.

Tools ▸ Macro

Macros are stored procedures that automate tasks that you do often. You can record a macro or create a procedure directly in Visual Basic.

Tools ▸ Macro ▸ Macros...

When you choose **Tools**, **Macro**, **Macros** or press **Alt+F8**, you open the Macros dialog box which enables you to run or manage your macros (see Figure 2.111).

Quick Choices RUN MACRO

1. Press **Alt+F8**. The Macro dialog box opens.

2. Double-click the macro name.

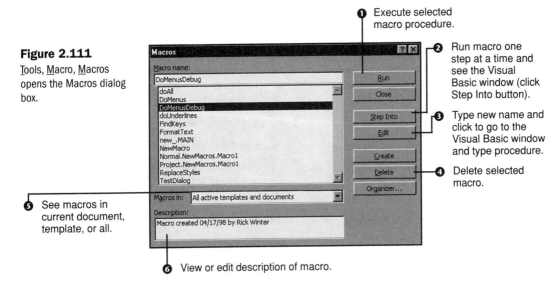

❶ Execute selected macro procedure.

❷ Run macro one step at a time and see the Visual Basic window (click Step Into button).

❸ Type new name and click to go to the Visual Basic window and type procedure.

❹ Delete selected macro.

Figure 2.111
Tools, Macro, Macros opens the Macros dialog box.

❺ See macros in current document, template, or all.

❻ View or edit description of macro.

When you click the **Organizer** button in the Macros dialog box, the Organizer dialog box opens to the **Macro Project Items** tab, enabling you to copy macros from one template or document to another (see Figure 2.112).

Figure 2.112
The Organizer button on the Macros dialog box opens the Organizer dialog box.

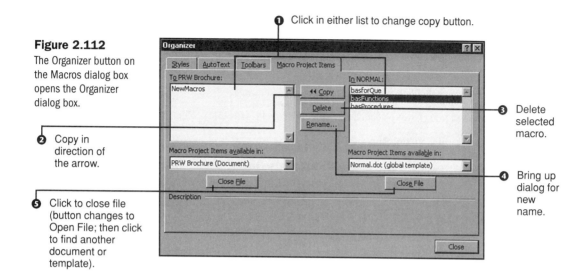

① Click in either list to change copy button.

② Copy in direction of the arrow.

⑤ Click to close file (button changes to Open File; then click to find another document or template).

③ Delete selected macro.

④ Bring up dialog for new name.

You can also copy styles (see **F̲ormat ▪ S̲tyle...**, page 178), AutoText (see **Insert ▪ A̲utoText**, page 101), and toolbars (see **V̲iew ▪ Toolbars**, page 66) between documents and templates.

T̲ools ▪ M̲acro ▪ R̲ecord New Macro...

You can record your keystrokes and menu choices and save the sequence of steps as a macro. Word automatically creates the Visual Basic procedure for you.

1. Choose **T̲ools**, **M̲acros**, **R̲ecord New Macro**. The Record Macro dialog box opens.

2. Type a name for the macro in the **Macro name** text box.

3. Choose the document or template to **Store macro in**. The Normal.dot template allows you to run the macro from any document. You can also choose to store the macro in the current document (or a template if the document is based on an additional template).

4. Type a **Description** for your macro. This box will start with your name and today's date.

5. You have an option of creating a button or shortcut key to your macro. If desired, do one of the following:

    - To create a button on a toolbar, click the **Toolbars** button. The Command tab of the Customize dialog box opens. Drag the macro name from the **Comman̲ds** column to a toolbar or menu and click **Close**. For more information, (see **V̲iew ▪ Toolbars ▪ C̲ustomize...**, page 87).

    - To assign a shortcut key to the macro, click the **Keyboard** button. The Customize Keyboard dialog box opens. Press your key combination while you are in the **Press n̲ew shortcut key** text box. If the key combination is already assigned, a message appears below this text box. Click **A̲ssign** and **Close** to assign this key. To add the keyboard later (see **V̲iew ▪ Toolbars ▪ C̲ustomize... K̲eyboard Button**, page 91).

    - ▪ Click **OK** to begin the recording without assigning either a button or a shortcut key.

6. You enter a document window with the Stop Recording toolbar open. Type the desired text. To move the insertion point, use the keyboard or choose a menu or buttons. You cannot record mouse movements on the screen.

7. If you want to pause recording and do something else, click the **Pause Recording** button . Click it again to resume recording.

8. When you're done recording your macro, click the **Stop Recording** button .

Tools ▸ Macro ▸ Visual Basic Editor

To edit a macro or see macro procedures, choose **Tools**, **Macro**, **Visual Basic Editor** or press Alt+F11. Microsoft Visual Basic Editor opens. Click the **Find** button . In the **Find What** text box, type your macro name and choose **Find Next** until you find your macro. For more information on Visual Basic for Applications, see Que's *Special Edition Using Visual Basic for Applications 5*.

Tools ▸ Templates and Add-Ins...

The Templates and Add-Ins dialog box (see Figure 2.113) enables you to manage which templates (see **File ▸ New...**, page 20) are attached to the current document and used during this session of Word. Add-ins are supplemental programs that add toolbars, menu items, and other features. You can buy supplemental add-ins from a third party, download them from Microsoft's Web site, or find them on the Microsoft Office 97 CD-ROM.

If you click **Organizer** on the Templates and Add-ins dialog box, the dialog box that opens is the same as the Macros dialog box (refer to Figure 2.112).

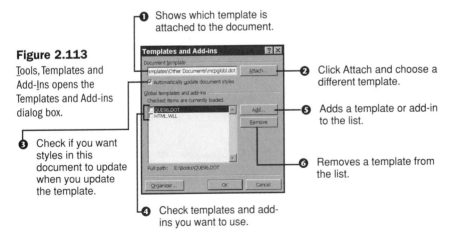

Figure 2.113
Tools, Templates and Add-Ins opens the Templates and Add-ins dialog box.

❶ Shows which template is attached to the document.

❷ Click Attach and choose a different template.

❸ Check if you want styles in this document to update when you update the template.

❹ Check templates and add-ins you want to use.

❺ Adds a template or add-in to the list.

❻ Removes a template from the list.

Tools ▸ Customize...

When you choose **Tools**, **Customize**, the Customize dialog box opens, enabling you to edit or create toolbars and menus. The same dialog box is shown in the **View ▸ Toolbars ▸ Customize...** section on page 87.

Tools ➥ Options...

The **Tools**, **Options** command modifies the way that various Word features work, including the screen appearance, printing, editing, spelling, and user identification. Some of the tabs on the Options dialog box can be accessed from other parts of Word. For each of the following tabs, see the designation section in this book:

Tab	Refer To
Print	**File** – **Print...**, page 42
Save	**File** – **Save As...**, page 29
Spelling and Grammar	**Tools** – **Spelling and Grammar...**, page 188
Track Changes	**Tools** – **Track Changes** – **Highlight Changes...**, page 196

The following sections describe the rest of the tabs on the Options dialog box.

Tools ➥ Options... View Tab

The items displayed on the View tab depend on which view you're in when you open the dialog box (see **View** – **Normal**, page 62; **View** – **Online Layout**, page 63; **View** – **Page Layout**, page 63; **View** – **Outline**, page 63). The third column of the following table specifies whether the item is available for each of the views: Normal (N), Page Layout (PL), Online Layout (OL), Outline (O).

Dialog Box Option	Description	N, PL, OL, O
Show Section		
Draft font	Check to speed up screen updating in documents with lots of formatting. Most character formatting is displayed as underlined and bold. Graphics displays as empty boxes.	N, O
Drawings	Clear to hide drawings. This Hiding may increase the speed of scrolling on your document and does not affect printing.	PL, OL
Object anchors	Check to see an anchor when an object is attached to a specific paragraph (only visible when **Show/Hide** button ¶ is selected).	PL, OL
Text boundaries	Check to display dotted lines around margins, text columns, and objects.	PL, OL
Picture placeholders	Check to display pictures as empty boxes and speed up displaying a document.	N, PL, OL, O
Animated text	When you format text with animation (see **Format** – **Font...**, page 160), check this box to show the	N, PL, OL, O

continues

Dialog Box Option	Description	N, PL, OL, O
	animation. Clear the box to see how the document will look when printed.	
ScreenTips	Check to display a yellow pop-up box with comments (see **Insert - Comment**, page 129), footnotes (see **Insert - Footnote...**, page 131), endnotes, or reviewers changes (see **Tools - Track Changes**, page 196) when you hover over one of those items.	N, PL, OL, O
Highlight	Check to show highlights inserted with the Highlight button on the Formatting toolbar.	N, PL, OL, O
Bookmarks	Check to show square brackets in the document where a bookmark is located (see **Insert - Bookmark...**, page 159).	N, PL, OL, O
Field codes	Check to see curly brackets, the field code, and any options as a code—for example, {DATE \@ "MMMM d, yyyy"}. Clear this box to see the results of the field (see **Insert - Field...**, page 106).	N, PL, OL, O
Field shading	Choose Always to see a gray highlight for all fields; or choose When selected to see the highlight when the insertion point is in the field.	N, PL, OL

Nonprinting Characters Section. The Show/Hide button ¶ on the Standard toolbar shows or hides all the characters below. Turn off the Show/Hide button and click the following to see only the characters below.

Tab characters	Check to see and arrow for each tab.	N, PL, OL, O
Spaces	Check to see a dot for a space.	N, PL, OL, O
Paragraph marks	Check to see a paragraph symbol when you press Enter and return arrow when you insert a manual line break (**Shift+Enter**).	N, PL, OL, O
Optional hyphens	Check to see a hyphen symbol for hyphenating words at the end of the line (see **Tools - Language - Hyphenation...**, page 193).	N, PL, OL, O
Hidden text	Check to see a dotted underline with hidden text (see **Format - Font...**, page 160).	N, PL, OL, O
All	Check to see all non-printing characters.	N, PL, OL, O

Window Section

Status bar	Check to see the Status bar on bottom of the screen.	N, PL, OL, O
Style area width	Use the spinner button or type a size for the style area to see a pane on the left side of the screen	N, O

Dialog Box Option	Description	N, PL, OL, O
	showing the names of all styles. After you choose this option and go to the document, you can drag the line between this pane and the document to make the area larger or smaller.	
Horizontal scroll bar	Check to see the scroll bar with view buttons on the bottom of the screen.	N, PL, OL, O
Vertical scroll bar	Check to see the scroll bar with browse buttons on the right side of the screen.	N, PL, OL, O
Wrap to window	Check to wrap text so you can see it all regardless of the size of the font. Clear this box to see how the document will wrap when you print.	N, OL, O
Vertical ruler	Check to see the ruler (see also **View - Ruler**, page 92).	PL
Enlarge fonts less than	Click the spinner buttons or type the font size in this text box to make small fonts appear larger on the screen.	OL

Tools - Options... General Tab

Dialog Box Option	Description
Background repagination	Check this box in normal view to automatically reset page numbers as you work. This is dimmed in page layout view because it occurs by default.
Help for WordPerfect users	Check this box to get help when you press a WordPerfect for DOS key combination. WPH appears in the status bar. You can double-click WPH to open the Help for WordPerfect dialog box.
Navigation keys for WordPerfect users	Check to change the functions of Page Up, Page Down, Home, End, and Esc keys to their WordPerfect equivalents.
Blue background, white text	Check for a blue background and white text (similar to WordPerfect for DOS screen).
Provide feedback with sound	If Microsoft Office Sounds is installed on your computer, this option provides sounds when you do perform certain events (close, maximize, menu popup). To change sounds associated with an event, choose the Windows **Start** button, **Settings**, **Control Panel**, and double-click on the Sounds icon.

continues

Dialog Box Option	Description
Provide feedback with animation	Check to show animated cursors when you are printing, repaginating, saving, or AutoFormatting.
Confirm conversion at Open	Check to verify the file converter to use to open a file created in another application. Clear to allow Word to select the converter (see **File - Open...**, page 21).
Update automatic links at Open	Check to update linked information when you open a document with information linked to another file (see **Insert - File...**, page 157 and **Insert - Object...**, page 158).
Mail as attachment	When you choose Send to Mail Recipient, Word attaches the current document as an attachment. Clear if you want Word to insert the contents of the current document into the message (see **File - Send To - Mail Recipient...**, page 45).
Recently used file list	Check and use spinner button to list up to 9 nine filenames at the bottom of your File menu (see **File - Recently Used File List**, page 48).
Macro virus protection	Check if you want to have Word warning you when you open a document that might have a virus because the document has macros or customized toolbars, menus, or shortcuts.
Measurement units	Choose Inches, Centimeters, Points, or Picas for the horizontal ruler and any measurements in dialog boxes (margins, paragraphs, and so on).

Tools - Options... Edit Tab

Dialog Box Option	Description
Typing replaces selection	Check for Word to replace selected text with what you type. Clear for Word to insert new text in front of selected text.
Drag-and-drop text editing	Check to allow you to drag selected text with a left-pointing arrow to a new location (press Ctrl to copy text). You can also drag with the right mouse button and then choose whether you want to **Move Here** or **Copy Here**.
When selecting, automatically select entire word	Check to select the word and space following word when dragging across a selection.
Use the INS key for paste	Check to use **Insert** key to paste contents of Clipboard.

Dialog Box Option	Description
Overtype mode	Check to replace one character for each character you type. OVR appears on the status bar. Double-click to turn it on or off.
Use smart cut and paste	Check to remove extra space when you delete text or add space when you paste text.
Tabs and backspace set left indent	Check to increase or decrease left indent marker when you press Tab or Backspace while on the margin.
Allow accented uppercase in French	Check when text is formatted as French (see **Tools - Language - Set Language...**, page 192) to allow Word to suggest accent marks for uppercase letters.
Picture editor	Choose from the drop-down list which program you want to use for your picture editor.

Tools - Options... User Information

User Information enables you to enter information one time and use it repeatedly. The following items are on this tab of the dialog box.

- **Name** Type the name that will appear by default in Properties (see **File - Properties**, page 46), letters and envelopes (see **Tools - Envelopes and Labels...**, page 213), track changes (see **Tools - Track Changes**, page 196), and comments (see **Insert - Comment**, page 129).

- **Initials** Type your initials for comment marks and built-in letter (see **Tools - Letter Wizard...**, page 217) and memo elements (see **File - New...**, page 20).

- **Mailing address** Type the mailing address to use as the default for envelopes and letters.

Tools - Options... Compatibility

Change compatibility options when you work with other word processing programs.

Dialog Box Option	Description
Font Substitution	When fonts in the document are not on this system, click this button to choose which fonts to substitute.
Recommended options for	Choose a word processing program to change options settings in the list below.
Options	Change any of the 30 options to display how the document appears and prints in Word:

- Combine table borders like Word 5.x for Windows

- Do full justification like WordPerfect 6.x for Windows

continues

Dialog Box Option	Description
	• Don't add automatic tab stop for hanging indent
	• Don't add extra space for raised/lowered characters
	• Don't add leading (extra space) between rows of text
	• Don't add space for underlines
	• Don't balance columns for Continuous section starts
	• Don't balance SBCS characters and DBCS characters
	• Don't blank the area behind metafile pictures
	• Don't center "exact line height" lines
	• Don't convert backslash characters into yen signs
	• Don't draw underline on trailing spaces
	• Expand character spaces on the line ending Shift+Return
	• Expand/condense by whole number of points
	• Lines wrap like Word 6.0
	• Print body text before header/footer
	• Print colors as black on noncolor printers
	• Set the width of a space like WordPerfect 5.x
	• Show hard page or column breaks in frames
	• Substitute fonts based on font size
	• Suppress extra line spacing at bottom of page
	• Suppress extra line spacing at top of page
	• Suppress extra line spacing at top of page like Word 5.x for the Mac
	• Suppress extra line spacing like WordPerfect 5.x
	• Suppress Space Before after a hard page or column break
	• Swap left and right borders on odd facing pages
	• Treat "\" as "" in mail merge data sources
	• Truncate font height
	• Use larger small caps like Word 5.x for the Macintosh
	• Use printer metrics to lay out document

Dialog Box Option	Description
	● Use Word 6.x/95 border rules
	● Wrap trailing spaces to next line
Default	Click to store the settings in the **Options** list as the defaults.

Tools ▪ Options... File Locations

Use the File Locations tab to change the default location in which documents and settings are stored.

Quick Choices   *SET FILE LOCATIONS*

1. Choose **Tools, Options**. The Options dialog box opens.
2. Click the **File Locations** tab.
3. Choose one of the items in the list (described in the following table) and click **Modify**. The Modify Location dialog box opens.
4. Use the Modify Location dialog box like the File Open dialog box (see **File ▪ Open...**, page 21) to find a folder (not file) in which you want to store the documents; then choose **OK**.

Item	Used For
Documents	Changes the default location when you open Word for the location for File Save (see **File ▪ Save As...**, page 29) and File Open (see **File ▪ Open...**, page 21).
ClipArt pictures	Changes where ClipArt pictures are stored. You can choose a folder on the Microsoft Office CD-ROM.
User templates	Changes to include the folder where templates are stored on this computer (see **File ▪ New...**, page 20).
Workgroup templates	If part of a networked group and you have an additional location for templates, change or add this information here. Templates appear on the tabs of the File New dialog box.
User options	Left over from previous versions. Doesn't do anything (according to Microsoft phone help).
AutoRecover files	Specifies a location in which files are stored when the computer crashes (**see Save AutoRecover info every** option on the Options Save tab in **File ▪ Save As...**, page 29). If this option has no folder selected, check for your AutoRecover files in the Window's Temp folder.
Tools	Left over from previous versions. Doesn't do anything (according to Microsoft phone help).
Startup	Changes the location of files that will launch when Word starts. If you want a document, template, or add-in to automatically load each time you start Word, place the file in this folder.

Table

Tables enable you to enter information in rows and columns. You can print the lines surrounding rows and columns. Tables are an alternative to setting tabs (see **Format ▪ Tabs...**, page 174).

Table ➥ Draw Table

In Word 97 you can draw a table with the mouse pointer.

Quick Choices   *DRAW A TABLE*

1. Click the **Tables and Borders** button 🔲 on the Standard toolbar, choose **Table, Draw Table**, or right-click in the document and choose **Draw Table**. The mouse pointer changes to a pencil, and the Tables and Borders toolbar displays. For a description of the buttons on the toolbar, see **View ▪ Toolbars ▪ Tables and Borders**, page 66.

2. Drag the pencil mouse pointer to draw a rectangle for the outer edge of your table.

3. Drag the pencil across the table from one edge to another to draw rows and down from top to bottom to draw columns. You can also draw between two columns or rows to draw a partial row or column.

4. If desired, click the **Eraser** button 🔲 on the Tables and Borders toolbar and drag to remove lines for rows or columns.

5. Click whichever button is turned on—**Eraser** 🔲 or **Draw Table** 🔲—to finish the table.

Table ➥ Insert Table...

If you know the number of rows and columns, you can also create a table by using the Insert Table toolbar button or menu item.

Quick Choices   *CREATE A TABLE*

1. Click the **Insert Table** button 🔲 on the Standard toolbar.

2. Drag down from this button into the grid to choose the number of rows and columns. The note on the bottom of the palette tells you how large the table will be (for example, a 4 × 2 Table will be four rows and two columns).

You can also choose **Table, Insert Table** to create a table. The dialog box in Figure 2.114 appears.

When you are in a cell of a table or have one or more rows selected, the Insert Table button on the toolbar and menu changes to Insert Rows. If you have one or more columns selected, the button and menu item changes to Insert Columns.

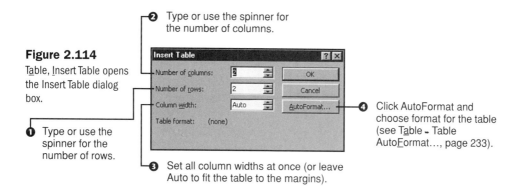

② Type or use the spinner for the number of columns.

Figure 2.114
Table, Insert Table opens the Insert Table dialog box.

④ Click AutoFormat and choose format for the table (see Table – Table AutoFormat…, page 233).

① Type or use the spinner for the number of rows.

③ Set all column widths at once (or leave Auto to fit the table to the margins).

Table—Keyboard Movement

After you create a table, you can use the mouse to click in the cell you want or use the following keys to move around or insert items in the table.

To Move To	Press
Next cell	**Tab**
Previous cell	**Shift+Tab**
Previous row	**Up arrow**
Next row	**Down arrow**
First cell in the row	**Alt+Home**
Last cell in the row	**Alt+End**
First cell in the column	**Alt+Page Up**
Last cell in the column	**Alt+Page Down**

To Insert	Press
New paragraph in the cell	**Enter**
Tab character in The cell	**Ctrl+Tab**
To split the table, or if in first cell, insert a blank paragraph above the table	**Ctrl+Shift+Enter**

Table ➙ Delete Cells...

To remove cells from a table, you can select rows (drag the white arrow to the left of table) or columns (drag the black down arrow above table) and choose **Table**, **Delete Rows** or **Table**, **Delete Columns**. These options are also available when you right-click a table selection.

If you have a partial row or column selected and choose **Table** or right-click, choose **Delete Cells**. The Delete Cells dialog box opens. You can then choose one of the following four options and click **OK**.

- **Shift cells <u>l</u>eft** (other cells in the row remain).
- **Shift cells <u>u</u>p** (other cells in the column remain).
- **Delete entire <u>r</u>ow** (if selection includes cells in more than one row, deletes multiple rows).
- **Delete entire <u>c</u>olumn** (if selection includes cells in more than one column, deletes multiple columns).

Ta<u>b</u>le ➥ <u>M</u>erge Cells

To combine multiple cells into one larger cell, do one of the following:

Quick Choices   *MERGE TABLE CELLS*

- Select two or more cells and click the **Merge Cells** button 📭 on the Tables and Borders toolbar.
- Select two or more cells and choose **Ta<u>b</u>le, Merge Cells**.
- Click the **Eraser** ✐ button on the Tables and Borders toolbar and click the line between two cells.

Ta<u>b</u>le ➥ <u>S</u>plit Cells...

To turn one or more selected cells into multiple cells, click the Split Cells button on the Tables and Borders toolbar or choose **Ta<u>b</u>le, <u>S</u>plit Cells**. The Split Cells dialog box opens with the following options:

- Type or use the spinner button to specify the **Number of <u>c</u>olumns** you want to make from the selected cell(s).
- Type or use the spinner button to specify the **Number of <u>r</u>ows** you want to make from the selected cell(s).
- If you have more than once cell selected, you can first **<u>M</u>erge cells before split** so that they are all the same size. Otherwise, each cell splits into the number of rows and columns you choose.

Click **OK** after choosing one of these options.

Quick Choices   *SPLIT CELLS WITH DRAW TABLE BUTTON*

- Click the **Draw Table** button ✐ on the Tables and Borders toolbar and draw new lines where you want to split the cells.

Ta<u>b</u>le ➥ <u>S</u>elect Row

To select the entire row the current cell is in (for deleting, inserting, and so on), choose **Table, Select <u>R</u>ow**. You can also move the mouse pointer to the left of the table (It becomes a right-facing white arrow) and click (or drag down to select more than one row).

You can also add borders around cells. Click the Borders or Shading Color buttons on the Tables and Borders toolbar (see **View ⇒ Toolbars ⇒ Tables and Borders**, page 82) or make a choice from the drop-down list (or see **Format ⇒ Borders and Shading...**, page 170).

Table ⇒ Select Column

To select the entire column the current cell is in (for deleting, inserting, and so on), choose **Table, Select Column**. You can also move the mouse pointer above the table (the pointer becomes a black down arrow) and click (or drag across to select more than one column). You can also hold **Alt** and click in a cell to select the column.

Table ⇒ Select Table

To select the entire table, choose **Table, Select Table,** or press **Alt + 5** on the numeric keypad (with Num Lock off). If you want to delete the table, choose **Table, Delete Rows**.

Table ⇒ Table AutoFormat...

To apply predesigned formats with shading, borders, fonts, and colors, click the **Table AutoFormat** button 📧 on the Tables and Borders toolbar, or choose **Table, Table AutoFormat**. The Table AutoFormat dialog box opens (see Figure 2.115).

Figure 2.115
Table, AutoFormat opens the Table AutoFormat dialog box.

❶ Choose a predefined format.

❷ Check boxes to apply borders, shading, font, and color shown in preview area.

❸ Check to make all columns fit largest text.

❺ Check to apply formats to last row and/or column (if box is clear, format does not show in preview).

❹ Check to apply formats for first row and/or column (if checked, format displays in preview).

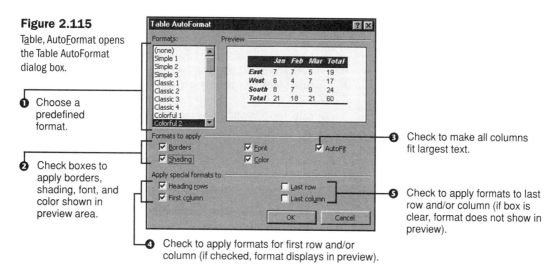

Table ⇒ Distribute Rows Evenly

When you draw a table with the **Draw Table** button 🖉, the rows often are not the same height. To make them the same height, select multiple rows and click the **Distribute Rows Evenly** button ⊞ on the Table and Borders toolbar, or choose **Table, Distribute Rows Evenly**.

Table ⇝ Distribute Columns Evenly

Columns also may not be the same width. To make them the same width, select multiple columns and click the **Distribute Columns Evenly** button ⊞ on the Table and Borders toolbar, or choose **Table, Distribute Rows Evenly**.

Table ⇝ Cell Height and Width...

You can change the row height or column width in your table.

Quick Choices   *CHANGE COLUMN WIDTH*

- ■ Without any cells selected, move to the line indicating a row or column. The mouse pointer changes to a double-headed arrow and double-headed line. Drag to change the row height or column width.

- ■ Double-click the double-headed line on a column for the column width to change to automatically fit the widest entry for the column.

To change the row height of all rows in a table or the column width of one or more columns, select what you want to change and then choose **Table, Cell Height and Width**. The Cell Height and Width dialog box opens with the following options:

Dialog Box Item	How to Use
Row Tab	
Height of rows	Choose the down arrow to make all rows At least (minimally) or Exactly the height shown in At text box. Optionally, choose Auto to adjust to the largest row. If you're trying to re-create a paper form, having the row height set to Exactly will prevent extra text from expanding the row and distorting the form.
At	Type or click the spinner buttons for a height for the At least or Exactly choices above.
Indent from left	Type or click the spinner buttons to show where the table starts from the left margin (if it is aligned **Left**).
Allow row to break across pages	If a row has many lines, clear this box to force a page break before the row.
Alignment	Click **Left**, **Center**, or **Right** to place the table between the margins.
Previous Row and **Next Row**	When you enter this dialog box, all rows are selected. Choose **Previous Row** or **Next Row** to choose one of the rows in the table.

Dialog Box Item	How to Use
Column Tab	
Width of column	Type or click the spinner buttons to change the width of the specified columns.
Space between columns	Type or click the spinner buttons to increase or decrease the space between columns.
Previous Column	Move to the column before the selected one.
Next Column	Move to the column after the selected one.
AutoFit	Change the width of the selected column(s) to fit the widest entry.

Note: You can enter measurements in units other than the default points. For example, type 2" (including the inch symbol).

Table ➥ Headings

If you have a large table and want the first row(s) to print on top of every page where the table continues, select the row (or first few rows) and choose **Table**, **Headings**. To unselect headings, choose the row(s) again and choose **Table**, **Headings** again to clear the checkmark next to the **Headings** item.

Table ➥ Convert Text to Table...

This command actually works both ways. If you have a list that is not in a table, you can convert it to a table (see Figure 2.116). If you have a table, you can convert it to a list (see Figure 2.117). The actual menu item depends on what you have selected (table or text).

❷ Verify or type a new number of columns.

❸ Verify or type a new number of rows.

Figure 2.116

Table, Convert Text to Table opens the Convert Text to Table dialog box.

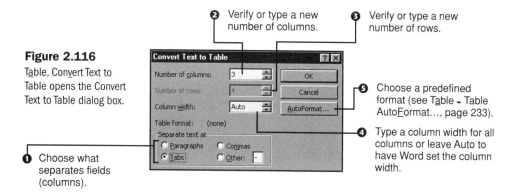

❺ Choose a predefined format (see Table – Table Auto**F**ormat..., page 233).

❹ Type a column width for all columns or leave Auto to have Word set the column width.

❶ Choose what separates fields (columns).

If you select a table and choose **Table, Convert Table to Text**, the Convert Table to Text dialog box appears (see Figure 2.117).

Figure 2.117
Table, Convert Table to Text opens the Convert Table to Text dialog box.

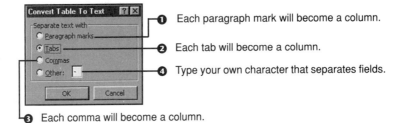

① Each paragraph mark will become a column.

② Each tab will become a column.

④ Type your own character that separates fields.

③ Each comma will become a column.

Table ➥ Sort...

Use Sort to order the rows in your table.

Quick Choices   SORT

■ To sort in A-to-Z or 1-to-9 order, click the column you want to use for sorting and click the **Sort Ascending** button 🔼 on the Tables and Borders toolbar.

■ To sort in reverse order, click the **Sort Descending** button 🔽.

If you want to sort on more than one column, choose **Table, Sort**. The Sort dialog box opens as shown in Figure 2.118.

① Choose which column to sort.

Figure 2.118
Table, Sort opens the Sort dialog box.

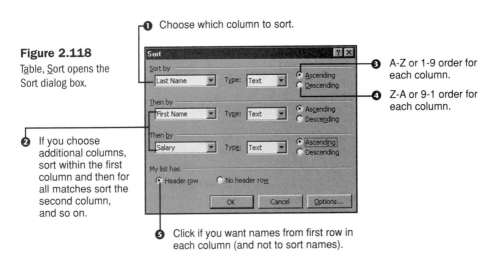

③ A-Z or 1-9 order for each column.

④ Z-A or 9-1 order for each column.

② If you choose additional columns, sort within the first column and then for all matches sort the second column, and so on.

⑤ Click if you want names from first row in each column (and not to sort names).

You can also use Sort if you are not in a table. You can sort paragraphs or tabbed items by using the **Options** button on the Sort dialog box (see Figure 2.119).

Figure 2.119
Table, Sort, Options opens the Sort Options dialog box.

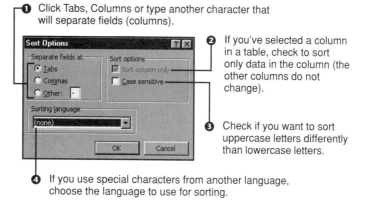

❶ Click Tabs, Columns or type another character that will separate fields (columns).

❷ If you've selected a column in a table, check to sort only data in the column (the other columns do not change).

❸ Check if you want to sort uppercase letters differently than lowercase letters.

❹ If you use special characters from another language, choose the language to use for sorting.

Table ➥ Formula...

While you're in a table you can calculate sums, averages, and create formulas in a cell.

Quick Choices *CREATE A TOTAL*

- Type numbers in your row or column, leaving the last row or column empty. Click in the last row or column and click the **AutoSum** button Σ on the Tables and Borders toolbar.

---

1. Position the insertion point where you want the formula to go.

2. Choose **Table, Formula**. The Formula dialog box opens.

3. If desired, click the drop-down arrow for **Paste function** and choose one of the following functions:

Function	Description and Example
ABS	Absolute value. Changes negative numbers to positive numbers. ABS(-5) = 5
AND	Returns 1 (true) if both expressions are true or 0 (false) if either expression is false. AND(3<4, 5<4) = 0
AVERAGE	Gives an average of a list of values. If AVERAGE(Above) is in the last row, this function will give the average of the contents of the column.
COUNT	Returns the number of items in the list. COUNT(A1,A2,A3) = 3 if all cells have numbers.

continues

Function	Description and Example
DEFINED	Returns 1 (true) if the expression can be computed or 0 (false) if it can't. DEFINED(a5)=0 if cell a5 does not exist.
FALSE	Returns 0.
IF	If condition is true, returns second argument. If condition is false, returns third argument. IF(A2<A3, True, False)=True if the value of cell A2 is less than A3.
INT	Returns the integer value of a number. INT(5.8) = 5.
MAX	Returns the largest item in the list. MAX(7,9,3) = 9.
MIN	Returns the smallest item in the list. MIN(3,4,1) = 1.
MOD	Returns the remainder when dividing one number by another. MOD(5,2) = 1.
NOT	Returns the opposite of the expression. NOT(True)=False.
OR	If either condition is true, returns true. If both conditions are false, returns false. OR(5<3,3>5)=True.
PRODUCT	Multiplies all items in list together. PRODUCT(2,4,5) = 40.
ROUND	Rounds the expression to the number of places in the second argument. ROUND(345.352,1) = 345.4
SIGN	If the number is positive, returns 1. If the number is negative, returns -1. SIGN(-34) = -1
SUM	Adds all items in a list. SUM(Left) sums all items in columns to the left.
TRUE	Returns 1.

4. After you choose a function, put the appropriate arguments in the parentheses. Arguments can be numbers, formulas, bookmark names, or cell references. Just like Excel, column 1 is identified with an A, column 2 a B, and so on. The first row is 1, the second is 2. Therefore, C4 specifies the cell at the intersection of column 3 and row 4. You can also use keywords like Left, Right, Above, and Below.

5. You can also put normal arithmetic formulas in the Formula box. Use + for addition, - for subtraction, * for multiplication, and / for division. Use parentheses to override the normal order. For example, =(5+3)*2 equals 30.

Notice that all formulas and functions start with the equal sign.

6. While you're in the **Formula** text box, you can use the Paste Bookmark drop-down arrow and choose a bookmark if you created one for a number (see **Insert ▪ Bookmark...**, page 159).

7. To change the way the number displays, click the Number format drop-down arrow and choose a format. A pound sign means the number is optional. A 0 means that the digit is required. 3212.5 formatted as #,##0.00 will display as 3,212.50.

8. Click **OK** to finish the formula.

Table ➡ Split Table

To split a table in two, click the row below where the split will occur and choose **Table**, **Split Table**, or press **Ctrl+Shift+Enter**.

Table ➡ Hide Gridlines

If you haven't set any borders (see **Format - Borders and Shading...**, page 170) for your table, you may want to see how the table will look when it's printed. Choose **Table**, **Hide Gridlines** to clear the dotted lines around the table. Choose **Table**, **Show Gridlines** to restore these lines so that you can easily identify cells.

Window

The Window menu organizes your document windows on the screen.

Window ➡ New Window

Choose **Window**, **New Window** to open another window for the same document. When you open a new window, the document name followed by a colon and a number appears in the title bar. You can position your insertion point at different parts of the same document for copying or editing. Switch between windows by using the bottom of the Window menu or pressing **Ctrl+F6**. Close the extra window by clicking the close button (X) for the window or by pressing **Ctrl+W**.

Window ➡ Arrange All

If you have two or more documents open (or one document with more than one window), choose **Window**, **Arrange All** to see smaller windows for each document. Click on the maximize button of a window to make it fill the screen again.

Window ➡ Split

When you want to look at two different parts of the same document for copying or editing, choose **Window**, **Split** or drag the split box above the up scroll arrow on the vertical scroll bar. You get a double-headed mouse pointer and can position the split anywhere on the screen. After you position the split bar, two vertical scroll bars enable you to move in the two parts of the document independently.

Window → [Open Documents]

The bottom of the Window menu shows you a list of all open documents. Click a document name or press **Ctrl+F6** to go to another open document.

Help

Help allows you to look up more information on the application.

Help → Microsoft Word Help

Quick **Choices**   *TO LAUNCH WORD HELP*

Do one of the following:

- ■ Press **F1**.
- ■ Click the **Office Assistant** button 🔲 on the Standard toolbar.
- ■ Choose **Help**, **Microsoft Word Help**.

The Office Assistant opens. If you are working on a task, the Assistant may offer context-sensitive suggestions (see Figure 2.120).

Figure 2.120
Help, Microsoft Word Help launches the Office Assistant.

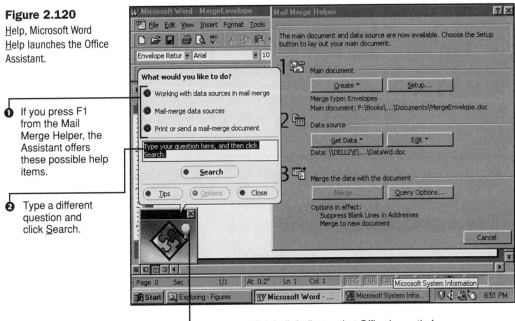

❶ If you press F1 from the Mail Merge Helper, the Assistant offers these possible help items.

❷ Type a different question and click Search.

❸ The yellow lightbulb indicates that Office has a tip for something you've been doing. Click Tips.

When you use the Assistant from a document rather than a dialog box, the **Options** button is not dimmed (as it is in Figure 2.120). When you click the **Options** button, the Office Assistant dialog box opens with the following options:

Office Assistant options

Dialog Box Item	How to Use
Assistant Capabilities Section	
Respond to F1 key	Check to show Office Assistant when you press **F1**. Clear to show the Help Topics contents and index dialog box instead.
Help with wizards	Check to display Office Assistant help with most of the wizards.
Display alerts	Check to display alert messages (for example, Do you want to save your document?) through the Office Assistant. Clear to display in a normal dialog box.
Search for both product and pro-gramming help when programming	When in the Visual Basic Editor, display help on Word and Visual Basic.
Move when in the way	Check to have the Office Assistant try to move out of the way of the area you're working in (such as dialog boxes) and shrink if you don't use it within five minutes.
Guess help topics	As shown in Figure 2.120, check to have Office Assistant guess topics depending on what you're doing.
Make sounds	Check to have the Office Assistant make sounds (for example, tap on your monitor when you need to save).
Show Tips About Section	
Using features more effectively	Check to display tips (the yellow lightbulb) about how to make better use of features you're using.
Using the mouse more effectively	Check to display tips about using the mouse to improve your performance.
Keyboard shortcuts	Check to show tips featuring keyboard shortcuts for actions you perform.
Other Tip Options	
Only show high priority tips	Check to show you only important tips, especially time-saving features.
Show the Tip of the Day at startup	Check to show a tip when you start Word.
Reset my tips	Click to reset tips so you can see them again.

Click the **Gallery** tab and choose **Back** or **Next** to choose another Office Assistant. You may have to insert the Office CD-ROM. Click **OK** when finished.

When you right-click the Office Assistant, you have a shortcut menu.

Right-click options	
Dialog Box Item	**How to Use**
Hide assistant	Click to close the Assistant. You can also click the X in the upper-right corner.
See **t**ips	Click to see the latest tips the Assistant wants to offer you. You can also click the lightbulb directly on the Assistant. When you do, you can click the **Back** and **Next** buttons to see other tips.
Options	Click to open the Office Assistant dialog box to the **Options** tab. These are the same options listed in the above table.
Choose assistant	Click to open the Office Assistant dialog box to the **Gallery** tab, which enables you to choose the Office Assistant as shown above.
Animate!	For Assistants that change, click to see one of the animations.

Help ➞ Contents and Index

For more control about what you look up in help, choose **Help, Contents and Index** (or if **Respond to F1 key** is cleared in the Office Assistant Options, press F1). The Help Topics dialog box opens with three tabs: Contents, Index, and Find.

Help ➞ Contents and Index, Contents Tab

To browse through help as though it were a table of contents for a book, choose **Help, Contents and Index**, and click the Contents tab (see Figure 2.121).

See **Help ‑ Contents and Index, Help Topic Window** for navigating in the resulting help topic window.

Help ➞ Contents and Index, Index Tab

To search through help as though you were looking for a word in the index in a book, choose **Help, Contents and Index**, and click the Index tab (see Figure 2.122).

See **Help ‑ Contents and Index, Help Topic Window** for navigating in the resulting help topic window.

Help ➞ Contents and Index, Find Tab

Of the three help tabs, the Find tab of the Help Topics window gives you the most detailed control for looking up help because it is an alphabetized list of every unique word in the help file. Choose **Help, Contents and Index**, and click the Find tab (see Figure 2.123). The exact options in the dialog box depend on which option you chose from the **Rebuild** button.

Figure 2.121

Help, Contents and Index, Contents opens the Help Topics dialog box to the Contents tab.

❶ Double-click a book icon to expand or collapse the category.

❷ Double-click a ? icon to see the topic.

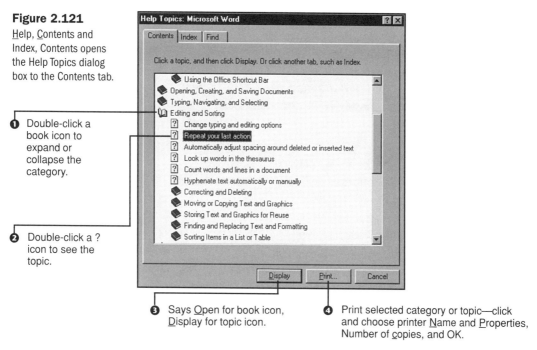

❸ Says Open for book icon, Display for topic icon.

❹ Print selected category or topic—click and choose printer Name and Properties, Number of copies, and OK.

Figure 2.122

Help, Contents and Index, Index tab opens the Help Topics dialog box to the Index tab.

❶ Begin typing the word.

❷ Double-click an entry (or click Display).

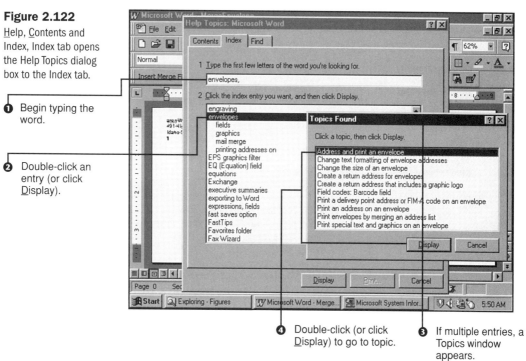

❹ Double-click (or click Display) to go to topic.

❸ If multiple entries, a Topics window appears.

Figure 2.123

Help, Contents and Index, Find opens the Help Topics dialog box to the Find tab.

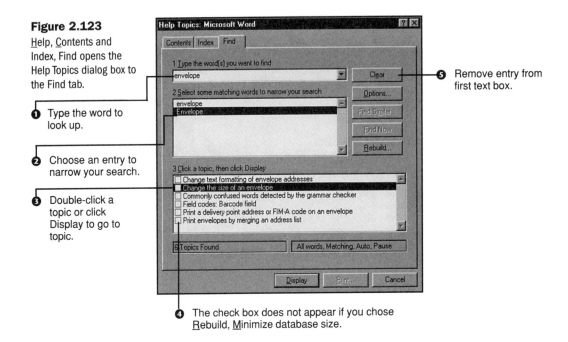

❶ Type the word to look up.

❷ Choose an entry to narrow your search.

❸ Double-click a topic or click Display to go to topic.

❺ Remove entry from first text box.

❹ The check box does not appear if you chose Rebuild, Minimize database size.

The additional options on the dialog box are described below.

When you click the **Rebuild** button, the Find Setup Wizard box opens with three options:

Find Setup Wizard

Dialog Box Item	How to Use
Minimize database size	Click to choose the smallest, quickest, but fewest options for your index.
Maximize search capabilities	Click to have the largest, slowest, but most options for your index.
Customize search capabilities	Click to choose which capabilities you want for your index: 1. Help Files (Word, Tips, Upgrade) 2. Untitled topics (for example, pop-up definitions) 3. Phrase searching (more than one word) 4. Matching phrases (find phrases while typing) 5. Find related topics (similarity searches)

If you choose option 5 (similarity searches) or **Maximize Search Capabilities**, check one or more of the boxes in the **Click a topic, then click Display** list box and then click **Find Similar** to display a window that shows related topics.

When you click the **Options** button, the Find Options dialog box opens with the following options:

Find options

Dialog Box Item	How to Use
Search for Topics Containing - Section	
All the words you typed in any order	Click to find help topics containing all the words you specify.
At least one of the words you typed	Click to find help topics containing any of the words you specify.
The words you typed in exact order	Click to find help topics that have words you type in the order you type them. You cannot choose this option if you chose **Minimize database size** from the **Rebuild** button.
Display matching phrases	You can only choose this option with **The words you typed in exact order**.
Show words that	Choose from the drop-down list to show words that match characters, contain the characters, end with the characters, or have the same root.
Begin Searching - Section	
After you click the Find Now button	Click to search only after you click Find Now.
Immediately after each keystroke	Click to start the search as soon as you start typing.
Wait for a pause before searching	Click to start the search as soon as you pause in your typing.
Files	Click to open a dialog box to allow you to search which help files (Word, Tips, Upgrade).

Help ‑ Contents and Index, Help Topic Window

After you choose one of the preceding methods (from the Contents, Index, or Find tabs) and double-click the topic of your choice, you enter a window that displays a help topic. If necessary, scroll down to read the entire topic. To use the help topic window, do any of the following:

- Click a single-arrow Show me button to have the program actually do the task for you.
- Click a dotted-green underline to display a pop-up window showing you a definition.
- Click a double-arrow button to go to a related topic.
- Click the **Back** button to return to the previous help topic.
- Click the **Help Topics** button to return to the Help Topics window with the Contents, Index, and Find tabs.
- Drag across text to select it; right-click and choose **Copy** to copy the text to the Clipboard. Go to a word processor and paste the text (see **Edit ‑ Paste**, page 51).

- Right-click in the window or click the **Options** button and choose the following other options:
    - Choose **Annotate** to open the Annotate dialog box. Type a note and choose **Save**. A paperclip displays in the upper-left corner of the help topic window. Click the paperclip to return to the annotation. In the Annotate window, you can also **Delete** the annotation or use **Copy** and **Paste**.
    - Choose **Print topic** to open the Print dialog box. Choose the printer **Name**, **Properties**, and the **Number of copies** you want.
    - Choose **Font** to display the size of the font for help topics (**Small**, **Normal**, or **Large**).
    - Choose **Keep Help on Top** to display a menu to allow you to choose the **Default** setting for your help topic, always keep help **On Top**, or **Not On Top** of other windows.
    - Choose **Use System Colors** to use the Windows colors for the help window.
    - Choose **Bookmarks** to see a list of placeholders you have in your help file. Double-click any bookmark to go to that help file.
    - If the current help topic is something you might want to return to, choose **Define Bookmarks**. The Bookmark Define dialog box opens. Keep the name of the help topic or type a new one in the **Bookmark name** text box and click the **OK** button. Return to this dialog box and click **Delete** to remove the highlighted bookmark.

Help ➥ What's This?

To learn about an item that you see on the screen, do one of the following:

- Press **Shift+F1**.
- Click the What's this button (?) on a dialog box.
- Choose **Help**, **What's This**?

After you use one of these options, your mouse pointer changes to an arrow with a question mark. Click a part of the screen or dialog box to display a yellow pop-up help box that describes the object. You can also click text to see a summary of paragraph formatting and font formatting.

Help ➥ Microsoft on the Web

Because these menu items are links to Internet Web pages, they change all the time. Sometimes the specific site that houses one of the following starting Web pages may be unavailable, so you may not go to the location mentioned. You could try again later to see whether it is available. By the time you get this book, the specific Web pages will be different, but the following general descriptions explain the function of each menu item.

Help - Microsoft on the Web - Free Stuff

This Web site often shows add-ins, product enhancements, and trial versions of (Microsoft and non-Microsoft) products that work with Word and other Office applications.

Help - Microsoft on the Web - Product News

This Web site gives information on patches and upgrades to Word and how to use the different platforms that support Word (Macintosh, Windows, NT). There also have been links to download different file converters so that you can translate some of your other word processing documents. (One converter enables people with older versions of Word to open files saved in Word 97 format). Also on this site are links to viewers for Word that enable someone to see your document without having Word loaded.

Help - Microsoft on the Web - Frequently Asked Questions

This Web site shows features, tips, and troubleshooting questions that people often ask.

Help - Microsoft on the Web - Online Support

Use online support to search for answers to your questions. You will find links to the Knowledge Base articles that Microsoft phone technicians use to answer questions when you call. There are also links to frequently asked questions, newsgroups, drivers, and how to contact Microsoft technical support.

Help - Microsoft on the Web - Microsoft Office Home Page

This Web page has included links to upgrades of applets that work within Microsoft Office (new Office Assistants and Microsoft Draw 98, for example), trial versions and upgrades of Office applications (Microsoft Outlook 98, for example), patches, and other news about the Office suite.

Help - Microsoft on the Web - Send Feedback...

If you want to tell Microsoft what you think of its software, offer suggestions for improvements, or give feedback on its Web site, this is the place to go.

Help - Microsoft on the Web - Best of the Web

This Web page has included interesting news of the day, current chats, and "best of the Web" links to Business, Computers, Education, Entertainment, Health, Home & Family, Lifestyles, News, Shopping & Services, Sports, and Travel.

Help - Microsoft on the Web - Search the Web...

This Web page enables you to search the Web for any text of your choosing and enables you to choose the search engine such as Yahoo or Lycos. You also have categories to search such as white pages, yellow pages, location guides, and newsgroups.

Help → Microsoft on the Web → Web Tutorial

This Web site shows you how to surf the Web and what the Internet is all about. Among the topics that have appeared on this site are an introduction, what you can find on the Internet, how to connect to the Internet, how to use your browser, how to search, how to communicate with others, and how to use Microsoft Internet Explorer.

Help → Microsoft on the Web → Microsoft Home Page

This Web page has included general announcements about Microsoft products, new releases, information for Microsoft channel partners, and special offers.

Help → WordPerfect Help...

If you are a WordPerfect user who wants some transition help, double-click the WPH box on the status bar or choose **Help, WordPerfect Help**. The Help for WordPerfect Users dialog box opens (see Figure 2.124).

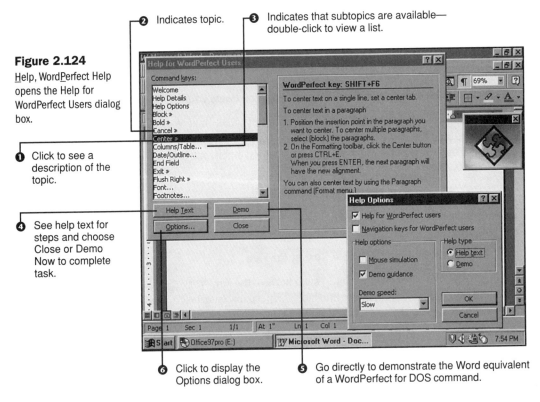

Figure 2.124
Help, WordPerfect Help opens the Help for WordPerfect Users dialog box.

❷ Indicates topic.

❸ Indicates that subtopics are available— double-click to view a list.

❶ Click to see a description of the topic.

❹ See help text for steps and choose Close or Demo Now to complete task.

❻ Click to display the Options dialog box.

❺ Go directly to demonstrate the Word equivalent of a WordPerfect for DOS command.

When you click the **Options** button, the Help Options dialog box opens with the following options:

Help options

Dialog Box Item	How to Use
Help for WordPerfect users	Check to automatically display help text or a demonstration when you press a WordPerfect for DOS key combination. WPH appears bold in the status bar.
Navigation keys for WordPerfect users	Check to change Page Up, Page Down, Home, End, and Esc to be what they are in WordPerfect instead of Word. WPN appears bold in the status bar. If both this and the above option are checked, WP appears.
Mouse simulation	Check to display the mouse pointer when a demo runs.
Demo guidance	Check to display help bubbles that offer additional help when a demo runs.
Help text or Demo	Choose Help text or Demo to display text or run the demo when you select a command on the Help for WordPerfect Users dialog box.
Demo speed	Choose Fast, Medium, or Slow to change the speed of Word demos.

Help ➡ About Microsoft Word

When you call Microsoft for help, technicians may ask you for your Product ID and the version of the program you're using. Choose **Help, About Microsoft Word** to find this and copyright information.

This dialog box has two additional buttons that can give you more help.

The **System Info** button opens the Microsoft System Information application (you can also press **Ctrl+Alt+F1**). This information is mostly used for Microsoft support personnel, who may ask for it when you call. The System Information tells you about your system configuration, printers, system Dynamic Link Libraries (DLLs), font, proofing tools, graphic filters, text converters, display configuration, multimedia capabilities, applications that are running, OLE settings for your computer, and active modules.

The **Tech Support** button opens the help file for technical support. The first help topic on the Contents tab, When You Have a Question, tells you the steps to take when you have a problem. The second help topic, Product Support Worldwide, gives contact information for technical support around the world. The third help topic opens to subtopics that give you technical support information for the United States and Canada. For telephone support, double-click Standard Support. Note as of this writing, the area code for most of the support numbers is no longer 206 (which still appears on some help files). The new area code is 425. The rest of the phone number remains the same. For example, the support number for Word is 425-462-9673.

Excel

The Excel Screen, Keyboard, and Mouse

The Screen

The Excel worksheet is like a giant Word table. The work area is divided into rows and columns. The intersection of a row and column is called a cell. You type and edit in the cell. One or more cells are referred to as a range. Among other things, ranges are used to change the way a group of cells looks (see **Format ▪ Cells...**, page 360), create formulas and functions (see **Insert ▪ Function**, page 313), and chart (see **Insert ▪ Chart**, page 306). You can have multiple worksheets in a workbook. Figure 3.1 shows a diagram of a new workbook with three worksheets.

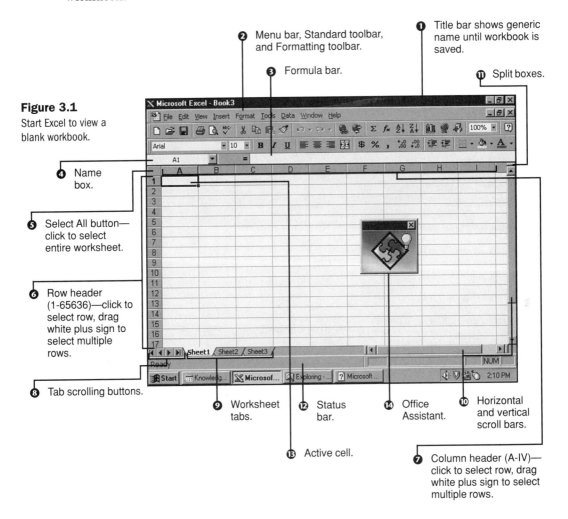

❷ Menu bar, Standard toolbar, and Formatting toolbar.

❶ Title bar shows generic name until workbook is saved.

❸ Formula bar.

⓫ Split boxes.

Figure 3.1
Start Excel to view a blank workbook.

❹ Name box.

❺ Select All button—click to select entire worksheet.

❻ Row header (1-65636)—click to select row, drag white plus sign to select multiple rows.

❽ Tab scrolling buttons.

❾ Worksheet tabs.

⓬ Status bar.

⓮ Office Assistant.

❿ Horizontal and vertical scroll bars.

⓭ Active cell.

❼ Column header (A-IV)—click to select row, drag white plus sign to select multiple rows.

Typing in an Excel Worksheet

Use the keyboard to type characters. First click the mouse or use the arrow keys to position the Active cell (square box surrounding a cell). When you type, characters appear in the cell and in the Formula bar. Press **Backspace** to remove characters you just typed.

Press **Enter** to confirm what you just typed into the cell. The Active cell moves down to the next cell. (You can change the behavior of **Enter**, see **Tools** ‑ **Options... Edit Tab**, page 402.) Instead of **Enter**, you can press any arrow key to enter the text into the cell and move the Active cell in the direction of the arrow. If you press **Esc** before you enter data, you cancel the entry. If you've already entered data, press **Delete** to remove the item. If you're using the mouse, you can also click the green check mark to confirm or the red X to remove the item.

The following shows additional tips for inserting data:

- To repeat text you've already typed in a list (column), begin typing the first few characters; Excel automatically completes the value if it is already in the list. You can turn this AutoComplete feature on and off (see **Tools** ‑ **Options... Edit Tab**, page 402).

- To enter a number in a cell, type it in. If you want to add a dollar sign, comma, or change the number of digits, you can use the Formatting toolbar or **Format** menu (see **View** ‑ **Toolbars** ‑ **Formatting**, page 291 or **Format** ‑ **Cells... Number Tab**, page 361).

- If you haven't entered anything in a cell yet, you can include formatting when you type a number. For example, type **$25.00** to include the dollar sign and decimal places.

- By default, numbers are aligned on the right side of the cell and text (any combination of letters and numbers) is aligned on the left side of the cell. To change the alignment, use the Formatting toolbar or **Format** menu (see **Format** ‑ **Cells... Alignment Tab**, page 366).

- Type a negative number with a minus sign (–) or by enclosing the number in parentheses.

- Type a number followed by a percent (%) sign to divide the number by 100 and display it as percent at the same time (the value for 25% is .25).

- If a scientific notation (1.23E+08) or pound signs (####) appear after you type a number, it means that your column isn't wide enough. Double-click the line after the column header (see **Format** ‑ **Column** ‑ **Width...**, page 370).

- To enter today's date, press **Ctrl+;** (semicolon).

- To enter the current time, press **Ctrl+Shift+:** (colon).

- To enter a carriage return in a cell, press **Alt+Enter** and continue typing.

Creating Formulas

You can create formulas (addition, subtraction, and so on) by typing them directly in the cell. Start a formula with an equal sign (=), type a number, cell reference, or click in a cell and type one of the arithmetic operators shown in the following table:

Arithmetic operators

Symbol	Meaning	Example
+ (plus sign)	Add	=B3+B4
– (minus sign)	Subtract	=C5–25
* (asterisk)	Multiply	=5*D1
/ (forward slash)	Divide	=D5/D6
% (percent sign)	Percent of	=56*25%
^ (caret)	Power of (exponentiation)	=3^3 (= 3*3*3)

Type another number, cell reference or click a cell. Continue the formula until it is complete and press **Enter** or click the green check mark when done. Functions enable you to enter formulas more quickly. You can type =SUM(B4..B8), instead of typing =B4+B5+B6+B7+B8 (see **Insert ‒ Function...**, page 313).

Order of Preference

If you have three or more numbers or cell references in the formula, the order that the formula calculates is first exponents, then multiplication and division, then addition and subtraction. 4+5*2 equals 14. If you want to override this natural order, add parentheses. (4+5)*2 equals 18.

Combining Text Phrases

If you want to add (concatenate) two text values together to produce a single piece of text, use the "&" ampersand. ="John" & " " & "Doe" produces "John Doe."

Absolute Reference

When you refer to a cell address in a formula and copy the cell, the address changes relative to where you copy it (see **Edit ‒ Copy**, page 273). =B4+B5 copied over one cell becomes =C4+C5. If you want to keep a cell in the formula static, make the cell absolute by putting dollar signs in front of the cell address. =$B$4+B5 copied one cell over becomes =$B$4+C5. You can add dollar signs by clicking the reference in the Formula bar and pressing **F4**. You can make a portion of the cell address absolute and the other part relative by continuing to press F4. (Cycle through the cell reference as follows: B4, $B$4, B$4, $B4, B4.)

Comparison Operators

In some cases, you need to compare one value with another one. The result of these formulas produces TRUE or FALSE. Comparison symbols that you can use are shown in the following table.

Comparison symbols

Symbol	Meaning	Example
=	Equals	=B3=B4
>	Greater than	=B3>B4
<	Less than	=B3<B4
>=	Greater than or equal to	=B3>=B4
<=	Less than or equal to	=B3<=B4
<>	Not equal to	=B3<>B4

Editing Text

To correct your worksheet, first move the Active cell to the cell that has text and click at the point you want to edit in the Formula bar. You can also double-click a cell to edit within the cell, click in the Formula bar, or press **F2** to enter the Formula bar. Even if text looks like it is in a cell, it might be a long item from a previous cell. Look in the Formula bar to make sure the text is in the cell. Then you can use the keys in the following table.

Keys used to delete text

Press	To
Backspace	Delete one character to the left of insertion point
Delete	Delete one character to the right of insertion point
Ctrl+Delete	Delete from insertion point to end of Formula bar
Ctrl+Z	Undo the last action
Ctrl+Y or F4	Repeat the last action

When you're editing a formula and you click in the Formula bar or press **F2**, a series of colored boxes highlights the ranges that are part of the formula. You can use the mouse to move or change the size of the ranges. Move the white arrow mouse pointer to the edge of one of the ranges and drag to move the range. The bottom-right corner of each colored range has a fill handle. Move the mouse pointer until it changes to a black plus sign and drag to change the size of the range.

Navigating

To move to a different worksheet, click the Sheet tab at the bottom of the worksheet. If the sheet is not visible, use the tab scrolling buttons. You can click to display to first, previous, next, and last Sheet tab. You can also hold down Shift and click a middle tab button to scroll several tabs at a time.

To type on the worksheet, you need to have the cell in which you want to enter text visible. After you move to where you should be, click the mouse pointer or use the keyboard to move the Active cell. In the following table, you see a list of navigational keyboard combinations.

Use the keyboard to move the active cell or insertion point

Press	To Move
Tab	To the next cell to the right
Shift+Tab	To the previous cell on the left
Ctrl+End	To end of a worksheet
Ctrl+Home	To beginning of a worksheet
Home	To beginning of a row (in Edit mode, to beginning of the entry)
End+ any arrow key	To the edge of the current range, next range, or end of the worksheet
End	In Edit mode, to the end of the entry
Left Arrow	A cell to the left (or a character to left in the Formula bar in the Edit mode)
Right Arrow	A cell to the right (or a character to right in the Formula bar in the Edit mode)
Up Arrow	Up a row
Down Arrow	Down a row
Ctrl+Backspace	Scroll window to display where the Active cell is
Ctrl+Left Arrow	To the left edge of the current range, next range, or left edge of the worksheet (in edit mode in the Formula bar, a word to the left)
Ctrl+Right Arrow	To the right edge of the current range, next range, or right edge of the worksheet (in edit mode in the Formula bar, a word to the right)
Page Up	Up one screen
Page Down	Down one screen
Alt+Page Up	Left one screen
Alt+Page Down	Right one screen
Ctrl+Page Up	Previous sheet in the workbook
Ctrl+Page Down	Next sheet in the workbook
Ctrl+F6 or Ctrl+Tab	Next workbook or window
Ctrl+Shift+F6 or Ctrl+Shift+Tab	Previous workbook or window
F6	Next window pane (see **Window - New Window**, page 443 or **Window - Split**, page 444)

Press	To Move
Shift+F6	Previous pane
F5+Cell address	To a cell (see **Edit - Go To...**, page 284)

Use the mouse to scroll on the screen

Click	To
Up scroll arrow	Scroll up one line
Down scroll arrow	Scroll down one line
Above the scroll box	Scroll up one screen
Below the scroll box	Scroll down one screen
And drag the vertical scroll box	Screen tip shows row while you scroll to a specific row
And drag the horizontal scroll box	Screen tip shows column while you scroll to a specific column
Left scroll arrow	Scroll left
Right scroll arrow	Scroll right
Left of horizontal scroll box	Scroll a screen left
Right of horizontal scroll box	Scroll a screen right

After you use the mouse to scroll, make sure you click to move the Active cell where you want to start editing.

Use Microsoft IntelliMouse

Do This	To
Rotate the wheel toward you.	Scroll down a few rows
Rotate the wheel away from you.	Scroll up a few rows
Hold down the wheel button and drag up, down, right, or left (the farther from the starting mark, the faster you pan).	Pan up, down, right, or left
Click the wheel button. Move mouse pointer above or below starting point in vertical scroll bar (or horizontal scroll bar) for direction. Excel starts scrolling down (the farther from the starting mark, the faster you scroll). Click mouse to stop scrolling.	Hands free scroll up or down (or right or left)
Hold **Ctrl** as you rotate the wheel toward you.	Zoom so view is smaller
Hold **Ctrl** as you rotate the wheel away you.	Zoom so view is magnified

Selecting Cells

Before you do major editing or formatting, you need to select a range (highlight the cells you want to change). After you select a range, you can press **Delete** to remove the text. See also the **Format** (page 360) and **Edit** (page 271) sections for many of the features you can use with the selected range.

See the navigation keys shown in the previous table. Select cells in a range by holding down the **Shift** key and using the movement keys (see **Navigating**, page 257). For example, hold **Shift** and press an arrow. You select one cell at a time. The following are some additional keys that you can use to select a range in the document.

Keyboard methods to select ranges

Press	To
Ctrl+A	Select the entire worksheet
Shift+ any arrow key	Extend the selection by one cell
F8+ any arrow key. Press **Esc** to cancel selection mode.	Select from the point at which you pressed **F8** to wherever you end up
Ctrl+Spacebar	Select the current column
Shift+Spacebar	Select the current row
Ctrl+Shift+* (asterisk)	Select the current range
Ctrl+Shift+O (letter O)	Select all cells with comments
Ctrl+[	Select all cells that are directly referred to within the formula (when Active cell is)
Ctrl+Shift+{	When Active cell is on a formula, selects all cells that are directly or indirectly referred to within the formula
Ctrl+]	Select all formulas that refer directly to active cell
Ctrl+Shift+}	Select all formulas that refer directly or indirectly to the active cell

Select with the mouse

Do This	To
Drag cells with the white plus	Select cells
Hold down **Ctrl** and click or drag mouse pointer	Select noncontiguous ranges of cells
Double-click in the Formula bar	Select a word
Click the graphic	Select a graphic
Click mouse pointer on row header or drag white plus sign in row headers	Select one or more rows

Do This	To
Click mouse pointer on column header or drag white plus sign in column headers	Select one or more columns
Click the Select All button above the row numbers and to the left of the column headers	Select all cells on the worksheet
Click at the start of the selection. Move to the end of the selection with mouse. Hold down **Shift** and click again.	Select a range of cells (use this method when the screen scrolls too fast to effectively select cells)

Selecting Cells Through a Dialog Box

When you want to identify a range in a dialog box, you can type the range address directly in the text box. However, most dialog boxes now have the Collapse Dialog button to the right of the text box (see Figure 3.2). Click the Collapse Dialog button. The dialog box shrinks. Drag to select the range on the worksheet, and then click the Collapse Dialog button again to return to the dialog box.

Figure 3.2
Choose File, Page Setup, Sheet tab to see three Collapse Dialog buttons.

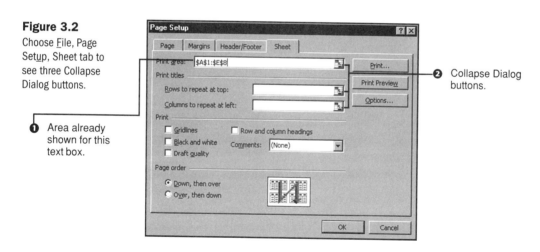

❶ Area already shown for this text box.

❷ Collapse Dialog buttons.

File

The **File** menu helps you manage the document; where it is stored, the size and formatting of paper, where you want to print or email it, and its summary information.

File ▸ New...

The first item on the **File** menu, ▸ New, is your first step to creating a blank workbook or a workbook with pre-existing text, formatting, and formulas. When you first start Excel or use the New toolbar button, the default workbook is based on the Workbook template (shown as

Workbook on the General tab of the dialog box). Excel offers different templates from Word when you start a new document. Word also enables you to create a new template from the dialog box (see Word's **File ▸ New...**, page 20). The following table shows the templates available when you open a new worksheet in Excel.

Excel templates available to start a new document		
Template	**Availability**	**Description**
Invoice	Typical Install	This creates a customer invoice. Enter text and amounts in this or other worksheets. Use the customized toolbar for help and click the **Customize** button to change the design.
Village Software	Typical Install	This is a company that makes Excel templates. Use this workbook to request more information or navigate to their Web site and see or order more templates.
Expense Statement	Complete Install	This creates an employee expense (reimbursement) statement.
Purchase Order	Complete Install	This is a purchase order form, similar to the invoice.
Budget	ValuPack	This is a family budget-planning workbook. When using this and other workbooks from the ValuPack in previous versions of Excel, you get a message that Visual Basic macro modules are now edited in the Visual Basic Editor. Click **OK**.
Crtrack	ValuPack	This is a (product or process) change request tracker.
Leasing	ValuPack	This workbook helps you evaluate options when leasing a vehicle.
Loan	ValuPack	This is a loan manager, which amortizes car or short-term loans and enables you to compare different types of loans.
Planner	ValuPack	This workbook is a business planner, which analyzes your current financial status and forecasts future cash flow.
Timecrd	ValuPack	This is an employee time card for the week.

File ▸ Open...

File, **Open** enables you to display and edit a file from a disk on your screen. Differences between Word and Excel appear in the **Files of type** drop-down box. Most of Word's files are word-processing applications, whereas most of Excel's are spreadsheet or database applications.

In Excel, when you open a file of a different type, you might enter an Import wizard dialog box. Fill out the options to give Excel the information it needs to open the file (see **Data – Text to Columns...**, page 419).

File → Close

To remove the current workbook from the screen, you use **File – Close**. If you haven't saved the file since your last change, Excel prompts you to do so. **File – Close** is the same in Word and Excel (see **File – Close**, page 263).

File → Save

If you already gave your workbook a name, **File – Save** saves the file changes to that workbook name on your disk; otherwise, the Save As dialog box opens. **File – Save** works the same way it does in Word (see Word's **File – Save**, page 29).

File → Save As...

Saving a file places a copy of what is onscreen to a location on a disk. The first time you save a file with **File, Save** or the **Save** button ![save icon], you enter the Save As dialog box. Thereafter, choose **File, Save As** or press **F12**. The two commands in Excel and Word (see Word's **File – Save As...**, page 29) are the same except for a couple of options on the Save As dialog box.

- If you want to save the workbook as a different file format, click the **Save as type** drop-down list and select another spreadsheet or database format. Type options include text, previous versions of Excel, CSV (Comma delimited), Lotus 1-2-3 (WK3, WK1, and so on), Quattro Pro, dBASE, DIF (Data Interchange Format), and SYLK (Symbolic Link).

- If you want to save the workbook as a template that you can use over and over (see **File – New...**, page 261), choose **Template**. Excel opens to the Templates folder. Double-click the **Spreadsheet Solutions** folder.

- If you want to create a default template for when you start Excel or use the **New** button ![new icon], change headers and footers, add text and formatting, and change any other defaults you want. Then save the workbook as Book.xlt in the XLStart folder.

- If you want to save to workbook as an add-in so you can use the features such as macros and toolbars, choose Microsoft Excel Add-In (see **Tools – Add-Ins...**, page 398).

For additional file-saving options, click the **Options** button (on the Save As dialog box) and do any of the following:

- To save the file with a password, type either a **Password to open** or a **Password to modify**. When you click **OK**, you are asked to verify the password. Type it again and click **OK**.

- If you select **Read-only recommended**, a dialog box appears when you open the file and asks you whether you want to open the file as read-only or allow changes.

- If you want to create a backup copy of the file on disk, check the **Always create backup** box.

File ➥ Save as HTML...

One of the new features of Office 97 gives you the ability to save workbooks in an HTML file format. After the file is in this format, you can load this on a Web server and others can view the workbook with a Web browser (either through an intranet or the Internet). In Typical setup, this item is not available on your menu. You might have to go through setup again to install this option.

1. If desired, select the range you want to save and choose **File**, **Save as HTML**. The Internet Assistant Wizard dialog box opens to Step 1. Optionally, do any of the following:
   - To add another range, click the **Add** button and select a new range to add to the HTML file and click **OK**.
   - To delete a range, select an existing range in the **Ranges and charts to convert** click the **Remove** button.
   - Click the up and down Move buttons to change the order for the ranges and charts.

2. Click on the **Next** button to go to Step 2 of the wizard. Choose whether you want to **Create an independent HTML file** or **Insert the data into an existing HTML file**. If you choose the second option, you need to know how to edit HTML code. Choose **Next**.

3. On Step 3 of the wizard, you have the following options:
   - To change the title bar of the window, type text in the **Title** text box.
   - Type text in the **Header** to create the first line that appears in the HTML file.
   - If desired, type a **Description below Header**.
   - You can enter a line after the description and before your data by checking **Insert a horizontal line before the converted data**.
   - If desired, check **Insert a horizontal line after the converted data**.
   - If desired, type a date you want displayed on the HTML page in the **Last Update on** text box.
   - You can also type your name in the **By** text box.
   - If you want your email displayed on the HTML page, type it in the **Email** text box.

4. Click **Next** to go to Step 4 of the wizard. You have these options:
   - **Which code page do you want to use for your Web page?** Generally, choose whichever option Excel chooses for you, unless you are using foreign language symbols. In that case, choose the appropriate language to display symbols properly.
   - If you have FrontPage, you can click **Add the result to my FrontPage Web**. Otherwise, choose **Save the result as an HTML file**.
   - Type the path and filename for your HTML file in **File path** or choose **Browse** and select the name of a file you want to overwrite.

5. Choose **Finish** to complete the wizard.

The next time you use **Save as HTML** with this file, the wizard remembers these settings.

File ➥ Save Workspace...

If you have a number of workbooks you use in conjunction with each other, use **File – Save Workspace** to save the workbooks and their positions on the screen (see **Window – Arrange...**, page 443). The Save Workspace dialog box, which looks similar to the Save dialog box, opens (see Word's **File – Save As...**, page 29). The **Save as type** option is Workspaces. Locate the folder in **Save in**, type in the **File name**, and click **Save**.

Open the saved Workspace file as you would any other file (see Word's **File – Open...**, page 21). In the Open dialog box, the icon for the file looks slightly different. It has multiple worksheets with the Excel icon.

File ➥ Page Setup...

The Page Setup dialog box has four tabs that control the formatting for the page, margins, headers and footers, and settings specific to the worksheet. Choose **File – Page Setup** and the Page Setup dialog box appears. Figure 3.3 shows the options for the Margins tab. Figure 3.4 shows the Header/Footer tab. The following table describes the rest of the options on the dialog box.

Figure 3.3
File, Page Setup opens the Page Setup dialog box; the Margins tab has been clicked.

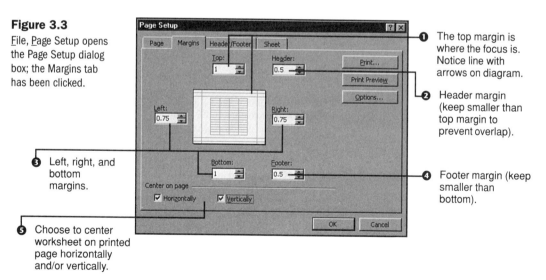

❶ The top margin is where the focus is. Notice line with arrows on diagram.

❷ Header margin (keep smaller than top margin to prevent overlap).

❸ Left, right, and bottom margins.

❹ Footer margin (keep smaller than bottom).

❺ Choose to center worksheet on printed page horizontally and/or vertically.

Page Setup options

Dialog Box Item	How to Use
All Tabs	
Print	Click to go to the Print dialog box (see **File - Print...**, page 268).
Print Preview	Click to go to the print preview window (see **File - Print Pre**v**iew**, page 268).
Options	Click to go to the Properties dialog box for the printer. Choose the default settings for paper size, layout, orientation, paper tray, and other options. (Make changes depending on your printer.)
Page Tab	
Por**trait**	Click to print across the short dimension of the paper.
Landscape	Click to print across the long dimension of the paper.
Adjust to	Click to magnify or shrink the print up or down by a percent.
Fit to	Click and change the number of **pages wide** and by the number of **tall** boxes to shrink your worksheet to fit on the indicated number of pages.
Paper siz**e**	Change the paper size from Letter to Legal, A4, or envelopes.
Print quality	For printers that support it, choose a higher resolution for better quality (but it takes longer to print).
Fir**st page number**	Leave **Auto** for automatic page numbering or type the new starting page number.
Sheet Tab	
Print area	Type a range name or range address. Alternatively, click the Collapse Dialog button (on the right of the text box) and select the range you want to print. For multiple ranges, hold down the **Ctrl** key and select additional ranges. Click the Collapse Dialog button again to return to the dialog box. See **File - Print Area** as an alternative to set the range to print.
Print Titles Section	
Rows to repeat at top	Type or use the Collapse Dialog button to identify the rows that will repeat on the top of every page.
Columns to repeat at left	Type or use the Collapse Dialog button to identify the rows that will repeat on the left of every page.
Print Section	
Gr**idlines**	Check this box to print the row and column grid on your paper.
Black and white	Check this box if you formatted the worksheet with colors but are printing with a black and white printer or to reduce time on a color printer.

Dialog Box Item	How to Use
Draft quality	Check to have Excel ignore gridlines and most graphics to increase printing speed.
Row and column headings	Check to print the column letters (A-IV) and row numbers with the worksheet.
Comments	Choose if you don't want comments or if you want to print them at end of sheet or as displayed on sheet.
Page Order Section	
Down, then over	For large ranges, click to print all ranges vertically first and then come to the next set of columns.
Over, then down	Click to print ranges horizontally across the range first.

Figure 3.4

File, Page Setup opens the Page Setup dialog box; click Header/Footer tab.

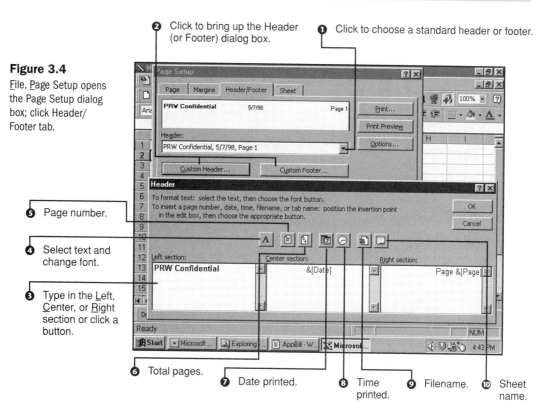

For more information on headers and footers, see **View ‒ Header and Footer...**, page 301.

File ➥ Print Area

You can use the Print area option on the Sheet tab of the Page Setup dialog box (see **File ▪ Page Setup...**, page 265), or instead, **File, Print Area** to set or clear the area you want to print. This is an alternative to printing the whole worksheet.

File ➥ Print Area ➥ Set Print Area

Quick Choices *SET YOUR PRINT RANGE*

1. Select the range you want to print.

2. Choose **File ▪ Print Area**.

Continue by printing the worksheet whenever you want (see **File ▪ Print...**, page 268). The print area for each worksheet is saved with the workbook.

File ➥ Print Area ➥ Clear Print Area

If you set the print area and want to print the whole worksheet, choose **File ▪ Print Area ▪ Clear Print Area**. This clears the print range whether you used the menu (see **File ▪ Print Area ▪ Set Print Area**, page 268) or the Page Setup dialog box (see **File ▪ Page Setup...**, page 265). Choose the **Print** button on the Standard toolbar 🖨 to print the entire worksheet.

File ➥ Print Preview

Print Preview lets you see a bird's-eye view of what your worksheet will look like when printed. You can graphically change margins or see more than one page at a time. Figure 3.5 shows a worksheet in Print Preview mode. If you want to work on the worksheet and see where pages will break, use Page Break Preview instead (see **View ▪ Page Break Preview**, page 288).

Click the **Print Preview** icon 🔍 or choose **File ▪ Print Preview** to display a worksheet in Preview mode.

File ➥ Print...

To send your worksheet to a printer, choose this option. See Figure 3.6 for a description of the screen elements. Click **OK** when you are ready to print.

Quick Choices *PRINT*

1. Click the **Print** button 🖨 on the Standard toolbar. The worksheet prints to the default printer.

To print a worksheet or multiple worksheets, do the following:

1. Click the worksheet you want to print. If you want to print multiple worksheets, click the first Sheet tab, hold down **Shift** and click the last Sheet tab. If the worksheets are not contiguous, hold down **Ctrl** and click each one.

2. Choose **File, Print** or press **Ctrl+P**. The Print dialog box displays (see Figure 3.6).

Figure 3.5

File, Print Preview shows a worksheet in Preview mode.

② Click to go to the previous or next page.

③ Click to go to the Print or Page Setup dialog boxes.

④ Click to show margins and column guides.

① Click Zoom to magnify the screen.

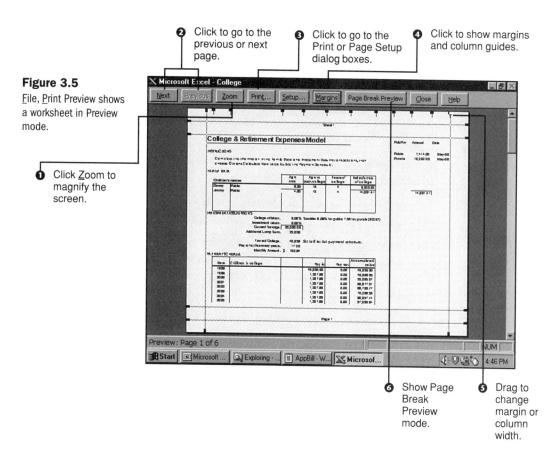

⑥ Show Page Break Preview mode.

⑤ Drag to change margin or column width.

Figure 3.6

File, Print opens the Print dialog box.

② Description of printer.

③ Which port the printer is attached to (use this port for Step 9).

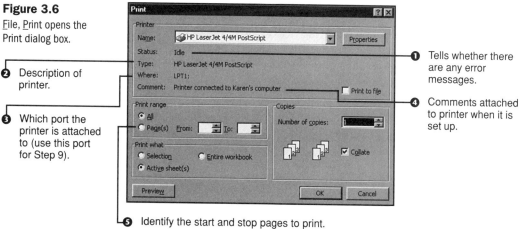

① Tells whether there are any error messages.

④ Comments attached to printer when it is set up.

⑤ Identify the start and stop pages to print.

3. To change the printer (or print to a fax) select from the **Name** drop-down list.

4. If you want to change Windows options for your printing, click the **Properties** button and change such things as paper size, paper orientation, where to get paper, and printer resolution. Many of these options you will want to change for the worksheet instead through **File**, **Page Setup** (see page 265).

5. To print a portion or all of resulting pages, choose one of the following:

   - Click **All** to print the entire worksheet.
   - Choose **Page(s)** and in the **From** text box, type a starting page number and in the **To** text box, type an ending page number.

6. Choose one of the following to print a portion of your worksheet.

   - Click **Selection** to print if you have selected cells and objects.
   - Click **Active sheet(s)** to print the selected sheets.
   - If you want to print all sheets whether they are selected or not, click **Entire workbook**. If a sheet has a print area (see **File - Print Area**, page 268), only that area prints.

7. To print more than one copy, use the spinner buttons or text box to reset the **Number of copies**.

8. If you have more than one copy and you want one entire set and then another copy set, check **Collate**. With this option unchecked, you print multiple copies of page 1, and then multiple copies of page 2, and so on (and printing is faster).

9. If you don't have the selected printer connected to your computer, choose to **Print to file** on your disk. When you choose **OK**, Excel opens the Print to file dialog box. Give the file a name and location and click **OK** again. Excel automatically gives the file a prn extension.

   When you want to print the file, click the Windows **Start** button, choose **Programs**, **MS-DOS Prompt**. From the DOS window, type **COPY /B filename port**. A specific example would be COPY /B c:\docs\print.prn lpt1. Note: When using print to file, you need to have the print driver for the destination printer installed, even if you are not attached to it.

10. If you want to see what the printing is going to look like, choose **Preview** (see **File - Print Preview**, page 268). Choose **Print** to print the range.

11. If you didn't do step 9, click **OK** to print the worksheet.

File ➥ Send To

The **File**, **Send To** menu enables you to transmit your workbook electronically to one or more email recipients. The submenus on Word and Excel are identical except that Word gives two more options—Fax Recipient and Microsoft PowerPoint (see Word's **File - Send To**, page 45).

File ➨ Properties

File properties enable you to identify and categorize your file in more detail than you can with just a name. You can add notes in many different fields (such as **Subject** and **Comments**). File properties also let you see more information about your file such as the number of words, the creation date, and the MS-DOS name. The dialog boxes for Word and Excel are almost identical with a couple of exceptions (see Word's **File ➨ Properties**, page 46):

- The bottom half of the Statistics tab in Word tells how many words, paragraphs, and so on that the document has, and in Excel this area is blank.
- Excel's Contents tab gives a list of all worksheets, charts, MS Excel 4.0 Macros, and MS Excel 5.0 Dialog sheets that are part of the workbook.

File ➨ Recent Used File List

To open one of your recently saved workbooks, choose **File** and then select one of the files on the bottom of the **File** menu. The hot keys are numbered for each of the files (**1**, **2**, **3**, and so on). The last file saved is indicated with the number 1. If the names do not display at the bottom of the **File** menu, follow these steps:

To display the recent files or change number displayed:

1. Choose **Tools**, **Options**. The Options dialog box displays.
2. Click the General tab.
3. Type or use the **Entries** spinner button to change number of files you want to see in the **Recently used file** list.
4. Click **OK**.

Excel displays up to the number of files you specified in step 3.

File ➨ Exit

To get out of Excel, you use **File**, **Exit.** Press **Alt+F4,** or click the **Close (X)** button in the upper-right corner of the application window. Excel prompts you to save each workbook that has changed since your last save. If you choose **Yes** and have not given the document a name, you enter the Save As dialog box (see Word's **File ➨ Save As...**, page 29).

Edit

The **Edit** menu enables you to make changes to the worksheet. It contains the Undo and Repeat, Cut, Copy and Paste commands. You can fill cells with information based on selected cells, clear cell contents, delete selected information, delete, move and copy whole worksheets, find specific information in a worksheet, replace information that has been found, create links, and edit objects.

Edit ► Undo...

The first item on the **Edit** menu enables you to **Undo** specific actions.

Quick Choices UNDO

- ■ Click the **Undo** button [↶ ▾] on the Standard toolbar.
- ■ Choose **Edit**, **Undo Action**. The bracketed action is the last action you performed.
- ■ Press **Ctrl+Z**.

  The last action you performed is undone.

Quick Choices UNDO MULTIPLE ACTIONS

- ■ Click the pull-down arrow on the **Undo** button [↶ ▾], and select the actions you want to undo. All the actions up to the one you select will be undone.

Edit ► Redo...

Edit, **Redo** is similar to **Edit**, **Undo**. It redoes something you have undone. It is a valuable tool to use with Undo.

Quick Choices REDO

- ■ Click the **Redo** button [↷ ▾] on the Standard toolbar.
- ■ Choose **Edit**, **Redo Action**. The bracketed action is the last action you undid.
- ■ Press **Ctrl+Y**.

  The last action you performed is undone.

Quick Choices REDO MULTIPLE ACTIONS

- ■ Click the pull-down arrow on the **Redo** button [↷ ▾], and select the actions you want to redo. All the actions up to the one you select will be redone.

Edit ► Repeat

Choose **Edit**, **Repeat** or press **F4** or **Ctrl+Y** to repeat the last action or command. **Edit**, **Repeat** replaces **Edit**, **Redo** when it is available. Actions such as formatting fonts, adding borders and so on enable **Edit**, **Repeat**.

Edit ► Cut

The **Cut** command enables you to remove selected text and place it on the Windows clipboard to **Paste** somewhere else. Select the cell or range of cells you want to cut; see **Typing in an Excel Worksheet** on page 255, and **Selecting Cells** on page 260 for more information.

Quick **Choices** *CUT*

- Click the **Cut** button 🔲 on the Standard toolbar.
- Press **Ctrl+X**.
- Choose **Edit, Cut**.
- Right-click the selection and choose **Cut**.
- Drag and drop—Point to the edge of the selected range, when the mouse pointer changes to a white arrow, click and drag the selection to the new location.
- Right-click and drag the selection to the new location, and then select from the following: **Move Here, Copy Here, Copy Here as Values Only, Copy Here as Formats Only, Link Here, Create Hyperlink Here, Shift Down and Copy, Shift Right and Copy, Shift Down and Move, Shift Right and Move,** or **Cancel**.

If the drag and drop operation isn't working, make sure the **Allow cell drag and drop** option is checked on the **Tools - Options... Edit Tab** (see page 402 for more information).

If you are cutting a range that includes an object and you want to cut the object with the range, check **Cut, Copy and sort objects with cells** on the **Tools Options... Edit Tab** (see page 402 for more information).

Edit ➥ Copy

The **Copy** command enables you to copy selected text and place it on the Windows clipboard to **Paste** somewhere else. Select the cell or range of cells you want to copy (see **Typing in an Excel Worksheet** on page 255, and **Selecting cells** on page 260 for more information).

Quick **Choices** *COPY*

- Click the **Copy** button 🔲 on the Standard toolbar.
- Press **Ctrl+C**.
- Choose **Edit, Copy**.
- Drag and drop—Point to the edge of the selected range, when the mouse pointer changes to a white arrow, hold down the **Ctrl** key and click and drag the selection to the new location.
- Right-click and drag the selection to the new location, and then select from the following: **Move Here, Copy Here, Copy Here as Values Only, Copy Here as Formats Only, Link Here, Create Hyperlink Here, Shift Down and Copy, Shift Right and Copy, Shift Down and Move, Shift Right and Move,** or **Cancel**.

If the drag and drop operation isn't working, make sure the **Allow cell drag and drop** option is checked on the **Tools - Options... Edit Tab** (see page 402 for more information).

If you are copying a range that includes an object and want to copy the object with the range, check **Cut, Copy and sort objects with cells** on the **Tools - Options... Edit Tab**; see page 402 for more information.

Edit ➥ Paste

The **Paste** command allows you to paste what is on the Windows clipboard at the location of the insertion point. Used with **Edit, Cut,** you move the original text. Used with **Edit, Copy,** you create a copy of the original text.

Quick Choices   PASTE

- Click the **Paste** button 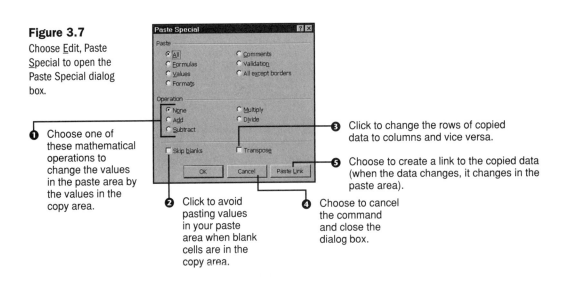 on the Standard toolbar.
- Press **Ctrl+V**.
- Choose **Edit, Paste**.
- Right-click where you want to insert the copied information and choose **Paste**.

Edit ➥ Paste Special...

The **Paste Special** command enables you to paste, link, or embed what is on the Windows clipboard (at the location of the insertion point) with the formatting you specify. If you are pasting information from within Excel, the choices are different than if you are pasting from another program.

To paste Excel information, follow these steps:

1. Cut or Copy the information you want to paste.

2. Move the insertion point where you want to paste the information.

3. Choose **Edit, Paste Special**. The Paste Special dialog box displays (see Figure 3.7). The options are different depending on what you are pasting, a range of data versus a chart.

Figure 3.7
Choose **E**dit, Paste **S**pecial to open the Paste Special dialog box.

❶ Choose one of these mathematical operations to change the values in the paste area by the values in the copy area.

❷ Click to avoid pasting values in your paste area when blank cells are in the copy area.

❸ Click to change the rows of copied data to columns and vice versa.

❹ Choose to cancel the command and close the dialog box.

❺ Choose to create a link to the copied data (when the data changes, it changes in the paste area).

4. Choose one of the Paste options described in the following table.

Paste options on the Paste Special dialog box

Option	Description
All	Pastes all cell contents and formatting. This is the same as **Edit, Paste**.
Formulas	Pastes only the formulas entered in the Formula bar.
Values	Pastes only the values displayed in the cells.
Formats	Pastes only cell formatting. This is the same as **Format Painter** 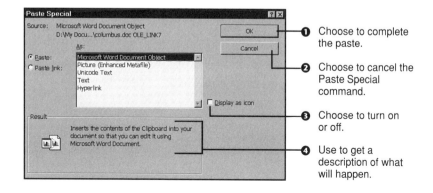.
Comments	Pastes only comments attached to cells.
Validation	Pastes data validation rules for the copied cells to the paste area. For more information on Data Validation, see **Data – Validation...**, page 414.
All except borders	Pastes all cell contents and formatting except borders.
If You Are Pasting a Chart	
Picture	Inserts the contents of the clipboard as a picture. This option takes the least amount of space to store and displays the quickest.
MS Office Drawing Object	Inserts the contents of the clipboard as an MS Office Drawing Object format.

5. Choose **OK** to complete the paste.

To paste information from another application, follow these steps:

1. In another application, Cut or Copy the information that you want to paste.

2. Switch to Excel and move the insertion point to where you want to paste the information.

3. Choose **Edit, Paste Special**. The Paste Special dialog box displays (see Figure 3.8).

Figure 3.8
Choose Edit, Paste Special to display the Paste Special dialog box.

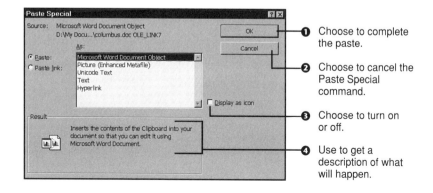

❶ Choose to complete the paste.

❷ Choose to cancel the Paste Special command.

❸ Choose to turn on or off.

❹ Use to get a description of what will happen.

4. Choose **Paste** or **Paste link**.

Depending on the source application, when you choose the **Paste** option the following formats and **Display as icon** options may be available:

Display as icon options (when choosing Paste)

Option	Format	Display as Icon—Active
Application Object	Inserts the object so you can edit it with the source application.	Yes
Picture (Enhanced Metafile)	Inserts the contents of the clipboard as an Enhanced Metafile.	No
Unicode Text	Inserts the contents of the clipboard as Unicode Text.	No
Text	Inserts the contents of the clipboard with no formatting.	No
Hyperlink	Inserts the contents of the clipboard as a hyperlink. Click the hyperlink to jump to the source.	No

When you choose the **Paste link** option, any changes in the source document are reflected in the active worksheet. Depending on the source application, the following formats and **Display as icon** options may be available:

Display as icon options (when choosing Paste Link)

Option	Format	Display as Icon—Active
Application Object	Inserts the object so you can edit it with the source application.	Yes
Picture (Enhanced Metafile)	Inserts the contents of the clipboard as an Enhanced Metafile.	Yes
Unicode Text	Inserts the contents of the clipboard as Unicode Text.	Yes
Text	Inserts the contents of the clipboard with no formatting.	Yes
Hyperlink	Inserts the contents of the clipboard as a hyperlink. Click the hyperlink to jump to the source.	Yes

Edit ‣ Paste as Hyperlink

The **Paste as Hyperlink** command enables you to paste clipboard contents as a hyperlink. A hyperlink creates a shortcut to the source document. Click the hyperlink to jump to the source document. If the application that created the hyperlink is not open, it opens and the document also opens.

Quick **Choices**   HYPERLINK

1. After you have cut or copied text to the clipboard, move the insertion point to the location you want to paste to.
2. Choose **Edit**, **Paste as Hyperlink**, or select the text to be moved; right-click and drag it to the new location and choose **Create Hyperlink Here**.

Edit ‣ Fill

The **Edit**, **Fill** command enables you to build forecasts, budgets, and trends. You can also fill cells with a series of dates, numbers, or text. To create your own custom lists to use with the fill command. See the **Tools ‣ Options... Customized List Tab** on page 405 for more information.

To use the fill handle, follow these steps:

1. Type numbers, dates, or text in at least two cells in the worksheet (to begin the series).
2. Select the range; click and drag over the cells of information.
3. Point to the black square on the bottom-right corner of the range. The mouse pointer changes to a thin black plus sign (see Figure 3.9).
4. Click and drag the range to be filled with the series.

Figure 3.9
This is an example of seven series using the fill handle.

❶ Beginning pattern.

❷ Fill handle.

❸ Mouse pointer.

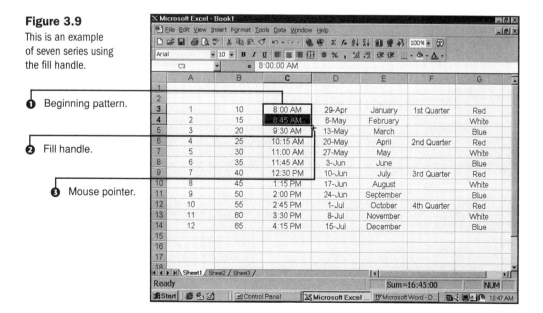

To use the right-mouse button with the fill handle, follow these steps:

1. Type numbers, dates, or text in at least one cell in the worksheet (to begin the series).
2. Select the range; click and drag over the cell or cells of information.
3. Point to the black square on the bottom-right corner of the range. The mouse pointer changes to a thin black plus sign.
4. Right-click and drag the range to be filled with the series.
5. Select one of the following commands from the shortcut menu.

Shortcut menu options

Command	Description
Copy Cells	Fills the selection with a copy of the original cell or cell contents.
Fill Series	Fills the selection with values that increase by one from the value in the first cell.
Fill Formats	Copies the format to the selection. If you have selected multiple cells with different formatting, the formatting for each cell is pasted with the same formula found in the original. Similar to **Format Painter** ; for more information about format painter, see **View - Toolbars - Standard**, **Format Painter** on page 290.
Fill Values	Fills the selection with values that increment by the value differential of the selected cells. This is the same as clicking and dragging with the left mouse button, see **Edit - Fill** on page 277.
Fill Days	Fills the selection with days that increase by one beginning with the day in the first cell.
Fill Weekdays	Fills the selection with weekdays that increase by one beginning with the day in the first cell.
Fill Months	Fills the selection with months that increase by one beginning with the month in the first cell.
Fill Years	Fills the selection with years that increase by one beginning with the year in the first cell.
Linear Trend	Fills the selection with linear regression (best fit) values. This command is available only when more than one cell is filled with a starting value.
Growth Trend	Fills the selection with values calculated from a growth (exponential) regression. This command is available only when more than one cell is filled with a starting value.
Series	Displays the Series dialog box; see **Edit - Fill - Series...** on page 280 for more information.

Edit - Fill - Down

You can use **Edit**, **Fill**, **Down** to enter a copy of cell contents going down. You have two options when using **Edit**, **Fill**, **Down**.

■ Enter data in one cell. Move to the cell below the data you entered, and choose **Edit**, **Fill**, **Down**. The cell you are in receives a copy of the data from above.

■ Enter data in one cell. Select that cell and the range you want to copy the data to; choose **Edit**, **Fill**, **Down**. The blank cells in the selection receive a copy of the data in the first cell.

Edit – Fill – Right

You can use **Edit**, **Fill**, **Right** to enter a copy of cell contents to the right of the active cell. You have two options when using **Edit**, **Fill**, **Right**.

■ Enter data in one cell. Move to the cell to the right of the data you entered, and choose **Edit**, **Fill**, **Right**. The cell you are in receives a copy of the data from the left.

■ Enter data in one cell. Select that cell and the range you want to copy the data to; choose **Edit**, **Fill**, **Right**. The blank cells in the selection receive a copy of the data in the first cell.

Edit – Fill – Up

You can use **Edit**, **Fill**, **Up** to enter a copy of cell contents going up. You have two options when using **Edit**, **Fill**, **Up**.

■ Enter data in one cell. Move to the cell above the data you entered, and choose **Edit**, **Fill**, **Up**. The cell you are in receives a copy of the data from below.

■ Enter data in one cell. Select that cell and the range you want to copy the data to; choose **Edit**, **Fill**, **Up**. The blank cells in the selection receive a copy of the data in the first cell.

Edit – Fill – Left

You can use **Edit**, **Fill**, **Left** to enter a copy of cell contents to the left of the active cell. You have two options when using **Edit**, **Fill**, **Left**.

■ Enter data in one cell. Move to the cell to the left of the data you entered, and choose **Edit**, **Fill**, **Left**. The cell you are in receives a copy of the data from the right.

■ Enter data in one cell. Select that cell and the range you want to copy the data to; choose **Edit**, **Fill**, **Left**. The blank cells in the selection receive a copy of the data in the first cell.

Edit – Fill – Across Worksheets...

You can use the **Edit**, **Fill**, **Across Worksheets** command to copy information from one worksheet to one or more worksheets in your workbook.

To use the **Edit**, **Fill**, **Across Worksheets** command:

1. Enter the information on one worksheet or, open the workbook that has the information you want to copy (see Figure 3.10).

2. Choose **Edit**, **Fill**, **Across Worksheets**.

Figure 3.10

The Edit, Fill, Across Worksheets command copies the selected data to the selected sheets.

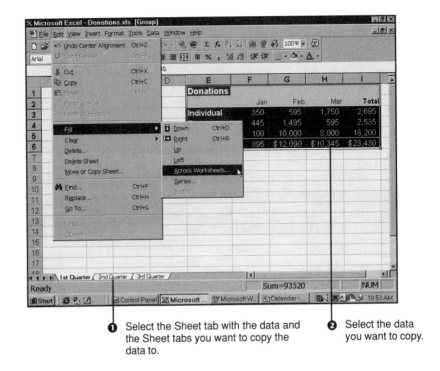

❶ Select the Sheet tab with the data and the Sheet tabs you want to copy the data to.

❷ Select the data you want to copy.

Edit ➥ Fill ➥ Series...

The **Edit**, **Fill**, **Series** command enables you to fill a selected range of cells with one or more series of numbers or dates. The contents in the first cell or cells are used as the starting value for the series.

To use the **Edit**, **Fill**, **Series** command, do the following:

1. Type the beginning of the series in one or more cells.

2. Select the range of cells to hold the series including the cells you typed.

3. Choose **Edit**, **Fill**, **Series** to display the Series dialog box (see Figure 3.11).

❶ Verify that this matches the type of range you want filled. This is determined by your range selection.

Figure 3.11

The Edit, Fill, Series command displays this dialog box.

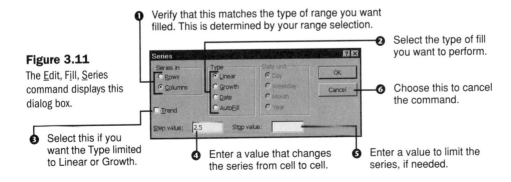

❷ Select the type of fill you want to perform.

❻ Choose this to cancel the command.

❸ Select this if you want the Type limited to Linear or Growth.

❹ Enter a value that changes the series from cell to cell.

❺ Enter a value to limit the series, if needed.

4. Choose **OK** to complete the series fill.

You can create your own custom lists to use with the fill command. (See the **Tools - Options... Custom Lists Tab** on page 405 for more information.)

Edit → Fill → Justify

Choose the **Edit, Fill, Justify** command to redistribute the text contents of cells to fill the selected range. Numbers or formulas cannot be filled and justified.

Edit → Clear

The **Edit, Clear** command gives you a choice of what to clear or erase instead of always deleting the entire cell contents. You can clear formats, contents, or just comments.

To use one of the **Edit, Clear** commands, follow these steps:

1. Select the range of cells you want to clear.
2. Choose **Edit, Clear** to display the Clear submenu.
3. Select one of the commands from the submenu as explained in the following table.

Edit, Clear submenu choices

Command	Description
Edit, **Clear**, **All**	Clears cell contents and comments, and returns the format to General.
Edit, **Clear**, **Formats**	Returns the format of the cells to the General format.
Edit, **Clear**, **Contents**	Clears the cell contents but does not change the formats or comments. This is the same as using the **Delete** key.
Edit, **Clear**, **Comments**	Clears the notes but does not change the contents or formats.

Edit → Delete...

The **Edit, Delete** command removes cells, rows, or columns from the worksheet. This is different from the **Edit, Clear** command because **Delete** completely removes the cells, rows, or columns and slides in other cells to fill the range.

To delete cells, rows, or columns, do the following:

1. Select the cells or range of cells, or select the cells in the column or row to be deleted.
2. Choose **Edit, Delete** or press **Ctrl+–** (minus); or right-click the selection and choose **Delete**. The Delete dialog box is displayed (see Figure 3.12).

If you selected a row or column heading, the dialog box is not displayed and the row or column is deleted.

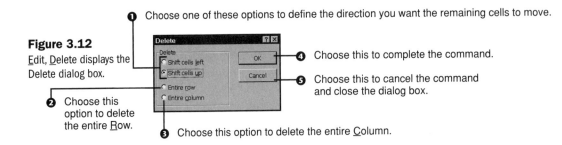

Figure 3.12
Edit, Delete displays the Delete dialog box.

❶ Choose one of these options to define the direction you want the remaining cells to move.

❹ Choose this to complete the command.

❺ Choose this to cancel the command and close the dialog box.

❷ Choose this option to delete the entire Row.

❸ Choose this option to delete the entire Column.

Edit ➥ Delete Sheet

The **Edit**, **Delete Sheet** command enables you to delete entire worksheets in your workbook.

Quick Choices TO DELETE WORKSHEET(S)

■ Point to the Sheet tab you want to delete and right-click; then choose **Delete** from the shortcut menu.

To delete worksheet(s) from the workbook, follow these steps:

1. Select the sheet or sheets you want to delete.

2. Choose **Edit**, **Delete Sheet**. A message box from Excel is displayed asking you to confirm the deletion.

3. Choose **OK** to delete the sheet or sheets.

Make certain you want to delete the worksheet or worksheets before you confirm the deletion. You cannot undo this action with the Undo command.

Edit ➥ Move or Copy Sheet...

The **Edit**, **Move or Copy Sheet** command enables you to copy or move worksheets to different workbooks as well as within the same workbook.

Quick Choices MOVE OR COPY A WORKSHEET

■ Select the sheet you want to move or copy.

■ To move it, click and drag the Sheet tab to the new location.

■ To copy it, hold down the **Ctrl** key while you click and drag the Sheet tab to the new location.

To move or copy a sheet, follow these steps:

1. Select the sheet you want to move or copy. If you are moving or copying to another workbook, open the workbook file.

2. Choose **Edit**, **Move or Copy Sheet** to display the Move or Copy dialog box (see Figure 3.13).

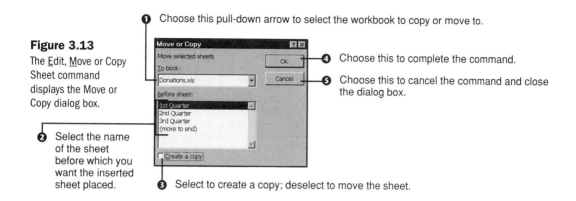

Figure 3.13
The Edit, Move or Copy Sheet command displays the Move or Copy dialog box.

❶ Choose this pull-down arrow to select the workbook to copy or move to.

❹ Choose this to complete the command.

❺ Choose this to cancel the command and close the dialog box.

❷ Select the name of the sheet before which you want the inserted sheet placed.

❸ Select to create a copy; deselect to move the sheet.

If you want to move or copy the sheet to a new workbook, select new book from the list on the **To book** pull-down list. A new workbook window opens with the copied sheet.

Edit ➥ Find...

The **Edit**, **Find** command enables you to search for characters you specify.

Quick Choices FIND

1. Press **Ctrl+F**.

2. Type what you are looking for in the **Find what** text box, and choose the **Find Next** button or press **Enter**.

   You may find that it is easier to press **Shift+F4** without the Find and Replace dialog box open, to repeat the last Find action. Using this shortcut enables you to see the document without the dialog box in the way.

To use the **Edit**, **Find** command, follow these steps:

1. Choose **Edit**, **Find** to display the Find dialog box (see Figure 3.14).

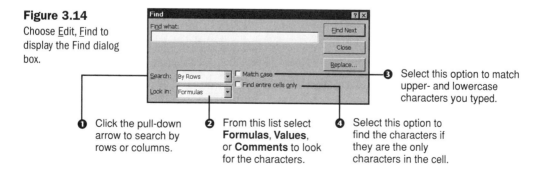

Figure 3.14
Choose Edit, Find to display the Find dialog box.

❶ Click the pull-down arrow to search by rows or columns.

❷ From this list select **Formulas**, **Values**, or **Comments** to look for the characters.

❹ Select this option to find the characters if they are the only characters in the cell.

❸ Select this option to match upper- and lowercase characters you typed.

2. Type what you want to search for in the **Find what** text box.

3. Choose the **Find Next** button.

4. When you get to the first occurrence of the item, you can choose **Find Next** again, **Close**, or click the **Replace** button. For more information about Replace, see the next section, **Edit ➥ Replace...**.

Edit ➥ Replace...

The **Edit**, **Replace** command enables you to search for characters you specify.

1. Press **Ctrl+H**.

2. Type what you are looking for in the **Find what** text box.

3. Type what you want to replace in the **Replace with** text box.

4. Select any additional options (refer to Figure 3.14).

5. Choose the **Find Next** button.

6. To replace the found text with the new text, choose the **Replace** button. To replace all occurrences of the found text with the new text, choose **Replace All.** To skip this occurrence of the found text and continue the search, choose the **Find Next** button. To end this session, choose the **Close** button.

Edit ➥ Go To...

The **Edit**, **Go To** command moves to a cell, range, or cells with special characteristics that you specify.

Quick Choices   *GO TO*

1. Press **Ctrl+G** or **F5** to open the Go To dialog box.

2. Enter the cell reference you want to go to or choose a range name or cell reference from the **Go To** list.

3. Choose **OK** or press **Enter**.

Edit ➥ Go To... Special...

1. Choose **Edit**, **Go To** to display the Go To dialog box.

2. Choose the **Special** button to display the Go To Special dialog box (see Figure 3.15).

3. Select any of the options that apply and click **OK**.

The following table describes the **Data validation** options.

Figure 3.15
Choose Edit, Go To, and select the Special button to display this dialog box.

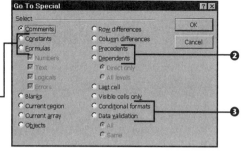

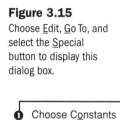

❶ Choose Constants or Formulas to activate the four check boxes under Formulas.

❷ Choose Precedents or Dependents to activate the choices under Dependents.

❸ Choose Conditional formats or Data validation to activate the options under Data validation.

Data validation options

Option	Description
Comments	Selects all comments on the active worksheet. (See **Insert – Comment** on page 129 and **View – Comments** on page 302 for more information.)
Constants	Selects all cells whose contents do not start with an equal sign or contain a formula. Further define the type of constant by selecting **Numbers**, **Text**, **Logicals**, or **Errors**.
Formulas	Selects all cells that contain formulas. Further define the type of formula by selecting **Numbers**, **Text**, **Logicals**, or **Errors**. For more information, see **Insert – Function...** on page 313.
Blanks	Selects all blank cells up to the last cell that contains data or formatting.
Current region	Selects a rectangular cell range around the active cell. Excel defines this range using blank rows and columns.
Current array	Selects the entire array, if the active cell is in an array.
Objects	Selects all graphic objects.
Row differences	Selects cells with contents different from the comparison cells in each row.
Column differences	Selects cells with contents different from the comparison cells in each column.
Precedents	Selects cells that are accessed by the formula in the current cell. Further define using **Direct Only** or **All levels**. For more information about Precedents, see **Tools – Auditing** on page 392.
Dependents	Selects cells that are referenced in a formula (see **Tools – Auditing** on page 392 for more information about Dependents).
Direct Only	Selects cells directly referred to by formulas (**Precedents**) or cells directly related to formulas (**Dependents**). For more information about Precedents and Dependents, see **Tools – Auditing** on page 392.

continues

Continued

Option	Description
All levels	Selects cells directly or indirectly referred to by formulas (**Precedents**) or cells directly or indirectly related to formulas (**Dependents**). See **Tools - Auditing** on page 392 for more information about Precedents and Dependents.
Last cell	Selects the last cell in the worksheet that contains data or formatting.
Visible cells only	Selects visible cells in a worksheet, not cells hidden in rows or columns.
Conditional formats	Selects only cells with conditional formats. Further define by choosing **All** or **Same** (see **Format - Conditional Formatting...** on page 372 for more information).
Data validation	Selects only cells with data validation applied. Further define by choosing **All** or **Same**. For more information, see **Data - Validation...** on page 414.
All	Selects all cells on the worksheet that have **Conditional formats** or **Data validation** applied.
Same	Selects only those cells that have the same **Conditional formats** or **Data validation** rules as the active cell.

Edit ⇒ Links...

Edit - Links remains dimmed until you have linked objects. For information on creating links, see **Edit - Paste Special...** on page 274 and **Edit - Paste as Hyperlink** on page 277. After you have linked objects, you might need to edit the information related to the object. If you move the source worksheet or document or change the name of the worksheet or document, the link will be broken and you get an error in the active worksheet.

To update or edit a link, follow these steps:

1. Choose **Edit**, **Links** to display the Links dialog box; see Figure 3.16.

Figure 3.16
Edit, Links opens the
Links dialog box.

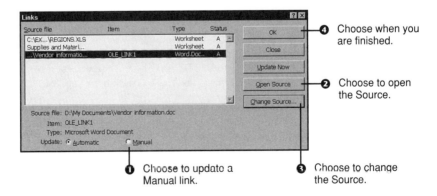

❹ Choose when you are finished.

❷ Choose to open the Source.

❶ Choose to update a Manual link.

❸ Choose to change the Source.

2. In the **Source file** list box, select the file or files you want to work with.

3. From the **Update** options, select one of the following:

- Choose **Automatic** to have the link updated every time the source file changes.
- Choose **Manual** to require updating through the **Update Now** choice or by selecting the link and pressing **F9**.

Change the Source

If you choose the **Change Source** button on the Links dialog box, the Change Links dialog box is displayed (see Figure 3.17).

Figure 3.17
Choose Edit, Links and then choose Change Source to display this dialog box.

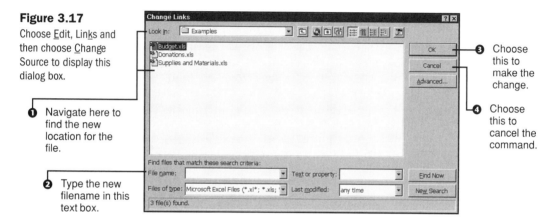

❶ Navigate here to find the new location for the file.

❷ Type the new filename in this text box.

❸ Choose this to make the change.

❹ Choose this to cancel the command.

Edit ➡ Object

Edit, **Object** is available if you have an object selected. The menu name and additional choices change to reflect the type of object that is selected. These menu commands might relate to the **Edit**, **Paste Special** choices and the **Edit**, **Links** choices. For more information, see the **Edit - Paste Special...** section on page 274, and the **Edit - Links...** section on page 286.

For information on inserting objects, see **Insert - Picture** on page 360, **Insert - Map...** on page 360, and **Insert - Object...** on page 360. The following table lists the choices available when you open **Edit**, **Object**.

Some of the Edit, Object choices

Command	Description
Edit	Opens the source application and enables you to edit the object in place.
Open	Opens the source application and enables you to edit the object in a separate window.
Replace	Opens the source application so you can replace the object.
Convert	Converts an OLE object from one type to another.

View

The View menu changes the way your screen looks. You can change the view to see headers and footers, make the view larger or smaller, and turn on or off certain screen items such as toolbars, the Status bar, and the Formula bar.

View ➡ Normal

For most tasks in Excel (especially typing, formatting, editing, and charting), you want to be in Normal view. Choose **View**, **Normal** to return to Normal view if you've switched views.

View ➡ Page Break Preview

Page Break Preview is new to Excel. This feature enables you to see and change where pages break on your document. This view displays the document in a shrunken view and the page numbers in a large nonprinting font on the screen (see Figure 3.18). If the order of the pages is incorrect (the pages should first go across the worksheet instead of down), choose **File**, **Page Setup**; click the Sheet tab, and choose **Over, then down** (see **File ➡ Page Setup...**, page 265).

Quick **Choices** *GET TO PAGE BREAK PREVIEW*

■ Choose **View**, **Page Break Preview**.

■ Choose **File**, **Print Preview** or click the **Print Preview** button on the Standard toolbar and click the **Page Break Preview** button.

Figure 3.18
Choose View, Page Break Preview to show page breaks and page numbers.

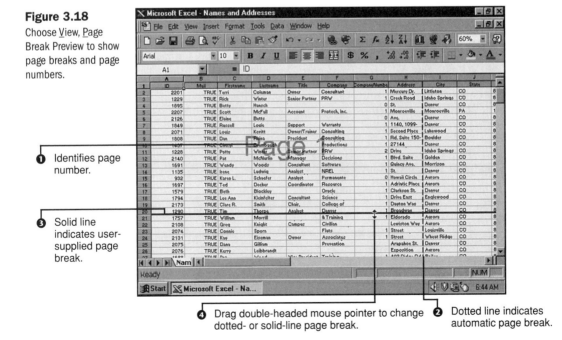

❶ Identifies page number.

❸ Solid line indicates user-supplied page break.

❹ Drag double-headed mouse pointer to change dotted- or solid-line page break.

❷ Dotted line indicates automatic page break.

View → Toolbars

To get many of your tasks done quickly, use a toolbar button rather than a menu item. The toolbar button (or a keyboard shortcut) usually is the quickest way to accomplish a task, whereas the corresponding menu item gives you more details. Many of the toolbars and the procedures for using them are the same or similar in Word and Excel (see Word's **View - Toolbars**, page 289).

All of the following toolbars are the same in both Word and Excel except the Visual Basic toolbar (see Word's **View - Toolbars Visual Basic**, page 84):

- Control
- Picture
- Visual Basic
- Web
- WordArt

In Excel, note the addition of the Resume Macro button. Click this button to continue the macro when the button appears pressed if Visual Basic is in Break mode.

View → Toolbars → Standard

The Standard toolbar is one of the two default toolbars that appear on your screen unless you turn them off. Some of the features you use the most (such as opening a file, saving, and printing are on this toolbar). See the following table for a complete list of buttons on the Standard toolbar. You can hide and display the Standard toolbar by pressing **Ctrl+7**.

Standard toolbar buttons

Button	Name	How to Use
	New	Click to create a new blank workbook.
	Open	Click to display the Open dialog box. Double-click the file you want to open (see Word's **File - Open...**, page 21).
	Save	Click to Save workbook with existing name or display Save As dialog box if no name has been given. Type the name in **File name** text box (see Word's **File - Save As...**, page 29).
	Print	Click to print the worksheet. For additional options, see **File - Print...**, page 268.
	Print Preview	Click to see what the worksheet will look like when printed (see **File - Print Preview**, page 268).
	Spelling	Click to open the Spelling dialog box. Click the **Change** button to make suggested change or **Ignore** to skip the word or phrase (see **Tools - Spelling...**, page 382).

continues

Continued

Button	Name	How to Use
	Cut	Click to place a copy of the selection into the clipboard (see **Edit - Cut**, page 272) and remove the selection after you paste.
	Copy	Click to place a copy of selection into the clipboard (see **Edit - Copy**, page 273).
	Paste	Click to paste what you cut or copied into the worksheet (see **Edit - Paste**, page 274).
	Format Painter	Click the text with the formatting you want to pick up. Then click the button and click the text to format. If you want to format multiple sections, double-click the button; then paint the sections you want to format. Click the Format Painter button again to turn it off.
	Undo	Click to cancel the last thing you did. You can cancel the last series of items you did by choosing them from the drop-down arrow (see **Edit - Undo**, page 272).
	Redo	Click to cancel the Undo for the last item. Alternatively, click the drop-down arrow for the last series of items.
	Insert Hyperlink	Click to open the Insert Hyperlink dialog box. Type the hyperlink in the **Link to File or URL** text box (see Word's **Insert - Hyperlink...**, page 159).
	Web Toolbar	Click to show or hide the Web toolbar (see Word's **View - Toolbars - Web**, page 85).
	AutoSum	Click in cell to right of row of numbers or below column of numbers. Click **AutoSum** button twice to place total in cell (see **Insert - Function...**, page 313).
	Paste Function	Click in cell to receive function and click the **Paste Function** button. In the Paste Function dialog box, choose Function name and click **OK**. Fill in arguments and click **OK** (see **Insert - Function...**, page 313).
	Sort Ascending	Click in column of a range and then click this button to sort the range by this column in A–Z, 1-9 order.
	Sort Descending	Click in column of a range and then click this button to sort the range by this column in Z–A, 9-1 order.
	Chart Wizard	Select the data you want to graph. Then click this button to open the Chart Wizard dialog box. Choose chart types and other settings on each of the dialog boxes (see **Insert - Chart...**, page 306).

Button	Name	How to Use
🌐	**Map**	Select geographic data to display. Click the **Map** button and drag plus mouse pointer into a rectangle to start **Microsoft Map** (see **Insert - Map...**, page 360).
✏️	**Drawing**	Click to show or hide the Drawing toolbar (see **View - Toolbars - Drawing**, page 293).
100% ▾	**Zoom**	Click on the drop-down arrow or type in the **Zoom** box to change the magnification of what you see on the screen. (This does not affect printing size.) For more details, see **View - Zoom...**, page 304.
❓	**Office Assistant**	Click and type a question for help. If you are in the middle of trying to do a task, choose from one of the bulleted items (see Excel's **Help**, page 445).

View ⟶ Toolbars ⟶ Formatting

Like the Standard toolbar, the Formatting toolbar also appears by default unless you turned it off. Most items are on the **Format** menu. The following tables list the buttons found on the Formatting toolbar.

Formatting toolbar buttons

Button	Name	How to Use
Arial ▾	**Font**	Select cells and click drop-down arrow to change font. For this button and the next buttons (through Comma Style), see more details at **Format - Cells...**, page 360.
10 ▾	**Font Size**	Select cells and click drop-down arrow to change size of the text.
B	**Bold**	Click to make selected cells (or characters) bold.
I	**Italic**	Click to make selected cells (or characters) italic.
U	**Underline**	Click to make selected cells (or characters) underlined.
≡	**Align Left**	Click to make text in selected cells line up on the left.
≡	**Center**	Click to make text in selected cells centered between the edges of the column.
≡	**Align Right**	Click to make text in selected cells line up on the right.
⊞	**Merge and Center**	Select multiple cells in a row. Click this button to center the text across all cells in the selection.
$	**Currency Style**	Click to change all numbers in selection to display and print dollar sign and two decimals.
%	**Percent Style**	Click to multiply all numbers in selection by 100 and add percent sign.

continues

Continued

Button	Name	How to Use
,	**Comma Style**	Click to change all numbers in selection to display and print commas for thousands placeholders with two decimals.
+.0 .00	**Increase Decimal**	Click to change selection to display and print more decimal places.
.00 +.0	**Decrease Decimal**	Click to change selection to display and print fewer decimal places.
	Decrease Indent	Click to remove spaces between left cell border and text.
	Increase Indent	Click to add spaces between left cell border and text.
	Borders	Click to add last border style to selected text. Click arrow to choose which edges of the cell and styles of the border to apply to the selection.
	Fill Color	Click to choose last fill color to create a background for the selected cells. Click the arrow to choose which color to apply. If you use the fill colors often, after you click the drop-down arrow, drag the top of the palette to create a new toolbar.
A	**Font Color**	Click to apply last font color to cells. Click the drop-down arrow to apply a different color. If you use the font colors often, after you click the drop-down arrow, drag the top of the palette to create a new toolbar.

<u>V</u>iew → <u>T</u>oolbars → Chart

The Chart toolbar appears when you select a chart, after you create one, or when you choose **<u>V</u>iew, <u>T</u>oolbars, Chart**. This toolbar helps change the graph type and characteristics. The available buttons are listed in the following table. For more information on creating a chart, see **Insert - C<u>h</u>art...**, page 306. For more information on modifying a chart, see **<u>C</u>hart**, page 445.

Chart toolbar buttons

Button	Name	How to Use
	Chart Objects	Click the down arrow on this button and choose a part of the chart to select. Small squares indicate the object is selected and it is ready to be edited or formatted. You can also click the chart objects directly to select them.

Button	Name	How to Use
	Format Selected Object	Open the Format dialog box. (The title bar and tabs change depending on the object selected.) Choose from options on the various tabs to change the text font and color; line and fill colors, styles, and patterns; tick marks, data labels and other features (see **F**ormat, **Chart Objects**, page 375).
	Chart Type	Click the **Chart Type** button to change the chart to the last used type. Click the drop-down arrow and choose another chart type (see also **Chart - Chart Type...**, page 446).
	Legend	Click to turn on or off the legend for the chart.
	Data Table	Click to turn on or off table showing data below the chart.
	By Row	Click to plot each data series using cells across range.
	By Column	Click to plot each data series using cells down the range.
	Angle Text Downward	When text is selected, click to change orientation of text so it's diagonally facing down. Click again to return to horizontal orientation.
	Angle Text Upward	When text is selected, click to change orientation of text so it's diagonally facing up. Click again to return to horizontal orientation.

View → Toolbars → Drawing

The Drawing toolbar is the same as Word's Drawing toolbar (see Word's **View** - **Toolbars** - **Drawing**, page 73) with a couple of exceptions:

■ Excel's adds the **Connectors** shapes from the **AutoShapes** button.

■ Word and Excel have slightly different menu options from the **Draw** button. Excel's additions are explained here.

- **Snap**—Choose to display the Snap menu. When you choose **To Grid**, objects move to these grid points when you drag an object. To override the grid, hold down **Alt** as you drag an object. Choose **To Shape** to draw ovals and rectangles to the size of the grid. Choose either of the menu choices to turn off the feature.

- **Reroute Connectors**—This feature makes flowcharts and organization charts easier by attaching the connector line to the best point on an object, taking the shortest route possible between objects.

View ⇝ Toolbars ⇝ External Data

The External Data toolbar appears when you insert external data into your worksheet, when you select an external data table on an existing worksheet, or when you choose **View**, **Toolbars**, **External Data** (see **Data ‑ Get External Data ‑ Create New Query...**, page 436). The following table lists the buttons available on the External Data toolbar.

External Data toolbar buttons

Button	Name	How to Use
	Edit Query	While in an external table, click to bring up the Query Wizard to choose new tables and fields, and for filtering, and sorting (see **Data ‑ Get External Data ‑ Edit Query...**, page 440).
	Data Range Properties	While in an external table, click to open the External Range Data Properties dialog box. This enables you to choose options for defining the query, changing when to refresh, and applying data layout options (see **Data ‑ Get External Data ‑ Data Range Properties**, page 440).
	Query Parameters	When you choose **View data or edit query in Microsoft Query** on the last step of the Query Wizard (see **Data ‑ Get External Data ‑ Edit Query...**, page 440), you can choose to have Excel prompt you each time you open the worksheet or refresh the data (see **Data ‑ Get External Data ‑ Parameters...**, page 441).
	Refresh Data	Click this button to rerun the commands necessary to get your data. If you have a query parameter prompt set, you will be re-prompted.
	Cancel Refresh	If your data is taking a long time to download or update, you can click this button to stop the refresh.
	Refresh All	Updates all external queries in the workbook.
	Refresh Status	If your data is taking a long time to refresh, click this button to open the Refresh Status dialog box to find out what is going on with your external table.

View ⇝ Toolbars ⇝ Forms

Forms enables you to fill in a text box, toggle a check box on or off, or select from a drop-down list. In addition to putting these controls on a worksheet, you can also add them to an MS Excel 5.0 dialog box. This dialog sheet is used for backward compatibility. For most of your worksheets, you should use the Control Toolbox instead (see Word's **View ‑ Toolbars ‑ Control Toolbox**, page 70).

Quick `Choices` *CREATING A FORM*

1. If you want to create your own dialog box, right-click Worksheet tab, choose **I**nsert, and double-click **MS Excel 5.0 Dialog Box**.

2. Create the controls listed in the two Forms Toolbar Buttons tables that follow. Click the button on the toolbar and then click in the sheet to place the item. You can also click and drag in the sheet to define the size of the control.

3. If desired, click the **Control Properties** button and fill out the options on the Control tab (see the following table).

4. If you want, click the **Edit Code** button button and type Visual Basic code to control what happens when you click the control.

The following table lists the buttons that are available for all of your sheets including worksheets, chart sheets, and dialog sheets. Some buttons are only available for dialog sheets.

Forms toolbar buttons—All sheets

Button	Name	Use and Additional Editing Notes
Aa	Label	This is a static label on the sheet that does not change. After adding this to the sheet, drag the mouse I-beam across text and retype to change the label.
	Group Box	Use this to surround and identify Option Buttons.
	Button	Use this to run macros. After you add this to a worksheet, the Assign Macro dialog box opens (if you are on a dialog sheet, right-click and choose **Assign Macro**). Double-click your macro to assign a macro to the button or use the generic name provided for you.
	Check Box	This is a box that you can check on or off.
	Option Button	This is a circle that you can check on or off, but is usually part of an option group. (Set **Cell link** property to the same cell for all those in the same option group.)
	List Box	This enables you to choose from a list of items.
	Combo Box	This is a combination of an edit box and combo box. The user types or chooses from a list.
	Scroll Bar	This enables you to increase or decrease values.
	Spinner	This enables you to increase or decrease values.
	Control Properties	Use this button in conjunction with all buttons listed previously and in the following table. The properties change depending on the selected object.

continues

Continued

Button	Name	Use and Additional Editing Notes
	Edit Code	When you click this button, you open the Visual Basic for applications window and go to the procedure for clicking the button. Type in Visual Basic statements.
	Toggle Grid	In a worksheet, turns on and off the worksheet grid. On a dialog sheet, turns on and off the dots representing the design grid.

Forms toolbar buttons—Dialog sheets only

Button	Name	Use and Additional Editing Notes
	Edit Box	After you click this button, click in the worksheet or dialog sheet to place a text box that enables you to type or edit your changes.
	Combination List-Edit	Creates two controls: an Edit Box and a List Box. To set their properties and program them, do each control separately.
	Combination Drop-Down Edit	Creates a combo box that is identical to the combo box in the previous table.
	Run Dialog	This displays the dialog in User view. To display this sheet from another macro, include the line **Application.Sheets("Dialog1").Show** where **Dialog1** can be replaced with the name of any dialog sheet.

Forms toolbar buttons—Control Properties—Control tab

Controls	Properties	How to Use
All except Command Button, Label, and Edit Box	Cell link	Type or click the Collapse Dialog button and go to the cell that will display the user's input from the dialog box you created.
On worksheet, all Command Button, Edit Box, and Label	3D shading	Check to give an engraved or sunken appearance.
Check Box and Option Button	Unchecked	When selected, the default value is blank.
Check Box and Option Button	Checked	When selected, the default value is filled.
Check Box	Mixed	When selected, the default is a grayed box.

Controls	Properties	How to Use
List Box and Combo Box	**Input range**	Type possible values for the list in a one column range on the worksheet. Type the range address or click the **Collapse Dialog** button and drag the cells that will display within the list.
List Box	**Single**	Click this option to allow just one choice to be selected in the list box.
List Box	**Multi**	Click this option to allow the user to click and save multiple choices in the list box.
List Box	**Extend**	Click this option to allow the user to choose multiple choices by holding down **Shift** for adjacent items or **Ctrl** for nonadjacent items.
Combo Box	**Drop down lines**	Type the number of rows that will display when the user clicks the down arrow of the combo box.
Scroll Bar and Spinner	**Current value**	Set the number for value of the control. This number changes when you click the arrows of the control.
Scroll Bar and Spinner	**Minimum value**	Type or use the up and down arrows to set the smallest number that the user can choose.
Scroll Bar and Spinner	**Maximum value**	Type or use the up and down arrows to set the largest number that the user can choose.
Scroll Bar and Spinner	**Incremental change**	Type or use the up and down arrows to set how much the **Current Value** will change when the user clicks the up or down arrow.
Scroll Bar	**Page change**	Type or use the up and down arrows to set how much the **Current Value** will change when the user clicks above or below the scroll box.
Command Buttons	**Default**	Check this option (for only one Command Button) to run when the user presses **Enter** (for dialog sheets only).
Command Buttons	**Cancel**	Check this option (for only one Command Button) to run when the user closes using **Esc** or the close button (for dialog sheets only).
Command Buttons	**Dismiss**	Check this option to run the macro and then close the dialog box (on dialog sheets only).
Command Buttons	**Help**	Check this option (for only one Command Button) to run when the user presses **F1**.
Command Button, Group Box, and Label	**Accelerator key**	Type a letter so the user can press **Alt+** the letter to run the command button, go to the group, or go to the control after the label. (To make and control, first you add a label, and then immediately you add the control.)

<u>V</u>iew ▾ <u>T</u>oolbars ▾ PivotTable

The PivotTable toolbar appears when you add a PivotTable to your worksheet (see **Data ▾ PivotTable Report...**, page 424) or choose **<u>V</u>iew**, **<u>T</u>oolbars**, **PivotTable**. For most of the buttons on the PivotTable toolbar to work, you need to have your Active cell within a PivotTable. The following table describes the button available on the PivotTable toolbar.

PivotTable toolbar buttons

Button	Name	How to Use
PivotTable ▾	PivotTable	Click this button to display a menu of choices explained in the following table.
	PivotTable Wizard	Return to Step 3 of the PivotTable Wizard. Drag fields on or off the Row, Column, Page, and Data areas. Double-click a field to show PivotTable Field dialog box. Choose Next and place PivotTable on a new or existing worksheet (see **Data ▾ PivotTable Report...**, page 424).
	PivotTable Field	Move to a row, column, or cell in the PivotTable and click this button. The PivotTable Field dialog box appears enabling you to change the field's format, hide values, and choose a different function associated with a Data field (see **PivotTable Fields**, page 428).
	Show Pages	Opens the Show Pages dialog box and displays a list of Page fields. Double-click a field to create a new worksheet for each value of the field.
	Ungroup	Move to a group and then click this button to ungroup the items.
	Group	Click the first field, hold down **Ctrl**, and select additional fields. Then click this button to create a group of items.
	Hide Detail	If you have items making up part of a subtotal in the PivotTable, click one of the items and then click this button to show only the subtotal.
	Show Detail	If you've hidden detail, click this button to display the items again.
	Refresh Data	Updates the PivotTable with any changes from the source data.
	Select Label	When you click in a row of the PivotTable, the text is selected.
	Select Data	When you click in a row of the PivotTable, the numbers are selected.
	Select Label and Data	When you click in a row of the PivotTable, both the data and label are selected.

The following table shows the menu choices on the PivotTable button of the PivotTable toolbar. Not shown are choices that also have a button on the PivotTable toolbar (see the previous table).

PivotTable toolbar—PivotTable button menu items

Menu Item	How to Use
Wizard	Same as clicking the PivotTable Wizard button.
Refresh Data	Same as clicking the PivotTable Refresh Data button.
Select	Click this button to display a submenu that contains some of the options that of the other buttons on this toolbar. You can select the **Entire Table** right now. Or, when you select a cell in the first column of the table, either the data, label, or row selects depending on you choice of **Label**, **Data**, or **Label and Data**. Choose **Enable Selection** to turn the value from selected options on or off. **Enable Selection** also enables you to select a range within the PivotTable.
Formulas	This item displays a submenu to create or manage additional fields (see **PivotTable Formulas**, page 431).
Field	Opens the PivotTable Field dialog box for changing the function, orientation or other options (see **PivotTable Fields**, page 428).
Options	Opens the PivotTable Options dialog box for formatting and data options for this table (see **PivotTable Options**, page 433).

View – Toolbars – Reviewing

You can use the Reviewing toolbar to navigate and edit comments you added (see **Insert – Comment**, page 359). You can also view a comment by hovering over the highlight in the text. The following table describes the buttons found on the Reviewing toolbar.

Reviewing toolbar buttons

Button	Name	How to Use
	New Comment	Click to add a comment. A yellow box opens with your name. Type the comment.
	Previous Comment	Click to move to and display the previous comment.
	Next Comment	Click to move to and display the next comment.
	Show Comment	Click the cell containing the comment. Then click the button to toggle back and forth between displaying and hiding the comment.
	Show All Comments	Toggle back and forth between displaying and hiding all comments.

continues

Continued		
Button	**Name**	**How to Use**
🖼	Delete Comment	Click the cell containing a comment or use the **Previous Comment** and **Next Comment** buttons and then click the **Delete Comment** button to remove it.
☑	Create Microsoft Outlook Task	Click to open Microsoft Outlook and create a task. The task area shows a shortcut to the workbook and enters the text of the comment.
🗐	Update File	Updates a shared file with changes from other users (see **Tools - Share Workbook...**, page 383) or changes a read-only file to reflect changes made to the original workbook since the read-only copy was opened.
✉	Send to Mail Recipient	Click to open up your email program with the current workbook as an attachment. The Subject becomes the name of the file.

View ⇒ Toolbars ⇒ Customize...

When you choose **View - Toolbars - Customize**, the Customize dialog box opens enabling you to edit or create toolbars and menus. This is the same dialog box shown in the Word's **View - Toolbars - Customize...** section (see page 87). The Excel version differs from Word in that Excel does not have the **Keyboard** option button. (Instead, you use **Options** button on the Macro dialog box.) Additionally, Excel's Options tab of the Customize dialog box does not have an option to display shortcut keys.

Excel does have an **Attach** button on the Toolbars tab that Word does not. Click this button to bring up the Attach Toolbars dialog box. Any Custom toolbars you have are listed on the left side of the dialog box. Click the **Copy** button to connect the toolbar with your current workbook. Then, even if you delete the custom toolbar later, this toolbar is available when you open the workbook.

Excel and Word also differ in how you attach a macro to a button or menu item. In Word, you need to do this as you create the button. (A dialog box appears when you drag a custom button to the toolbar.) In Excel, you can right-click a button or menu item and choose **Assign Macro** to open up the Macro dialog box. Double-click the macro name to assign it to the button.

View ⇒ Formula Bar

Choose **View, Formula Bar** or **Tools, Options, View tab, Formula bar** to display or hide the Formula bar. This bar appears under the menu and toolbars. The bar consists of a Name text box, edit buttons, and a box that enables you to create or edit text or formulas.

Quick **Choices** *USE THE FORMULA BAR FOR RANGES, EDITING, OR FORMULAS*

- Click the drop-down arrow of the Name text box and choose an existing range name to move to and select the range.
- Type a cell address (for example, A6) in the Name box text to go to that cell (see also **E̲dit ‑ G̲o To...**, page 284).
- Type a range address (for example, E8:E15) in the Name text box to select that range.
- Select a range and type a name in the Name text box to create a range name for that range (see also **I̲nsert ‑ N̲ame ‑ D̲efine...**, page 356).
- Move to a cell with data. Drag the mouse pointer to select text in the Formula bar. Then type new text as a replacement, press **Delete** to remove the text, or choose a font format option on the Formatting toolbar to format selected text.
- Move to a cell to receive a formula. Click the equal sign **=** in the Formula bar to begin a formula. The formula palette opens and displays the results of your formula as you build it. Click the first cell or type a number in the formula, type an operator (such as +, -, *, or /), and then click on another cell or type another number. Continue until the formula is built. Then do one of the following:
  - Press **Enter**, and click **OK** on the formula palette, or click the green check mark ✓ to complete the formula.
  - Press **Esc**, click **Cancel** on the formula palette, or click the red X ✗ to omit the formula.
- Move to a cell below the range of data you want to create a function for. Click on the equal sign **=**. The Name box turns into the Function box with the most recent function used on the button. Click the **Function** button or choose a common function and then fill in the arguments for the function in the function palette (see **I̲nsert ‑ F̲unction...**, page 313).

Vi̲ew ‑ Status Bar

The Status bar is at the bottom of the screen and shows whether certain keys are pressed (Caps Lock, Scroll Lock, Num Lock). If you have a range with numbers selected, the Status bar also shows the total or other statistics. Right-click and choose one of the functions to display on the Status bar (**A̲verage**, **C̲ount**, **Co̲unt Nums**, **M̲ax**, **Mi̲n**, **S̲um**, or choose **None** to not display an AutoCalculate result).

Choose either **View**, **Status Bar** or **T̲ools**, **O̲ptions**, **View tab**, **S̲tatus bar** to turn on or off the Status bar.

Vi̲ew ‑ H̲eader and Footer...

Headers and footers print at the top and bottom of your document.

Quick **Choices** *CREATE HEADER OR FOOTER*

1. Choose **View**, **Header and Footer**. The Page Setup dialog box opens to the Header/ Footer tab (see **File** ‑ **Page Setup...**, page 265).
2. Choose a preset **Header** from the drop-down box.
3. Choose a preset **Footer** from the drop-down box.
4. The example boxes show what the header and footer will look like. Choose **OK** and then **Print** 🖨 or **Print Preview** 🔍 the document.

While you are in the Page Setup dialog box, you can create a **Custom Header** or **Customer Footer**. When you click either of these buttons, a Header or Footer dialog box opens with the following options:

Header or Footer dialog box

Item	Code	How to Use
Left section		Type any text you want repeated on left side of header or footer or click one of the following buttons.
Center section		Type or click a button for items in the middle of the header or footer.
Right section		Type or click a button for items aligned on the right side of the header or footer.
A		Opens Font dialog box allowing you to choose font, style, size, underline, and other effects for this section of the header or footer.
🔢	&[Page]	Click to place a code for the page number.
🔢	&[Pages]	Click to place a code for the total number of pages.
📅	&[Date]	Click to insert a code that prints the date when the document is printed.
🕐	&[Time]	Click to insert a code that prints the time when the document is printed.
📄	&[File]	Click to place a code for the name of the file.
🗔	&[Tab]	Click to place a code for the name of the worksheet.

View ‑ Comments

Comments enables you to add a note directly to a cell. When you hover your mouse pointer over a comment (indicated by a red triangle in the upper-right corner of a cell), the note appears as a ScreenTip (see **Insert** ‑ **Comment**, page 359 to add a comment). **View**, **Comments** also displays the Reviewing toolbar (see **View** ‑ **Toolbars** ‑ **Reviewing**, page 299). Choose **View**, **Comments** again or click the **Hide All Comments** button 🖳 on the Reviewing toolbar to turn off comments.

You can also change the view of comments by choosing **Tools**, **Options** and clicking the View tab. Under the Comments section, click **None** for no indication of a comment. Click **Comment indicator only** to see the red triangle in the upper-right corner of the cell indicating a comment, or click **Comment and indicator** to see the comment and red-triangle indicator both.

View ➥ Custom Views...

The Views feature enables you to save different print settings or hidden items with separate names. Choose **View**, **Custom Views** to bring up the Custom Views dialog box (see Figure 3.19).

Figure 3.19
View, Custom Views opens the Custom Views dialog box.

❶ Choose a view and double-click to show the view.

❷ Click to show any view you select.

❹ Click to create another view.

❸ Click to remove the selected view.

When you choose the **Add** button in the Custom Views dialog box, the Add View dialog box opens (see Figure 3.20).

Figure 3.20
View, Custom Views, Add button opens the Add View dialog box.

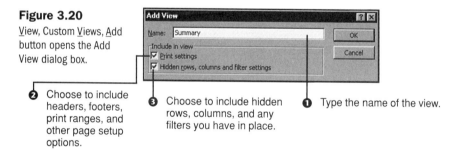

❷ Choose to include headers, footers, print ranges, and other page setup options.

❸ Choose to include hidden rows, columns, and any filters you have in place.

❶ Type the name of the view.

View ➥ Report Manager...

The Report Manager takes the Custom Views feature a step further by enabling you to add views (see **View ▪ Custom Views...**, page 303), and scenarios (see **Tools ▪ Scenarios...**, page 389). You also can choose which sheets you want to print as a set. Choose **View**, **Report Manager** to open the Report Manager dialog box (see Figure 3.21).

If you did a typical install of Office or Excel, you need to install the Report Manager.

Figure 3.21

View, Report Manager opens the Report Manager dialog box.

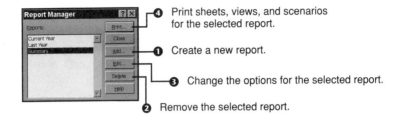

④ Print sheets, views, and scenarios for the selected report.

① Create a new report.

③ Change the options for the selected report.

② Remove the selected report.

When you choose the **Edit** button on the Report Manager dialog box, the **Edit** Report dialog box opens (see Figure 3.22).

Figure 3.22

View, Report Manager, Add button opens the Add Report dialog box.

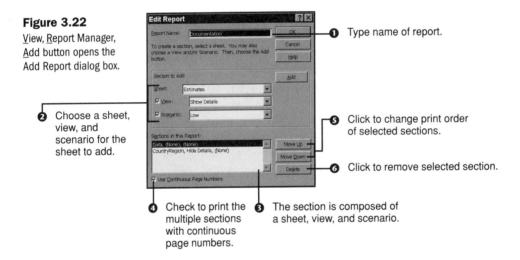

① Type name of report.

② Choose a sheet, view, and scenario for the sheet to add.

⑤ Click to change print order of selected sections.

⑥ Click to remove selected section.

④ Check to print the multiple sections with continuous page numbers.

③ The section is composed of a sheet, view, and scenario.

View ➡ Full Screen

Full screen hides most of the elements on the screen, such as toolbars and the Status bar, so you can see more of your screen. Click the **Close Full Screen** button or choose **View**, **Full Screen** again to close the Full Screen view.

View ➡ Zoom...

Zoom enables you see more or less of your worksheet at one time. The magnification of the worksheet changes on the screen but does not affect printing.

Click the **Zoom** button 100% ▼ on the Standard toolbar and choose a magnification from the drop-down list or type a value in the box. Select a range of cells and choose **Selection** to shrink the screen so all cells are visible. Alternatively, you can choose **View**, **Zoom** to make changes on the Zoom dialog box (see Figure 3.23).

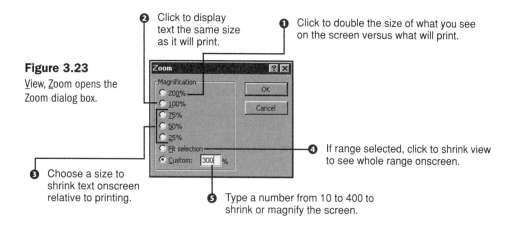

Figure 3.23
View, Zoom opens the
Zoom dialog box.

❶ Click to double the size of what you see
on the screen versus what will print.

❷ Click to display
text the same size
as it will print.

❸ Choose a size to
shrink text onscreen
relative to printing.

❹ If range selected, click to shrink view
to see whole range onscreen.

❺ Type a number from 10 to 400 to
shrink or magnify the screen.

Insert

The **Insert** menu gives you commands to insert worksheet items such as cells, rows, columns, worksheets, charts, and functions. You can also create names for ranges, insert page breaks and comments, and create geographical maps. You can insert objects, from other programs such as clip art pictures, PowerPoint slides, organization charts, and many others objects depending on what you have installed on your computer.

Insert ➥ Cells...

The **Insert**, **Cells** command enables you to insert cells, rows, or columns in the worksheet.

To insert cells, rows, or columns, do the following:

1. Select a cell or range of cells where you want the new cells inserted, or select a cell in the column or row to be inserted.

2. Choose **Insert**, **Cells** or press **Ctrl++**(plus sign); or right-click the selection and choose **Insert**. The Insert dialog box is displayed (see Figure 3.24).

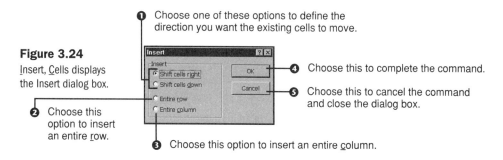

Figure 3.24
Insert, Cells displays
the Insert dialog box.

❶ Choose one of these options to define the
direction you want the existing cells to move.

❷ Choose this
option to insert
an entire row.

❸ Choose this option to insert an entire column.

❹ Choose this to complete the command.

❺ Choose this to cancel the command
and close the dialog box.

If you select a row or column heading, the dialog box is not displayed and a row or column is inserted, shifting the existing row down and the existing column to the right.

Insert ➥ Rows

Select the number of row headings or cells for the number of rows you want to insert. Choose **Insert**, **Rows**. The selected rows or cells will be pushed down to make room for the inserted rows.

Insert ➥ Columns

Select the number of column headings or cells for the number of columns you want to insert. Choose **Insert**, **Columns**. The selected columns or cells will be pushed to the right to make room for the inserted columns.

Insert ➥ Worksheet

Select the Worksheet tab to the right of where you want the new worksheet; choose **Insert**, **Worksheet**. A new worksheet is inserted to the left of the selected sheet.

Insert ➥ Chart...

The **Insert**, **Chart** command displays the first dialog box in the Chart Wizard. You can use this command to create a chart on a new sheet or insert an embedded chart on the worksheet you select. To modify a chart, see **Chart**, page 445.

Quick Choices *TO CREATE A CHART*

■ Select the data to be charted; press **F11**. A chart sheet is inserted to the left of the active worksheet. See **Selecting Cells** on page 260 for more information about selecting worksheet data. See **View ▪ Toolbars ▪ Chart** on page 292 for information on changing chart elements.

Follow these basic steps to create a chart using the Chart Wizard:

1. Select the worksheet data you want to chart. See **Selecting Cells** on page 260 for more information about selecting worksheet data.
2. Choose **Insert**, **Chart** or click ▦ on the Standard toolbar to display the first dialog box in the Chart Wizard.
3. Make your selections on the dialog boxes.
4. If necessary, click a tab on the dialog box to make changes to additional options.
5. Choose one of the buttons listed on the following table.

Chart Wizard buttons

Button	Action
Cancel	Return to the worksheet without creating a chart. You can also press the **Esc** key.
Back	Go to the previous dialog box in the Chart Wizard process. Not available on the first step.
Next	Go to the next dialog box in the Chart Wizard process.
Finish	Complete the chart with the selections made so far. Skips the rest of the dialog boxes.

6. When you are finished making selections in the Chart Wizard, choose the **Finish** button to insert the chart.

Chart Wizard—Step 1 of 4—Chart Type

Use this dialog box to select the chart type (see Figure 3.25).

Figure 3.25
Choosing Insert, Chart displays the Chart Wizard—Step 1 of 4— Chart Type dialog box.

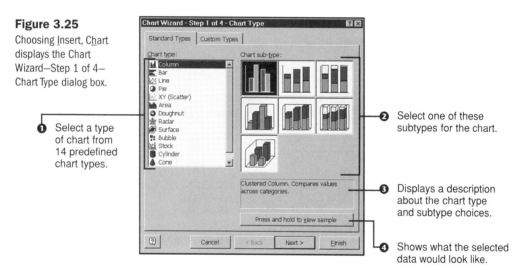

❶ Select a type of chart from 14 predefined chart types.

❷ Select one of these subtypes for the chart.

❸ Displays a description about the chart type and subtype choices.

❹ Shows what the selected data would look like.

See **Chart - Chart Type...** on page 446 for more information.

Chart Wizard—Step 1 of 4—Chart Type ➥ Custom Types Tab

Choose the Custom Types tab to display a list of custom chart types (see Figure 3.26).

Figure 3.26

Choose Insert, Chart and click the Custom Types tab to display this dialog box.

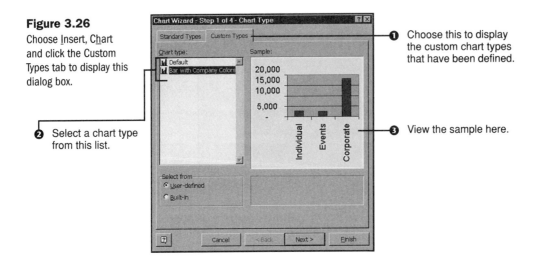

❶ Choose this to display the custom chart types that have been defined.

❸ View the sample here.

❷ Select a chart type from this list.

Chart Wizard—Step 2 of 4—Chart Source Data

Use this dialog box to define or redefine the data for the chart (see Figure 3.27).

Figure 3.27

Chart Wizard—Step 2 of 4—Chart Source Data dialog box—Data Range tab.

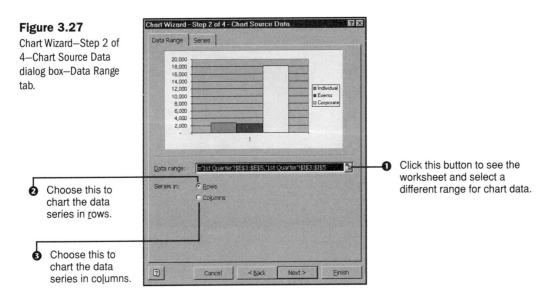

❶ Click this button to see the worksheet and select a different range for chart data.

❷ Choose this to chart the data series in rows.

❸ Choose this to chart the data series in columns.

See **Chart - Source Data...** on page 447 for more information.

Chart Wizard—Step 2 of 4—Chart Source Data—Series Tab

Choose the Series tab to add more options to the series information (see Figure 3.28).

Figure 3.28
Chart Wizard—Step 2
of 4—Chart Source
Data dialog box—Series
tab.

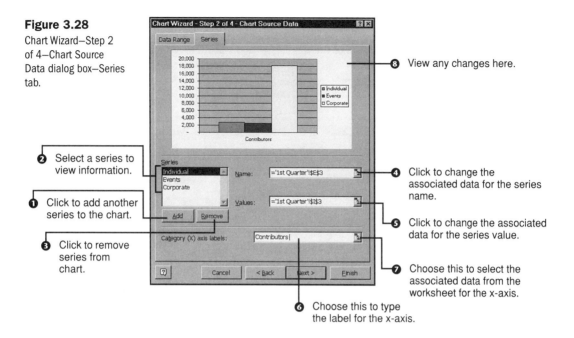

❷ Select a series to
view information.

❶ Click to add another
series to the chart.

❸ Click to remove
series from
chart.

❽ View any changes here.

❹ Click to change the
associated data for the series
name.

❺ Click to change the associated
data for the series value.

❼ Choose this to select the
associated data from the
worksheet for the x-axis.

❻ Choose this to type
the label for the x-axis.

Chart Wizard—Step 3 of 4—Chart Options

Use this dialog box to add or change chart options such as Titles, Axis information, Gridlines,
Legend placement, Data Labels, and a Data Table (see Figure 3.29).

❶ Click here to type the chart title.

Figure 3.29
Chart Wizard—Step 3
of 4—Chart Options
dialog box—Titles tab.

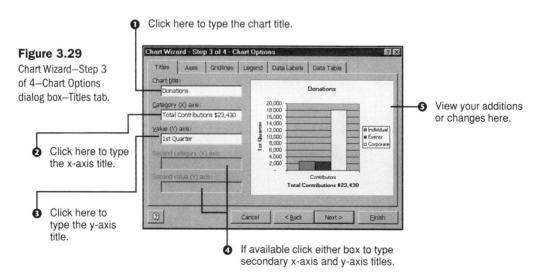

❷ Click here to type
the x-axis title.

❸ Click here to
type the y-axis
title.

❺ View your additions
or changes here.

❹ If available click either box to type
secondary x-axis and y-axis titles.

See **Chart - Chart Options...** on page 447 for more information.

Chart Wizard—Step 3 of 4—Chart Options—Axes Tab

Choose the Axes tab to turn on or off the display of the primary axes (see Figure 3.30).

❷ Click to display the x-axis labels as dates if they are formatted as dates in the worksheet (default option).

❶ Click to turn display of x-axis on or off.

Figure 3.30
Chart Wizard—Step 3 of 4—Chart Options—Axes tab.

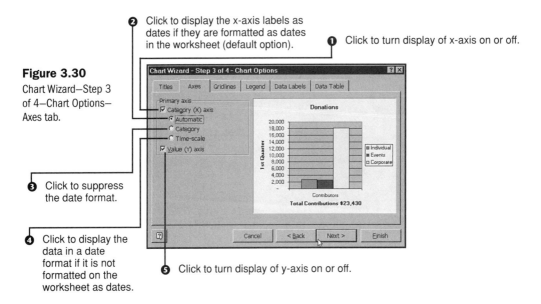

❸ Click to suppress the date format.

❹ Click to display the data in a date format if it is not formatted on the worksheet as dates.

❺ Click to turn display of y-axis on or off.

Chart Wizard—Step 3 of 4—Chart Options—Gridlines Tab

Choose the Gridlines tab to turn on or off the display of major and minor gridlines for both the x and y axes (see Figure 3.31).

❶ Click to display gridlines at major intervals on the x-axis.

Figure 3.31
Chart Wizard—Step 3 of 4—Chart Options—Gridlines tab.

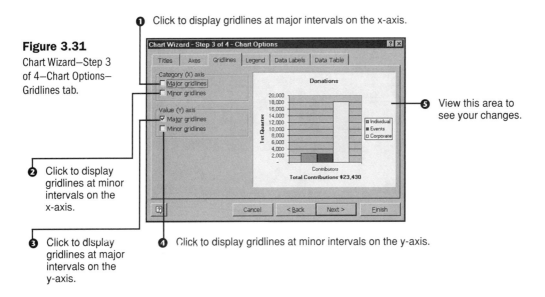

❺ View this area to see your changes.

❷ Click to display gridlines at minor intervals on the x-axis.

❸ Click to display gridlines at major intervals on the y-axis.

❹ Click to display gridlines at minor intervals on the y-axis.

Chart Wizard—Step 3 of 4—Chart Options—Legend Tab

Choose the Legend tab to decide to display the legend and if so where on the chart you want it to appear (see Figure 3.32).

Figure 3.32
Chart Wizard—Step 3 of 4—Chart Options—Legend tab.

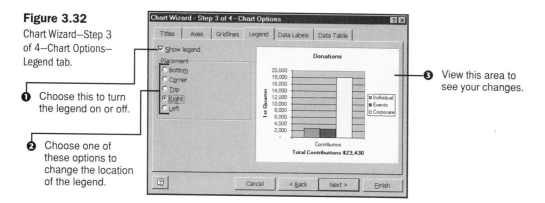

❶ Choose this to turn the legend on or off.

❷ Choose one of these options to change the location of the legend.

❸ View this area to see your changes.

Chart Wizard—Step 3 of 4—Chart Options—Data Labels Tab

Choose this tab to define options regarding the data labels (see Figure 3.33).

❸ If you are creating a pie or doughnut chart, select this option to display the percent of the total on all data points.

❷ Choose this option to display the value on all data points.

❶ Choose this option to delete labels from all the data points.

Figure 3.33
Chart Wizard—Step 3 of 4—Chart Options—Data Labels tab.

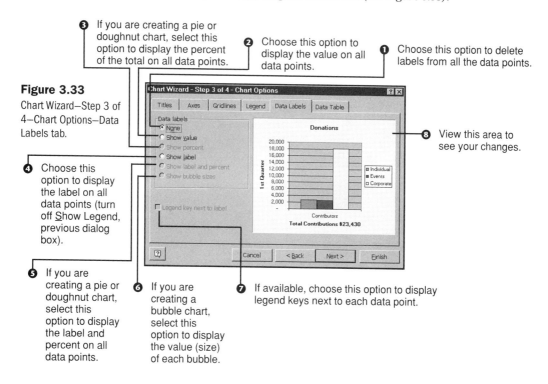

❹ Choose this option to display the label on all data points (turn off Show Legend, previous dialog box).

❺ If you are creating a pie or doughnut chart, select this option to display the label and percent on all data points.

❻ If you are creating a bubble chart, select this option to display the value (size) of each bubble.

❼ If available, choose this option to display legend keys next to each data point.

❽ View this area to see your changes.

Chart Wizard—Step 3 of 4—Chart Options—Data Table Tab

Choose this tab to determine whether you want to show the data table on the chart (see Figure 3.34).

Figure 3.34
Chart Wizard—Step 3 of 4—Chart Options—Data Table dialog tab.

① Choose this option to show the data table.

② Choose this option to show legend keys in the data table.

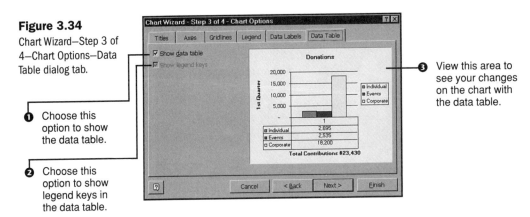

③ View this area to see your changes on the chart with the data table.

Chart Wizard—Step 4 of 4—Chart Location

Use this dialog box to specify whether you want to embed the chart in the worksheet or create a separate chart sheet (see Figure 3.35).

Figure 3.35
Chart Wizard—Step 4 of 4—Chart Location dialog box.

① Select this option to create a chart sheet.

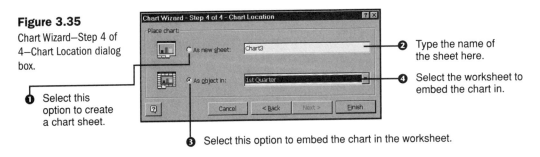

② Type the name of the sheet here.

④ Select the worksheet to embed the chart in.

③ Select this option to embed the chart in the worksheet.

See **Chart - Location...** on page 450 for more information. Also see the **Chart** menu section beginning on page 445 for more information about creating and changing charts.

Insert ➥ Page Break

Select the cell below where you want the page break to occur. Then choose **Insert, Page Break** to insert a manual page break above the selected cell. A long dashed line indicates a manual page break.

This command changes to **Remove Page Break** when the active cell is below a cell with a manual page break.

Insert ⇝ Reset All Page Breaks

When you select the entire worksheet, you can choose **Insert**, **Reset All Page Breaks** to delete all the manual page breaks.

Insert ⇝ Function...

The **Insert**, **Function** command displays the Paste Function dialog box to help you enter functions and their arguments. Functions are predefined formulas that enable you to perform simple to complex calculations. For information about formulas, see **Creating Formulas** on page 255.

Quick **Choices** *TO ENTER FUNCTIONS*

1. Position the active cell where you want the result of a calculation.
2. Do one of the following:
   - Click ∑ on the Standard toolbar to sum a column or row of numbers. See **View ⇝ Toolbars ⇝ Standard** for more information on AutoSum.
   - Click *fx* on the Standard toolbar to display the Paste Function dialog box. Proceed through the formula palette to create the formula. For more information, see the detail steps that follow.
   - Type the function yourself.
   - Type an equal sign (=) or click the equal sign (=) on the Formula bar, then type the function you want to use, or click the **Function** button to the left, and choose one of the most recent functions you have used.

To enter a function using Paste Function:

1. Position the active cell where you want the result of a calculation to appear.
2. Choose **Insert**, **Function** or click *fx* on the Standard toolbar to display the Paste Function dialog box (see Figure 3.36).

Figure 3.36
Choose Insert, Function to display the Paste Function dialog box.

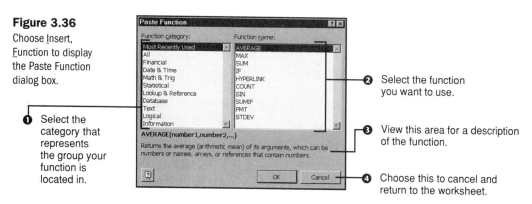

❶ Select the category that represents the group your function is located in.

❷ Select the function you want to use.

❸ View this area for a description of the function.

❹ Choose this to cancel and return to the worksheet.

3. Choose **OK** to continue and display the Formula palette as shown in Figure 3.37. The Formula palette is different depending on the function you are using.

4. If you need to see the worksheet behind the Formula palette, point to any gray area on the palette, click and drag to move it out of the way.

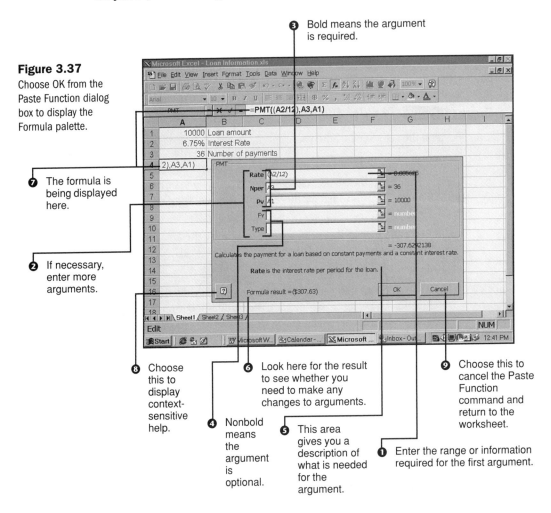

❸ Bold means the argument is required.

Figure 3.37
Choose OK from the Paste Function dialog box to display the Formula palette.

❼ The formula is being displayed here.

❷ If necessary, enter more arguments.

❽ Choose this to display context-sensitive help.

❹ Nonbold means the argument is optional.

❻ Look here for the result to see whether you need to make any changes to arguments.

❺ This area gives you a description of what is needed for the argument.

❾ Choose this to cancel the Paste Function command and return to the worksheet.

❶ Enter the range or information required for the first argument.

5. When you are finished entering arguments, choose **OK**. The result of the formula is displayed in the active cell, with the formula visible on the Formula bar.

Function List

The following is a list of the functions available if you did the Typical setup of Office 97 or Excel 97. Remember that all functions must start with = (equal sign) and have parentheses surrounding any arguments. Include the parentheses even if there are no arguments. In the following descriptions of the functions, bold indicates when an argument is required and italic indicates that the argument is optional. You can type the function directly in a cell, but it is often easier to use the Paste Function button because Excel gives you instructions on the function and its arguments. A description is provided for each function. Examples are provided in some cases.

Financial Functions

Some financial functions use common arguments: *rate, per, nper, pmt, pv, fv,* and *type*. *Rate* is the interest rate for each period. *Per* is the current period (this can be any number from 1 to nper). *Nper* is the number of payment periods. *Pmt* is the payment (interest and principal) for the loan or investment. *Pv* is the present value—how much the future payments would be worth right now. *Fv* is the future value—how much the series of payments would be worth in the future. *Type* indicates when payments are due. *Type* is 0 (this is the default if not included) for payments due at the end of the period and 1 for payments due at the beginning of the period. Make sure that your time periods are consistent. If the *rate* is an annual interest rate (12%, for example) and your loan *nper* is for 60 months, change the interest rate to monthly interest ($12\%/12 = 1\%$) to calculate monthly payments. For cash you pay out (for example, a deposit to a mutual fund), values are negative numbers. For cash you receive (such as dividends), values are positive numbers.

- DB(**cost, salvage, life, period,** *month*)—Declining balance depreciation.

  Calculates depreciation (using fixed-declining balance method) of an asset with an initial **cost**. Value at the end of depreciation is equal to **salvage**; number of periods the asset is being appreciated is equal to **life**; current period is equal to **period**; and optionally, the number of months in the first year is equal to *month*. **Life** and **period** must be the same units (such as years). If *month* is not included, it is assumed to be 12.

  DB(100000,10000,6,1,7)= $18,608

- DDB(**cost, salvage, life, period,** *factor*)—Double-declining balance depreciation.

  Calculates depreciation (using double-declining balance method) of an asset with an initial **cost**. Value at the end of depreciation is equal to **salvage**; number of periods the asset is being appreciated is equal to **life**; current period is equal to **period**; and the rate the balance declines is equal to *factor*. **Life** and **period** must be the same units (such as years). If *factor* is not included, it is assumed to be 2 (the double-declining balance method).

  DDB(100000,10000,6,1,2)=$33,333

- FV(**rate, nper, pmt,** *pv, type*)—Future value.

  How much will a lump-sum investment (*pv*) be worth in the future if you add constant payments (**pmt**) given an interest **rate** and number of periods (**nper**)?

  FV(10%/12,36,–200,1000,0)=$7,008

- IPMT(**rate, per, nper, pv,** *fv, type*)—Interest payment.

  Calculates how much interest you are paying (receiving) for a given loan (investment) at a specific period.

IPMT(7%/12,5,360,100000) = ($581). (The interest in the 5th month you pay on a $100,000, 30-year loan at 7% interest is $581).

■ IRR(**values,** *guess*)—Internal rate of return.

Estimates what interest rate you are earning (or paying) based on a series of cash flows consisting of payments (negative values) and income (positive values). The cash amounts can be different amounts, but the periods must be spaced evenly (such as months or years). **Values** represents a range of cells. *Guess* is a number you can use to estimate the internal rate of return (and if not included, it is assumed to be 10%). If the formula gives a #NUM! error, try a different *guess*. If B1 through B6 contains the following—5000, −1000, −1500, −750, −1250, 12000 representing your original deposit, annual contributions, and the amount you took out at the end—then IRR(B1:B6)=6%.

■ MIRR(**values, finance_rate, reinvest_rate**)—Modified internal rate of return.

If you have different interest rates for the money you pay (**finance_rate**) and you receive (**reinvest_rate**), MIRR calculates the rate of return. If you borrowed $100,000 five years ago at 15% interest to start your business (enter—100,000 in B1) and earned profits of $10,000, $15,000, $30,000, $50,000, and $55,000 (entered in B2 through B6) and reinvested the profits earning 10% annually, your return would be MIRR(B1:B6, 15%, 10%)=13%.

■ NPER(**rate, pmt, pv,** *fv, type*)—Number of periods for an investment.

Calculates how many payments you would need to make if you had a loan (**pv**) at the interest **rate**, and made consistent periodic payments (**pmt**). If your loan was $100,000, your interest rate was 8% per year, and you paid $1000 per month, you would need to make 165.3 payments to pay off the loan: NPER(8%/12, −1000, 100000) = 165.3.

■ NPV(**rate, value1,** *value2, ...*)—Net present value.

Calculates how much your series of cash flows (payments received are positive values, payments made are negative values) is worth in today's dollars. PV calculates the same value, but NPV can have different amounts of cash flows (PV has to be consistent). PV can calculate based on payments at the beginning or end of the period. NPV is based on payments at the end of the period. Consider the **rate** (of discount) as inflation or the rate of a competing investment.

NPV(8%, −$1000, $500, $500, $2000) = $1370 (note the $1000 would be paid at the end of the first year).

■ PMT(**rate, nper, pv,** *fv, type*)—Payment.

Calculates periodic (for example, monthly) payments on a loan based on a constant interest rate.

PMT(6%/12, 60, 20000)=$387 (your monthly payments on that $20,000 minivan you want, even at 6% interest for 5 years).

■ PPMT(**rate, per, nper, pv,** *fv, type*)—Principal payment.

See IPMT for the interest portion of a payment. PPMT is how much of your principal you pay for the given period.

PPMT(7%/12,5,360,100000)=($83.90). You are only paying $83.90 in principal in the 5th month of your house payment (compared to $581 in interest).

■ PV(**rate, nper, pmt**, *fv, type*)—Present value.

Calculates how much your series of constant payments is worth in today's dollars (see NPV above).

PV(10%/12, 60, 100) = ($4707). If you are considering selling your car to a friend (not a good idea) and he or she offers to pay you $5,000 cash or $100 a month for 60 months and you know you could make 10% in mutual funds over that period, you should take the cash. (Even if PV was greater than 5000, maybe you should take the cash depending on how reliable your friend is.)

■ RATE(**nper, pmt, pv**, *fv, type, guess*)—Interest rate.

Calculates what the interest rate is for a loan given the number of payments (**nper**), payment amount (**pmt**), and present value (of borrowed amount). If you omit *guess*, it is assumed to be 10%. If the formula gives a #NUM! error, try a different *guess*.

RATE(360,–1200,150000)= .74% (monthly interest rate). To figure annual interest rate: .74% * 12 = 8.9%. Remember that payments (1200) above are only interest and principal and do not include taxes, insurance, and any other fees.

■ SLN(**cost, salvage, life**)—Straight-line depreciation.

Calculates how much you can depreciate an asset for each period (year) when you use a consistent amount of depreciation each year. If you buy a computer for $3000 that will have a value $300 after three years (bummer, isn't it?), you can depreciate 900 dollars per year. See DB for description of arguments.

SLN(3000, 300, 3) = $900

■ SYD(**cost, salvage, life, per**)—Sum-of-years' digits depreciation.

If you're not using straight-line depreciation, you can figure out what the depreciation is for each period (**per**). See DB for description of arguments.

SYD(3000, 300, 3, 1) = $1,350 in first year

SYD(3000, 300, 3, 2) = $900 in second year

SYD(3000, 300, 3, 3) = $450 in third year

■ VDB(**cost, salvage, life, start_period, end_period**, *factor, no_switch*)—Variable declining balance.

If you need more control over depreciation to include periods such as months, days, or any portion of time, use VDB. **Life** is the total number of periods, **start_period** is the beginning period to calculate, **end_period** is the ending period to calculate, and all must be in the same time units. *Factor* equals the rate at which the balance declines. It is assumed to be 2 (double-declining balance method if you don't include it). If *no_switch* is FALSE (the default), you to go to straight-line depreciation when depreciation is greater than the declining balance calculation.

If you buy a truck for $30,000 that has a lifetime of 10 years and salvage value of $500:

VDB(30000,500,12*10,0,1)= $500 (the first month's depreciation)

VDB(30000,500,12*10,118,120)= $348 (months 118–120 depreciation)

Date and Time Functions

When you're using date and time functions, Excel often uses the serial number of the date for an argument or to return a value. The serial number is the number of time units (usually days) since the starting point (for Excel for Windows: 1/1/1900; for Excel for the Macintosh: 1/2/1904). Excel automatically converts the date to the correct format when you open a Macintosh file on Windows. You can override this: Choose **Tools**, **Options**, Calculation tab, and check **1904 date system**. When you work with serial numbers, you will often want to format them in Date format (see **Format - Cells... Number Tab**, page 361, and use Date or Time **Category**). For some of the following examples, we're using Friday, January 1, 1999's serial number of 36161 in many cases. You can also enter a serial number as text (for example, "1/1/99" or "4:24 pm").

- DATE(**year, month, day**)—Date of given year, month, and day. Serial number of a particular date. DATE(99,12,1) = 12/1/99. (The actual value is 36495, but Excel formats this automatically.)

- DATEVALUE(**date_text**)—Date value of text. Converts a date in the form of text to a serial number, if it is in a Microsoft Excel date format.

  DATEVALUE("January 1, 1999") = 36161, which can be formatted to 1/1/99.

- DAY(**serial_number**)—Day of month.

  Converts a serial number to a day of the month. The serial_number argument can also be text.

  DAY(36161) = 1

  DAY("10-Oct-1998") = 10

  DAY("12/25/2005") = 25

- DAYS360(**start_date, end_date,** *method*)—Number of days between dates based on 360-day year. The 360-day year (12 months, 30-days each) is used in some accounting systems. *Method* is TRUE (European) or FALSE (U.S. and this is the default if not included). For the European method, starting or ending dates that occur on the 31st become equal to the 30th of the month. The United States sometimes has the ending date equal to the 1st of the next month. If cell D1 has date 1/30/97 and D2 has 2/1/97, then DAYS360(D1,D2)=1.

N O T E   To determine number of days on a normal year, use subtraction. In this example, D2-D1=2. ■

- HOUR(**serial_number**)—Hour of serial number.

  HOUR(.25) = 6 (1/4 of a day would be 6 o'clock).

- MINUTE(**serial_number**)—Minute of serial number.

  MINUTE("4:24 pm")=24

MINUTE(.2)=48

■ MONTH(**serial_number**)—Month of serial number.

MONTH(36161)=1

MONTH("5/27/89") = 5

■ NOW( )—Current date and time.

NOW( )= 36161 if today is Jan 1, 1999 (Excel would automatically enter as 1/1/99). If this is at 2 p.m. and the number is formatted with date and time, the result would be 36161.58 and formatted as 1/1/99 14:00.

■ SECOND(**serial_number**)—Second of serial number.

SECOND("5:05:25 pm") = 25

SECOND(3/(24*60*60)) = 3 (24 hours in a day * 60 minutes in an hour * 60 seconds in a minute).

■ TIME(**hour, minute, second**)—Hour of serial number.

TIME(6,30,30) = .27 (Excel automatically formats this as 6:30 AM.)

■ TIMEVALUE(**time_text**)—Time value of a text entry.

TIMEVALUE("6:30:30 AM") = .27

■ TODAY( )—Current date.

TODAY( )= 36161.00 (no hours) but would automatically be entered as 1/1/99.

■ WEEKDAY(**serial_number,** *return_type*)—Day of the week.

Returns 1 for Sun., 2 for Mon., through 7 for Sat., if *return_type* is not included or is a 1. For *return type* =2, Monday=1, Sunday=2. For *return_type* =3, Monday = 0, Saturday = 6.

WEEKDAY(36161)=6 (Friday)

WEEKDAY("12/25/2000") = 2 (Monday)

■ YEAR(**serial_number**)—Year of serial number.

YEAR(36161)=1999

YEAR("5/27/89") = 1989

Math and Trigonometry Functions

When functions ask for an array, this array can be a cell range such as B2:B10, a named range, or an array constant. Array constants include numbers in curly brackets. If the arrays consist of more than one dimension, separate the dimensions with a semicolon (;). For example, {1,2,3} is a 3-column by 1-row array and {1,2,3;4,5,6;7,8,9;10,11,12} is a 3-column by 4-row array.

■ ABS(**number**)—Absolute value.

Changes negative numbers to positive numbers (positive numbers stay positive).

ABS(–5) = 5

■ ACOS(**number**)—Arccosine.

Number is the cosine of the angle (must be between –1 and 1). The result is in radians (to convert to degrees, multiply by 180/PI( ) or use the DEGREES function).

ACOS(0.5)= 1.05

ACOS(–1)=PI( )

ACOS(1)=0

■ ACOSH(**number**)—Inverse hyperbolic cosine.

Number is greater than or equal to 1. ACOSH(COSH(**number**))=**number**.

ACOSH(1)=0

ACOSH(5)=2.29

■ ASIN(**number**)—Arcsine.

Number is angle whose sine is **number** (and must be between –1 and 1). Returned value is an angle in radians (from –PI( )/2 to PI( )/2). To convert radians to degrees, multiply by 180/PI( ) or use the DEGREES function.

ASIN(0)=0

ASIN(1)=1.57

■ ASINH(**number**)—Inverse hyperbolic sine.

ASINH(SINH(**number**))=**number**.

ASINH(0)=0

ASINH(1)=.88

■ ATAN(**number**)—Arctangent.

Number is tangent of angle. Result is in radians (from –PI( )/2 to PI( )/2). To convert radians to degrees, multiply by 180/PI( ) or use the DEGREES function.

ATAN(0)=0

ATAN(1)=.79 (formatted to 2 decimal places which is 1/4 of PI( ))

■ ATAN2(**x_num, y_num**)—Arctangent from x- and y-coordinates.

X_num and **y_num** are x- and y-coordinates of end point of line (which begins at origin (0.0)). The result is an angle given in radians between –PI( ) and PI( ).

ATAN2(0,1) = PI( )/2 (1.57 formatted to 2 decimal places)

ATAN2(1,1) = PI( )/4 (.79 formatted to 2 decimal places)

■ ATANH(**number**)—Inverse hyperbolic tangent.

Number is any number between 1 and –1. ATANH(TANH(**number**))=**number**.

ATANH(0)=0

ATANH(.5)=.55

■ CEILING(**number, significance**)—Round up to nearest multiple of **significance**.

To round up to the nearest quarter, type .25 for **significance**. See also FLOOR.

CEILING(1.13,.25)=1.25

CEILING(131,25)=150

- COMBIN(**number, number_chosen**)—Number of combinations for a given number of objects.

    Number is the number of items and **number_chosen** is the items in each combination. If you have four people and want to place two people in a group, then you have six different possible combinations. See also PERMUT.

    COMBIN(4,2)=6

    COMBIN(9,3)=84

- COS(**number**)—Cosine.

    Number is an angle in radians. To convert degrees to radians, multiply by PI( )/180 or use RADIANS function.

    COS(1)=.54

    COS(0)=1

- COSH(**number**)—Hyperbolic cosine.

    COSH(1)=1.54

- DEGREES(**angle**)—Convert radians to degrees.

    DEGREES(1)=57.30

    DEGREES(PI( ))=180

- EVEN(**number**)—Round up to the nearest even integer.

    EVEN(3.2)=4

    EVEN(6.1)=8

- EXP(**number**)—Exponent applied to base e.

    This calculates e raised to the power of a given number. The constant e is 2.71828182845904 (the base of the natural logarithm). To calculate exponents of other bases, use ^ (caret—for example, 10^2 = 100).

    EXP(1)=2.72 (this is e—formatted to 2 decimal places)

    EXP(3)=20.09

- FACT(**number**)—Factorial.

    Number is a non-negative number. Nonintegers are truncated to their integer number. A factorial is when you take the product of all numbers up to and including the number (starting with 1). The factorial of 0 is 1.

    FACT(3)=6 (1*2*3)

    FACT(8.1) = 40320 (1*2*3*4*5*6*7*8)

- FLOOR(**number, significance**)—Round down to nearest multiple of **significance**.

    To round down to the nearest quarter, type .25 for **significance**. See also CEILING.

    FLOOR(1.53,.25)=1.50

    FOOR(186,50)=150

- INT(**number**)—Integer.

The integer portion of a **number**.

INT(5.8) = 5.

- LN(**number**)—Natural logarithm.

  Number is a positive number. Natural logarithms are based on e (2.71828...).

  LN(1)=0

  LN(2.71828)=1

  LN(100)=4.61

- LOG(**number**, *base*)—Logarithm of a number.

  Number is a positive number. *Base* is the base of the logarithm and, if not included, is assumed to be 10. LOG asks *base* to the power of what equals your **number**.

  LOG(100)=2 (10^2 = 100)

  LOG(16,2)=4 (2^4 = 16)

- LOG10(**number**)—Base-10 logarithm.

  Number is a positive number. 10 to the power of what equals your **number**.

  LOG10(1000)=3

  LOG10(150)=2.18

- MDETERM(**array**)—Matrix determinant.

  Array is a numeric array with an equal number of rows and columns (no cells can be empty or contain text). MDETERM(A1:C3) = A1*(B2*C3-B3*C2) + A2*(B3*C1-B1*C3) + A3*(B1*C2-B2*C1)

  MDETERM({1,3,2;1,2,3;4,5,6}) = 9

- MINVERSE(**array**)—Matrix inverse.

  MINVERSE({1,3,2;1,2,3;4,5,6}) = −.33

- MMULT(**array1**, **array2**)—Matrix product.

  Multiply each corresponding cell in a matrix together. You will get a #VALUE! error unless the number of rows in **array1** equals the number of columns as **array2** or if any cells are empty or contain text.

  MMULT({1,3,4,1;2,4,6,8;3,1,2,2},{3,2,1;3,1,2;4,5,6;1,1,1})=29

- MOD(**number**, **divisor**)—Remainder when dividing two numbers.

  The result has the same sign as the **divisor**.

  MOD(5,2) = 1

  MOD(26,−4)=−2

- ODD(**number**)—Round up number to nearest odd integer.

  ODD(27.2)=29

- PI( )—Pi constant value.

  PI( ) = 3.14159265358979

- POWER(**number, power**)—Number raised to a power.

  You can use the ^ (caret) operator instead to also do exponentiation.

  POWER(10,2) = 100 (10^2 or 10*10)

  POWER(5,3) = 125 (5^3 or 5*5*5)

- PRODUCT(**number1,** *number2,...*)—Product of items in list.

  Multiply all items in list together.

  PRODUCT(2,4,5) = 40.

- RADIANS(**angle**)—Convert degrees to radians.

  RADIANS(180) = 3.14 (=PI( )—formatted to 2 decimal places)

  RADIANS(90) = 1.57 (=PI( )/2—formatted to 2 decimal places)

- RAND( )—Random number.

  Calculates a random number between 0 and 1. Every time a new entry is added to the worksheet, the number recalculates. (If you don't want the number to recalculate, click on **RAND( )** in the Formula bar and press **F9**.) To generate a random number between 0 and 10, use RAND( )*10. To generate a random number between 30 and 40, use RAND( )*(40–30)+30.

- ROMAN(**number,** *form*)—Roman number.

  Converts a **number** to a roman numeral. There are different types of roman numerals determined by the *form* argument (use 0–4, True, or False). If you leave off the form argument or type 0, the classic roman numeral style is used.

  ROMAN(1999)= MCMXCIX

  ROMAN(1999,4)=MIM

- ROUND(**number, num_digits**)—Round to number of digits.

  Rounds the expression to the number of places in the second argument. For **num_digits** greater than 0, the calculation is to the number of digits to the right of the decimal point. If **num_digits** is less than 0, the calculation is to the left of the decimal point.

  ROUND(345.352,1) = 345.4

  ROUND(345.352,–2) = 300

- ROUNDDOWN(**number,** *num_digits*)—Round down.

  ROUNDDOWN(345.352,1) = 345.3

  ROUNDDOWN(345,–1) = 340

- ROUNDUP(**number,** *num_digits*)—Round up.

  ROUNDUP(345.352,1) = 345.4

  ROUNDUP(345.352,–2) = 400

- SIGN(**number**)—Sign.

  If number is positive, 1. If the number is negative, –1.

  SIGN(–34) = –1

- SIN(**number**)—Sine of angle.

Number is an angle in radians. To convert degrees to radians, multiply by PI( )/180 or use RADIANS function.

SIN(1) = 0.84

SIN(0) = 0

- SINH(**number**)—Hyperbolic sine.

SINH(1)=1.18

- SQRT(**number**)—Square root.

The result times itself equals the **number**. **Number** needs to be positive or you will get the #NUM! error.

SQRT(25)=5

- SUBTOTAL(**function_num, ref1,** *ref2,*...)—Subtotal in a list.

You can also create this function using the Subtotals command (see **Data ▸ Su̱btotals,** page 414) and then edit the resulting function. Unlike the SUM function, the SUBTOTAL function ignores any subtotals in its calculation. (If you had a grand total, you could use SUBTOTAL across the whole range.) Also, if you filter data (see **Data ▸ Filter,** page 411), SUBTOTAL ignores hidden rows. (SUM does not.)

The **function_num** argument determines what kind of function you want to use (see entries for AVERAGE, COUNT, COUNTA, MAX, MIN, PRODUCT, STEDEV, STDEVP, SUM, VAR, and VARP).

SUBTOTAL(9,B4:B7) and SUBTOTAL(9,B10:B14) use the SUM function for subtotals.

SUBTOTAL(9,B4:B14) with the above subtotals still use SUM but do not include these two values so the numbers in the range will still be totaled once.

SUBTOTAL(4,B4:B14) finds the largest (MAX) number in the range.

- SUM(**number1,** *number2,*...)—Sum total.

Adds all items in a list. You can use numbers, cells, ranges, or arrays for each of the **number** arguments.

SUM(2,3,4)=9

SUM(A5:A9) is the total of all numbers in the range A5:A9.

- SUMIF(**range, criteria,** *sum_range*)—Sum for given criteria.

Criteria is a number or expression that the function uses to choose which cells to sum. For example, you could sum all the sales for those values less than 17000.

If B2:B5 includes the following values—$10,000; $20,000; $15,000; $18,000—then SUMIF(B2:B5,"<17000") = $25,000.

Sum_range is optional, but if included, this is the actual range of cells to sum. (This range corresponds to the **range**.) In the previous example, if C2:C5 includes the values 2,3,7,8, then SUMIF(B2:B5,"<17000",C2:C5) = 9.

- SUMPRODUCT(**array1, array2,** *array3,*...)—Sum product of each array.

Each array must have the same dimensions or you will get a #VALUE! error. The first cell in **array1** is multiplied by the first cell in **array2**. This result is added to the second cell in **array1** multiplied by the second cell in **array1**, and so forth.

SUMPRODUCT({1;2;3},{3;5;2})=19

■ SUMSQ(**number1,** *number2,...*) Sum of the squares.

This takes each number, squares the number, and then adds it to the square of the next number.

SUMSQ(2,3)=13

SUMSQ(1,3,5)=35

■ SUMX2MY2(**array_x, array_y**)—Sum of the difference of squares.

Both arrays have to have the same number of values (otherwise you get the #N/A error value). This takes the first cell in **array_x** and squares the value. Then it takes the first cell in **array_y**, squares the value and subtracts the two squares, and so forth. (Hint: read the formula as **Sum X^2 Minus Y^2.**)

SUMX2MY2({1;2;3},{3;5;2}) = –24

■ SUMX2PY2(**array_x, array_y**)—Sum of the sum of squares.

Both arrays have to have the same number of values (otherwise you get the #N/A error value). This takes the first cell in **array_x** and squares the value. Then it takes the first cell in **array_y**, squares the value and adds the two squares, and so forth. (Hint: read the formula as **Sum X^2 Plus Y^2.**)

SUMX2PY2({1;2;3},{3;5;2}) = 52

■ SUMXMY2(**array_x, array_y**)—Sum of squares of differences.

Both arrays have to have the same number of values (otherwise you get the #N/A error value). This takes the first cell in **array_x** and then subtracts the first cell in **array_y**. Then the formula squares this result. The formula continues with the next cells and adds the square of this difference. (Hint: read the formula as **Sum** of (**X Minus Y**)^2.)

SUMXMY2({1;2;3},{3;5;2}) = 14

■ TAN(**number**)—Tangent.

Number is an angle in radians. To convert degrees to radians, multiply by PI( )/180 or use RADIANS function. This equals SIN(**number**)/COS(**number**).

TAN(1)=1.56

■ TANH(**number**)—Hyperbolic tangent.

TANH(1)=0.76

■ TRUNC(**number,** *num_digits*)—Truncate a number to an integer.

Takes off the last part of the number. The default value for *num_digits* is 0, which means remove all decimals.

TRUNC(3.7) = 3
TRUNC(–3.723,1) = –3.7

Statistical Functions

- AVEDEV(**number1**, *number2,...*)—Average of the absolute deviations of data points from their mean.

  You can use numbers, cells, ranges, or arrays for each of the **number** arguments. This is one of the functions that gives you an idea of how much the points vary from the mean. The larger the number, the more deviation there is.

  AVEDEV(4,5,6,4,4,6,3,7)=1.125

  AVEDEV(4,4,4)=0

- AVERAGE(**number1**, *number2,...*)—Average (arithmetic mean) of list of values.

  You can use numbers, cells, ranges, or arrays for each of the **number** arguments. When you include cells with 0, the average drops because that item is counted. When you include blank cells, the average does not drop because the blank is not counted. AVERAGE(range)= SUM(range)/COUNT(range).

  If cells B1=2, B2=4, B3=6 and B4="we"

  AVERAGE(B2:B3) = 4

  AVERAGE(B2:B4) = 4

- AVERAGEA(**value1**, *value2,...*)—Average of all items.

  Average of its arguments, including numbers, text, and logical values. Unlike AVERAGE, which would exclude text in the count of items, AVERAGEA includes text in the count of items (when summing numbers, text counts as 0).

  If cells B1=2, B2=4, B3=6 and B4="we"

  AVERAGEA(B2:B3) = 4

  AVERAGEA(B2:B4) = 3

- BETADIST(**x, alpha, beta,** *A, B*)—Cumulative beta probability density.

  X is the value between A and B to evaluate. **Alpha** and **beta** are parameters to the distribution and must be greater than 0 (or you get the #NUM! error value). A and B are optional upper and lower bounds to **x**. If you don't include A and B, Excel uses the standard cumulative beta distribution (A=0 and B=1). All arguments must be a number (or you get #VALUE! error value).

  BETADIS(4,1,3,0,10) = 0.784

- BETAINV(**probability, alpha, beta,** *A, B*)—Inverse of the cumulative beta probability density.

  If BETADIST(**x**...) = **probability**, then BETAINV(**probability**...) = **x**.

  Probability is the result of the beta distribution function (BETADIST). The other arguments are the same as for BETADIST.

  BETAINV(0.784,1,3,0,10) = 4

- BINOMDIST(**number_s, trials, probablity_s, cumulative**)—Individual term binomial distribution probability.

Use BINOMDIST to calculate probability when you have two possible answers (for example, yes and no or male and female). **Number_s** is the number of times you want to test for a success in the total number of times tried (**trials**). **Probability_s** is the success for an individual trial. If **cumulative** is FALSE (probability mass function), then BINOMDIST determines the probability for getting exactly the **number_s** in the number of **trials**. If **cumulative** is TRUE, then the function will return the probability of the most successes that could happen.

BINOMDIST(1,2,0.5,FALSE) = 0.5 (the chances of getting just 1 girl in two tries is 50%).

BINOMDIST(1,2,0.5,TRUE) = 0.75 (the chances of getting 0 or 1 girls in two tries is 75%).

■ CHIDIST(**x, deg_freedom**)—One-tailed probability of the chi-squared distribution.

Both arguments need to be a number (or you get a #VALUE! error). The **deg_freedom** is degrees of freedom and has to do with your total number of responses in the sample and how many different answers are possible for each response.

CHIDIST(20,10) = .03

■ CHIINV(**probability, deg_freedom**)—Inverse of the one-tailed probability of the chi-squared distribution.

If CHIDIST(**x**...) = **probability**, then CHIDIST(**probability**...) = **x**.

CHIINV(.03,10) = 19.92

■ CHITEST(**actual_range, expected_range**)—Chi-squared distribution.

This test will help you determine how well a range of data matches an expected range of data. Both ranges have to have the same number of points. The result ranges from 0 to 1. The closer the result is to 1, the closer is the match (a 0 is no match). If you expected 100 people to answer a survey equally yes and no, the following are the chi-squared results when 49 out of 100 answer yes and 60 and of 100 answer yes.

CHITEST({49,51},{50,50}) = 0.84

CHITEST({60,40},{50,50}) = 0.05

■ CONFIDENCE(**alpha, standard_dev, size**)—Confidence interval for a population mean.

Alpha is (1—confidence level) or the significance level. **Standard_dev** is the population standard deviation (STDEVP) and **Size** is the sample size.

If our sample includes 25 students, and the average score on a test is 75 with a population standard deviation of 20, then CONFIDENCE(.05,20,25) = 7.84. Therefore we can be 95% (1-alpha) sure that the population mean is in the interval 75 +/-7.84.

■ CORREL(**array1, array2**)—Correlation coefficient.

Determines if two sets of data are related to each other. Both arrays have to have the same number of data points (or you'll get the #N/A error value). The closer to 1, the more the data is related. If the result is –1, then they are inversely related. If the result is 0, then the data sets are not related.

CORREL({1,2,3,4},{2,4,6,8}) = 1

CORREL({1,2,3,4},{8,6,4,2}) = –1

CORREL({1,2,3,4},{1,3,3,10}) = .88

- COUNT(**value1**, *value2*,...)—Count all numbers in list.

You can use numbers, cells, ranges, or arrays for each of the **number** arguments.

COUNT(A1,A2,A3) = 3 if all cells have numbers. If there is a blank or text in cell A2, then the count would be 2.

- COUNTA(**value1**, *value2*,...)—Count all items.

Counts how many values are in the list of arguments including text.

COUNT(A1,A2,A3) = 3 if the cells have any contents. If there is text in A2, the count is still 3. However, if A2 is blank, then the count is 2.

- COUNTBLANK(**range**)—Count of empty cells.

COUNTBLANK(A1,A2,A3) = 0 if all cells have any contents. If A2 is blank, then the count is 1.

- COUNTIF(**range, criteria**)—Count based on criteria.

This function counts the number of nonblank cells within a range that meet the given criteria. **Criteria** is a number or expression that the function uses to choose which cells to sum. For example, you could count all the sales for those values less than 17000. See also SUMIF.

If B2:B5 includes the following values—$10,000; $20,000; $15,000; $18,000—then COUNTIF(B2:B5,"<17000") = 2.

- COVAR(**array1**, **array2**)—Covariance (average of the products of paired deviations).

Use this function to see how two data sets are related. Both arrays need to have the same number of data points (or you'll get a #N/A error value).

COVAR({3,5,7,9},{5,6,9,11})=5.25

- CRITBINOM(**trials, probability_s, alpha**)—Cumulative binomial distribution.

Trials is the number of Bernoulli trials, **probability_s** is probability of success, and **alpha** is the criterion value.

CRITBINOM(8,0.33,0.75)=4

- DEVSQ(**number1**, *number2*,...)—Sum of squares of deviations.

You can use numbers, cells, ranges, or arrays for each of the **number** arguments. If all numbers are the same, then there would be no deviation.

DEVSQ({5,5,5,5})=0

DEVSQ({4.5,5.5,5,5.25}) = .55

- EXPONDIST(**x, lambda, cumulative**)—Exponential distribution.

X and **lambda** need to be positive values (or you'll get the #NUM! error value). **Cumulative** is TRUE (cumulative distribution function) or FALSE (probability density function).

EXPONDIST(0.5,5,FALSE) = 0.41

■ FDIST(**x, deg_freedom1, deg_freedom2**)—F probability distribution.

Use this function to see if two sets of data vary differently.

All arguments must be numbers (or you'll get the #VALUE! error value).

FDIST(25,10,2)=0.04

■ FINV(**probability, deg_freedom1, deg_freedom2**)—Inverse of the F probability distribution.

If the FDIST(**x**...) = **probability**, then FINV(**probability**...) = **x**.

All arguments must be numbers (or you'll get the #VALUE! error value).

FINV(.04,10,2)=24.40

■ FISHER(**x**)—Fisher transformation.

X is the correlation coefficient and must be a number (or you'll get the #VALUE! error value) and between –1 and 1 (or you'll get the #NUM! error value).

FISHER(0.88)=1.38

■ FISHERINV(**y**)—Inverse of the Fisher transformation.

Y must be a number (or you'll get the #VALUE! error value). If **y**=FISHER(**x**), then **x**=FISHERINV(**y**).

FISHERINV(1.38) = 0.88

■ FORECAST(**x, known_y's, known_x's**)—Forecast of a value along a linear trend.

Assuming you have a line where each y (in **known_y's**) is plotted against a given x (in **known_x's**), find the value of y given a new **x**. **Known_y's** and **known_x's** must have the same number of data points (or you'll get the #N/A error value). Say that sales have been rising at a constant rate for the last five years. You can make a forecast for the eighth year (assuming that the trend continues).

FORECAST(8,{2,4,6,8,10},{1,2,3,4,5})=16

■ FREQUENCY(**data_array, bins_array**)—A frequency distribution as a vertical array.

You can count the values that fall between—range of numbers.

Suppose you have the following test scores: 75, 71, 77, 89, 88, 98, 76, 88, 62, 91 in cells F3:F12—and you want to count how many fall in the following categories—0–69, 70–79, 80–89, 90–99. In cells G3:G6, type **69, 79, 89, 99**. Then place the cell pointer in H3 and type **=FREQUENCY(F3:F12, G3:G6)** and press **Ctrl+Shift+Enter** to enter the formula as an array. The result will show 1,4,3,2 in cells H3 through H6.

■ FTEST(**array1, array2**)—F-test.

This function tests the variances of both arrays (how much they deviate from the mean) and compares the two variances. If both data sets vary by the same amount, the result is 1. If one data set has a large variation compared to the other, you'll get a number closer to 0. You have to have 2 or more data points in each array and the variance of both arrays cannot be 0 (or you'll get the #DIV/0! error value).

FTEST({500,500,500,500,502},{40,40,40,40,42}) = 1

FTEST({500,500,500,500,502},{41,45,42,43,42}) = .33

- **GAMMADIST(x, alpha, beta, cumulative)**—Gamma distribution.

  X, alpha, and **beta** need to be numbers (or you get the #VALUE! error value). **Cumulative** is TRUE (cumulative distribution function) or FALSE (probability mass function). The data can be skewed (and not perfectly normal).

  GAMMADIST(15,10,3,FALSE) = 0.012

  GAMMADIST(15,10,3,TRUE) = 0.032

- **GAMMAINV(probability, alpha, beta)**—Inverse of the gamma cumulative distribution.

  If **probability** = GAMMADIST(**x**...), then GAMMAINV(**probability**...) = **x**.

  GAMMAINV(0.032,10,3) = 15.01

- **GAMMALN(x)**—Natural logarithm of the gamma function, G(x).

  X needs to be a number (or you'll get a #VALUE! error value) and greater than 0 (or you'll get a #NUM! error value).

  GAMMALN(3) = 0.69

- **GEOMEAN(number1, *number2*, ...)**—Geometric mean.

  Unlike the arithmetic mean (AVERAGE), none of the **numbers** can be less than or equal to 0 (or you'll get a #NUM! error value). The GEOMEAN is calculated by multiplying all the numbers and taking the *n*th root of the result (*n* is the number of items in the list). The GEOMEAN is always equal to or less than the AVERAGE.

  GEOMEAN(2,4,6) = 3.63

- **GROWTH(known_y's, *known_x's, new_x's, const*)**—Forecast values along an exponential trend.

  Given **known_y** values (in the equation y = b*m^x), you can optionally add *known_x* values. *New_x's* are x-values for which you want Excel to calculate the corresponding y-values. Type **TRUE** for the *const* to have Excel calculate the b constant of the line (b) normally, otherwise type **FALSE** to set the b value to 1.

  GROWTH({1,3,7,11}) = 1.17

- **HARMEAN(number1, *number2*, ...)**—Harmonic mean.

  Unlike the arithmetic mean (AVERAGE), none of the numbers can be less than or equal to 0 (or you'll get a #NUM! error value). The HARMEAN is calculated by taking 1/**number1** + 1/*number2*, and so on and taking the reciprocal of this result and multiplying it by the number of items in the list. This is always equal to or less than the GEOMEAN.

  HARMEAN(2,4,6) = 3.27

- **HYPGEOMDIST(sample_s, number_sample, population_s, number_population)**—Hypergeometric distribution.

  The result is the probability of the sample response (**sample_s**), given the size of the sample (**number_sample**), population response (**population_s**), and size of the population (**number_population**). The response is either yes or no (success or failure). All arguments have to be a number (or you'll get the #VALUE! error value). Because you need to know both the total population and the population response rate, it is advantageous to work with a small population. Given that there are 50 males in the senior class of 90 students, there is a 21% probability that a random group of 9 students will have 4 males.

HYPGEOMDIST(4,9,50,90) = 21%

■ INTERCEPT(**known_y's, known_x's**)—Intercept of the linear regression line.

This function calculates where the line plotted through the **known_x** and **known_y** values will cross the y-axis (when x = 0). You can use numbers, cells, ranges, or arrays for each of the arguments. However, both arguments must contain the same number of data points (or you'll get a #N/A error value).

INTERCEPT({50,60,70,80},{1,2,3,4}) = 40

■ KURT(**number1,** *number2, ...*)—Kurtosis of a data set.

This describes how peaked (positive result) or flat (negative result) the distribution is relative to a normal distribution. You can use numbers, cells, ranges, or arrays for each of the **number** arguments. You need at least 4 data points (or you'll get a #DIV/0! error value).

KURT({1,3,3,3,5}) = 2

KURT({1,1,2,3,4,5}) = –1.5

■ LARGE(**array, k**)—K-th largest value.

K has to be greater than 0 and less than or equal to the number of items. LARGE (array, 1) is the same as the maximum (MAX) while LARGE(array, number of items) = smallest number (MIN). See also SMALL.

LARGE({11,12,13,14,15,16,17,18},2) = 17 (the second largest number).

LARGE({11,12,13,14,15,16,17,18},5) = 14 (fifth largest number).

■ LINEST(**known_y's,** *known_x's, const, stats*)—Least squares array that describes a straight line.

Each **known_y** can be dependent on multiple *known_x's*. If not included, *known_x's* are assumed to be 1,2,3,4,... (through the number of **known_y's**). If *const* is not included or TRUE, b (the y-intercept) is calculated normally. If *const* is FALSE, the line crosses the y-axis at 0. If *stats* is TRUE, return additional statistics such as standard error values and regression of sum of the square. Before you create the function, select a range, define the function, and press **Ctrl+Shift+Enter**.

Select one cell in each of two columns, type =**LINEST({3,5,7,9},{1,2,3,4})**, and press **Ctrl+Shift+Enter**. Excel enters a 2 in the first cell and 1 in the cell to the right (the slope of the line (m) = 2 and a y-intercept (b) = 1 [the line equation is y = mx + b].

■ LOGEST(**known_y's,** *known_x's, const, stats*)—Parameters of an exponential trend.

The arguments are the same as LINEST but LOGEST calculates an exponential curve to fit the data.

LOGEST({3,5,7,9},{1,2,3,4}) would place 1.44 and 2.34 in the first two cells.

■ LOGINV(**probability, mean, standard_dev**)—Inverse of the lognormal distribution.

If **probability** = LOGNORMDIST(**x**...), then LOGINV(**probability**...) = **x**. **Probability** is the probability associated with the lognormal distribution. **Mean** and **standard_dev** are the mean and standard deviation of the natural logarithm of **x**. All arguments must be numbers (or you'll get a #VALUE! error value).

LOGINV(0.10,5,2.1) = 10.06

■ LOGNORMDIST(**x, mean, standard_dev**)—Cumulative lognormal distribution.

X is the value to evaluate, **mean** and **standard_dev** are the mean and standard deviation of the natural logarithm of **x**. All arguments must be numbers (or you'll get a #VALUE! error value).

LOGNORMDIST(10,5,2.1) = 0.10

■ MAX(**number1,** *number2, ...*)—Maximum.

The function finds the largest item in the list. You can use numbers, cells, ranges, or arrays for each of the **number** arguments. Any text is not included.

MAX(7,9,3) = 9.

■ MAXA(**value1,** *value2, ...*)—Maximum of all items.

Maximum value in a list of arguments, including numbers, text, and logical values. Any text counts as 0. If –1, –3, –4, "dog" are in cells A1:A4, then

MAXA(A1:A4) = 0.

■ MEDIAN(**number1,** *number2, ...*)—Median.

50% of the numbers are above the result and 50% are below. If there are an even number of values, the result is the average of the two middle values. You can use numbers, cells, ranges, or arrays for each of the **number** arguments.

MEDIAN({1,1,1,1,5,6,7,8,9}) = 5

MEDIAN({1,1,1,1,5,7,8,9,10,11}) = 6

■ MIN(**number1,** *number2, ...*)—Minimum.

The function finds the smallest item in the list. You can use numbers, cells, ranges, or arrays for each of the **number** arguments. Any text is not included.

MIN(3,4,1) = 1.

■ MINA(**value1,** *value2, ...*)—Minimum of all items.

Smallest value in a list of arguments, including numbers, text, and logical values.

Any text counts as 0. If 1, 3, 4, "dog" are in cells A1:A4, then

MINA(A1:A4) = 0.

■ MODE(**number1,** *number2, ...*)—Mode.

The most common value in the data.

MODE({1,1,1,3,3,6,7,8,9}) = 1

■ NEGBINOMDIST(**number_f, number_s, probability_s**)—Negative binomial distribution.

Given the **probability_s** of success for each trial, this function calculates the probability that there will be **number_f** failures before the **number_s** success. The difference with BINOMDIST is that in NEGBINOMDIST the number of trials is variable and the number of successes is fixed. All arguments must be numbers (or you'll get the #VALUE! error value). **Probability_s** must be between 0 and 1 (or you'll get the #NUM! error value).

If your probability of hitting the nail on the head is 90%, and it takes 10 successful hits to sink the nail, what is the probability of hitting your finger once before all 10 hits?

NEGBINOMDIST(1,10,90%) = 35% (you at least better wear a glove).

■ NORMDIST(**x, mean, standard_dev, cumulative**)—Normal cumulative distribution.

X is the value you want to test, **mean** is the arithmetic mean (AVERAGE) of the distribution and **standard_dev** (STDDEV) of the distribution. **Cumulative** is TRUE (cumulative distribution function—adding probabilities) or FALSE (probability mass function—one time probability). If **mean** = 0 and **stardard_dev** = 1, then this is the standard normal distribution (NORMSDIST). All arguments must be numbers (or you'll get the #VALUE! error value).

If the mean height of all men is 70 inches, and the standard deviation is 10 inches, what is the probability that a man would be any height up to 50 inches?

NORMDIST(50,70,10,TRUE) = 0.023

■ NORMINV(**probability, mean, standard_dev**)—Inverse of the normal cumulative distribution.

All arguments must be numbers (or you'll get the #VALUE! error value). **Probability** must be between 0 and 1 (or you'll get the #NUM! error value).

If **probability** = NORMDIST(**x**...), then **x**=NORMINV(**probability**).

NORMDIST(0.023,70,10,TRUE) = 50.05

■ NORMSDIST(**z**)—Standard normal cumulative distribution.

This is the same function as NORMDIST except the mean is 0 and standard deviation is 1.

NORMSDIST(0.5) = 0.69

■ NORMSINV(**probability**)—Inverse of the standard normal cumulative distribution.

If **probability** = NORMSDIST(**z**), then **z**=NORMSINV(**probability**). **Probability** must be a number (or you'll get the #VALUE! error value) and between 0 and 1 (or you'll get the #NUM! error value).

NORMSINV(0.69) = 0.5

■ PEARSON(**array1, array2**)—Pearson product moment correlation coefficient.

This function measures the linear relationship between two sets of data. Both arrays must have the same number of data points (or you'll get the #N/A error value). You can use numbers, cells, ranges, or arrays for each of the **array** arguments. The result ranges from –1 to 1 (for strong negative or positive correlation). If the result is 0, then there is no correlation.

PEARSON({1,2,3,4,5},{2,4,6,8,10}) = 1

PEARSON({1,2,3,4,5},{10,9,8,7,6}) = –1

PEARSON({1,2,3,4,5},{2,1,6,3,2}) = 0.16

- PERCENTILE(**array, k**)—K-th percentile of values in a range.

  This is similar to the LARGE and SMALL functions, but this estimates the result within the percentile. **K** must be a number (or you'll get the #VALUE! error value) between 0 and 1 (or you'll get the #NUM! error value).

  PERCENTILE({1,2,3,4,5},10%) = 1.4

  PERCENTILE({1,2,3,4,5}, 90%) = 4.6

- PERCENTRANK(**array, x,** *significance*)—Percentage rank of a value in a data set.

  Use this function to find what percent **x** is within the **array**. *Significance* is optional and determines the number of decimal places to use (if not included, it is 3).

  PERCENTRANK({97,89,76,90,32,57,88,91,77,50},90,2) = 0.77 (which means given these test scores, a 90 is only in the 77th percentile).

  PERCENTRANK({97,89,76,90,32,57,88,91,77,50},92,2) = 0.9 (however, a 92 is in the 90 percentile).

- PERMUT(**number, number_chosen**)—Permutations for a given number of objects.

  This function is similar to COMBIN. In PERMUT the order of the items is important. In COMBIN it is not. Both arguments need to be a number (or you'll get the #VALUE! error value).

  PERMUT(32,4) = 863,040 (If your lottery requires you to get 4 numbers in the correct order and each number can be from 1 to 32, then your chances of getting a winning ticket are 1 in 863 thousand. Buy stock instead.)

- POISSON(**x, mean, cumulative**)—Poisson distribution.

  X is the number of events, and **mean** is the arithmetic average of events happening in a given time period. If **cumulative** is TRUE, then cumulative Poisson probability (adding probabilities from 0 to **x**). If **cumulative** is FALSE, then Poisson probability mass function (probability for just **x**). **X** and **mean** need to be numbers (or you'll get the #VALUE! error value).

  If the average number of people that go into the mall on a Tuesday is 6 per minute, what is the probability that 4 will go in on this Tuesday in a minute?

  POISSON(4,6,TRUE) = 0.29 (there will only be 0–4 people)

  POISSON(4,6,FALSE) = 0.13 (there will be exactly 4)

- PROB(**x_range, prob_range, lower_limit,** *upper_limit*)—Probability that values in a range are within two limits.

  X_range is a series of values each related to a probability in the **prob_range**. If *upper_limit* is not included, the probability is just for the value of the **lower_limit**. Otherwise, the probability is for values between the two limits.

  The values in the **prob_range** have to be between 0 and 1 and total 1 (or you'll get the #VALUE! error value).

  PROB({0,1,2,4},{0.3,0.2,0.4,0.1},2) = 0.2

  PROB({0,1,2,4},{0.3,0.2,0.4,0.1},3) = 0

  PROB({0,1,2,4},{0.3,0.2,0.4,0.1},1,2) = 0.6

■ QUARTILE(**array, quart**)—Quartile of a data set.

There are four quartiles (25 percent proportions) in a population. This function finds the value for each of the quartiles. The values for **quart** are as follows: 0 (minimum = MIN), 1 (first quartile—25th percentile), 2 (second quartile—50th percentile = MEDIAN), 3 (third quartile—75th percentile), and 4 (maximum value or 100 percent = MAX). If **quart** isn't one of these values, then you get the #NUM! error value. You can use a range or array for the **array** argument.

QUARTILE({71,73,74,85,87,89,90,93,93,95},1) = 76.75

■ RANK(**number, ref,** *order*)—Rank of a number in a list of numbers.

This function returns the position of the item if the list were sorted. **Number** is the item in the list you want to check and **ref** is the range or array of numbers. If *order* is 0 or not included, the largest number would be ranked first. If *order* is any nonzero number, the smallest number would be ranked first. If you have duplicates, they are ranked the same, but subsequent numbers would skip the number of duplicates there are. If the range A1:A6 contain the numbers 10, 5, 6, 3, 11, and 12, then

RANK(6,A1:A6) = 4 (4th highest value)

RANK(6,A1:A6,1) = 3 (3rd lowest value)

■ RSQ(**known_y's, known_x's**)—R-squared (square of the Pearson product moment correlation coefficient).

The RSQ function gives you an idea of how much of the **known_y's** variability is due to the variability in **known_x's**. The closer to 1, the more you can explain the **known_y** variability due to **known_x**. If the result is 0, there is no correlation. Both arguments need the same number of data points (or you'll get the #N/A error value).

RSQ({2,4,6,8,10},{1,2,3,4,5}) = 1

RSQ({2,4,6,8,10},{1,2,6,3,5}) = 0.47

■ SKEW(**number1,** *number2, ...*)—Skewness of a distribution.

A normal distribution is symmetrical around the mean. SKEW measures how asymmetrical the distribution is. A tailing of responses may be toward the values greater than the mean (positive skew) or toward the values less than the mean (negative skew). You can use numbers, cells, ranges, or arrays for each of the **number** arguments. You need at least three values and some variance in the data (or you'll get the #DIV/0! error value).

SKEW(1,2,2,2,3,3,4,5,6) = 0.68

SKEW(1,2,2,3,3,3,4,4,5) = 0 (normal distribution)

■ SLOPE(**known_y's, known_x's**)—Slope of the linear regression line.

This function returns the rate of change along the line (the vertical distance between two points divided by the horizontal distance). The arguments can be ranges or arrays and need the same number of data points (or you'll get the #N/A error value).

SLOPE({2,4,6,8,10},{1,2,3,4,5}) = 2

■ SMALL(**array, k**)—K-th smallest value in a data set.

K has to be greater than 0 and less than or equal to the number of items. SMALL(array, 1) is the same as the smallest (MIN) while SMALL(array, number of items) = largest number (MAX). See also LARGE.

SMALL({11,12,13,14,15,16,17,18},2) = 12 (the second smallest number).

SMALL({11,12,13,14,15,16,17,18},5) = 15

■ STANDARDIZE(**x, mean, standard_dev**)—Normalized value.

This function tells how many standard deviation units away from the **mean x** is given the **standard_dev** of the distribution.

STANDARDIZE(47,50,1.5) = –2

■ STDEV(**number1,** *number2, ...*)—Sample standard deviation.

The standard deviation measures how widely the sample data varies from the mean (AVERAGE). You can use numbers, cells, ranges, or arrays for each of the **number** arguments. Text and logical values (TRUE and FALSE) are counted as blanks and are not included. The data assumes that the arguments are part of a sample of a larger population. If your data is the entire population, then use STDEVP. The average of the values in the example that follows is 4. The standard deviation tells us that if the sample is a normal distribution, 2/3 of the data is 1 standard deviation above and below the mean 4+/–1.6 (2.4 to 5.6). For larger samples, 95% of the data is within 2 standard deviations and 99% of the data is within 3 standard deviations.

STDEV(1,2,2,3,3,3,4,4,4,5,5,5,6,6,7) = 1.63.

■ STDEVA(**value1,** *value2, ...*)—Sample standard deviation of all items.

This is the same as STDEV except numbers, text, and logical values are included. Text counts as 0s. TRUE counts as 1 and FALSE counts as 0.

If all the values in the STDEV example are in cells and the first cell's contents is TRUE, then the STDEVA would equal STDEV.

■ STDEVP(**number1,** *number2, ...*)—Population standard deviation.

This function is the same as STDEV except that the arguments here assume that this is the entire population you are looking at (not a sample). You can use numbers, cells, ranges, or arrays for each of the **number** arguments.

STDEVP(1,2,2,3,3,3,4,4,4,5,5,5,6,6,7) = 1.58.

■ STDEVPA(**value1,** *value2, ...*)—Population standard deviation of all items.

This is the same as STDEVP except numbers, text, and logical values are included. Text counts as 0s. TRUE counts as 1 and FALSE counts as 0.

If all the values in the STDEVP example are in cells and the first cell's contents is TRUE, then the STDEVPA would equal STDEVP.

■ STEYX(**known_y's, known_x's**)—Standard error of the predicted y-value for each x in the regression.

Each set of values must have the same number of data points (or you'll get the #N/A error value). If the two samples are 100% correlated (they have an RSQ of 1), then you get the error value #DIV/0!. This function gives you an estimate of how each y value varies around the predicted line.

STEYX({1,2,3,4,5,6},{2,4,5,6,8,10})= 0.27

■ TDIST(**x, deg_freedom, tails**)—Student's t-distribution.

This function is to test your hypothesis for small samples. Use this function instead of looking up a t-value in a t-distribution table. The result will tell you the level of significance for the t-value. **X** is the t-value to evaluate and **deg_freedom** is the degrees of freedom (determined by the number of items and formulas). **Tails** is either 1 or 2. 1 is for a one-tailed distribution test and 2 is for two-tailed distribution. All arguments must be numeric (or you'll get the #VALUE! error value). The **deg_freedom** must be greater than 1 (or you'll get the #NUM! error value).

TDIST(2.447,6,2) = 0.05

■ TINV(**probability, deg_freedom**)—Inverse of the Student's t-distribution.

If **probablity**=TDIST(**x**...), then **x**=TINV(**probability**). **Probability** is the probability associated with the two-tailed Student's t-distribution.

TINV(0.05,6) = 2.447

■ TREND(**known_y's,** *known_x's, new_x's, const*)—Predict new values for a trend line.

Given a set of *known_x* independent data (if not included is 1,2,3, etc.) and the **known_y** dependent data, what will the new y values be for each *new_x*? If *const* is FALSE, the place where the line crosses the y-axis is 0. Otherwise if *const* is TRUE or not included, then b (the y-intercept is calculated normally). Before you create the formula, select a range with as many values as *new_x's*, create the formula, and press **Ctrl+Shift+Enter**.

In the example, the first 9 numbers represent the last 9 months of computer prices. The second set of numbers (10–12) request that the formula make a prediction for the next three months. Select three cells and press **Ctrl+Shift+Enter** to display the results of 2821, 2782, and 2744.

TREND({3150;3125;3115;3110;3000;2900;2950;2900;2875},,{10;11;12})

■ TRIMMEAN(**array, percent**)—Mean of the interior of a data set.

Use this function to calculate a mean when you want to remove outlyers (data that is at the top or bottom extremes). **Percent** is what proportion from the data to remove from the top and from the bottom.

TRIMMEAN({0,11,12,13,14,15,16,17,18,1000},.1)=14.5

■ TTEST(**array1, array2, tails, type**)—Probability associated with a Student's t-test.

This is to test whether two samples are likely to have come from the two populations with the same mean.

Each **array** can be a range, range name, or array. **Tails** is either 1 or 2. 1 is for a one-tailed distribution test and 2 is for two-tailed distribution. There are three **type**s of t-tests: 1 = paired, 2 = two-sample equal variance, and 3 = two-sample unequal variance.

TTEST({0,1,1,1,1,1,2,2,3,6},{0,1,1,1,1,1,2,2,3,7},2,2) = .90

■ VAR(**number1,** *number2,...*)—Sample variance.

The variance is the square of the standard deviation and also measures how much data is dispersed about the mean.

You can use numbers, cells, ranges, or arrays for each of the **number** arguments.

VAR({0,1,1,1,1,1,2,2,3,6}) = 2.84

■ VARA(**value1**, *value2*, ...)—Sample variance of all items.

This is the same as VAR except numbers, text, and logical values are included. Text counts as 0. TRUE counts as 1 and FALSE counts as 0.

If all the values in the VAR example are in cells and the first cell's contents is FALSE, then VARA would equal VAR.

■ VARP(**number1**, *number2*,...)—Population variance.

This function is the same as STDEV except that the arguments here assume that this is the entire population you are looking at (not a sample). You can use numbers, cells, ranges, or arrays for each of the **number** arguments.

VARP({0,1,1,1,1,1,2,2,3,6}) = 2.56

■ VARPA(**value1**, *value2*, ...)—Population variance of all items.

This is the same as VARP except numbers, text, and logical values are included. Text counts as 0. TRUE counts as 1 and FALSE counts as 0.

If all the values in the VARP example are in cells and the first cell's contents is FALSE, then VARPA would equal VARP.

■ WEIBULL(**x, alpha, beta, cumulative**)—Weibull distribution.

This gives you an idea how reliable your equipment is (how long until it fails).

If **cumulative** is TRUE, then this adds probabilities from 0 to **x**. If **cumulative** is FALSE, then this is just the probability for **x**.

X, **alpha**, and **beta** all need to be numbers (or you'll get the #VALUE! error value).

WEIBULL(50,10,50,TRUE) = 0.63

■ ZTEST(**array, x,** *sigma*)—Two-tailed P-value of a z-test.

This test returns a standard score showing the likelihood a value (**x**) is part of a particular population defined by the **array**. *Sigma* is the known population standard deviation. If you don't include it, then Excel uses the sample standard deviation of the **array**.

ZTEST({1,1,1,2,2,2,3,4},2) = 0.5

Lookup and Reference Functions

■ ADDRESS(**row_num, column_num,** *abs_num, a1, sheet_text*)—Single cell text reference on a worksheet.

Row_num is the row number and **column_num** is the column number (A=1, B=2, etc.). *Abs_num* tells whether to return an absolute (1—the default); absolute row, relative column (2); relative row, absolute column (3); or relative (4) reference. If *a1* is TRUE or not included, then the reference is in the A1 style. If *a1* is FALSE, then the reference is in R1C1 style. If desired, use *sheet_text* to refer to the name of the sheet.

ADDRESS(1,2) = "$B$1"

ADDRESS(1,2,3) = "$B1"

ADDRESS(1,2,3,FALSE) = "R[1]C2"

ADDRESS(1,2,1,FALSE, "Sheet1") = "Sheet1!R1C2"

ADDRESS(1,2,1,TRUE, "[Budget.xls]Sheet1") = "[Budget.xls]Sheet1!B1"

■ AREAS(**reference**)—Areas in a reference.

Reference can be range address(es) or a range name. If you have more than one range, enclose the whole reference in parentheses, so Excel doesn't think there are multiple arguments.

AREAS((A1:B5,C3,E7:E9,database)) = 4 (if database is one contiguous range).

■ CHOOSE(**index_num, value1**, *value2*)—Choose a value from a list.

Index_num determines which **value** (**value1**, *value2*, and so on) to return. You can have up to 29 values in the list. If **Index_num** is greater than the last value, you get a #VALUE! error value.

CHOOSE(3,"Sun","Mon","Tue","Wed","Thu","Fri","Sat") = "Tue"

SUM(B2:CHOOSE(3,B5,B8,B14)) = SUM(B2:B14) which will return the sum of this range

■ COLUMN(*reference*)—Column number.

COLUMN(B20) = 2

COLUMN(D5) = 4

COLUMN() = 1 (returns column of active cell—if in A3, returns 1)

Select three horizontal cells, type **=COLUMN(B2:D3)** and press **Ctrl+Shift+Enter** and 2, 3, and 4 will be displayed in the three cells.

■ COLUMNS(**array**)—Number of columns.

Array can be a range of cells or array formula.

COLUMNS(B6:F18) = 5

COLUMNS({11,12,34;32,4,5}) = 3

■ HLOOKUP(**lookup_value, table_array, row_index_num**, *range_lookup*)—Horizontal lookup. Figure 3.38 shows an HLOOKUP range.

Figure 3.38
Range for HLOOKUP.

	A	B	C	D
1		1	5	10
2	727	40	55	62
3	737	50	65	72
4	747	60	75	82
5	767	70	85	92
6	DC10	80	95	102
7	L1011	90	105	112
8	A310	100	115	122

HLOOKUP(1,A1:D8,7,FALSE) = 90

HLOOKUP(6,A1:D8,3,TRUE) = 65

Lookup_value is the column label to look for (in the first row). In the first example, Excel looks for a 1 (in B1) and then looks down that column (7 rows). In the second example, Excel looks for a 6. Because *range_lookup* is TRUE, then Excel doesn't have to match values exactly and looks for the next lowest value (which is 5 in C1). If *range_lookup* were FALSE, Excel would have to find an exact match. Because it would not find a match, the #N/A error value would display. If you use FALSE, the columns need to be in ascending order (see **Data ▪ Sort** and click the **Options** button and choose **Sort left to right**, page 410).

Table_array is the table you use to look up the values. This table includes the row and column headings in the first row and first column. In the example it is the range A1:D8.

Row_index is the number of the row you want to look in. Starting from the top of **table_array** (including the column headings), count down. In the first formula, come down to row 7 (L1011). In the second formula, come to row 3 (737). Find the intersection of this row and the **lookup_value** column.

■ HYPERLINK(**link_location,** *friendly_name*)—Hyperlink.

It is easier to use **Insert ▪ Hyperlink** (see page 360) to create a hyperlink, but you can also use this function to create a shortcut that opens a document stored on a network server, an intranet, or the Internet. **Link_location** is the name of the URL or path (including network server). The path includes the filename and can include a location in the document (such as a range name in Excel or bookmark in Word). *Friendly_name* is optional and, if included, displays whatever text you type. Otherwise, the path or URL is displayed.

HYPERLINK("c:\data\stats.xls")—open stats.xls from hard drive

HYPERLINK("[c:\data\stats.xls]Pearson!F10")—open and go to Pearson sheet and select cell **F10**

HYPERLINK("[c:\data\stats.xls]Database")—open and select Database range

HYPERLINK("\\finance\stats.xls")—open from shared network folder finance

HYPELINK("c:\data\stats.xls","Click to open file")—show "Click to open file" for hyperlink

HYPERLINK("http://www.prw.com/reports/stats.xls")—open from Internet (from location **www.prw.com/reports**)

■ INDEX(**array,** *row_num, column_num, area_num*)—choose a value from a reference or array.

Array is a range of cells or array constant. Use *row_num* and *column_num* to find the row and column intersection to return a value. Use 0 for either of the arguments to return the entire row or column as an array when you press **Ctrl+Shift+Enter**). If you have multiple ranges in the **array**, enclose them in parentheses and type the number of the range in *area_num*.

If you are using the HLOOKUP example (refer to Figure 3.38),

INDEX(A1:D8,7,1) = "L1011"

INDEX(A1:D8,7,3) = 105

Select four horizontal cells, type **=INDEX(A1:D8,7,0)** and press **Ctrl+Shift+Enter** and the values "L1011", 90, 105, and 112 appear in these cells.

INDEX((A1:D5,A8:D8),1,1,2) = "A310"

You can also use the INDEX function to return a reference.

SUM(B7:INDEX(A1:D8,7,3)) = SUM(B7:C7) which will return 195

- INDIRECT(**ref_text,***a1*)—Reference indicated by a text value.

  Ref_text is a cell (a1 or R1C1 style reference), range name, or reference to cell as text string. If **ref_text** is not a valid cell reference, you'll get #REF!. If *a1* is TRUE or not included, then **ref_text** is an A1-style reference. If it is FALSE, **ref_text** is an R1C1 reference. If the referred cell contains the name of a cell or one cell range name, then the result is the value of the referred cell or range name.

  If the "B2" is in A1, 1.45 is in B2, "Planes" is in B3, and 3.5 is in B4,

  INDIRECT(A1) = 1.45.

  Change A1 to be "B3" and INDIRECT(A1) = "Planes"

  Change A1 to be "R4C2" and INDIRECT(A1,FALSE) = 3.5

- LOOKUP(**lookup_value, lookup_vector, result_vector**)—Lookup value.

  Lookup_value is a number, text, logical value or range name. **Lookup_vector** is either a row or column of data where the **lookup_value** will be checked and needs to be sorted in ascending order (see **Data ➔ Sort**, page 410). **Result_vector** is the same size as the **lookup_vector**. Excel searches in the **lookup_vector** for the **lookup_value**. If there is a match, the result will be the same row or column in the **result_vector**. It there is no match, Excel goes to the next smallest value in the **lookup_vector** and displays the corresponding value from the **result_vector**. If the **lookup_value** is smaller than the smallest **lookup_vector** value, then #N/A is displayed. You can also use the Lookup Wizard to lead you through the process of finding values (see **Tools ➔ Wizard ➔ Lookup**, page 408). Figure 3.39 shows a LOOKUP range.

Figure 3.39
Range for LOOKUP.

	A	B
1	Score	Grade
2	10	F
3	68.125	D
4	77.250	C
5	89.500	B
6	100.000	A

LOOKUP(79,A2:A6,B2:B6) = "C"

LOOKUP(9,A2:A6,B2:B6) = #N/A (the scores only go down to 10)

■ MATCH(**lookup_value, lookup_array,** *match_type*)—Match value in array.

Whereas LOOKUP, VLOOKUP, or HLOOKUP gives you a value, MATCH gives you the position of an item in the range instead of the item itself. **Lookup_value** is the value you want to look up. **Lookup_array** is the location where you're looking up something. *Match_type* is one of three values. Use 1 (the default if not included) for *match_type* to find the largest value less than or equal to the **lookup_value** (**lookup_array** needs to be in ascending order). Use 0 for *match_type* to find an exact match. Use –1 for *match_type* to find the smallest value that is greater than or equal to the **lookup_value** (**lookup_array** needs to be in descending order).

Using the figure in the LOOKUP example (refer to Figure 3.39),

MATCH(79,A2:A6,1) = 3 (3rd item in list)

MATCH("E",B2:B6,–1) = 1

MATCH(89.5,A2:A6,0) = 4

MATCH(79,A2:A6,–1) = #N/A (because *match_type* of –1 requires A2:A6 to be in descending order)

■ OFFSET(**reference, rows, cols,** *height, width*)—Reference offset from a given reference.

The result will be a range that is the number of **rows** and **cols** away from the original **reference**. You can optionally include the number of rows in the new range with *height* and number of columns in the new range with *width*.

If cells A4 through A7 have the values 2, 4, 6, and 8,

OFFSET(A1,3,0) = 2 (this displays the value of cell A4)

OFFSET(A7,–1,0) = 6 (the value of A6)

SUM(OFFSET(A1,3,0,4,1)) = 20 (The reference A4:A7 is returned by the OFFSET function and so the formula becomes SUM(A4:A7) which is 20.)

■ ROW(**reference**)—Row number.

ROW(B20) = 20

ROW(D5) = 5

ROW() = 3 (returns row of active cell—if in A3, returns 3)

Select two vertical cells, type **=ROW(B2:D3)** and press **Ctrl+Shift+Enter,** and 2 and 3 will be display in the two cells.

■ ROWS(**array**)—Number of rows.

Array can be a range of cells or array formula.

ROWS(B6:F18) = 13

ROWS({11,12,34;32,4,5}) = 2

■ TRANSPOSE(**array**)—Transpose an array.

Change a horizontal array to vertical and vice versa.

If A1:D1 contain 2, 4, 6, and 8, and you select cells A4:A7, type in **=TRANSPOSE (A1:D1)** and press **Ctrl+Shift+Enter.** 2, 4, 6, and 8 values display in A4 through A7.

■ VLOOKUP(**lookup_value, table_array, col_index_num,** *range_lookup*)—Vertical lookup (see Figure 3.40).

Figure 3.40

Range for VLOOKUP.

	A	B	C	D
1		1	5	10
2	727	40	55	62
3	737	50	65	72
4	747	60	75	82
5	767	70	85	92
6	DC10	80	95	102
7	L1011	90	105	112
8	A310	100	115	122

VLOOKUP("DC10",A1:D8,4, FALSE) = 102

VLOOKUP("747A",A1:D8,2,TRUE) = 60

Lookup_value is the row label to look for (in the first column). In the first example, Excel looks for a "DC10" (in A6) and then looks across that row. In the second example, Excel looks for a "747A". Because *range_lookup* is TRUE, Excel doesn't have to match values exactly and looks for the next lowest value (which is 747 in A4). Because there is a mix of numbers and text in the first column, each value in A2 through A5 is entered as text (with an apostrophe before the number). If *range_lookup* were FALSE, Excel would have to find an exact match in column A. Because it would not, the #N/A error value would display for the second function. If you use FALSE, the values need to be in ascending order (see **Data** ▪ **Sort**, page 410).

Table_array is the table you use to lookup the values. This table includes the row and column headings in the first row and first column. In the example it is the range A1:D8.

Col_index _num is the number of the column you want to look in. Starting from the left of **table_array** (including the column headings), count across. In the first formula come across to column 4 (10 years). In the second formula come to column 2 (1 year). Find the intersection of this column and the **lookup_value** row.

Database and List Management Functions

Use the 12 database functions to get statistics from a particular subset of a database. All these functions have a paired function that gets the statistics for the entire list. The paired function is the same name without the D (DSUM is related to SUM).

A database is organized so that the first row contains labels identifying each column; the subsequent rows are in one record for a person, place, or thing for each row (see Figure 3.41). You can type data directly in the worksheet or use data generated from an external source (see **Data** ▪ **Get External Data**, page 435) or a PivotTable (see **Data** ▪ **PivotTable Report**, page 424).

The database functions have the same arguments:

Dfunction(**database, field, criteria**)

Figure 3.41
Range for database
functions.

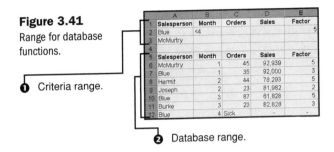

① Criteria range.

② Database range.

Database is the range with the row of labels and data mentioned previously. You can use cell references or a range name. If you use multiple database functions, it's easier to use a range name (see **Insert ▪ Name**, page 355). In the previous example, a range name DATABASE was created for the range A5:E12.

Field tells you which column to use in the function. Field can be text enclosed in double quotation marks or a number representing a column. In the example, you can use "Sales" or 4 to indicate column D.

Criteria filters which records you want to include in your results. The criteria range includes label(s) identical to the first row of the database and one or more rows with values you want to match. You can use cell references or a range name for the criteria. The following are some examples of the criteria:

- A1:A2 would find the salesperson Blue (rows 7, 10, 12).
- A1:A3 is an "or" condition when you have multiple rows below the labels. The results would be for Blue and McMurtry's records (rows 6, 7, 10, 12).
- A1:B2 is an "and" condition where both conditions have to be true. The results would be for Blue when the month is less than 4 (rows 7, 10).
- If the criteria is A1:E2, row 10 is evaluated.
- A1:B3 is a combination of "and" and "or." Excel would look at both conditions of each row. The result would be Blue less than 4th month (rows 7, 10) and McMurtry's record (row 6). So rows 6, 7, and 10 would be evaluated.

In the examples for each database function, notice that the criteria range uses absolute references. Although this is not required, copying and then modifying the functions is easier.

The following database functions use the example in Figure 3.41.

- DAVERAGE(**database, field, criteria**)—Database average.
  DAVERAGE(Database, "Sales",$A$1:$B$2) = 76,914
- DCOUNT(**database, field, criteria**)—Database count.
  This function counts the cells that contain numbers.
  DCOUNT(Database, "Month",$A$1:$A$2) = 3

- DCOUNTA(**database, field, criteria**)

  This function counts the cells that contain any nonblank cell.

  DCOUNTA(Database,"Salesperson",$A$1:$A$3) = 4

- DGET(**database, field, criteria**)—Get database record.

  DGET(Database,"Month",$A$1:$E$2) = 3

- DMAX(**database, field, criteria**)—Database maximum.

  DMAX(Database,"Sales",$A$1:$A$3) = 92,939

- DMIN(**database, field, criteria**)—Database minimum.

  DMIN(Database,"Orders",$A$1:$A$3) = 35

- DPRODUCT(**database, field, criteria**)—Database product.

  This function multiplies the values in a particular field.

  DPRODUCT(Database,"Factor",$A$1:$B$2) = 15

- DSTDEV(**database, field, criteria**)—Database sample standard deviation.

  See STDDEV.

  DSTDEV(Database,"Sales",$B$1:$B$2) = 11,316

- DSTDEVP(**database, field, criteria**)—Database population standard deviation.

  See STDEVP.

  DSTDEVP(Database,"Sales",$B$1:$B$2) = 10,330

- DSUM(**database, field, criteria**)—Database sum.

  DSUM(Database,"Sales",$A$1:$B$2) = 153,828

- DVAR(**database, field, criteria**)—Database sample variance.

  See VAR.

  DVAR(Database,"Orders",$B$1:$B$2) = 561

- DVARP(**database, field, criteria**)—Database population variance.

  See VARP.

  DVARP(Database,"Orders",$B$1:$B$2) = 467

- GETPIVOTDATA(**pivot_table, name**)—Get data from PivotTable.

  Pivot_table is a cell within the PivotTable, a range name of the PivotTable, or the range address of the PivotTable. **Name** is a text string in double quotes that refers to a cell in the PivotTable and can be a combination of multiple labels (see Figure 3.42).

Figure 3.42
PivotTable example.

	A	B	C	D	E	F
1	Month	(All) ▼				
2						
3	Sum of Value	Expense				
4	Division	Fuel	Other	Personnel	Supplies	Grand Total
5	Northern	50	200	400	100	750
6	Pacific		704	1232	440	2376
7	Southern		640	1120	400	2160
8	African		768	1344	480	2592
9	Grand Total	50	2312	4096	1420	7878

GETPIVOTDATA(B5,"Other") = 2312

GETPIVOTDATA(PT1,"Northern") = 750 (PT1 is the range name for A1:F9)

GETPIVOTDATA(B5,"African Supplies") = 480

Text Functions

■ CHAR(**number**)—Character.

Depending on the character set specified by your computer, this returns a character from the ANSI character set (Windows) or Macintosh character set.

CHAR(97) = "a"

■ CLEAN(**text**)—Clean text.

Removes all nonprintable characters from text.

CLEAN(Char(1) & "PrintMe" & Char(1)) = "PrintMe"

■ CODE(**text**)—Numeric code.

This shows the code for the letter (for the first character in a text string). This is the inverse of CHAR.

CODE("a") = 97

CODE("alligator") = 97

■ CONCATENATE(**text1, text2, ...**)—Concatenate.

Joins several text items into one text item. You can use up to 30 text items in this statement. Alternatively, you can use the & sign to concatenate text. If B2 contained 35, then you could type "Mileage is" & B2 & " cents/mile" or the following:

CONCATENATE("Mileage is" ,B2, "cents/mile") = "Mileage is 35 cents/mile"

■ DOLLAR(**number,** *decimals*)—Convert a number to text, using currency format.

Number can be a number or cell reference containing a number or formula. If *decimals* is left off, 2 is assumed. You can round to the left of the decimal point if you place a negative number for *decimals*. You can also format the number if you don't want to convert it to text (see **Format ▪ Cells... Number Tab**, page 361).

DOLLAR(3) = "$3.00"

DOLLAR(3,0) = "$3"

DOLLAR(123456,−3) = "$123,000"

■ EXACT(**text1, text2**)—Check to see whether two text values match.

If they match, TRUE is returned. If they don't, FALSE is returned. The function is case sensitive. You can also use Validation to check whether an entry matches text or numbers (see **Data ▪ Validation**, page 414).

EXACT("Test1","test1") = FALSE

■ FIND(**find_text, within_text,** *start_num*)—Finds one text value within another.

If **find_text** is somewhere **within_text**, then the result is the position that the text starts in the string. *Start_num* is optional and tells what position to start in **within_text**. If

Start_num is not included, it is assumed to be 1. This function is case sensitive.

FIND ("verif","Check 1 verified") = 9

FIND ("verif","Check 1 Verified") = #VALUE! (case sensitive)

FIND ("verif","verification is necessary",2) = #VALUE! (if can't find in string)

If you had strings with last name and comma ("Winter, Patty" and "Van Buren, Chris" in cells A2 and A3) and wanted to display only the last name, you could use these formulas.

MID (A2,1,FIND (",",A2)–1) = "Winter"

MID (A3,1,FIND (",",A3)–1) = "Van Buren"

■ FIXED (**number,** *decimals, no_commas*)—Formats a number as text with a fixed number of decimals.

Number can be a number or cell reference containing a number or formula. If *decimals* is left off, 2 is assumed. You can round to the left of the decimal point if you place a negative number for *decimals*. If you leave off *no_commas* or type FALSE, then commas are included. If you type TRUE, then the text string will not include commas. You can also format the number if you don't want to convert it to text (see **Format ‑ Cells... Number Tab**, page 361).

FIXED (3) = "3.00"

FIXED (3,0) = "3"

FIXED (123456,–3) = "123,000"

FIXED (1123.456,2,TRUE) = "1123.47"

■ LEFT (**text,** *num_chars*)—Leftmost characters.

If *num_chars* is not included, then only the first character is returned.

LEFT ("EN1234",2) = "EN"

LEFT ("EN1234") = "E"

■ LEN (**text**)—Number of characters in a string.

LEN ("Now is the time") = 15 (spaces are included)

■ LOWER (**text**)—Convert to lowercase.

See also PROPER and UPPER.

LOWER ("HELP ME I'M CAUGHT") = "help me i'm caught"

■ MID (**text, start_num, num_chars**)—Extract middle part of string.

Starting at **start_num** for **num_chars**, return that portion of the **text** string.

MID ("12345XT789",6,2) = "XT"

MID ("ABC",6,2) = "" (empty text when **start_num** is greater than length)

■ PROPER (**text**)—Convert to proper case.

Proper case is where the first letter of each word is capitalized. See also UPPER and LOWER.

PROPER ("old woman and young thing") = "Old Woman And Young Thing"

PROPER("Jerry McManus") = "Jerry Mcmanus" (PROPER's not always perfect)

PROPER("76trombones") = "76Trombones" (also capitalizes after numbers)

■ REPLACE(**old_text, start_num, num_chars, new_text**)—Replace characters within text.

Starting at **start_num** for **num_chars**, take out the **old_text** and add the **new_text**.

REPLACE("1000 dollars is enough",6,7,"pounds") = "1000 pounds is enough"

■ REPT(**text, number_times**)—Repeat text.

REPT("!*",6) = !*!*!*!*!*!*

■ RIGHT(**text,** *num_chars*)—Rightmost characters.

If *num_chars* is not included, then only the last character is returned.

RIGHT("EN1234D",2) = "4D"

RIGHT("EN1234D") = "D"

■ SEARCH(**find_text, within_text,** *start_num*)—Search within text.

See also FIND (which is case sensitive, while SEARCH is not).

SEARCH("verif","Check 1 verified") = 9

SEARCH("verif","Check 1 Verified") = 9 (not case sensitive)

SEARCH("verif","verification is necessary",2) = #VALUE! (if can't find in string)

■ SUBSTITUTE(**text, old_text, new_text,** *instance_num*)—Substitute new text for old text in a text string.

Instance_num tells you which instance of **old_text** you want replaced. If *instance_num* is not included, all instances of the **old_text** are replaced. REPLACE are used to replace any text, while SUBSTITUTE is used to replace specific text. If you want to do this through commands, see **Edit ▪ Replace**, page 284.

SUBSTITUTE("Mary Jones got married","Jones","Wilcox") = "Mary Wilcox got married"

■ T(**value**)—Convert to text.

This function is used for compatibility with other spreadsheet programs. Excel automatically converts values to text. If **value** is not text (for example, it is 25), then an empty string is returned.

T("Love Needed") = "Love Needed"

T(25) = "" (empty string)

■ TEXT(**value, format_text**)—Format number and convert to text.

This is more general than DOLLAR and FIXED. **Format_text** is a custom option for formatting numbers (see **Format ▪ Cells... Number Tab**, page 361). You cannot use General or asterisk (*).

TEXT(25, "$0.00") = $25.00

TEXT("1/1/99","mmmm d, yyyy") = "January 1, 1999"

■ TRIM(**text**)—Trim spaces from text.

Removes all spaces before and after text and all except one space between words.

TRIM(" Total values are : ") = Total values are :

■ UPPER(**text**)—Convert to uppercase.

See also PROPER and LOWER.

UPPER("help me i'm caught") = "HELP ME I'M CAUGHT"

■ VALUE(**text**)—Convert text to a number.

If Excel does not recognize a number, the #VALUE! error value is returned. This function is used for compatibility with other spreadsheet programs. (Excel automatically converts something entered as text to a number.)

VALUE("$2,000") = 2000

Logical Functions

■ AND(**logical1**, *logical2, ...*)

Returns TRUE if both (all) expressions are true or FALSE if either expression is false. You can have up to 30 expressions as arguments.

AND(3<4, 5<4) = FALSE

FALSE()

Returns the logical value FALSE. You can also type FALSE without the parentheses into a cell or formula and Excel interprets this as the logical value FALSE.

■ IF(**logical_test,** value_if_true, value_if_false)

If condition is true, second argument. If condition is false, third argument.

IF(A2<A3, "Buy", "Sell")="Buy" if the value of cell A2 is less than A3.

■ NOT(**logical**)

The opposite of the expression.

NOT(TRUE)=FALSE

NOT(3>4)=TRUE

■ OR(**logical1**, **logical2**, ...)

If any condition is true, TRUE. If all conditions are false, FALSE.

OR(5<3,5>3)=TRUE

■ TRUE()

Returns the logical value TRUE. You can also type TRUE without the parentheses into a cell or formula and Excel interprets this as the logical value TRUE.

Information Functions

■ CELL(**info_type, reference**)—Cell information.

Use this function to return all sorts of information about the formatting (see **Format** - **Ce̲lls...**, page 360), location, or contents of the cell in the upper-left corner of the **reference** (which can be a cell, range name, or range address).

The **info_type** argument can be any of the following:

"address"	Cell address (as absolute reference, becomes text).
"col"	Column number.
"color"	1 if formatted in color for negative numbers, 0 otherwise.
"contents"	What is included in the cell.
"filename"	Full path with name of current file. If file not yet saved, empty string ("").
"format"	Text value showing a cell format code (see below).
"parentheses"	1 if cell is formatted with parentheses for all values or positive numbers, 0 otherwise.
"prefix"	Label prefix of cell (from old Lotus 1-2-3 prefixes). Apostrophe (') for left-aligned, quote (") for right-aligned, caret (^) for center aligned, backslash (\) for fill-aligned, and empty string ("") for anything else.
"row"	Row number.
"type"	Type of data in the cell: "b" for blank or empty cell, "l" for label or text, "v" for value for numbers or formulas.
"width"	Column width rounded to an integer.

The following is the list of codes for the format **info_type**. For a description of the Excel formats in the second column, see **Format ⁓ Cells...**, page 360.

G	General
F	Fixed (no commas)
,	, (comma)
C	Currency
P	Percent
S	Scientific
2	Number of decimals (can be another number)
-	(Dash) formatted in color for decimal values
()	(Parentheses) cell formatted with parentheses for positive or all values

You can have a combination of results returned. For example, "F2" is a fixed with 2 decimal places. "C2-" is currency format with 2 decimal places, and negative numbers are formatted in red.

In addition, you can have the following codes for dates:

D1	d-mmm-yy or dd-mmm-yy
D2	d-mmm or dd-mmm
D3	mmm-yy
D4	m/d/yy or m/d/yy h:mm or mm/dd/yy
D5	mm/dd

D6	h:mm:ss AM/PM
D7	h:mm AM/PM
D8	h:mm:ss
D9	h:mm

- ERROR.TYPE(**error_value**)—Error type.

  This number gives you a number corresponding to an error type (which you can use in an IF function, for example). **Error_value** is a cell containing an error value (but can also be the error value itself).

  ERROR.TYPE(#NULL!) = 1

  ERROR.TYPE(#DIV/0!) = 2

  ERROR.TYPE(#VALUE!) = 3

  ERROR.TYPE(#REF!) = 4

  ERROR.TYPE(#NAME?) = 5

  ERROR.TYPE(#NUM!) = 6

  ERROR.TYPE(#N/A!) = 7

  ERROR.TYPE(B6) = 3 (if #VALUE! is in B6)

  ERROR.TYPE(B7) = #N/A (if there is no error in B7)

- INFO(**type_text**)—Information about the operating environment.

  Type_text is one of the following:

"directory"	Path of the current folder.
	INFO("directory") = "C:\DATA\"
"memavail"	How much memory is available in bytes.
"memused"	How much memory is used for data.
"numfile"	Number of active worksheets (note: not workbooks; this also includes sheets in hidden workbooks like the Personal.xls and Add-ins you have loaded).
"origin"	Address of top left visible cell with "$A:" added as a prefix (for example, "$A:B500"). This is used for Lotus 1-2-3 release 3.x compatibility.
"osversion"	The current operating system version.
	INFO("osversion") = "Windows (32-bit) 4.00"
"recalc"	Shows "Automatic" or "Manual" for current recalculation mode (see **Tools ➥ Options..., Calculation Tab**, page 401).
"release"	Current version of Microsoft Excel.
	INFO("release") = "8.0" (this is Excel 97)
"system"	For Windows will say "pcdos", for Macintosh will say "mac".
"totmem"	memavail + memused (total memory).

IS Functions

The following 11 functions all have the same argument (**value**). This can be a cell reference, text, number, or range name.

- ISBLANK(**value**)—Is value blank?

  ISBLANK(C47) = TRUE (if cell C47 is blank)

- ISERR(**value**)—Is value an error (except #N/A)?

  If **value** is any error value except #N/A, this returns TRUE.

  ISERR(#REF!) = TRUE

  ISERR(#N/A) = FALSE (ISERR returns TRUE any error value except #N/A)

- ISERROR(**value**)—Is value an error?

  Value is actually what is typed in parentheses, not a cell reference to a cell that has an error (unlike ISERR and other IS funcitons). Returns TRUE for #N/A, #VALUE!, #REF!, #DIV/0!, #NUM!, #NAME?, or #NULL!.

  ISERROR(#REF!) = TRUE

  ISERROR(#N/A) = TRUE

- ISLOGICAL(**value**)—Is value a logical value?

  ISLOGICAL(FALSE) = TRUE

- ISNA(**value**)—Is value #N/A?

  ISNA(#N/A) = TRUE

  ISNA(C47) = FALSE (if C47 is anything but #N/A)

- ISNONTEXT(**value**)—Is value not text?

  ISNONTEXT("test") = FALSE

  ISNONTEXT(1) = TRUE

- ISNUMBER(**value**)—Is value a number?

  ISNUMBER("test") = FALSE

  ISNUMBER (1) = TRUE

  ISNUMBER(FALSE) = FALSE

  ISNUMBER("1") = FALSE (Unlike most other functions, text values are not converted to their appropriate data type in IS functions.)

- ISREF(**value**)—Is value a cell or range reference?

  ISREF(C47) = TRUE

  ISREF(Database) = TRUE (if range name Database exists, otherwise = FALSE)

- ISTEXT(**value**)—Is value text?

  ISTEXT("test") = TRUE

  ISTEXT(1) = FALSE

■ N(**value**)—Convert to number.

Generally you do not need to use this function because Excel automatically converts a value to a number when it is typed into a cell. This function is provided for compatibility with other spreadsheet programs.

N(10) = 10

N(1/1/99) = 0.01 (1 divided by 1 divided by 99)

N(B47) = 36161 (if B47 has 1/1/99 entered as a date)

N(TRUE) = 1

N(FALSE) = 0

N("76Sunset") = 0

NA()—Error no value available (#N/A).

The error value #N/A can also be typed directly in the cell. When you have a formula that refers to a cell that has #N/A, the formula cell also displays #N/A.

■ TYPE(**value**)—Data type.

TYPE returns a number indicating the data type of a value. **Value** can be a number, text, logical value, or cell reference.

TYPE(200) = 1 (number)

TYPE("Test") = 2 (text)

TYPE(FALSE) = 4 (logical value)

TYPE(C5) = 1 (if C5 contains a formula that evaluates to a number)

TYPE(#VALUE!) = 16 (error value)

TYPE({1,2,3}) = 64 (array)

These 231 functions are available when you do Typical setup when installing Office 97 or Excel 97. There are an additional 94 functions available when you use Custom setup. The following table shows the additional number of functions in each category.

Financial Functions	37
Date and Time	5
Math and Trigonometry	10
Information	3
Engineering (new category)	39

Define a Function in Visual Basic

You can also create your own functions in Visual Basic to use in your worksheets. You can create a function that you will use in multiple workbooks or one specifically for this workbook. The following procedure is a brief description of how you create a simple function in Visual Basic. For more information, see Que's *Special Edition Using Visual Basic for Applications 5*.

1. Choose **Tools**, **Macro**, **Macros** (or press **Alt+F8**). The Macro dialog box opens.

2. Type the name of the new function in the **Macro Name** text box.

3. In the **Macros in** drop-down, choose **This Workbook** to create the function for use in the current workbook or **PERSONAL.XLS** to store the macro for use in all workbooks.

4. Click the **Create** button. The Microsoft Visual Basic window opens with your new procedure displayed. Figure 3.43 shows the Visual Basic window with two completed functions.

Figure 3.43

Choose Tools, Macro, Macros; fill in Macro Name, and click Create to open the Visual Basic window to create a procedure.

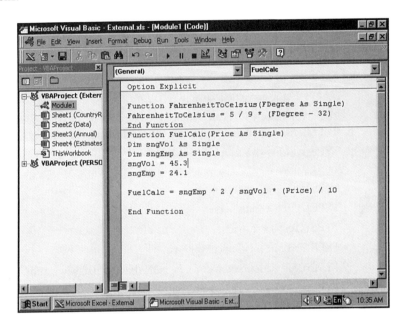

5. Remove the word Sub (sub procedure) and type **Function** in its place. (End Sub will automatically change to End Function when you move off the first line.)

6. Do one or more of the following:

   - Between the parentheses after the function name, type names of any arguments you want and their data types (in the form *argumentname* as Type). Type can be Single (decimals), String (text), Boolean (true or false), Integer (whole numbers) and others.

   - If it is necessary to use variables in your calculation, dimension (identify) those variables with the statement Dim *variablename* as Type (using the types previously listed).

7. In the last line of the procedure (before End Function), type the function name, an equal sign, and a formula that defines the function.

8. Choose **File, Close and Return to Microsoft Excel** or press **Alt+Q**.

9. To use the function in Excel, do one of the following:

- If the function is on the current workbook, type = and the name of the function and values for any arguments.

- Click the **Paste Function** button ƒ*x* on the Standard toolbar. In the **Function category** of the Paste Function dialog box, select **User Defined**. Double-click your function in the **Function name** list box. Fill in the values for the arguments in the function helper (see **Insert ⮕ Function**, page 313).

Insert ⮕ Name

The **Insert, Name** command enables you to create and modify names that refer to one cell, a group of cells (a range), and even frequently used formulas and constants. Names make formulas easier to recognize and maintain; they help reduce errors in formulas and commands and make moving around in a workbook easier. Additionally they are easier to remember than cell references.

You don't need to use range names in formulas. Instead you can use the labels at the beginning of the row or top of the column. For instance: Type **=sum(January)** to get the total for the January column. For more information, see **Insert ⮕ Name ⮕ Label...** on page 358 to define numbers as labels.

To create a name you need to remember a few rules:

- Names must start with a letter or an underscore; after that, you can use any character except a space or hyphen. Use an underscore (_) or period(.) instead of a space.

- Names can be up to 255 characters, although it is better to limit the names to 15 or less characters (for display and formula purposes).

- You can type names in upper- or lowercase letters. Excel keeps the capitalization, but it does not distinguish between upper- and lowercase. For instance, YTD_Expenses and ytd_expenses would be the same name. The second one would overwrite the first one.

To define names using the name box on the workbook, follow these steps:

1. Select the cell or range of cells you want to name.
2. Click the Name text box on the left side of the Formula bar; the active cell appears in the Name text box and is highlighted.
3. Type in the name and press **Enter**.

If you type a name that is already being used, you move to the cell or range with that name instead of creating a new name. If you want to redefine the name to reflect the new range, you need to use the **Insert, Name, Define** command (see the following section).

To use column or row headings in a formula, follow these steps:

1. Position the Active cell where you want the formula.
2. Type the formula using the name of the column or row. For example

- If the Active cell is at the bottom of the Feb column, type **=Sum(Feb)**. Excel knows to sum the Feb column.

- If the Active cell is to the right of the Payroll row, type **=Average(Payroll)**. Excel knows to find the average in the Payroll row.

Insert ➡ Name ➡ Define...

The **Insert**, **Name**, **Define** command displays the Define Name dialog box to enable you to create new names, delete names you don't need, and change cell references for names.

To create names, do the following:

1. Select the cell, range, or multiple ranges you want to name.
2. Choose **Insert**, **Name**, **Define**. The Define Name dialog box is displayed (see Figure 3.44).

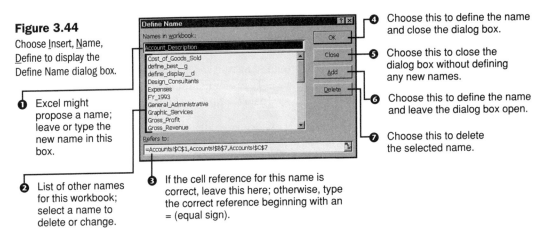

Figure 3.44

Choose Insert, Name, Define to display the Define Name dialog box.

❶ Excel might propose a name; leave or type the new name in this box.

❷ List of other names for this workbook; select a name to delete or change.

❸ If the cell reference for this name is correct, leave this here; otherwise, type the correct reference beginning with an = (equal sign).

❹ Choose this to define the name and close the dialog box.

❺ Choose this to close the dialog box without defining any new names.

❻ Choose this to define the name and leave the dialog box open.

❼ Choose this to delete the selected name.

3. If you chose the **Add** button to leave the dialog box open, you can type a new name in the **Names in workbook** text box.
4. Click in the **Refers to** text box and do one of the following:
   - Type the reference beginning with an equal sign (=).
   - Move the dialog box out of the way and select the range in the worksheet that you are referring to.
5. Choose **Add** to define the new name and repeat the process. Choose **OK** to define the name and close the dialog box.

Insert ➡ Name ➡ Paste...

The **Insert**, **Name**, **Paste** command can be used to insert a name in a formula.

Quick Choices *PASTE NAMES*

- Type the formula; where you want to insert the name, press **F3** or choose **Insert**, **Name**, **Paste**, and then select the name from the **Paste Name** list and choose **OK.**

■ Type the formula and type the name instead of a cell reference.

■ Type the formula; where you want to insert the name, click the down-arrow on the **Name** drop-down list box and select the name you want to paste.

Insert ~ Name ~ Create...

The **Insert**, **Name**, **Create** command enables you to create one name or many names at a time.

1. Select the range(s) you want to name, including the row or column heading(s), as shown in Figure 3.45.

2. Choose **Insert**, **Name**, **Create** to display the Create Names dialog box (see Figure 3.45).

Figure 3.45
The Insert, Name, Create command displays the Create Names dialog box.

❷ Column headings become the name.

❶ Selected columns for names.

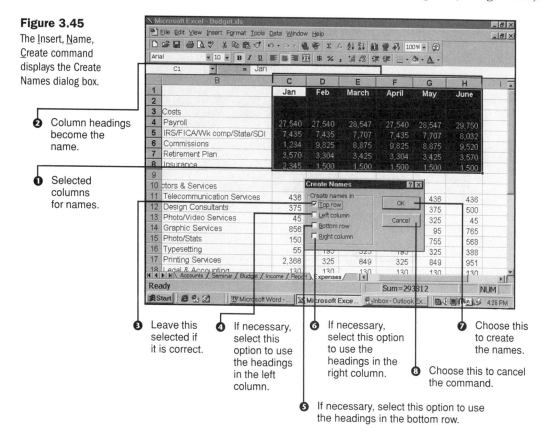

❸ Leave this selected if it is correct.

❹ If necessary, select this option to use the headings in the left column.

❻ If necessary, select this option to use the headings in the right column.

❼ Choose this to create the names.

❽ Choose this to cancel the command.

❺ If necessary, select this option to use the headings in the bottom row.

3. If you have selected a range that is different than the original range associated with a name, you see a message box asking **Replace existing definition of 'Name'?** for each name in question.

4. Choose **Yes** to redefine the name, **No** to leave the name intact, or **Cancel** to cancel the command (none of the names will be created).

<u>I</u>nsert ▸ <u>N</u>ame ▸ <u>A</u>pply...

The **<u>I</u>nsert**, **<u>N</u>ame**, **<u>A</u>pply** command gives you the capability to apply names to the formulas you have already created.

1. Select one cell if you want to apply names to the whole worksheet, or select a range (including the row and column headings and cells with formulas) to apply names to the formulas in the range.

2. Choose **<u>I</u>nsert**, **<u>N</u>ame**, **<u>A</u>pply** to display the Apply Names dialog box (see Figure 3.46).

Figure 3.46

The <u>I</u>nsert, <u>N</u>ame, <u>A</u>pply command displays the Apply Names dialog box.

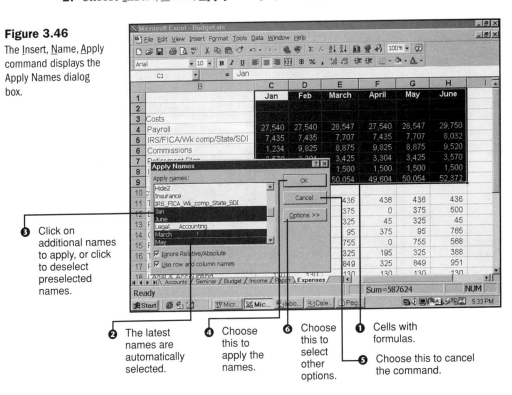

❸ Click on additional names to apply, or click to deselect preselected names.

❷ The latest names are automatically selected.

❹ Choose this to apply the names.

❻ Choose this to select other options.

❶ Cells with formulas.

❺ Choose this to cancel the command.

<u>I</u>nsert ▸ <u>N</u>ame ▸ <u>L</u>abel...

The **<u>I</u>nsert**, **<u>N</u>ame**, **<u>L</u>abel** command is a process to make the Natural Language Formulas function work with numbers. The difference between this and **<u>I</u>nsert**, **<u>N</u>ame** is that this is used for typing formulas using English, not cell references.

Normally a label is text when you are identifying rows or columns, for example **Personnel** or **January**. However, you might have a number that you want to act as a label, for instance 1999 or 2000, that would identify the year for a column or row. To have Excel treat these numbers as labels, use the **<u>I</u>nsert**, **<u>N</u>ame**, **<u>L</u>abel** command by following these steps:

1. Select the range of column or row headings you want to define as labels.

2. Choose **Insert**, **Name**, **Label** to display the Label Ranges dialog box (see Figure 3.47).

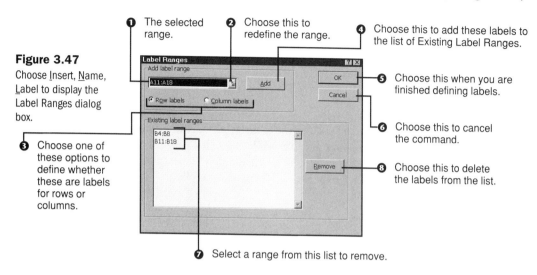

❶ The selected range.

❷ Choose this to redefine the range.

❹ Choose this to add these labels to the list of Existing Label Ranges.

Figure 3.47
Choose Insert, Name, Label to display the Label Ranges dialog box.

❸ Choose one of these options to define whether these are labels for rows or columns.

❺ Choose this when you are finished defining labels.

❻ Choose this to cancel the command.

❽ Choose this to delete the labels from the list.

❼ Select a range from this list to remove.

After you perform the previous procedure, you can type a Natural Language formula, **=sum(1999)**, and Excel converts this to the proper Natural Language formula **=sum('1999')**.

Insert ➥ Comment

The **Insert**, **Comment** command gives you the ability to write comments to yourself or someone else.

Quick **Choices** *TO INSERT A COMMENT*

1. Move the active cell to the place on the worksheet you want the comment.
2. Press **Shift+F2**, right-click and choose **Insert Comment**, or click 🖼 on the Reviewing toolbar, or choose **Insert**, **Comment**.
3. Type your comment in the text box that displays.
4. Click outside the comment box to close it. A red triangle in the top-right corner indicates a comment.

To edit comments, follow these steps:

1. Right-click the cell that contains a comment to display the shortcut menu.
2. Choose **Edit**, **Comment** to open the comment box.
3. Make changes to the comment, and click outside the box to close it.
4. To go to the next comment, turn the Reviewing toolbar on (right-click any toolbar and choose **Reviewing**).

5. Click the **Next Comment** button on the Reviewing toolbar to go to the next comment.

To delete comments, follow these steps:

1. Right-click the cell that contains a comment to display the shortcut menu.
2. Choose **Delete**, **Comment**.

Insert ➟ Picture

The **Insert**, **Picture** command enables you to insert pictures from many outside sources, such as drawing programs, scanners, and clip art collections. You can also insert pictures using Excel's built-in tools: AutoShapes, WordArt, Organization Chart, and the Drawing toolbar. For detailed information see Word's **Insert** ‑ **Picture** on page 149.

Insert ➟ Map...

The **Insert**, **Map** command creates a map based on the selected data. The data must contain geographical references in the left column, such as abbreviations of countries or states, and values in the right column.

1. Type the data for the map.
2. Select the data, and then choose **Insert**, **Map**.
3. With the crosshair mouse pointer, drag in your worksheet to set the location and size of the map.
4. Use the Map toolbar and the Microsoft Map Control to create your map.
5. Click back in the worksheet when you are finished.

Insert ➟ Object...

The **Insert**, **Object** command inserts an object, such as a drawing, WordArt text effect, or an equation, at the location of the insertion point. See Word's **Insert** ‑ **Object** on page 158 for more information.

Insert ➟ Hyperlink...

The **Insert**, **Hyperlink** command enables you to insert or edit the hyperlink you specify. See Word's **Insert**, **Hyperlink** on page 159 for more information.

Format

Formatting enables you to change how the text and figures look on the page.

Format ➟ Cells...

After you select a range, use **Format**, **Cells**, Press **Ctrl+1**, or right-click the range and choose **Format Cells** to apply a format to the selection. The Format Cells dialog box appears with six tabs (Number, Alignment, Font, Border, Patterns, and Protection) which are discussed next.

If the sheet is protected (see **Tools ▾ Protection ▾ Protect Sheet...**, page 387) and the cells are locked (see **Format ▾ Cells... Protection Tab**, page 369), **Format**, **Cells** will not be available.

Format ▾ Cells... Number Tab

When you format numbers, the value of data does not change, just the way the numbers display. For example, 1.234 may display as $1.23, but Excel still uses the 1.234 in calculations. To change the number format, first select the range you want to change and then do any of the following. (Note: This is not true when **Precision as Displayed** is checked on the Calculation tab of the Options dialog box; see **Tools ▾ Options... Calculation Tab**, page 401).

Quick Choices *CHANGE THE FORMAT OF SELECTED TEXT*

What Style	Example	Button on Formatting Toolbar	Keyboard Shortcut
General	No format		**Ctrl+Shift+~**
Currency	$1,234.00		**Ctrl+Shift+$**
Accounting	$1,234.00	**$**	
Percent	.45 becomes 45%	**%**	**Ctrl+Shift+%**
Comma	1,234.00	**,**	**Ctrl+Shift+!**
Increase Decimal	34.00 becomes 34.000	**+.0 .00**	
Decrease Decimal	34.49 becomes 34.5	**.00 +.0**	
Exponential format	123.45 becomes 1.23E+02		**Ctrl+Shift+^**
Date—Day, Month, Year	1/27/99 becomes 27-Jan-99		**Ctrl+Shift+#**
Time—Hour, Minute, AM or PM	.61 becomes 2:38 PM		**Ctrl+Shift+@**

In addition to the quick choices mentioned previously, you can also use the Number tab of the Format Cells dialog box (see Figure 3.48) and the following table.

Figure 3.48

Format, Cells... Number tab opens the Format Cells dialog box for formatting the display of numbers.

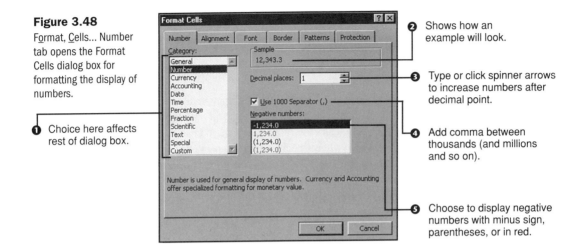

❶ Choice here affects rest of dialog box.

❷ Shows how an example will look.

❸ Type or click spinner arrows to increase numbers after decimal point.

❹ Add comma between thousands (and millions and so on).

❺ Choose to display negative numbers with minus sign, parentheses, or in red.

Format cells—Number tab

Category	Description	Dialog Box Options
General	No formatting	None
Number	General display of numbers 1035.231 becomes 1,035.23	**Decimal places, Use 1000 Separator, Negative numbers**
Currency	Monetary values 1035.231 becomes $1,035.23	**Decimal places, Symbol, Negative numbers**
Accounting	Lines up currency symbols and decimal places in a column	**Decimal places, Symbol**
Date	Shows serial numbers as date values 36161 becomes 1/1/99	**Type**—choose one of date examples such as 3/4, 3/4/97, 4-Mar-97 and so on
Time	Shows serial numbers as time values .3 becomes 7:12 AM	**Type**—choose one of time examples such as 13:30, 1:30 PM, 30:55.7, 3/4/97 1:30 PM
Percent	Multiplies value by 100 and shows a percent	**Decimal places**

Category	Description	Dialog Box Options
	symbol .3 becomes 30	
Fraction	Displays one number over another .4 becomes 2/5	**Type**—choose 1-3 digits or standard fractions (halves, quarters, eighths, sixteenths, tenths, hundredths)
Scientific	Expresses number in powers of 10 110 becomes 1.1E+02 .011 becomes 1.1E-02	**Decimal places**
Text	Numbers treated as text—displays exactly as shown and is left aligned in cell	None
Special	For data that is often associated with names and addresses 1234 becomes 01234 (zip) 5554567 becomes 555-4567 (Phone) 1234567890 becomes 123-456-7890 (Social Security)	**Type**—choose one of the formats for zip code, Phone, Social Security
Custom	Enables you to create your own detailed format A trick with custom formats is to choose the type of formatting (time) first, and the choose custom to refine it	**Type**—choose built-in or custom format from list or type in codes for your own format See next table for codes **Delete**—remove selected custom format from list (cannot delete built-in formats)

Click the down arrow and choose the currency symbol for the country. Or, with Num Lock on, press Alt and one of the following to create a currency symbol:

0162   ¢

0163	£
0165	¥

When you create a custom format, you can include up to four parts for the format. Each part is separated by semicolons (;). The four sections are positive numbers, negative numbers, zeros, and text format. For example **#,###; [Red](#,###);0.00;"invalid entry"** displays 1234 as 1,234; –1234 as (1,234) in red; 0 as 0.00; and displays any text such as "abc" as *invalid entry*. The following tables shows the codes you can enter for numbers, dates, and times.

Number format codes

Code	Description	Example Format	Example
#	Significant digits, do not display insignificant zeros	#,##0	1234 is 1,234
	Displays insignificant 0s	0.000	.3 is 0.300
?	Space for insignificant zeros (to get numbers to line up)	?.00	1.20 .20
,	Comma separator	#,###	1234 is 1,234
,	Comma separator at end leaves off each set of 1000s	0.0, #,,	12000 is 12.0 12000000 as 12
[Color]	Include color name in brackets for only following colors: Black, Cyan, Magenta, White, Blue, Green, Red, Yellow	[Blue] ; [Red]- # ; [Green]	Display positive numbers in blue, negatives in red, and zero as green
[condition]	Shows condition in one format and other numbers in another format (see also **Format – Conditional Formatting…**, page 372)	[<=99999] 00000 ; 00000- 0000	1234 becomes 01234, 804561234 becomes 80456-1234

Code	Description	Example Format	Example
m	Months (1-12)	m-d-yy	1-1-99
mm	Months (01-12)	mm-dd-yy	01-01-99
mmm	Months (Jan-Dec)	mmm-yy	Jan-99
mmmm	Months (January-December)	mmmm yyyy	January 1999
mmmmm	First letter of month	mmmmm/yy	J/99
d	1 or 2 digit days (1-31)	m/d/yy	1/1/99
dd	2 digit days 01-31	mm/dd/yy	01/01/99
ddd	Days Sun-Sat	ddd m/d	Sat 1/1
dddd	Days Sunday-Saturday	dddd m/d	Saturday 1/1
yy	2 digit years 00-99	m d yy	1 2 99
yyyy	4 digit years (1900-1999)	m d yyyy	1 2 1999
h	1 digit hours (0-23)	h:mm	23:09
hh	2 digit hours (00-23)	hh:mm	03:09
m	1 digit minutes (0-59) m after h codes or before ss codes (otherwise months)	h:m	23:9
mm	2 digit minutes (00-59)	h:mm	3:09
s	1 digit seconds (0-59)	h:mm.s	3:09.9
ss	2 digit seconds (00-59)	h:mm.ss	3:09.59
AM/PM	AM or PM	h AM/PM	4 AM
am/pm	am or pm	h:mm am/pm	3:04 PM
a/p	a or p (am or pm)	h:mm a/p	3:09 p
[h]	elapsed hours	[h]	3:04 PM as 15
[mm]	elapsed minutes	[mm]	3:04 PM as 904
[ss]	elapsed seconds	[ss]	3:04 PM as 54250

Text and Spacing format codes

Code	Description	Example Format	Example
" "	Include text	h "o'clock"	5 o'clock
@	Display any text (last of 4 format sections)	#.0;(#.0);0;@ #.0;(#.0);0;	abc as abc abc as blank
_	Keep space for width of following character	#_);(#)	1 (1)
*	Repeat next character to fill column width	*-	- - - - - - -

Format → Cells... Alignment Tab

Aligning is to place text in a position in the cell. The alignment can be horizontal (right, left, center) or vertical (top, bottom, center) or angled within the cell.

Quick Choices   CHANGE THE ALIGNMENT OF SELECTED TEXT

Button on Formatting Toolbar	How to Use
▤	Click to align characters on left of selected cells.
▤	Click to position characters in the middle of selected cells.
▤	Click to align characters on right of selected cells.
▤	Select a title and surrounding cells. Click to merge all cells as one and center (or left or right align) characters across all cells depending on which of the three previous buttons selected.
▤	Click to reduce the indent within the selected cells.
▤	Click to increase the indent within the selected cells.

In addition to the quick choices mentioned above you can also use the Alignment tab of the Format Cells dialog box (see Figure 3.49).

Format → Cells... Font Tab

Font is the way characters are printed on the page and appear on the screen. Font includes the type style, size, and effects such as strikethrough or underline. To set the default font style and size see **Standard Font** and **Size** on the options dialog box (see **Tools → Options... General Tab**, page 403).

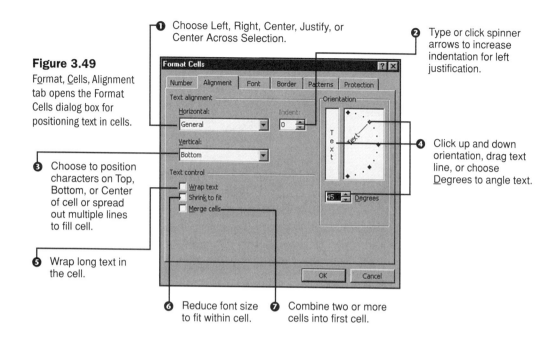

Figure 3.49
Format, Cells, Alignment tab opens the Format Cells dialog box for positioning text in cells.

1 Choose Left, Right, Center, Justify, or Center Across Selection.

2 Type or click spinner arrows to increase indentation for left justification.

3 Choose to position characters on Top, Bottom, or Center of cell or spread out multiple lines to fill cell.

4 Click up and down orientation, drag text line, or choose Degrees to angle text.

5 Wrap long text in the cell.

6 Reduce font size to fit within cell.

7 Combine two or more cells into first cell.

Quick Choices **CHANGE THE FORMAT OF SELECTED TEXT**

Do What	Button on	Keyboard Shortcut Formatting Toolbar
Bold	**B**	**Ctrl+B**
Italicize	*I*	**Ctrl+I**
Underline	U	**Ctrl+U**
Strikethrough		**Ctrl+5 (on the number row, not on the number keypad)**
Change font face	Arial	**Ctrl+Shift+F then use up or down arrow**
Change font size	10	**Ctrl+Shift+P then use up or down arrow**
Font color	**A**	
Highlight (background color)		

In addition to the quick choices, you can also use the Font tab of the Format Cells dialog box (see Figure 3.50).

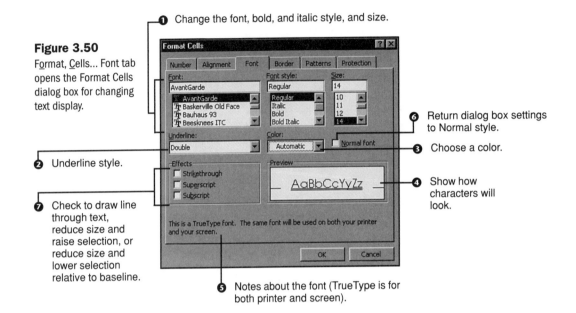

Figure 3.50
Format, Cells... Font tab opens the Format Cells dialog box for changing text display.

❶ Change the font, bold, and italic style, and size.

❷ Underline style.

❼ Check to draw line through text, reduce size and raise selection, or reduce size and lower selection relative to baseline.

❻ Return dialog box settings to Normal style.

❸ Choose a color.

❹ Show how characters will look.

❺ Notes about the font (TrueType is for both printer and screen).

Format ⇥ Cells... Border Tab

Borders enable you to draw lines around sides of the cells.

Quick Choices   DRAW BORDERS AROUND CELLS

1. Select the cells.

2. Click the **Borders** button [⊞▾] on the Formatting toolbar to choose the last border option or click the drop-down arrow and choose one of the borders for the selection. If you use borders a lot, you can tear off the border palette by dragging the dark bar on top of the palette.

3. If you want to remove gridlines from printing to see the borders better on your paper, choose **File**, **Page Setup**; then click the Sheet tab, and clear **Gridlines**.

4. If you want to remove the gridlines from the screen to see borders better, choose **Tools**, **Options**; then click the View tab, and clear **Gridlines**.

In addition to the quick choices, you can also use the Borders tab of the Format Cells dialog box (see Figure 3.51).

Figure 3.51
Format, Cells... Borders tab opens the Format Cells dialog box for drawing lines around the selection.

❸ Choose preset for no border, border around selection, or internal lines.

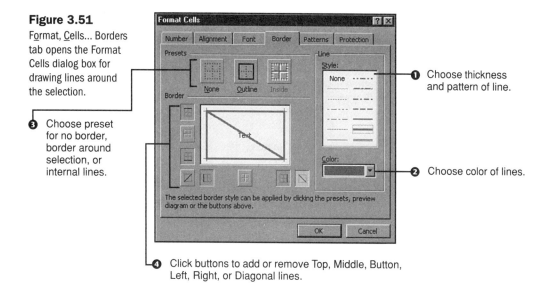

❶ Choose thickness and pattern of line.

❷ Choose color of lines.

❹ Click buttons to add or remove Top, Middle, Button, Left, Right, or Diagonal lines.

Format ➥ Cells... Patterns Tab

You can add a background color or pattern to the selected cells to make them stand out compared to your other cells. Click the **Fill Color** button ![Fill Color button] on the Formatting toolbar to choose the last color, or click the drop-down arrow to choose a different color. You could also choose **Format, Cells**; then click the Patterns tab and choose a **Color**. If desired, you could also click the **Pattern** drop-down arrow and choose a pattern and color for the lines or dots on the pattern.

Format ➥ Cells... Protection Tab

The Protection tab on the Format Cells dialog box has two check boxes. Check or clear the **Locked** box. Then protect the worksheet (see **Tools - Protection - Protect Sheet...**, page 387). If you choose **Contents** on the Protect Sheet dialog box, you won't be able to edit or format the cells you locked. You can change cells you did not lock. If you check **Hidden** on the Format Cells dialog box, you cannot view the formula in the Formula bar when you select the cell and the worksheet is protected.

Format ➥ Row

The **Format, Row** commands enables you to change the height and hide or unhide rows.

Format ➥ Row ➥ Height...

Position the double-headed mouse pointer between two row headers and drag to change the row height. You can also choose **Format, Row, Height** or right-click a row header and choose **Row Height** to open the Row Height dialog box. Type the row height in points (about two or three points larger than the font size is usually appropriate).

To change multiple row heights at the same time, also select multiple rows (drag the white plus across row headers) before using one of the previous methods.

Format ➥ Row ➥ AutoFit

Position the double-headed mouse pointer between two row headers and double-click to change the height to the tallest entry. You can also choose **Format, Row, AutoFit.**

Format ➥ Row ➥ Hide

You can hide one or more rows with one of the three methods:

Quick **Choices**   *HIDE ROWS*

- ▪ Select cells in any rows and press **Ctrl+9** (on the numbers row—not the numeric keypad).
- ▪ Select cells in any rows and choose **Format, Row, Hide**.
- ▪ Drag the white plus mouse pointer on row headers, right-click the selection, and choose **Hide**.

Format ➥ Row ➥ Unhide

To unhide rows, the key is to select the hidden rows first. You can tell you have hidden rows because the row header numbers are not continuous. Position the white plus mouse pointer starting above the hidden row(s) and drag to a row below the hidden rows to select the rows. Then do one of the following:

- ▪ Right-click and choose **Unhide**.
- ▪ Press **Ctrl+Shift+(**.
- ▪ Choose **Format, Row, Unhide**.

To unhide all hidden rows, you can also click the Select All button above row header 1 (and to the left of column A) and choose either of the last two options.

Format ➥ Column

The **Format, Column** commands enable you to change the width and hide or unhide columns.

Format ➥ Column ➥ Width...

Position the double-headed mouse pointer between two column headers and drag to change the column width. You can also choose **Format, Column, Width** or right-click a column header and choose **Column Width** to open the Column Width dialog box. Type the column width (a number from 0 to 255 to indicate the number of characters that you can display with the standard font). Note: You can actually enter 32,000 characters in a cell, but the only way to see more than 255 characters is to have text wrap on (**Format, Cells... Alignment Tab, Wrap Text**).

You can also select multiple columns. Drag the white plus sign across column headers before you use one of the previous methods to change multiple column widths at the same time.

Format ➥ Column ➥ AutoFit Selection

Position the double-headed mouse pointer between two column headers and double-click to change the column width to the widest entry. You can also choose **Format**, **Column**, **AutoFit Selection.**

Format ➥ Column ➥ Hide

You can hide one or more columns with one of the three methods:

- Select cells in any rows and press **Ctrl+0** (zero on the numbers row—not the numeric keypad).
- Select cells in any rows and choose **Format**, **Column**, **Hide**.
- Drag the white plus sign mouse pointer on column headers, right-click the selection, and choose **Hide**.

Format ➥ Column ➥ Unhide

Just like rows, to unhide columns, the key is to select the hidden columns first. You can tell you have hidden columns because the column header letters are not continuous. Position the white plus mouse pointer starting to the left of the hidden column(s) and drag to a column past the hidden columns. Then do one of the following:

- Right-click and choose **Unhide**.
- Press **Ctrl+Shift+)**.
- Choose **Format**, **Column**, **Unhide**.

To unhide all hidden columns, you can also click the **Select All** button above row header 1 (and to the left of column A) and choose either of the last two options.

Format ➥ Column ➥ Standard Width...

To change the width of rest of the columns you have not manually changed, choose **Format**, **Column**, **Standard Width** and type the number of characters in the Standard Width dialog box.

Format ➥ Sheet

To change the name, hide or unhide a worksheet, or display a background picture, use the **Format**, **Sheet** commands.

In order to move to a sheet, you may need to use the Tab scrolling buttons to the left of the horizontal scroll bar. The first button (line with an arrow) displays the first sheet, the second button displays the previous sheet, the third button displays the next sheet, and the fourth button (arrow with a line) displays the last sheet. You can also press **Ctrl+Page Up** and **Ctrl+Page Down** to move to other sheets. To scroll several sheets at a time, hold **Shift** down as you click the middle two buttons.

Format ⇥ Sheet ⇥ Rename

The generic names for worksheets are Sheet1, Sheet2, Sheet3 and so forth. If you use many sheets (see **Insert ⇥ Worksheet**, page 306), you will probably want to give each a more useful name.

To highlight the sheet name, do one of the following:

- Double-click the Sheet tab.
- Right-click the Sheet tab and choose **Rename**.
- For the current sheet, choose **Format**, **Sheet**, **Rename**.

After you have the sheet name highlighted, type the new name and press **Enter**.

Format ⇥ Sheet ⇥ Hide

To make a sheet invisible to the user, choose **Format**, **Sheet**, **Hide**. If you want to make unhiding (or hiding) unavailable, protect the workbook (see **Tools ⇥ Protection ⇥ Protect Workbook...**, page 388).

Format ⇥ Sheet ⇥ Unhide...

To make a sheet visible again, choose **Format**, **Sheet**, **Unhide**. The Unhide dialog box appears showing a list of all hidden sheets. Double-click the hidden sheet. Repeat this command for each sheet you want to unhide.

Format ⇥ Sheet ⇥ Background...

The new Background feature enables you to display a graphic on your worksheet. The image is repeated (tiled) to cover up the whole sheet but does not print. Choose **Format**, **Sheet**, **Background**. The Sheet Background dialog box displays and is like the Open dialog box (see Word's **File ⇥ Open...**, page 21). Navigate to a picture file and double-click. To remove the background, choose **Format**, **Sheet**, **Delete Background**.

Format ⇥ AutoFormat...

The AutoFormat command enables you to choose from built-in formats to a cell range or PivotTable. To start, click a cell within a range that you've been working on or select the range. For PivotTables, click within the table. Then choose **Format**, **AutoFormat** to bring up the AutoFormat dialog box (see Figure 3.52).

Format ⇥ Conditional Formatting...

Conditional Formatting is a new feature that enables you to choose formatting depending on the values that are in the cell. This feature is much easier than custom formatting (see **Format ⇥ Cells... Number Tab**, page 361). Choose **Format**, **Conditional Formatting** to open the Conditional Formatting dialog box (see Figure 3.53).

Figure 3.52
Format, AutoFormat
opens the AutoFormat
dialog box.

❶ Choose one of the
formats and see the
sample.

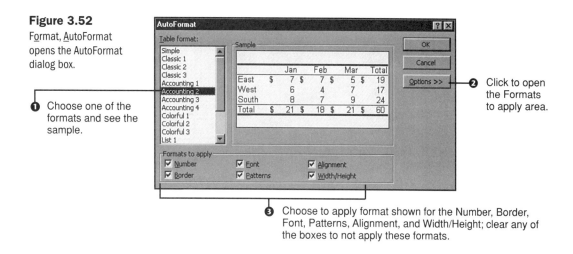

❷ Click to open
the Formats
to apply area.

❸ Choose to apply format shown for the Number, Border,
Font, Patterns, Alignment, and Width/Height; clear any of
the boxes to not apply these formats.

❷ Choose Cell Value
Is or Formula Is.

❸ Choose comparisons.

Figure 3.53
Format, Conditional
Formatting opens the
Conditional Formatting
dialog box.

❶ You can include
up to three
conditions.

❻ Click to add
condition two or
condition three.

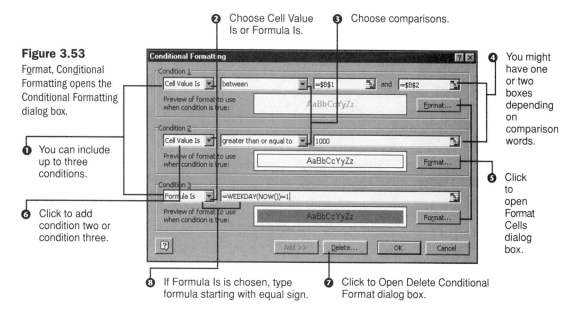

❹ You might
have one
or two
boxes
depending
on
comparison
words.

❺ Click
to
open
Format
Cells
dialog
box.

❽ If Formula Is is chosen, type
formula starting with equal sign.

❼ Click to Open Delete Conditional
Format dialog box.

Format → Style...

Style enables you to format with a number of formatting options at once. If you change the
formatting applied to the style, all ranges with that style also change. Select the range you want
to change formatting for and choose **Format**, **Style**. The Style dialog box opens (see Figure
3.54).

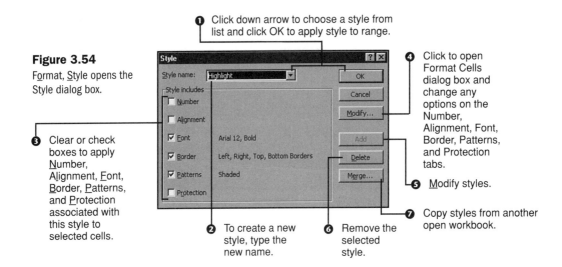

Figure 3.54
Format, Style opens the Style dialog box.

① Click down arrow to choose a style from list and click OK to apply style to range.

③ Clear or check boxes to apply Number, Alignment, Font, Border, Patterns, and Protection associated with this style to selected cells.

② To create a new style, type the new name.

④ Click to open Format Cells dialog box and change any options on the Number, Alignment, Font, Border, Patterns, and Protection tabs.

⑤ Modify styles.

⑥ Remove the selected style.

⑦ Copy styles from another open workbook.

Format ➡ Object...

If you have an object selected such as a picture or AutoShape, the **Format**, **Cells** menu item changes to **Format**, **Object** or **Format** and the name of the type of object (**Picture**, **WordArt**, **AutoShape**). Generally, this is something you've added by pasting from the clipboard or through the **Insert** menu (see **Insert ‑ Object...**, page 360 or **Insert ‑ Picture**, page 360). If you want to change colors for all objects on the workbook at the same time, see **Tools ‑ Options... Color Tab**, page 406.

Most of the options for formatting an object are the same as they are for Word (see Word's **Format ‑ Object**, page 183). The following table shows what is added for Excel.

Format Object dialog box—Differences from Word

Dialog Box Item	How to Use
Protection Tab	
Locked	Check this option to prevent changes to the object if the worksheet is protected (see **Tools ‑ Protection ‑ Protect Sheet...**, page 387).
Properties Tab	
Move and size with cells	If surrounding cells move or change size (width or height), also reposition and size this graphic.
Move but don't size with cells	If surrounding cells move or change size (width or height), only reposition this graphic.
Don't move or size with cells	If surrounding cells move or change size, don't do anything with this graphic.
Print object	Check this box to print the graphic with the worksheet.

Dialog Box Item	How to Use
Margins Tab (Text Box, Comment, and Callout Objects)	
Automatic	Have Excel calculate the internal margin.
Internal margin	Type or use the **L**eft, **R**ight, **T**op, and **B**ottom spinner boxes to indicate the amount of space between text and the box.
Alignment Tab (Text Box, Comment, and Callout Objects)	
Horizontal	Choose to have the text Left aligned, Centered, Right aligned, or both left and right aligned (Justify) within the text box.
Vertical	Choose to have your text at the Top, Center, or Bottom of your text box or spread between the top and bottom (Justify).
Orientation	Click one of the four example orientations to have your text left to right or different variations of up and down.
Automatic size	Check this box to change the size of the shape to fit the text.
Font tab (Text Box, Comment, and Callout Objects)	This is the same tab as on the Format Cells dialog box (see **Format - Cells... Font Tab**, page 366).

Format ➙ Chart Objects

When you are on a chart sheet or have an embedded chart object selected, the first item on the **Format** menu changes to whatever part of the chart is selected. To format an object you first select the object and then bring up Format dialog box:

To select a chart object do one of the following:

- Click the object.
- Click the **Chart Objects** drop-down button [_____ ▼] on the Chart toolbar.
- To select a data point (one bar, column, and so on) first click the data series and then click the specific data point. Small rectangles surround the data point.
- After a chart object is selected, press any arrow key to select other chart objects.

To open the Format dialog box do one of the following:

- Double-click the object.
- Right-click the object and choose the **Format** menu item.
- Click the **Format Selected Object** button on the Chart toolbar.
- Press **Ctrl+1** (on the number key row and not numeric keypad).
- Choose **Format** and the **Selected** chart object menu item.

After you are in the Format dialog box (the title is specific to the chart object), you have up to six tabs, each of which is described in the following sections.

Format ⇝ Chart Objects... Patterns Tab

Any chart object that has lines (such as an axis, or data table) or color (for example, title text boxes; plot areas; walls; floors; data series; data points for bar charts, column charts, area charts, and so on) will have a Patterns tab in its Format dialog box. In most Pattern tabs, there are three sections: a Border (or Line) section, an Area section, and a Sample section (see Figure 3.55).

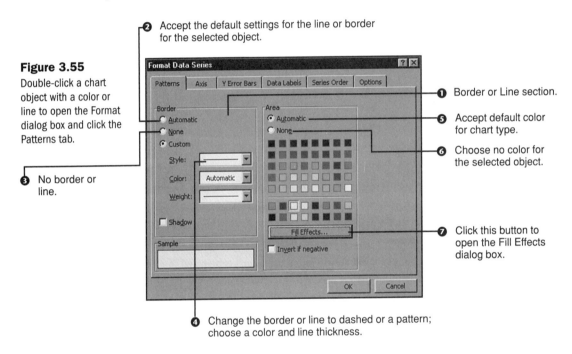

② Accept the default settings for the line or border for the selected object.

Figure 3.55
Double-click a chart object with a color or line to open the Format dialog box and click the Patterns tab.

❸ No border or line.

❶ Border or Line section.

❺ Accept default color for chart type.

❻ Choose no color for the selected object.

❼ Click this button to open the Fill Effects dialog box.

❹ Change the border or line to dashed or a pattern; choose a color and line thickness.

Specific Notes About the Patterns Tab for Data Series and Data Points

- The Area section of the Patterns tab appears for all chart types except line charts (Line, XY Scatter, and the parts of Radar and Stock charts that are lines only).

- Most two-dimensional charts (except Stock and line charts) have a **Shadow** check box to place a shadow on the bottom and right side of the selected object.

- For charts that have some height to the data series (2- and 3-D Columns, Bars, Cylinder, Cone, and Pyramids), check **Invert if negative** to change the color of the data point for values less than 0.

- Line, XY Scatter, and the Radar charts with lines, have an additional section, **Marker**, that can place a shape at each data point. Choose **Automatic** to choose the default settings for this chart type or **None** to place no marker (leave a line). If you want a specific marker, choose the shape in the **Sty_l_e** drop-down list and the **_F_oreground** and **_B_ackground** colors. You can also change the **Si_z_e** of the marker and check the box to give it a **Sha_d_ow**.

▪ Line, XY Scatter, and Radar charts with lines also have a **S_m_oothed Line** check box to take out the jagged edges in lines.

▪ For a Bubbles chart, check **_3_-D effect** to vary the color to make the bubbles appear three-dimensional.

If you want to change colors for all charts on the workbook at once, see **_T_ools ▪ _O_ptions... Color Tab**, page 406.

Patterns Tab for Data Table (Additions)

When you add a Data Table to a chart, you can turn on and off **Show _l_egend keys** to show the legend colors or markers within the table. You can also choose which lines you want to display for the table (**_H_orizontal**, **_V_ertical**, and **_O_utline**).

Patterns Tab for Axis (Additions)

You set major and minor divisions for your numbers on your axes on the Scale tab (see **Format ▪ Chart Objects... Scale Tab**, page 378). The Patterns tab enables you to determine marks you place on the scale. These are called tick marks. The major tick marks are those for categories on the x-axis and usually whole numbers on the y-axis. Minor tick marks are usually smaller units between the major tick marks.

For **_M_ajor tick mark types** and **Mino_r_ tick mark types**, you can choose to have no tick mark (**None**). You also can choose to have the tick mark on the **Inside** part of the chart, the **Outside** part of the chart, or crossing the axis (**Cross**).

For the **_T_ick mark labels** associated with a major tick mark, you can choose to have no label (**None**) or have the label **Next to axis**. If you choose **Low**, the labels appear on the same side of the chart as the axis (usually bottom or left side). If you choose **High**, the labels appear on the opposite side of the chart (usually top or right side).

Format ▪ Chart Objects... Font Tab

When you format any text (title, axis, data label, and so on) on your chart, there is a Font tab in the Format dialog box. This is the same as the Format Cells dialog box (see **Format ▪ Cells... Font Tab**, page 366) with the addition of the **Au_t_o scale** check box. Check this box to have the text change size when you change the size of the whole chart.

Format ▪ Chart Objects... Alignment Tab

You can change the justification of text on your chart with the Alignment tab of the Format dialog box (see Figure 3.56).

Figure 3.56

Double-click a text chart object to open the Format dialog box and click the Alignment tab.

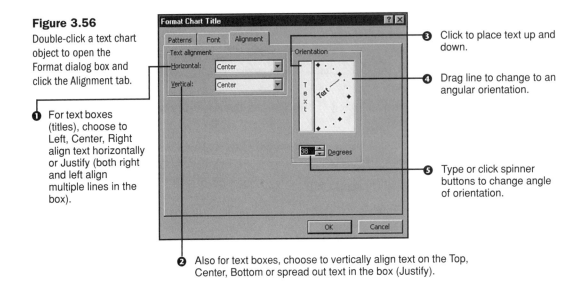

① For text boxes (titles), choose to Left, Center, Right align text horizontally or Justify (both right and left align multiple lines in the box).

③ Click to place text up and down.

④ Drag line to change to an angular orientation.

⑤ Type or click spinner buttons to change angle of orientation.

② Also for text boxes, choose to vertically align text on the Top, Center, Bottom or spread out text in the box (Justify).

Quick **Choices**   *CHANGE ALIGNMENT OF TEXT ON CHART*

1. Select text or an axis on the chart.

2. Click the **Angle Text Downward** 🔧 or **Angle Text Upward** button 🔧 on the Chart toolbar.

Format ￫ Chart Objects... Placement Tab

There is no Alignment tab on the Format Legend dialog box when you format a legend. Alternatively, you can use the Placement tab to change the location of the legend to the **Bottom**, **Corner**, **Top**, **Right**, or **Left** side of the chart. If there are many items in the legend, the shape might change to accommodate the placement (narrow rectangle on the sides or long rectangle on top or bottom). After you place the legend on the chart, you can also drag the legend to another location on the chart.

Format ￫ Chart Objects... Scale Tab

The Scale tab of the Format Axis dialog box is available when you format any of the axes. When you format the value axis (Y scale in 2-D charts or Z scale in 3-D charts), the following dialog box appears (see Figure 3.57).

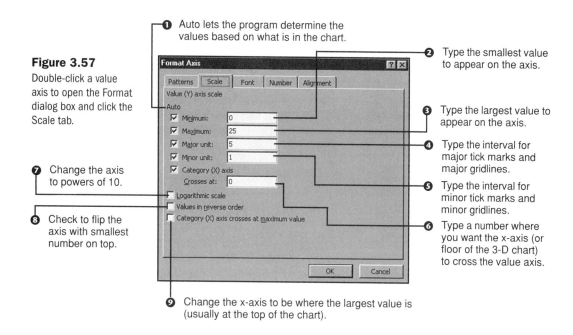

Figure 3.57
Double-click a value axis to open the Format dialog box and click the Scale tab.

❶ Auto lets the program determine the values based on what is in the chart.

❷ Type the smallest value to appear on the axis.

❸ Type the largest value to appear on the axis.

❹ Type the interval for major tick marks and major gridlines.

❼ Change the axis to powers of 10.

❺ Type the interval for minor tick marks and minor gridlines.

❽ Check to flip the axis with smallest number on top.

❻ Type a number where you want the x-axis (or floor of the 3-D chart) to cross the value axis.

❾ Change the x-axis to be where the largest value is (usually at the top of the chart).

When you format the category axis (usually the horizontal axis), the following dialog box appears (see Figure 3.58). Depending on the chart, not all the options appear.

To place gridlines with this scale (see **Chart – Chart Options... Gridlines Tab**, page 449).

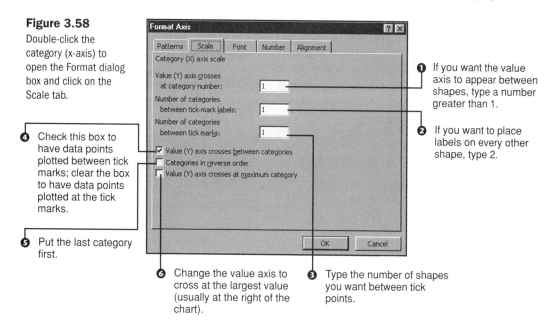

Figure 3.58
Double-click the category (x-axis) to open the Format dialog box and click on the Scale tab.

❹ Check this box to have data points plotted between tick marks; clear the box to have data points plotted at the tick marks.

❺ Put the last category first.

❶ If you want the value axis to appear between shapes, type a number greater than 1.

❷ If you want to place labels on every other shape, type 2.

❻ Change the value axis to cross at the largest value (usually at the right of the chart).

❸ Type the number of shapes you want between tick points.

Format ➥ Chart Objects... Axis Tab

This Axis tab is available for a data series. When you double-click a bar or chart, the Format Data Series dialog box opens. Click the Axis tab. For the data series you selected, you can choose to plot the series on the **Primary axis** or the **Secondary axis**. You might need to plot the data on the second axis if it is significantly different than the other data. For example, you might want to plot sales units and total revenue on the same chart. Because units and revenue have different measurements, you can use two different axes.

Format ➥ Chart Objects... Shape Tab

If you want to change the 3-D shape for one of the data series in certain charts—3-D Column, Bar, Cylinder, Cone, or Pyramid charts—double-click the data series and click the Shape tab. Choose one of the six shapes: blocks, full and cut pyramids, cylinders, and full and cut cones.

Format ➥ Chart Objects... Y Error Bars and X Error Bars Tabs

Error bars tell you the range of values you can expect for each data point in a series (the maximum and minimum value). You can add error bars for Area, Bar, Column, Line, XY Scatter, and Bubble charts. For XY Scatter charts you can add error bars for either or both dimensions (Y Error Bars and X Error Bars). Figure 3.59 shows the Y Error Bars tab on the Format Data Series dialog box.

Figure 3.59
Double-click a chart; open the Format dialog box and click the Y Error Bars or X Error Bars tab.

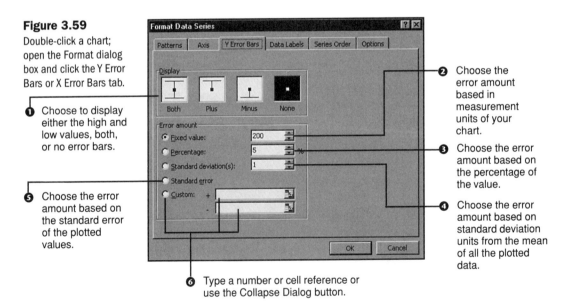

❶ Choose to display either the high and low values, both, or no error bars.

❺ Choose the error amount based on the standard error of the plotted values.

❻ Type a number or cell reference or use the Collapse Dialog button.

❷ Choose the error amount based in measurement units of your chart.

❸ Choose the error amount based on the percentage of the value.

❹ Choose the error amount based on standard deviation units from the mean of all the plotted data.

Format ▾ Chart Objects... Series Order Tab

If you want to change the order of the columns, bars, and so on on you chart, double-click one of them and click the Series Order tab on the Format Data Series dialog box. Click on the series in the **Series order** list box and choose the **Move Up** or **Move Down** button.

Format ▾ Chart Objects... Options Tab

All data series except Stock charts have an Option tab on the Data Series Format dialog box. This tab changes the placement of the data points on the x-axis, the thickness of 3-D shapes, starting point and colors of pie slices, and other options. These options are described in the following table.

Dialog Box Option	Chart Types	How to Use
Overlap	Column, Bar	Type or click the spinner buttons to change how much the columns or bars overlap each other at each category. A positive number overlaps shapes; a negative number spreads out shapes.
Gap depth	3-D Column, 3-D Bar, 3-D Area, Cylinder, Cone, Pyramid	Type (0-500) or click spinner buttons to specify the amount of space between categories of data markers (similar to Overlap).
Gap width	2-D and 3-D Column, Bar	Type or click spinner buttons to change space between categories.
Series lines	2-D Stacked Bar and Column charts	Check this box to draw lines between each category for the series.
Chart depth	All 3-D charts except Pie	Type or click spinner button to increase or decrease the thickness of shapes on the chart (how deep the chart is relative to its width).
Vary colors by point	For a single data series in 2-D and 3-D Bar and Column charts, Line, XY Scatter, Cylinder, Cone, Pyramid	Check to change color for each data point of the series.
Vary colors by slice	Pie, 3-D Pie, Doughnut	Check to make sure each slice is a different color.
Drop lines	Line, Area, 3-D Area, Ribbon	Check this box to create lines from the data point to the x-axis.

continues

Dialog Box Option	Chart Types	How to Use
High-low lines	Line	Check this box to create lines from the highest value to lowest value for each category.
Up-down bars	Line	Check this box to create a rectangle from the highest value to lowest value for each category.
Angle of first slice Degrees	Pie, 3-D Pie, Doughnut	Type (0-360) or click spinner buttons to specify starting angle for the first pie slice.
Doughnut hole size %	Doughnut	Type (10-90) or click spinner buttons to specify the size of the hole in the middle of the doughnut.
Category labels	Radar	Check this box to place category labels on each data point.
Area of bubbles or Width of bubbles	Bubble	Click to change the bubble size and proportion to be relative to their area or width.
Scale bubble size to % of default	Bubble	Type (0-300) to enlarge or shrink bubbles to a percentage of their default size.
Show negative bubbles	Bubble	Check this box to display bullets with negative values in a different color (white).

Tools

The Tools menu is a grab bag of options including working with words, managing revisions, macros, and setting the Excel environment.

Tools ➥ Spelling...

The Spelling dialog box checks the spelling of each word in your document.

1. Open the Spelling and Grammar dialog box one of the following ways:
   - Click the **Spelling and Grammar** button ⬛ on the Standard toolbar.
   - Press **F7**.
   - Choose **Tools, Spelling**.

2. If you don't want to check words in capital letters, check **Igno_r_e UPPERCASE**.

3. Words that are not in the dictionary display in the top of the dialog box. Do one of the following:

   - Click **Ignore** to skip the misspelled word.

   - Click **Ignore All** to skip this word throughout the document. Unlike Word, Excel does not maintain an internal list of words for the document. Each time you run spell check, Excel stops at the word (unless you choose **Add**).

   - Click **Add** to add the word to the dictionary (and not check it for other documents).

   - Choose from the **Suggestions** and click **Change** to correct your document, **Change All** to change every occurrence in your document, or **AutoCorrect** (see the section below to correct this mistake every time you type the word this way).

   - Check **Always suggest** to have Excel suggest spellings when you first come to a misspelled word. If you want additional words for the current misspelling, choose a word in the Suggestions list box and click **Suggest**.

4. If you accidentally made a correction, click **Undo Last** to go back to the last change.

5. Continue checking the document, and click **Close** when you are finished.

Tools ➥ AutoCorrect...

The AutoCorrect dialog box enables Excel to fix mistakes as you type and expand abbreviations for words. Excel's AutoCorrect dialog box has one tab—AutoCorrect. Word has this same tab with the same options, but also has additional tabs (see Word's **Tools ➥ AutoCorrect**, page 195).

Tools ➥ Look Up Reference...

Microsoft Office comes with Bookshelf Basics, which is a collection of reference tools that include a dictionary, thesaurus, and quotations. Bookshelf Basic also includes previews of an encyclopedia, almanac, atlas, Internet directory, chronology, and an address builder that finds zip codes.

Select a word on your document and choose **Tools**, **Look Up Reference** to open the Look Up Reference dialog box. Depending on what you have installed, choose the title you want to view and click **Keyword** to search only article titles, **Full Text** to check the whole reference, or **None** to open up the reference without searching.

Tools ➥ Share Workbook...

The Share Workbook feature lets multiple people edit and save changes to the same workbook. Choose **Tools**, **Share Workbook**. The Share Workbook dialog box opens (see Figure 3.60).

Figure 3.60

Tools, Share Workbook opens the Share Workbook dialog box.

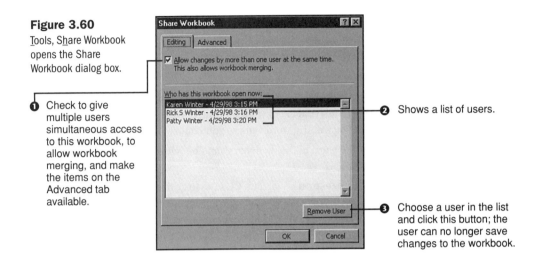

❶ Check to give multiple users simultaneous access to this workbook, to allow workbook merging, and make the items on the Advanced tab available.

❷ Shows a list of users.

❸ Choose a user in the list and click this button; the user can no longer save changes to the workbook.

The following are options on the Advanced tab. They are only enabled when the **Allow changes by more than one user at the same time** box is checked.

Share Workbook Advanced Tab

Dialog Box Option	How to Use
Track Changes Section	
Keep change history for	Click this option and type number of **days** or click spinner arrows to have Excel keep information about changes made during past sessions. (To view changes, see **Tools - Track Changes - Highlight Changes...**, page 385.)
Don't keep change history	Click to not record changes.
Update Changes Section	
When file is saved	Click this option to provide the current user with updates from other users on **File, Save**.
Automatically every minute	Instead of the previous option, click this option to automatically receive other's changes at the interval in **m**inutes.
Save my **c**hanges and see others' changes	If **Automatically every** is checked, click this option to save your changes and receive changes from others.
Just see other users' changes	If **Automatically every** is checked, click this option to receive changes from others (without saving your changes automatically).

Dialog Box Option	How to Use
Conflicting Changes Between Users Section	
A<u>s</u>k me which changes win	When two people edit the same cell, click this option to open the Resolve Conflicts dialog box shown in Figure 3.61.
<u>T</u>he changes being saved win	When two people edit the same cell, click this option to have changes determined by the last person to save.
Include in Personal View Section	
<u>P</u>rint settings	For each different user, check this box to allow them to separately define print settings (see **File - Page Setup...**, page 265).
<u>F</u>ilter settings	For each different user, check this box to allow them to separately keep filter settings (see **Data - Filter**, page 411).

If two users change the same cell(s), the second user to save the workbook sees the Resolve Conflicts dialog box (see Figure 3.61).

Figure 3.61
When two users edit the same cell, the Resolve Conflicts dialog box appears when the second user tries to save the file.

❶ Shows location and discrepancy between the current and other user.

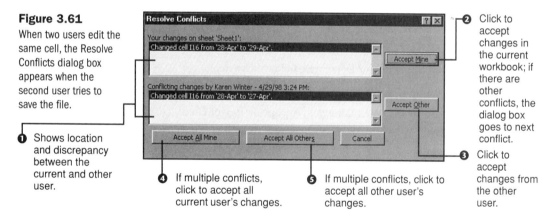

❷ Click to accept changes in the current workbook; if there are other conflicts, the dialog box goes to next conflict.

❸ Click to accept changes from the other user.

❹ If multiple conflicts, click to accept all current user's changes.

❺ If multiple conflicts, click to accept all other user's changes.

Tools ➥ Track Changes

You can use the Track Changes feature if you want to keep track of your edits, additions, and deletions. This is especially helpful if you send your document out to other people for review.

Tools ➥ Track Changes ➥ Highlight Changes...

Highlight changes enables you to see editing on your document. If you've selected the **Keep change history** option on the Advanced tab of the Share Workbook dialog box (see **Tools - Share Workbook...**, page 383), you can see any changes you or other users have made. Choose **Tools, Track Changes, Highlight Changes**. The Highlight Changes dialog box opens (see Figure 3.62).

Figure 3.62

Tools, Track Changes, Highlight Changes opens the Track Changes dialog box.

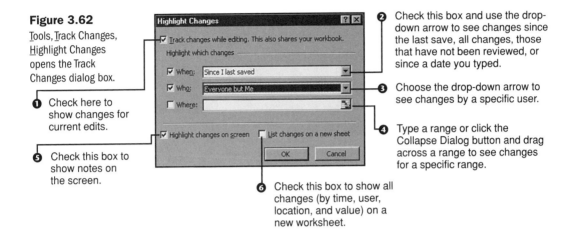

❶ Check here to show changes for current edits.

❺ Check this box to show notes on the screen.

❷ Check this box and use the drop-down arrow to see changes since the last save, all changes, those that have not been reviewed, or since a date you typed.

❸ Choose the drop-down arrow to see changes by a specific user.

❹ Type a range or click the Collapse Dialog button and drag across a range to see changes for a specific range.

❻ Check this box to show all changes (by time, user, location, and value) on a new worksheet.

If you want to prevent users from clearing the **Track changes while editing** box, see **Tools** ▪ **Protection** ▪ **Protect and Share Workbook...**, page 388.

Tools ▪ Track Changes ▪ Accept or Reject Changes...

After you've recorded changes (see **Tools** ▪ **Track Changes** ▪ **Highlight Changes...**, page 385), you can choose to keep or remove the changes.

To Review Changes in Your Document, follow these steps:

1. Press **Ctrl+Home** to move to the top of the document.

2. Choose **Tools, Track Changes, Accept or Reject Changes**. The Select Changes to Accept or Reject dialog box opens.

3. Choose the changes you want to see by **When, Who,** and **Where** (similar to Figure 3.62) and click **OK**. The Accept or Reject Changes dialog box opens.

4. Click one of the changes in the **Select a value for cell** list.

5. If you want to keep the change, click **Accept** or if you want to disregard the change, click **Reject**. Word automatically goes to the next or previous change (this depends on which Find button you last chose).

6. You can also deal with all changes at the same time. Click **Accept All** to keep all corrections or **Reject All** to turn the document back the way it was before changes.

7. When finished, choose **Close**.

Tools ▪ Merge Workbooks...

If you want to keep two (or more) separate copies of the same workbook for editing at different times, you can use the Merge Workbooks feature. Maybe one workbook is on a laptop and another is at the office. Before you make a copy of the workbook, first turn on the Share

Workbook feature (see **Tools - Share Workbook...**, page 383). Then use **File, Open** to go to the Open dialog box. Right-click the file and chose **Open as Copy**. When you're finished editing the file you can save it with a different name if you want (see **File - Save As...**, page 263).

After you've set up the copy of the workbook and made changes to both copies, do the following to merge the copies together:

1. Open the workbook where you want to merge into.

2. Choose **Tools, Merge Workbooks**. The Select Files to Merge Into Current Workbook dialog box appears.

3. Select the file. You can hold down **Ctrl** and click additional files if you want. Click **OK** when ready.

The files merge together with comments for cells that were added (see **View - Comments**, page 302).

Tools - Protection

Protection enables you to prevent changes to a worksheet or workbook. You can assign a password to the protection so unauthorized users cannot turn off the protection. If your workbook is shared (see **Tools - Share Workbook...**, page 383), the first two menu items (Protect Sheet and Protect Workbook) are disabled.

Tools - Protection - Protect Sheet...

In some cases, you will want to allow the user to edit some cells (such as a data entry area) and not allow the user to edit other areas (such as formulas or labels). You first have to unlock or lock cells or objects and then turn on protection.

To unlock cells and objects and protect the worksheet, follow these steps:

1. Select a range you want to unlock. You can hold down **Ctrl** and select multiple ranges.

2. Choose **Format, Cells**, click the Protection tab, and uncheck **Locked**. This box is checked by default. If you want to prevent edits in the cell, check **Locked**. If you want formulas to not show in the Formula bar, check **Hidden**. Choose **OK**.

3. If you want to unlock an object, right-click the object and choose the **Format** menu item (**Object, Picture, AutoShape**, and so on). Uncheck **Locked** on the Protection tab. If the object can accept text, you can also uncheck **Lock text** so you can make changes to text in the callout or text box. Choose **OK**.

4. After you've unlocked or locked all ranges and objects, choose **Tools, Protection, Protect Sheet**. The Protect Sheet dialog box opens.

5. Do any of the following:

    - To prevent edits to all unlocked cells, check **Contents**.
    - To prevent edits to all unlocked objects, check **Objects**.
    - To prevent changes to scenarios (see **Tools - Scenarios...**, page 389), check **Scenarios**.

6. If you want a **P**assword, type it in the text box. (Write this down and keep it somewhere safe. You cannot unprotect the worksheet without it.)

7. Click **OK**. If you typed a password in step 6, type it again and click **OK**.

If someone tries to edit a locked cell or object, he or she gets a message that the item is locked. Many of the menu items are also disabled. To unprotect the sheet, choose **Tools**, **P**rotection, **U**nprotect Sheet. If you set a password, type the **P**assword and click **OK**.

Tools ➠ Protection ➠ Protect Workbook...

If you want to prevent users from changing sheets, protect your workbook. Users will not be able to delete, move, hide, unhide, rename, or insert sheets. You can also protect windows from being moved or resized.

To protect window and sheet structures, follow these steps:

1. Choose **Tools**, **P**rotection, **Protect W**orkbook. The Protect workbook dialog box opens.

2. Do any of the following:
   - To prevent deletions, additions, and changes to all sheets in the workbook, check **Structure**.
   - To prevent moving and sizing of windows, check **W**indows.

3. If you want a **P**assword, type it in the text box. (Write this down and keep it somewhere safe. You will not be able to unprotect the workbook without it.)

4. Click **OK**. If you typed a password in step 3, type it again and click **OK**.

Tools ➠ Protection ➠ Protect and Share Workbook...

You can prohibit users from turning off the tracking history (see **Tools ➠ Track Changes ➠ Highlight Changes...**, page 385) and from sharing the workbook (see **Tools ➠ Share Workbook...**, page 383).

1. Choose **Tools**, **P**rotection, **Protect and Share Workbook.** (This menu item is named **Protect Shared Workbook** if the workbook is already shared.) The Protect Shared Workbook dialog box opens.

2. Check **Sharing with Track Changes**.

3. If you want a **P**assword, type it in the text box. (Write this down and keep it somewhere safe. You cannot unprotect the workbook without it.)

4. Click **OK**. If you typed a password in step 3, type it again and click **OK**.

Tools ➡ Goal Seek...

If you have a formula that depends on certain input cells, you can work backwards and choose a result you want for the formula by having Excel automatically adjust one of the input cells. Excel keeps recalculating the formula by changing the input value multiple times. You can set the number of times Excel calculates by changing the iteration values on the options dialog box (see **Tools – Options... Calculation Tab**, page 401). Move to the formula cell and choose **Tools, Goal Seek**. The Goal Seek dialog box opens (see Figure 3.63).

Figure 3.63

Tools, Goal Seek opens the Goal Seek dialog box.

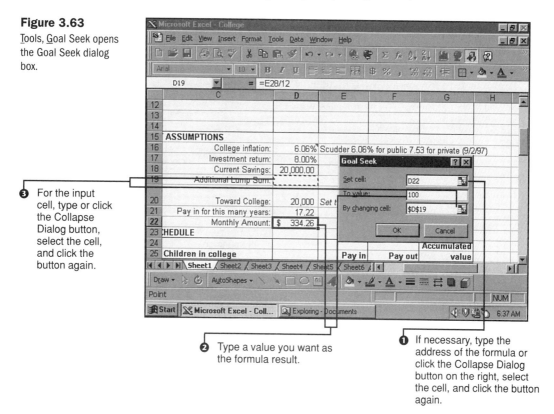

❸ For the input cell, type or click the Collapse Dialog button, select the cell, and click the button again.

❷ Type a value you want as the formula result.

❶ If necessary, type the address of the formula or click the Collapse Dialog button on the right, select the cell, and click the button again.

After you click **OK**, the Goal Seek Status dialog box opens (see Figure 3.64).

Tools ➡ Scenarios...

If you have multiple input cells that you want to change and see the results, use the Scenarios feature. This is great for managing your what-if analyses. To start, choose **Tools, Scenarios**. The Scenario Manager dialog box opens (see Figure 3.65).

6 Click Cancel to return worksheet to original numbers before Goal Seek.

Figure 3.64
Click OK on the Goal Seek dialog box to open the Goal Seek Status dialog box.

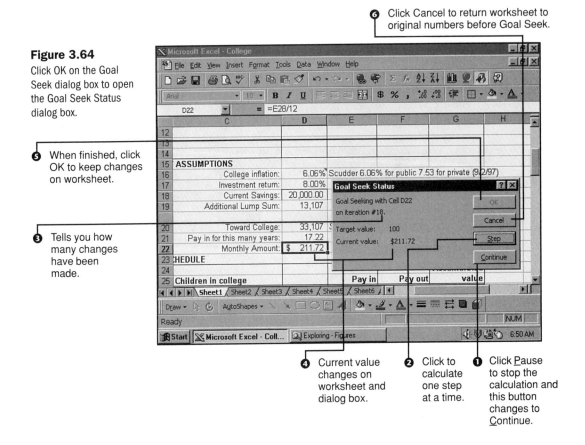

5 When finished, click OK to keep changes on worksheet.

3 Tells you how many changes have been made.

4 Current value changes on worksheet and dialog box.

2 Click to calculate one step at a time.

1 Click Pause to stop the calculation and this button changes to Continue.

2 Display results for highlighted scenario.

Figure 3.65
Tools, Scenarios opens the Scenario Manager dialog box.

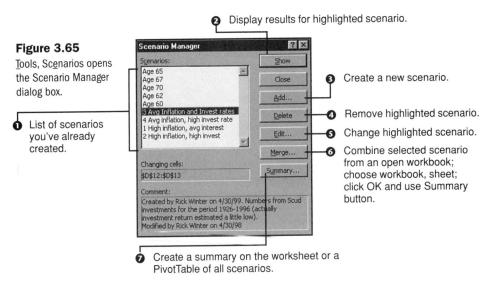

1 List of scenarios you've already created.

3 Create a new scenario.

4 Remove highlighted scenario.

5 Change highlighted scenario.

6 Combine selected scenario from an open workbook; choose workbook, sheet; click OK and use Summary button.

7 Create a summary on the worksheet or a PivotTable of all scenarios.

To create a new scenario, click the **Add** button on the Scenario Manager dialog box. The Add Scenario dialog box opens (see Figures 3.66 and 3.67). This dialog box is almost identical to the Edit Scenario dialog box (except for the title bar).

Figure 3.66

Click Add on the Scenario Manager dialog box to open the Add Scenario dialog box.

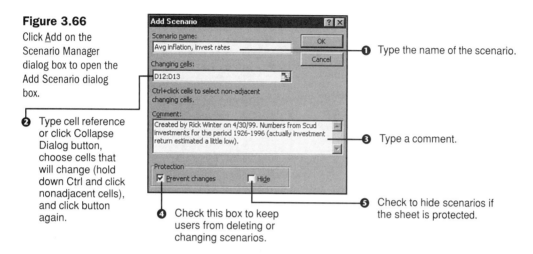

❷ Type cell reference or click Collapse Dialog button, choose cells that will change (hold down Ctrl and click nonadjacent cells), and click button again.

❶ Type the name of the scenario.

❸ Type a comment.

❺ Check to hide scenarios if the sheet is protected.

❹ Check this box to keep users from deleting or changing scenarios.

After you choose **OK** from the Add (or Edit) Scenario dialog box, the Scenario Values dialog box opens. Type the value of each of your changing cells and click **OK**. On a new sheet, list input cells on the left side of the table and result cells as columns (see Figure 3.68).

❶ Create a summary on a new sheet that lists scenarios and input and result cells (use for one set of changing cells provided by one user).

Figure 3.67

Click Summary on the Scenario Manager dialog box to open the Add Scenario dialog box.

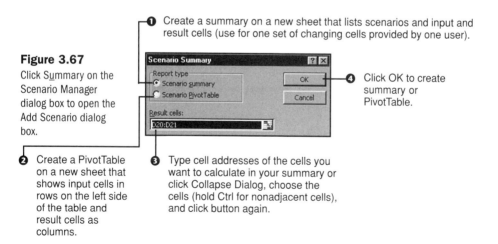

❹ Click OK to create summary or PivotTable.

❷ Create a PivotTable on a new sheet that shows input cells in rows on the left side of the table and result cells as columns.

❸ Type cell addresses of the cells you want to calculate in your summary or click Collapse Dialog, choose the cells (hold Ctrl for nonadjacent cells), and click button again.

Figure 3.68
On Scenario Summary dialog box, choose Scenario PivotTable and click OK to see these results.

❷ Labels were originally cell addresses; new meaningful labels were typed.

❸ If you want to format cells (and keep the format), select the cells and choose the PivotTable button on the PivotTable toolbar; then choose Select, Enable Selection.

❶ Click drop-down arrow to choose changes by different users.

❹ Use the PivotTable toolbar.

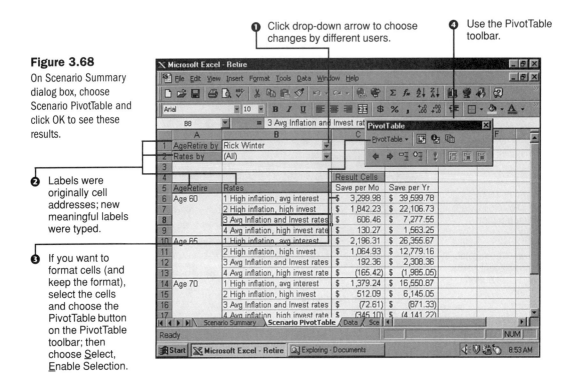

Tools ➥ Auditing

The Auditing features of Excel enable you to see cells that are part of a formula (precedents) or formulas that depend on cells (dependents). You can also see cells that cause an error.

In addition to the auditing features mentioned in this section, Excel also the new Range Finder feature. When you edit a formula by (pressing **F2**) or clicking in the Formula bar, Excel highlights the precedent cells of the formula.

Tools ➥ Auditing ➥ Trace Precedents

A precedent is a cell that is required for a formula. To draw an arrow to the cells that make up a formula, choose **Tools, Auditing, Trace Precedents** or click the **Trace Precedents** button on the Auditing toolbar. Click **Trace Precedents** again to see if there are cells that are precedents to the precedents.

To remove the arrows, click **Remove Precedent Arrows** or **Remove All Arrows** or choose **Tools, Auditing, Remove All Arrows**.

If you want to select all precedent cells, press **Ctrl+[** for direct precedents or **Ctrl+Shift+{** for direct or indirect precedents.

Tools – Auditing – Trace Dependents

Dependents are formula cells that depend on data from the active cell. The formula depends on this cell. To see if any formulas depend on the current cell, choose **Tools, Auditing, Trace Dependents** or click the **Trace Dependents** button 🔳 on the Auditing toolbar. Click **Trace Dependents** 🔳 again to see if there are cells that are dependents to the dependents.

To remove the arrows, click **Remove Dependent Arrows** 🔳 or **Remove All Arrows** 🔳 or choose **Tools, Auditing, Remove All Arrows**.

If you want to select all dependent cells, press **Ctrl+]** for direct dependents or **Ctrl+Shift+}** for direct or indirect dependents.

Tools – Auditing – Trace Error

If the current cell has an error (such as #Value, #Div/0, or #Name?), choose **Tools, Auditing, Trace Error** or click the **Trace Error** button on the Auditing toolbar to draw arrows to cells that make up the formula.

Tools – Auditing – Remove All Arrows

To get rid of precedent, dependent, or error arrows, choose **Tools, Auditing, Remove All Arrows** or click the **Remove All Arrows** 🔳 button on the Auditing toolbar.

Tools – Auditing – Show Auditing Toolbar

To turn the Auditing toolbar on or off, choose **Tools, Auditing, Show Auditing Toolbar**. The first six buttons are discussed in the previous paragraphs. The toolbar contains the following remaining buttons:

Button	Name	How to Use
🔳	**New Comment**	Click to add a comment (see **Insert – Comment**, page 359).
🔳	**Circle Invalid Data**	If there is any data that is outside the limits you set through Validation, circle this data (see **Data – Validation...**, page 414).
🔳	**Clear Validation Circles**	Remove circles you added with Circle Invalid Data button.

Tools – AutoSave...

AutoSave automatically saves your open workbook(s) during the time period you specify. However you should still use **File, Save** (see page 263) after you've done some difficult procedures.

The AutoSave feature is not turned on during the Typical installation of Excel 97 or Office 97. If this option is not on the **Tools** menu, first try **Tools, Add-Ins**; check AutoSave and click **OK**. If this option is not in the Add-Ins dialog box, go through the Custom setup to install. After the add-in is installed, choose **Tools, AutoSave**. The AutoSave Dialog box displays (see Figure 3.69).

Figure 3.69

Tools – AutoSave opens the AutoSave dialog box.

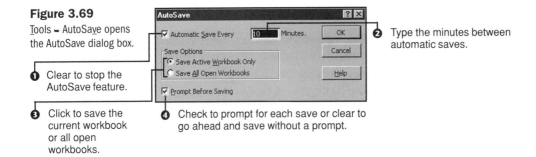

❶ Clear to stop the AutoSave feature.

❷ Type the minutes between automatic saves.

❸ Click to save the current workbook or all open workbooks.

❹ Check to prompt for each save or clear to go ahead and save without a prompt.

Tools ➥ Solver...

Unlike Goal Seek, which changes one input cell for a formula, Solver can change multiple cells to maximize, minimize, or set the value calculated by a formula. Changing the value of the input cells has to change the value of the formula. (Although the formula could be tied indirectly to the input cell through an intermediate formula or formulas.)

Goal Seek is not available in the Typical installation of Excel 97 or Office 97. You might need to go through the Custom setup to install this feature and then choose **Tools, Add-Ins**, and check **Solver Add-In** and click **OK**. After the add-in is installed, choose **Tools, Solver**. The Solver Parameters Dialog box displays (see Figure 3.70).

❶ Type or use Collapse Dialog button to Set Target Cell where the formula you want to evaluate is.

❾ Click to open Solver Results dialog box.

Figure 3.70

Tools, Solver opens the Solver Parameters dialog box.

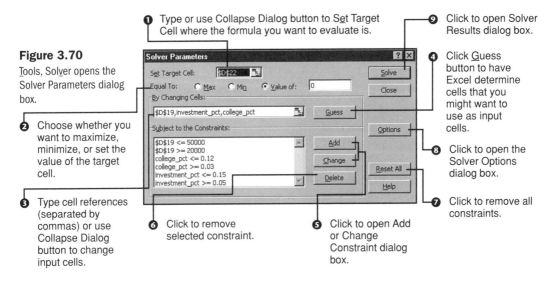

❹ Click Guess button to have Excel determine cells that you might want to use as input cells.

❷ Choose whether you want to maximize, minimize, or set the value of the target cell.

❽ Click to open the Solver Options dialog box.

❸ Type cell references (separated by commas) or use Collapse Dialog button to change input cells.

❼ Click to remove all constraints.

❻ Click to remove selected constraint.

❺ Click to open Add or Change Constraint dialog box.

After opening the Add or Change Constraint dialog box, type or use Collapse Dialog button to fill in **Cell Reference** box, use middle drop-down button to set operator to <=, =, >=, int (integer), bin (binary - yes or no), and type or use Collapse Dialog button to fill in **Constraint** if you use one of the first three operators. Click **Add** to add the constraint and keep Change Constraint dialog box open. Choose **OK** to return to the Solver Parameters dialog box.

The Solver Results dialog box is shown in Figure 3.71; the Solver Options dialog box is shown in Figure 3.72.

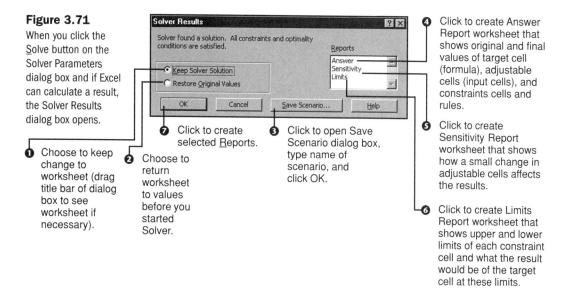

Figure 3.71

When you click the Solve button on the Solver Parameters dialog box and if Excel can calculate a result, the Solver Results dialog box opens.

① Choose to keep change to worksheet (drag title bar of dialog box to see worksheet if necessary).

② Choose to return worksheet to values before you started Solver.

⑦ Click to create selected Reports.

③ Click to open Save Scenario dialog box, type name of scenario, and click OK.

④ Click to create Answer Report worksheet that shows original and final values of target cell (formula), adjustable cells (input cells), and constraints cells and rules.

⑤ Click to create Sensitivity Report worksheet that shows how a small change in adjustable cells affects the results.

⑥ Click to create Limits Report worksheet that shows upper and lower limits of each constraint cell and what the result would be of the target cell at these limits.

The following are additional options on the Solver Options dialog box:

Option	How to Use
Assume Linear Model	Check if all relationships are linear and to speed up solution.
Assume Non-Negative	Check to have all constraint cells not set with lower limit to stop at 0.
Use Automatic Scaling	Check if input cells and target cell have large difference in magnitudes (for example, millions and ones).
Show Iteration Results	Click to pause for each intermediate solution. In the Show Trial Solution dialog box, click **Continue** to go to next solution, **Stop** to see current result, or **Save Scenario** to save dialog box settings.
Estimates	If the equations relating the data are linear, click **Tangent**, otherwise click **Quadratic**. (If you don't like the results, try **Quadratic**.)
Derivatives	For most problems, use **Forward**. If Solver gives you a message that a solution could not be improved, you may want to try **Central**. (This may work when constraints change rapidly near the limits.)
Search	For most problems, use **Newton**. If Solver takes a long time or you get a memory error, you can try **Conjugate**.

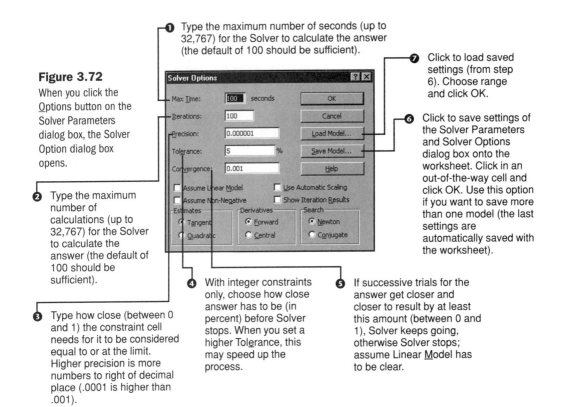

❶ Type the maximum number of seconds (up to 32,767) for the Solver to calculate the answer (the default of 100 should be sufficient).

❼ Click to load saved settings (from step 6). Choose range and click OK.

Figure 3.72
When you click the Options button on the Solver Parameters dialog box, the Solver Option dialog box opens.

❻ Click to save settings of the Solver Parameters and Solver Options dialog box onto the worksheet. Click in an out-of-the-way cell and click OK. Use this option if you want to save more than one model (the last settings are automatically saved with the worksheet).

❷ Type the maximum number of calculations (up to 32,767) for the Solver to calculate the answer (the default of 100 should be sufficient).

❹ With integer constraints only, choose how close answer has to be (in percent) before Solver stops. When you set a higher Tolerance, this may speed up the process.

❺ If successive trials for the answer get closer and closer to result by at least this amount (between 0 and 1), Solver keeps going, otherwise Solver stops; assume Linear Model has to be clear.

❸ Type how close (between 0 and 1) the constraint cell needs for it to be considered equal to or at the limit. Higher precision is more numbers to right of decimal place (.0001 is higher than .001).

Tools ➥ Macro

Macros are stored procedures that automate tasks that you do often. You can record a macro or create a procedure directly in Visual Basic.

Tools ➥ Macro ➥ Macros...

When you choose **Tools**, **Macro**, **Macros** or press **Alt+F8**, you open the Macros dialog box, which enables you to run or manage your macros (see Figure 3.73).

Quick Choices RUN MACRO

1. Press **Alt+F8**. The Macro dialog box opens.
2. Double-click the macro name.

Tools ➥ Macro ➥ Record New Macro...

You can record your keystrokes and menu choices and save it as a macro. Excel automatically creates the Visual Basic procedure for you.

1. Choose **Tools**, **Macros**, **Record New Macro**. The Record Macro dialog box displays.
2. Type the name in the **Macro name** text box.

❸ Type new name and click to go to Visual Basic window and type procedure.

❶ Execute selected macro procedure.

Figure 3.73
Tools, **M**acro, **M**acros opens the Macro dialog box.

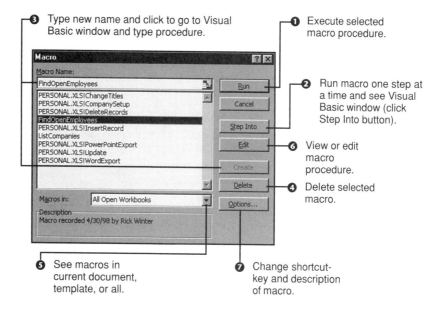

❷ Run macro one step at a time and see Visual Basic window (click Step Into button).

❻ View or edit macro procedure.

❹ Delete selected macro.

❺ See macros in current document, template, or all.

❼ Change shortcut-key and description of macro.

3. If you want to create a shortcut to run the macro, type the letter, number, or symbol in the **Shortcut <u>k</u>ey** text box.

4. Choose the workbook to **<u>S</u>tore macro in**. To make the macro available to all workbooks, choose Personal Macro Workbook. If you're going to send the workbook to someone else, make sure you store the macro with This Workbook.

5. Type a **<u>D</u>escription** for your macro. This box starts with your name and today's date.

6. Click **OK**. You enter a worksheet window with the Stop Recording toolbar open. The second button on the toolbar, **Use Relative References** , enables you to record each cell address you move to (**Absolute Addresses**—button is not pressed) or record the number of cells away from the starting cell (**Relative Addresses**—button is pressed).

7. Type text; move the insertion point, or choose menu or toolbar buttons. Unlike Word, you can record mouse movements.

8. When you're done recording your macro, click the **Stop Recording** button .

<u>T</u>ools ~ <u>M</u>acro ~ <u>V</u>isual Basic Editor

If you want to edit a macro or see macro procedures, choose **Tools**, **<u>M</u>acro**, **<u>V</u>isual Basic Editor** or press **Alt+F11**. Microsoft Visual Basic Editor opens. Click the **Find** button. In the **Find What** text box, type your macro name and choose **Find <u>N</u>ext** until you find your macro. For more information on Visual Basic for Applications, see Que's *Special Edition Using Visual Basic for Applications 5*.

Tools ➥ Add-Ins...

Add-ins extend the capabilities of Excel. They can add new functions, new menu items, and new toolbars. To activate an add-in, choose **Tools**, **Add-Ins**. The Add-Ins dialog box opens. Check each add-in you want or click the **Browse** button and double-click on any add-in file you would like to add.

The following table lists the available add-ins. Some of these might be not installed and so you might have to go through setup again to include them in this dialog box.

List of add-ins		
Add-In	**Used For**	**Changes to Program**
Installed During Typical Setup		
Analysis ToolPak	This is a collection of additional financial, statistical, and engineering functions.	To the **Data** menu, adds **Data Analysis.** When you choose **Insert, Function**, additional functions (and the Engineering category) are shown in the Paste Function dialog box.
AutoSave	Enables you to save your workbooks automatically at a specified time interval.	To the **Tools** menu, adds **AutoSave**.
Conditional Sum Wizard	Allows you to create a sum formula for data that matches criteria you specify.	See **Tools ‑ Wizard ‑ Conditional Sum...**, page 407.
Lookup Wizard	Steps you through the process of creating a formula to look up values in a list based on using a known value in the list.	See **Tools ‑ Wizard ‑ Lookup...**, page 408.
Microsoft Bookshelf Integration	Allows you to look up a word in the online thesaurus, dictionary, and other reference books.	See **Tools ‑ Look Up Reference...**, page 383.
Template Utilities	This add-in provides utilities used by the built-in templates.	
Update Add-in Links	If you had links to add-in features in earlier versions of Excel that are now built in to Excel 97, this updates those links.	

Add-In	Used For	Changes to Program
Installed with Complete or Custom Setup		
File Conversion Wizard	You can convert multiple files at one time to Excel.	To the **Tools, Wizard** menu, adds **File Conversion**.
Internet Assistant Wizard	Opens a wizard that enables you to save an Excel worksheet as an HTML file.	To the **File** menu, adds **Save as HTML**.
Microsoft AccessLinks Add-In	This enables you to create Access forms and reports to work with Excel data.	Adds the following items to your **Data** menu: **MS Access Form**, **MS Access Report**, and **Convert to MS Access**.
MS Query Add-In for Excel 5 Compatibility	If you have external Excel 97 data ranges, converts these ranges to Excel 5.0/95 format. This is necessary if you created macros in these previous versions.	
ODBC Add-In	Enables you to use Open Database Connectivity drivers.	
Report Manager	Enables you to combine print settings, custom views, and scenarios into a report for printing.	To the **View** menu, adds **Report Manager**.
Solver Add-In	Enables you to Calculate multiple input cells for a formula.	To the **Tools** menu, adds **Solver**.
Template Wizard with Data Tracking	This wizard steps you through the process of creating a template that records entries in a separate database.	To the **Data** menu, adds **Template Wizard**.
Web Form Wizard	This wizard steps you through the process of creating a form on a Web server so that data added to the form is added to a database.	To the **Tools, Wizard** menu, adds **Web Form**.

Tools ➥ Customize...

When you choose **Tools, Customize**, the Customize dialog box opens enabling you to edit or create toolbars and menus. This is the same dialog box shown in the Word's **View – Toolbars – Customize...** (see page 87). For differences between Word and Excel, see **View – Toolbars – Customize...** (see page 300).

Tools ➟ Options...

The **Tools**, **Options** command modifies how Microsoft Excel works including screen appearance, transition from Lotus 1-2-3, editing, user identification, and other options.

The following sections describe the tabs on the Options dialog box.

Tools ➟ Options... View Tab

The following table lists the available options on the View tab of the **Tools**, **Options** menu.

Dialog Box Option	How to Use
Show Section	
Formula bar	Check to display bar used for editing and creating formulas (see **View** - **Formula Bar**, page 300).
Status bar	Check to display the bar on the bottom of the screen (see **View** - **Status Bar**, page 301).
Comments Section	
None	Click to display no comments.
Comment **i**ndicator only	Click to display the red triangle in the upper-right corner of the cell. Hover over the comment to show the comment in a ScreenTip (see **View** - **Comments**, page 302).
Co**m**ment & indicator	Click to see all comments and their indicators.
Objects Section	
Show **a**ll	Click to see graphic objects such as pictures and charts.
Show **p**laceholders	Click to show (or print) a gray hatched box for pictures and charts to speed up viewing.
Hi**d**e all	Click to hide all graphic objects such as pictures, AutoShapes, text boxes, and buttons to really speed up viewing.
Window Options Section	
Page brea**k**s	Check to see page breaks on the screen as a dotted line (see **Insert** - **Page Break**, page 312).
For**m**ulas	Check to view and print functions and formulas instead of the resulting value for the formulas (see **Insert** - **Function...**, page 313).
Gridlines	Check to see gridlines on the screen or clear to hide gridlines. To print gridlines, choose **F**ile, Page Set**u**p, Sheet tab, **G**ridlines.

Dialog Box Option	How to Use
Color	Click drop–down arrow and choose the color for the **Gridlines**. Choose Automatic for normal gridlines.
Row & column headers	Check to show the 1,2,3 and A,B,C, (and so on) on the right side and top of the grid.
Outline symbols	If the worksheet contains an outline (see **Data – Group and Outline**, page 422), display the left edge with outline symbols.
Zero values	Check this box to display a zero (or selected format—see **Format – Cells... Number Tab**, page 361) for values that evaluate to 0 or clear this box to hide all 0s.
Horizontal scroll bar	Check to see the scroll bar that enables you to use the mouse to see more columns.
Vertical scroll bar	Check to see the split box and the bar that enables you to see more rows.
Sheet tabs	Check to see the tabs on the bottom of the worksheet and the Tab scrolling buttons.

Tools – Options... Calculation Tab

The following table lists the available options on the Calculation tab of the **Tools**, **Options** menu.

Dialog Box Option	How to Use
Calculation Section	
Automatic	Click to have Excel recalculate formulas every time you enter new values.
Automatic except tables	Click to have Excel recalculate all formulas automatically except data tables (see **Data – Table...**, page 418).
Manual	Click to not have Excel recalculate formulas automatically. Warning: the values in your formulas will be incorrect until you press **F9**.
Recalculate before save	If you chose **Manual**, check this option to have Excel calculate all formulas when you save the workbook.
Calc Now (F9)	Click to calculate all formulas and update charts.
Calc Sheet	Click to calculate formulas and update charts on the current worksheet only.
Iteration	Check this box to limit the number of calculations Excel uses for goal seeking (see **Tools – Goal Seek...**, page 389) and resolving circular references.

continues

Dialog Box Option	How to Use
Maximum iterations	If **Iteration** is checked, type the maximum number of calculations used for goal seeking and circular references.
Maximum change	If **Iteration** is checked, type the amount that goal seek and circular references will use to stop calculations.

Workbook Options

Dialog Box Option	How to Use
Update remote references	If you use a remote reference (the formula looks like =Application|Filename!Range or field), check this box to have Excel calculate the values.
Precision as displayed	Check this box to convert all numbers to the number of digits they actually display (1.234 will become 1.23 if formatted for 2 decimal places). For formatting, see **Format - Cells... Number Tab**, page 361.
1904 date system	The default starting date is January 1, 1900. If formatted in comma format, 1/1/99 is 36,161 which is the number of days from 1/1/1900. Check this box to use 1/2/1904 as the starting date. (Excel for the Macintosh uses this as the starting date.)
Save external link values	If your worksheet takes a long time to open or is very large, clearing this box might save time or reduce disk size.
Accept labels in formulas	If the top or left cell in a list is a label and you check this box, you can type the name of the label in a formula (such as =**Sum(April)**).

Tools ▸ Options... Edit Tab

The following table lists the available options on the Edit tab of the **Tools, Options** menu.

Dialog Box Option	How to Use
Edit directly in cell	Check this box if you want to double-click a cell to position the insertion point for editing.
Allow cell drag and drop	With this box checked, you can select a range. Then move the mouse pointer to the border around the range until it is a white left-leaning arrow and drag to move the range. (Hold down **Ctrl** to copy the range.)
Alert before overwriting cells	If you check the **Allow cell drag and drop** box, make sure you check this box to get a warning message if you drop the selection where there is any data.
Move selection after Enter	After you press **Enter** the Active cell will go Down, Right, Up, or Left depending on what you choose in **Direction**. Clear this box if you want to remain in the cell you are editing when you press **Enter**.

Dialog Box Option	How to Use
Fi<u>x</u>ed decimal	Check this box if you want to automatically enter a decimal point at the number of <u>P</u>laces when you enter numbers. For example, if 2 is in <u>P</u>laces, Excel will enter .01 when you type a 1. If –2 is in <u>P</u>laces, Excel will automatically enter 100. You have to manually enter the decimal place to override this option (or clear this box).
Cut, copy, and sort <u>o</u>bjects with	If you have graphic cells objects in a range and check this box, the object will move with the range.
Ask to <u>u</u>pdate automatic links	When you open a workbook that contains links to other files, Excel asks you if you want to update the links if this box is checked. Keep the box checked if the links are to a computer or drive that might not always be available.
Provide feedback with A<u>n</u>imation	If your screen update is slow, you might want to clear this box. If the box is checked, you see worksheet action for deleting and inserting columns, rows, and cells.
Enable Auto<u>C</u>omplete for cell	If this box is checked, Excel uses the first unique letters you type in a list to automatically suggest an entry based on a previous item in the column.

<u>T</u>ools ⁻ <u>O</u>ptions... General Tab

The following table lists the available options on the General tab of the **Tools**, **Options** menu.

Dialog Box Option	Description
R1<u>C</u>1 reference style	Check this box to change column headers to numbers rather than letters. When you refer to a cell, you use the row and column number. C5 becomes R5C3. Clear this box for normal A1 style references.
<u>I</u>gnore other applications	Clear to allow exchange of data with other applications that use Dynamic Data Exchange (DDE).
Macro virus pro<u>t</u>ection	Check if you want a warning when you open a document that might have a virus because the document has macros, customized toolbars, menus, or shortcuts.
<u>R</u>ecently used file list	Check this box and type or click spinner arrows in the **Entries** to indicate up to 9 file names to show on the bottom of the File menu (see **File ⁻ Recent Used File List**, page 271).
<u>P</u>rompt for workbook properties	When you save a workbook (see **File ⁻ Save**, page 263), Excel prompts you with the Properties dialog box (see **File ⁻ Proper<u>t</u>ies**, page 271) if this box is checked.

continues

Dialog Box Option	Description
Provide **f**eedback with sound	If Microsoft Office Sounds is installed on your computer, this provides sounds when you do certain events (close, maximize, menu popup). To change sounds associated with an event, choose the Windows **Start** button, **S**ettings, **C**ontrol Panel, and double-click the Sounds icon.
Zoom on roll with IntelliMouse	When this box is checked, the screen magnifies when you roll the Intellimouse button away from you and shrinks when you roll it toward you. Clear this box to have the screen scroll up and down when you roll the Intellimouse button.
S**h**eets in new workbook	Type a number from 1 to 255 or click the spinner buttons to identify the number of sheets that appear when you create a new workbook.
St**a**ndard font	Click the drop-down arrow to choose the default font for new workbooks and worksheets. To change the font for a selected range, see F**o**rmat - C**e**lls... Font Tab, page 366.
Si**z**e	Click the drop-down arrow to choose the default font size for new workbooks and worksheets.
Default file location	When you first start Excel, the File Open dialog box (see **File - Open...**, page 262) defaults to this location and stays there until you look in another folder. Examples include **C:\My Documents** or **\\FinanceServer\SharedFolders**.
Alternate start file **l**ocation	If the **Default file location** is unavailable, the File Open dialog box opens to this folder.
User **n**ame	Type a name to be used for comments (see **Insert - Co**mment, page 359) and as the default for the **Author** in Properties (see **File - Proper**ties, page 271).

Tools ⇨ **O**ptions... Transition Tab

The following table lists the available options on the Transition tab of the **T**ools, **O**ptions menu.

Dialog Box Option	How to Use
Save E**x**cel files as	Click the drop-down arrow to change the default file type for saving. You can override this by changing the **Save as type** on the File, Save As dialog box (see **File - Save A**s..., page 263). To save as an Excel 97 file, choose Microsoft Excel Workbook.

Settings Tab

Microsoft Excel **m**enu or Help key	Type a key to use to access the Excel menu with the keyboard (in addition to **F10**) or start Lotus 1-2-3 help.

Dialog Box Option	How to Use
Microsoft Excel menus	Click this button to use the key mentioned in the previous entry to access Excel menus. After you access the menu, you can press **Tab** or **Shift+Tab** to move on the menu or **Ctrl+Tab** to move to a different menu or toolbar.
Lotus 1-2-3 Help	Click this button to display Lotus 1-2-3 Help instead of accessing the Excel menu when you press the **Microsoft Excel menu** or **Help** key. You can also access this help with **Help – Lotus 1-2-3 Help...**, see page 445.
Transition navigation keys	Check this box to use Lotus 1-2-3 movement keys (such as **Home** to go to A1 instead of **Ctrl+Home**).
Sheet Options	
Transition formula evaluation	If this box is checked, more of your formulas from Lotus 1-2-3 work correctly. Text strings evaluate as 0; true/false expressions become 0 or 1, and database criteria use Lotus 1-2-3 rules.
Transition formula entry	Excel converts most formulas that you type in Lotus 1-2-3 style into what it needs. For example, @Sum(C5..C10) becomes =Sum(C5:C10). However, if you type a function that does not have arguments such as @NOW, Excel gives you an error message unless you have this box checked.

Tools – Options... Custom Lists Tab

The Custom Lists tab enables you to create a list for use when you drag the fill handle (see **Edit – Fill**, page 277) and for sorting (see **Data – Sort...**, page 410). If you start with one item, the other items automatically appear with the fill handle. To create a list, choose **Tools**, **Options**, and click the Custom Lists tab. The Options dialog box displays (see Figure 3.74).

Tools – Options... Chart Tab

The following table lists the available options on the Chart tab of the **Tools**, **Options** menu.

Dialog Box Option	How to Use
Active Chart Section (Only Enabled When Chart Is Selected)	
Not plotted (leave gaps)	For line and ribbon charts, click this button if you don't want to see anything where there are blank values.
Zero	For line and ribbon charts, click this button if you want to see the line go to zero where there are blank values.
Interpolated	For line and ribbon charts, click this button if you want to have Excel automatically connect the line to the previous and next values for data points where there are blank values.

continues

Dialog Box Option	How to Use
Plot visible cells only	If you hide a row or column with data in a chart, Excel does not show this data if this box is checked. To see all values on the chart, clear this box.
Chart sizes with window frame	When you change the size of the workbook's window, the chart shrinks or grows if this box is checked. This does not affect printing.
Chart Tips Section	
Show names	Check this box to display a ScreenTip with the name of the part of the chart as you hover the arrow over it.
Show values	Check this box to display a ScreenTip with the value of a data point when you hover the arrow over it.

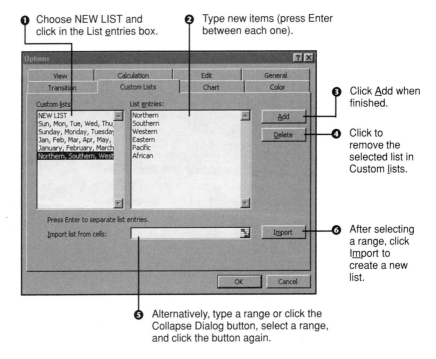

❶ Choose NEW LIST and click in the List entries box.

❷ Type new items (press Enter between each one).

❸ Click Add when finished.

❹ Click to remove the selected list in Custom lists.

❺ Alternatively, type a range or click the Collapse Dialog button, select a range, and click the button again.

❻ After selecting a range, click Import to create a new list.

Figure 3.74
Tools, Options, Custom Lists tab opens the Options dialog box to enable you to create lists for the fill handle.

Tools ➞ Options... Color Tab

For any objects in the workbook, Excel has a palette of colors. You can change all of one color to another one throughout the workbook. For example if a series of AutoShapes is red, you can change it to pink. If the first series of bars in all the charts is blue, you can change it to dark green.

The following table lists the available options on the Color tab of the **Tools**, **Options** menu.

Dialog Box Option	How to Use
Standard colors	For objects on the workbook (excluding charts), click the color you want to replace and choose the **Modify** button.
Chart fills	To change the first (second, and so on) color for all filled (bar, column, area, pie) chart series in the workbook, click a color and choose the **Modify** button.
Chart lines	To change the first (second, and so on) color for all line chart series in the workbook, click a color and choose the **Modify** button.
Copy colors from	If you want to use the palette from another open workbook, click the drop-down arrow and choose the workbook.
Modify	When you click this button for all colors, the Colors dialog box opens. You can choose a color from the Standard or Custom tab (see **Format – Object...** Colors).
Reset	Click this button to return the palette to Excel's default colors.

Tools ➥ Wizard

When you install various add-ins, they appear on the Tools, Wizard menu. These wizards help you perform functions that are difficult on their own or add completely new features to Excel. The following two wizards are installed in the Typical setup. When you use Complete setup during installation, you get additional wizards.

Tools ➥ Wizard ➥ Conditional Sum...

This wizard steps you through the process of summing a list if the items meet condition(s). You can also create the formula with a combination of the SUM and IF functions but it is tedious.

Although this wizard is installed with the default Typical setup, you can turn it on and off by checking or clearing the box on the Add-Ins dialog box (see **Tools ➥ Add-Ins...**, page 398).

To create a conditional sum, follow these steps:

1. Click in the list that has the numbers and choose **Tools, Wizard, Conditional Sum**. The first step of the Conditional Sum Wizard opens.

2. If the range isn't correct, drag the mouse pointer across the range. Include both labels and numbers in the range. If the dialog box is in the way, use the **Collapse Dialog** button; drag across the range, and then click the **Collapse Dialog** button again. Choose **Next**.

3. On Step 2 of the wizard, choose which **Column to sum** (the values you want to total) from the drop-down list. The entry will either contain the label at the top of the column or the first number if there is no label.

4. In the **Column** drop-down list, choose a column header. Choose the comparison operator in the **Is** column (<> is not equal, >= is greater than or equal to, and so on). Type or select a value in the **This value** drop-down list. Click the **Add Condition** button.

5. If you want to remove a condition, click it and choose **Remove Condition**.

6. Repeat step 4 until you have all conditions you want and choose **Next**.

7. Choose **Copy the formula to a single cell** or **Copy the formula and the conditional values**. Choose **Next**.

8. In the next dialog boxes, choose where you want the results to go. Type in the text box or click the worksheet. Click **Finish** when you are done.

Tools ▾ Wizard ▾ Lookup...

The Lookup function is difficult to write without a wizard. The resulting function is really a combination of INDEX and MATCH functions. This procedure allows you to look up the value in a list by knowing the row and column headers.

To look up a value using a row and column heading, follow these steps:

1. Click in the list that has the numbers and choose **Tools, Wizard, Lookup**. The first step of the Lookup Wizard opens.

2. If the range isn't correct, drag the mouse pointer across the range. Include both labels and numbers in the range. If the dialog box is in the way, you can use the **Collapse Dialog** button, drag across the range, and then click the **Collapse Dialog** button again. Choose **Next**.

3. Identify the column and row you need in Step 2 of the wizard.

4. Choose **Copy just the formula to a single cell** or **Copy the formula and lookup parameters**. Choose **Next**.

5. In the next dialog boxes, choose where you want the results to go. Type in the text box or click the worksheet. Click **Finish** when you are done.

Tools ▾ Wizard ▾ Web Form...

Although you can save a worksheet as an HTML document (see **File ▾ Save as HTML**, page 264), you can also have Excel create a Web input form for you and save the results in an Access database.

This feature is not available in the Typical installation of Excel 97 or Office 97. You might need to go through the Custom setup to install this feature and then choose **Tools, Add-Ins**, check **Web Form Wizard**, and click **OK**. After the add-in is installed, do the following:

1. Choose **Tools, Wizard, Web Form**. The first step of the Web Form Wizard opens. Choose **Next**.

2. Click **Add a Cell**; choose a cell in the workbook that the user will be typing information in, and click **OK**. If you add the wrong cell, click the reference in the **Controls and cells** list and click **Remove**. To make the names of the input cells easier to identify, click the reference, type the **Field name of the selected control** and click **Change Name**. After you add all the input cells, click **Next**.

3. On Step 3 of the Web Form Wizard, choose whether your Internet server is **Microsoft Internet Information Server with Internet Database Connector** or **Common Gateway Compliant (CGI) Web Server**, and then choose **Next**.

4. Choose whether you want to save the result to an Excel worksheet or to your **FrontPage Web**. Type or use the **Browse** button to set the name of the Excel worksheet and click **Next**. If you choose **FrontPage Web**, FrontPage launches (unless it is already running).

5. On Step 5 of the Web Form Wizard, type in information you want users to see after they click the **Submit** button. This includes the title bar, first line of the dialog box (header), and text of the message. Also type the URL address of where you want to collect the data.

6. On Step 6 of the Web Form Wizard, Excel gives you a message about the files that were created and about the files sent to your System Administrator. If you want more information, click **Help**. When you are done reading this step, click **Finish** to complete the procedure.

Tools ▾ Wizard ▾ File Conversion...

The File Conversion Wizard enables you to convert multiple files from a different spreadsheet or database program to Excel. Although you can open (see **File ▾ Open...**, page 262) individual files and save (see **File ▾ Save As...**, page 263) them, this procedure is quicker when you have many files you want to convert in one folder.

This feature is not available in the Typical installation of Excel 97 or Office 97. You might need to go through the Custom setup to install this feature and then choose **Tools, Add-Ins**, check **File Conversion Wizard**, and then click **OK**. After the add-in is installed, do the following:

1. Choose **Tools, Wizard, File Conversion**. The File Conversion Wizard box displays Step 1 of 3.

2. Type or use the **Browse** button to choose the folder location of the files to convert.

3. Choose the **File format** of the files to convert. They can be **Lotus 1-2-3**, **Quattro Pro**, **MS Works**, **dBase**, **SYLF**, **Data Interchange Format**, or older versions of **Microsoft Excel**. These options might vary depending on what data filters you included in your installation.

4. Click **Next** to go to Step 2 of the wizard.

5. Click the check box beside each of the files you want to convert (or choose **Select All**) and click **Next**.

6. Type or use the **Browse** button to choose the folder location of where you want to store the Excel files (you can also create a **New Folder** for the files).

7. Choose **Finish** to complete the procedure. When the process is complete, Excel creates a new workbook showing the results of the conversion (and whether each file succeeded).

Tools ➥ Update Add-in Links...

If you used add-ins for some of the functionality of Excel in previous versions, some of those add-ins are now built directly in Excel. In your old workbooks, use the **Update Add-in Links** command to link those functions to the functions now provided by Excel. Open the workbook(s) you want to convert. Choose **Tools**, **Update Add-in Links** and choose whether you want to modify the **Active Document** or **All open documents** and click **OK**. When you are finished, save your workbook in the Excel 97 format (see **File ➥ Save As**, page 263).

This feature is not available in the Typical installation of Excel 97 or Office 97. You might need to go through the Custom setup to install this feature and then choose **Tools**, **Add-Ins**, check **Update Add-In Links**, and then click **OK**.

Data

The **Data** menu treats your worksheets as databases. Each column in your worksheet becomes a field, and each row becomes a record. To be set up as a database, the worksheet has labels on the top row of the range and values on the next and subsequent rows. **Data** menu items enable you to sort, filter, input, summarize, and validate the database.

Data ➥ Sort...

Sorting the worksheet data means changing the order in which the rows appear.

Quick Choices SORT

1. Click in the column within the range you want to sort.

2. Do one of the following:

   - Click the **Sort Ascending** button 🔼 on the Standard toolbar to sort the range based on values in the column from the lowest values to the highest values (1–9 and A–Z).

- Click the **Sort Descending** button 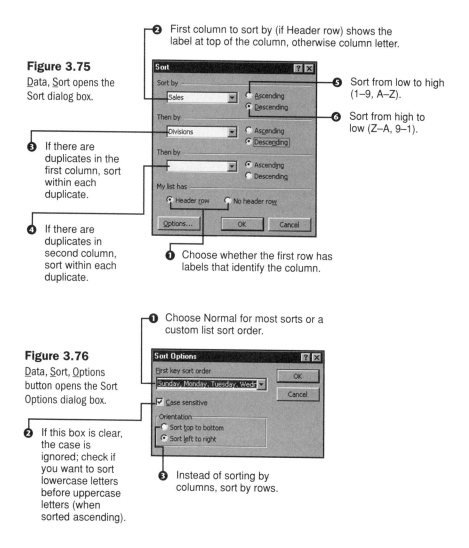 to sort from highest to lowest (Z–A and 9–1).

You can sort by more than one column if you use **Data, Sort**. The Sort dialog box opens (see Figure 3.75). The Sort Options dialog box is shown in Figure 3.76.

Figure 3.75
Data, Sort opens the Sort dialog box.

❷ First column to sort by (if Header row) shows the label at top of the column, otherwise column letter.

❺ Sort from low to high (1–9, A–Z).

❻ Sort from high to low (Z–A, 9–1).

❸ If there are duplicates in the first column, sort within each duplicate.

❹ If there are duplicates in second column, sort within each duplicate.

❶ Choose whether the first row has labels that identify the column.

Figure 3.76
Data, Sort, Options button opens the Sort Options dialog box.

❶ Choose Normal for most sorts or a custom list sort order.

❷ If this box is clear, the case is ignored; check if you want to sort lowercase letters before uppercase letters (when sorted ascending).

❸ Instead of sorting by columns, sort by rows.

Data ➥ Filter

Filtering your data enables you to see only a portion of data. For example, if you want to see only values from one division or employee and hide the rest of the rows, you use a filter. For numeric data, you can also choose to see the top 10 values in the list.

Data → Filter → AutoFilter

AutoFilter is a quick way to choose which items you want to see in a list.

Quick Choices *DRAW BORDERS*

1. Position your Active cell in the range you want to filter.
2. Choose **Data, Filter, AutoFilter**. Excel puts a drop-down arrow on the label at the top of each column for the range.
3. Click the drop-down arrow. Each item from the column's values in the range is shown once. Choose one of the values. All other rows are hidden and the arrow turns blue to indicate there is a filter in that column.

You can repeat the previous procedures to filter on more than one column. You can also select two choices in the AutoFilter list that will bring up dialog boxes. For a numeric column, choose **(Top 10)**. In the Top 10 AutoFilter dialog box, choose **Top** or **Bottom**, the number you want, and whether you want items or percent. The resulting worksheet shows the top or bottom values from your list.

When you choose **(Custom...)**, the Custom AutoFilter dialog box opens (see Figure 3.77).

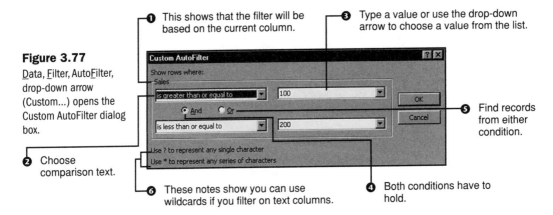

1 This shows that the filter will be based on the current column.

3 Type a value or use the drop-down arrow to choose a value from the list.

Figure 3.77
Data, Filter, AutoFilter, drop-down arrow (Custom...) opens the Custom AutoFilter dialog box.

2 Choose comparison text.

5 Find records from either condition.

6 These notes show you can use wildcards if you filter on text columns.

4 Both conditions have to hold.

To remove a filter for a column, click the blue drop-down arrow and choose **(All)**. To turn off AutoFilter completely, choose **Data, Filter, AutoFilter** again. The check mark next to the AutoFilter indicates AutoFilter is on, no check mark indicates that it's off.

Data → Filter → Show All

While in AutoFilter or Advanced Filter mode, to display all the values in the list, choose **Data, Filter, Show All** or click each blue drop-down arrow you filtered and choose **(All)**.

Data ~ Filter ~ Advanced Filter...

Advanced Filter enables you to set up a criteria range for multiple fields. Position your Active cell in the range you want to filter and choose **Data**, **Filter**, **Advanced Filter**. The Advanced Filter dialog box opens (see Figure 3.78).

Figure 3.78

Data, Filter, Advanced Filter opens the Advanced Filter dialog box.

❶ Create a criteria range on your worksheet with labels from the columns; include comparison operators and values in the second row of the criteria range.

❺ Verify the correct range as the source.

❷ Position your Active cell in the list.

❸ Hide items that don't meet the criteria in the list.

❹ Place the results somewhere else.

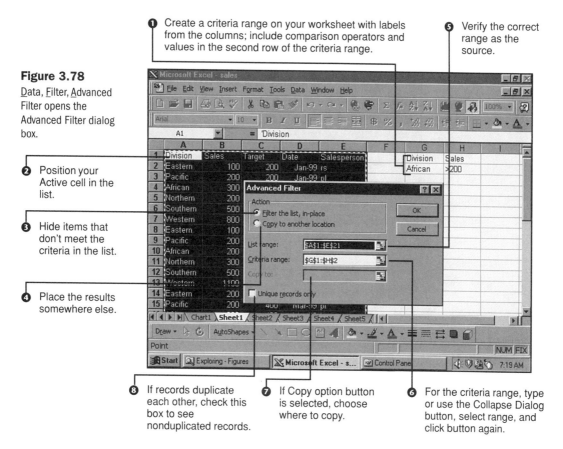

❽ If records duplicate each other, check this box to see nonduplicated records.

❼ If Copy option button is selected, choose where to copy.

❻ For the criteria range, type or use the Collapse Dialog button, select range, and click button again.

Data ~ Form...

If you have many columns in your list and want to see or input them all at the same time, you can use the Data Form feature to see the values from one row at a time. Position the Active cell in the list and choose **Data**, **Form**. The Data Form dialog box opens (see Figure 3.79).

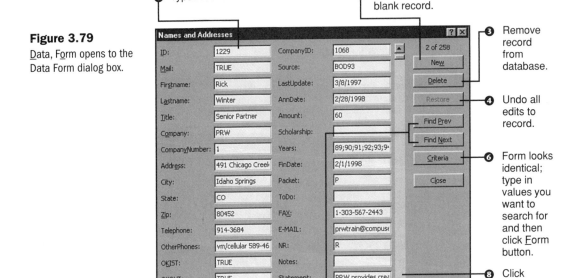

Figure 3.79
Data, Form opens to the Data Form dialog box.

① Type in boxes to edit.

② Save changes and open new, blank record.

③ Remove record from database.

④ Undo all edits to record.

⑥ Form looks identical; type in values you want to search for and then click Form button.

⑧ Click below or above scroll box to move 10 records at a time.

⑤ Go to the next or previous record based on what is in the criteria.

⑦ Click on up or down arrow to move one record at a time.

Data ➥ Subtotals...

Instead of manually adding a sum or count after every group in your worksheet, you can have Excel automatically create subtotals for you. First sort the database list in the order you want to break for each grouping. For example, if you are going to subtotal by each division, first sort by the subdivision (see **Data ➥ Sort...**, page 410). Then position your Active cell in the list and choose **Data**, **Subtotals**. The Subtotal dialog box opens (see Figure 3.80).

After you create subtotals, the left side of the screen shows the outline area (refer to Figure 3.80). Click the minus (–) button to hide the details for that group. The minus turns to a plus (+). Click the plus (+) to show the details. Additionally, there are numbers at the top of the outline. Click the 1 to show just the total for all the items. In Figure 3.80, if you clicked on the 2, you would just see totals for each month. In the example, if you clicked on 3, you would see all the detail. In other examples, you might have more levels. For working with the outline, see **Data**, **Group and Outline**, page 422.

Data ➥ Validation...

Excel now enables you to verify your data as you enter it. You can add an input help message or an error message if the user enters data incorrectly. Choose **Data**, **Validation** to open the Data Validation dialog box (see Figure 3.81). After you set data validation on existing data, you can use the Auditing toolbar to find cells that no longer have valid data (see **T**ools ‑ A**u**diting ‑ **S**how Auditing Toolbar, page 393).

Figure 3.80
Data, Su**b**totals opens the Subtotal dialog box.

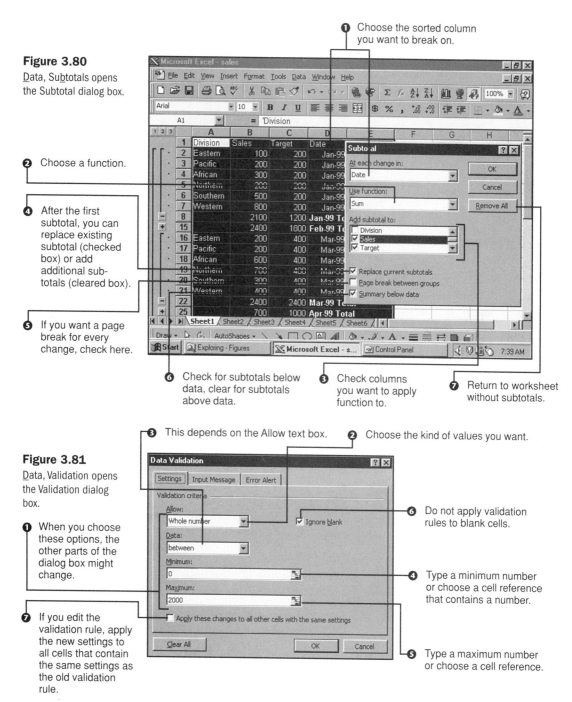

❶ Choose the sorted column you want to break on.

❷ Choose a function.

❹ After the first subtotal, you can replace existing subtotal (checked box) or add additional sub-totals (cleared box).

❺ If you want a page break for every change, check here.

❻ Check for subtotals below data, clear for subtotals above data.

❸ Check columns you want to apply function to.

❼ Return to worksheet without subtotals.

❸ This depends on the Allow text box.

❷ Choose the kind of values you want.

Figure 3.81
Data, Validation opens the Validation dialog box.

❶ When you choose these options, the other parts of the dialog box might change.

❼ If you edit the validation rule, apply the new settings to all cells that contain the same settings as the old validation rule.

❻ Do not apply validation rules to blank cells.

❹ Type a minimum number or choose a cell reference that contains a number.

❺ Type a maximum number or choose a cell reference.

The options on the Settings tab of the Validation dialog box change depending on what you choose in the **Allow** drop-down list. The following table describes these options.

Allow choices on the Data Validation dialog box

Allow Choice	Effects on Other Choices and How to Use
Any value	There are no longer restrictions on entering data. Use this to remove a validation rule or to display an input message and not check for valid entries.
Whole number	All entries must be integers (see the following table for **Data** choices).
Decimal	All entries can be any number (see the following table for **Data** choices).
List	All values must be one of the items in a list you give in the **Source** box. Check **In-cell dropdown** to allow the user to use the drop-down arrow to make a choice from entries in this list. You can use the **Collapse Dialog** button to select the list on the worksheet. You can also type the values (for example Low, Medium, High) separated by the Windows list separator character. To change the character, click the Windows **Start** button, choose **Settings**, **Control Panel**, double-click the Regional Settings icon, click the Number tab, and type a character in the **List separator** box.
Date	All entries must be a valid date (see the following table for **Data** choices).
Time	All entries must be a valid time (see the following table for **Data** choices).
Text length	The number of characters must be in the range specified for the **Data** choices (see the following table for **Data** choices).
Custom	Enter a formula starting with an equal sign (=). If the formula evaluates to True, the data is valid. If the formula evaluates to False, the data is invalid.

Data choices for whole, decimal numbers, date, time, text length

Data Choice	Effects on Other Choices
Between	Type **Minimum** and **Maximum** numbers. **Between** includes both the minimum and maximum number. For Date and Time in the **Allow** drop-down list, the names of these options are **Start Date** and **End Date** or **Start Time** and **End Time**.
Not between	Type the same options as for **Between**.
Equal to	Type the **Value** that must match. For Date and Time in the **Allow** drop-down list, the name of this option is **Date** or **Time**.
Not equal to	Type the **Value** that all entries must not match. For Date and Time in the **Allow** drop-down list, the name of this option is **Date** or **Time**.
Greater than	Type the **Minimum** number that all entries must exceed. For Date and Time in the **Allow** drop-down list, the name of this option is **Start Date** or **Start Time**.

Data Choice	Effects on Other Choices
Less than	Type the **Maximum** number that all entries must not exceed. For Date and Time in the **Allow** drop-down list, the name of this option is **End Date** or **End Time**.
Greater than or equal to	Type the **Minimum** number that all entries must exceed or match. For Date and Time in the **Allow** drop-down list, the name of this option is **Start Date** or **Start Time**.
Less than or equal to	Type the **Maximum** number that all entries must match or not exceed. For Date and Time in the **Allow** drop-down list, the name of this option is **End Date** or **End Time**.

For all these choices you can type a number or use the Collapse Dialog button; click a cell containing a value, and then click Collapse Dialog button to return to the Data Validation dialog box.

The Input Message tab of the Data Validation dialog box is shown in Figure 3.82. When input and error messages appear, if your Office Assistant is active, they appear in the Office Assistant. Otherwise, the messages appear in a dialog box.

❶ Whenever you enter a cell with these data validation settings, show the input message; if this box is clear, no input message appears.

Figure 3.82

Data, Validation, Input Message tab opens the Data Validation dialog box to enable you to show the user a message.

❷ The title of the dialog box or Office Assistant balloon.

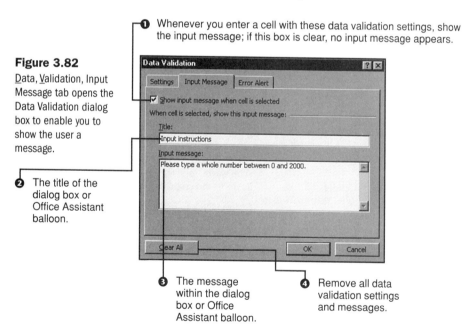

❸ The message within the dialog box or Office Assistant balloon.

❹ Remove all data validation settings and messages.

The Error Alert tab of the Data Validation dialog box is shown in Figure 3.83.

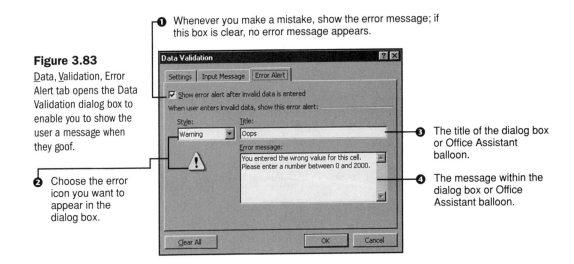

Figure 3.83

Data, Validation, Error Alert tab opens the Data Validation dialog box to enable you to show the user a message when they goof.

❶ Whenever you make a mistake, show the error message; if this box is clear, no error message appears.

❷ Choose the error icon you want to appear in the dialog box.

❸ The title of the dialog box or Office Assistant balloon.

❹ The message within the dialog box or Office Assistant balloon.

Depending on your choice in the Style drop-down list, the user receives different options and command buttons.

Style choices for the Error Alert on Data Validation

Style Choice	Buttons	What Happens
Stop	Retry	You can't have an invalid number. Return to the cell for editing.
	Cancel	Restores the original value.
Warning	OK	Gives you the message but enables you to enter the value.
	Cancel	Restores the original value.
Information	Yes	Gives you the message but enables you to enter the value.
	No	Return to the cell for editing.
	Cancel	Restores the original value.

Data ➥ Table...

The Data Table feature enables you to see what will happen with a formula if you change one or two input values. You can also accomplish this task with additional features by using Scenarios (see **Tools ➥ Scenarios...**, page 389).

The first step is to create a formula and the input cells that will be changing. If you have one input cell, the first column is changing values for that input cell. At the top of the second column is a formula where one of the cells in the formula will change. The results for the formula go below the formula and to the right of the changing values. Select the range that includes the changing values, formula, and blank cells to the right of each changing input value. Then choose **Data**, **Table** and choose the changing **Column input cell**. Figure 3.84 shows the Table dialog box for two input cells (and the results) after **OK** was clicked and the values formatted.

Figure 3.84

Data, Table opens the Table dialog box.

❷ Value in first row of range that is changing.

❹ Formula goes in upper-left corner of range.

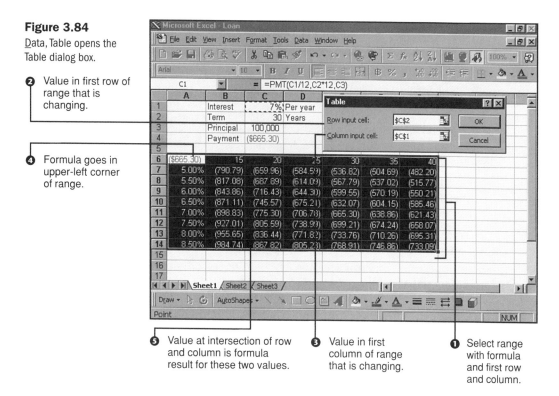

❺ Value at intersection of row and column is formula result for these two values.

❸ Value in first column of range that is changing.

❶ Select range with formula and first row and column.

Data ➥ Text to Columns...

If you've imported or copied text into your worksheet, you might want to convert the text into columns. You can use the Convert Text to Columns Wizard if the text is already in your worksheet or use the Open dialog box and change the **Files of type** to **Text Files**. The Text Import Wizard opens, which is essentially the same wizard with a different title (see **File ➥ Open...**, page 262).

To convert text to columns, follow these steps:

1. Select the 1-column range that contains the text to convert.

2. Choose **Data**, **Text to Columns** to start the Convert Text to Columns Wizard.

3. Choose **Delimited** if you have some character (such as a comma) identifying columns or **Fixed width** if the columns start at predetermined positions. Click **Next**.

4. If you chose **Delimited** on Step 1 of the wizard, do the following:

- Check one or more of the separators between columns (**Tab**, **Semicolon**, **Comma**, **Space**) or check **Other** and type a character.

- If you have multiple separators indicating one column, check **Treat consecutive delimiters as one**.

- Normally text is indicated by quotes. Choose this, an apostrophe, or {none} from the **Text Qualifier** drop-down list.

- Your data shows with column breaks in the data preview section. You can use the horizontal and vertical scrollbars to check to make sure the columns are breaking in the right places.

5. If you chose **Fixed width** on Step 1 of the wizard, you verify or set your column breaks. Click the ruler to add a break line, drag a line to move it, and double-click to delete a line.

6. After you choose **Next** from either of the previous options, you reach Step 3 of the wizard. If you want to change the data type, choose one of the data formats (**General**, **Text**, **Date**, or **Do not import column (Skip)**. If you choose **Date**, you can also choose how the date is formatted.

7. Type the location you want to copy the results to in the **Destination** box (or use the **Collapse Dialog** button to select the range).

Data ↦ Template Wizard...

The Template Wizard enables you to create a template that accepts user input and stores it in a database. The database can be an Excel worksheet, Access table, or another database.

This feature is not available in the Typical installation of Excel 97 or Office 97. You might need to go through the Custom setup to install this feature and then choose **Data**, **Add-Ins**, check **Template Wizard with Data Tracking**, and click **OK**. After the add-in is installed, follow these steps:

1. Choose **Tools**, **Template Wizard**. The first step of the Template Wizard opens up. Select the name of an open workbook you want to create a template from in the drop-down list; Type a name for the template in the text box, and click **Next**.

2. In Step 2 of the wizard, choose a database type from the drop-down list (**Excel**, **Access**, **dBase**, or **FoxPro**), type or use the **Browse** button to choose a name and location for the database and choose **Next**.

3. In Step 3 of the wizard, type a table name. Type a cell address or use the **Collapse Dialog** button to choose a **Cell** for input into the database. In the second column, type a **Field Name** that will be created in the database table. Repeat this step to choose all the cells you want for fields. When you are finished, choose **Next**.

4. On Step 4 of the wizard, choose whether to include information from additional Excel workbooks (where cells you're going to import are in the same location as the current workbook).

If you choose **Yes**, **include**, and **Next**, Step 4 of the wizard changes to enable you to select files. Click the **Select** button and choose the workbook(s) you want to include from the File dialog box and click **Open**. If you add a wrong workbook, select the workbook on Step 4 of the Template Wizard and choose **Delete**. Click **Preview** to make sure the data from the highlighted file is in the right location.

Choose **Next** to continue.

5. On Step 5 of the wizard, Excel gives you information about where your template and database are stored. If you want to send this template each time a new workbook is created from the template, click **Add Routing Slip** and choose the people you want to send the template to. When you are finished with this last step, choose **Finish**.

Data ▸ Consolidate...

The powerful consolidation feature enables you to total (or count, average, and so on) multiple ranges from different worksheets and workbooks into one combined range. Move to one of the ranges and choose **Data**, **Consolidate**. The Consolidate dialog box opens (see Figure 3.85).

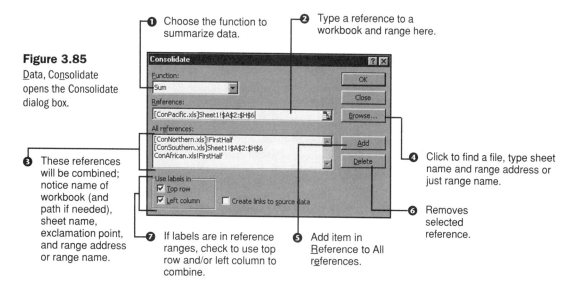

Figure 3.85
Data, Consolidate opens the Consolidate dialog box.

❶ Choose the function to summarize data.

❷ Type a reference to a workbook and range here.

❸ These references will be combined; notice name of workbook (and path if needed), sheet name, exclamation point, and range address or range name.

❹ Click to find a file, type sheet name and range address or just range name.

❺ Add item in Reference to All references.

❻ Removes selected reference.

❼ If labels are in reference ranges, check to use top row and/or left column to combine.

If you check the **Use labels in Top row** and **Left column** boxes, you do not need to have any labels in the consolidation range. For those items that have duplicated labels, Excel adds values. For those items that are unique, Excel adds new rows or columns. If you clear these check boxes, you need to have each of the reference ranges set up in the same order.

If you check the **Create links to source data** check box, Excel creates an outline of your data with the detail rows hidden. You can expand the outline or sections of the outline (see **Data ▸ Group and Outline**, page 422). The contents of the hidden details are cell references to the ranges from the **All references** section of the Consolidate dialog box. The subtotals are functions determined by the **Function** in the dialog box.

The options in the **Function** drop-down list are included in the following table.

Consolidation functions	
Function	**Use**
Sum	Finds the total.
Count	Counts number of all items.
Average	Finds average.
Max	Finds largest number.
Min	Finds smallest number.
Product	Multiplies all numbers together.
Count Nums	Counts only numbers in corresponding ranges.
StdDev	Finds standard deviation based on sample (how much do values vary).
StdDevp	Finds standard deviation based on entire population.
Var	Finds variance based on sample (another measure of how values vary).
Varp	Finds variance based on population.

Data ➥ Group and Outline

An outline enables you to see an overview of your data without details, some of the details, or all of the details and totals. You can create outlines manually through the menu items on the Group and Outline submenu, or automatically with Auto Outline (see **Data ➥ Group and Outline ➥ Auto Outline**, page 423), Subtotals (see **Data ➥ Subtotals...**, page 414), and Consolidation (see **Data ➥ Consolidate...**, page 421).

Data ➥ Group and Outline ➥ Hide Detail

After you have an outline or PivotTable created, you can show or hide the details that go into a total. To hide details, do one of the following:

- For outlines, click the minus (–) in the Outline bar to the left of the row numbers beside the row you want to hide.

- For outlines or PivotTables, click the **Hide Detail** button ▣ on the PivotTable toolbar.

- For outlines or PivotTables, choose **Data, Group and Outline, Hide Detail**.

- You can hide multiple sets of detail. Select multiple rows and click the **Hide Detail** button ▣ or choose **Data**, **Group and Outline**, **Hide Detail**.

- If you want to hide all levels of detail in an outline, click the 1 button in the Outline bar. To see successive levels, click the other numbered buttons.

Data ⁃ Group and Outline ⁃ Show Detail

To show details in an outline or PivotTable, do one of the following:

- For outlines, click the plus (+) in the Outline bar to the left of the row numbers beside the row you want to hide.

- For outlines or PivotTables, click the **Show Detail** button ▣ on the PivotTable toolbar.

- For outlines or PivotTables, choose **Data**, **Group and Outline**, **Show Detail**.

- You can show multiple sets of detail. Select multiple rows and click the **Show Detail** button ▣ or choose **Data**, **Group and Outline**, **Show Detail**.

- If you want to show all levels of detail in an outline, click the largest number button in the Outline bar.

Data ⁃ Group and Outline ⁃ Group...

To create an additional level in an outline or PivotTable, select multiple rows and click the **Group** button ▣ on the PivotTable toolbar or choose **Data**, **Group and Outline**, **Group**. In a PivotTable, a new cell appears in the column to the left of the detail rows. If you want, type a name for the group instead of the generic "**Group1**" name Excel adds for you.

Data ⁃ Group and Outline ⁃ Ungroup...

To ungroup data you grouped with the Group command, select the row(s) with the group and click the **Ungroup** button ▣ on the PivotTable toolbar or choose **Data**, **Group and Outline**, **Ungroup**.

Data ⁃ Group and Outline ⁃ Auto Outline

If you want Excel to automatically create an outline, use the Auto Outline feature. First select a cell in the worksheet; to outline a specific range, select a range. Then choose **Data**, **Group and Outline**, **Auto Outline** (see Figure 3.86).

Any totals you have become a higher level. For example, if you have three divisions with subtotals for each division and a grand total, Auto Outline produces three levels to the left of the row headers. Similarly, if you have quarter totals and an annual total, the Auto Outline adds buttons above the column headers.

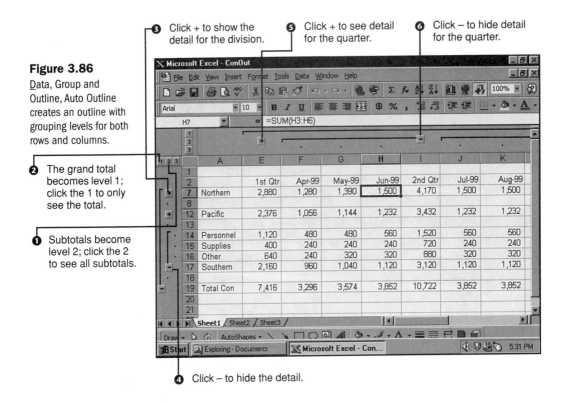

Figure 3.86
Data, Group and
Outline, Auto Outline
creates an outline with
grouping levels for both
rows and columns.

❸ Click + to show the
detail for the division.

❺ Click + to see detail
for the quarter.

❻ Click − to hide detail
for the quarter.

❷ The grand total
becomes level 1;
click the 1 to only
see the total.

❶ Subtotals become
level 2; click the 2
to see all subtotals.

❹ Click − to hide the detail.

Data ▸ Group and Outline ▸ Clear Outline

To get rid of the outline group levels, choose **Data**, **Group and Outline**, **Clear Outline**. If a range was selected, only the outline for that area is removed. If only a cell was selected, the outline is removed for the whole worksheet.

Data ▸ Group and Outline ▸ Settings...

Normally your totals in a worksheet are below the detail and to the right of column detail. Sometimes the summary rows will be above or to the left of the detail. After you create your outline, you might want to have the summary or detail rows stand out by applying a style. Use the Settings dialog box to change the location where Excel looks for the summary rows and apply styles. Choose **Data**, **Group and Outline**, **Settings** to bring up the Settings dialog box (see Figure 3.87).

Data ▸ PivotTable Report...

A PivotTable enables you to summarize a large amount of information. PivotTables are interactive in that you can change the structure by dragging rows and columns to different locations, you can filter what you see by displaying different pages, and show or hide details (see **Data ▸ Group and Outline ▸ Hide Detail**, page 422). Use the PivotTable toolbar to help you work with these tables (see **View ▸ Toolbars ▸ PivotTable**, page 298).

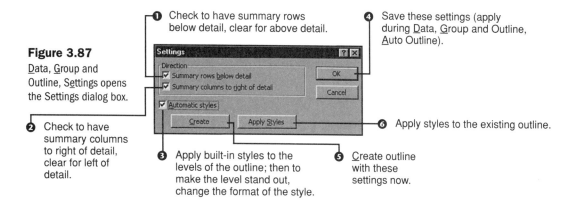

Figure 3.87
Data, Group and Outline, Settings opens the Settings dialog box.

❶ Check to have summary rows below detail, clear for above detail.

❹ Save these settings (apply during Data, Group and Outline, Auto Outline).

❷ Check to have summary columns to right of detail, clear for left of detail.

❸ Apply built-in styles to the levels of the outline; then to make the level stand out, change the format of the style.

❺ Create outline with these settings now.

❻ Apply styles to the existing outline.

You can create a PivotTable from the following:

- Excel list or database (see the following procedure).

- Multiple Excel worksheets.

- External database (see the last step of **Data ~ Get External Data ~ Create New Query...**, page 436).

- Another PivotTable.

To create a PivotTable from an Excel worksheet, follow these steps:

1. Click within a worksheet that contains an Excel list with column labels at the top and each row is a separate record.

2. Choose **Data**, **PivotTable Report**. The PivotTable Wizard opens to the first step.

3. Click **Microsoft Excel list or database** and choose **Next**.

4. Excel attempts to determine your range. If the range is incorrect, do one of the following:

   - Type the new **Range** address. You can type the address from the current worksheet (such as **A1:M1079**); the sheet name, an exclamation point and the range (such as **Pacific!A1:M1079**); or another workbook, sheet, and range (such as **[Sales99]Pacific!A1:M1079**). A range name can replace the range address or sheet name, range address combination in any of these cases (for example, **[Sales99]Data**).

   - Click the **Collapse Dialog** button at the right of the **Range** text box. If necessary, choose a Window and go to another open workbook. Then click the Worksheet tab and drag across the range. Click the **Collapse Dialog** button again to return to the PivotTable Wizard.

   - Click the **Browse** button. Navigate to another file and double-click to enter the name in the **Range** text box. Then add the sheet name and range address shown in the first bullet above.

5. Choose **Next** to go to Step 3 of 4 of the PivotTable Wizard (see Figure 3.88).

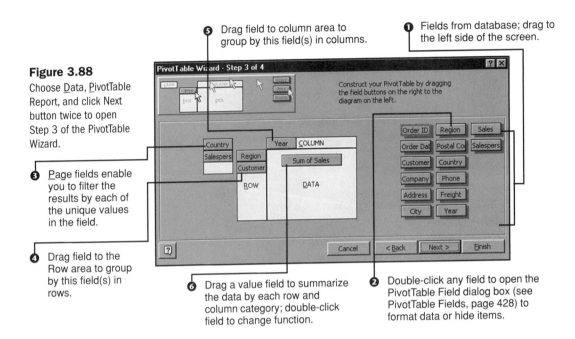

Figure 3.88
Choose Data, PivotTable Report, and click Next button twice to open Step 3 of the PivotTable Wizard.

❺ Drag field to column area to group by this field(s) in columns.

❶ Fields from database; drag to the left side of the screen.

❸ Page fields enable you to filter the results by each of the unique values in the field.

❹ Drag field to the Row area to group by this field(s) in rows.

❻ Drag a value field to summarize the data by each row and column category; double-click field to change function.

❷ Double-click any field to open the PivotTable Field dialog box (see PivotTable Fields, page 428) to format data or hide items.

6. Choose **Next** to go to Step 4 of 4 of the PivotTable Wizard. You can place the PivotTable on a **New worksheet** or **Existing worksheet** (type or choose location with the **Collapse Dialog** button. You can also click **Options** (see **PivotTable Options**, page 433). Choose **Finish** when you are done.

The PivotTable appears on your worksheet. For an example, see Figure 3.89.

PivotTable—Other Sources of Data

In Step 1 of the PivotTable Wizard, you have four choices for your data. The previous procedure shows what happens for an Excel list (see **Data ▪ PivotTable Report...**, page 424). The following shows the differences for the other three choices on Step 1:

- **External data source**—On Step 2 of the wizard, choose the **Get Data** button. The Choose Data Source dialog box opens just as it does when you are getting external data (see **Data ▪ Get External Data ▪ Create New Query...**, page 436). Follow the same steps to get the external data. After you click **Finish** on the Query Wizard, click **Next** on the PivotTable Wizard to get to Step 3. From here, the procedure is the same as mentioned in **Data ▪ PivotTable Report**.

- **Another PivotTable**—You can use the same data source from one PivotTable for another PivotTable. On Step 2 of the wizard, choose the PivotTable in the current workbook that contains the data you want and choose **Next**. From Step 3 on, the wizard is the same as before (see **Data ▪ PivotTable Report**, page 424).

■ **Multiple consolidation ranges**—When you use this option, the row and column labels should match. Think of a budget for each division of a company. The row labels would be items such as Personnel, Supplies, and so on. The column labels would be months. When you consolidate the ranges, the summary sheet contains totals for all divisions for Personnel in each month and so forth.

❶ Page fields—click and choose a value to filter the data.

❺ Double-click any field (or click PivotTable Field button) to open PivotTable Fields dialog box.

❼ PivotTable toolbar.

Figure 3.89
Choose Data,
PivotTable Report, fill
out all steps and
choose Finish to create
a PivotTable.

❹ Drag any field to a new location to restructure the PivotTable.

❷ Row fields.

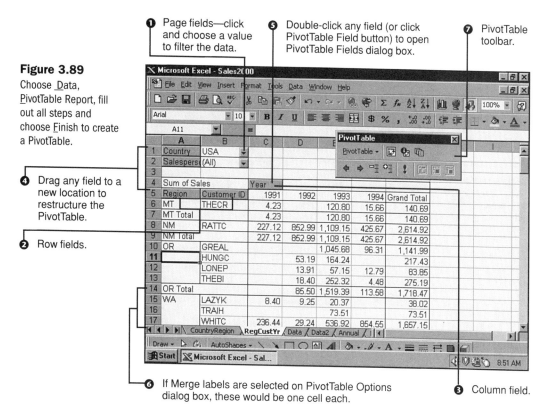

❻ If Merge labels are selected on PivotTable Options dialog box, these would be one cell each.

❸ Column field.

After you choose **Next** on Step 1 of the PivotTable Wizard, the wizard opens up to Step 2a. Choose whether you want Excel to **Create a single page field for me** or **I will create the page fields**. Click **Next**. Step 2b of the wizard opens (see Figure 3.90).

When you choose **Next** after Step 2b, the wizard is the same as before (see **Data ‑ PivotTable Report**, page 424).

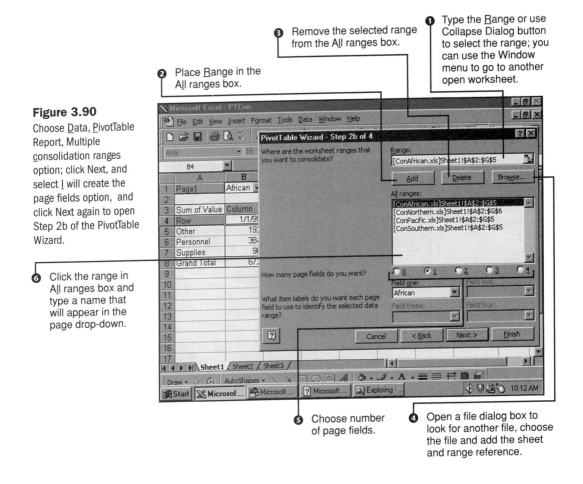

❸ Remove the selected range from the All ranges box.

❶ Type the Range or use Collapse Dialog button to select the range; you can use the Window menu to go to another open worksheet.

❷ Place Range in the All ranges box.

Figure 3.90

Choose Data, PivotTable Report, Multiple consolidation ranges option; click Next, and select I will create the page fields option, and click Next again to open Step 2b of the PivotTable Wizard.

❻ Click the range in All ranges box and type a name that will appear in the page drop-down.

❺ Choose number of page fields.

❹ Open a file dialog box to look for another file, choose the file and add the sheet and range reference.

PivotTable Fields

You can change the way fields are formatted, functions for totals, orientation, and hide items with the PivotTable Field dialog box. There are a number of ways to get to this dialog box. Do any of the following:

- Double-click a field button within the PivotTable Wizard.
- Double-click on a field button in the PivotTable.
- Right-click a field button in a PivotTable and choose **Field**.
- Select the field and click the **PivotTable** button [PivotTable ▾] on the PivotTable toolbar.
- Click the **PivotTable** button on the PivotTable toolbar and choose **Field**.

Regardless of the way you bring up the PivotTable Field dialog box, you get one of two types of boxes. One dialog box is for fields you are using for grouping (see Figure 3.91). The other dialog box is for the data field that you are totaling (see Figure 3.92).

Figure 3.91

Double-clicking a row, column, or page field opens the PivotTable Field dialog box.

❷ Change location for field (you can also drag the field in the PivotTable).

❶ Type a label for the field.

❺ Remove this field from the PivotTable.

❸ If not the last column or row, show subtotals; you can click on multiple functions or choose <u>N</u>one.

❼ If field is numeric, click to open Number tab of Format Cells dialog box.

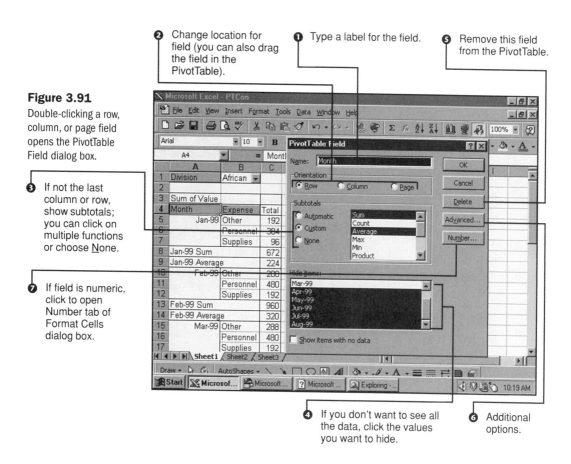

❹ If you don't want to see all the data, click the values you want to hide.

❻ Additional options.

You have additional options for your PivotTable fields, as shown in the following table. Click the **Advanced** button on row, column, and page fields.

PivotTable field Advanced options

Option	How to Use
Page Field Options (Only available if the selected field is a page field and the data source is an external database)	
<u>R</u>etrieve external data for all page field items	Click this option for faster calculation (all page items are retrieved into memory).
<u>Q</u>uery external data source as you select each page field item	If you have problems with your memory (you get error messages saying you cannot create or change the PivotTable), click this option so Excel looks up the external database every time you change the

continues

Continued

Option	How to Use
	page field. However, you will not be able to select All or click the **Show Pages** 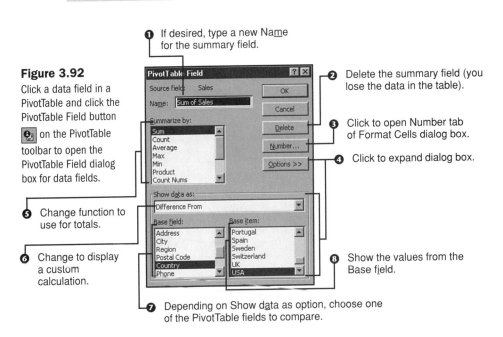 button on the PivotTable toolbar.
Disable pivoting of this field	If you choose **Query external data source as you select each page field item**, you can check this box to not allow you to drag the page field.

AutoSort Options (For column and row fields)

Manual	Let Excel determine the sort order.
Ascending	Sort the PivotTable in the 1–9, A–Z order by the field in **Using field**.
Descending	Sort the PivotTable in the Z–A, 9–1 order by the field in **Using field**.

AutoShow Options (For column and row fields)

Manual	Show all data determined by the other PivotTable settings.
Automatic	Use the **Show** and **Using field** options.
Show	Display the Maximum or Minimum values based on the field in the **Using field** drop-down box. Type the number of values you want to see.

Figure 3.92

Click a data field in a PivotTable and click the PivotTable Field button on the PivotTable toolbar to open the PivotTable Field dialog box for data fields.

➊ If desired, type a new Name for the summary field.

➋ Delete the summary field (you lose the data in the table).

➌ Click to open Number tab of Format Cells dialog box.

➍ Click to expand dialog box.

➎ Change function to use for totals.

➏ Change to display a custom calculation.

➐ Depending on Show data as option, choose one of the PivotTable fields to compare.

➑ Show the values from the Base field.

Show Data As—Choices in Data field's PivotTable Field dialog box

Show Data As	Explanation
Normal	The numeric total.
Difference From	The numeric difference from this value. Choose one of the **Base fields** from the source data and one of the values of the field from the **Base item**.
% Of	The percent of the data from this value. Choose one of the **Base fields** from the source data and one of the values of the field from the **Base item**.
% Difference From	The percent difference of the data from this value. Choose one of the **Base fields** from the source data and one of the values of the field from the **Base item**.
Running Total in	Choose a **Base field** that is a PivotTable field. Then continually add one item's value in the field to the next item.
% of row	The percent of each item compared to the total of the row.
% of column	The percent of each item compared to the total of the column.
% of total	The percent of each item compared to the total of all rows and columns.
Index	Gives you a weighting for each item relative to its position among all items in its column and its row.

PivotTable Formulas

You can add formulas to your PivotTable by creating a new data field or create a new item, which can be an additional row or column in the PivotTable.

PivotTable Formulas – Calculated Field

To create a new field, right-click anywhere in the PivotTable and choose **Formulas**, **Calculated Field**. The Insert Calculated Field dialog box opens (see Figure 3.93).

PivotTable Formulas – Calculated Item

To insert a calculated column or row in the PivotTable, right-click an existing column or row header and choose **Formulas**, **Calculated Item**. The Insert Calculated Item dialog box opens (see Figure 3.94).

PivotTable Formulas – Solve Order

If the order of the items is important (you need to calculate one item before another because it is used in the second formula), right-click in the PivotTable and choose **Formulas**, **Solve Order**. The Calculated Item Solve Order dialog box opens (see Figure 3.95).

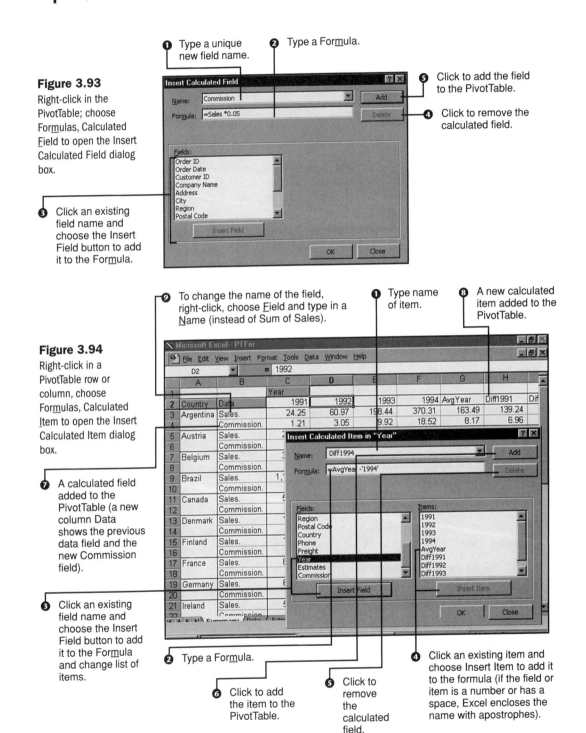

Figure 3.93
Right-click in the PivotTable; choose Formulas, Calculated Field to open the Insert Calculated Field dialog box.

❶ Type a unique new field name.

❷ Type a Formula.

❺ Click to add the field to the PivotTable.

❹ Click to remove the calculated field.

❸ Click an existing field name and choose the Insert Field button to add it to the Formula.

Figure 3.94
Right-click in a PivotTable row or column, choose Formulas, Calculated Item to open the Insert Calculated Item dialog box.

❼ A calculated field added to the PivotTable (a new column Data shows the previous data field and the new Commission field).

❸ Click an existing field name and choose the Insert Field button to add it to the Formula and change list of items.

❾ To change the name of the field, right-click, choose Field and type in a Name (instead of Sum of Sales).

❶ Type name of item.

❽ A new calculated item added to the PivotTable.

❷ Type a Formula.

❻ Click to add the item to the PivotTable.

❺ Click to remove the calculated field.

❹ Click an existing item and choose Insert Item to add it to the formula (if the field or item is a number or has a space, Excel encloses the name with apostrophes).

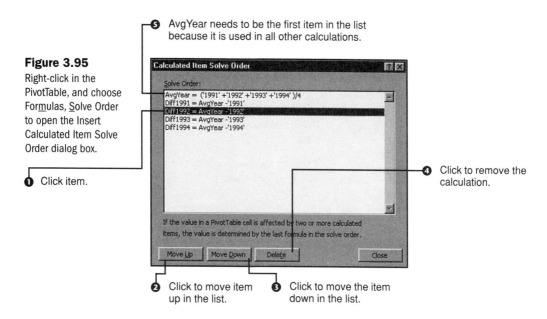

⑤ AvgYear needs to be the first item in the list because it is used in all other calculations.

Figure 3.95
Right-click in the PivotTable, and choose For_mulas, _Solve Order to open the Insert Calculated Item Solve Order dialog box.

① Click item.

④ Click to remove the calculation.

② Click to move item up in the list.

③ Click to move the item down in the list.

PivotTable For_mulas ▾ _List Formulas

To see a list of your calculated fields and calculated items on a new worksheet, right-click in the PivotTable and choose **Formulas**, **List Formulas**.

PivotTable Options

When you click **Options** on Step 4 of the PivotTable Wizard (see **Data ▾ PivotTable Report**, page 424) or click the **PivotTable** button `PivotTable ▾` on the PivotTable toolbar and choose **Options**, the PivotTable Options dialog box opens with the following choices:

PivotTable Options dialog box

Option	How to Use
Format Options	
G_rand totals for columns	Check this box to create sums (or whatever the function is for the Data field) for all columns.
Grand _totals for rows	Check this box to create sums (or whatever the function is for the Data field) for all rows.
_AutoFormat table	Check to have Excel figure out an appropriate format with fonts and borders for this table. You can also choose another AutoFormat (see **Fo_rmat ▾ _AutoFormat...**, page 372).

continues

Continued

Option	How to Use
Subtotal <u>h</u>idden page items	Check this box if you want to include hidden page items in subtotals. To hide items, double-click a page field to open the PivotTable Field dialog box (see **PivotTable Fields**, page 428).
<u>M</u>erge labels	Check this box to merge labels into one cell (refer to Figure 3.89).
<u>P</u>reserve formatting	If you use the **Num<u>b</u>er** button on the PivotTable Field dialog box, keep the formatting for the field (see **PivotTable Fields**, page 428).
Page <u>l</u>ayout	If you have more than one-page layout field, choose the order (Down, then Over or Over, then Down).
<u>F</u>ields per column (or row)	Depending on your choice in **Page <u>l</u>ayout**, you see column or row. Type or choose the number of page fields that can appear in one column (or row) before Excel places fields in the next column (or row). If you want all page fields in one column, choose 0.
For error <u>v</u>alues, show	Check the box on the left and type in the box on the right what you want displayed (such as **Error** or **NA**) when the formula calculates an error for data values.
For empty <u>c</u>ells, show	Check the box and type a number (such as **0**) or a label (such as **NA**) to display when there are empty cells in the PivotTable.

Data Source Options

Option	How to Use
Save data <u>w</u>ith table layout	Check this box to save a copy of the external database with the worksheet. If this box is clear, you must first click the **Refresh Data** button [!] on the PivotTable toolbar to reattach the external data.
Enable <u>d</u>rilldown	Check this box so you can double-click a data cell in the PivotTable to show a new worksheet that shows the detail that makes up this total.
<u>R</u>efresh on open	Check this box to update the table with any changes in the source data when you open the workbook.

External Data Options (only available if data source is an external database)

Option	How to Use
<u>S</u>ave password	Check this box to keep the password with the query so you don't need to retype the password when you **Refresh** the PivotTable.
<u>B</u>ackground query	If you check this box with an external database, Excel runs the query in background so you can continue working on other areas of your worksheet while Excel is getting the data.

Option	How to Use
Optimize memory	If you get an error message that the system doesn't have enough memory to create the PivotTable, check this box and try again. If you still get the message, try reducing the number of PivotTable fields or PivotTables in the Workbook.

PivotTable – Summary of Right-Click Menu Items

The menu items for right-clicking in a PivotTable have been summarized in other sections of this chapter. Here are the locations:

PivotTable right-click cross-reference

Menu Item	Cross-reference
Format Cells	**F**ormat – **C**ells... (page 360)
Insert	On data, inserts Calculated field, see **PivotTable Formulas** –**Calculated Field** (page 431). On row or column field, inserts blank calculated item, see **PivotTable For**m**ulas** – **Calculated Item** (page 431) to edit.
Delete	Remove field from PivotTable.
Wizard	**V**iew – **T**oolbars – **PivotTable** (page 298) ⬚
Refresh Data	**D**ata – **R**efresh Data (page 442)
Select submenu	**V**iew – **T**oolbars – **PivotTable** (page 298) [PivotTable ▾]
Group and Outline submenu	**D**ata – **G**roup and Outline, page 422
For**m**ulas submenu	**PivotTable Formulas**, page 431
Field	**PivotTable Fields**, page 428
O**p**tions	**PivotTable Options**, page 433
Show **P**ages	**V**iew – **T**oolbars – **PivotTable** (page 298) ⬚

Data → Get External Data

The Get External Data menu option enables you to grab data from nonExcel data sources such as Microsoft Access, dBASE, and the Internet. The commands to return the information into your worksheet are stored in queries. You can run a saved query or create a new one.

Data – Get External **D**ata – Run **W**eb Query...

You can run a previously saved query that reads data off the Internet (or an intranet). To do so, follow these steps:

1. Connect to the Internet (or your intranet).

2. Choose **Data, Get External Data, Run Web Query**. The Run Query dialog box opens with Web Queries (*.iqy) selected in the **Files of type** drop-down list.

3. Double-click the query you want. The Return External Data to Microsoft Excel dialog box opens.

4. Choose where you want to place the data (in the **Existing Worksheet** at displayed location or create a **New Worksheet**).

5. If you click the **Properties** button, you go to the External Data Range Properties dialog box (see **Data ‣ Get External Data ‣ Data Range Properties**, page 440). Choose **OK** to get back to the Return External Data to Microsoft Excel dialog box.

6. Choose **OK** to return the information into your worksheet. The External Data toolbar appears to enable you to manage the data (see **View ‣ Toolbars ‣ External Data**, page 294).

One of the saved queries that comes with Excel 97 is a query that returns other queries that people have sent Microsoft as of today's date. Double-click **Get More Queries** in the Run Query dialog box. After the query returns the data to Excel, follow the instructions in your worksheet.

Data ‣ Get External Data ‣ Run Database Query...

If you saved a database query (**Data ‣ Get External Data ‣ Create New Query...**, page 436), you can run the query when you need it.

1. Choose **Data, Get External Data, Run Database Query**. The Run Query dialog box opens with **Database Queries** (*.dqy) selected in the **Files of type** drop-down list.

3. Double-click the query you want. The Return External Data to Microsoft Excel dialog box opens.

4. Choose where you want to place the data (in the **Existing Worksheet** at the displayed location or create a **New Worksheet**). You can also create a new **PivotTable Report**.

5. If you click the **Properties** button, you go to the External Data Range Properties dialog box (see **Data ‣ Get External Data ‣ Data Range Properties**, page 440). Choose **OK** to get back to the Return External Data to Microsoft Excel dialog box.

6. Choose **OK** to return the information into your worksheet.

Depending on your choice in step 4, you see the External Data toolbar (see **View ‣ Toolbars ‣ External Data**, page 294) or PivotTable toolbar (see **View ‣ Toolbars ‣ PivotTable**, page 298).

Data ‣ Get External Data ‣ Create New Query...

When you create a new query, you use Microsoft Query, which is a standalone program that is also integrated with Excel through this menu option. The easiest way to retrieve the data from the external data source is to use the Query Wizard to walk you through the steps you need to accomplish.

N O T E   If you did not install Microsoft Query when you installed Excel, you might need to go through
Setup again. This section is limited to using the Query Wizard to use Microsoft Access as an
external database. For more information on accessing external databases and using Microsoft Query,
see Que's *Special Edition Using Microsoft Excel 97*. ▓

To create a query to get data from Access, follow these steps:

1. Position your Active cell in a worksheet where you want to place the data and choose
   Data, **Get External Data**, **Create New Query**. The Choose Data Source dialog box
   opens (see Figure 3.96). If you already have a data source created, double-click the name
   and go to step 5 below.

Figure 3.96

Data, Get External Data,
Create New Query
opens the Choose Data
Source dialog box.

❻ Create a new
   query.

❶ Double-click an
   existing data
   source.

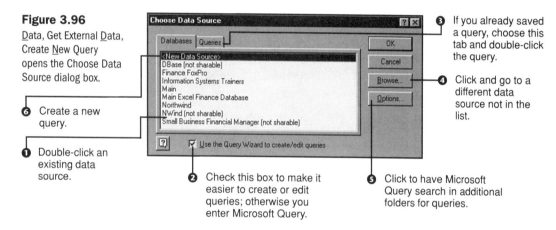

❸ If you already saved
   a query, choose this
   tab and double-click
   the query.

❹ Click and go to a
   different data
   source not in the
   list.

❷ Check this box to make it
   easier to create or edit
   queries; otherwise you
   enter Microsoft Query.

❺ Click to have Microsoft
   Query search in additional
   folders for queries.

2. If you chose **<New Data Source>** you enter the Create Data Source dialog box. Fill out
   the dialog box as shown in Figure 3.97.

❶ Type the name you want to appear on the Databases tab of
   the Choose Data Source dialog box.

Figure 3.97

Data, Get External Data,
Create New Query,
<New Data Source>
opens the Create New
Data Source dialog box.

❸ Click Connect to
   open the dialog
   box specific for the
   driver in above.

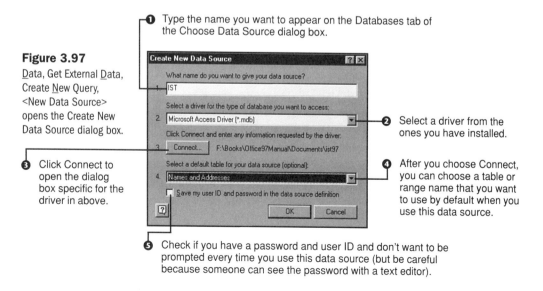

❷ Select a driver from the
   ones you have installed.

❹ After you choose Connect,
   you can choose a table or
   range name that you want
   to use by default when you
   use this data source.

❺ Check if you have a password and user ID and don't want to be
   prompted every time you use this data source (but be careful
   because someone can see the password with a text editor).

3. When you click the **Connect** button on the Create Data Source dialog box you enter the ODBC Application Setup dialog box. The options change depending on which database driver you're using. For Access, fill out the dialog box as shown in Figure 3.98.

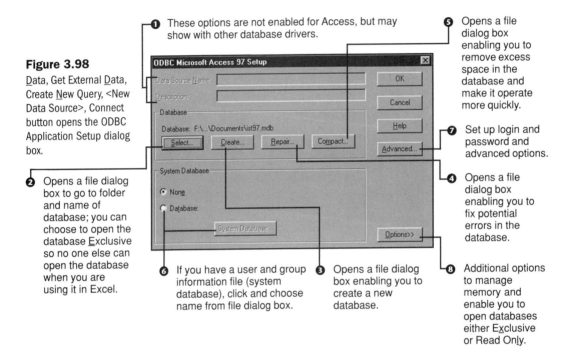

❶ These options are not enabled for Access, but may show with other database drivers.

❺ Opens a file dialog box enabling you to remove excess space in the database and make it operate more quickly.

Figure 3.98
Data, Get External Data, Create New Query, <New Data Source>, Connect button opens the ODBC Application Setup dialog box.

❷ Opens a file dialog box to go to folder and name of database; you can choose to open the database Exclusive so no one else can open the database when you are using it in Excel.

❼ Set up login and password and advanced options.

❹ Opens a file dialog box enabling you to fix potential errors in the database.

❻ If you have a user and group information file (system database), click and choose name from file dialog box.

❸ Opens a file dialog box enabling you to create a new database.

❽ Additional options to manage memory and enable you to open databases either Exclusive or Read Only.

4. After you create a new database driver, select the driver on the Choose Data Source dialog box and choose **OK**.

5. The Query Wizard goes to the Choose Columns dialog box. You also enter this step if you double-clicked an existing data source in step 1. Fill in the figure as shown in Figure 3.99.

6. Choose **Next** to go to the Filter Data dialog box. If desired, choose which records you want to see as shown in Figure 3.100.

7. Choose **Next** to go to the Sort Order dialog box. If desired, click the **Sort by** drop-down arrow and choose a field to sort the external data. If there are duplicates in this field, you can choose two additional sort levels.

8. Choose **Next** to go to the Finish dialog box. You can choose the following options:

   • Click the **Save Query** button and type the **File name** and click **Save**. If you save the query, you can use it again (see **Data ▸ Get External Data ▸ Run Database Query...**, page 436).

   • Click **Return Data to Microsoft Excel** and choose **Finish** to load the data into your worksheet.

- Click **View data** or **Edit query** in **Microsoft Query** to open Microsoft Query and choose **Finish** so you can add additional query options or edit the data. When you are finished, choose **File**, **Return Data to Microsoft Excel**.

After you make a choice, you enter the Returning External Data to Microsoft Excel dialog box.

❷ Click + to expand table and show fields. ❺ Use buttons to add or remove fields. ❻ Double arrow is to move all fields.

Figure 3.99

Choose Data, Get External Data, Create New Query, and double-click a data source name to open the Query Wizard–Choose Columns dialog box.

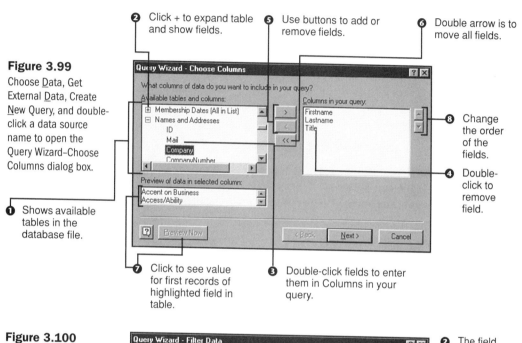

❶ Shows available tables in the database file.

❼ Click to see value for first records of highlighted field in table.

❸ Double-click fields to enter them in Columns in your query.

❽ Change the order of the fields.

❹ Double-click to remove field.

Figure 3.100

Choose Data, Get External Data, Create New Query, and select a data source name, and then select Next to open the Query Wizard–Filter Data dialog box.

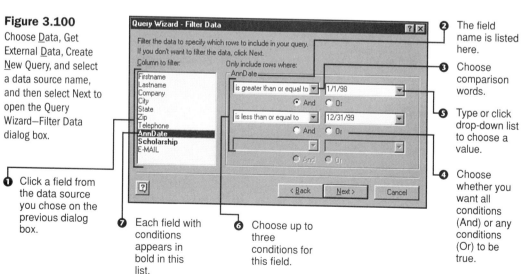

❶ Click a field from the data source you chose on the previous dialog box.

❷ The field name is listed here.

❸ Choose comparison words.

❺ Type or click drop-down list to choose a value.

❹ Choose whether you want all conditions (And) or any conditions (Or) to be true.

❼ Each field with conditions appears in bold in this list.

❻ Choose up to three conditions for this field.

9. Choose where you want to place the data (in the **E̲xisting Worksheet** at displayed location or in a **N̲ew Worksheet**). You can also create a new **P̲ivotTable Report**.

10. If you click the **Pr̲operties** button, you go to the External Data Range Properties dialog box (see **Data ▪ Get External D̲ata ▪ Da̲ta Range Properties**, page 440). Choose **OK** to get back to the Return External Data to Microsoft Excel dialog box.

11. Choose **OK** to return the data to your worksheet.

Data ▪ Get External D̲ata ▪ E̲dit Query...

For database queries (not Web queries), you can edit columns, filter, and sort information. Position your Active cell somewhere in the query results, and choose **Data, Get External Data, Edit Query**. You enter the Query Wizard. Choose Columns dialog box (see **Data ▪ Get External D̲ata ▪ Create N̲ew Query...**, page 436). Continuing from this point, it is the same as if you were creating a new query.

Data ▪ Get External D̲ata ▪ Da̲ta Range Properties

Choose **Data Range Properties** to save the query with the worksheet, choose when data is refreshed, and change the layout of the external database range. When you choose **Data, Get External D̲ata, Da̲ta Range Properties**, the following options are included in the dialog box:

External Database Range Properties dialog box options

Dialog Box Option	How to Use
N̲ame	Type a new name if you want to name the external data range. Microsoft automatically names the range the name of the saved query or a generic name such as ExternalData1, ExternalData2, and so forth.
Query Definition Section	
Save qu̲ery definition	Check this box to save the query for the external data with the worksheet so you can refresh the data if the external data changes.
Save p̲assword	Check this box to save the password with the query so you don't have to enter the password each time you refresh the query.
Refresh Control Section	
Enable b̲ackground refresh	Check this box so you can continue working on other areas of the worksheet while Excel is getting the data.
Refresh data on fi̲le open	Check this box to get the latest source data when you open the workbook. **Save qu̲ery definition** must be checked.

Dialog Box Option	How to Use
Remove external data from worksheet before saving	Check this box to get rid of the external data when you save the file. Because **Refresh data on file** open must by checked to select this box, updated values appear when you open the workbook again.

Data Layout Section

Include field names	Check this box to include the field names from the external data source. If you use your own field names, type the labels above where you start the external data range and clear this check box.
Include row numbers	Check this box to add row numbers in the first column for each row you import (starting with 0).
Autoformat data	Check this box to have Excel figure out an appropriate format with fonts and borders for this external database. You can also choose another AutoFormat (see **Format, AutoFormat...**, page 372).
Autofit column width	For Web queries, this option appears instead of **Autoformat data**. Check this box to automatically change the column width to the widest entry for the data.
Import HTML table(s) only	Clear this box to import all parts of the Web query to the worksheet (including nontabular text). Check this box to return only tabular text to Excel.
If the number of rows in the data range changes upon refresh	When you refresh data, choose whether you want to insert new cells or entire rows or replace existing data.
Fill down formulas in columns adjacent to data	If you have formulas created based on external data to the right of the external data range, check this box to have the formulas copied all the way down to the end of the data.

Data ⁃ Get External Data ⁃ Parameters...

If your query requires parameters (inputs) to run, you can set a value for a parameter, or change the dialog box prompt that appears when you refresh the data. Choose **Data**, **Get External Data**, **Parameters** or click the **Query Parameters** button on the External Data toolbar to open the Parameters dialog box (see Figure 3.101).

Figure 3.101

Data, Get External Data, Parameters opens the Parameters dialog box.

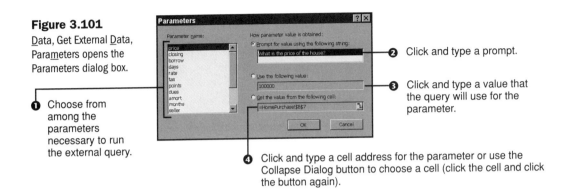

❶ Choose from among the parameters necessary to run the external query.

❷ Click and type a prompt.

❸ Click and type a value that the query will use for the parameter.

❹ Click and type a cell address for the parameter or use the Collapse Dialog button to choose a cell (click the cell and click the button again).

After you fill in the parameters, you need to refresh the range to use the new values or run the prompts (see **Data ‑ Refresh Data**, page 442).

Data ➥ Refresh Data

If your source data changes, click the **Refresh Data** button 🛢 on the PivotTable toolbar or choose **Data**, **Refresh Data** to recalculate your PivotTable or bring changes to your external data.

Data ➥ MS Access Form...

If you have Microsoft Access installed, you can create an Access form for entering data into the worksheet. Position the active cell in an Excel database range and choose **Data**, **MS Access Form**. Microsoft Access launches the Form Wizard. Through the wizard, add fields you want on the form, select the form layout and form style, and type a form name. When you finish, a button appears on your worksheet, which opens the form in the Access database.

This feature and the other Access menu items (**Data**, **MS Access Report** and **Data**, **Convert to Access**) are not available in the Typical installation of Excel 97 or Office 97. You might need to go through the Custom setup to install these feature and then choose **Tools**, **Add-Ins**, and check **Microsoft AccessLinks Add-In** and click **OK.**

Data ➥ MS Access Report...

In addition to creating an Access form, you can also create an Access report from your Excel worksheet. Position the active cell in an Excel database range and choose **Data**, **MS Access Report**. The Access Report Wizard starts and asks you to add fields, group and sort the fields, choose report layout and style, and give the report a name. When you finish, a button appears on your worksheet that opens the report in Print Preview in the Access database.

Data ➥ Convert to Access...

You can also convert the Excel database range to an Access table. Position the active cell in an Excel database range and choose **Data**, **Convert to Access**. Choose whether to add the Excel information to a new or existing database. Access then opens its Import Spreadsheet Wizard that asks you for row headings, a name for the new table (or existing table), field information, whether to set a primary key, and a name for the table.

<u>W</u>indow

The Window menu organizes your document windows on the screen.

<u>W</u>indow ➡ <u>N</u>ew Window

Choose **<u>W</u>indow**, **<u>N</u>ew Window** to open another window for the same document. When you open a new window, the document name followed by a colon and a number appears in the title bar. You can position your Active cell at different parts of the same document for copying or editing. Switch between windows by using the bottom of the Window menu or pressing **Ctrl+F6**. Close the extra window by clicking the close button (X) for the window or pressing **Ctrl+W**.

<u>W</u>indow ➡ <u>A</u>rrange...

If you have two or more workbooks open (or one workbook with more than one window), choose **<u>W</u>indow**, **<u>A</u>rrange** to see smaller windows for each document. The Arrange Windows dialog box opens (see Figure 3.102).

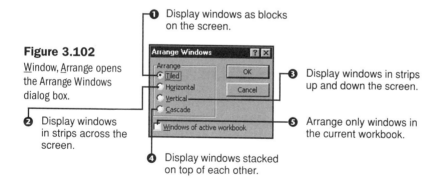

❶ Display windows as blocks on the screen.

Figure 3.102
<u>W</u>indow, <u>A</u>rrange opens the Arrange Windows dialog box.

❷ Display windows in strips across the screen.

❸ Display windows in strips up and down the screen.

❹ Display windows stacked on top of each other.

❺ Arrange only windows in the current workbook.

Click the maximize button of a window to make it full screen again.

<u>W</u>indow ➡ <u>H</u>ide

If you do not want to show the current window onscreen, but still want to keep it in memory, choose **<u>W</u>indow**, **<u>H</u>ide**. The window disappears and it is no longer on the bottom of the Window menu. However, you can still use the macros associated with the workbook.

Window ➥ Unhide...

If you want to display a hidden workbook, choose **Window**, **Unhide**. The Unhide dialog box opens with a list of hidden workbooks. If you have the Personal workbook listed, that is where your global macros are stored. Double-click any name in the Unhide workbook list to display it. If you unhide the Personal workbook, hide it again (see **Window ‒ Hide**, page 443) after you're finished modifying it.

Window ➥ Split

When you want to look at two different parts of the same workbook for copying or editing, do one of the following:

- Position the Active cell in the workbook where you want the split to occur and choose **Window**, **Split**. If you position the Active cell in the middle of the first row, the workbook splits into two vertical panes. If you position the Active cell in the middle of the first column, the workbook splits into two horizontal panes. If you position the Active cell in the middle of the screen, the workbook splits into four panes.

- With the double-headed mouse pointer, drag one of the split boxes above the vertical scrollbar or to the right of the horizontal scrollbar.

After you position the split bar, you have scrollbars that enable you to move in the different panes of the workbook independently of each other. You can press **F6** to move between panes or **Shift+F6** to move backward between panes.

To get rid of the split, choose **Window**, **Remove Split**.

Window ➥ Freeze Panes

In addition to splitting the window you can also freeze panes. This is useful when you have labels at the top or left of the worksheet that help you identify what's in the columns or rows. If you have a large worksheet, you can keep these labels visible so you can continue to identify the data in rows and columns that are not near the top or left edge of your range. This is similar to splitting the window (see **Window ‒ Split**, page 444).

1. First scroll the screen so that the rows you want displayed are at the top of the screen and the columns you want are on the left edge.

2. Position the Active cell below any rows you want to keep displayed and to the right of any columns.

3. Choose **Window**, **Freeze Panes**. Now when you scroll down or right, the rows and/or columns stay on the screen.

4. To reset the window, choose **Window**, **Unfreeze Panes**.

Window ➥ [Open Workbooks]

The bottom of the Window menu shows you a list of all open workbooks. Click a workbook name or press **Ctrl+F6** to go to another open workbook.

Chart | 445

Help

Help enables you to look up more information on the application. The only major difference between Word and Excel's Help is the Lotus 1-2-3 Help menu item (see Word's **Help**, page 240). The first and last menu items, say Microsoft Excel Help and About Microsoft Excel instead of Word, but they and all other menu items work the same. The Tech Support information is also the same, but Excel's help phone number is (425) 635-7070.

Help ➥ Lotus 1-2-3 Help...

If you are a Lotus 1-2-3 user and want some transition help, choose **Help**, **Lotus 1-2-3 Help**. The Help for Lotus 1-2-3 Users dialog box displays (see Figure 3.103).

Figure 3.103

Help, Lotus 1-2-3 Help opens the Help for Lotus 1-2-3 Users dialog box.

❷ Indicates topic.

❹ Paste instructions on the worksheet.

❸ Indicates that there are subtopics; double-click to view list.

❶ Click to see a description of the topic.

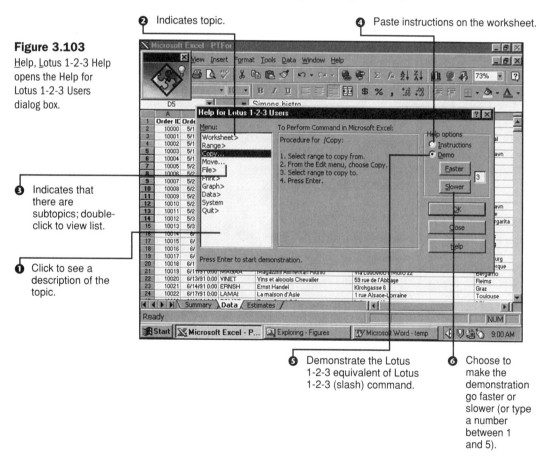

❺ Demonstrate the Lotus 1-2-3 equivalent of Lotus 1-2-3 (slash) command.

❻ Choose to make the demonstration go faster or slower (or type a number between 1 and 5).

Chart

The **Chart** menu only appears when you are on a chart sheet or have selected an embedded chart (and replaces the **Data** menu). This menu enables you to change the chart type, add data, and modify the chart. To insert a chart, see **Insert ▸ Chart...**, page 306. To format a chart, see **Format ▸ Chart Objects**, page 375. For additional settings for a chart (such as what to do with empty cells), see **Tools ▸ Options... Chart Tab**, page 405.

Chart ▸ Chart Type...

Depending on your needs, you can change your chart to a column, line, pie, or one of many different kinds.

Quick Choices   *CHANGE CHART TYPE*

1. Click a chart or a data series within the chart.

2. Click the drop-down arrow of the **Chart Type** button ▥ ▾ on the Chart toolbar and click a chart type.

Choose **Chart**, **Chart Type** to bring up the Chart Type dialog box (see Figure 3.104). This is the same dialog box as Step 1 of the Chart Wizard (see **Chart Wizard ▸ Step 1 of 4 ▸ Chart Type**, page 307). For some charts, you can click a data series and change the chart type of just the series. You can't mix 2-D and 3-D series on one chart, though.

Figure 3.104
Chart, Chart Type opens the Chart Type dialog box.

❶ Choose 1 of the 14 chart types.

❸ If you selected a data series, check this box to apply the chart type just to the series or clear the box to apply the type to the entire chart.

❹ Check the box to remove any formatting you added to the chart.

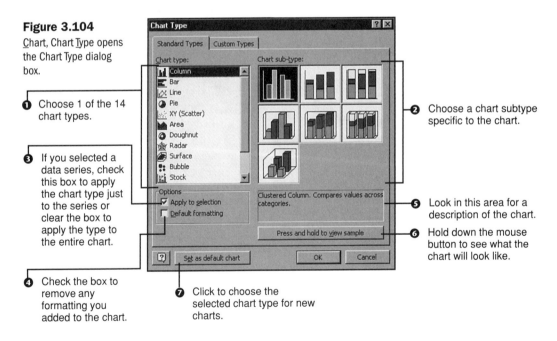

❷ Choose a chart subtype specific to the chart.

❺ Look in this area for a description of the chart.

❻ Hold down the mouse button to see what the chart will look like.

❼ Click to choose the selected chart type for new charts.

Figure 3.104 shows the first chart type, a Column chart. To choose another chart type, click the desired type from the Chart type list; then select a subtype from the Chart subtype list. Click **OK**.

Chart ▸ Source Data...

If you need to add or remove values, x-axis labels, or y-axis labels, choose **Chart**, **Source Data** to bring up the Source Data dialog box. This is the same dialog box that appeared in Step 2 of the Chart Wizard (see **Chart Wizard ▸ Step 2 of 4 ▸ Chart Source Data**, page 308). Do any of the following:

On the Data Range tab:

■ Type a new **Data range** or click the **Collapse Dialog** button, select the new range with labels and click the **Collapse Dialog** button again.

■ If the legend and x-axis seem reversed in the chart example at the top of the dialog box, try changing the **Series in** to **Rows** or **Columns**. You can also change the orientation from the Chart toolbar by clicking the **By Row** 📊 or **By Column** 📊 buttons.

On the Series tab:

■ The **Series** show in the list box. Each line, bar, column and so on is a series. Click each row to see the existing settings for the **Name** and **Values**.

■ Type a new label in the **Name** text box for the highlighted series (which will appear in the legend) or click the **Collapse Dialog** button and choose a cell on the worksheet.

■ Type a new range address in the **Values** text box for the highlighted series (which is the height or length of columns, lines and so on) or click the **Collapse Dialog** button and select a range on the worksheet.

■ Click the **Add** button to add another line, bar, and so on to the chart and fill in the **Name** and **Values** text boxes for this new series.

■ Click **Remove** to delete the selected series from the chart.

■ Type a new range address in the **Category (x) axis labels** box for x-axis (horizontal axis for most charts) or click the **Collapse Dialog** button and select a range on the worksheet. The x-axis is often a time period or a list of categories.

Chart ▸ Chart Options...

The Chart Options dialog box enables you to add text, axes, gridlines, legends, data labels, and a data table to the chart as well as modify the look and position of some of these options. The dialog box has different options and a different number of tabs depending on the chart type. This dialog box is the same as Step 3 of the Chart Wizard (see **Chart Wizard ▸ Step 3 of 4 ▸ Chart Options**, page 309). Each of the tabs is explained in sections that follow.

Chart ▸ Chart Options... Titles Tab

You can add text to your chart that is floating or assigned to the chart title or an axis.

Quick Choices *ADD TEXT*

1. With the chart selected, type text. As you type the text, it appears in the Formula bar.
2. Press **Enter**. The text moves into a text box on the chart.
3. Drag the text to the location you want.

You can also attach text to the chart title or one of the axes. Choose **Chart**, **Chart Options**, and click the Titles tab. On this tab of the Chart Options dialog box you have the following options:

Chart Options dialog box—Titles tab

Options	How to Use
Chart title	The chart title appears at the top of the chart. For this or any other title, type in the text box. If you want a line break, click in the text box in the chart and press **Enter**.
Category (X) axis	For most charts (except Bar), the category axis is the horizontal axis and usually has time or category labels.
Series (Y) axis	This is only available for 3-D charts (Ribbon, 3-D-Area, Surface) when there is also a Value (Z) axis. This labels the same axis where the series appear.
Value (Y) axis	For 2-D charts, this labels the axis where the numeric values go (usually on the left side of the chart).
Value (Z) axis	For 3-D charts, this labels the axis where the numeric values go.
Second category (X) axis	For mixed charts (Line and Bar, for example), you can have another x-axis (usually at the top of the chart).
Second value (Y) axis	For mixed charts, you can have a second y-axis (usually on the right of the chart.

Chart ➤ Chart Options... Axes Tab

The Axes tab enables you to display or hide any of the axes. Choose **Chart**, **Chart Options**, and click the Axes tab. On this tab of the Chart Options dialog box you have the following options:

Chart Options dialog box—Axes tab

Options	How to Use
Category (X) axis	Check the box to display axis for categories (usually bottom of the chart). Clear this box to hide the values and titles associated with the axis.
Automatic	Choose **Category** for nontime formatted values, and **Time-scale** for time formatted values.
Category	Even if the data is date formatted, displays data with a label for each x-axis value. If monthly data and months are skipped, does not show missed months.

Options	How to Use
Time-scale	Click to display the category axis tick marks evenly spaced across the x-axis based on major and minor units of time. For example, if monthly data and months are skipped, this shows labels on the x-axis for the missed months.
Value (Y) axis	Check this box to display the axis for values for 2-D charts (usually the left edge). Clear this box to hide the values and titles associated with the axis.
Series (Y) axis	This is only available for 3-D charts (Ribbon, 3-D-Area, Surface) when there is also a Value (Z) axis. Check the box to display the axis; clear it to hide the axis.
Value (Z) axis	Check this box to display the axis for values for 3-D charts. Clear this box to hide the values and titles associated with the axis.
Secondary axis section	In mixed charts (Line and Bar, for example), you can have a Secondary axis with same options as the previous entry (Category (X) axis, and Value (Y) axis).

Chart ▾ Chart Options... Gridlines Tab

Each of the axes can have their own gridlines (lines going up and down or across the chart). As mentioned in the previous two sections, 2-D charts and 3-D charts have different axes available. For each of these axes you can check **Major gridlines** and **Minor gridlines** to display either or both. Each scale has a major and minor unit set through **Format**, **Selected Axis**, Scale tab.

Chart ▾ Chart Options... Legend Tab

The legend displays a key for what each bar, line, or pie slice means.

Quick **Choices** *TURN ON AND OFF LEGEND*

1. Click the **Legend** button 🖾 on the Chart toolbar to turn the legend on or off.
2. If the legend displays, drag the legend where you want it to go on the chart.

You can also position the legend on the chart and change the shape by choosing **Chart**, **Chart Options**, and clicking the Legend tab. If you check **Show legend**, you can choose the placement on the chart to be on the **Bottom**, **Corner**, **Top**, **Right**, or **Left** of the chart. Unlike the other tabs of the Chart Options dialog box, this tab's options do not change depending on the chart type selected.

Chart ▾ Chart Options... Data Labels Tab

Data labels are the labels that appear with each data point. Choose **Chart**, **Chart Options**, and click the Data Labels tab to select the kind of labels you want.

For all charts except Surface charts, you can choose to have no labels (**None**), display the number associated with the data point (**Show value**), or display the category (x-axis) label associated with each data point (**Show label**). If you show the value or label, you can display the color or marker next to the label by checking **Legend key next to label**.

For pie and doughnut charts you can also elect to show what percent the slice makes up out of the whole by choosing one of two additional options: **Show percent** or **Show label and percent**.

Pie charts also have an additional option—when you choose a data label, you can choose to **Show leader lines**, which is a line from the data label to the pie slice.

Bubble charts have an extra choice, **Show bubble sizes**. The third value plotted on a bubble chart is the size of the bubble.

Chart ⇨ Chart Options... Data Table Tab

If you want to place a table beneath your chart that shows the data values used to calculate the chart, choose **Chart**, **Chart Options**, click the Data Table tab, and check **Show data table**. After you've checked this option, you can also check **Show legend keys** if you want to see the color or marker for each data series represented in the table. The data table option is available for 2-D and 3-D column, bar, line, area and stock, cylinder, cone, and pyramid charts.

Quick **Choices**   *TURN DATA TABLE ON AND OFF*

■ Click the **Data Table** button ⊞ on the Chart toolbar to display or hide the data table.

Chart ⇨ Location...

To relocate the chart from an embedded chart to a chart sheet or visa-versa, choose **Chart**, **Location**. In the Chart Location dialog box type a sheet name in the **As new sheet** text box or choose the sheet name in the **As object in** drop-down list.

Chart ⇨ Add Data...

After you create the chart, you can place additional data on the chart.

Quick **Choices**   *ADD NEW DATA BY COPY AND PASTE*

1. On the worksheet, select the new row or column of data you want to add.
2. Click the **Copy** button 🖹 on the Standard toolbar.
3. Click in the chart and click the **Paste** button 📋 on the Standard toolbar.

Quick **Choices**   *ADD NEW DATA THROUGH THE MENU*

1. Choose **Chart**, **Add Data**. The Add Data dialog box opens.
2. In the **Range** text box, type the range address or click the **Collapse Dialog** button, select the range you want to add, click the **Collapse Dialog** button again, and choose **OK**.

Chart ➥ Add Trendline...

A trendline smoothes out the fluctuations of your data. You might be able to use the trendline to make predictions of your data. Click a data series and choose **Chart**, **Add Trendline**. The Add Trendline dialog box opens with two tabs (see Figures 3.105 and 3.106).

❶ Draws straight line connecting the points.

❷ Draws curved line assuming more growth at beginning.

❸ Draws waved line.

Figure 3.105
Chart, Add Trendline, Type tab opens the Add Trendline dialog box where you can choose which kind of line you want.

❺ Draws curved line assuming more constant growth.

❻ Draws curved line assuming accelerating growth.

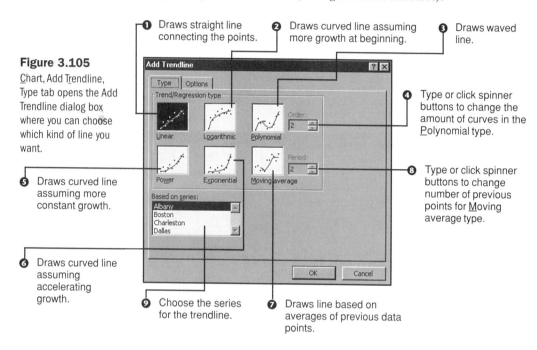

❹ Type or click spinner buttons to change the amount of curves in the Polynomial type.

❽ Type or click spinner buttons to change number of previous points for Moving average type.

❾ Choose the series for the trendline.

❼ Draws line based on averages of previous data points.

❶ Automatically give series name to trendline or type in your own name that will appear in the legend.

Figure 3.106
Chart, Add Trendline, Options tab opens the Add Trendline dialog box where you can forecast and display information.

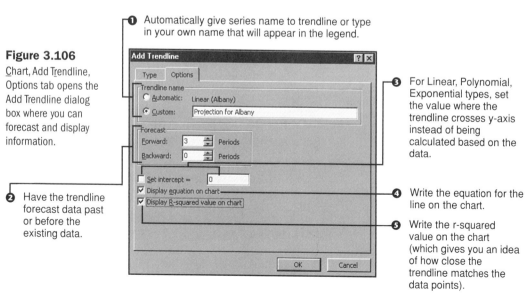

❸ For Linear, Polynomial, Exponential types, set the value where the trendline crosses y-axis instead of being calculated based on the data.

❷ Have the trendline forecast data past or before the existing data.

❹ Write the equation for the line on the chart.

❺ Write the r-squared value on the chart (which gives you an idea of how close the trendline matches the data points).

To modify the trendline after you've created it, double-click the trendline to go to the Format Trendline dialog box. In addition to the two tabs mentioned previously, you also have the Patterns tab. You can change the line **Style** (dashed or patterned line), **Color**, and **Weight** (thickness).

Chart ➥ 3-D View...

The 3-D view enables you to tilt and rotate your three-dimensional chart. With a 3-D chart selected, choose **Chart**, **3-D View**. The 3-D View dialog box appears (see Figure 3.107).

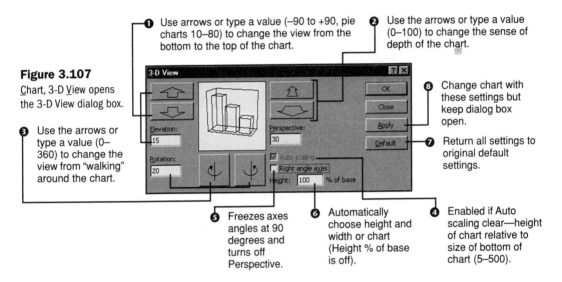

❶ Use arrows or type a value (–90 to +90, pie charts 10–80) to change the view from the bottom to the top of the chart.

❷ Use the arrows or type a value (0–100) to change the sense of depth of the chart.

Figure 3.107

Chart, 3-D View opens the 3-D View dialog box.

❸ Use the arrows or type a value (0–360) to change the view from "walking" around the chart.

❽ Change chart with these settings but keep dialog box open.

❼ Return all settings to original default settings.

❺ Freezes axes angles at 90 degrees and turns off Perspective.

❻ Automatically choose height and width or chart (Height % of base is off).

❹ Enabled if Auto scaling clear—height of chart relative to size of bottom of chart (5–500).

PowerPoint

The PowerPoint Screen, Keyboard, and Mouse

Starting PowerPoint

Unlike Word, which starts with a blank document, and Excel, which starts with a blank workbook, PowerPoint opens a dialog box to start with (see Figure 4.1).

❶ AutoContent Wizard displays a series of dialog boxes that ask you what type of presentation you will give, what type of output you'll require, and input for the title slide. Then PowerPoint builds a number of slides with suggested content that you can edit.

Figure 4.1
Windows Start button, Programs, Microsoft PowerPoint opens the PowerPoint dialog box.

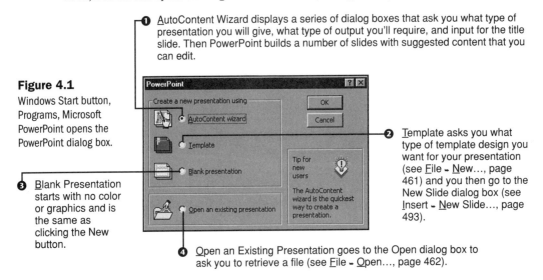

❷ Template asks you what type of template design you want for your presentation (see File – New..., page 461) and you then go to the New Slide dialog box (see Insert – New Slide..., page 493).

❸ Blank Presentation starts with no color or graphics and is the same as clicking the New button.

❹ Open an Existing Presentation goes to the Open dialog box to ask you to retrieve a file (see File – Open..., page 462).

AutoContent Wizard

If you choose the AutoContent Wizard from the startup dialog box, the dialog box that opens shows you Start and Finish and the steps that you will be performing. You can also choose **File**, **New**, click the Presentations tab, and double-click AutoContent Wizard. Click the **Next** button and choose the Presentation type (see Figure 4.2).

❶ This area shows the steps of the wizard and where you currently are.

❷ Click a button to narrow the scope of the list.

❸ Choose a presentation type.

❹ For all buttons except All and Carnegie Coach, click Add to add another template to the list and Remove to delete the selected item.

Figure 4.2
Choose AutoContent Wizard from the opening dialog box and click Next to open the Presentation type section of the AutoContent dialog box.

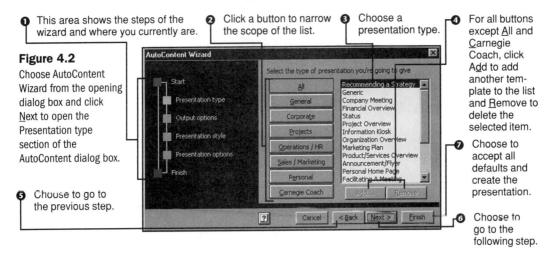

❼ Choose to accept all defaults and create the presentation.

❺ Choose to go to the previous step.

❻ Choose to go to the following step.

The next step asks what kind of output you'll have. The steps following depend on this step. Choose one of the following kinds of presentations:

Presentations, informal meetings, handouts (generally, with a speaker)

1. Click one of the output options: **On-screen presentation, Black and white overheads, Color overheads,** or **35mm slides**.
2. Click whether you will print handouts and choose **Next**.
3. On the Presentation options step, type the text that you want to appear on your first slide: **Presentation title, Your name,** and any **Additional information** you want to appear on the slide. Choose **Next** and **Finish** to create your presentation.

Internet, kiosk (generally, without a speaker)

1. Check if you want a **Copyright notice on each page** and type the text for the notice.
2. Check if you want to include the **Date last updated**.
3. If you want, check and type your **E-mail address** in the format of user@domain. Choose **Next** and **Finish** to create your presentation.

Regardless of the presentation options you chose, you enter Outline view after PowerPoint creates the presentation (see **View** ▬ **Outline**, page 475). You can switch to the other views using the buttons to the left of the horizontal scrollbars (see **View** ▬ **Slide Sorter**, page 477 and **View** ▬ **Notes Page**, page 478). If you want to run the presentation, see **View** ▬ **Slide Show**, page 478.

The Screen

PowerPoint screen views are significantly different from each other. See the references to the Outline, Slide Sorter, and Slide show in the paragraph above. The Slide view is the most common and is shown in Figure 4.3.

Typing in PowerPoint

The first step to typing in PowerPoint is to position the insertion point where you want to type. Click a section of a slide, outline, or on notes pages. You see the blinking vertical line (insertion point) where your type is inserted. When you create a new slide, you see prompts such as Click to Add Title and Click to Add Text to guide you.

Use the keyboard to type characters. When you type, any characters after the insertion point are pushed to the right. Press **Backspace** to remove characters before the insertion point.

The slide generally has two areas: the title area and text area. The text area often has bullets. After you type the first bullet, press **Enter** and you are at the second bullet. If you press **Tab** you get an indented bullet. Instead of pressing **Enter**, press **Shift+Enter** to create a line break and indent the text under the same bullet item.

Figure 4.3
Click the Slide view button to see and edit a slide.

❶ Standard toolbar (see <u>V</u>iew - <u>T</u>oolbars - Standard, page 484).

❺ Click the Up or Down arrow to move up and down pages or lines depending on the view and Zoom setting (see <u>V</u>iew - <u>Z</u>oom…, page 492).

❷ Formatting toolbar (see <u>V</u>iew - <u>T</u>oolbars - Formatting, page 484).

❾ The current placeholder shows with a hatched pattern.

❸ View buttons: Slide, Outline, Slide Sorter, Notes, Slide Show.

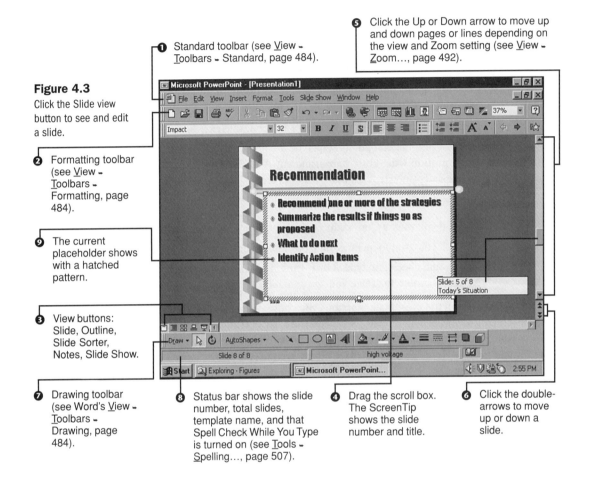

❼ Drawing toolbar (see Word's <u>V</u>iew - <u>T</u>oolbars - Drawing, page 484).

❽ Status bar shows the slide number, total slides, template name, and that Spell Check While You Type is turned on (see <u>T</u>ools - <u>S</u>pelling…, page 507).

❹ Drag the scroll box. The ScreenTip shows the slide number and title.

❻ Click the double-arrows to move up or down a slide.

Editing Text

To correct your document, use the following keys.

Delete text

Press	To
Backspace	Delete one character to the left of insertion point, or the selected text
Delete	Delete one character to the right of insertion point, or the selected text
Ctrl+Backspace	Delete one word to the left
Ctrl+Delete	Delete one word to the right
Ctrl+Z	Undo the last action

Editing Objects

You insert objects through many choices on the Insert menu (see especially **Insert - Picture** page 496, **Insert - Chart...** page 498, and **Insert - Object...**) or by double-clicking on an object placeholder when you choose that kind of AutoLayout (see **Insert - New Slide...**, page 493).

To move the object, move the mouse pointer to the object. The mouse pointer changes to a four-headed arrow. Drag the object to where you want to go.

To size the object, click it. Small square handles appear around the object. Move the mouse pointer to one of the squares. The mouse pointer changes to a double-headed arrow. Drag the handle to resize the object.

To delete a graphic object, click the object and press **Delete**.

Navigating

To type on a slide, you need to position the insertion point where you want to edit.

Use the keyboard to move the insertion point in the selected area

Press	To Move
Left Arrow	A character to the left on an outline, slide, or note. To the next slide in Slide Sorter view.
Right Arrow	A character to the right on an outline, slide, or note. To the previous slide in Slide Sorter view.
Up Arrow	Up a line in an outline, slide, or note. To the previous row of slides in Slide Sorter view.
Down Arrow	Down a line in an outline, slide, or note. To the next row of slides in Slide Sorter view.
Ctrl+Left Arrow	A word to the left in an outline, slide, or note.
Ctrl+Right Arrow	A word to the right in an outline, slide, or note.
Ctrl+Up Arrow	A paragraph up in a note.
Ctrl+Down Arrow	A paragraph down in a note.
Tab	To the tab stop in a note. Demote the bullet in an outline and slide.
Shift+Tab	To the tab stop in an outline and slide.
End	To end of a line.
Home	To beginning of a line.
Page Up	Up one screen in Outline view. In full Slide view, to previous slide.
Page Down	Down one screen in Outline view. In full Slide view, to next slide.
Ctrl+Home	To first slide.
Ctrl+End	To last slide.

After you use the mouse to scroll, make sure that you click to move the insertion point where you want to start editing.

Use mouse to scroll on the screen

Click	To
Up scroll arrow	Go to previous slide (or up a line if slide does not take up full screen) in Slide view. Scroll up one line in an outline.
Down scroll arrow	Go to next slide (or down a line if slide does not take up full screen) in Slide view. Scroll down one line in an outline.
Above the scroll box	Scroll up one screen or to previous slide.
Below the scroll box	Scroll down one screen or to next slide.
Drag the scroll box	Screen tip shows slide number and title.
Left scroll arrow	Scroll left.
Right scroll arrow	Scroll right.
Double-arrow on bottom of vertical scrollbar	To previous or next slide.
Double-click slide icon in Outline view	To open slide in Slide view.
Double-click slide in Slide Sorter view	To open slide in Slide view.

Use Microsoft IntelliMouse

Do This	To
Rotate the wheel toward you	Scroll down a few lines in Outline view to the next slide in Slide view.
Rotate the wheel away from you	Scroll up a few lines in Outline view to the previous slide in Slide view.
Hold **Ctrl** as you rotate the wheel toward you	Zoom so view is smaller.
Hold **Ctrl** as you rotate the wheel away you	Zoom so view is magnified.

Selecting Text

Before you do major editing or formatting, you need to select text first. After you select text, you can press **Delete** to remove the text. (See also the **Format** (page 499) and **Edit** (page 469) sections for many of the features you can do with selected text.)

See the navigation keys with the keyboard above. Select text by holding down the **Shift** key and using the movement keys (see Navigating, page 459). For example, hold **Shift** and press **Ctrl+Right** arrow. You select one word at a time. The following are some additional keys to select text in the document.

Press **Ctrl+A** to select the whole presentation in Outline, and Slide Sorter views. Press **Ctrl+A** to select all objects on the current slide in Slide view. In Notes Pages view, press **Ctrl+A** to select all objects on the slide and the notes.

Select with the mouse

Do This	To Select
Drag over the text	Any text
Double-click	A word
Click the graphic	A graphic
Click mouse pointer and drag down	One or more lines
Ctrl + click in a sentence	A sentence
Click at the start of the selection. Move to the end of the selection with mouse. Hold down **Shift** and click again.	A block of text (use this method when the screen scrolls too fast to effectively select a large block of text)

File

The **File** menu helps you manage the document as a whole: where it is stored, the size and formatting of paper, where you want to print or email the document, and summary information.

File – New...

The first item on the **File** menu——**New**—is your first step to creating a blank presentation or a presentation with preexisting text and formatting. When you first start PowerPoint or use the New toolbar button, the default presentation is based on the Blank Presentation template (shown as Blank Presentation on the General tab of the dialog box). The only differences between Word and PowerPoint are the templates available to start a new document and that you can create a new document or template with Word while you can only create a new document in PowerPoint from the dialog box (see Word's **File – New...**, page 20).

After you choose the template, PowerPoint may ask for the layout of the first slide. Double-click the layout of the slide you want.

File ▸ Open...

File, **Open** enables you to open a file stored on a disk and display and edit it on your screen. The only difference between Word and PowerPoint is the list in the **Files of type** drop-down box (see Word's **File ▸ Open...**, page 21). You can open PowerPoint presentations, templates, add-ins, and HTML documents.

Also, one of the items in **Files of Type** is All Outlines. Use this to open a Word Outline document. Each Heading 1 becomes the title of the slide. Each Heading 2 and lower level headings become bullets and subbullets of the slides. If you open an Excel workbook, each row becomes a slide. You can also open a plain text file and each line becomes a slide. Other presentation files such as Harvard Graphics can also be opened, depending on which converters have been installed.

File ▸ Close

To remove the current presentation from the screen, use **File**, **Close**. If you haven't saved the file since your last change, PowerPoint prompts you to save. File, Close is also the same in Word and PowerPoint (see **File ▸ Close**, page 462).

File ▸ Save

If you already gave your presentation a name, **File**, **Save** or **Shift+F12** saves changes to that presentation name on your disk (otherwise, the Save As dialog box opens). This command works the same way it does in Word (see Word's **File ▸ Save**, page 29).

File ▸ Save As...

Saving a file places a copy of what is on the screen to a location on a disk. The first time you save a file with **File**, **Save** or the **Save** button 🖫, you enter the Save As dialog box. Thereafter, choose **File**, **Save As** or press **F12.** The two commands in PowerPoint and Word (see Word's **File ▸ Save As...**, page 462) are the same except for a couple of the following options on the Save As dialog box:

- Check **Embed TrueType** to add the fonts to the document. If you open the presentation on another computer, that computer does not have to have the fonts installed.

- In the **Save as type** drop-down, choose from among the following:

  The **Save as type** for PowerPoint is listed as Presentation. If you want to save the presentation as a different file format, click the **Save as type** drop-down and select a previous version of PowerPoint, a graphic format (such as Windows Metafile, Portable Network Graphics, CompuServe GIF, or JPEG File Interchange Format).

  If you want to save the presentation as a template that you can use over and over (see **File ▸ New...**, page 461), choose Presentation Template. PowerPoint opens to the Templates folder. Double-click the Presentations folder.

  If you want to save to presentation as an add-in so that you can use the features such as macros and toolbars, choose PowerPoint Add-In (see **Tools ▸ Add-Ins...**, page 515).

If you want to save the presentation as an outline, choose Outline/RTF. When you open this file in Word, the slide titles become Heading 1 style, bullets become Heading 2, 3, and so on.

You can save the presentation as a PowerPoint Show. Then, when you double-click the file name from the Windows Explorer, the file automatically opens in Slide Show view. When you finish the Slide Show, PowerPoint closes. If you want to edit the file, open it through the Open dialog box.

File → Save as HTML

If you want to save your presentation as HTML files for use on the Web, choose **File, Save as HTML**. The Save as HTML Wizard opens, enabling you to choose browser frames, the graphics format (GIF, JPEG, or PowerPoint animation), monitor resolution, home page identification, page colors and buttons styles, and location of your files. In typical installation, this item is dimmed on your menu. You may have to go through setup again to install this option.

File → Pack and Go...

The Pack and Go Wizard enables you to copy your file for use on another computer. The wizard compresses the file and enables you to place one file on more than one disk if necessary. The wizard also asks you whether you want to include the PowerPoint Viewer, which is a free program that enables the user to look at your presentation, but not edit it.

Copy the file with the Pack and Go Wizard

1. Open the file you want to copy and choose **File, Pack and Go**. The Pack and Go Wizard dialog box opens, listing the steps you need to take. Click the **Next** button to start.

2. The Pick Files to Pack Step appears. You can check the **Active presentation** (the one on the screen). You can also check **Other presentation(s)** and type or use the **Browse** button to choose another presentation. If you want more than one, hold down the **Ctrl** key while you click each presentation and click **Select** to return to the wizard. Click the **Next** button.

3. On the Choose destination step, click the **A:\drive** or **B:\drive**. Alternatively, you can click the **Choose destination** option button and type or use the Browse button to choose a folder or disk to store the presentation(s). Click the **Next** button.

4. The Links step asks you whether you want to **Include linked files**—other applications' files you may have inserted (see **Insert → Object...**, page 498). You can also check if you want to **Embed TrueType fonts** so that the presentation looks the same on another computer even if the computer doesn't have the same fonts installed. Click the **Next** button.

5. The next step asks whether you want to include the PowerPoint **Viewer for Windows 95 or NT**. This Viewer enables people without PowerPoint to see but not edit your presentation. Otherwise, click **Don't include the Viewer**. Click the **Next** button.

6. If you told the wizard to store the presentation on a removable disk, insert the disk in the disk drive and click **Finish**. If the presentation and files don't fit on the disk, PowerPoint prompts you for additional disks as needed.

When you give the disks to the other users, tell them to double-click the Pngsetup (Pack and Go Setup) file on the disk. The wizard asks for a destination and then prompts for each of the disks.

File ⮚ Page Setup...

The Page Setup dialog box controls the size of slides and printed output and page numbers. Choose **File**, **Page Setup** and the Page Setup dialog box appears (see Figure 4.4).

❶ Choose what kind of size you want for the slides: Onscreen Show, Letter Paper, A4 Paper, 35mm Slides, Overhead, Banner, or Custom.

Figure 4.4

File, Page Setup opens the Page Setup dialog box.

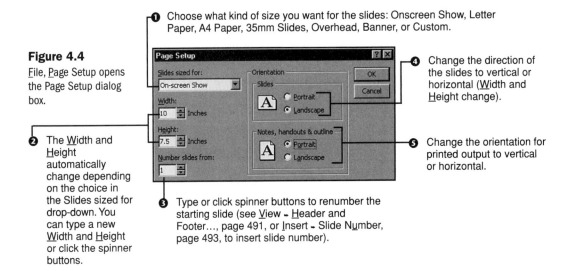

❹ Change the direction of the slides to vertical or horizontal (Width and Height change).

❷ The Width and Height automatically change depending on the choice in the Slides sized for drop-down. You can type a new Width and Height or click the spinner buttons.

❺ Change the orientation for printed output to vertical or horizontal.

❸ Type or click spinner buttons to renumber the starting slide (see View ⮚ Header and Footer..., page 491, or Insert ⮚ Slide Number, page 493, to insert slide number).

File ⮚ Print...

To send your slides, notes pages, handouts, or outline to a printer, choose this option.

Quick **Choices**   *PRINT*

■ Click the **Print** button 🖶 on the Standard toolbar. The slides print to the default printer.

To print slides or other items to the printer, follow these steps:

1. Choose **File**, **Print** or press **Ctrl+P**. The Print dialog box displays (see Figure 4.5).
2. To change the printer (or print to a fax) select from the **Name** drop-down.

❶ Indicates any error messages.

Figure 4.5
File, Print opens the
Print dialog box.

❷ Description of
printer.

❹ Comments
attached to printer
when it is set up.

❺ Identify the range
of slides to print.

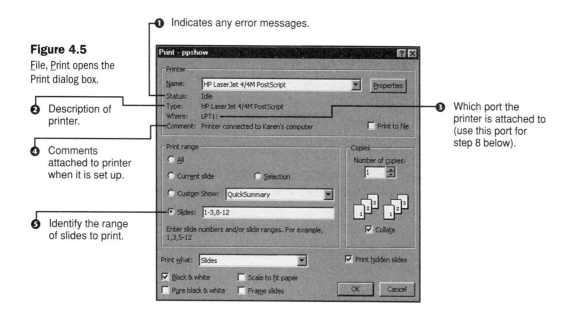

❸ Which port the
printer is attached to
(use this port for
step 8 below).

3. If you want to change Windows options for your printing, click the **Properties** button and change such things as paper size, paper orientation, where to get paper, and printer resolution. You want to change some of these options for the presentation through **File**, **Page Setup** (see page 464).

4. To print a portion or all resulting slides, choose one of the following:

   - Click **All** to print the entire presentation.

   - Click to print just the **Current slide**.

   - If you've selected multiple slides (in Slide Sorter view, hold down **Shift** as you click slides) or a portion of an outline, click to print the **Selection**.

   - If you've created a **Custom Show** (see **Slide Show – Custom Shows...**, page 533), choose it from the drop-down list.

   - To print specific slides, type the slide numbers in the Slides text box. For example, 2-4,6,9,13-15.

5. In the **Print what** drop-down, choose whether you want to print Slides, Handouts (2, 3, or 6 per page), Notes Pages, or the Outline view.

6. To print more than one copy, use the spinner buttons or text box to reset the **Number of copies**.

7. If you have more than one copy and you want one entire set and a copy set, check **Collate**. With this option unchecked, printing can be faster, and you print multiple copies of page 1, then page 2, and so forth.

8. If you don't have the selected printer connected to your computer, choose to **Print to file** on your disk. When you choose **OK**, PowerPoint opens the Print to file dialog box. Give the file a name and location and click **OK** again. PowerPoint automatically gives the file a PRN extension.

   When you want to print the file, click the Windows **Start** button, choose **Programs**, **MS-DOS Prompt**. From the DOS window, type **COPY /B filename port**. A specific example would be **COPY /B c:\docs\print.prn lpt1**. (When using print to file, you need to have the print driver for the destination printer installed, even if you are not attached to it.)

9. Check one or more of the following check boxes on the bottom of the Print dialog box (the defaults can be set, see **Tools ⁃ Options... Print Tab**, page 515):

   - Check **Black & white** to make color slides look as good as possible on a black and white printer. Prints colors as shades of gray.
   - Check **Pure black & white** to only print black and white and no shades of gray (you can't have both this and the box above checked at the same time). Use to print draft copies on a color printer and quick speaker's notes and handouts.
   - Check **Scale to fit paper** to reduce or enlarge the slides so that they fit on a printed page.
   - Check **Frame slides** to add a thin border around slides on slides, handouts, and notes pages.
   - Check **Print hidden slides** if you want to print slides that you hid (see **Slide Show ⁃ Hide Slide**, page 533).

10. Click **OK** to print the presentation with your choices.

File ⁃ Send To

The **File**, **Send To** menu enables you to transmit your presentation electronically to one or more email recipients. The first three items on the **Send To** submenus are the same as Word's. (For **Mail Recipient**, **Routing Recipient**, and **Exchange Folder**, see Word's **File ⁃ Send To**, page 45.) PowerPoint has two additional options—**Microsoft Word** and **Genigraphics**.

File ⁃ Send To ⁃ Microsoft Word...

You can export your notes, handouts, or outline to Microsoft Word and then use Word as an editor. If you export the outline to Word and edit it, you can then import it back into PowerPoint (see Word's **File ⁃ Send To ⁃ Microsoft PowerPoint**, page 46). Choose **File**, **Send To, Microsoft Word** to open the Write-Up dialog box (see Figure 4.6).

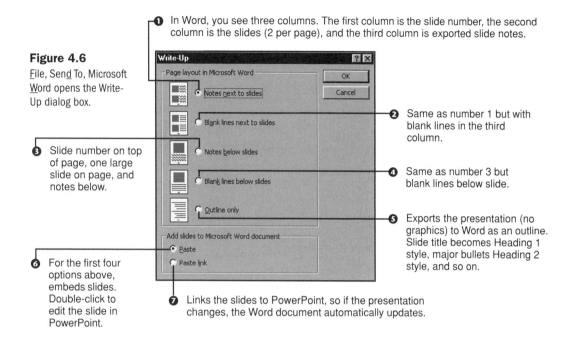

Figure 4.6
File, Send To, Microsoft Word opens the Write-Up dialog box.

❶ In Word, you see three columns. The first column is the slide number, the second column is the slides (2 per page), and the third column is exported slide notes.

❷ Same as number 1 but with blank lines in the third column.

❸ Slide number on top of page, one large slide on page, and notes below.

❹ Same as number 3 but blank lines below slide.

❺ Exports the presentation (no graphics) to Word as an outline. Slide title becomes Heading 1 style, major bullets Heading 2 style, and so on.

❻ For the first four options above, embeds slides. Double-click to edit the slide in PowerPoint.

❼ Links the slides to PowerPoint, so if the presentation changes, the Word document automatically updates.

File ~ Send To ~ Genigraphics...

Genigraphics is a company that can take your PowerPoint file and produce 35-mm slides, color prints, color overheads, posters, and other services. Use **File**, **Send To**, **Genigraphics** to open the Genigraphics Wizard so that you can package your file, identify your order specifications, and transmit your order by modem. In Typical setup, this item is dimmed on your menu. You may have to go through setup again to install this option.

File ~ Properties

File properties enable you to identify and categorize your file in more detail than you can with just a name. You can add notes in many different fields (such as **Subject** and **Comments**). File properties also enable you to see more information about your file, such as the number of words, the creation date, and the MS-DOS name. The dialog boxes for Word and PowerPoint are almost identical with the following exceptions (see Word's **File ~ Properties**, page 46):

■ The bottom half of the Statistics tab in Word tells how many words, paragraphs, and so on the document has. In PowerPoint, this area adds how many slides, hidden slides, and Multimedia clips there are.

■ PowerPoint's Contents tab is much more thorough than Word's (see Figure 4.7).

Figure 4.7
File, Properties, opens the Properties dialog box. Click the Contents tab to see details of your presentation.

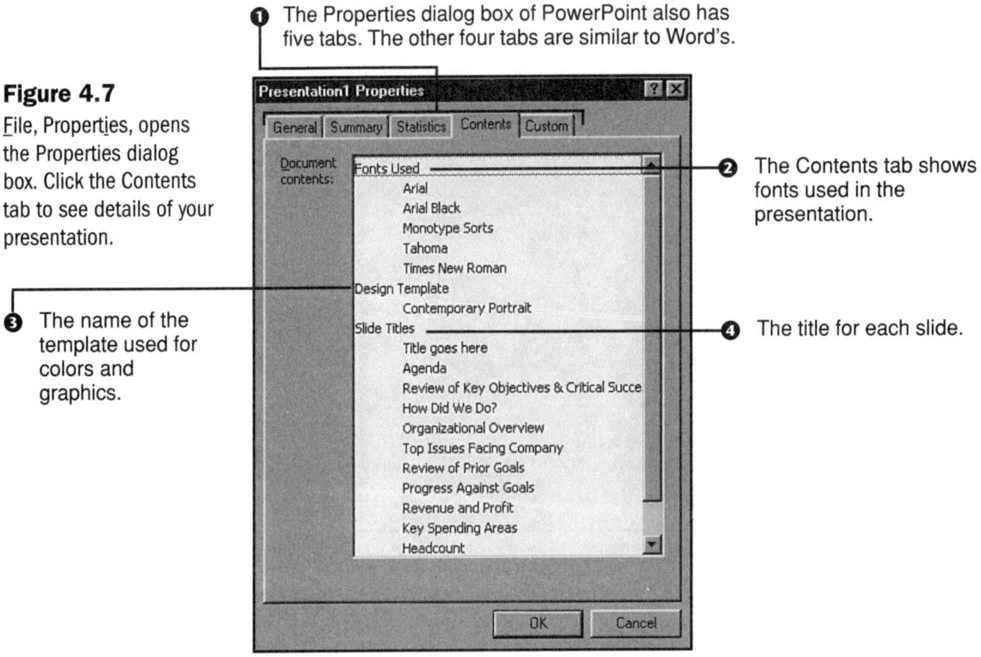
The Properties dialog box of PowerPoint also has five tabs. The other four tabs are similar to Word's.
Presentation1 Properties
General
Summary
Statistics
Contents
Custom
Document contents:
Fonts Used
Arial
Arial Black
Monotype Sorts
Tahoma
Times New Roman
Design Template
Contemporary Portrait
Slide Titles
Title goes here
Agenda
Review of Key Objectives & Critical Succe
How Did We Do?
Organizational Overview
Top Issues Facing Company
Review of Prior Goals
Progress Against Goals
Revenue and Profit
Key Spending Areas
Headcount
OK
Cancel
The Contents tab shows fonts used in the presentation.
The name of the template used for colors and graphics.
The title for each slide.

File ➡ Recently Used File List

To open one of your last saved presentations, choose **File** and then select one of the files on the bottom of the file menu. The hot keys are numbered for each of the files (**1**, **2**, **3**, and so on), with the last file saved indicated with number 1. If the names do not display at the bottom of the **File** menu, do the following procedure.

To display the recent files or change the number displayed, do the following:

1. Choose **Tools**, **Options**. The Options dialog box displays.
2. Click the General tab.
3. Type or use the **entries** spinner button to change number of files that you want to see in the **Recently used file list**.
4. Click **OK**.

PowerPoint displays up to the number of files you chose in step 3.

File ➡ Exit

To get out of PowerPoint, you use **File**, **Exit** or press **Alt+F4**. PowerPoint prompts you if you want to save each presentation changed since your last save. If you choose **Yes** and have not given the document a name, you enter the Save As dialog box (see Word's **File ➡ Save As...**, page 29).

Edit

The **E**dit menu enables you to make changes to the presentation as a whole: undo and repeat commands, cut, copy and paste information, clear and delete selected information, duplicate slides, find specific information in a presentation, replace information that has been found, create links, and edit objects.

Edit – Undo...

The first item on the **E**dit menu enables you to **U**ndo specific actions.

Quick Choices   UNDO

- Click the **Undo** button on the Standard toolbar.
- Choose **E**dit, **U**ndo Action. The bracketed action is the last action you performed. For instance, Typing, Formatting, Duplicate, and so on.
- Press **Ctrl+Z**.

  The last action that you performed is undone.

Quick Choices   UNDO MULTIPLE ACTIONS

- Click the pull-down arrow on the **Undo** button , and select the actions that you want to undo. All the actions up to the one you select are undone.

Edit – Redo...

Edit, **R**edo is similar to **E**dit, **U**ndo. It redoes something that you have undone. It is a valuable tool to use with Undo.

Quick Choices   REDO

- Click the **Redo** button on the Standard toolbar.
- Choose **E**dit, **R**edo Action. The bracketed action is the last action you undid. For instance, Typing, Formatting, Duplicate, and so on.
- Press **Ctrl+Y**.

  The last action you undid is redone.

Quick Choices   UNDO MULTIPLE ACTIONS

- Click the pull-down arrow on the **Redo** button , and select the actions that you want to redo. All the actions up to the one you select are redone.

Edit → Repeat

Choose **Edit**, **Repeat** or press **F4** or **Ctrl+Y** to repeat the last action or command. **Edit**, **Repeat** replaces **Edit**, **Redo** when it is available. Actions such as formatting fonts, formatting slide color, and so on enable **Edit**, **Repeat**.

Edit → Cut

The **Cut** command enables you to remove selected text and place it on the Windows Clipboard to **Paste** somewhere else. Select the text or slide that you want to cut (see **Typing in PowerPoint** on page 457 and **Selecting Text** on page 460 for more information).

Quick Choices   CUT

■ Click the **Cut** button ✂ on the Standard toolbar.

■ Press **Ctrl+X**.

■ Choose **Edit**, **Cut**.

■ Right-click the selection and choose **Cut**.

■ Drag and drop—Point to the selected text; when the mouse pointer changes to a white arrow, click and drag the selection to the new location.

■ Right-click and drag the selection to the new location, and select **Move Here**, **Copy Here**, **Create Hyperlink Here**, or **Cancel**.

If the drag-and-drop operation isn't working, make sure that the **Drag-and-Drop text editing** option is checked on the **Tools** → **Options…** **Edit Tab** (see page 517 for more information).

Edit → Copy

The **Copy** command enables you to copy selected text and place it on the Windows Clipboard to Paste somewhere else. Select the text or slide(s) that you want to copy (see **Typing in PowerPoint** on page 457 and **Selecting Text** on page 460 for more information).

Quick Choices   COPY

■ Click the **Copy** button ▣ on the Standard toolbar.

■ Press **Ctrl+C**.

■ Choose **Edit**, **Copy**.

■ Right-click the selection and choose **Copy**.

■ Drag and drop—Point to the selection; when the mouse pointer changes to a white arrow, hold down the **Ctrl** key, and click and drag the selection to the new location.

■ Right-click and drag the selection to the new location, and then select **Move Here**, **Copy Here**, **Create Hyperlink Here**, or **Cancel**.

If the drag-and-drop operation isn't working, make sure that the **Drag-and-Drop text editing** option is checked on the **Tools** → **Options…** **Edit Tab** (see page 515 for more information).

Edit ~ Paste

The **Paste** command enables you to paste what is on the Windows Clipboard at the location of the insertion point. Used with **Edit, Cut,** you move the original text. Used with **Edit, Copy,** you create a copy of the original text.

Quick Choices PASTE

- Click the **Paste** button 📋 on the Standard toolbar.
- Press **Ctrl+V.**
- Choose **Edit, Paste.**
- Right-click where you want to insert the copied information, and choose **Paste.**

Edit ~ Paste Special...

The **Paste Special** command enables you to paste, link, or embed what is on the Windows Clipboard (at the location of the insertion point) with the formatting you specify.

1. **Cut** or **Copy** the information you want to paste.
2. Move the insertion point where you want to paste the information.
3. Choose **Edit, Paste Special.** The Paste Special dialog box displays (see Figure 4.8).

Figure 4.8
Choose Edit, Paste Special to display the Paste Special dialog box.

❸ If available, choose to turn this on or off.

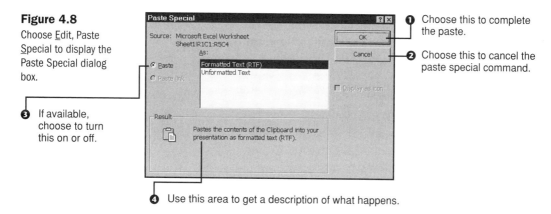

❶ Choose this to complete the paste.

❷ Choose this to cancel the paste special command.

❹ Use this area to get a description of what happens.

4. Choose **Paste** or **Paste link.**

For more information about Paste Special, see Word's **Edit ~ Paste Special...** on page 52.

Edit ~ Paste as Hyperlink

The **Paste as Hyperlink** command enables you to paste Clipboard contents as a hyperlink. A hyperlink creates a shortcut to the source document. Click the hyperlink to jump to the source document. If the application that created the hyperlink is not open, it opens and the document also opens.

Quick **Choices**   *HYPERLINK*

1. After you have cut or copied text to the Clipboard, move the insertion point to the location you want to paste to.

2. Choose **Edit**, **Paste as Hyperlink**.

   or

   Select the text to be moved, right-click it, drag it to the new location, and choose **Create Hyperlink Here**.

Edit ‣ Clear

The **Edit**, **Clear** command deletes the selected text or object without putting it on the Clipboard.

1. Select the text or object you want to clear.

2. Choose **Edit**, **Clear**.

Edit ‣ Select All

Choose **Edit**, **Select All** or press **Ctrl+A** to select the whole presentation.

Edit ‣ Duplicate

Select the object that you want to duplicate and choose **Edit**, **Duplicate** or press **Ctrl+D** to make a copy of the object. Choose **Edit**, **Duplicate** again to make additional copies of the object.

Edit ‣ Delete Slide

The **Edit**, **Delete Slide** command deletes the current slide in Slide or Notes view or deletes the selected slides in Slide Sorter or Outline view from the presentation.

Edit ‣ Find...

The **Edit**, **Find** command enables you to search for text you specify.

Quick **Choices**   *FIND*

1. Press **Ctrl+F**.

2. Type what you are looking for in the **Find what** text box, and choose the **Find Next** button or press **Enter**.

Without the Find dialog box open, press **Shift+F4** to repeat the last Find action without opening the Find dialog box. (For more information, see Excel's **Edit ‣ Find...** on page 283.)

Edit ▸ Replace...

The **Edit**, **Replace** command enables you to search for and replace characters you specify.

1. Press **Ctrl+H**.
2. Type what you are looking for in the Find what text box.
3. Type what you want to replace in the Replace with text box.
4. Select Match Case or Find Whole Words Only to turn those options on or off.
5. Choose the **Find Next** button.
6. To replace the found text with the new text, choose the **Replace** button. To replace all occurrences of the found text with the new text, choose **Replace All.** To skip this occurrence of the found text and continue the search, choose the **Find Next** button. To end this session, choose the **Close** button.

Edit ▸ Go To Property...

The **Edit**, **Go To Property** command enables you to move to a specific location in your presentation, similarly to Word's **Edit ▸ Go To** (see page 58). To enable the **Edit**, **Go To Property** command, you need to define **File**, **Properties** with a link to the location, which is similar to creating a Bookmark in Word.

To mark a location in your presentation, follow these steps:

1. Select the text you want to mark.
2. Choose **File**, **Properties** and select the Custom tab to display the *Filename*.ppt Properties dialog box (see Figure 4.9).

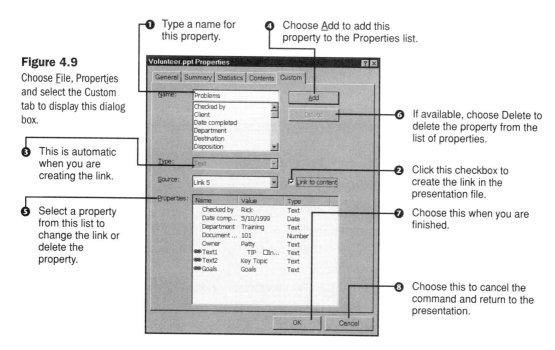

Figure 4.9

Choose File, Properties and select the Custom tab to display this dialog box.

❶ Type a name for this property.

❸ This is automatic when you are creating the link.

❺ Select a property from this list to change the link or delete the property.

❹ Choose Add to add this property to the Properties list.

❻ If available, choose Delete to delete the property from the list of properties.

❷ Click this checkbox to create the link in the presentation file.

❼ Choose this when you are finished.

❽ Choose this to cancel the command and return to the presentation.

To use the Go to Property command, follow these steps:

1. Choose **Edit, Go to Property** to open the Properties dialog box (see Figure 4.10).

Figure 4.10

Choose Edit, Go to Property to open the Properties dialog box.

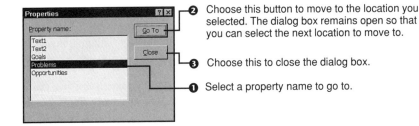

➋ Choose this button to move to the location you selected. The dialog box remains open so that you can select the next location to move to.

➌ Choose this to close the dialog box.

➊ Select a property name to go to.

Edit ▾ Links...

Edit, Links remains dimmed until you have linked objects. (For information on creating links, see Excel's **Edit ▾ Paste Special...** on page 274 and **Edit ▾ Paste as Hyperlink** on page 277.) After you have linked objects, you may need to edit the information related to the object. If you move the source presentation or document or change the name of the presentation or document, the link is broken and you get an error in the active presentation. (See Excel's **Edit ▾ Links** on page 286 for more information. The only option that is different in PowerPoint is the addition of the **Break Link** button.)

Choose the **Break Link** button to break the link between the source document and your presentation, and change the object to an unlinked embedded object. Because the connection is no longer a link, when the source information changes, your presentation remains the same.

Edit ▾ Object

Edit, Object is available if you have an object selected. The menu name and additional choices change to reflect the type of object that is selected. These menu commands may relate to the **Edit, Paste Special** choices and the **Edit, Links** choices. (For more information see **Excel's Edit ▾ Paste Special...** section on page 274, and Excel's **Edit ▾ Links...** section on page 286.)

To use the shortcut menu to edit an object, right-click an object and select one of the following commands:

Edit commands on the shortcut menu

Command	Description
Add Text	Places the insertion point in the object so that you can type text.
Edit Text	Selects the added text for you to edit. **Add Text** and **Edit Text** replace each other on the shortcut menu.
Font	Opens the Font dialog box (see **Format ▾ Font...** on page 499).
Bullet	Opens the Bullet dialog box (see **Format ▾ Bullet...** on page 501).

Command	Description
Grouping	If you have more than one object selected, this gives you the grouping submenu options: **Group**, **Ungroup**, and **Regroup**.
Order	Displays the submenu options: **Bring to Front**, **Send to Back**, **Bring Forward**, and **Send Backward**.
Set AutoShape Defaults	Sets formatting for all the AutoShapes you insert to these settings (see **Format** ￫ **Object...** on page 505).
Custom Animation	Opens the Custom Animation dialog box (see **Slide Show** ￫ **Preset Animation**, page 527, and **Slide Show** ￫ **Custom Shows**, page 533).
Action Settings	Opens the Action Settings dialog box (see **Slide Show** ￫ **Action Settings...**, page 525).
Format AutoShape	Opens the Format AutoShape dialog box (see **Format** ￫ **Object...** on page 505).

For information on inserting objects, see Word's **Insert** ￫ **Picture** on page 149 and Word's **Insert** ￫ **Object...** on page 158.

View

The **View** menu changes the way your screen looks. You can change the view to see slides, the outline, notes, and preview the slide show. You can also see headers and footers, make the view larger or smaller, and turn on or off certain screen items such as toolbars, the ruler, guides, and comments.

View ￫ Slide

For most tasks in PowerPoint (especially typing, formatting and editing), you want to be in Slide view. Choose **View**, **Slide** or click the **Slide View** button 🔲 on the bottom left of the horizontal scrollbar to go to Slide view.

View ￫ Outline

Outline view in PowerPoint works similar to Outline view in Word (see Word's **View** ￫ **Outline**, page 63). Click the **Outline View** button 📇 on the bottom left of the screen or choose **View**, **Outline** to turn on Outline view. Type on a line, and it becomes the title of the slide. Press **Enter**, and PowerPoint is ready to type the next slide title. Press **Tab**, and the line becomes the first bullet on the slide. Type the text, press **Enter**, and you're ready to type the next bullet. Press **Tab** again, and you can type subbullets. Double-click the slide icon to go to Slide view. You can also use the following toolbar buttons:

Outlining toolbar buttons

Button	Name	How to Use
	Promote	Click to move the heading to one level higher (subbullet[1] becomes a bullet or first-level bullet becomes slide title). You can also press **Shift+Tab, Alt+Shift+Left Arrow** or drag the bullet to the left.
	Demote	Click to move heading to one level lower. You can also press **Tab, Alt+Shift+Right Arrow** or drag the bullet or slide the icon to the right.
	Move Up	Click to move the current line up one row. You can also use the four-headed mouse pointer to drag a slide title (and all its bullets) or drag one bullet up a row. Alternatively, press **Alt+Shift+Up Arrow.**
	Move Down	Click to move the current line down a row. You can also use the four-headed mouse pointer to drag a slide title (and all its bullets) or drag one bullet down a row. Alternatively, press **Alt+Shift+Down Arrow.**
	Collapse	Click to hide all bullets on a selected slide or press **Alt+Shift+Minus**. Hidden text is represented by a gray line.
	Expand	Click to show all bullets on a selected slide or press **Alt+Shift+Plus**.
	Collapse All	Click to show only slide titles.
	Expand All	Click to show all slide titles and bullets. You can also press **Alt+Shift+A** (available only in Outline view).
	Summary Slide	This creates a summary slide with the bullets being the titles of the selected slides. Click the first slide for the summary, hold down **Shift**, and click the last slide. Then click this button. Edit the title of the new summary slide (available only in Outline view).
	Show Formatting	Click to show or hide formatting such as bold, italic, and underline. You can also press / (slash) on the numeric keypad (available only in Outline view).

[1] *In the table above, the bullet rows do not have to display the bullets. In the table, we're using "bullets" also to mean subordinate items. You can click the Bullets button on the Formatting toolbar to turn the display of bullets on or off.*

View - Slide Sorter

Slide Sorter displays miniatures of your slides and enables you to move the slides around. You can also create transitions, animation effects, and set slide timings. Click the **Slide Sorter View** button 88 on the bottom-left of the screen or choose **View**, **Slide Sorter**.

To move one or more slides in Slide Sorter view, follow these steps:

1. To select slides you want to move, do one of the following:

   - Click the slide you want to move.
   - Press the arrow keys to go to the slide you want to move.
   - Click the first slide, hold down **Shift**, and click additional slides.
   - Move the mouse pointer in an area not occupied by a slide and draw a rectangle choosing the slides you want (you don't have to completely enclose the slides, just touch part of a slide).

2. The selected slides have a darker outline than the other slides. Drag in the middle of the selection to the area before a slide. The mouse pointer changes to an arrow with a box, and a vertical line appears where the slides will go. Release the mouse pointer. If you hold down **Ctrl** when you drag the mouse, you copy the slides.

You can also use Cut (see **Edit - Cut**, page 470) and Paste (see **Edit - Paste**, page 471) to move your slides.

Double-click a slide to return to Slide view for that slide. The following toolbar appears in Slide Sorter view.

Slide Sorter toolbar buttons

Button	Name	How to Use
🔲	**Slide Transition**	Click this button to open the Slide Transition dialog box. Choose the transition **Effect** and click **Apply** for this slide or **Apply to All** for all slides (see **Slide Show - Slide Transition...**, page 529).
Blinds Horizontal ▾	**Slide Transition Effects**	Instead of using the Slide Transition dialog box, click the drop-down arrow and choose transition effect for all the selected slides.
Appear ▾	**Text Preset Animation**	Click the drop-down arrow and choose an effect for the bullets on the slide (see **Slide Show - Preset Animation**, page 527).
🔲	**Hide Slide**	Click to hide or display the selected slides (see **Slide Show - Hide Slide**, page 533).
☝	**Rehearse Timings**	Click this button to display Slide Show view with the Rehearsal dialog box with a timer. Click the arrow when you think there has been enough time to show

continues

Continued		
Button	**Name**	**How to Use**
		the slide to your potential audience (see **Slide Show - Rehearse Timings**, page 520). Finish the slide show or press **Esc**. Choose **Yes** to record your timings. The time for each slide appears below the slide in Slide Sorter view.
	Summary Slide	This creates a summary slide with the bullets being the titles of the selected slides. Click the first slide for the summary, hold down **Shift**, and click any slides you want. Then click this button. Double-click the summary slide and edit the title.
	Show Formatting	Click this button to show only unformatted slide titles and no text, especially if it takes a long time to redraw your screen. Click the button again to show the slide miniatures with text and graphics.

View – Notes Page

To add notes that don't show during the presentation, click the **Notes Page View** button on the bottom left of the screen or choose **View**, **Notes Page**. The screen shows the slide on the top half of the screen and an area to write notes on the bottom half. You may need to change your **Zoom percent** `100%` to see your typing as you add notes. Instead of using this view, you can choose **View**, **Speaker Notes** to add notes in Slide view. To print your slides with speaker notes, choose **File**, **Print** and choose Notes Pages in the **Print what** drop-down box.

View – Slide Show

To see how your slide show will look when it is presented, do one of the following:

- Click the **Slide Show** button on the bottom-left of the screen.
- Choose **View**, **Slide Show**.
- Choose **Slide Show**, **View Show**.

If you have any automatic timings (see **Slide Show - Slide Transition...**, page 529), the slides advance. If there are no timings, click the screen to go to the next slide or next animation
effect.

While the slide show is on the screen, you can use any of the following to displays slides or create special effects.

Keyboard and mouse options during a slide show

Keyboard or Mouse	Effect
Number, Enter	Go to the slide.
Hold down both left and right mouse buttons for 2 sec.	Return to first slide.
Left-click, Spacebar, N, Right arrow, Down arrow, Enter, or Page Down	Advance to next slide.
Backspace, P, Left arrow, Up arrow, Page Up	Go to previous slide.
Esc, Ctrl+Break, – (minus)	Stop the slide show.
B or . (period)	Black or unblack the screen.
W or , (comma)	White or unwhite the screen
A or = (equals)	Show or hide white arrow mouse pointer.
S or + (plus)	If automatic timing is set, stop or restart the slide show.
E	Erase screen drawing.
H	Go to hidden slide (see **Slide Show – Hide Slide**, page 533).
Ctrl+P	Show pen for mouse pointer to enable presenter to drag on the screen to draw.
Ctrl+A	Return to arrow mouse pointer to advance to next screen and display button.
Ctrl+H	Hide both arrow and pop-up menu button on bottom-left of screen.
Ctrl+L	Turn off arrow and button permanently for this viewing of the presentation (press **Ctrl+A** to turn it back on).

Right-mouse click or pop-up menu button items

Menu Item	Effect
Next	Go to the next slide.
Previous	Go to the previous slide.
Go	Display a submenu with the following items.

continues

Continued

Menu Item	Effect
Go, **H**idden **Slide**	If the next slide is a hidden slide, go to that slide; otherwise, this item is dimmed.
Go, **Slide** **N**avigator	Slide Navigator opens a dialog box with a list of all slides (hidden slides are in parentheses). Double-click any slide to go to the slide. If custom shows available, they are listed in the **Sh**ow drop-down box.
Go, **By** **T**itle	Displays titles of all the slides in the presentation. Click a slide to go to.
Go, **C**ustom **Show**	Displays a list of all custom shows. Go to the slides in that show (see **Slide Show - Custom Shows...**, page 533).
Go, **P**reviously **Viewed**	When you jump to another part of the presentation because of the action settings (see **Slide Show - Action Settings...**, page 525) on an action button or graphic, choose this to go back to the slide from which you jumped.
Meeting Minder	Opens the Meeting Minder dialog box that enables you to take notes during a presentation (see **Tools - Meeting Minder...**, page 512).
Speaker Notes	Opens Speaker Notes dialog box so that you and everyone else viewing the presentation can see your notes (see **View - Speaker Notes...**, page 484).
Slide Meter	Compare the actual speed of your presentation with the rehearsed timings (to not use timings, **Slide Show**, **Set Up Show**, **Manually**). See Figure 4.11 for a description of the meter.
Arrow	Turn arrow mouse pointer on (turns pen off).
Pen	Turn pen on (turns arrow off). When on, drag mouse pointer to draw on a slide (the drawing does not show next time slide appears).
Pointer Options	Opens a submenu with which to hide the mouse pointer; choose **Hide Now** (move mouse to unhide). To hide the mouse pointer even when the mouse is moving, choose **Hide Always**. You can also change the **Pen Color** to one of the colors on the submenu or **Reset** to the original color.
Screen	Opens a submenu to **Pause** a presentation with automatic timings (choose **Screen**, **Resume** to start the presentation again). Choose **Screen**, **Erase Pen** to remove all pen marks on the current slide.
End Show	Return to editing the show or location that opened the slide show.

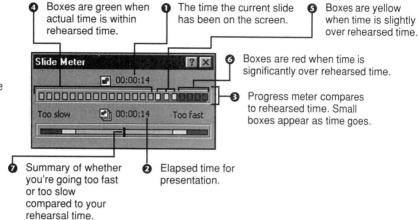

Figure 4.11

Right-click during a slide show and choose Slide Meter to display the Slide Meter.

❹ Boxes are green when actual time is within rehearsed time.

❶ The time the current slide has been on the screen.

❺ Boxes are yellow when time is slightly over rehearsed time.

❻ Boxes are red when time is significantly over rehearsed time.

❸ Progress meter compares to rehearsed time. Small boxes appear as time goes.

❼ Summary of whether you're going too fast or too slow compared to your rehearsal time.

❷ Elapsed time for presentation.

Note: You can have the right-click menu or the pop-up menu turned off (see **Tools - Options... View Tab**, page 515).

View - Master

Masters enable you to change all pages of one type of view at once (slides, handouts, or notes). You add text or a graphic so that it prints on every page. While you are in a master view, you can do the following:

- Select the text indicating the style area and format the font (see **Format - Font...**, page 499).

- Type text in an area on the slide or insert a text box (see **Insert - Text Box**, page 496).

- Insert a picture or other graphic (see **Insert - Picture**, page 496 and **Insert - Object...**, page 498).

- With the four-headed arrow mouse pointer, drag the Header, Date, Footer, or Number area to change the position.

When you display all four masters, the following toolbar displays.

Master toolbar buttons

Button	Name	How to Use
⊞	**Slide Miniature**	Show a small window showing the current slide (see **View - Slide Miniature**, page 483).
Close	**Close**	Click this button to get out of the master view and back where you were when you got in.

View ▸ Master ▸ Slide Master

The Slide Master enables you to edit the default layout and formatting for all slides except title slides (see **View ▸ Master ▸ Title Master**, page 482). Hold down **Shift** and click the **View Slide Master** button 🔲 on the bottom left of the screen or choose **View, Master, Slide Master** to get to this view.

In addition to the procedures you can do (mentioned in **View ▸ Master** above), you can change the format of a bullet (see **Format ▸ Bullet...**, page 501). To add headers and footers to the slides, see **View ▸ Header and Footer...**, page 491.

Any slides that you already changed do not change to the new master format. If, however, you want to apply the slide master format to a slide with a different format, click the **Slide Layout** button 🔳 on the Standard toolbar and choose the same slide type as the current slide (see **Format ▸ Slide Layout...**, page 503).

View ▸ Master ▸ Title Master

The Title Master sets the default layout and formatting for title slides only. Choose the procedures mentioned in **View ▸ Master** above. To add a new title slide, see **Insert ▸ New Slide...**, page 493, and double-click the first slide in the New Slide dialog box.

View ▸ Master ▸ Handout Master

The Handout Master enables you to see what the position of the slides will be on handouts (see the toolbar buttons below). For handouts and the outline, you can also change the formatting and location of items as mentioned in **View ▸ Master** above. Hold down **Shift** and click the **View Handout Master** button 🔳 on the bottom left of the screen, or choose **View, Master, Notes Master** to get to this view.

Handout Master toolbar buttons	
Button	**Purpose**
🔲	Show positioning of 2-per-page handouts
🔳	Show positioning of 3-per-page handouts
🔳	Show positioning of 6-per-page handouts
🔳	Show positioning of outline

View ▸ Master ▸ Notes Master

The Notes Master enables you to see the layout and formatting of speaker notes pages (see **View ▸ Master**, page 481). Hold down **Shift** and click the **View Notes Master** button 🔳 on the bottom left of the screen or choose **View, Master, Notes Master** to get to this view.

View – Black and White

Instead of showing the presentation in color, click the **Black and White** button ![icon] on the Standard toolbar or choose **View, Black and White** to see and print the presentation in black, white, and shades of gray. The changes you make while working in this view do not affect colors in your presentation. Change the settings for black and white while in this view by right-clicking an object on the slide and choosing **Black and White** and one of the following options. (To change Slide Master to change all slides at once, see **View – Master**, page 481.)

Black and White settings

Menu Item	Description
Automatic	Show only text and graphics and hide textured or shaded background.
Grayscale	Print and display the selected object in shades of gray.
Light Grayscale	Print and display the selected object in lighter shades of gray than **Grayscale**.
Inverse Grayscale	Print and display the selected object in reverse shades of gray—lighter shades appear darker.
Gray with White Fill	Print and display text, lines, and shape outlines in gray and everything else in white.
Black with Grayscale Fill	Print and display text, lines, and shape outlines in black and everything else in shades of gray.
Black with White Fill	Print and display text, lines, and shape outlines in black and everything else in white.
Black	Print and display selected object in black.
White	Print and display selected object in white (doesn't show on a white background).
Don't Show	Do not print or display the selected object.

View – Slide Miniature

When you're done setting the Black and White settings, you can use the Slide Miniature to see what your presentation will look like when you print it on a non-color printer. Choose **View, Slide Miniature** to display a small window with your slide.

By default, the miniature is in opposite mode to the slide. If the slide is in color, the miniature is in black and white and shows what the image will look like when printed. When you click the **Black and White** button ![icon], the slide toggles to black and white while the miniature goes to color. You can right-click the miniature and override this by choosing either **Black and White View** or **Color View**.

Click the slide or right-click and choose Animation Preview to see any animation settings and transitions you have for the slide or text (see **Sli̲de Show ▪ Preset Animation...**, page 527, and **Sli̲de Show ▪ Slide T̲ransition...**, page 527).

V̲iew ▪ Spea̲ker Notes...

Instead of using notes pages (see **V̲iew ▪ Notes Page**, page 478), open a dialog box for notes by choosing **V̲iew, Spea̲ker Notes**. Type your notes in the **Sl̲ide** text box. Although they are unformatted, they are easier to read than they are on notes pages. Navigate to each slide and add notes as you want. Click **C̲lose** to remove the dialog box from the screen.

V̲iew ▪ T̲oolbars

To get many of your tasks done quickly, use a toolbar button rather than a menu item. The toolbar button (or a keyboard shortcut) usually is the quickest way to accomplish a task, while the corresponding menu item gives you more details. Many of the toolbars and the procedures for using them are the same or similar in Word and PowerPoint (see Word's **V̲iew ▪ T̲oolbars**, page 66).

The following toolbars are the same in both Word and PowerPoint (see the description in Word for a list of the buttons):

- ■ Control (Word has two extra buttons: Design Mode and Image)
- ■ Picture
- ■ Visual Basic (except that Word has an extra button for Design Mode)
- ■ Web
- ■ WordArt

The Drawing toolbar for Excel matches PowerPoint's Drawing toolbar more closely than Word's does (see both Excel's and Word's **V̲iew ▪ T̲oolbars ▪ Drawing**, page 293 and page 73).

V̲iew ▪ T̲oolbars ▪ Standard

The Standard toolbar is one of the two default toolbars that appear on your screen unless you turn them off. Some of the features you use most, such as opening a file, saving, and printing, are on this toolbar.

Standard toolbar buttons

Button	Name	How to Use
	New	Click to create a new blank presentation.
	Open	Click to display the Open dialog box. Double-click the file you want to open (see Word's **File ▪ O̲pen...**, page 21).
	Save	Click to save presentation with existing name or

Button	Name	How to Use
		display Save As dialog box if no name yet given. Type name in File n̲ame text box (see Word's **Fi̱le – Save A̲s...**, page 29).
	Print	Click to print the slide. For additional options, see **Fi̱le – P̲rint...**, page 464.
	Spelling	Click to open the Spelling dialog box. Click the **C̲hange** button to make the suggested change or **I̲gnore** to skip the word or phrase (see **T̲ools – S̲pelling...**, page 507).
	Cut	Click to place a copy of the selection into the Clipboard (see **Edi̱t – Cu̱t**, page 470) and remove the selection after you paste.
	Copy	Click to place a copy of the selection into the Clipboard (see **Edi̱t – C̲opy**, page 470).
	Paste	Click to paste what you cut or copied into the slide (see **Edi̱t – P̲aste**, page 471).
	Format Painter	Click the text or object whose format you want to pick up. Then click the button and click some text or an object to format. If you want to format multiple sections, double-click the button, then paint the sections you want to format. Click the **Format Painter** button again to turn it off.
	Undo	Click to cancel the last thing you did. You can cancel the last series of items you did by choosing them from the drop-down arrow (see **Edi̱t – U̲ndo**, page 469).
	Redo	Click to cancel the Undo for the last item. Alternatively, click the drop-down arrow for the last series of items.
	Insert Hyperlink	Click to open the Insert Hyperlink dialog box. Type the hyperlink in the L̲ink to File or URL text box (see Word's **Insert – Hyperli̱nk...**, page 159).
	Web Toolbar	Click to show or hide the Web toolbar (see Word's **Vi̱ew – T̲oolbars – Web**, page 85).
	Insert Microsoft Word Table	Click the button and drag to determine the number of rows and columns. Microsoft Word opens with a new table. Type and format the table as desired (see Word's **T̲able**, page 230, and **Vi̱ew – T̲oolbars – Tables** and **Borders**, page 82). When finished with the table, choose Word's **Fi̱le** menu and click **C̲lose & Return** to your presentation.

continues

Continued

Button	Name	How to Use
	Insert Microsoft Excel Worksheet	Click the button and drag to determine the number of rows and columns. Microsoft Excel opens with a new worksheet. Type within the worksheet and add any other worksheet features (see Excel's Typing in an Excel Worksheet, page 255).When finished, choose Excel's File menu and click Close & Return to your presentation.
	Insert Chart	If you have Microsoft Graph installed, choose this button to create a graph (see **Insert - Chart...**, page 498).
	Insert Clip Art	Click to open the Clip Art Gallery and double-click the graphic, sound, or motion picture you want (see **Insert - Picture - Clip Art...**, page 496).
	New Slide	Click this button and double-click the layout you want for a new slide (see **Insert - New Slide...**, page 493).
	Slide Layout	To reapply the master style to the current slide or change the layout of the slide, click this button and choose a type of slide (see **Format - Slide Layout...**, page 503).
	Apply Design	To choose a layout from another template, click this button and double-click a presentation template file (see **Format - Apply Design...**, page 505).
	Black and White view	Click this button to toggle between color and black and white for the slide. The Black and White view shows what the slides will look like when printed on a non-color printer (see **View - Black and White**, page 483).
100% ▼	**Zoom**	Click the drop-down arrow or type in the box to change the magnification of what you see on the screen (does not affect printing). For more details, see **View - Zoom...**, page 492.
	Office Assistant	Click and type a question for help. If you are in the middle of trying to do a task, choose from one of the bullet items (see **Help**, page 535).

View – Toolbars – Formatting

Like the Standard toolbar, the Formatting toolbar also appears by default unless you've turned it off. Most items are also on the Format menu.

Formatting toolbar buttons

Button	Name	How to Use
Times New Roman	**Font**	Select cells and click the drop-down arrow to change the font. For this button, the next buttons (through Shadow), and the font size buttons below, see more details at **Format – Font…**, page 499.
44	**Font Size**	Select cells and click the drop-down arrow to change size of the text.
B	**Bold**	Click to make selected characters bold.
I	**Italic**	Click to make selected characters italic.
U	**Underline**	Click to make selected characters underlined.
S	**Shadow**	Click to give selected characters a shadow format.
▤	**Left Alignment**	Click to make selected text line up on the left.
▤	**Center Alignment**	Click to make text in selected cells centered between the edges of the text frame.
▤	**Right Alignment**	Click to make text in selected cells line up on the right.
▤	**Bullets**	Select bulleted or unbulleted text on a slide or slide master (see **View – Master – Slide Master**, page 482), and click this button to turn bullets on or off.
▤	**Increase Paragraph Spacing**	Select multiple lines of text on a slide or on the notes page. Click this button to increase the space between the lines (see **Format – Line Spacing…**, page 502).
▤	**Decrease Paragraph Spacing**	Select multiple lines of text on a slide or on the notes page. Click this button to decrease the space between the lines.
A	**Increase Font Size**	Click to increase the size of selected characters.
A	**Decrease Font Size**	Click to decrease the size of selected characters.
←	**Promote**	Click a line in the text part of a slide or outline to give the text less indent and give a higher level bullet (if bullets are turned on).

continues

Continued

Button	Name	How to Use
	Demote	Click a line in the text part of a slide or outline to give the text more indent and give a lower level bullet (if bullets are turned on).
	Animation Effects	Turns the Animation Effects toolbar on and off (see **View** - **Toolbars** - **Animation Effects**, page 488).

View - Toolbars - Animation Effects

Animation effects move text or objects in Slide Show view. You can turn this toolbar on or off with the **Animation Effects** button on the Formatting toolbar or through **View**, **Toolbars**, **Animation Effects**. Most of these items are also on the **Slide Show**, **Present Animation** submenu.

Animation Effects toolbar buttons

Button	Name	Description (and Sound if Sound Board Installed)	Works with Graphic Objects*
	Animate Title	Title of slide flies from top (turn on or off).	
	Build Slide Text	Each click of the mouse displays a new bullet item.	
	Drive-in Effect	Object flies from right with a car sound.	Yes
	Flying Effect	Object flies from left with a whoosh sound.	Yes
	Camera Effect	Object starts from center outward with a camera sound.	Yes
	Flash Once	Flashes the object on and then off.	Yes
	Laser Text Effect	Drops one letter at a time from top right with a laser sound.	
	Typewriter Effect	Adds one letter at a time with a typewriter sound.	
	Reverse Order	Quickly builds text from left to right. If bullets are selected, reverses order of bullets (builds from bottom to top).	
	Drop-in	Drops down one word at a time.	
1	Animation Order	If multiple objects are on a slide, chooses order for each animation effect.	Yes

Button	Name	Description (and Sound if Sound Board Installed)	Works with Graphic Objects*
	Animation Settings	Opens Animation Settings dialog box, which shows existing settings and gives more options than other buttons on Animation Effects dialog box alone (see **Slide Show – Action Buttons**, page 524).	Yes

* All items in above table work with text. Those indicated with Yes in fourth column work with pictures, clip art, and drawn objects.

View – Toolbars – Common Tasks

The Common Tasks toolbar is a small toolbar with three of the most common procedures.

Common Tasks toolbar buttons

Name	Alternative
New Slide	Click this button and double-click the layout you want for a new slide (see **Insert – New Slide...**, page 493). Also press **Ctrl+M** or click .
Slide Layout	To reapply the master style to the current slide or change the layout of the slide, click this button an choose a type of slide (see **Format – Slide Layout...**, page 503). Also click .
Apply Design	To choose a layout from another template, click this button and double-click a presentation template file (see **Format – Apply Design...**, page 505). Also click .

View – Toolbars – Reviewing

You can use the Reviewing toolbar to add or edit comments (see **Insert – Comment**, page 494).

Reviewing toolbar buttons

Button	Name	How to Use
	Insert Comment	Click to add a comment. A yellow box opens with your name. Type the comment.
	Show/Hide Comments	Toggle back and forth between displaying and hiding all comments.
	Create Microsoft Outlook Task	Click to open Microsoft Outlook and create a task. The task area shows a shortcut to the presentation and enters the text of the comment.
	Mail Recipient	Click to open your email program with the current presentation as an attachment. The Subject becomes the name of the file.

View ▸ Toolbars ▸ Customize...

When you choose **View ▸ Toolbars ▸ Customize**, the Customize dialog box opens, enabling you to edit or create toolbars and menus. This is the same dialog box shown in Word's **View ▸ Toolbars ▸ Customize...** section (see page 87). The only difference in PowerPoint is that you do not have the **Keyboard** option button.

View ▸ Ruler

The ruler in PowerPoint in similar to the ruler in Word. You can see where you are on the document from the side and top in inches. You can also use the horizontal ruler to set indents and tabs (see Figure 4.12). In PowerPoint, **Tab** demotes text to the next level in PowerPoint (or creates a new level with additional indents). Use **Shift+Tab** to move to the tab stop. Another difference between PowerPoint and Word is that tabs and indents are set for the entire text section (in the hatched box) rather than just the selected rows.

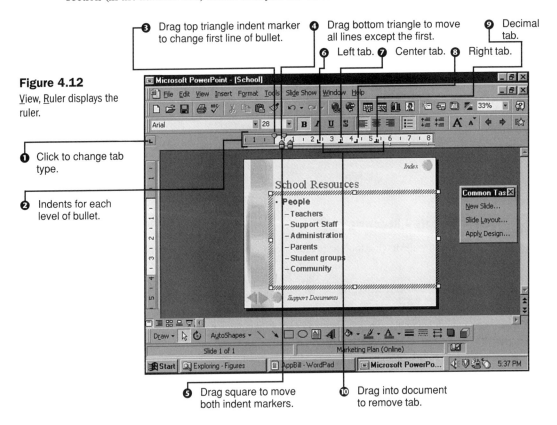

Figure 4.12
View, Ruler displays the ruler.

❸ Drag top triangle indent marker to change first line of bullet.
❹ Drag bottom triangle to move all lines except the first.
❾ Decimal tab.
❻ Left tab. ❼ Center tab. ❽ Right tab.

❶ Click to change tab type.

❷ Indents for each level of bullet.

❺ Drag square to move both indent markers.

❿ Drag into document to remove tab.

View ▸ Guides

Guides are dotted lines across or up and down the slide that help you line up text or objects. To turn the guides on or off, choose **View, Guides**. You can do the following procedures with the guides.

CREATE, DELETE, AND USE GUIDELINES

■ You can drag a guide by moving the tip of the white arrow mouse pointer onto the dotted line and dragging. As you drag, a number shows how far you are from the center line.

■ To create another guideline, hold down **Ctrl** as you drag a line.

■ To delete a guideline, drag it off the slide.

■ To line up objects, drag the object until its edge or center is near the guideline. When you release, the object automatically aligns with the guideline.

■ If you want to override aligning with the guideline, hold down **Alt** as you drag the object.

View – Header and Footer...

Headers and footers print at the top and bottom of your documents. You can have headers and footers on slides, handouts, note pages, and outlines. Choose **View**, **Header and Footer**. The Header and Footer dialog box opens (see Figure 4.13).

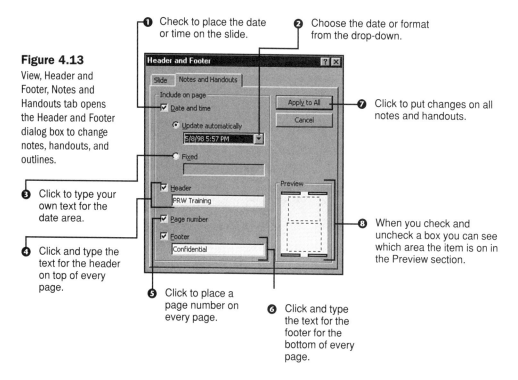

Figure 4.13
View, Header and Footer, Notes and Handouts tab opens the Header and Footer dialog box to change notes, handouts, and outlines.

❶ Check to place the date or time on the slide.

❷ Choose the date or format from the drop-down.

❼ Click to put changes on all notes and handouts.

❸ Click to type your own text for the date area.

❹ Click and type the text for the header on top of every page.

❺ Click to place a page number on every page.

❻ Click and type the text for the footer for the bottom of every page.

❽ When you check and uncheck a box you can see which area the item is on in the Preview section.

The Slide tab is essentially the same as the Notes and Handouts tab shown in Figure 4.13 except that you cannot place a header on the slide. This tab also has a check box for **Slide number** instead of **Page number**. The slide tab also gives you the option **Don't show on title slide** so that there is no footer or other items on the first slide.

To change the location of the footer, header, page number, or date box or to add additional text or graphics on every slide or page, use the master (see **View - Master**, page 481).

View ⇀ Comments

Comments enable you to add a note directly to a slide. A comment is a small yellow box that puts your name (set through **Tools**, **Options**, **General Tab**, **Name** text box) and any text about a slide that you want to add to it. Comments print when you print the slide. Use the Reviewing toolbar to work with comments (see **View - Toolbars - Reviewing**, page 489).

Quick Choices   ADD AND DISPLAY OR HIDE COMMENTS

- To turn comments on or off, choose **View**, **Comments** or click the **Show/Hide Comments** button ▨ on the Reviewing toolbar.

- To add a comment, choose **Insert**, **Comment** or click the **Insert Comment** button ▨ on the Reviewing toolbar.

- To move a comment, drag it with the four-arrow mouse pointer.

- To change the fill color for a comment, double-click the comment, click the Colors and Lines tab of the Format Comment dialog box and choose a **Color** from the drop-down box.

View ⇀ Zoom...

Zoom enables you to see more or less of your slide, notes, handout, or outline at one time. The magnification changes on the screen but does not affect printing.

Click the **Zoom** button 100% ▾ on the Standard toolbar and choose a magnification from the drop-down list or type a value in the box. In Slide view, choose fit to see the whole slide on the screen. Alternatively, you can choose **View**, **Zoom** to make changes on the Zoom dialog box (see Figure 4.14).

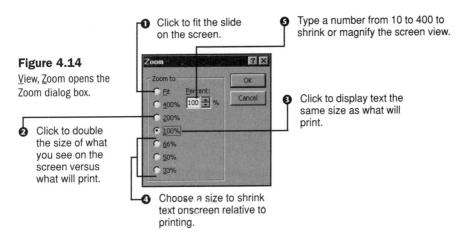

Figure 4.14
View, Zoom opens the Zoom dialog box.

❶ Click to fit the slide on the screen.

❺ Type a number from 10 to 400 to shrink or magnify the screen view.

❸ Click to display text the same size as what will print.

❷ Click to double the size of what you see on the screen versus what will print.

❹ Choose a size to shrink text onscreen relative to printing.

Insert

The **Insert** menu gives you options for inserting slides, the date and time, tabs, symbols, comments, slides from other files, slides from a Word outline, objects from other programs such as clip art pictures, Excel spreadsheets or charts, Word tables, organization charts, and many others depending on what you have installed on your computer.

Insert ➥ New Slide...

The **Insert**, **New Slide** command opens the New Slide dialog box so that you can select a slide layout for the new slide that is inserted after the active slide. You can also press **Ctrl+M** instead of using the menu commands.

Insert ➥ Duplicate Slide

The **Insert**, **Duplicate Slide** command inserts a copy of the slide you are on after the current slide. You can also press **Ctrl+Shift+D**.

Insert ➥ Slide Number

The **Insert**, **Slide Number** command adds the slide number to an individual slide at the location of the insertion point. If you want to add the slide number to every slide, use the Header and Footer command (see **View** – **Header and Footer...** on page 491).

Insert ➥ Date and Time...

The **Insert**, **Date and Time** command adds the current date and time to an individual slide at the location of the insertion point using the format you choose. If you want to add the date and time to every slide, use the Header and Footer command (see **View** – **Header and Footer...** on page 491).

Insert ➥ Tab

The **Insert**, **Tab** command enables you to insert a tab at the location of the insertion point. When you press the Tab key, you change the outline level of the line you are on. Therefore, this enables you to insert a tab to move text over on the line.

Insert ➥ Symbol...

The **Insert**, **Symbol** command enables you to insert symbols and special characters in your text based on the fonts you have installed on your computer. You can insert foreign language characters, decorative characters, scientific characters, or even special characters for sports, transportation, holidays, and many more. When you insert a symbol, it is inserted into a text box; therefore, when you paste the symbol, it is pasted into its own text box.

To insert symbols, take these steps:

1. Move the insertion point to wherever you'd like to place the symbol you need.

2. Choose **Insert**, **Symbol** to display the Symbol dialog box (see Figure 4.15).

❶ Click a font to display its
symbol set in this grid.

❷ Select a symbol to insert.

Figure 4.15

Choose Insert, Symbol
to display the Symbol
dialog box.

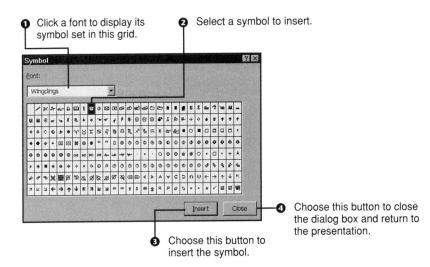

❹ Choose this button to close
the dialog box and return to
the presentation.

❸ Choose this button to
insert the symbol.

- Double-clicking a symbol is the same as selecting the symbol and choosing the **Insert** button.

- Click and drag the Title bar to move the Symbol dialog box out of your way.

- You can also use the Character Map application that comes with Windows to see the codes for characters. Choose the Windows **Start** button and **Run**. Type CHARMAP and press **Enter**. The Character map dialog box is displayed with the ANSI code for a selected symbol in the lower right corner.

Insert ➥ Comment

The **Insert**, **Comment** command gives you the capability to write comments to yourself or someone else.

Quick Choices **TO INSERT A COMMENT:**

1. Switch to Slide view and position the insertion point where you want the comment.

2. Choose **Insert**, **Comment** to open the comment box.

3. Type your comment in the box that displays.

4. Click outside the comment box to go back to the presentation. The comment box stays open and the Reviewing toolbar is displayed.

To Edit Comments

1. Turn on the Reviewing toolbar if it is not visible. Right-click any visible toolbar and select Reviewing.
2. Click ▣ to turn the comments on.
3. Click inside the comment box and make changes to the comment.

To Delete Comments

1. Turn on the Reviewing toolbar if it is not visible. Right-click any visible toolbar and select Reviewing.
2. Click ▣ to turn the comments on.
3. Click the comment you want to delete, click the hashed outline around the comment box, and press **Delete**.

Insert ⟶ Slides from Files...

The **Insert**, **Slides from Files** command enables you to select slides from other presentations to insert into the current presentation.

1. Move the insertion point where you want the inserted slide(s) to appear.
2. Choose **Insert**, **Slides from Files** to display the Slide finder dialog box (see Figure 4.16).

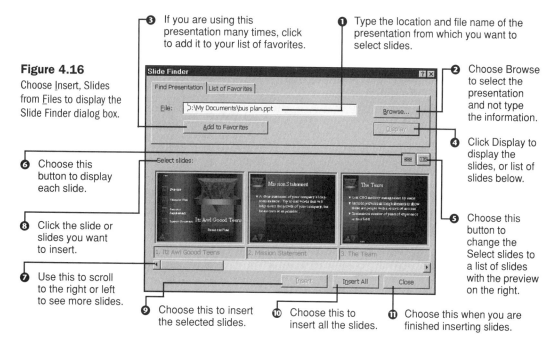

❸ If you are using this presentation many times, click to add it to your list of favorites.

❶ Type the location and file name of the presentation from which you want to select slides.

Figure 4.16
Choose Insert, Slides from Files to display the Slide Finder dialog box.

❷ Choose Browse to select the presentation and not type the information.

❹ Click Display to display the slides, or list of slides below.

❻ Choose this button to display each slide.

❺ Choose this button to change the Select slides to a list of slides with the preview on the right.

❽ Click the slide or slides you want to insert.

❼ Use this to scroll to the right or left to see more slides.

❾ Choose this to insert the selected slides.

❿ Choose this to insert all the slides.

⓫ Choose this when you are finished inserting slides.

When you use the **Browse** button, the Insert Slides from Files dialog box opens. Navigate to the folder and file you want to use. For more information on navigating in the dialog box, see Word's **File ▸ Open...** on page 21. The slides are inserted after the active slide.

Insert ▸ Slides from Outline...

The **Insert**, **Slides from Outline** command enables you to insert slides from outlines created in other programs into the current presentation.

1. Move the insertion point where you want the inserted slide(s) to appear.

2. Choose **Insert**, **Slides from Outline** to display the Insert Outline dialog box (see Figure 4.17).

Insert ▸ Picture

Figure 4.17
Choose Insert, Slides from Outline to display the Insert Outline dialog box.

❶ Navigate to the folder where the outline is saved.

❷ Select the outline you want to insert.

❸ Choose this button to insert the outline slides after the current slide.

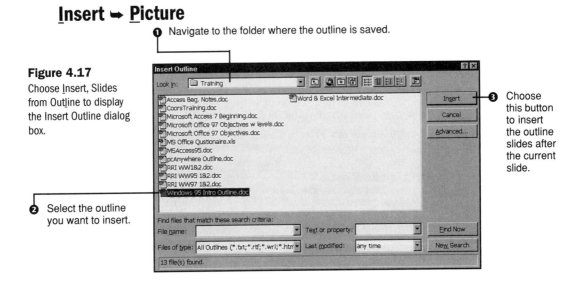

The **Insert**, **Picture** command enables you to insert pictures from many outside sources, such as drawing programs, scanners, and clip art collections. You can also insert pictures using PowerPoint's built-in tools: AutoShapes, WordArt, Organization Chart, Microsoft Word Table, and the drawing toolbar. (For detailed information, see Word's **Insert ▸ Picture** on page 149.)

Insert ▸ Text Box

The **Insert**, **Text Box** command enables you to insert a text box object. (For more information, see Word's **View ▸ Toolbars ▸ Drawing** Text Box on page 73.)

Insert ➡ Movies and Sounds

The **Insert, Movies and Sounds** command opens the Microsoft Clip Gallery 3.0 dialog box to enable you to insert videos, sounds, pictures, and clip art. (See Word's **Insert - Picture - Clip Art...** on page 149.)

Insert ➡ Movies and Sounds ➡ Movie from Gallery...

See Word's **Insert - Picture - Clip Art...** on page 149.

Insert ➡ Movies and Sounds ➡ Movie from File...

See Word's **Insert - Picture - From File...** on page 152.

Insert ➡ Movies and Sounds ➡ Sound from Gallery...

See Word's **Insert - Picture - Clip Art...** on page 149.

Insert ➡ Movies and Sounds ➡ Sound from File...

See Word's **Insert - Picture - From File...** on page 152.

Insert ➡ Movies and Sounds ➡ Play CD Audio Track...

The **Insert, Movies and Sounds, Play CD Audio Track** inserts an audio track from a CD in the slide so that you can play it during a slide show.

1. Move the insertion point where you want the inserted audio to reside.

2. Choose **Insert, Movies and Sounds, Play CD Audio Track** to display the Play Options dialog box (see Figure 4.18).

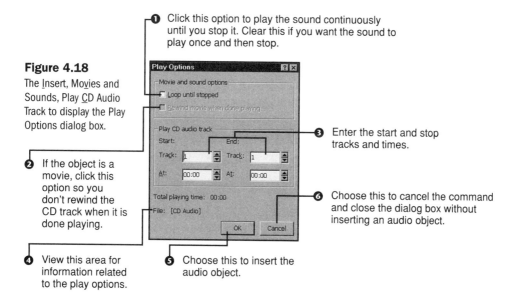

❶ Click this option to play the sound continuously until you stop it. Clear this if you want the sound to play once and then stop.

Figure 4.18
The Insert, Movies and Sounds, Play CD Audio Track to display the Play Options dialog box.

❸ Enter the start and stop tracks and times.

❷ If the object is a movie, click this option so you don't rewind the CD track when it is done playing.

❻ Choose this to cancel the command and close the dialog box without inserting an audio object.

❹ View this area for information related to the play options.

❺ Choose this to insert the audio object.

Insert ► Movies and Sounds ► Record Sound

The **Insert, Movies and Sounds, Record Sound** enables you to Record a sound or comment on the active slide. Choose **Insert, Movies and Sounds, Record Sound** to display the Record Sound dialog box (see Figure 4.19).

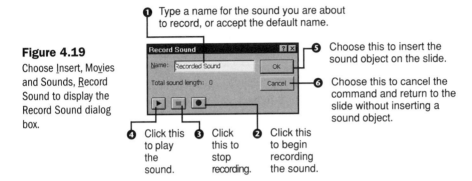

❶ Type a name for the sound you are about to record, or accept the default name.

Figure 4.19
Choose Insert, Movies and Sounds, Record Sound to display the Record Sound dialog box.

❺ Choose this to insert the sound object on the slide.

❻ Choose this to cancel the command and return to the slide without inserting a sound object.

❹ Click this to play the sound.

❸ Click this to stop recording.

❷ Click this to begin recording the sound.

After you have inserted the sound, double-click the sound icon to play it while you are on the slide.

By default, PowerPoint assigns the name *RecordingN*.**wav**, where *N* is a number. PowerPoint embeds this sound on the current slide and adds the name to the Sounds list in the Custom Animation and Slide Transition dialog boxes. (See **Slide Show ► Custom Shows...** on page 533, and **Slide Show ► Slide Transition...** on page 529 for more information.)

Insert ► Chart...

The **Insert, Chart** command opens the Microsoft Graph 97 Chart applet. This is a quick way to create a simple chart. (See Word's **Insert ► Picture ► Chart...** on page 156 for more information.)

> **N O T E**   If you don't have Microsoft Graph installed or, if you know Excel, create a chart in Excel and copy and paste it to your slide in PowerPoint. (See Excel's Chart menu on page 445) ■

Insert ► Object...

The **Insert, Object** command gives you a choice of inserting many types of objects in your document. The choices are related to the software you have installed on your computer. (For more information, see Word's **Insert ► Object...**, page 158.)

Insert ► Hyperlink...

The **Insert, Hyperlink** command enables you to create or edit a link to a document on your computer, network, or Internet (see Word's **Insert ► Hyperlink...**, page 159).

Format

Formatting enables you to change the text and how figures look on the page.

Format ➥ Font...

Font is the way characters are printed and viewed on the slide. Font includes the type style, size, and effects such as bold or underline. To change the font, first select the text you want to change and then do any of the following. If you want to change the font throughout your presentation, change the slide master or title master (see **View** ➤ **Master**, page 481).

Quick Choices   *CHANGE THE FORMAT OF SELECTED TEXT*

Do What	Button on Formatting Toolbar	Keyboard Shortcut
Bold	**B**	**Ctrl+B**
Italicize	*I*	**Ctrl+I**
Underline	U	**Ctrl+U**
Shadow	S	
Change font face	Times New Roman	**Ctrl+Shift+F then use Up or Down arrow**
Change font size	44	**Ctrl+Shift+P then use Up or Down arrow**
Increase font size	A	**Ctrl+Shift+>**
Decrease font size	A	**Ctrl+Shift+<**
Subscript		**Ctrl+=**
Superscript		**Ctrl+Shift+=**
Cycle through uppercase, title case, and lowercase		**Shift+F3**

To change multiple font characteristics at a time, first select the text that you want to change and then choose **Format, Font** or press **Ctrl+T**. The Font dialog box appears (see Figure 4.20).

The following table includes additional notes about the Font dialog box not shown in the next figure.

❶ Change the font, bold and italic style, and size.

Figure 4.20

Format, Font opens the Font dialog box.

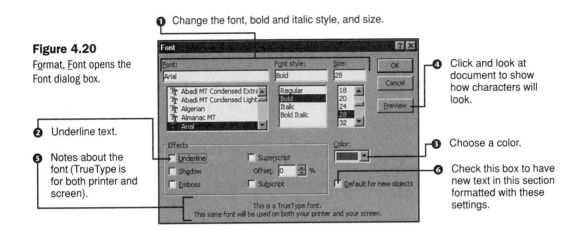

❹ Click and look at document to show how characters will look.

❷ Underline text.

❺ Notes about the font (TrueType is for both printer and screen).

❸ Choose a color.

❻ Check this box to have new text in this section formatted with these settings.

Dialog Box Item	What It Looks Like and Notes
Superscript	Like the 2 in $E=MC^2$
Subscript	Like the 2 in H_2O
Offset	Type a number or click the spinner arrows to tell how much text falls above or below the baseline. Positive numbers will be superscript. Negative numbers will be subscript.
Shadow	This effect makes text look like it is floating over the page.
Emboss	This effect makes text look like it has been "pushed up" on the page.

To work with fonts, you can also do the following:

- ■ To copy text formatting, select the text formatting you want to copy and do one of the following:
  - • Click the **Format painter** button 🖌 on the Standard toolbar. The mouse pointer changes to a paintbrush with an I-beam. Select the text you want to change.
  - • Double-click the Format painter button and continue selecting multiple areas for format. Click the Format painter button again to turn off the copy.
  - • Press **Ctrl+Shift+C** to copy the format. Select the text to accept the format and press **Ctrl+Shift+V**.
- ■ To remove manual formatting, press **Ctrl+Spacebar**.

Format → Bullet...

Bullets are special characters before a line of text that summarize key points. Usually each level of bullets has different shaped bullets. The most common bullets are filled circles and dashes, but you have a choice of many different shapes.

Quick Choices USE BULLETS

■ To turn bullets on or off for selected text, click the **Bullets** button ▤ on the Formatting toolbar.

To change bullet shapes, take these steps:

1. Do one of the following:

   ● Select the text on one slide.

   ● To change all bullets on all slides, hold down **Shift** and click the **Slide Master** button ▭ to the left of the horizontal scrollbar. Click one of the bullet lines.

2. Choose **Format, Bullet**. The Bullet dialog box opens (see Figure 4.21).

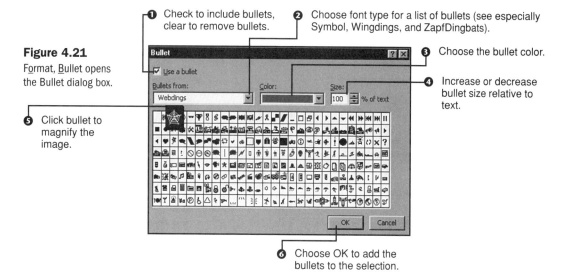

Figure 4.21
Format, Bullet opens the Bullet dialog box.

❶ Check to include bullets, clear to remove bullets.

❷ Choose font type for a list of bullets (see especially Symbol, Wingdings, and ZapfDingbats).

❸ Choose the bullet color.

❹ Increase or decrease bullet size relative to text.

❺ Click bullet to magnify the image.

❻ Choose OK to add the bullets to the selection.

Format → Alignment

Alignment places text in a horizontal position on the page. In some software programs, alignment is called justification.

Format → Alignment → Left

Select the text to align on the left margin of the page and click the **Left Alignment** button ▤ on the Formatting toolbar, press **Ctrl+L**, or choose **Format, Alignment, Left**.

Format ▸ Alignment ▸ Center

Select the text to center between the left and right margins and click the **Center Alignment** button ▤ on the Formatting toolbar, press **Ctrl+E**, or choose **Format**, **Alignment**, **Center**.

Format ▸ Alignment ▸ Right

Select the text to align on the right margin and click the **Right Alignment** button ▤ on the Formatting toolbar, press **Ctrl+R**, or choose **Format**, **Alignment**, **Right**.

Format ▸ Alignment ▸ Justify

Justify works for multiple lines of a paragraph or one bullet item. When you justify, both the left and the right edges of the line are lined up on the margin. The alternative is sometimes called ragged right or ragged left. Select the text to justify and choose **Format**, **Alignment**, **Justify**.

Format ▸ Line Spacing...

Line spacing is the distance between paragraphs of text. Normally each bullet is one line, but the text can wrap to the second or additional lines. You can format an individual slide or note area or change the formatting for all slides or notes (see **View ▸ Master**, page 481). Select multiple paragraphs of text (usually the bullet area on the slide) and then choose **Format**, **Line Spacing**. The Line Spacing dialog box displays (see Figure 4.22).

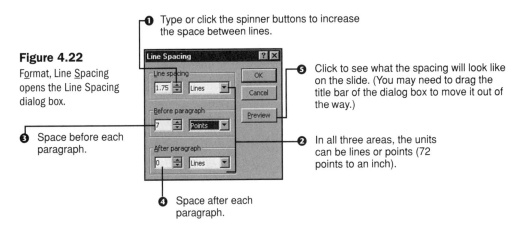

❶ Type or click the spinner buttons to increase the space between lines.

Figure 4.22
Format, Line Spacing opens the Line Spacing dialog box.

❺ Click to see what the spacing will look like on the slide. (You may need to drag the title bar of the dialog box to move it out of the way.)

❸ Space before each paragraph.

❷ In all three areas, the units can be lines or points (72 points to an inch).

❹ Space after each paragraph.

Format ▸ Change Case...

To change the capitalization of selected text, press **Shift+F3** until it is the case you want. You can also choose **Format**, **Change Case**, and choose whether you want the text **Sentence case** (only first letter in line capitalized), **lowercase**, **UPPERCASE**, **Title Case** (first letter of every word capitalized), or **tOGGLE cASE** (change all uppercase to lowercase and vice versa).

Format ➥ Replace Fonts...

If you have one font throughout your presentation and want to change it to another font, choose **Format**, **Replace Fonts** to open the Replace Font dialog box. In the **Replace** drop-down list, choose the font you want to change. In the **With** drop-down list, choose the new font and click the **Replace** button.

Format ➥ Slide Layout...

If you want to change the organization of your slide, you can choose the Slide Layout feature. For example, you may have a bullet list and want to put the bullets on the left side and a chart on the right side.

Change layout of a slide with these steps:

1. Do one of the following:
   - Move to a slide in Slide view.
   - Go to **Slide Sorter** view and hold down **Shift** as you click each slide to select multiple slides you want to change.

2. Open the Slide Layout dialog box (see Figure 4.23) through one of the following methods:
   - Click the **Slide Layout** button on the Standard toolbar.
   - Click the **Slide Layout** button on the Common Task toolbar.
   - Right-click the background of the slide and choose **Slide Layout**.
   - Choose **Format**, Slide **Layout**.

Figure 4.23
Format, Slide Layout, opens the Slide Layout dialog box.

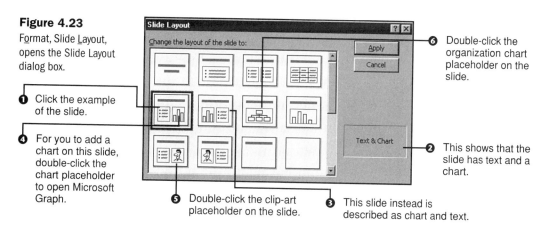

❶ Click the example of the slide.

❹ For you to add a chart on this slide, double-click the chart placeholder to open Microsoft Graph.

❺ Double-click the clip-art placeholder on the slide.

❸ This slide instead is described as chart and text.

❻ Double-click the organization chart placeholder on the slide.

❷ This shows that the slide has text and a chart.

Format ➥ Slide Color Scheme...

The color scheme is the set of colors that you use for text, graphic objects, and the background. You can change the color scheme for one slide or for the whole presentation. Choose **Format, Slide Color Scheme** or right-click the background of the slide and choose **Slide Color Scheme**. The Color Scheme dialog box opens with two tabs (see Figures 4.24 and 4.25).

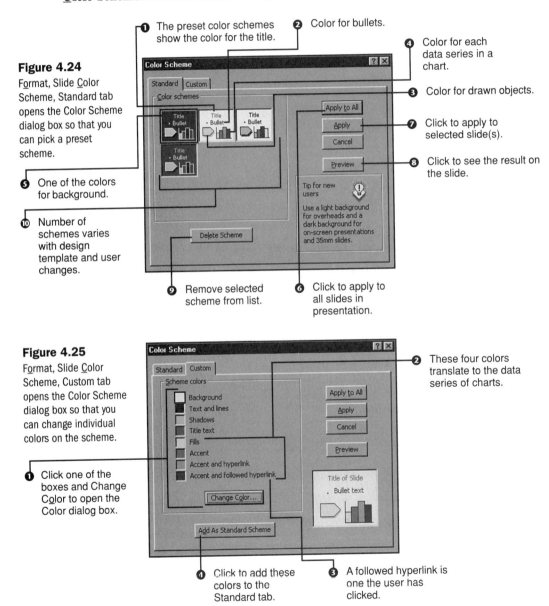

❶ The preset color schemes show the color for the title.

❷ Color for bullets.

❹ Color for each data series in a chart.

Figure 4.24
Format, Slide Color Scheme, Standard tab opens the Color Scheme dialog box so that you can pick a preset scheme.

❸ Color for drawn objects.

❼ Click to apply to selected slide(s).

❺ One of the colors for background.

❽ Click to see the result on the slide.

❿ Number of schemes varies with design template and user changes.

❾ Remove selected scheme from list.

❻ Click to apply to all slides in presentation.

Figure 4.25
Format, Slide Color Scheme, Custom tab opens the Color Scheme dialog box so that you can change individual colors on the scheme.

❷ These four colors translate to the data series of charts.

❶ Click one of the boxes and Change Color to open the Color dialog box.

❹ Click to add these colors to the Standard tab.

❸ A followed hyperlink is one the user has clicked.

Format ➥ Background...

In addition to using **Format**, **Slide Color Scheme** for the background, you have more control with the background feature as far as gradients of colors and patterns when you choose **Format**, **Background**. The Background dialog box displays (see Figure 4.26).

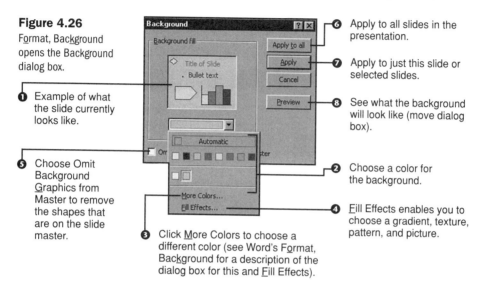

Figure 4.26
Format, Background opens the Background dialog box.

❶ Example of what the slide currently looks like.

❺ Choose Omit Background Graphics from Master to remove the shapes that are on the slide master.

❸ Click More Colors to choose a different color (see Word's Format, Background for a description of the dialog box for this and Fill Effects).

❻ Apply to all slides in the presentation.

❼ Apply to just this slide or selected slides.

❽ See what the background will look like (move dialog box).

❷ Choose a color for the background.

❹ Fill Effects enables you to choose a gradient, texture, pattern, and picture.

Format ➥ Apply Design...

The Apply Design feature enables you to apply the color scheme and master settings from a template file or another PowerPoint presentation. Choose **Format**, **Apply Design** to open the Apply Design dialog box. This dialog box has all the features of any open file dialog box for looking for a file (see Word's **File ‑ Open**, page 21). The dialog box opens to the Presentation Designs folder. You can preview the designs of each of the files. Click **Apply** to change the design of your active presentation.

Format ➥ Colors and Lines...

To change the color and style of lines or borders around figures, choose **Format**, **Colors and Lines**. The Format dialog box opens to the Colors and Lines tab. You can also get to this dialog box through the **Format**, **Object** command below.

Format ➥ Object...

If you have an object selected such as a picture or AutoShape, the **Format**, **Object** menu item changes to the name of the type of object (**Picture**, **WordArt**, **AutoShape**). Generally, this is something you've added by pasting from the Clipboard, through the **Insert** menu (see **Insert ‑ Object...**, page 498 or **Insert ‑ Picture**, page 496), or by double-clicking the object on an AutoLayout slide (see **Insert ‑ New Slide...**, page 493).

Most of the options for formatting an object are the same as they are for Word (see Word's **Format ▸ Object...** page 183). The following table shows what is added for PowerPoint.

Format Object dialog box—differences from Word	
Dialog Box Item	**How to Use**
Colors and Lines tab	
Co**n**nector	If the object is an AutoShape connector, this option is enabled. Choose whether you want the connector <u>S</u>traight, <u>E</u>lbow (angled), or <u>C</u>urved.
De**f**ault for new objects	If the object is an AutoShape or drawing, use the settings on this tab for new shapes you create in this presentation.
Size tab	
Best scale for slide show	If the object is a picture, adjust the picture size for ideal viewing of the picture in a slide show. When this box is checked, change the Res<u>o</u>lution to what the screen monitor will be for showing the presentation.
Position tab	
Horizontal	For the location across the slide for the shape, type or click the spinner buttons to change the distance and choose <u>F</u>rom the Top Left Corner or Center of the slide.
Vertical	For the location down the slide for the shape, type or click the spinner buttons to change the distance and choose <u>F</u>rom the Top Left Corner or Center of the slide.
Picture tab	
Recolor	Click this button to open the Recolor dialog box (see Figure 4.27) and change colors of items in the selected picture.
Text Box tab	
Text **a**nchor point	Within the text box, choose where you want the text (Top, Middle, Bottom, or Top Centered, Middle Centered, Bottom Centered). This doesn't show unless you have Resize autoshape to <u>f</u>it text cleared.
<u>W</u>ord wrap text in autoshape	Check to have text automatically come to the next line when the width of the text box is reached. Clear for one long line of text.

Dialog Box Item	How to Use
Resize autoshape to fit text	Make the shape smaller or larger depending on how much text is in the text box.
Rotate text within the autoshape by 90°	Have the text appear rotated and running from top to bottom of the text box, instead of left to right.

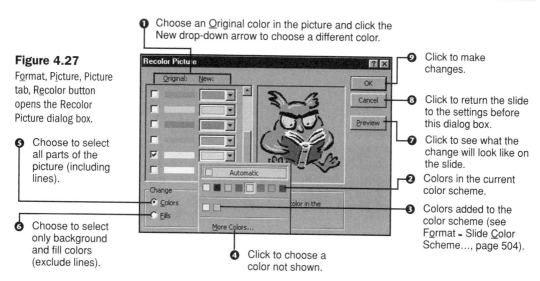

Figure 4.27
Format, Picture, Picture tab, Recolor button opens the Recolor Picture dialog box.

❶ Choose an Original color in the picture and click the New drop-down arrow to choose a different color.

❺ Choose to select all parts of the picture (including lines).

❻ Choose to select only background and fill colors (exclude lines).

❹ Click to choose a color not shown.

❾ Click to make changes.

❽ Click to return the slide to the settings before this dialog box.

❼ Click to see what the change will look like on the slide.

❷ Colors in the current color scheme.

❸ Colors added to the color scheme (see Format – Slide Color Scheme..., page 504).

Tools

The **Tools** menu provides quick access to Office's spell checker, AutoCorrect, and other handy features that improve the quality and presentation of all your Office documents. In PowerPoint, the Tools menu provides additional tools such as the Style Checker, AutoClipArt, and the Meeting Minder to help you organize and improve your slide shows.

Tools ➡ Spelling...

The Spelling dialog box checks the spelling of each word in your presentation. Spelling in Excel and PowerPoint are essentially the same (see Excel's **Tools – Spelling...**, page 382). Excel has a couple of extra options on the Spelling dialog box (**Ignore UPPERCASE**, **Always Suggest**, and **Undo Last**). In PowerPoint, if you want to undo the last spelling change that you made, click the **Undo** button on the Standard toolbar. To set some of the other options for spelling, see the Spelling tab of the Options dialog box (see **Tools – Options... Spelling Tab**, page 519).

Spell check also runs when you choose the Style Checker. (See the following section.)

Tools → Style Checker...

The Style Checker checks your presentations for spelling, for ease of reading (visual clarity), for proper use of upper- and lowercase, and for proper punctuation.

To use the Style Checker, do the following:

1. Choose **Tools, Style Checker**. The Style Checker box appears with the option to check for **Spelling, Visual Clarity, Case and end punctuation**, or any combination of the three. Click **Options...**.

2. In the Style Checker Options dialog box on the Case and End Punctuation page (see Figure 4.28), establish any conventions or standards you've used throughout the presentation that may contradict traditional spelling, usage, and punctuation. The Style Checker recognizes and accepts these customized conventions.

❶ Customize case styles for slide titles and body text.

Figure 4.28
Tools, Style Checker, Options button, Case and End Punctuation tab opens the Style Checker Options dialog box and enables you to check for punctuation and case consistency.

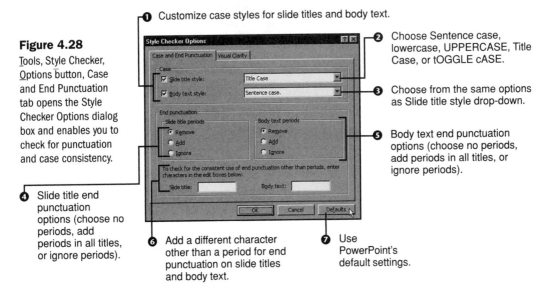

❷ Choose Sentence case, lowercase, UPPERCASE, Title Case, or tOGGLE cASE.

❸ Choose from the same options as Slide title style drop-down.

❺ Body text end punctuation options (choose no periods, add periods in all titles, or ignore periods).

❹ Slide title end punctuation options (choose no periods, add periods in all titles, or ignore periods).

❻ Add a different character other than a period for end punctuation on slide titles and body text.

❼ Use PowerPoint's default settings.

3. Click the Visual Clarity tab (see Figure 4.29).

4. In the Style Checker dialog box, click **Start** to begin the Style Checker. The Spelling dialog box appears (see Figure 4.30) where you can change, ignore, and otherwise manage the Spelling check in progress.

5. After the spelling check is complete, the Style Checker automatically proceeds to the Visual Clarity, Case, and End Punctuation checks. Choose to **Ignore** or **Change** each of the discrepancies. When all three checks are complete, PowerPoint displays the Style Checker Summary dialog box pointing out the possible inconsistencies. Click **OK** to return to the main PowerPoint window where you can manually correct these inconsistencies if you want.

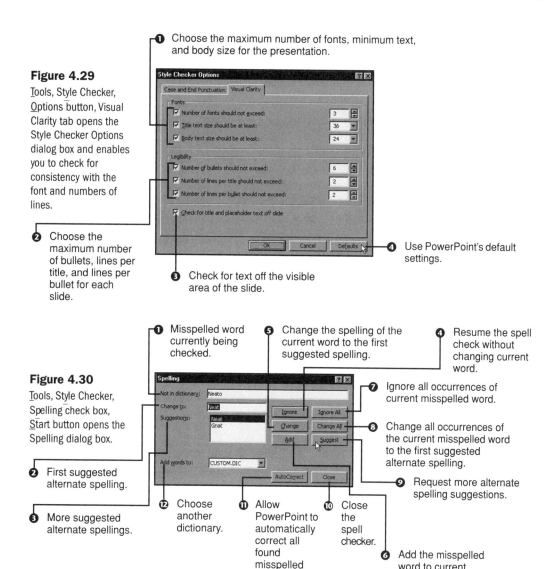

① Choose the maximum number of fonts, minimum text, and body size for the presentation.

Figure 4.29
Tools, Style Checker, Options button, Visual Clarity tab opens the Style Checker Options dialog box and enables you to check for consistency with the font and numbers of lines.

② Choose the maximum number of bullets, lines per title, and lines per bullet for each slide.

③ Check for text off the visible area of the slide.

④ Use PowerPoint's default settings.

① Misspelled word currently being checked.

⑤ Change the spelling of the current word to the first suggested spelling.

④ Resume the spell check without changing current word.

Figure 4.30
Tools, Style Checker, Spelling check box, Start button opens the Spelling dialog box.

⑦ Ignore all occurrences of current misspelled word.

⑧ Change all occurrences of the current misspelled word to the first suggested alternate spelling.

② First suggested alternate spelling.

⑨ Request more alternate spelling suggestions.

③ More suggested alternate spellings.

⑫ Choose another dictionary.

⑪ Allow PowerPoint to automatically correct all found misspelled words.

⑩ Close the spell checker.

⑥ Add the misspelled word to current dictionary.

Tools ⇒ Language...

If you want spelling to skip a selection of text or to set a specific language for a selection of text, choose **Tools, Language**. The Language dialog box is the same as it is in Word (see Word's **Tools - Language - Set Language...**, page 192).

Tools ➥ AutoCorrect...

The AutoCorrect dialog box enables PowerPoint to fix mistakes as you type and expand abbreviations for words. PowerPoint's AutoCorrect dialog box has one tab—AutoCorrect. Word has this same tab with the same options, but also has additional tabs (see Word's **Tools ➥ AutoCorrect...**, page 195).

Tools ➥ Look Up Reference...

Microsoft Office comes with Bookshelf Basics, which is a collection of reference tools that includes a dictionary, thesaurus, and quotations. Bookshelf Basic also includes previews of an encyclopedia, almanac, atlas, Internet directory, chronology, and an address builder that finds zip codes.

Select a word on your presentation and choose **Tools, Look Up Reference** to open the Look Up Reference dialog box. Depending on what you have installed, choose the title that you want to view and click **Keyword** to search only article titles, **Full Text** to check the whole reference, or **None** to open the reference without searching.

Tools ➥ AutoClipArt...

AutoClipArt scans your presentation for important keywords and makes clip art suggestions based on its findings. You can insert a suggested piece of clip art, search the entire Microsoft Gallery for something appropriate, or ignore the AutoClipArt findings and continue building your presentation.

Quick **Choices** **TO USE AUTOCLIPART**

▪ Click the **Insert Clip Art** button 🖼 on the Standard toolbar.

Automatically add ClipArt to your presentation with the following steps:

1. Choose **Tools, AutoClipArt...**. PowerPoint automatically compares the content of your presentation with its collection of clip art to determine any matches. The AutoClipArt dialog box shows you PowerPoint's recommendations based on keywords in your presentation (see Figure 4.31).

2. Click **View Clip Art** to see PowerPoint's recommendations. The Microsoft Clip Art Gallery opens, showing you PowerPoint's suggestions for clip art, pictures, sounds, or video that match the key words that it found in your presentation (see Figure 4.32). If you want to insert some clip art you see previewed, click the image to highlight it and then click **Insert**. PowerPoint inserts the art into the corresponding slide.

3. After you insert selected clip art or close the Gallery without changing your presentation, PowerPoint returns you to the AutoClipArt dialog box. Choose another keyword or slide from the drop-down box to view other clip art possibilities, or click **Close**.

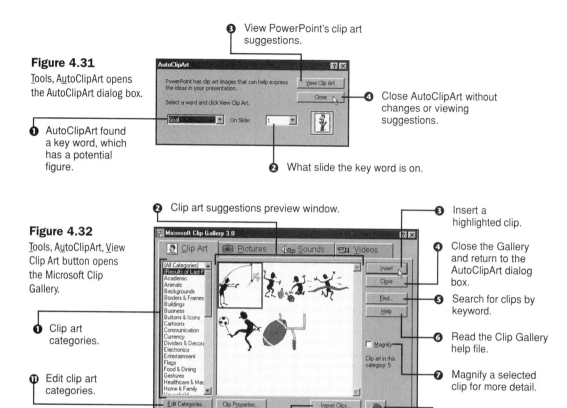

View PowerPoint's clip art suggestions.

Figure 4.31

Tools, AutoClipArt opens the AutoClipArt dialog box.

Close AutoClipArt without changes or viewing suggestions.

AutoClipArt found a key word, which has a potential figure.

What slide the key word is on.

Clip art suggestions preview window.

Figure 4.32

Tools, AutoClipArt, View Clip Art button opens the Microsoft Clip Gallery.

Insert a highlighted clip.

Close the Gallery and return to the AutoClipArt dialog box.

Search for clips by keyword.

Clip art categories.

Read the Clip Gallery help file.

Edit clip art categories.

Magnify a selected clip for more detail.

Keywords used to choose selected clip art.

Properties of the highlighted clip.

Import clips from another gallery or folder.

Search the Web for more clips.

Tools ⇒ PowerPoint Central

PowerPoint Central is a larger, more robust Help feature, downloadable from Microsoft's Web site. It contains upgrade information including patches and plug-ins, tips, usability information, and much more than regular PowerPoint Help.

To use PowerPoint Central, do the following:

1. Choose **Tools**, **PowerPoint Central**. PowerPoint may ask whether you'd like to update PowerPoint Central if it has been any significant length of time since you did so. (If you choose to update, establish an Internet connection first, because Office attempts to download the latest version of PowerPoint Central from the Microsoft Web site.)

2. The PowerPoint Central document looks and acts like a PowerPoint presentation or a Web page. Click any of the options along the top to read more about PowerPoint and install free stuff downloadable from the Internet. When you're through, close the document like any other presentation.

Tools → Presentation Conference

Presentation Conference helps you establish and manage a conferenced PowerPoint presentation—from gathering all participants together on the phone to customizing your connection options. If you are scheduling a presentation conference, make certain that everyone involved runs the Presentation Conference tool before joining in so that each person is properly set up.

To use Presentation Conference, follow these steps:

1. Choose **Tools ‑ Presentation Conference**. The Presentation Conference Wizard launches (see Figure 4.33). Follow the instructions in the first step and click **Next**, or choose any step by clicking its corresponding box in the progress chart.

Figure 4.33

Tools, Presentation Conference opens the Presentation Conference Wizard.

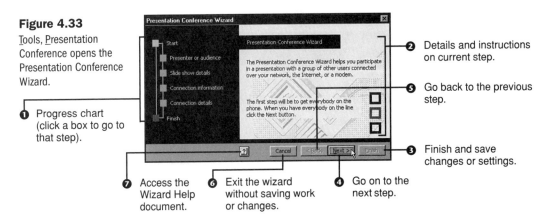

❶ Progress chart (click a box to go to that step).

❷ Details and instructions on current step.

❺ Go back to the previous step.

❸ Finish and save changes or settings.

❼ Access the Wizard Help document.

❻ Exit the wizard without saving work or changes.

❹ Go on to the next step.

2. In the **Presenter** or **Audience** step, click the appropriate option button if you're leading the presentation or just viewing it. Click **Next**.

3. In the Slide Show Details step, decide whether you want PowerPoint to display all the slides in the open presentation. (To make changes, you have to exit the wizard and choose **Slide Show**, **Set Up Show** or some similar PowerPoint feature—you can't customize the slide sequence here.) Click **Next**.

4. In the Connection Information step, connect to the Internet. Click **Next**.

5. In the Connection Details step, enter the computer name or Internet address of all the presentation participants as they each specify. Use the **Add** or **Remove** buttons to include or exclude individuals, use the **Open List** button to import a preestablished conference list, and use the **Save List** button to save the current list to your hard drive. Click **Finish**.

Tools → Meeting Minder

Meeting Minder enables you to take notes during a presentation and make a list of any discussed tasks or goals and who will be responsible for getting them done.

To Use Meeting Minder, do the following:

1. Choose **Tools** - **Meeting Minder**. Type any notes here on the Meeting Minutes page (see Figure 4.34).

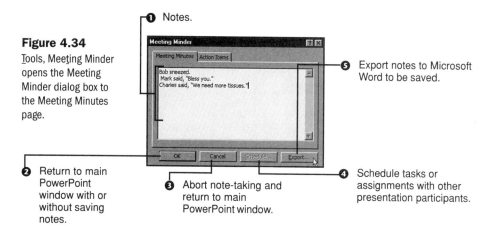

Figure 4.34
Tools, Meeting Minder opens the Meeting Minder dialog box to the Meeting Minutes page.

❶ Notes.

❺ Export notes to Microsoft Word to be saved.

❷ Return to main PowerPoint window with or without saving notes.

❸ Abort note-taking and return to main PowerPoint window.

❹ Schedule tasks or assignments with other presentation participants.

2. Click the Action Items tab. List any tasks or assignments mentioned during the meeting, who will complete them, and when (see Figure 4.35). Click **OK** when finished.

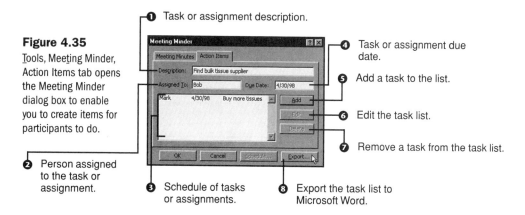

Figure 4.35
Tools, Meeting Minder, Action Items tab opens the Meeting Minder dialog box to enable you to create items for participants to do.

❶ Task or assignment description.

❹ Task or assignment due date.

❺ Add a task to the list.

❻ Edit the task list.

❼ Remove a task from the task list.

❷ Person assigned to the task or assignment.

❸ Schedule of tasks or assignments.

❽ Export the task list to Microsoft Word.

Tools ➥ Expand Slide

Expand Slide takes the bulleted items on an existing slide and creates a new slide for each. This feature enables you to quickly create more detailed slides in a presentation when you want to include more information without losing the flow or train of thought.

To expand a slide, take these steps:

1. Click the **Slide View** button 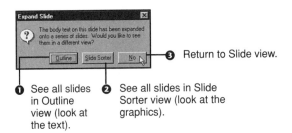 to choose the slide that you want to expand. Choose **Tools ‣ Expand Slide**. PowerPoint automatically creates new slides based on the selected slide's information.

2. In the Expand Slide dialog box (see Figure 4.36), you have the option to view the new slides in sequence using the Outline view where you can easily add new text, or the Slide Sorter view where you can easily add graphics or animation.

Figure 4.36
Tools, Expand Slide opens the Expand Slide dialog box.

❶ See all slides in Outline view (look at the text).   ❷ See all slides in Slide Sorter view (look at the graphics).   ❸ Return to Slide view.

Tools ‣ Macro

Macros are stored procedures that automate tasks you do often. You can record a macro or create a procedure directly in Visual Basic.

Tools ‣ Macro ‣ Macros...

When you choose **Tools, Macro, Macros** or press **Alt+F8**, you open the Macros dialog box, which enables you to run or manage your macros (see Figure 4.37).

Quick **Choices**   *RUN MACRO*

1. Press **Alt+F8**. The Macro dialog box opens.
2. Double-click the macro name.

Tools ‣ Macro ‣ Record New Macro...

You can record your keystrokes and menu choices and save them as a macro. PowerPoint automatically creates the Visual Basic procedure for you.

1. Choose **Tools, Macros, Record New Macro**. The Record Macro dialog box displays.
2. Type the name in the **Macro name** text box.
3. Choose the workbook to **Store macro in**. To make the macro available to all work-books, choose Personal Macro Workbook.
4. Type a **Description** for your macro. This box starts with your name and today's date.
5. Click **OK**. You enter the presentation window with the Stop Recording toolbar open.
6. Type text, move the insertion point, or choose menu or toolbar buttons. Unlike Word, you can record mouse movements.
7. When you're done recording your macro, click the **Stop Recording** button ■.

Figure 4.37
Tools, Macro, Macros opens the Macros dialog box.

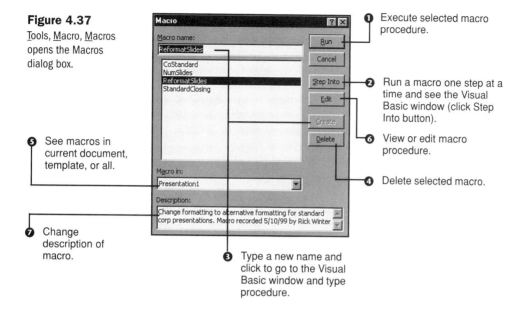

● Execute selected macro procedure.

❷ Run a macro one step at a time and see the Visual Basic window (click Step Into button).

❻ View or edit macro procedure.

❹ Delete selected macro.

❺ See macros in current document, template, or all.

❼ Change description of macro.

❸ Type a new name and click to go to the Visual Basic window and type procedure.

Tools ➜ Macro ➜ Visual Basic Editor

If you want to edit a macro or see macro procedures, choose **Tools**, **Macro**, **Visual Basic Editor** or press **Alt+F11**. Microsoft Visual Basic Editor opens. Click the **Find** button 🔍. In the **Find What** text box, type your macro name and choose **Find Next** until you find your macro. For more information on Visual Basic for Applications, see Que's *Special Edition Using Visual Basic for Applications 5*.

Tools ➜ Add-Ins...

Add-ins extend the capabilities of PowerPoint. They can add new functions, new menu items, and new toolbars. To activate an add-in, choose **Tools**, **Add-Ins**. The Add-Ins dialog box opens. Check each add-in that you want, or click the **Add New** button and double-click any add-in file that you would like to add. Click **Unload** to save memory if you aren't going to use the add-in soon. Click **Remove** to delete the add-in from the list.

Tools ➜ Customize...

When you choose **Tools**, **Customize**, the Customize dialog box opens enabling you to edit or create toolbars and menus. This is the same dialog box shown in the Word's **View - Toolbars - Customize...** (see page 87). For differences between Word and PowerPoint, see **View - Toolbars - Customize...** (see page 490).

Tools ➜ Options...

The **Tools**, **Options** command modifies how PowerPoint works including screen appearance, printing, editing, spelling, and other options.

<u>T</u>ools ⇀ <u>O</u>ptions... View Tab

Dialog Box Option	How to Use
Show section	
Startup dialog	Check to have PowerPoint display the startup dialog box asking whether you want to create a new presentation or open an existing presentation when you launch PowerPoint.
New slide dialog	Check to display the New Slide dialog box each time you insert a new slide; otherwise, PowerPoint inserts the last slide type used. Also, check to have PowerPoint prompt you for a layout for the first slide when you create a new presentation. If **Startup dialog** is clear, presentation starts with the New Slide dialog box. If both of these two options are clear, the presentation starts with a blank title slide.
Status bar	Check to see the Status bar on bottom of the screen.
Vertical ruler	Check to see the vertical ruler whenever the horizontal ruler is in view (see also **<u>V</u>iew ⁃ Ruler**, page 490).
Slide show section	
Popup menu on right mouse click	While in a Slide Show view, enable a right-click to bring up the pop-up menu to choose the slide to go to, arrow and pen options, and other choices (see **View ⁃ Slide Show**, page 478).
Show popup menu button	While in Slide Show view, show button on bottom left of screen.
<u>E</u>nd with black slide	After the last slide, place a blank slide, which can be either black or white depending on the template of the presentation.

<u>T</u>ools ⇀ <u>O</u>ptions... General Tab

Dialog Box Option	How to Use
Provide feedback with sound to screen elements	If Microsoft Office Sounds is installed on your computer, it provides sounds when you do certain events (close, maximize, menu popup). To change sounds associated with an event, choose the Windows **Start** button, **Settings**, **Control Panel**, and double-click the Sounds icon.
Recently used file list	Check and use **entries** spinner button to list up to nine file names at the bottom of your File menu (see **File ⁃ Recently Used File List**, page 468).

Dialog Box Option	How to Use
Macro virus protection	Check this if you want a warning when you open a presentation that might have a virus, because the file has macros or customized toolbars, menus, or shortcuts.
Link sounds with file size greater than	Instead of embedding large sound files, link the sound to the file on disk if the sound file is greater than the size you choose.
Name	Type the name that appears by default in Properties (see **File – Properties**, page 467) and comments (see **Insert – Comment**, page 494).
Initials	Type your initials.

Tools – Options... Edit Tab

Dialog Box Option	How to Use
Replace straight quotes with smart quotes	Check this box to replace straight up and down quotes with curly quotes.
Automatic word selection	Check to select the word and space following a word when dragging across a selection.
Use smart cut and paste	Check to remove extra space when you delete text or add space when you paste text.
Drag-and-drop text editing	Check to enable you to drag selected text with a left-pointing arrow to a new location (press **Ctrl** to copy text).
New charts take on PowerPoint font	Clear this box to keep the fonts on inserted charts. Check this box to use 18-point Arial for fonts on inserted charts.
Maximum number of undos	To save memory, limit the number of actions you can reverse at one time with the **Undo** button.

Tools – Options... Print Tab

Dialog Box Option	How to Use
Printing options	
Background printing	If you want to be able to continue working while the presentation is printing, check this box.

continues

Dialog Box Option	How to Use
Print <u>T</u>rueType font as graphics	Instead of downloading TrueType fonts to your printer, check this box (if available for your printer) to print the fonts as graphics for faster printing (but maybe lower quality).
Print <u>i</u>nserted objects at printer resolution	Print all objects at the resolution of the printer (which may be lower than the object resolution). This may speed up printing and make the presentation more uniform, but it may reduce the quality of some graphics.

Options for current document only

Dialog Box Option	How to Use
Use the most <u>r</u>ecently used print settings	Print the presentation with the last used settings (see **File ▪ Print...**, page 464).
Use the following <u>d</u>efault print settings	Activates the following choices. You can change these options when you choose **File**, **Print** or set the defaults here.
Print <u>w</u>hat	In the drop-down box, choose whether you want to print Slides, Handouts (2, 3, or 6 per page), Notes Pages, or the Outline view
Print <u>h</u>idden slides	If you want to print the slides that you hide (see **Slide Show ▪ Hide Slide**, page 533).
<u>B</u>lack and white	Check to make color slides look as good as possible on a black-and-white printer. Prints colors as shades of gray.
<u>P</u>ure black and white	Check to only print black and white and no shades of gray (you can't have both this and the box above checked at the same time). Use to print draft copies on a color printer and quick speaker's notes and handouts.
Scale to <u>f</u>it paper	Check to reduce or enlarge the slides so that they fit on a printed page.
Fra<u>m</u>e slides	Check to add a thin border around slides on slides, handouts, and notes pages.

<u>T</u>ools ▪ <u>O</u>ptions... Save Tab

Dialog Box Option	How to Use
Allow <u>f</u>ast saves	Speeds up saving files by only saving what is new to the disk. You cannot use this option with **Always create <u>b</u>ackup copy**. The general consensus, however, is not to use fast save; it tends to corrupt documents.

Dialog Box Option	How to Use
Prompt for file properties	After you save the document, PowerPoint displays the Properties dialog box (see **File – Properties**, page 467).
Full text search information	Check this option to save text search information with the document so that the find features of the file dialog boxes are quicker (see Word's **File – Open... Find a File**, page 24).
Save AutoRecover info every	If the computer crashes, the AutoRecover file automatically opens the next time you start PowerPoint and displays presentations you had open when the last AutoRecover save event happened. Enter a number in the **minutes** spinner box for this save frequency.
Save PowerPoint files as	Changes the default **Save as type** option in the Save As dialog box (see **File – Save As...** on page 462) when you first save a file.

Tools – Options... Spelling Tab

Dialog Box Item	How to Use
Check spelling as you type section	
Spelling	With the next option unchecked, check this box to show you a spelling error as soon as you press space or **Enter** after the word.
Hide spelling errors	Check to hide the (nonprinting) red wavy underline on words that you spell wrong as you type. If this box is cleared, right-click the misspelled word to display suggested words.
Suggest section	
Always	Check to always try to display a list of suggestions in the Spelling and Grammar dialog box (even if you really messed up the word). If the spell checker can't find a close word, the **Suggestions** text box displays "no spelling suggestions" rather than be blank.
Ignore section	
Words in UPPERCASE	Check to skip words in uppercase.
Words with numbers	Check to skip words that have a number.

<u>T</u>ools ⇥ <u>O</u>ptions... Advanced Tab

Dialog Box Item	How to Use
Picture section	
Render 24-bit <u>b</u>itmaps at highest quality	For viewing, check this box to display 24-bit images at the highest quality (it may take longer to see them).
Export pictures	When you export your presentation, choose whether pictures are exported **Best for printing** or **Best for on-screen viewing**.
File locations section	
<u>D</u>efault file location	When you first start PowerPoint, the File Open dialog box (see **File ⁃ Open...**, page 462) defaults to this location and stays until you look in another folder. Examples include **C:\My Documents** or **\\FinanceServer\SharedFolders**.

Slide Show

The Sli<u>d</u>e Show menu helps you prepare and customize individual slides in a presentation: with viewing and rehearsal options; with timing and rehearsals; with adding Action Buttons, animation, and other effects; and creating custom slide shows.

Sli<u>d</u>e Show ⇥ <u>V</u>iew Show

This **Sli<u>d</u>e Show**, **<u>V</u>iew Show** menu item is identical to **<u>V</u>iew**, **Slide Sho<u>w</u>** (see **<u>V</u>iew ⁃ Slide Sho<u>w</u>**, page 478).

Sli<u>d</u>e Show ⇥ <u>R</u>ehearse Timings

<u>R</u>ehearse Timings opens the current presentation at full screen size along with a clock control dialog box for stopping, pausing, and restarting the presentation, a pop-up menu button for choosing pen and pointer options, access to the Meeting Minder and any related presentation Notes, and more.

To rehearse timings with a slide show, follow these steps:

1. Choose **Sli<u>d</u>e Show**, **<u>R</u>ehearse Timings**. The current presentation begins, and the clock control and pop-up menu button appear (see Figure 4.38).

2. To go to the next slide, click the **Play/Proceed** button or choose **Next** from the Rehearsal pop-up menu, displayed in the lower-left corner of the screen during rehearsals (see Figure 4.39).

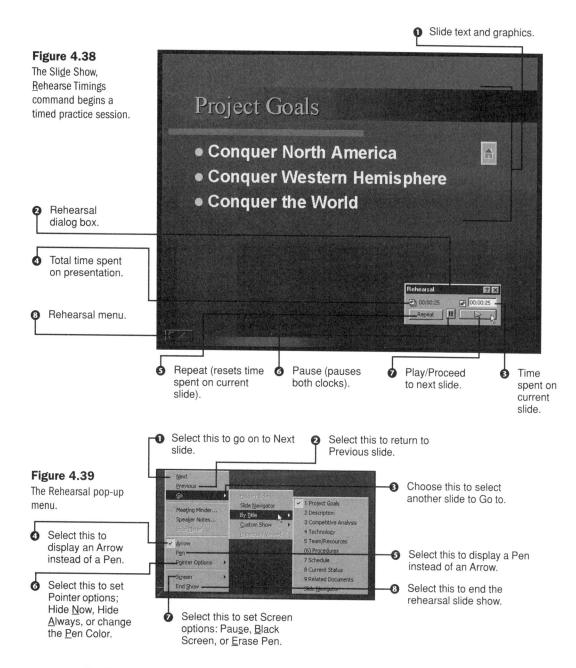

Figure 4.38
The Slide Show, Rehearse Timings command begins a timed practice session.

❶ Slide text and graphics.

❷ Rehearsal dialog box.

❹ Total time spent on presentation.

❽ Rehearsal menu.

❺ Repeat (resets time spent on current slide).

❻ Pause (pauses both clocks).

❼ Play/Proceed to next slide.

❸ Time spent on current slide.

Figure 4.39
The Rehearsal pop-up menu.

❶ Select this to go on to Next slide.

❷ Select this to return to Previous slide.

❸ Choose this to select another slide to Go to.

❹ Select this to display an Arrow instead of a Pen.

❺ Select this to display a Pen instead of an Arrow.

❻ Select this to set Pointer options; Hide Now, Hide Always, or change the Pen Color.

❽ Select this to end the rehearsal slide show.

❼ Select this to set Screen options: Pause, Black Screen, or Erase Pen.

3. Repeat a current slide by clicking the **Repeat** button on the Rehearsal dialog box.

4. Close the current practice session by choosing **End Show** from the Rehearsal pop-up menu, or by clicking the left mouse button once at the end of a rehearsal. PowerPoint shows you the elapsed time and asks whether you want to save your progress.

Keyboard commands while in rehearsal

T	After the first time through rehearsal, run rehearsal again. Press **T** for new time shown.
O	After the first time through rehearsal, run rehearsal again. Press **O** to use original time.
M	After the first time through rehearsal, run rehearsal again. Press **M** to remove time and advance on a mouse click.

Slide Show ➥ Record Narration...

Record Narration enables you to record a voiceover for the presentation in progress. This is also where you establish the narration recording quality, format, and various other attributes such as stereo/mono sound.

To record narration, take the following steps:

1. Choose **Slide Show, Record Narration...**. The Record Narration dialog box appears (see Figure 4.40).

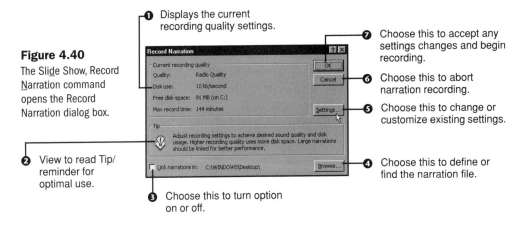

❶ Displays the current recording quality settings.

❼ Choose this to accept any settings changes and begin recording.

Figure 4.40

The Slide Show, Record Narration command opens the Record Narration dialog box.

❻ Choose this to abort narration recording.

❺ Choose this to change or customize existing settings.

❷ View to read Tip/reminder for optimal use.

❹ Choose this to define or find the narration file.

❸ Choose this to turn option on or off.

2. Choose **Settings...** to display the Sound Selection dialog box (see Figure 4.41).

3. The presentation is shown at full screen size and begins recording your narration. Use the left mouse button to move from slide to slide, and to close out the presentation when you have finished. PowerPoint asks whether you want your narrations saved. Click **OK** to accept or click **Cancel** to decline.

Slide Show ➥ Set Up Show...

Set Up Show enables you to customize certain presentation features with regard to the intended audience, runtime, and customizable display parameters.

To set up the slide show, choose **Slide Show, Set Up Show...** (see Figure 4.42).

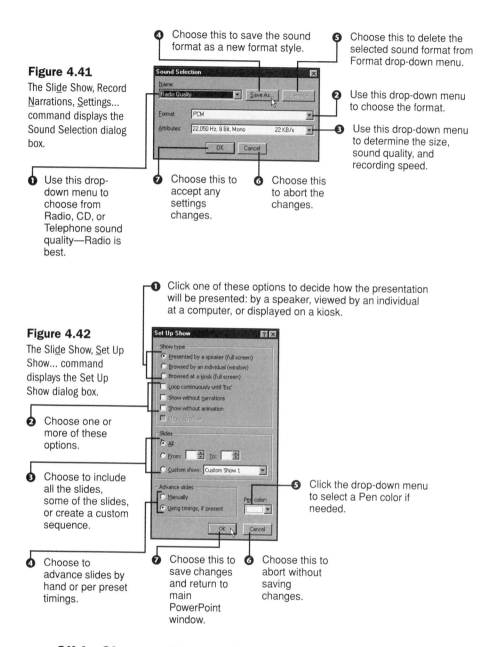

④ Choose this to save the sound format as a new format style.

⑤ Choose this to delete the selected sound format from Format drop-down menu.

Figure 4.41
The Slide Show, Record Narrations, Settings... command displays the Sound Selection dialog box.

② Use this drop-down menu to choose the format.

③ Use this drop-down menu to determine the size, sound quality, and recording speed.

① Use this drop-down menu to choose from Radio, CD, or Telephone sound quality—Radio is best.

⑦ Choose this to accept any settings changes.

⑥ Choose this to abort the changes.

① Click one of these options to decide how the presentation will be presented: by a speaker, viewed by an individual at a computer, or displayed on a kiosk.

Figure 4.42
The Slide Show, Set Up Show... command displays the Set Up Show dialog box.

② Choose one or more of these options.

③ Choose to include all the slides, some of the slides, or create a custom sequence.

④ Choose to advance slides by hand or per preset timings.

⑤ Click the drop-down menu to select a Pen color if needed.

⑦ Choose this to save changes and return to main PowerPoint window.

⑥ Choose this to abort without saving changes.

Slide Show → View on Two Screens

View on Two Screens enables the presentation to be viewed simultaneously on two computers, one for the presenter and another for the audience. PowerPoint enables you to see the presentation running on two screens—a larger size for the audience and a smaller size for the speaker—so you can familiarize yourself with this feature before you give the real thing.

To view on two screens, do the following:

1. Choose **Sli̲de Show, View on T̲wo Screens** (see Figure 4.43).

   The Trying to Connect dialog box appears as PowerPoint attempts to make the connection between the speaker's and the audience's computers.

2. Repeat the process to set up the second computer by choosing **A̲udience** instead of **Presenter** (or vice versa).

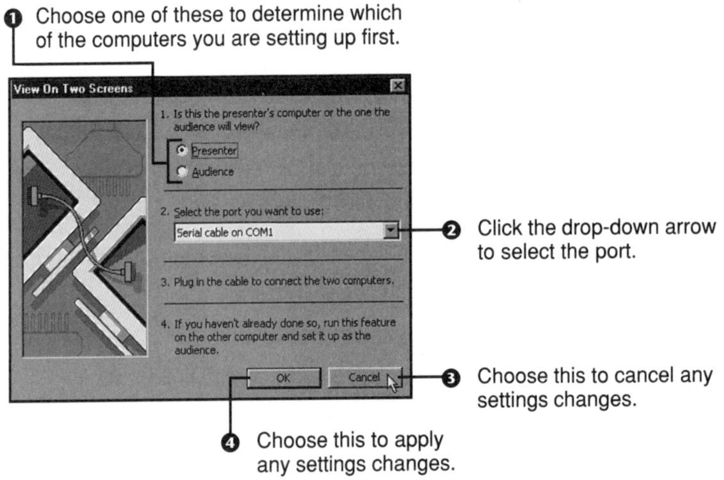

❶ Choose one of these to determine which of the computers you are setting up first.

Figure 4.43

The Sli̲de Show, View On T̲wo Screens command opens the View on Two Screens dialog box.

❷ Click the drop-down arrow to select the port.

❸ Choose this to cancel any settings changes.

❹ Choose this to apply any settings changes.

Sli̲de Show ➥ Action Butt̲ons

Action Butt̲ons enables you to choose from and drag and drop a group of custom or preset icons into each or all the individual slides in your presentation.

To insert an action button, follow these steps:

1. Click the **Slide View** button to the left of the horizontal scrollbar to view the presentation slides.

2. Choose **Sli̲de Show, Action Butt̲ons** and select an **Action Butt̲on** to insert into the current slide.

You have twelve Action Butt̲ons from which to choose

Button Name	Purpose
Action Button: Custom	Adds an action button that you can customize on the Action Settings dialog box (see **Sli̲de Show ‐ Action Settings**, page 525)
Action Button: Home	Adds a button that returns the viewer to the main or Home presentation page

Button Name		Purpose
🕯	**Action Button: Help**	Adds a button that directs the viewer to a Help page
ⓘ	**Action Button: Information**	Adds a button that directs the viewer to an Information page
◁	**Action Button: Back or Previous**	Adds a button that takes the viewer back to the page viewed previously
▷	**Action Button: Forward or Next**	Adds a button that takes the viewer to the next slide in the presentation
◁|	**Action Button: Beginning**	Adds a button that returns the viewer to the first slide in the presentation
▷|	**Action Button: End**	Adds a button that returns the viewer to the last slide in the presentation
↩	**Action Button: Return**	Adds a button that returns the viewer to the previous presentation page
▯	**Action Button: Document**	Adds a button that directs the viewer to a document
◁:	**Action Button: Sound**	Adds a button that plays a sound
▭	**Action Button: Movie**	Adds a button that plays a movie

3. After you select the type of button that you want to insert, a set of crosshairs appear on the slide; drag the cursor over the area where you want to insert the **Action Button** and release the left mouse key.

4. The Action Settings dialog box appears. See the following section, **Slide Show – Action Settings** to understand the choices on this dialog box.

Slide Show → Action Settings

Action Settings opens the Action Settings dialog box, enabling you to change the Mouse Click and Mouse Over options for a selected Action Button. (To add action buttons, see the previous section, **Slide Show – Action Buttons** on page 524.)

To create an action setting, follow these steps:

1. If necessary, change to **Slide View** using 🗖 to the left of the horizontal scrollbar.

2. Click the **Action** button you want to customize and choose **Slide Show, Action Settings** or right-click the action button and choose **Action Settings**. The Action Settings dialog box is displayed (see Figure 4.44).

Figure 4.44
The Slide Show, Action Settings command opens the Action Settings dialog box.

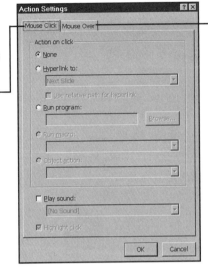

❶ Select the Mouse Click tab if you want the action to take place when you click the button.

❷ Select the Mouse Over tab if you want the action to take place when you move the mouse over the button.

Mouse Click and Mouse Over options

Option	Description
None	Click to remove an action from the action button.
Hyperlink to	Click to define the hyperlink connected to this button—a slide in this presentation or another presentation, a file, or a URL address.
Use relative path for hyperlink	If this option is available, clicking it uses the relative path to the hyperlink. The link has no specific instruction for the drive or folder, just the filename. If you leave this unchecked, the path is absolute. This means that the link includes the drive or folder instructions. If you move the file, the link is broken.
Run program	Enables you to run a program. You can select the **Browse** button to locate the program.
Run macro	Enables you to run a macro you select from the list.
Object action	Enables you to open, edit, or play the object you select from the list.
Play sound	Enables you to play a sound you select from the list.
Highlight click	Highlights the selected object when you click it or move the mouse over it. This is not available if the selected object is text.

Slide Show ↝ Preset Animation

Slide Show, **Preset Animation** enables you to add preset animation effects to the way that text appears on the slides in your presentation.

To apply a preset animation, do the following:

1. If necessary, change to **Slide Sorter View** 🔲 or **Outline View** 🔲 (buttons to the left of the horizontal scrollbar).

2. Select the slide or slides that you want to affect.

   Open the Animation Effects toolbar (choose **View, Toolbars, Animation Effects**) and click either the **Animate Title** 🔲 or **Animate Slide Text** 🔲 button. (See **View ▪ Toolbars ▪ Animation Effects** on page 488 for a description of the tools on this toolbar.)

   Choose **Slide Show, Preset Animation** and select a preset animation from the submenu. The first eight choices (not including Off) are on the Animation Effects toolbar. (To see a description of what the choices are, see **View ▪ Toolbars ▪ Animation Effects** on page 488.)

Additional animation effects choices

Effect	Description
Off	Is the default animation setting. The highlighted slide has no special text effects.
Wipe Right	Makes the text appear word by word, forming in position in a silent, horizontal unrolling motion from right to left.
Dissolve	Makes the text slowly appear in position line by line in a reverse, silent dissolve.
Split Vertical Out	Makes the text appear word by word, forming in position in a vertical motion like shutters opening silently.
Appear	Makes the text appear silently in position.

To create a custom animation, do the following:

1. Change the view from **Outline View** to **Slide View** 🔲 to the left of the horizontal scrollbar. Choose **Slide Show, Custom Animation** (see Figure 4.45).

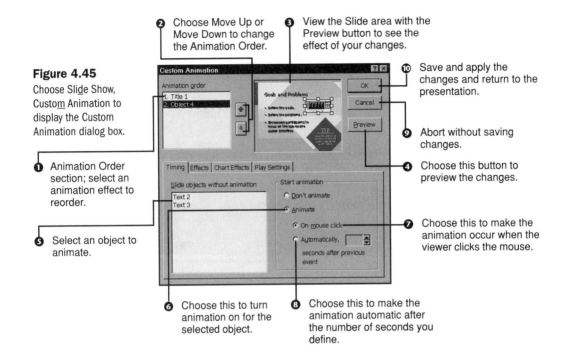

Figure 4.45
Choose Slide Show, Custom Animation to display the Custom Animation dialog box.

❷ Choose Move Up or Move Down to change the Animation Order.

❸ View the Slide area with the Preview button to see the effect of your changes.

❿ Save and apply the changes and return to the presentation.

❶ Animation Order section; select an animation effect to reorder.

❾ Abort without saving changes.

❹ Choose this button to preview the changes.

❺ Select an object to animate.

❼ Choose this to make the animation occur when the viewer clicks the mouse.

❻ Choose this to turn animation on for the selected object.

❽ Choose this to make the animation automatic after the number of seconds you define.

2. Click the Effects tab (see Figure 4.46).

3. If there is a chart in the presentation, click the Chart Effects tab. Decide how to introduce the chart's individual elements with the **Introduce chart elements** drop-down menu, plus the **Entry animation and sound** and **After animation** effect via their drop-down menus.

4. Finally, click the Play Settings tab to establish timing options in the **Play using animation order** section, such as when or if the animation should play or pause and when it should stop altogether. Click **Preview** to view the settings in full-screen size and then click **OK** to save or **Cancel** to abort.

Slide Show ➧ Animation Preview

Slide Show, Animation Preview enables you to preview animations on a slide in the Slide view or Outline view by opening a small preview window.

Figure 4.46

Choose Sli**d**e Show, Cust**o**m Animation and click the Effects tab to display this portion of the dialog box.

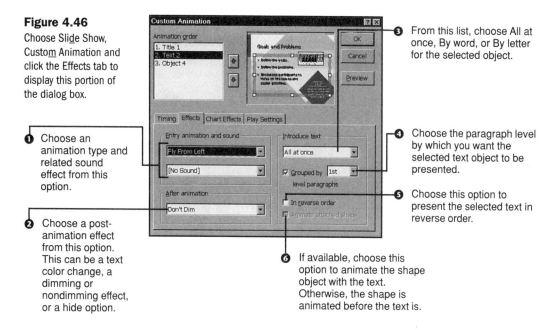

❶ Choose an animation type and related sound effect from this option.

❷ Choose a post-animation effect from this option. This can be a text color change, a dimming or nondimming effect, or a hide option.

❸ From this list, choose All at once, By word, or By letter for the selected object.

❹ Choose the paragraph level by which you want the selected text object to be presented.

❺ Choose this option to present the selected text in reverse order.

❻ If available, choose this option to animate the shape object with the text. Otherwise, the shape is animated before the text is.

To see an Animation Preview, do the following:

Quick **Choices**   *PREVIEWING AN ANIMATION*

■ Choose **Sli**d**e Show, Animation Pr**e**view.** PowerPoint opens a smaller preview window and begins the animation immediately.

Sli**d**e Show ▸ Slide **T**ransition

Slid**e Show, Slide **T**ransition** enables you to add effects one by one or as a whole to the transitions between slides in a presentation.

To create a slide transition, take these steps:

1. Select the slide or slides to which you want to apply a transition.

2. Choose **Sli**d**e Show, Slide **T**ransition,** or right-click the selected slides and choose **Slide **T**ransition** to display the Slide Transition dialog box (see Figure 4.47).

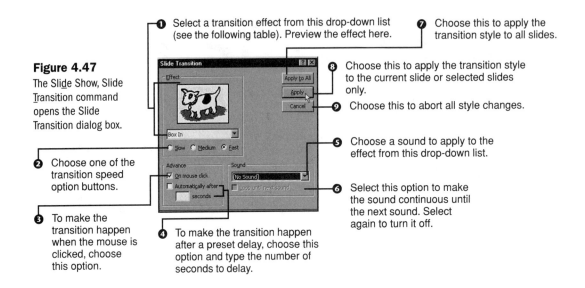

Figure 4.47
The Slide Show, Slide Transition command opens the Slide Transition dialog box.

❶ Select a transition effect from this drop-down list (see the following table). Preview the effect here.

❼ Choose this to apply the transition style to all slides.

❽ Choose this to apply the transition style to the current slide or selected slides only.

❾ Choose this to abort all style changes.

❺ Choose a sound to apply to the effect from this drop-down list.

❷ Choose one of the transition speed option buttons.

❻ Select this option to make the sound continuous until the next sound. Select again to turn it off.

❸ To make the transition happen when the mouse is clicked, choose this option.

❹ To make the transition happen after a preset delay, choose this option and type the number of seconds to delay.

The Transition Effect drop-down menu options are

Name	How to Use
No Effect	No effects applied
Appear	Slide appears in position
Fly from Bottom	Slide flies up from the bottom edge of the screen into position
Fly from Left	Slide flies into position from the left side of the screen
Fly from Right	Slide flies into position from the right of the screen
Fly from Top	Slide flies down from the top of the screen into position
Fly from Bottom-Left	Slide flies into position from an angle at the bottom-left corner of the screen
Fly from Bottom-Right	Slide flies into position from an angle at the bottom-right corner of the screen
Fly from Top-Left	Slide flies into position from an angle at the top-left corner of the screen
Fly from Top-Right	Slide flies into position from an angle at the top-right corner of the screen
Blinds Horizontal	Slide appears in position using a horizontal window blind effect
Blinds Vertical	Slide appears in position using a vertical window blind effect
Box In	Slide appears in position using a fill-in rectangular box-shaped effect

Name	How to Use
Box Out	Slide appears in position using an expanding rectangular box-shaped effect
Checkerboard Across	Slide appears in position using a left-to-right fill-in checkerboard effect
Checkerboard Down	Slide appears in position using a top-to-bottom fill-in checkerboard effect
Crawl from Bottom	Slide slowly flies up from the top of the screen into position
Crawl from Left	Slide slowly flies into position from the left side of the screen
Crawl from Right	Slide slowly flies into position from the right side of the screen
Crawl from Top	Slide slowly flies into position down from the top of the screen
Dissolve	Slide slowly appears in position in a reverse dissolve
Flash Once, Fast	Slide appears in position, flashes once quickly, and disappears
Flash Once, Medium	Slide appears in position, flashes once at moderate speed, and disappears
Flash Once, Slow	Slide appears in position, flashes once slowly, and disappears
Peek from Bottom	Slide appears word by word, rising up from its line of position on the screen
Peek from Left	Slide appears word by word, sliding out from left to right into its line of position on the screen
Peek from Right	Slide appears word by word, sliding out from right to left into its line of position
Peek from Top	Slide appears word by word, descending into its line of position
Random Bars Horizontal	Slide appears word by word, forming in position from randomly sized horizontal bars
Random Bars Vertical	Slide appears word by word, forming in position from randomly sized vertical bars
Spiral	Slide swoops into position in a spiraling motion
Split Horizontal In	Slide forms in position in a horizontal motion like shutters closing
Split Horizontal Out	Slide forms in position in a horizontal motion like shutters opening
Split Vertical In	Slide forms in position in a vertical motion like shutters closing
Split Vertical Out	Slide forms in position in a vertical motion like shutters opening

continues

Name	How to Use
Stretch Across	Slide forms in position in a horizontal unfolding motion
Stretch from Bottom	Slide forms in position in a horizontal upward-tilting motion
Stretch from Left	Slide forms in position in a horizontal swinging motion from left to right
Stretch from Right	Slide forms in position in a horizontal swinging motion from right to left
Stretch from Top	Slide forms in position in a horizontal downward-tilting motion
Strips Left-Down	Slide forms in position in a horizontal unrolling motion from the upper-right to lower-left corner
Strips Left-Up	Slide forms in position in a horizontal unrolling motion from the lower-right to upper-left corner
Strips Right-Down	Slide forms in position in a horizontal unrolling motion from the upper-left to lower-right corner
Strips Right-Up	Slide forms in position in a horizontal unrolling motion from the lower-left to upper-right corner
Swivel	Slide forms in position with a horizontal pivoting motion
Wipe Down	Slide forms in position in a horizontal unrolling motion from top to bottom
Wipe Left	Slide forms in position in a horizontal unrolling motion from right to left
Wipe Right	Slide forms in position in a horizontal unrolling motion from left to right
Wipe Up	Slide forms in position in a horizontal unrolling motion from bottom to top
Zoom In	Slide forms in position in a zooming motion
Zoom In from Screen Center	Slide forms from the center of the screen and moves into position in a zooming motion
Zoom In Slightly	Slide forms in position in a slower zooming motion
Zoom Out	Slide forms by dropping down and moving into position in a zooming motion
Zoom Out from Screen Bottom	Slide forms from the bottom of the screen and moves into position in a zooming motion
Zoom Out Slightly	Slide forms by dropping down and moving into position in a slower zooming motion
Random Effects	Slide forms with PowerPoint applying a different, random

animation effect each time the slide loads, or in between each
slide if this effect is applied to the entire presentation

Slide Show ➥ Hide Slide

Slide Show, **Hide Slide** enables you to remove a slide from the presentation lineup or hide it
temporarily from view. When a slide is hidden, it does not appear in sequence when you practice or run the presentation. This feature enables you to vary or customize slightly the content
of the same presentation for two different audiences.

To hide a slide, do the following:

Quick Choices *HIDING SLIDES*

- Change to **Slide Sorter View** using 🔲, to the left of the horizontal scrollbar, and
  choose **Slide Show**, **Hide Slide**.
- Choose **Hide Slide** from the Shortcut menu while using the Rehearsal Settings option.

Slide Show ➥ Custom Shows

Slide Show, **Custom Shows** enables you to create custom, shorter presentations based on a
single, longer presentation by selecting and working a handful of existing slides. This feature
goes one step beyond **Slide Show - Hide Slide** if you want to alter an existing presentation.

To create a custom show, do the following:

1. Choose **Slide Show**, **Custom Shows** to display the Custom Shows dialog box (see
   Figure 4.48).

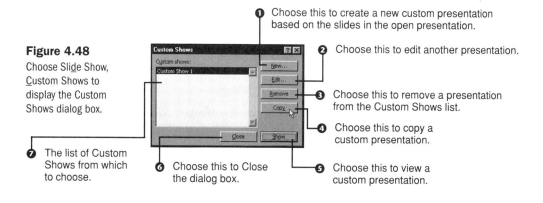

Figure 4.48
Choose Slide Show,
Custom Shows to
display the Custom
Shows dialog box.

❶ Choose this to create a new custom presentation
based on the slides in the open presentation.

❷ Choose this to edit another presentation.

❸ Choose this to remove a presentation
from the Custom Shows list.

❹ Choose this to copy a
custom presentation.

❺ Choose this to view a
custom presentation.

❻ Choose this to Close
the dialog box.

❼ The list of Custom
Shows from which
to choose.

2. When you choose **New** to create a new custom show, the Define Custom Show dialog box is displayed (see Figure 4.49).

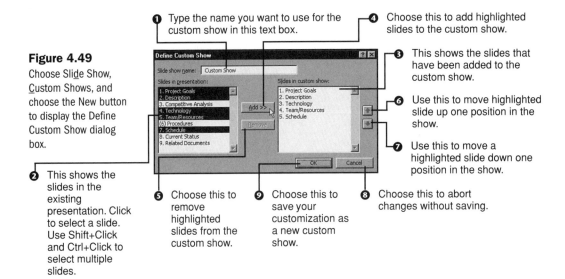

① Type the name you want to use for the custom show in this text box.

④ Choose this to add highlighted slides to the custom show.

Figure 4.49

Choose Slide Show, Custom Shows, and choose the New button to display the Define Custom Show dialog box.

③ This shows the slides that have been added to the custom show.

⑥ Use this to move highlighted slide up one position in the show.

⑦ Use this to move a highlighted slide down one position in the show.

② This shows the slides in the existing presentation. Click to select a slide. Use Shift+Click and Ctrl+Click to select multiple slides.

⑤ Choose this to remove highlighted slides from the custom show.

⑨ Choose this to save your customization as a new custom show.

⑧ Choose this to abort changes without saving.

To select multiple slides to add or remove use **Shift+Click** and **Ctrl+Click**.

- **Shift+Click**—Click the first slide in a group of slides, point to the last slide in the group, hold down **Shift**, and click the last slide in the group.

- **Ctrl+Click**—Click the first slide you want to select, hold down **Ctrl**, and click the next and subsequent slides that you want to select.

Window

The Window menu organizes your document windows on the screen.

Window ➡ New Window

Choose **Window**, **New Window** to open another window for the same document. You can display different slides or different views of the same presentation for copying or editing (for example, a slide view and outline view). Switch between windows by using the bottom of the **Window** menu or by pressing **Ctrl+F6**. Close the extra window by clicking the close button (x) for the window or pressing **Ctrl+W**.

Window ➥ Arrange All

If you have two or more presentations open (or one presentation with more than one window), choose **Window**, **Arrange All** to see smaller windows for each document. If there are two presentations open, one window is on the left and one on the right. Click the maximize button of a window to make it full screen again.

Window ➥ Cascade

If you have two or more presentations open, choose **Window**, **Cascade** to have the windows stacked one on top of another. Click the title bar (or any other portion of the window) of any window to bring that window on top. Click the maximize button of a window to make it full screen again.

Window ➥ Fit to Page

Fit to Page restores the window of all presentations so that they are no longer maximized. Each window has its own title bar, scrollbars, and view buttons. Click any part of a window to bring it in front.

Window ➥ [Open Presentations]

The bottom of the Window menu shows you a list of all open presentations. Click a presentation name (or type the number **1**, **2**, and so on to the left of the document name). You can also press **Ctrl+F6** to cycle through open presentations.

Help

Help enables you to look up more information on the application. The only major difference between Word and PowerPoint help is that Word has the WordPerfect Help, and PowerPoint does not have an equivalent item (see Word's **Help**, page 240). The first and last menu items say Microsoft PowerPoint Help and About Microsoft PowerPoint instead of Word, but they and all other menu items work the same. The Tech Support information is also the same but PowerPoint's help phone number is (425) 635-7145.

See Word's **Help**, page 240, for detailed information regarding the Help menu, which is standard across all Office applications.

Outlook 98

In this chapter

Outlook Overview

Outlook, sometimes referred to as a Messaging and Collaboration Client, is a versatile tool you can use to keep your business and personal life organized. You can use Outlook to

- Send and receive e-mail and faxes
- Share information with other people
- Participate in electronic meetings with groups
- Maintain your calendar
- Organize meetings
- Keep a personal to-do list
- Ask other people to take on tasks
- Build and maintain your address book
- Access pages on the World Wide Web
- Participate in Internet newsgroups
- Keep a journal of your activities
- Save instant notes

This is only a partial list. The things you can get accomplished with Outlook are limited only by your personal creativity.

Outlook's Installation Options

You can install Outlook in the following three configurations:

- **No E-Mail Usage:** Choose this configuration if you want to use Outlook only as a personal information manager (PIM). You have full access to Outlook's capabilities to maintain your personal calendar, information about your contacts, your to-do list, and your journal, as well as to use Outlook to manage your computer environment.

- **Internet Only:** Choose this configuration if you send and receive e-mail only by way of the Internet. You also have all the facilities provided by the No E-Mail Usage configuration. This configuration may be the best choice for people who use Outlook at home or in a small business that doesn't have a computer network.

- **Corporate/Workgroup:** Choose this configuration if you send and receive e-mail by way of a local area network (LAN) or peer-to-peer network. With this configuration, you can use Messaging Application Programming (MAPI) services. You can set up various information services to use Exchange Server, Microsoft Mail, an Internet mail server, cc:Mail, or other e-mail systems. You also have all the facilities provided by the No E-Mail Usage configuration.

If you work in an environment that has a LAN, consult your LAN administrator before deciding which Outlook configuration to install.

This chapter assumes you're using the Corporate/Workgroup configuration, though much of the information applies to the other configurations. Significant differences between the three configurations are noted throughout the chapter.

Using Outlook as a Client for Exchange Server

To use Outlook as a client for Exchange Server, you must have installed the **Corporate/Workgroup** configuration, and you must have the Microsoft Exchange Server information service in your profile. In addition to the capabilities listed at the beginning of this chapter, you can use Outlook to

- Recall messages you've sent to recipients, but those recipients haven't yet read.
- Track messages so that you know when messages are received and read by recipients.
- Use a remote computer to read and send e-mail messages.
- Send multiple-choice questions with a message, and see summarized responses.
- Synchronize your offline folders and address book on a remote computer with information on the server.
- Give other people access to your folders and allow those people to send e-mail on your behalf.
- Plan meetings at times when the people you want to attend have openings on their calendars and when conference rooms and equipment are available.
- Use public folders to share information with other people.
- Collect Web pages for a group to share.

How Outlook Is Organized

Outlook comes with various folders, one for each type of information—messages you receive, messages you've sent, calendar information (appointments, meetings, and so on), tasks, and several others. Each piece of information is known as an item. A mail message is a message item; the information about a person is a contact item; the information about an appointment is a calendar item; and so on. Outlook displays the items in a folder in what's called an Information viewer.

In turn, each type of item contains specific fields of information—in most cases, many more fields than you ever want to use. With only a few exceptions, however, you can leave fields empty.

But Outlook is much more than a set of folders. Although it doesn't appear so and isn't marketed as such, Outlook is a database application. It contains the mechanism that enables you to easily manage the information in those folders.

Viewing Outlook Items

You can choose among several standard views of information in each Information viewer. You can choose various table views for all types of information. Some table views simply list all items in a folder; others group items by categories (see **Edit** ▪ **Categories**, page 567, and **Assigning Categories to Items**, page 593). You can easily display a table view of items sorted in ascending or descending order based on any field just by clicking the field name at the top of a column.

In addition to table views, Outlook has views you can use to display specific items in convenient ways. For example, you can display calendar items in a view that looks like a conventional calendar, containing details for one or more days, one or more weeks, or for a month. You can display contact items in a card view that shows contact information as it might appear on a business card.

Outlook provides a timeline view for several types of items. You can use this view to look for e-mail that you received on a certain date, or to show your activities over a specific period.

Entering Outlook Items

Items get into Outlook's folders by two principal ways: entering them yourself and arriving as messages from other people.

Outlook provides onscreen forms you use to enter specific information about an item. Each type of Outlook item has a separate form—a message form for creating messages, an appointment form for creating an appointment, and a contact form for entering information about a contact.

Using Outlook to Send and Receive Messages

If you have installed the **Internet Only** Outlook configuration, you can send and receive e-mail by way of an Internet service provider, such as America Online, CompuServe, or a local Internet provider. If you have installed the **Corporate/Workgroup** Outlook installation, you can send and receive e-mail by way of various types of mail servers, such as Microsoft Exchange and Lotus cc:Mail.

To send a message, create the message in the Message form. When you choose Send, Outlook places the message in your Outbox ready to be sent. Outlook sends the message on its way as soon as a connection to the appropriate mail server becomes available. If your computer is connected to the mail server by way of a LAN, Outlook attempts to connect to the mail server at intervals you specify. If you use a dial-up connection to a mail server, Outlook can make this connection at intervals you specify, or you can establish the connection manually. When Outlook successfully sends a message, it automatically keeps a copy of that message in your Sent Items folder.

Outlook receives e-mail messages whenever it establishes a connection to a mail server on which messages are waiting for you. Incoming messages are saved in your Inbox folder.

You can reply to messages you've received and you can forward messages, with annotations if you like, to other people.

How Outlook Uses Folders

Outlook saves items of information in folders that are either on your local computer or on the mail server. If you have chosen the **No E-Mail Usage** or **Internet Only** installation, Outlook creates a Personal Folders file on your hard disk. That file contains several folders, one for each type of item.

It's important to understand that Outlook folders are not the same as folders on your hard disk. Folders on your hard disk are containers for files. In contrast, Outlook folders are containers for Outlook items. Your Personal Folders file contains several of these folders.

If you're using a **Corporate/Workgroup** installation and have the Microsoft Exchange Server information service in your profile, you have a choice of where Outlook saves items. You can choose to save items in your Personal Folders file on your local hard drive. More likely, though, you'll save your Outlook items within a store on Exchange Server. Doing so enables you to take advantage of several Exchange capabilities, such as sharing your Outlook items with other people.

The Outlook Window

The principal Outlook Window has three panes, as shown in Figure 5.1.

Figure 5.1

This is a typical Outlook window.

❶ Menu bar.

❺ Information viewer.

❷ Standard toolbar.

❸ Outlook Bar.

❹ Status bar.

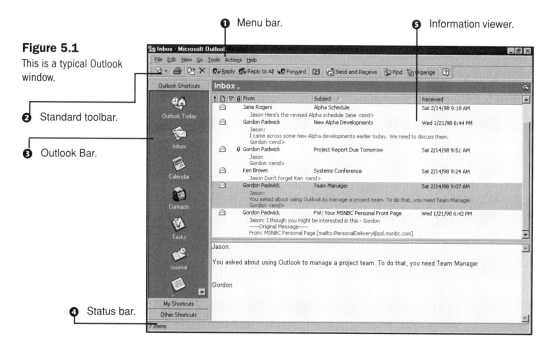

The menu bar contains seven menus, each providing access to various menu items. The menus have the same name no matter which Information viewer you select. The items in each menu, though, are different for each Information viewer. All the menus and menu items are described subsequently in this chapter.

The Standard toolbar contains various buttons, each of which provide fast access to a specific Outlook facility. You can use toolbar buttons instead of choosing from menus. Different toolbar buttons are available according to the Information view you have selected. When you move the mouse pointer onto a toolbar button and pause for a moment, a ToolTip appears giving you a brief explanation of the button's purpose.

The Outlook Bar provides fast access to Information viewers. (See the following section, Outlook Bar, for detailed information about the Outlook Bar.)

The status bar at the bottom of the Outlook window indicates how many items are in the currently accessed folder. When you have the Inbox Information viewer displayed, the status bar shows how many of the messages in the Inbox are unread.

An Information viewer pane occupies most of the Window. The viewer displays detailed information about items in the currently accessed folder.

Outlook Bar

The Outlook Bar at the left side of the Outlook window contains shortcuts you can click to gain fast access to folders and facilities. These shortcuts are arranged in three groups: Outlook Shortcuts, My Shortcuts, and Other Shortcuts.

Right-click within the Outlook Bar (but not on a shortcut) to display a context menu that contains these items:

Outlook bar context menu options

Item Name	Purpose
Large Icons	Display large icons for shortcuts on the Outlook Bar.
Small Icons	Display small icons for shortcuts on the Outlook Bar.
Add New Group	Add new group of shortcuts to the Outlook Bar.
Remove Group	Remove the currently selected group of shortcuts from the Outlook Bar.
Rename Group	Rename the currently selected Outlook Bar group of shortcuts.
Outlook Bar Shortcut	Add a new shortcut to the currently selected Outlook Bar group of shortcuts.
Hide Outlook Bar	Hide the Outlook Bar. Subsequently, choose **View**, **Outlook Bar** to redisplay the Outlook Bar.

Right-click an Outlook Bar shortcut to display a context menu that contains the items in the folowing table:

Outlook bar shortcuts

Item Name	Purpose
Open Folder	Close the currently open folder and open the folder associated with the shortcut.
Open in a New Window	Leave the currently open folder displayed and open the folder associated with the shortcut in a new window.
Advanced Find	Open the Advanced Find dialog box.
Remove from Outlook Bar	Remove the shortcut from the Outlook Bar.
Rename Shortcut	Rename the shortcut.
Properties	Open the Properties dialog box to examine the properties of the folder that the shortcut opens. If you choose the My Computer shortcut, your system properties are displayed. If you choose the My Documents or Personal shortcut, the properties of the file folder are displayed. If you choose the Favorites shortcut, the properties of the Favorite shell are displayed.

Outlook Shortcuts Group

The following shortcuts on the Outlook Bar's Outlook Shortcuts group are those you most often use:

Outlook bar—Outlook shortcuts

Shortcut	Purpose
Outlook Today	Displays the Outlook Today Information viewer in which you can see your appointments, meetings, and events for the next few days and also information about current messages and tasks.
Inbox	Displays the Inbox Information viewer that lists messages in the Inbox folder. A number in parentheses represents the number of unread messages in the Inbox.
Calendar	Displays the Calendar Information viewer that shows items in the Calendar folder.
Contacts	Displays the Contacts Information viewer that shows items in the Contacts folder.
Tasks	Displays the Tasks Information viewer that shows items in the Tasks folder.
Journal	Displays the Journal Information viewer that shows items in the Journal folder.
Notes	Displays the Notes Information viewer that shows items in the Notes folder.
Deleted Items	Displays the Deleted Items Information viewer that shows items in the Deleted Items folder (items you've deleted from other Outlook folders).

The following shortcuts in the Outlook Bar's My Shortcuts group provide access to message folders:

Outlook Bar—My Shortcuts	
Shortcut	**Purpose**
Drafts	Displays the Drafts Information viewer that lists items in the Drafts folder (e-mail messages you've prepared but haven't yet sent). A number in parentheses represents the number of drafts in the folder.
Outbox	Displays the Outbox Information viewer that lists items in the Outbox folder (e-mail messages you've sent but haven't yet been transmitted to a mail server). A number in parentheses represents the number of messages in the folder.
Sent Items	Displays the Sent Items Information viewer that lists items in the Send Items folder (e-mail messages you've transmitted to a mail server).

The following shortcuts in the Outlook Bar's Other Shortcuts group provide access to your computer's file system and to public folders:

Outlook Bar—Other Shortcuts	
Shortcut	**Purpose**
My Computer	Displays the My Computer Information viewer that lists the disks your computer has access to and can be used to access files on those disks. This is similar to the information displayed when you choose **My Computer** on the Windows desktop.
My Documents	Displays the My Documents (or Personal) Information viewer that lists files in your My Documents (or Personal) folder. (This shortcut is named My Documents if you're using Windows 95; it's named Personal if you're using Windows NT.)
Favorites	Displays the Favorites Information viewer that lists items, documents, folders, and URLs in your Favorites shell. If you use Internet Explorer to browse the Web, URLs you select as favorites are saved in this shell.
Public Folders	This shortcut is available only if you have the Exchanger Server information service in your profile. Displays the Public Folders Information viewer that lists public folders to which you have access on Exchange Server.

File

The File menu contains menu items you can use to manage Outlook items. Some of these menu items are available only when you have certain Information viewers selected.

File → New

Move the pointer onto **File**, **New** to see a menu. The top section of this menu contains one or more menu items relating to the currently selected Information viewer. The remaining menu items are more general.

With the Outlook Today Information Viewer Selected

The top section contains the following two menu items.

Menu Item	Purpose
Mail Message	Display the Message form in which you can create a new mail message. (Refer to **Message Form**, page 667, later in this chapter for information about this form.)
Outlook **B**ar Shortcut	Display the Add to Outlook Bar dialog box shown in Figure 5.2 in which you can add a new shortcut to the Outlook Bar.

Figure 5.2

Use this dialog box to add new shortcuts to the Outlook Bar.

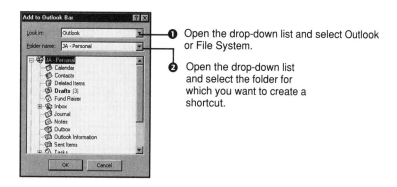

❶ Open the drop-down list and select Outlook or File System.

❷ Open the drop-down list and select the folder for which you want to create a shortcut.

With the Inbox, Deleted Items, Drafts, Outbox, Sent Items, or Public Folders Information Viewer Selected

The top section of the menu contains the following two menu items.

Menu Item	Purpose
Mail Message	Display the Message form in which you can create a new mail message. (Refer to **Message Form**, page 667, later in this chapter for information about this form.)
Post in This Folder	Display the Discussion form in which you can create an item other than a mail message. (Refer to **Discussion Form**, page 664, later in this chapter for information about this form.)

With the Calendar Information Viewer Selected

The top section of the menu contains the following two menu items.

Menu Item	Purpose
Appointment	Display the Appointment form in which you can create a new appointment or event. (Refer to **Appointment Form**, page 646, later in this chapter for information about this form.)
Meeting Request	Display the Meeting form in which you can create an invitation to a meeting. (Refer to **Meeting Form**, page 675, later in this chapter for information about this form.)

With the Contacts Information Viewer Selected

The top section contains one menu item.

Menu Item	Purpose
Contact	Display the Contact form in which you can create a contact item. (Refer to **Contact Form**, page 657, later in this chapter for information about this form.)

With the Tasks Information Viewer Selected

The top section contains the following two menu items.

Menu Item	Purpose
Task	Display the Task form in which you can create a new task. (Refer to **Task Form**, page 679, later in this chapter for information about this form.)
Task Request	Display the Task form in which you can create a task for someone else. (Refer to **Task Request Form**, page 684, later in this chapter for information about this form.)

With the Journal Information Viewer Selected

The top section contains one menu item.

Menu Item	Purpose
Journal Entry	Display the Journal Entry form in which you can create a journal item. (Refer to **Journal Entry Form**, page 665, later in this chapter for information about this form.)

With the Notes Information View Selected

The top section contains one menu item.

Menu Item	Purpose
Note	Display a Note form ready for your use. (Refer to **Note Form**, page 677, later in this chapter for information about this form.)

With the My Computer, My Documents, Personal, or Favorites Information Viewer Selected

The top section contains one menu item.

Menu Item	Purpose
Office **Document**	Display the New Office Document dialog box (shown in Figure 5.3) in which you can choose a template or form.

Figure 5.3

Use the New Office Document dialog box to select a template or form.

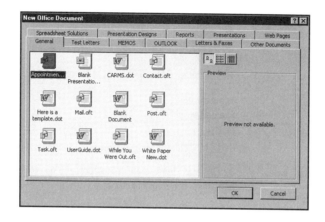

Quick Choices START A DOCUMENT

- You can also choose the **New Office Document** button ⏷ or press **Ctrl+N** to display the New Office Document dialog box.

With the Any Information Viewer Selected

The second section contains the following two menu items.

Menu Item	Purpose
Fold**er**	Display the Create New Folder dialog box (shown in Figure 5.4) in which you can create a new Outlook folder.
Outlook **Bar** Shortcut	Display the Add to Outlook Bar dialog box (refer to Figure 5.2) in which you can create a new Outlook Bar shortcut.

With the Outlook Today Information viewer selected, the Outlook Bar Shortcut is in the first section of the menu. There is no second section.

The third section contains seven or eight menu items. The following table lists nine items. In each case, menu items in the first section are omitted from the third section.

Figure 5.4

Use the Create New Folder dialog box to create a new Outlook folder.

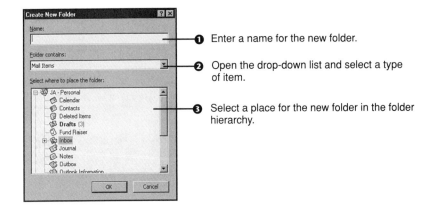

❶ Enter a name for the new folder.

❷ Open the drop-down list and select a type of item.

❸ Select a place for the new folder in the folder hierarchy.

Menu Item	Purpose
Appointment	Display the Appointment form in which you can create a new appointment or event. (Refer to **Appointment Form**, page 646, later in this chapter.)
Mail Message	Display the Message form in which you can create a new message. (Refer to **Message Form**, page 667, later in this chapter.)
Meeting Request	Display the Meeting form with which you can invite someone to a meeting. (Refer to **Meeting Form**, page 675, later in this chapter.)
Contact	Display the Contact form in which you can create a new contact item. (Refer to **Contact Form**, page 657, later in this chapter.)
Task	Display the Task form in which you can create a new task. (Refer to **Task Form**, page 679, later in this chapter.)
Task **R**equest	Display the Task Request form in which you can create a task for someone else. (Refer to **Task Request Form**, page 684, later in this chapter.)
Journal Entry	Display the Journal Entry form in which you can create a journal item. (Refer to **Journal Entry Form**, page 665, later in this chapter.)
Note	Display a Note form. (Refer to **Note Form**, page 677, later in this chapter.)
Office **D**ocument	Display the New Office Document dialog box (refer to Figure 5.3) in which you can choose which type of Office document to create.

The fourth and fifth sections each contain one menu item.

Menu Item	Purpose
Ch**o**ose Form	Display the Choose Form dialog box (shown in Figure 5.5) in which you can choose a form.
Personal Folders **F**ile	Display the Create Personal Folders dialog box (shown in Figure 5.6) in which you can create a new Personal Folders file.

Figure 5.5

Use the Choose Form dialog box to choose a form.

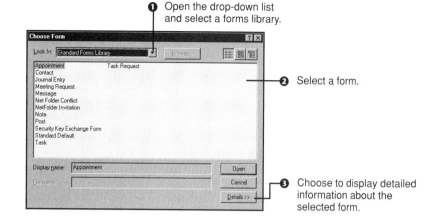

❶ Open the drop-down list and select a forms library.

❷ Select a form.

❸ Choose to display detailed information about the selected form.

Figure 5.6

Use the Create Personal Folders dialog box to create a new Personal Folders file.

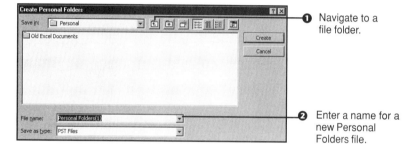

❶ Navigate to a file folder.

❷ Enter a name for a new Personal Folders file.

The Choose Form and Personal Folders File menu items are not available when the My Computer, My Documents, Personal, or Favorites Information viewer is displayed.

File ➜ Open

Move the pointer onto **File, Open** to see a menu. It is not available when My Computer, My Documents, Personal, or Favorites Information viewer is selected. The following table lists the items available in Outlook's **Open** option.

File ➜ Open menu options

Menu Item	Purpose
Selected Items	Select items in any view and then choose this. Each selected item opens in a separate window. This is not available when the Outlook Today Information viewer is selected.
Other User's Folder	Displays the Open Other User's Folder dialog box (shown in Figure 5.7) in which you can choose the name of another user and one of that user's Outlook folders. Only available if you're using the Corporate/Workgroup Outlook configuration and you have the Microsoft Exchange Server

continues

Continued	
Menu Item	**Purpose**
	information service in your profile. Users can allow or deny access to their folders.
P̲ersonal Folders File	Displays the Open Personal Folders dialog box (shown in Figure 5.8) in which you can choose among various Personal Folders files you may have created, including the one you use for archiving.

Figure 5.7
Use the Open Other User's Folder dialog box to open one of another person's Personal Folders files.

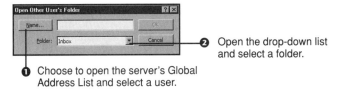

❷ Open the drop-down list and select a folder.

❶ Choose to open the server's Global Address List and select a user.

❶ Navigate to the folder that contains the Personal Folders file.

Figure 5.8
Use the Open Personal Folders dialog box to access one of another user's folders.

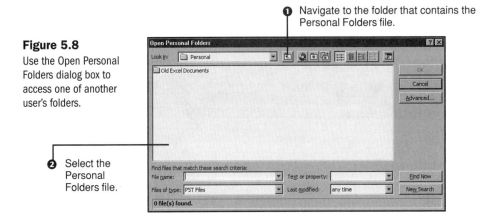

❷ Select the Personal Folders file.

File ➭ Clos̲e All Items

Choose **F̲ile**, **Clos̲e All Items** to close all open Outlook items.

Not available when My Computer, My Documents, Personal, or Favorites Information viewer is selected.

File ➭ Save A̲s

Choose **F̲ile**, **Save A̲s** to display the Save As dialog box (shown in Figure 5.9) in which you can save an item with a specific file name, in a specific location, and in a specific file format. For example, you can select a message in the Inbox Information viewer, and save that message (including all attachments) as a file in Text Only, Rich Text Format, Message Format, or Word Document Format. You can also save the message as an Outlook template.

This dialog box is not available when the Outlook Today, My Computer, My Documents, Personal, or Favorites Information viewer is displayed.

Figure 5.9

Use the Save As dialog box to save an item as a file.

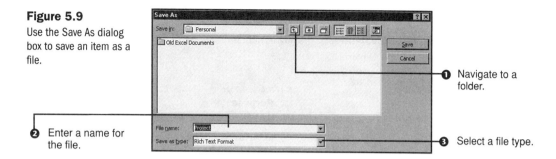

❶ Navigate to a folder.

❷ Enter a name for the file.

❸ Select a file type.

File ➜ Save Attachments

Choose **File**, **Save Attachments** to display a menu that lists the attachments to the selected Outlook item and also All Attachments (available if the selected file has two or more attachments). Choose an individual attachment to display the Save Attachment dialog box (shown in Figure 5.10) in which you can choose where to save the attachment. Alternatively, choose **All Attachments** to display the Save All Attachments dialog box (shown in Figure 5.11) in which you can select one or more specific attachments to save. After you've chosen one or more attachments, choose **OK** to display another dialog box named Save All Attachments in which you can choose where you want to save those attachments.

Figure 5.10

Use the Save Attachment dialog box to save an attachment in a specific location.

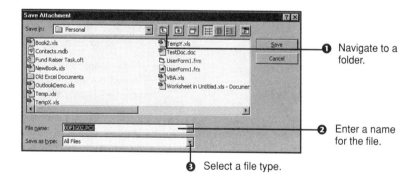

❶ Navigate to a folder.

❷ Enter a name for the file.

❸ Select a file type.

Figure 5.11

Use the Save All Attachments dialog box to choose which attachments to save. This is not available if the selected item has less than two attachments.

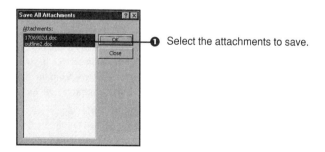

❶ Select the attachments to save.

The Save All Attachments dialog box is not available when the Outlook Today, My Computer, My Documents, Personal, or Favorites Information viewer is displayed.

File ➡ Folder

Move the pointer onto **File**, **Folder** to display a menu.

File ➡ Folder menu items	
Menu Item	**Purpose**
New Folder	Displays the Create New Folder dialog box (refer to Figure 5.4) in which you can create a new folder within your folder structure.
Move "Inbox"	Available only if a custom folder is selected. Displays the Move Folder dialog box (shown in Figure 5.12) in which you can choose where you want to move the selected folder within your folder structure.
Copy "Inbox"	Displays the Copy Folder dialog box (shown in Figure 5.13) in which you can choose where you want to create a copy of the selected folder within your folder structure.
Copy Folder Design	Displays the Copy Design From dialog box (shown in Figure 5.14) in which you can choose one or more of Permissions, Rules, Description, and Forms & Views from one folder to apply to the selected folder.
Delete "Inbox"	Available only if a custom folder is selected. Deletes the selected folder and moves its contents into the Deleted Items folder.
Rename "Inbox"	Available only if a custom folder is selected. Displays the Rename dialog box (shown in Figure 5.15) in which you can rename the selected folder.
Add to Public Folder Favorites	Available only if you have the Exchange Server information service in your profile. Moves selected items to the Favorites folder in Public Folders on Exchange Server.
Remove From Public Folder Favorites	Available only if you have the Exchange Server information service in your profile. Removes selected items from the Favorites folder in Public Folders on Exchange Server.
Properties for "Inbox"	Displays the Properties dialog box that has five tabs (shown in Figures 5.16 through 5.21) in which you can examine and change the selected folder's properties.

Figure 5.12

Use the Move Folder dialog box to move the selected folder within your folder structure.

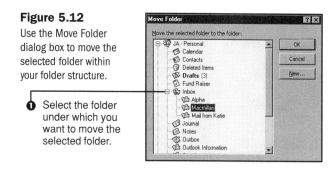

➊ Select the folder under which you want to move the selected folder.

Figure 5.13

Use the Copy Folder dialog box to copy the selected folder to another location within your folder structure.

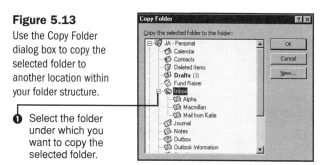

➊ Select the folder under which you want to copy the selected folder.

Figure 5.14

Use the Copy Design From dialog box to copy design elements from one folder to another.

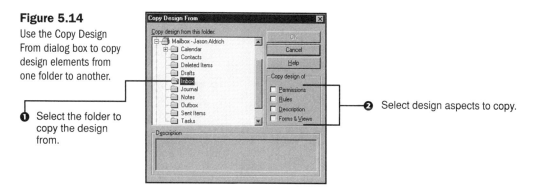

➊ Select the folder to copy the design from.

➋ Select design aspects to copy.

Figure 5.15

Use the Rename dialog box to change the name of a folder.

➊ Replace the old folder name with a new name.

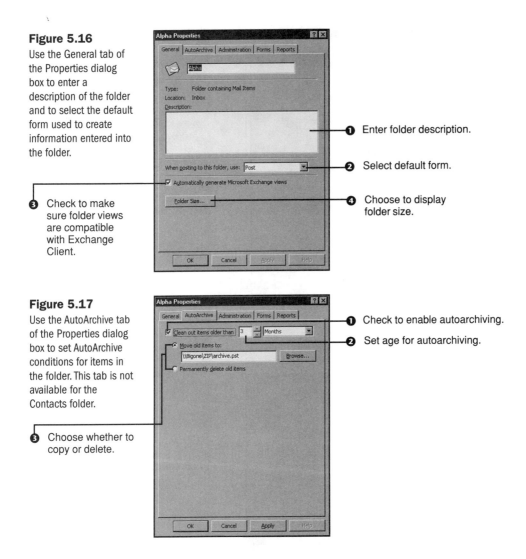

Figure 5.16
Use the General tab of the Properties dialog box to enter a description of the folder and to select the default form used to create information entered into the folder.

❶ Enter folder description.

❷ Select default form.

❸ Check to make sure folder views are compatible with Exchange Client.

❹ Choose to display folder size.

Figure 5.17
Use the AutoArchive tab of the Properties dialog box to set AutoArchive conditions for items in the folder. This tab is not available for the Contacts folder.

❶ Check to enable autoarchiving.

❷ Set age for autoarchiving.

❸ Choose whether to copy or delete.

The preceding information describes menu items as they appear when the Inbox Information viewer is selected. If a different Information viewer is selected, Inbox is replaced with that viewer's name.

This is not available when the Outlook Today, My Computer, My Documents, Personal, or Favorites Information viewer is displayed.

File ➡ Share

Share lets you create Net Folders you can use to share information in your folders with people to whom you can send e-mail. You can share Outlook items with people who use Outlook to receive e-mail. You can share only text items with people who use different applications to receive e-mail.

Figure 5.18

Use the Outlook Address Book tab of the Properties dialog box to choose whether the items in the Contacts folder should be used as an Outlook Address Book, and if so, provide a name for the Outlook Address Book. This tab is available only for the Contacts folder.

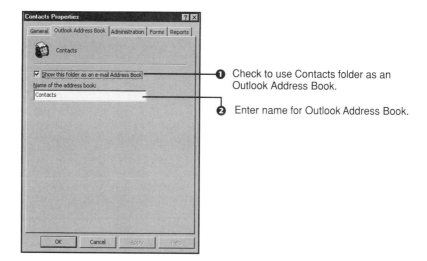

① Check to use Contacts folder as an Outlook Address Book.

② Enter name for Outlook Address Book.

Figure 5.19

Use the Administration tab of the Properties dialog box to choose an initial view of the folder and to set properties (if the selected folder is a public folder).

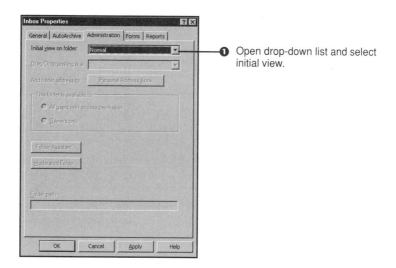

① Open drop-down list and select initial view.

You must have the Net Folders Add-In installed to use Net Folders. (See **Add-In Manager** later in this chapter for information about installing the Net Folders Add-In.)

Move the pointer onto **File, Share** to see the following four menu items.

File ➥ Share menu options

Menu Item	Purpose
Calendar	Displays the Net Folder Wizard's first dialog box (shown in Figure 5.22) in which you can start the process of creating a list of people with whom you want to share your Calendar folder and specify the permissions each person has.

continues

Continued

Menu Item	Purpose
<u>T</u>asks	Displays the Net Folder Wizard's first dialog box, similar to that shown in Figure 5.22, in which you can start the process of creating a list of people with whom you want to share your Tasks folder and specify the permissions each person has.
C<u>o</u>ntacts	Displays the Net Folder Wizard's first dialog box, similar to that shown in Figure 5.22, in which you can start the process of creating a list of people with whom you want to share your Contacts folder and specify the permissions each person has.
T<u>h</u>is Folder	Displays the Net Folder Wizard's first dialog box, similar to the one shown in Figure 5.22, in which you can start the process of creating a list of people with whom you want to share the selected custom folder and specify the permissions each person has.

Figure 5.20

Use the Forms tab of the Properties dialog box to manage forms associated with the folder.

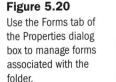
② List of available forms.

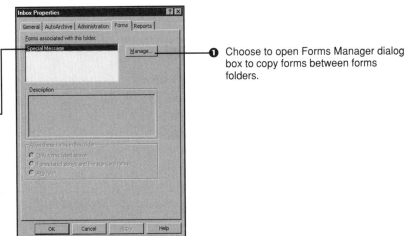

① Choose to open Forms Manager dialog box to copy forms between forms folders.

Figure 5.21

Use the Reports tab of the Properties dialog box to define reports that can be created based on items in the folder.

① List of available reports.

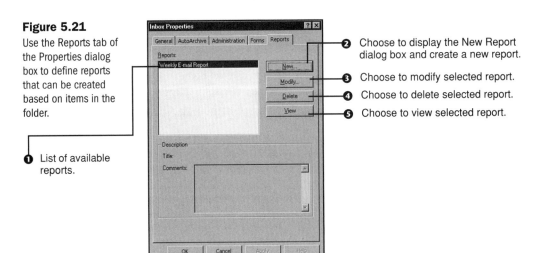

② Choose to display the New Report dialog box and create a new report.

③ Choose to modify selected report.

④ Choose to delete selected report.

⑤ Choose to view selected report.

Figure 5.22
Use the Net Folder Wizard dialog box to share items by way of a Net Folder.

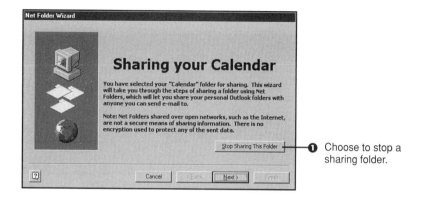

❶ Choose to stop a sharing folder.

The Net Folder Wizard dialog box is not available when the Outlook Today, My Computer, My Documents, Personal, or Favorites Information viewer is displayed.

File ➥ Import and Export

You can import information from many sources into Outlook and export Outlook information in many formats. Choose **File**, **Import and Export** to display the Import and Export Wizard's first dialog box (shown in Figure 5.23) that contains a list of actions Outlook can perform.

Figure 5.23
Use the Import and Export Wizard to import and export Outlook items.

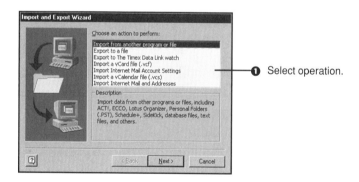

❶ Select operation.

Outlook Import and Export Options

Action	Purpose
Import from another program or file	Import data from such programs and files as Access, ACT!, dBASE, ECCO, Excel, Foxpro, Lotus Organizer, Microsoft Mail, Outlook Personal Address Book, Outlook Personal Folders file, Schedule+, Sidekick. You can also import files with comma-separated values or tab-separated values.

continues

Continued

Action	Purpose
Export to a file	Export data to such programs and files as Access, dBASE, Excel, Foxpro, Outlook Personal Folders file. You can also export files with comma-separated values or tab-separated values.
Export to The Timex Data Link watch	Export calendar, contact, and task items to a Timex Data Link watch.
Import a vCard file	Import contents of a vCard (Virtual Card) file to the contacts folder.
Import Internet mail account settings	Import Internet e-mail account settings from other e-mail applications.
Import a vCalendar file	Import contents of a vCalendar (Virtual Calendar) file to the calendar folder.
Import Internet Mail and Addresses	Import e-mail messages and e-mail addresses from other e-mail applications.

After choosing one of these actions, choose **Next** and follow subsequent steps in the wizard.

File ➥ Archive

You can enable Outlook to archive items automatically or you can choose manual archiving. To archive manually, choose **File**, **Archive** to display the Archive dialog box (shown in Figure 5.24).

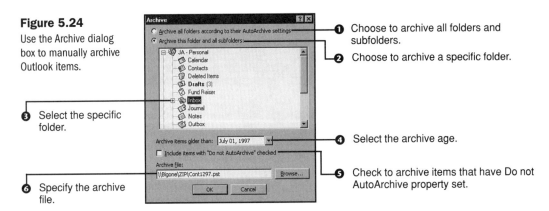

Figure 5.24
Use the Archive dialog box to manually archive Outlook items.

❶ Choose to archive all folders and subfolders.

❷ Choose to archive a specific folder.

❸ Select the specific folder.

❹ Select the archive age.

❺ Check to archive items that have Do not AutoArchive property set.

❻ Specify the archive file.

You can choose to do the following:

- Archive all folders according to their AutoArchive settings.
- Select a specific folder (including its subfolders) and archive items older than a specific date.

File ➡ Page Setup

Use this command to select the styles in which Outlook prints items in folders. The styles available are determined by the view in which items are displayed in an Information viewer. Choose **File**, **Page Setup** to display the following available printing styles:

Outlook printing styles

Folder	View	Styles
Inbox	Table	Table, Memo
Inbox	Timeline	Memo
Calendar	Day/Week/Month	Daily, Weekly, Monthly, Tri-fold, Calendar Details, Memo
Calendar	Table	Table, Memo
Contacts	Card	Card, Small Booklet, Medium Booklet, Memo, Phone Directory
Contacts	Table	Table, Memo
Tasks	Table	Table, Memo
Tasks	Timeline	Memo
Journal	Table	Table, Memo
Journal	Timeline	Memo
Notes	Icon	Memo
Notes	Table	Table, Memo
Deleted Items	Table	Table, Memo
Deleted Items	Timeline	Memo
Drafts	Table	Table, Memo
Drafts	Timeline	Memo
Outbox	Table	Table, Memo
Outbox	Timeline	Memo
Sent Items	Table	Table, Memo
My Computer	Table	Table
My Computer	Icon	None
My Documents	Table	Table
My Documents	Icon	None
My Documents	Timeline	None

continues

Continued

Folder	View	Styles
Personal	Table	Table
Personal	Icon	None
Personal	Timeline	None
Favorites	Table	Table
Favorites	Icon	None
Favorites	Timeline	None

File, Page Setup is not available when the Outlook Today Information viewer is selected.

Move the mouse pointer onto **File**, **Page Setup** and choose **Define Print Styles** to customize a print style for a specific folder using the Define Print Styles dialog box (shown in Figure 5.25).

Figure 5.25

The styles available in the Define Print Styles dialog box depend on which Information viewer is selected. The print styles available for Contacts items are shown here.

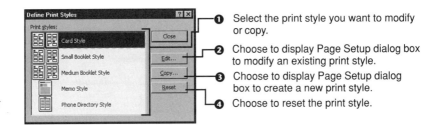

❶ Select the print style you want to modify or copy.

❷ Choose to display Page Setup dialog box to modify an existing print style.

❸ Choose to display Page Setup dialog box to create a new print style.

❹ Choose to reset the print style.

Select a Print Style and choose **Edit** to display the Page Setup dialog box (shown in Figure 5.26) in which you can customize the style by choosing fonts, paper type, page size, margins, orientation, and also create a header and footer.

Figure 5.26

Use the Page Setup dialog box to modify style details. The choices available in this box vary according to the Information viewer and print style you have previously selected.

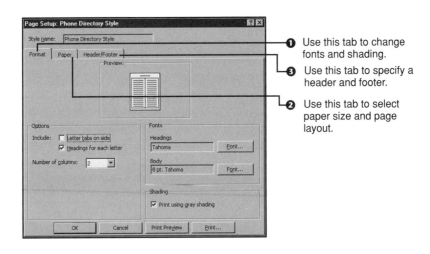

❶ Use this tab to change fonts and shading.

❸ Use this tab to specify a header and footer.

❷ Use this tab to select paper size and page layout.

Instead of choosing **Edit**, choose **Copy** to display the Page Setup dialog box (refer to Figure 5.26) in which you can create a new print style based on an existing style. After you do so, the Define Print Styles dialog box contains the new style. When you select the new print style, the button previously named Reset is named Delete. Choose this button to delete the new style.

File ➡ Print Preview

Choose **File**, **Print Preview** to display a preview of the default, or, if you have selected a specific print style, the selected print style such as that shown in Figure 5.27 is displayed.

Figure 5.27
This is an example of a Print Preview window. This preview shows Contact items in a card view.

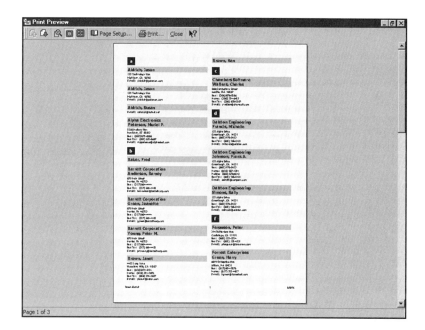

Choose **Close** on the toolbar to close the preview window. (Refer to **Print Preview**, page xx, later in this chapter for information about the other toolbar buttons available in the Print Preview window.)

Not available if the Outlook Today Information viewer is selected.

File ➡ Print

Choose **File**, **Print** to print items from the selected Information viewer.

Quick **Choices**   *PRINT ITEMS*

■ You can also choose the **Print** button 🖨 or press **Ctrl+P** to display the Print dialog box.

Outlook displays the Print dialog box (shown in Figure 5.28) in which you can choose a print style and define that style. You can also choose to print all items in the open folder, or only items you have selected in that folder. You can choose to print all pages, odd-numbered pages, or even-numbered pages, and how many copies to print.

Figure 5.28

The Print dialog box is quite similar to that displayed by other Office applications.

❶ Open the drop-down list and select a printer.

❷ Select a print style.

❸ Select all pages, even-numbered pages, or odd-numbered pages.

❹ Specify number of copies.

❺ Select all items or selected items.

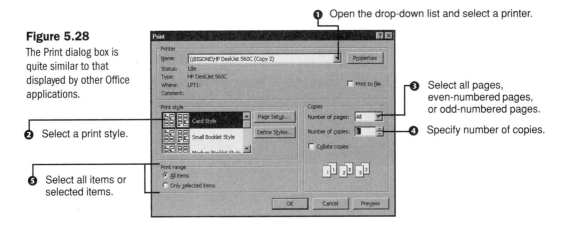

If you choose to print the Outlook Today folder, the Print dialog box gives you the capability to print all linked documents or a table of links to those documents.

File ➟ Exit

Choose **File**, **Exit** to close Outlook. If you are using any messaging services, you should use File, Exit and Log Off to close Outlook.

File ➟ Exit and Log Off

Choose **File**, **Exit and Log Off** to close Outlook and log off from all messaging services.

Edit

You can use the Edit menu for such purposes as editing items, moving and copying items between Outlook folders, marking messages as read or unread, and customizing your personal master category list. In most cases, commands such as **Undo**, **Cut**, **Copy**, and **Paste** work in Outlook just as they do in other Office applications, such as Word. (See Chapter 2, "Word," for more information about these standard Office commands.)

Edit ➟ Undo

Choose **Edit**, **Undo** to reverse the most recent command or to delete the last entry you typed.

Quick **Choices** *UNDO*

- You can press **Ctrl+Z** to undo the most recent command or delete the last entry you typed.

Unlike Word, Outlook doesn't keep a list of recent operations. You can Undo only the most recent operation. After you've used Undo, the menu item changes to Redo. Choose **Edit, Redo** to reverse the undo.

Edit ➥ Cut

Choose **Edit, Cut** to delete selected text or selected objects and place them on the Clipboard.

Quick **Choices** *CUT*

- You can also press **Ctrl+X** to cut selected text or objects and place them on the Clipboard.

Edit ➥ Copy

Choose **Edit, Copy** to copy selected text or selected objects, and place them on the Clipboard.

Quick **Choices** *COPY*

- You can also press **Ctrl+C** to copy selected text or objects to the Clipboard.

Edit ➥ Paste

Choose **Edit, Paste** to insert the contents of the Clipboard at the insertion point. If you have previously selected text or objects, the insertion replaces the selection.

Quick **Choices** *PASTE*

- You can also press **Ctrl+V** to insert the contents of the Clipboard at the insertion point.

Edit ➥ Clear

Choose **Edit, Clear** to delete selected text or objects. The deleted text or objects are not placed on the Clipboard.

Quick **Choices** *CLEAR*

- You can also press the Delete key to delete selected text or objects.

Edit ➥ Select All

Choose **Edit, Select All** to select all items in the open Information viewer.

■ Alternatively, to select all, press **Ctrl+A**.

Edit ➥ Delete

Choose **Edit**, **Delete** to move selected items from the open information viewer to the Deleted Items folder. If you select items in the Deleted Items folder, these items are permanently deleted.

■ Alternatively, press **Ctrl+D** or choose the **Delete** button ⊠ on the Standard toolbar to delete items.

Edit ➥ Move to Folder

Choose **Edit**, **Move to Folder** to move selected items to another Outlook folder. Outlook displays the Move Items dialog box (shown in Figure 5.29) in which you can select the folder to which you want to move items.

■ You can also press **Ctrl+Shift+V** to display the Move Items dialog box.

Figure 5.29
Use the Move Items dialog box to move selected items to another folder.

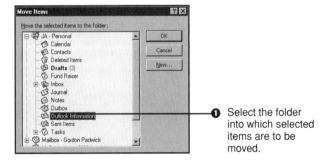

❶ Select the folder into which selected items are to be moved.

■ An alternative way to move items is to select the items and choose the Move to Folder button 🗗 in the Standard toolbar to display a list of folders. Select the folder to which you want to move the selected items.

Edit ⇥ Copy to Folder

Choose **Edit, Copy to Folder** to copy selected items to another Outlook folder. Outlook displays the Copy Items dialog box (shown in Figure 5.30) in which you can select the folder to which you want to copy items.

Figure 5.30

Use the Copy Items dialog box to copy selected items to another folder.

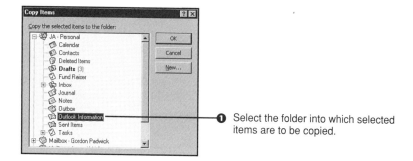

❶ Select the folder into which selected items are to be copied.

Edit ⇥ Mark as Read

Choose **Edit, Mark as Read** to remove the bold formatting in message headers to indicate that the selected messages have been read. If AutoPreview is selected, this command also hides the first three lines of those messages in the Inbox Information viewer.

Quick Choices   **MARK AS READ**

▪ You can also press **Ctrl+Q** to mark selected messages as read.

Edit ⇥ Mark as Unread

Choose **Edit, Mark as Unread** to enable bold formatting in message headers to indicate that the selected messages have not been read. If AutoPreview is selected, this command also displays the first three lines of those messages in the Inbox Information viewer (but not if those messages are encrypted).

Edit ⇥ Mark All as Read

Choose **Edit, Mark All as Read** to remove bold formatting in all message headers to indicate that all messages have been read. If AutoPreview is selected, this command also hides the first three lines of all messages displayed in the Inbox Information viewer.

Edit ⇥ Categories

Choose **Edit, Categories** to display the Categories dialog box (shown in Figure 5.31), which lists your personal master categories. You can use this dialog box to add, delete, or edit category names.

Figure 5.31

The Categories dialog box lists your available categories.

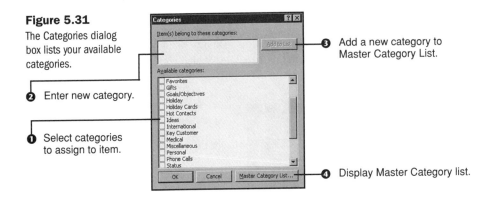

❷ Enter new category.

❶ Select categories to assign to item.

❸ Add a new category to Master Category List.

❹ Display Master Category list.

Select one or more categories and then choose **OK** to assign those categories to the selected items.

Choose **Master Category List** to display the Master Category List dialog box (shown in Figure 5.32).

Figure 5.32

Use the Master Category List dialog box to maintain your master category list.

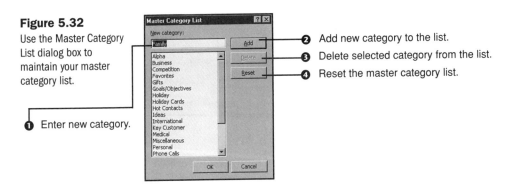

❶ Enter new category.

❷ Add new category to the list.

❸ Delete selected category from the list.

❹ Reset the master category list.

The following operations are performed in the Master Category List dialog box.

Master Category List operations

Operation	What to Do
Add new category	Enter a new category in the **New Category** box and then choose **Add**.
Delete category	Select a category and then choose **Delete**.
Reset the category list	Choose **Reset** to restore the master category list to what it was immediately after you installed Outlook.

When you reset the master category list, all categories you've added are removed from the list. However, all categories you've assigned to items remain assigned to those items, even though they are no longer in your master category list.

<u>V</u>iew

You can use the View menu to choose what Outlook displays.

<u>V</u>iew → Current <u>V</u>iew

Choose **<u>V</u>iew**, **Current <u>V</u>iew** to see a list of views available for the open Information viewer and to modify and create new views.

As first installed, Outlook provides certain views for each Information viewer, as listed below.

Outlook Today View

Outlook provides only the standard view of Outlook Today, although alternative views of Outlook Today can be created by methods that are beyond the scope of this book.

Inbox, Deleted Items, Drafts, Outbox, Sent Items, and Public Folders Views

With the Inbox, Deleted Items, Drafts, Outbox, Send Items, or Public Folders Information viewer selected, choose **<u>V</u>iew**, **Current <u>V</u>iew** to display the following list of views.

Inbox, Deleted Items, Drafts, Outbox, Sent Items and Public Folders views	
View Name	**Purpose**
Messages	Displays all received messages in table format without AutoPreview text.
Messages with AutoPreview	Displays all received messages in table format with AutoPreview text for unread messages.
By Follow Up Flag	Displays all received messages in table format grouped by flag. Flags may be send with the message or added by the recipient.
Last Seven Days	Displays all messages received during the last seven days in table format.
Flagged for Next Seven Days	Displays all messages flagged for action during the next seven days in table format. Flags may be sent with the message or added by the recipient.
By Conversation Topic	Displays all messages in table format grouped by conversation topics—the subjects of messages.
By Sender	Displays all messages in table format grouped by the name of the sender.
Unread Messages	Displays all unread messages in table format.
Sent To	Displays all messages in table format listed in order of date sent, with the most recent at the top.
Message Timeline	Displays all messages in Timeline format.

Calendar Views

With the Calendar Information viewer selected, choose **View**, **Current View** to display the following list of views.

View Name	Purpose
Calendar views	
Day/Week/Month	Displays all calendar items in calendar format and enables you to choose Day, Work Week, Week, or Month views
Day/Week/Month with AutoPreview	Displays all calendar items in calendar format and enables you to choose Day, Work Week, Week, or Month views
Active Appointments	Displays all future appointments and meetings in table format grouped by recurrence pattern
Events	Displays all events in table format in order of start of the recurrence range
Annual Events	Displays all annual events in table format in order of start of the recurrent range
Recurring Events	Displays all events in table format grouped by recurrence pattern
By Category	Displays all calendar items grouped by category

Contacts Views

With the Contacts Information viewer selected, choose **View**, **Current View** to display the following list of views.

View Name	Purpose
Contacts views	
Address Cards	Displays basic information for all contacts in card format
Detailed Address Cards	Displays extended information for all contacts in card format
Phone List	Displays all contacts with business phone, business fax, home phone, and mobile phone numbers in table format
By Category	Displays all contacts grouped by category in table format
By Company	Displays all contacts grouped by company in table format
By Location	Displays all contacts grouped by country in table format
By Follow Up Flag	Displays all contacts grouped by flag in table format

Tasks Views

With the Tasks Information viewer selected, choose **View**, **Current View** to display the list of views.

Tasks views	
View Name	**Purpose**
Simple List	Displays basic information for all tasks in table format
Detailed List	Displays extended information for all tasks in table format
Active Tasks	Displays all uncompleted tasks in table format
Next Seven Days	Displays all tasks due to be completed within the next seven days in table format
Overdue Tasks	Displays all uncompleted tasks due on or before yesterday in table format
By Category	Displays all tasks grouped by category in table format
Assignment	Displays tasks assigned by you to another person in table format
By Person Responsible	Displays all tasks grouped by task owner in table format
Completed Tasks	Displays completed tasks in table format
Task Timeline	Displays all tasks in timeline format

Journal Views

With the Journal Information viewer selected, choose **View**, **Current View** to display the following list of views.

Journal views	
View Name	**Purpose**
By Type	Displays all journal items grouped by entry type in table format
By Contact	Displays all journal items grouped by contact in table format
By Category	Displays all journal items grouped by category in table format
Entry List	Displays all journal items in order of start time in table format
Phone Calls	Displays phone call journal items in order of start time in table format

Notes Views

With the Notes Information viewer selected, choose **View**, **Current View** to display the following list of views.

Notes views	
View Name	**Purpose**
Icons	Displays all notes in icon format. You can click buttons in the Standard toolbar to choose large icons, small icons, or list (small icons with subject text).
Notes List	Displays all notes in table format.
Last Seven Days	Displays notes created or edited during the last seven days in table format.
By Category	Displays all notes grouped by category in table format.
By Color	Displays all notes grouped by color in table format.

My Computer Views

With the My Computer Information viewer selected, choose **View**, **Current View** to display the following list of views.

My Computer views	
View Name	**Purpose**
Icons	Displays all disks accessible to your computer in icon format. You can click buttons on the Standard toolbar to choose large icons, small icons, or small icons in a list.
Details	Displays all disks accessible to your computer with type information in table format.
By Type	Displays all disks accessible to your computer grouped by type in table format.

My Documents, Personal, and Favorites Views

With the My Documents, Personal, or Favorites Information viewer selected, choose **View**, **Current View** to display the following list of views.

My Documents, Personal, and Favorites views	
View Name	**Purpose**
Icons	Displays icons representing all folders, files, and shortcuts. You can click buttons in the Standard toolbar to choose large icons, small icons, or small icons in a list.
Details	Displays all folders, files, and shortcuts in table format.
By Author	Displays all folders, files, and shortcuts grouped by author in table format.
By File Type	Displays all folders, files, and shortcuts grouped by type in table format.

View Name	Purpose
Document Timeline	Displays all folders, files, and shortcuts in timeline format.
Programs	Displays, in table format, files having an EXE or COM extension.

View – Current View – Customize Current View

Choose **View**, **Current View** and choose **Customize Current View** to display the View Summary dialog box (shown in Figure 5.33) in which you can examine details of the currently selected view and make changes to it.

Figure 5.33

The View Summary dialog box provides a summary of the selected view and has buttons you can choose to make changes to that view.

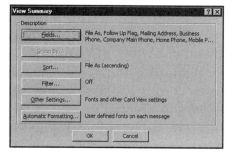

Choose buttons in the View Summary dialog box as follows.

View Summary buttons

Button Name	Purpose
Fields	Display the Show Fields dialog box (shown in Figure 5.34), which shows a list of fields in the current view and the fields you can add to the view. You can add fields, remove fields, and create custom fields in the view.
Group By	Display the Group By dialog box (shown in Figure 5.35). You can use this dialog box to select fields by which the current view is to be grouped. Fields not displayed in the view can be selected. Up to four levels of grouping can be specified. You can also specify whether groups are expanded or collapsed when the view is chosen. This button is available only for table and timeline views.
Sort	Display the Sort dialog box (shown in Figure 5.36) in which you can select fields by which the current view is to be sorted. Fields not displayed in the view can be selected. Up to four levels of sorting can be specified. For each level, ascending or descending sort order is available. This button is not available for timeline views.

continues

Continued

Button Name	Purpose
Filter	Display the Filter dialog box (shown in Figure 5.37) where you can specify conditions by which items are to be filtered. Select criteria for items to be included in the view. Criteria include text in specific fields, the time in one of the time fields, categories assigned, values in conditional fields, and defined selection conditions.
Other Settings	Display the Other Settings dialog box (shown in Figure 5.38) in which you can specify fonts to be used in different regions of the view. You can also modify certain aspects of the view layout.
Automatic Formatting	Display the Automatic Formatting dialog box (shown in Figure 5.39) in which you can specify rules that determine how Outlook displays specific items in a view. For example, text colors can be specified for messages from certain people.

❸ Add field to the view.

❹ Remove field from the view.

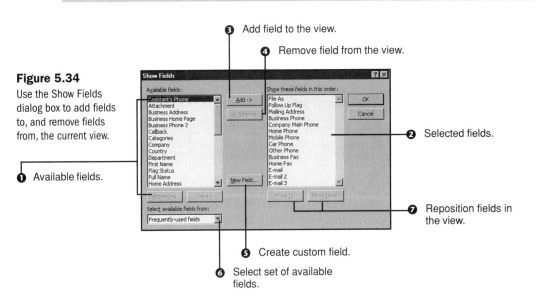

Figure 5.34
Use the Show Fields dialog box to add fields to, and remove fields from, the current view.

❷ Selected fields.

❶ Available fields.

❼ Reposition fields in the view.

❺ Create custom field.

❻ Select set of available fields.

① Open the drop-down list and
select a first-level grouping.

Figure 5.35

Use the Group By dialog
box to select fields by
which items in an
Information viewer are
to be grouped. This is
available only in table
and timeline views.

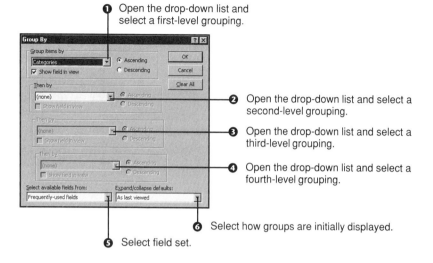

② Open the drop-down list and select a
second-level grouping.

③ Open the drop-down list and select a
third-level grouping.

④ Open the drop-down list and select a
fourth-level grouping.

⑥ Select how groups are initially displayed.

⑤ Select field set.

① Open the drop-down list and
select a first-level sorting.

Figure 5.36

Use the Sort dialog box
to select fields by which
items in an Information
viewer are to be sorted.

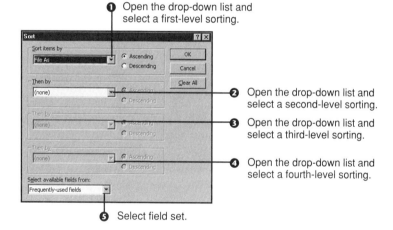

② Open the drop-down list and
select a second-level sorting.

③ Open the drop-down list and
select a third-level sorting.

④ Open the drop-down list and
select a fourth-level sorting.

⑤ Select field set.

4 Use this tab to specify categories and other item properties.

5 Use this tab to specify advanced criteria.

Figure 5.37

Use the Filter dialog box to specify how items are to be filtered. This dialog box has three tabs, the first of which is named according to the type of items in the current Information viewer.

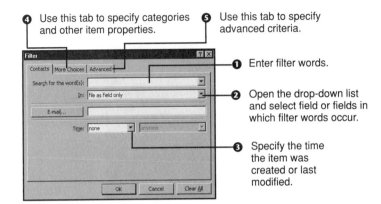

1 Enter filter words.

2 Open the drop-down list and select field or fields in which filter words occur.

3 Specify the time the item was created or last modified.

Figure 5.38

Use the Other Settings dialog box to specify fonts to be used in a view.

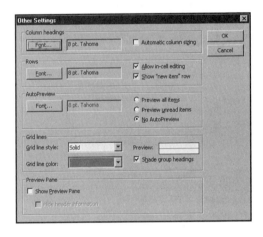

1 Enable or disable rules to use.

Figure 5.39

Use the Automatic Formatting dialog box to specify rules that control how items are displayed in a view.

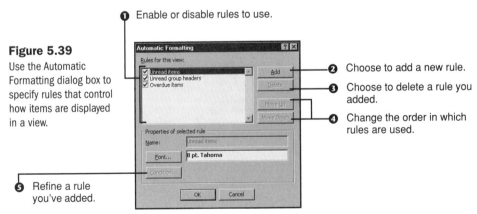

2 Choose to add a new rule.

3 Choose to delete a rule you added.

4 Change the order in which rules are used.

5 Refine a rule you've added.

View ⇒ Current View ⇒ Define Views

Choose **View**, **Current View**, **Define Views** to display the Define Views dialog box (shown in Figure 5.40).

Figure 5.40
Use the Define Views dialog box to define a new view.

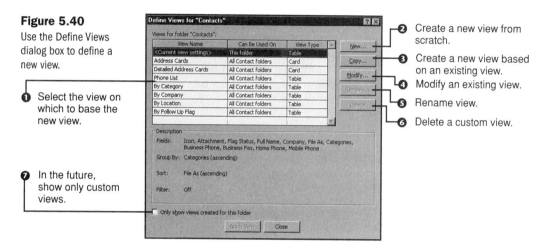

❶ Select the view on which to base the new view.

❷ Create a new view from scratch.

❸ Create a new view based on an existing view.

❹ Modify an existing view.

❺ Rename view.

❻ Delete a custom view.

❼ In the future, show only custom views.

In this view, you can

- Choose **New** to create a custom view from scratch.
- Choose **Copy** to create a custom view based on an existing view.
- Choose **Modify** to modify an existing view.
- Choose **Rename** to rename a custom view. You can't rename a view supplied with Outlook.
- Choose **Reset** to reset a view supplied with Outlook to its original configuration. You can't reset a custom view.
- Choose **Delete** to delete a custom view. You can't delete a view supplied with Outlook.
- Choose **Only show views created in this folder** to set Outlook so that only custom views are available when a user chooses **View**, **Custom View**.

View ⇒ Outlook Bar

Choose **View**, **Outlook Bar** to hide the Outlook bar if it is displayed, or to display the Outlook Bar if it is hidden.

View ⇒ Folder List

Choose **View**, **Folder List** to display the folder list if it is hidden, or to hide the folder list if it is displayed. You can also hide the folder list by clicking the **x** at the right end of the displayed folder list's title bar.

Depending on the information services in your profile, you may have one or more top-level folders in your folder list, each containing several subsidiary folders. The top-level folders may be expanded or collapsed. If a top-level folder is collapsed, click the + (plus) at the left side of the folder name to expand it so that you can see its subsidiary folders. If a top-level folder is expanded, click the – (minus) at the left of the folder name to collapse it so that the subsidiary folders are hidden.

One of the top-level folders in your folder list is the currently active one in which Outlook automatically saves items. This folder is indicated on the list by an image of a house superimposed on its icon in the list. (See **Delivering Information**, page 602, later in this chapter for information about changing the currently active top-level folder.)

<u>V</u>iew ➡ <u>Day</u>

This view is available only if the Day/Week/Month view of the Calendar Information Viewer or a timeline view of the Journal Information viewer is selected. Choose **<u>V</u>iew**, **<u>D</u>ay** to display a day view of the calendar or journal such as that shown in Figure 5.41.

❷ Date Navigator.

Figure 5.41
This is a typical Day view of a calendar.

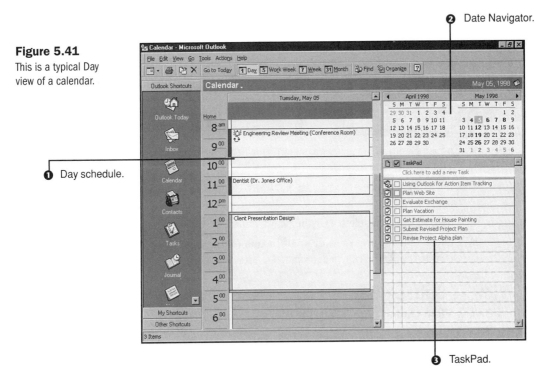

❶ Day schedule.

❸ TaskPad.

View ➤ Work Week

This view is available only if the Day/Week/Month view in the Calendar Information viewer is selected. Choose **View**, **Work Week** to display a work week view of the calendar such as that shown in Figure 5.42.

Figure 5.42
This is a typical Work Week view of a calendar.

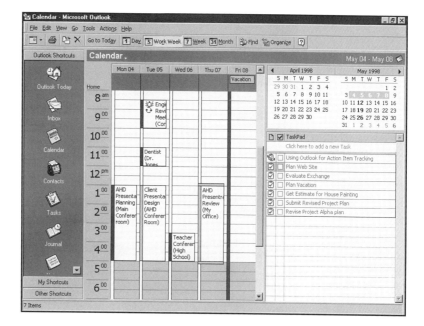

View ➤ Week

This view is available only if the Day/Week/Month view of the Calendar Information viewer or a timeline view of the Journal Information viewer is selected. Choose **View**, **Week** to display a week view of the calendar or journal such as that shown in Figure 5.43.

View ➤ Month

This view is available only if the Day/Week/Month view of the Calendar Information viewer or a timeline view of the Journal Information viewer is selected. Choose **View**, **Month** to display a month view of the calendar or journal such as that shown in Figure 5.44.

Figure 5.43

This is a typical Week view of a calendar.

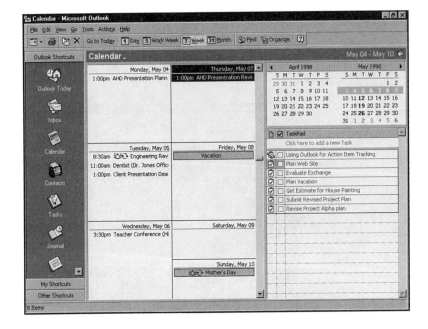

Figure 5.44

This is a typical Month view of a calendar.

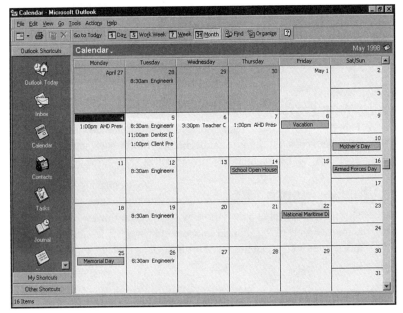

View ➥ TaskPad View

This view is available only when the Day/Week/Month view of the Calendar Information viewer is selected. Choose **View, TaskPad View** to display the following list of Taskpad views.

Taskpad views

View Name	Purpose
All Tasks	Display all tasks.
Today's Tasks	Display today's tasks.
Active Tasks for Selected Days	Tasks that are active for days selected in the Date Navigator.
Tasks for Next Seven Days	Tasks that are active for the next seven days.
Overdue Tasks	Tasks that are currently overdue.
Tasks Completed on Selected Days	Tasks that were completed on days selected in the Date Navigator.

By default, task views that refer to tasks by date include tasks that have no due date. To exclude tasks with no due date, choose **View, Include Tasks With No Due Date** to remove the check mark.

View ➥ Preview Pane

Although this menu item is available with most Information viewers, it is relevant only with the Inbox, Deleted Items, Drafts, Outbox, or Sent Items Information viewer selected. Choose **View, Preview Pane** to split the Information viewer into two panes. The lower pane shows details of the item selected in the upper pane. Make the same choice to hide the lower pane. Figure 5.1 shows the Inbox Information viewer with the Preview pane displayed.

When Outlook receives a digitally signed or sealed (encrypted) message, the preview pane doesn't display the contents of that message. Displaying such a message in the preview pane would defeat the purpose of signing or sealing the message.

View ➥ AutoPreview

Although available when certain other Information viewers are selected, this is principally useful when the Inbox Information viewer is selected. With the current view of the Inbox Information viewer set to Messages with AutoPreview, choose **View, AutoPreview**. Now, unread messages in the Inbox are displayed showing a header line and the first three lines of text; only the header line is shown for messages you've read. Make the same choice again to display only the header line for all messages.

<u>V</u>iew ➥ E<u>x</u>pand/Collapse Groups

This is available only when the selected view for an Information viewer displays items in groups.

Choose <u>V</u>iew, E<u>x</u>pand/Collapse Groups to display a menu.

Expand/Collapse Groups menu items	
Menu Item	**Purpose**
<u>C</u>ollapse This Group	Collapse the group selected in the Information viewer.
<u>E</u>xpand This Group	Expand the group selected in the Information viewer.
Collapse All	Collapse all groups.
Expand All	Expand all groups.

<u>V</u>iew ➥ <u>T</u>oolbars

Choose <u>V</u>iew, <u>T</u>oolbars to display a menu with the options in the following table.

Toolbars menu	
Menu Item	**Purpose**
Standard	Choose to hide or display the Standard toolbar.
Advanced	Choose to hide or display the Advanced toolbar. This toolbar contains supplementary buttons that are principally of interest to advanced Outlook users.
Remote	Choose to hide or display the Remote toolbar (available only when the Inbox, Deleted Items, Drafts, Outbox, or Sent Items Information viewer is selected). This toolbar contains buttons that are useful when you're using Outlook for remote e-mail.
<u>C</u>ustomize	Choose to display the Customize dialog box, which you can use to customize a toolbar or the menu bar.

<u>V</u>iew ➥ <u>S</u>tatus Bar

Choose <u>V</u>iew, <u>S</u>tatus Bar to hide or display the status bar at the bottom of the Outlook window.

Go

You can use the Go menu to move backwards and forwards among Information viewers you've previously selected, to select the folder that contains the items displayed by Information viewers, to select an Information viewer, and to access newsgroups, open your Web browser, and start an Internet Call.

Go ➥ Back

Choose **Go**, **Back** to select the Information viewer that was selected immediately before the one currently displayed during the present Outlook session. You can choose this command repeatedly to move back through a sequence of previously selected Information viewers.

This command is not available when you first open Outlook because, at that time, you have not previously selected Information viewers.

Go ➥ Forward

After you have chosen **Go**, **Back** to select a previously selected Information viewer, you can choose **Go**, **Forward** to return to the Information viewer that was selected prior to choosing **Go**, **Back**. You can choose this command repeatedly to move forward through a sequence of previously selected Information viewers.

This command is not available when you first open Outlook. It only becomes available after you have selected two or more Information viewers in the current Outlook session and have chosen **Go**, **Back**.

Go ➥ Up One Level

Choose **Go**, **Up One Level** to open the folder one level above the currently open folder. This command is useful only if you have created a hierarchy of folders and are currently accessing a folder that is at least one level below a top-level folder. If you are currently accessing a top-level folder, this command is still available in the menu. When you choose the command, Outlook displays a message that reads: You are at the highest level. There are no folders above this one.

Go ➥ Go to Folder

Choose **Go**, **Go to Folder** to display the Go To Folder dialog box (shown in Figure 5.45) in which you can choose any folder within your hierarchy of folders. If you are using Outlook as a client for Exchange Server, you can use this command to access Public Folders.

Quick Choices   *GO TO FOLDER*

■   You can also press **Ctrl+Y** to display the Go to Folder dialog box.

Figure 5.45
Use the Go To Folder
dialog box to select a
folder and display items
in that folder in the
Information viewer.

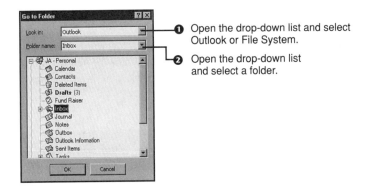

❶ Open the drop-down list and select
Outlook or File System.

❷ Open the drop-down list
and select a folder.

Go ➥ Outlook Today

Choose **Go**, **Outlook Today** to select the Outlook Today Information viewer. This command
has the same effect as clicking the Outlook Today shortcut in the Outlook Shortcuts section of
the Outlook Bar.

Go ➥ Inbox

Choose **Go**, **Inbox** to select the Inbox Information viewer. This command has the same effect
as clicking the Inbox shortcut in the Outlook Shortcuts section of the Outlook Bar.

Quick Choices *GO TO INBOX*

■ You can also press **Ctrl+Shift+I** to display the Inbox Information viewer.

Go ➥ Drafts

Choose **Go**, **Drafts** to select the Drafts Information viewer. This command has the same effect
as clicking the Drafts shortcut in the My Shortcuts section of the Outlook Bar.

Go ➥ Calendar

Choose **Go**, **Calendar** to select the Calendar Information viewer. This command has the same
effect as clicking the Calendar shortcut in the Outlook Shortcuts section of the Outlook Bar.

Go ➥ Contacts

Choose **Go**, **Contacts** to select the Inbox Information viewer. This command has the same
effect as clicking the Contacts shortcut in the Outlook Shortcuts section of the Outlook Bar.

Go ➥ Tasks

Choose Go, **Tasks** to select the Tasks Information viewer. This command has the same effect
as clicking the Tasks shortcut in the Outlook Shortcuts section of the Outlook Bar.

Go ➥ News

Choose **Go**, **News** to select your default newsreader. If you have not set up a different newsreader, Outlook opens the Outlook Newsreader shown in the Outlook Express News Information viewer. You can use this Information viewer (shown in Figure 5.46) to access Internet Newsgroups. Choose **File**, **Exit** in this Information viewer to return to the most recently selected Outlook Information viewer.

Figure 5.46

Use the Outlook Express News Information viewer to access Internet newsgroups.

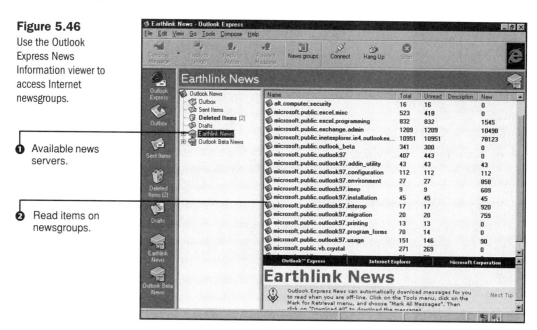

❶ Available news servers.

❷ Read items on newsgroups.

Go ➥ Web Browser

Choose **Go**, **Web Browser** to open your Web browser to access Web sites. If your browser is Internet Explorer, choose **File**, **Close** to close the browser and return to the most recently selected Outlook Information viewer.

Although you must install Internet Explorer before you can install Outlook, you can subsequently use a different browser to access the Internet.

Go ➥ Internet Call

Choose **Go**, **Internet Call** to begin communicating with someone by way of the Internet. Choose either

- **From Address Book** to select an Internet address from one of your address books
- **Internet Call** to open Microsoft NetMeeting to place and manage your call

Tools

The Tools menu provides access to a variety of Outlook facilities including:

- Manually sending and receiving messages from various mail servers
- Managing address books
- Finding and organizing information items
- Creating rules
- Using facilities available in specific information services
- Managing forms
- Installing, modifying, and deleting information services
- Setting Outlook's options

Tools ➥ Send

Choose **Tools**, **Send** to immediately send the current item. You must previously select the Inbox, Deleted Items, Drafts, Outbox, or Send Items Information viewers.

Tools ➥ Send and Receive

Use this command to manually send and receive messages. You must previously select the Inbox, Calendar, Deleted Items, Drafts, Outbox, or Send Items Information viewer.

If you're using the Corporate/Workgroup Outlook configuration, move the pointer onto **Tools**, **Send and Receive** to display a menu that lists the information services in your profile that can be used to send and receive messages. This list may include the following:

- The name of dial-up networking phonebook entry you use to access an Internet account or remote mailbox
- Microsoft Mail (if you have the Microsoft Mail information service in your profile)
- Microsoft Exchange Server (if you have the Microsoft Exchange Server information service in your profile)
- Fax Mail Transport (if you have the Fax Mail Transport information service installed in your profile) or a different fax information service

Several other information services may be listed. In this list, choose any information service to cause Outlook to immediately attempt to send all messages in the Outbox appropriate for that information service and also to receive any waiting messages.

In addition to choosing an individual information account, you can choose **All Accounts**. When you do this, Outlook accesses all accounts to which you are currently connected; however, it accesses only the first account that requires a dial-up connection.

If you're using the Internet Only Outlook configuration when you choose **Tools, Send and Receive**, you see a list of accounts. By default, these accounts include your own Internet account, a general Internet mail account, and the Symantec Winfax Starter Edition account. You can choose one of these accounts to work with Internet e-mail or to send faxes.

Tools ➡ Synchronize

This command is available only if you're using the Corporate/Workgroup Outlook configuration and you have the Microsoft Exchange Server information service in your profile.

You can copy folders from Exchange Server to your computer and use these folders remotely while you're not connected to the server. The folders on your computer are known as offline folders.

Choose **Tools, Synchronize** to update offline folders and server folders so that the most recent information is available on both. In the menu, choose from the following:

- **All Folders** to synchronize all offline folders
- **This Folder** to synchronize one selected offline folder
- **Download Address Book** to update the address book on your computer with the one on the server

Tools ➡ Remote Mail

You can use remote mail to send messages to and receive messages from a mail server. The mail server can be Exchange Server or another mail server. This is only available if you have installed the Corporate/Workgroup Outlook configuration.

Choose **Tools, Remote Mail** to display a menu with the following:

Remote mail menu

Menu Item	Purpose
Connect	Open the Remote Connection Wizard in which you can choose the remote mail service to which you want to connect.
Disconnect	Disconnect from the remote mail service to which you are currently connected.
Mark to Retrieve	After connecting to a remote mail service, mark the message you want to retrieve.
Mark to Retrieve a Copy	After connecting to a remote mail service, mark the message you want to copy, leaving the original message on the server.

continues

Continued

Menu Item	Purpose
Delete	After connecting to a remote mail service and selecting a message, delete the message.
U**n**mark	After connecting to a remote mail service and marking a message, unmark that message.
U**n**mark All	After connecting to a remote mail service, unmark all messages.
Remote Tools	Display the Remote toolbar.

Tools → Address Book

Choose **Tools**, **Address Book** to display the Address Book dialog box (shown in Figure 5.47) in which you can access information in any of your address books.

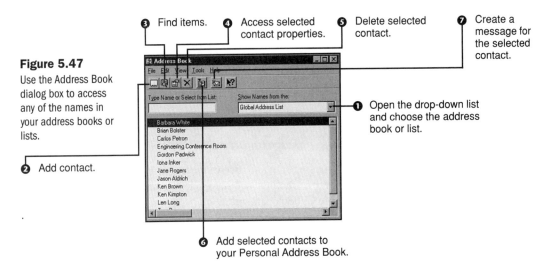

Figure 5.47
Use the Address Book dialog box to access any of the names in your address books or lists.

❸ Find items. **❹** Access selected contact properties. **❺** Delete selected contact. **❼** Create a message for the selected contact.

❶ Open the drop-down list and choose the address book or list.

❷ Add contact.

❻ Add selected contacts to your Personal Address Book.

Quick Choices *ADDRESS BOOK*

- Alternatively, press **Ctrl+Shift+B** to open the Address Book dialog box.

You can select a specific address book, and then add contacts to it, delete contacts from it, or edit information about an existing contact.

Tools → Find

With any Information viewer displayed, choose **Tools**, **Find** to display a pane such as that shown in Figure 5.48 in which you can define what you want to find within the folder displayed by that Information viewer. For example, if you have the Inbox Information viewer displayed, enter the text you want to find in messages into the **Look for** box and then choose **Find Now**.

Outlook searches the messages in your Inbox and displays a list of those that contain the text you specified.

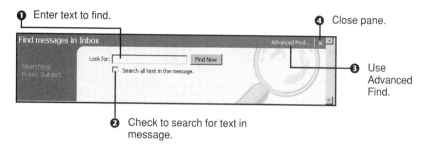

Figure 5.48
Use the Find pane to specify information you want to find. The Find pane shown here is displayed when you're using the Inbox Information viewer. If you have a different Information viewer selected, the Find pane is somewhat different.

By default, with the Inbox viewer selected, Outlook looks for the text you specified in the subject and text of the message. If you want to search only in the subject of the message, remove the check mark from **Search all text in the message**.

After the search is complete, Outlook offers the following:

- **Go to Advanced Find**. Choose this to open the Advanced Find dialog box described in the next section.
- **Clear Search**. Choose this to clear the display of found items and return to the previously displayed Information Viewer.

Double-click any found item to display the details of that item in a form.

When you've finished using Find, click the **x** at the right end of the Find Messages pane to hide that pane. Alternatively, you can click **Advanced Find** in the title bar to open the Advanced Find dialog box described in the next section.

<u>T</u>ools ➥ A<u>d</u>vanced Find

Choose **<u>T</u>ools**, **A<u>d</u>vanced Find** to display the Advanced Find dialog box (shown in Figure 5.49) in which you can create a detailed specification of items you want to find.

Quick **Choices**   *ADVANCED FIND*

- Alternatively, press **Ctrl+Shift+F** to open the Advanced Find dialog box.

The top part of this form contains the **Loo<u>k</u> for** box that identifies the type of item you're looking for. If you have the Inbox Information viewer selected when you start, this box contains "Messages"—the type of item in the Inbox.

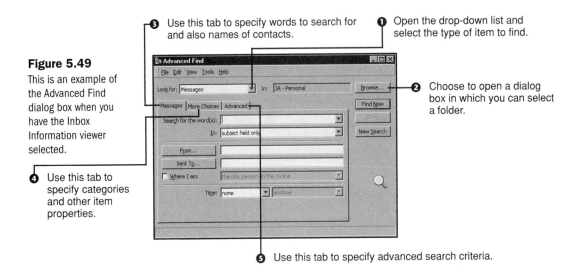

Figure 5.49

This is an example of the Advanced Find dialog box when you have the Inbox Information viewer selected.

❸ Use this tab to specify words to search for and also names of contacts.

❶ Open the drop-down list and select the type of item to find.

❷ Choose to open a dialog box in which you can select a folder.

❹ Use this tab to specify categories and other item properties.

❺ Use this tab to specify advanced search criteria.

If you want to look for a different type of item, Open the **Look for** list. You can choose from among the following:

- Any type of Outlook item
- Appointments and Meetings
- Contacts
- Files
- Files (Outlook/Exchange)
- Journal Entries
- Messages
- Notes
- Tasks

The top part of the dialog box also identifies the folder in which you want to search. If you start from the Inbox Information viewer, Outlook initially assumes you want to search in the Inbox folder. If you want to search in a different folder, choose **Browse** to open the Select Folders dialog box in which you can specify any folder in your Outlook folder structure.

The Advanced Find dialog box also contains a subform with three tabs, the first of which has the name of the type of item in the currently selected Information viewer. For example, if you have the Inbox Information viewer selected, the first tab is labeled "Messages." The other two tabs are labeled "More Choices" and "Advanced." The following sections assume you're starting from the Inbox Information viewer.

When you're using Advanced Find, remember that Outlook takes account of whatever is specified in all three tabs, even though only one tab is visible at a time. With any of the three tabs displayed, you can choose **New Search** to remove all the search criteria in all three tabs. Outlook ignores all search criteria that are not specified.

The Inbox Tab

The first tab contains the name of the type of items in the current Information viewer—Messages in this case. The layout of this tab is somewhat different according to the Information viewer you have selected. If you have the Inbox Information viewer selected, the tab provides boxes in which you can specify the following:

- Words to search for
- The fields in which to search
- Whom the message is from
- Whom the message is sent to
- Your involvement with the message
- Any time constrictions on the message you want to search for

If you have a different Information viewer selected, or select a different type of item to search for, the tab asks for different types of information.

More Choices

The More Choices tab is shown in Figure 5.50.

Figure 5.50

Use the More Choices tab to specify additional find criteria.

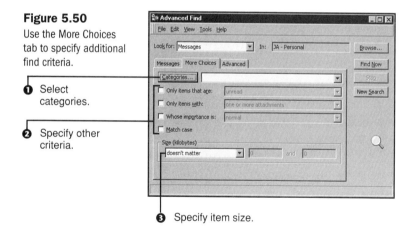

❶ Select categories.

❷ Specify other criteria.

❸ Specify item size.

You can use this tab to specify the following:

- One or more item categories.
- Specific conditions about an item. (These vary according to the type of item you're searching for.)
- Whether any text you're searching for should match case with the text in items (uppercase or lowercase).
- Lower and upper limits of size of the item you're searching for.

Advanced

You can use the Advanced tab (shown in Figure 5.51) to specify one or more criteria for various fields in items.

Figure 5.51

Use the Advanced tab to specify more search criteria.

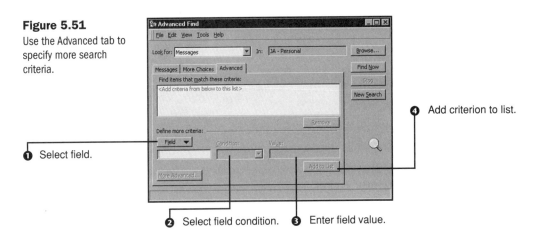

❶ Select field.

❷ Select field condition.   ❸ Enter field value.

❹ Add criterion to list.

To set the Advanced Find options, do the following:

1. Choose **Field** to open a list of field types, and point onto one of those types to display a list of fields.
2. Choose the field for which you want to specify a criterion.
3. Open the **Conditions** drop-down list to display a list of conditions and choose a condition.
4. If the condition you've chosen requires a value, enter a value in the **Value** box.
5. Choose **Add to List** to place the criterion in the **Find Items that match these criteria** box.
6. Repeat Steps 1 through 5 to create additional search criteria.

When you've finished specifying search criteria in the three tabs, choose **Find Now** to initiate the search. Outlook displays the result of the search in an Information viewer. Double-click any item in that Information viewer to display its details in a form.

Tools ➥ Organize

With this command, you can organize your Outlook items in several ways. (This command is not available when you have the Outlook Today Information viewer displayed.) The following available ways to organize depend on the types of items with which you're dealing:

- By moving selected items to specific folders or subfolders
- By displaying and printing items that satisfy certain criteria in specific colors
- By specifying rules that automatically place certain kinds of incoming messages in specific folders or subfolders, or by automatically deleting them
- By creating categories for specific types of items

You can also use the Organize command to change the current view of items.

After you've finished using the Organize pane, close it by choosing the **x** at the right end of the pane's title bar.

Moving Items to Specific Folders

Instead of keeping all items of a specific type in one folder, you can create any number of folders and move specific items to those folders. For example, instead of keeping all inbox items in the Inbox folder, you can organize your tasks by project. You can use the method outlined here to organize other types of items in specific folders. You can use the same method to move other types of items to specific folders.

Follow these steps to move specific inbox items into a separate folder:

1. Open the Inbox Information viewer and select the tasks you want to move to another folder.

2. Choose **Tools**, **Organize** to display the **Ways to Organize Inbox** pane (shown in Figure 5.52).

① Select the target folder.

Figure 5.52
You can use the Ways to Organize Inbox pane to organize tasks in several ways.

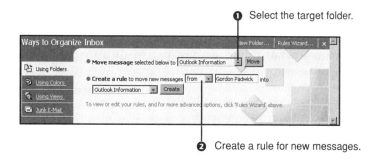

② Create a rule for new messages.

3. Choose **Using Folders** at the left side of the pane.

4. Open the **Move message selected below to** drop-down list to display a list of some of your folders.

5. If the name of the folder to which you want to move the selected messages is displayed, select that folder. If it isn't displayed, choose **Other folder** to display the Select Folder dialog box in which you can select any of your folders and subfolders.

6. With the target folder selected, choose **Move** to move the selected messages to that folder.

You can also choose New Folder in the pane's title bar to open the Create New Folder dialog box in which you can create a new folder or subfolder.

Assigning Categories to Items

You can assign categories to items when you create items and you can assign categories subsequently by individually opening items one at a time. The Organize command provides a way to assign one category to any number of items simultaneously. The following steps refer to task items, but you can use the same method for other types of items.

1. Open the Information viewer and select items to which you want to assign a category.
2. Choose **Tools**, **Organize** to display the **Ways to Organize Tasks** pane.
3. Choose **Using Categories** at the left side of the pane.
4. Open the **Add tasks selected below to** drop-down list and choose the category you want to assign to the selected items.
5. Choose **Add** to assign the category to the selected items.

After Step 3 you can, if you like, add a new category to your personal master category list. To do so, enter that category in the **Create a new category called** box, and choose **Create**. The name of the new category appears in the **Add tasks selected below to** box. Choose **Add** if you want to assign the new category to the selected items.

Changing the Current View

You can use the Organize command to change the view of items. The following steps are described in terms of the Tasks Information viewer, but you can use the same method for other Information viewers.

1. With any Information viewer selected, choose **Tools**, **Organize** to display the Ways to Organize Tasks pane.
2. Choose **Using Views** at the left side of the pane. Outlook displays a partial list of the views available. If necessary, use the scrollbar at the right side of the list to locate a specific view.
3. Select a view from the list. The Information viewer pane immediately changes to the new view.

You can choose **Customize Current View** in the pane's title bar to open the View Summary dialog box in which you can modify the current view.

Tools ➥ Rules Wizard

You can use the Rules Wizard to create rules that control how Outlook handles messages you receive and send. This command is available only when you have the Inbox, Deleted Items, Drafts, Outbox, or Sent Items Information viewer selected.

Using the Rules Wizard to Create New Rules

Choose **Tools**, **Rules Wizard** to start creating rules or to examine existing rules. The wizard's first window opens as shown in Figure 5.53. If you have previously created rules, those rules are listed. Otherwise, the list of rules is empty.

To create a rule, do the following:

1. Choose **New** to see a list of types of rules. Select any rule in the list to see a description of that rule. After you've selected a type of rule, choose **Next** to display the wizard's second window.
2. This window contains a list of conditions available for the type of rule you selected in the first window. The description box initially contains a description of the type of rule you

chose in Step 1. Place a check box next to one or more of the conditions. Each time you check a condition, Outlook adds a description of that condition to the description of the rule in the lower box. After you've chosen the appropriate conditions, choose **Next** to display the third window.

Figure 5.53

Use the Rules Wizard to create rules for how Outlook handles messages.

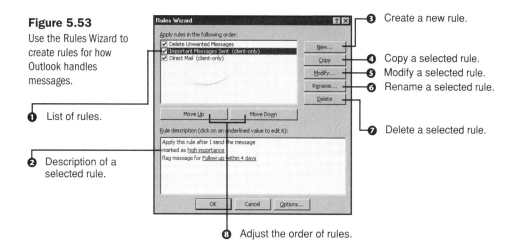

❸ Create a new rule.

❹ Copy a selected rule.
❺ Modify a selected rule.
❻ Rename a selected rule.

❶ List of rules.

❼ Delete a selected rule.

❷ Description of a selected rule.

❽ Adjust the order of rules.

Some conditions contain underlined words displayed in blue. These conditions require additional information you must supply. After you've chosen such a condition and a description of that condition appears in the description box, click the underlined text in the description. Outlook opens a dialog box in which you can select or supply the required additional information. The information you supply replaces the original underlined text in the description box.

3. Use the third window to choose what you want to do with a message that satisfies the rule defined in Steps 1 and 2. Place a check mark next to one or more of the available actions. Each time you check an action, Outlook adds a description of that action to the description of the rule in the lower box. After you've chosen appropriate actions, choose **Next** to display the fourth window.

Many actions contain underlined words displayed in blue. These actions require additional information you must supply. After you've chosen such an action and a description of that action appears in the description box, click the underlined text in the description. Outlook opens a dialog box in which you can select or supply the required additional information. The information you supply replaces the original underlined text in the description box.

4. In the fourth window, you can specify any exceptions to the conditions under which the rule you've specified should be acted on. You don't have to choose any exceptions. If you do check one or more exceptions, a description of these exceptions is added to the description of the rule. After you've chosen any required exceptions, choose **Next** to open the fifth window.

Some exceptions contain underlined words displayed in blue. These exceptions require additional information you must supply. After you've chosen such an exception and a description of that exception appears in the description box, click the underlined text in the description. Outlook opens a dialog box in which you can select or supply the required additional information.

5. Enter a name for the new rule in the fifth window. Make sure **Turn on this rule** is checked; otherwise, Outlook won't use the rule. Verify the full description of the rule as it appears in the description box. If you're satisfied defining the rule, choose **Finish** to display the name of the rule in the first wizard window.

   If you need to correct any aspect of the rule, choose **Back** one or more times to return to any of the previous wizard windows, make the correction, and choose **Next** as many times as necessary to return to the final window.

6. Repeat steps 1 through 5 to create additional rules. Each rule you create is listed in the first wizard window.

After you've created several rules, you can use the buttons at the right side and bottom edge of the first wizard window to manipulate those rules:

Rules Wizard buttons

Button Name	Purpose
New	Create a new rule from scratch.
Copy	Create a new rule by copying an existing rule, and then modifying the copy.
Modify	Modify an existing rule.
Rename	Rename an existing rule.
Delete	Delete an existing rule.
Move Up	Move a rule up one position in the list of rules.
Move Down	Move a rule down one position in the list of rules.

Outlook executes rules in the order they are listed. You must make sure your rules are listed in the order that achieves your intended objective.

Exporting and Importing Rules

You can export rules you've created to a file and you can import rules that you or someone else has created from a file. Choose **Tools**, **Rules Wizard** to open the first wizard window that contains a list of rules, if any, in Outlook. To export a set of rules as a file, do the following:

1. Choose **Options** to display the Options dialog box shown in Figure 5.54.

2. Choose **Export Rules** to display the Save Exported Rules as dialog box (shown in Figure 5.55).

3. Navigate to the folder in which you want to save the rules file.

4. Enter a name for the rules file in the **File Name** box.

5. Choose **Save** to save the file. Outlook saves the file with the filename extension .RWZ.

Figure 5.54

Use the Options dialog box to choose what you want to do.

❶ Update rules on Exchange Server.

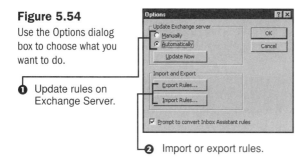

❷ Import or export rules.

❶ Navigate to a folder.

Figure 5.55

Use the Save Exported Rules as dialog box to choose where you want to save your set of rules and to give the set a filename.

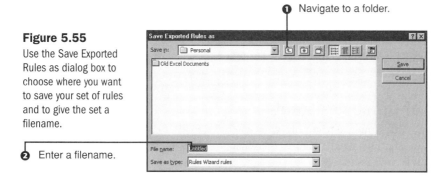

❷ Enter a filename.

To import a set of rules from a file, do the following:

1. Choose **Options** to display the Options dialog box (refer to Figure 5.54).

2. Choose **Import Rules** to display the Import Rules from dialog box (shown in Figure 5.56).

Figure 5.56

Use the Import Rules from dialog box to select the set of rules you want to import.

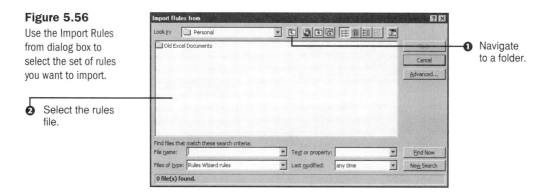

❶ Navigate to a folder.

❷ Select the rules file.

3. Navigate to the folder that contains the rules file.

4. Select the rules file.

5. Choose **Open** to import the file.

Updating Rules on Exchange Server

The information in this section applies only if you have installed the Corporate/Workgroup Outlook configuration, have the Microsoft Exchange Server information service in your profile, and you are using an Exchange Server store as the place where your messages are saved. Under these circumstances, many of the rules you create in Outlook can be copied to your Exchange Server so that the actions specified in those rules occur on Exchange Server instead of on your local computer. These rules are acted on even when your computer isn't turned on.

To update rules on Exchange Server, do the following:

1. Choose **Options** to display the Options dialog box (refer to Figure 5.54).

2. In the Update Exchange server section of the dialog box, choose **Manually** if you want to control when the rules on Exchange Server are updated, or choose **Automatically** if you want any changes you make to your rules automatically copied to Exchange Server.

3. If you chose **Manually** in Step 2, choose **Update Now** whenever you want to update rules on your Exchange Server.

Tools ➥ Out of Office Assistant

The information in this section applies only when you're using the Corporate/Workgroup Outlook configuration, you have the Microsoft Exchange Server information service in your profile, and you save your messages in an Exchange Server store.

The Out of Office Assistant is a specific rule running on Exchange Server that automatically sends a reply to messages you receive while you are out of the office.

Choose **Tools**, **Out of Office Assistant** to display the Out of Office Assistant dialog box (shown in Figure 5.57).

❶ Choose whether you're in or out of the office.

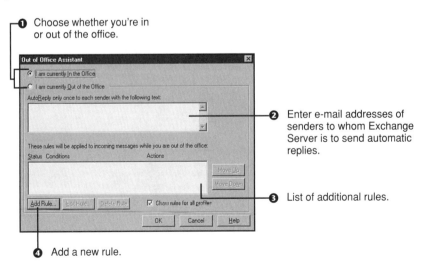

Figure 5.57

Use the Out of Office Assistant dialog box to indicate to Outlook whether you're In or Out and, if you're out, what Exchange is to do with messages addressed to you.

❷ Enter e-mail addresses of senders to whom Exchange Server is to send automatic replies.

❸ List of additional rules.

❹ Add a new rule.

Choose one of the following:

- **I am currently in the office** if you want to receive messages in the normal manner
- **I am currently out of the office** if you want Exchange Server to send an automatic response to messages sent to you

After you make the second choice, enter text for the automatic response in the upper text box. You can also, if you want, create additional rules that define actions that Exchange Server is to take when you are out of the office. For example, you might want to create a rule that directs Exchange Server to forward certain kinds of messages to specific people. To create rules such as this, display the Edit Rule dialog box in which you can define conditions and actions.

Tools ➥ Microsoft Mail Tools

The information in this section applies only if you have the Microsoft Mail information service in your profile and have an e-mail account on a Microsoft Mail post office.

Move the mouse pointer onto **Tools**, **Microsoft Mail Tools** to display a menu with the following:

Microsoft Mail tools menu

Menu Item	Purpose
Change Mailbox Password	Display a dialog box in which you can change your Microsoft Mail post office password.
Download Address Lists	Download address lists from the Microsoft Mail post office to your computer.
Schedule Remote Mail Delivery	Display a dialog box in which you can inspect the current remote mail delivery schedule or create a new one.
Set Dialing Location	Display a dialog box in which you can select a dialing location or create a new one.
View Session Log	Display a log of your Microsoft Mail sessions in Windows Notepad.

Tools ➥ Empty "Deleted Items" Folder

Whenever you delete items or subfolders from any folder except the Deleted Items folder, Outlook moves those items to the Deleted Items folder. You can permanently delete items from the Deleted Items folder, or you can use this command to permanently delete all items from the Deleted Items folder.

Choose **Tools**, **Empty "Deleted Items" Folder**. Outlook displays a message that reads: Are you sure you want to permanently delete all the items and subfolders in the "Delete Items" folder? Choose **Yes** or **No**.

Tools ➜ Recover Deleted Items

This capability is available only if you are using Outlook as a client for Exchange version 5.5 or later, if you save your Outlook items in an Exchange Server store, and the Exchange Server administrator has enabled the capability to recover deleted items.

Choose **Tools, Recover Deleted Items** to display a list of deleted items. Select the items you want to retrieve, and then choose **Recover Selected Items**.

Tools ➜ Forms

Move the mouse pointer onto **Tools, Forms** if you want to choose a special form such as one provided by an Outlook Add-In, or if you want to design a form. Outlook displays a menu:

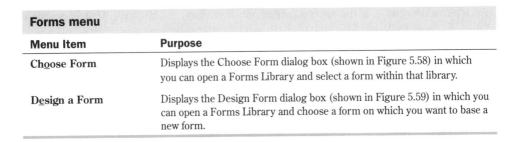

Forms menu	
Menu Item	**Purpose**
Choose Form	Displays the Choose Form dialog box (shown in Figure 5.58) in which you can open a Forms Library and select a form within that library.
Design a Form	Displays the Design Form dialog box (shown in Figure 5.59) in which you can open a Forms Library and choose a form on which you want to base a new form.

Figure 5.58
Use the Choose Form dialog box to select the form you want to use.

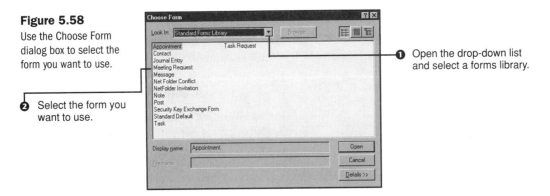

❶ Open the drop-down list and select a forms library.

❷ Select the form you want to use.

Tools ➜ Services

The Corporate/Workgroup and Internet Only configurations of Outlook uses one or more information services to access and save information. If you're using **Corporate/Workgroup** Outlook installation, you may have several information services at your disposal.

Listing Information Services

Choose **Tools, Services** to display the Services dialog box (shown in Figure 5.60). This is available only if you're using the Corporate/Workgroup Outlook configuration.

Figure 5.59

Use the Design Form dialog box to select the form on which you want to base the design of a new form.

❶ Open the drop-down list and select a forms library.

❷ Select the form you want to use as the basis of a new form.

Figure 5.60

The Services dialog box opens with the Services tab selected, showing a list of information services in your profile.

❸ Remove the selected information service.

❹ Display the properties of the selected information service.

❶ Installed information services.

❷ Add a new information service.

❺ Copy the selected information service to another profile.

❻ Display information about the selected information service.

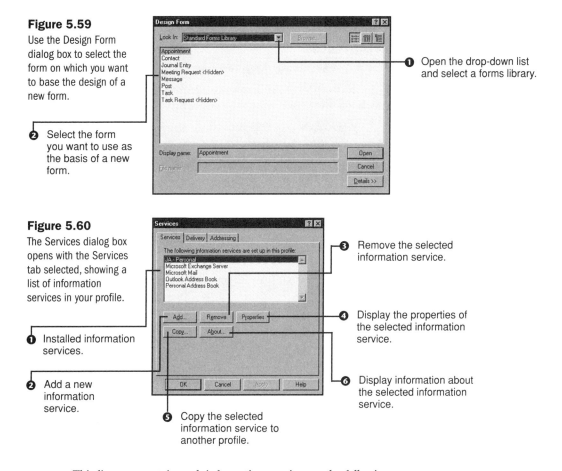

This list may contain such information services as the following:

Services dialog box options

Profile Name	Purpose
FAX Address Book	An address book that contains fax numbers
FAX Mail Transport	The functionality that sends and receives faxes by way of your modem
Internet	The functionality that sends and receives e-mail messages by way of the Internet
Microsoft Exchange Server	The functionality that provides access to Exchange Server for saving Outlook items, sending and receiving messages, and for collaborating with other people

continues

Continued

Profile Name	Purpose
Microsoft Mail	The functionality that provides access to a Microsoft Mail post office
Outlook Address Book	An address book that contains information about your contacts who have e-mail addresses or fax numbers
Personal Address Book	An address book that contains your personal list of contacts that you've created from scratch or copied from other address books
Personal Folders	The functionality Outlook can use to save items in a Personal Folders file on your computer

If you have some Outlook Add-Ins installed, you may have other information services in your profile.

Managing Information Services

With the Services dialog box's Services tab displayed, you can manage information services by choosing the following buttons:

Services tab buttons

Button Name	Purpose
Add	Add an information service to your profile. You can add one of the information services provided with Outlook or one that you've received from another source and is available on disk.
Remove	Remove an information service from your profile.
Properties	Open the Properties dialog box in which you can examine and set properties for an information service. The properties dialog box has one or more tabs, depending on the type of information service.
Copy	Copy an information service to another profile.
About	Display information about an information service.

Delivering Information

The topic of delivering information covers the following:

■ Where Outlook delivers items you create or receive

■ Which information services Outlook uses to send messages

Outlook can save items in several locations. For example, you can save Outlook items within your Personal Folders file on your own computer or, if you have access to Exchange Server, you can save items in an Exchange Server store.

To choose where Outlook saves items, choose the Services dialog box's Delivery tab and open the **Deliver** <u>n</u>**ew mail to the following location** drop-down list. Select one of the items in that list. If you have the Microsoft Exchange Server information service in your profile and want to save Outlook items in an Exchange Server store, select the location that has a name starting with Mailbox. If you want to save Outlook items in your Personal Folders file, select Personal Folders. After you change the delivery location, you must close and restart Outlook for the new location to take effect.

When you send an e-mail message, Outlook is normally smart enough to detect how the message should be sent by referring to each recipient's e-mail address. There are some circumstances, however, when there is ambiguity. Perhaps your profile contains an Internet information service and the Microsoft Exchange Server information service. When you send a message to an Internet address, do you want the message to be sent by way of the Internet information service on your computer or by way of Exchange Server's Internet service?

To resolve this problem, look at the <u>R</u>**ecipient addresses are processed by these information services in the following order** list. This list shows available information services in the order Outlook attempts to use them. You can use the two buttons (one with an up-pointing arrow and one with a down-pointing arrow) to change the order in which services are listed. If you want Internet messages to be sent by the Internet information service on your computer, make sure this service is listed above the Microsoft Exchange Transport service.

Addressing E-mail

The Corporate/Workgroup Outlook configuration can use several address books as the source of e-mail addresses, street addresses, telephone numbers, and fax numbers. These address books include the following:

Address Books

Table	Contents
Contacts	Outlook Contact items in the Contacts folder
Personal Address Book	Information you have created in, or copied into, a personal address book
Postoffice Address List	Information in the Microsoft Mail, or other e-mail system, post office
Global Address List	Information maintained by Exchange Server

You can use the Services dialog box's Addressing tab to specify how Outlook uses these, and other, sources of addresses.

The <u>S</u>**how this address list first** box contains the name of the address source Outlook initially uses when you choose **To** or **Cc** in the Messages form. Open the drop-down list to select a different address source.

The <u>K</u>**eep personal addresses in** box contains the name of the personal address book Outlook uses when you add names. You can open the drop-down list to select a different personal address book.

The **When sending mail, check names using these address lists in the following order** box contains a list of address sources Outlook uses when you enter a name in the Message form's **To** or **Cc** boxes. Choose the Check Names button on the Standard toolbar to check the validity of the name. You can change the order in which Outlook looks at address sources to validate names.

You can use the three buttons at the bottom of the Addressing tab as follows:

Addressing tab buttons

Button Name	Purpose
A**d**d	Add an address source to the list of those that can be used to validate addresses.
R**e**move	Remove an address source from the list of those that can be used to validate addresses.
P**r**operties	Display the properties of an address source.

Tools ➡ Accounts

The Internet Only Outlook configuration's **Tools** menu contains the **Accounts** menu item. Move the mouse pointer to **Tools**, **Accounts** to display the Internet Accounts dialog box that has the following three tabs:

- The All tab to display a list of available mail and news accounts
- The Mail tab to display a list of mail accounts
- The Directory Service tab to display a list of directory services

Tools ➡ Options

Outlook has many optional settings. If you install Outlook by downloading it from Microsoft or from a CD-ROM, you start off with certain default settings. If you install Outlook from your organization's LAN (Local Area Network), however, you might have completely different settings chosen by your LAN administrator.

The options available depend on which type of Outlook installation you have: **Corporate/ Workgroup**, **Internet Only**, or **No E-Mail Usage**. Also, any Outlook Add-Ins you have installed can affect the options available.

N O T E This section covers the Outlook options you most likely have available. You may not have some of those mentioned, and you may have others that are not mentioned. This section also assumes that you have installed **Corporate/Workgroup** Outlook. Options not available to **Internet Only** users are noted. Of course, if you've installed the **No E-Mail Usage** option, none of the e-mail options documented here applies to you. ∎

Choose **Tools**, **Options** to display the Options dialog box that has several tabs, the most common of which are covered in the following pages.

You are most likely concerned with only a few of Outlook's options. If you're using Outlook on a standalone computer, the options set when you install Outlook are probably what you need. If you're using Outlook as a network client, your network administrator has probably set the options appropriate for the network. In either case, you should use caution when working with Outlook's options. If you are in a network setting, it is best to ask your network administrator about changing Outlook options.

Preferences Options

Use the Preferences tab shown in Figure 5.61 to set your preferences for each of the Outlook items types.

Figure 5.61

This tab contains five sections in which you can set options for the major types of Outlook items.

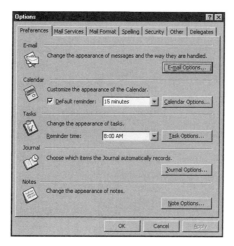

E-mail

In the E-mail section of the Preferences tab, choose **E-mail Options** to display the E-mail Options dialog box (shown in Figure 5.62), which has two sections.

The dialog box shown here is displayed by Corporate/Workgroup Outlook. Internet Only Outlook displays a similar dialog box, one difference being the addition of a check box labeled **Automatically put people I reply to in**. Also, the Internet Only dialog box does not contain the **Tracking Options** button.

Message Handling

Open the **After moving or deleting an open item** drop-down list and choose from the following:

- Open the previous item
- Open the next item
- Return to the Inbox

Figure 5.62

Use this dialog box to define how you want Outlook to handle messages.

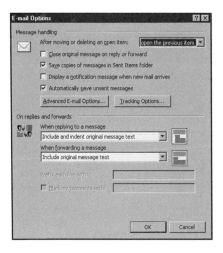

Check or uncheck the four check boxes:

- **Close original message on reply or forward**
- **Save copies of messages in Sent Items folder**
- **Display a notification message when new mail arrives**
- **Automatically save unsent messages**

Choose **Advanced E-mail Options** to display the dialog box shown in Figure 5.63 in which you can specify even more detailed actions relating to messages.

Figure 5.63

Use this dialog box to further customize how Outlook handles messages.

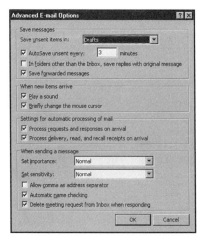

This illustration shows the dialog box displayed by Corporate/Workgroup Outlook. The equivalent Internet Only dialog box is almost identical; the check box labeled **Process delivery, read, and recall receipts on arrival** is not included because the functionality referred to depends on using Exchange as a mail server.

Choose **Tracking Options** (not available in Internet Only Outlook) to display the dialog box (shown in Figure 5.64) in which you can specify whether and how Outlook is to indicate when the messages you send are received.

Figure 5.64

Use this dialog box to request notification about message delivery.

The tracking options depend on the functionality of recipients' e-mail software and their e-mail servers. These options are primarily intended to work when people use Outlook as their e-mail client and Exchange as their mail server.

On Replies and Forwards

This section of the E-mail options dialog box deals with how you want to reply to, and forward, messages.

Open the **When replying to a message** drop-down list and choose from the following:

- Do not include original message
- Attach original message
- Include original message text
- Include and indent original message text
- Prefix each line of the original message

Open the **When forwarding a message** drop-down list and choose the following:

- Attach original message
- Include original message text
- Include and indent original message text
- Prefix each line of the original message

If you choose to prefix each line of the original message, either for messages to which you reply or for messages you forward, you can specify the character used as a prefix in the **Prefix each line with** box (but not if you're using Microsoft Word as your message format).

You can add comments to a message to which you reply or forward, and you can identify those comments with your name or other text. To change the identification, check **Mark my comments with** and enter the identification you want to use in the adjoining box.

When you reply to or forward a message, Outlook attempts to use the message format in which the original message was sent.

The Internet Only Outlook E-mail Options dialog box contains the check box labeled **Auto-matically put people I reply to in**. After you check this box, Outlook checks to see whether a contact item exists for the person to whom you're replying and, if not, creates a new contact item. You can choose **Folder** to open the Select Folder dialog box in which you select a folder other than your Contacts folder. (Refer to **Receiving a Message**, page 674, later in this chapter for information about how Corporate/Workgroup Outlook can save senders' names.)

Calendar

In the Calendar section of the Preferences tab (refer to Figure 5.61), you can choose whether or not you want Outlook to create reminders automatically. Check **Default Reminder** if you want automatic reminders. After you do check this, you can open the adjacent drop-down list and choose the period prior to calendar events that you want to be reminded.

Choose **Calendar Options** to display the dialog box shown in Figure 5.65.

Figure 5.65

The Calendar Options dialog box contains three sections.

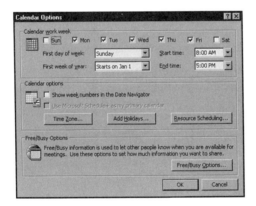

Calendar Work Week

In this section, check those days of the week you want Outlook to consider as working days. Open the **Start time** drop-down list and choose the time your working day starts. Open the **End time** drop-down list and choose the time your working day ends. The times you set in these boxes affect the Calendar Information viewer when you use the Day view.

Instead of choosing from the drop-down lists, you can enter times. You need to do so if the times you want are not in the drop-down lists.

Open the **First day of week** drop-down list and choose the day that you want the Date Navigator (displayed in the Calendar Information viewer) to show as the first day of the week.

Open the **First week of year** drop-down list and choose how you want the calendar to select the first week of the year. You can choose from the following:

- Starts on Jan 1
- First 4-day week
- First full week

Calendar Options

Check **Show week numbers in the Date Navigator** if you want weeks to be numbered.

If, when you installed Outlook on your computer, you enabled Schedule+, you can check **Use Microsoft Schedule+ as my primary calendar**, if that's what you want to do.

Choose **Time Zone** to display the dialog box (shown in Figure 5.66) in which you can select your primary time zone and, optionally, an additional time zone. In both cases, you can check a box to enable Outlook to adjust for daylight saving time. If you choose an additional time zone, Outlook shows times for both zones in the Day view of the calendar.

Figure 5.66

Use the Time Zone dialog box to specify your current time zone and, optionally, an additional time zone.

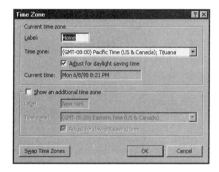

Choose **Add Holidays** if you want Outlook to automatically add holidays to your calendar; Outlook displays the dialog box shown in Figure 5.67.

Figure 5.67

Use this dialog box to select locations or cultures for which you want Outlook to create holiday items in your calendar.

You can choose one or more geographic locations or cultures and Outlook adds holidays appropriate for them. Beware, though, of the following limitations:

- Outlook adds most holidays as one-time events, not as recurring events.
- Outlook adds holidays for only a few years.
- If you choose two or more locations or cultures and the same holidays are listed for more than one of them, you have those holidays marked several times in your calendar.
- Outlooks assigns the category Holiday to all items, whether or not they really are holidays.

Instead of using **Add Holidays**, consider manually adding holidays as recurring events, and assigning appropriate categories to each of them.

Consider using the category Holiday only for those days that really are holidays, and using the category Special Day for other recognized days that are not holidays.

Alternatively, you can modify the list of holidays Outlook adds to your calendar when you choose **Add Holidays**. The holidays Outlook adds are listed in a text file named Outlook.txt. You can display this list and edit it in WordPad or another text editor.

Choose **Resource Scheduling** if you are responsible for coordinating resources; Outlook displays the dialog box shown in Figure 5.68.

Figure 5.68

You can make choices about how Outlook automatically responds to requests for resources.

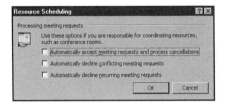

Free/Busy Options

These options operate only if you share calendar information with other people by way of Exchange or Net Folders.

Choose **Free/Busy Options** to open the dialog box shown in Figure 5.69.

Figure 5.69

Use this dialog box to specify how many months ahead you want to publish your calendar information on the server.

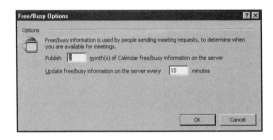

The dialog box shown in Figure 5.69 is the one displayed by Corporate/Workgroup Outlook. You can use it to specify how often you want Outlook to send updated calendar information to the server.

The corresponding Internet Only dialog box contains the following additional boxes:

- **Publish my free/busy information**. Check this box if you want to publish your free/busy information in a Net Folder.

- **Publish at this URL**. Enter the Uniform Resource Locator (URL) of the Internet server where the Net Folder is to be published.

■ **Search at the URL**. Enter the URL of the Internet server in which you want to search for other people's free/busy Net Folders.

Tasks

In the Tasks section of the Preferences tab (previously shown in Figure 5.61) you can specify the reminder time you want to appear in task items. Open the **Reminder Time** drop-down list and select a time.

Choose **Task Options** to display the dialog box shown in Figure 5.70.

Figure 5.70
Use this dialog box to select colors in which tasks are displayed.

Open the **Overdue tasks** drop-down list and select the color in which you want overdue tasks to be displayed. Open the **Completed tasks** drop-down box and select the color in which you want completed tasks to be displayed.

Journal

In the Journal section of the Preferences tab (refer to Figure 5.61), choose **Journal Options** to display the dialog box shown in Figure 5.71.

Figure 5.71
Use this dialog box to select the journal items Outlook creates automatically.

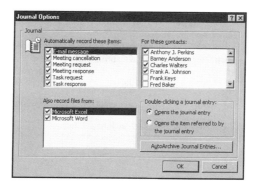

You can choose one or more of the following types of Outlook message items:

■ E-mail item
■ Meeting cancellation
■ Meeting request
■ Meeting response
■ Task request
■ Task response

You must also choose the people from whom these messages are received. The dialog box contains a list of the names of all the people in your Contacts folder. Outlook creates automatic journal items only for the types of message items you've selected, and only from those people you check in the list of names.

In addition to creating automatic journal items based on messages you receive, Outlook can also create a journal item each time you use one of the Office or Office-compatible applications to work with a file. You must check those applications for which you want Outlook to create journal items.

You can also choose what you want Outlook to do when you double-click a journal item in the Journal Information viewer. You can choose the following:

- **O̲pen the journal entry**
- **O̲pen the item referred to by the journal entry**

If you're using Outlook on a computer that has limited resources, such as a small memory or a slow microprocessor, you may be able to make Outlook run considerably faster by minimizing the number of journal items Outlook creates.

Choose **A̲utoArchive Journal Entries** to display the Journal Properties dialog box, which has the following five tabs (similar to the dialog box shown previously in Figure 5.16):

Journal properties dialog box tabs

Tab Name	Purpose
General	Contains general information about the journal folder.
AutoArchive	Provides the facilities to specify how often autoarchiving occurs and where you want to save autoarchived items.
Administration	Set access permissions.
Forms	Provide access to forms associated with the Journal folder.
Reports	Create reports based on Journal items.

Notes

In the Notes section of the Preferences tab (refer to Figure 5.61), choose **N̲ote Options** to display the dialog box shown in Figure 5.72.

Figure 5.72

Use this dialog box to specify the appearance of notes.

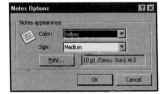

Open the **Color** drop-down list and select a default color for notes.

Open the **Size** drop-down list and select a default size for notes.

Choose **Font** to open a dialog box in which you can select the font to be used in notes.

Mail Services Options

Use the Mail Services tab of the Options dialog box (shown in Figure 5.73) to set your preferences for Outlook startup settings and mail options. Available only in Corporate/Workgroup Outlook.

Figure 5.73

The Mail Services tab contains two sections.

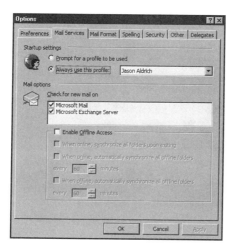

Startup Settings

This section contains two option buttons:

Startup settings	
Option Button	**Purpose**
Prompt for a profile to be used	Choose this if you want Outlook to offer a choice of profiles when it starts.
Always use this profile	Choose this if you want Outlook to always start using a specific profile. Open the drop-down list and select the profile you want Outlook to use.

Mail Options

The **Check for new mail on** list contains the names of all the information services in your profile that are capable of sending and receiving mail. Check those that you want Outlook to check for mail (checking, in this context, means receiving and sending).

The **Enable Offline Access** set of options have to do with the situation in which you may be using Outlook on a computer that is sometimes connected, and sometimes not connected, to Exchange. If your computer is permanently connected by way of a LAN to Exchange, this check box should be unchecked. If your computer is only sometimes connected to the server, check this box and then choose the conditions under which you want your offline folders to be synchronized with your folders in the Exchange store. These options are displayed only if you have the Microsoft Exchange Server information service in your profile and your computer currently has access to Exchange Server.

Synchronizing is the process of copying items between your local folders and the Exchange store so that the most recent information is saved on both.

Mail Delivery Options

Use the Mail Delivery tab (shown in Figure 5.74) to manage e-mail accounts and dial-up networking. This is available only in Internet Only Outlook.

Figure 5.74

This tab has three sections, two of which are used to manage e-mail accounts and one of which sets dial-up networking parameters.

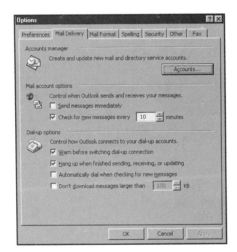

Accounts Manager

Choose **Accounts** to display the Internet Accounts dialog box (shown in Figure 5.75).

Figure 5.75

This dialog box initially displays a list of currently available Internet e-mail accounts.

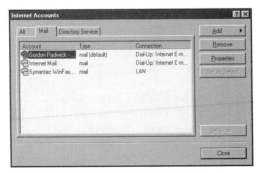

The Mail tab, initially displayed, shows a list of e-mail accounts. You can select the Directory Service tab to display a list of directory services, or the All tab to see e-mail accounts and directory services. With the Mail or All tab selected, your current default e-mail account is marked with the word default in the Type column.

With any tab selected, choose the following buttons to modify the list or items in a list:

- **Add**. Select Mail or Directory Service. When you choose Mail, Outlook displays the first Internet Connection Wizard window. Follow the steps in this wizard to define a new e-mail address to add to the list. When you choose Directory Service, Outlook displays the first Internet Connection Wizard window (different from the one displayed after you select Mail). Follow the steps in this wizard to define an Internet directory (LDAP) server to which you have access.

- **Remove**. Select an e-mail account or directory service in the list, and then choose **Remove** to remove that item from the list.

- **Properties**. Select an e-mail account or directory service in the list, and then choose **Properties** to display the Properties dialog box. Use this dialog box to examine or modify the properties of that account or delivery service.

- **Set as Default**. Available only if the All or Mail tab is selected and an e-mail account name, other than your current default e-mail account, is selected in the Account column. Choose **Set as Default** to set the selected e-mail account as your default account.

Mail Account Options

Use this section of the dialog box to specify when Outlook sends and receives messages.

Check **Send messages immediately** if you want Outlook to attempt to establish a connection to your Internet mail server as soon as you choose **Send** in the Message form's Standard toolbar. If this box is not checked, Outlook places messages in your Outbox folder and sends them when you choose **Send** or **Send and Receive** on the Tools menu.

Check **Check for new messages every** if you want Outlook to connect to your Internet mail server at regular intervals, send messages waiting in your Outbox to the server, and receive messages waiting on the server for you. Specify the interval at which Outlook should attempt to connect to the mail server in the adjacent box.

Dial-up Options

Check the boxes in this section according to your preferences:

- **Warn before switching dial-up connection**. Check this box if you want to get a confirmation message before you change dial-up connections.

- **Hang up when finished sending, receiving, or updating**. Check this box if you want to terminate a dial-up connection as soon as current activities are complete. It's advisable to check this box, particularly when you're using a dial-up connection for which you're charged for the time you use.

- **Automatically dial when checking for new messages**. Check this box if you want Outlook to dial your connection number when you check for new messages.

- **Don't download messages larger than**. Check this box if you want to specify the maximum size of messages you want to receive. After you check this box, enter the maximum message size in the adjacent box.

Mail Format Options

Use the Mail Format tab of the Options dialog box (shown in Figure 5.76) to set your preferences for message format and related subjects.

Figure 5.76

This tab has three sections, two of which are always present and one of which depends on which message format you have selected.

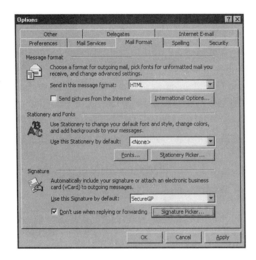

Message Format

In this section, you can choose one of four formats for messages you create:

Message formats

Message Format	Purpose
HTML	Use this format if you send messages to recipients who use an e-mail application that can accept HTML. This format provides easy-to-use message formatting that appears on recipients' screens as you intend.
Microsoft Outlook Rich Text	Use this format if you send messages to recipients who use an e-mail application that can accept Microsoft Rich Text.
Plain Text	Use this format if you send messages to recipients who may be using a text-based e-mail application.
Microsoft Word	Use this format if you send messages to recipients who use Word 97. You can use all of Word's formatting capabilities and be sure recipients receive your messages as you intend.

If you choose HTML message format, the **Send Pictures from the Internet** check box is checked. With this box checked, all pictures, including background images, are sent with your messages. If this box is unchecked, only references (pointers) to pictures are sent.

If you're using a non-English version of Outlook, you can send English versions of message headers, even though the text of the message is in a different language. To do so, choose **International Options** and then check **Use US English for message headers on replies and forwards**.

Stationery and Fonts

Stationery and Fonts are available if you have selected HTML, Microsoft Outlook Rich Text, or Plain Text as your message format.

Stationery refers to an overall design of a message, including a background pattern. Open the **Use this stationery by default** drop-down list and select the stationery you want (<None> is strongly recommended!).

Choose **Fonts** to display the dialog box shown in Figure 5.77.

Figure 5.77
Use this dialog box to select the default fonts you want to use in your messages.

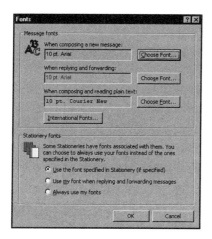

In the Fonts dialog box, you can also choose to override the fonts specified in some stationeries. Choose **Stationery Picker** to open the dialog box shown in Figure 5.78.

WordMail Templates

This is available if you have selected Microsoft Word as your message format. Open the **Use this template by default** drop-down list to display a list of Word templates you can use for your messages. Select the template you want to use. Choose **Fonts** to display the dialog box, shown previously in Figure 5.77, in which you can select the fonts you want to use in your messages. Choose **Template Picker** to open the WordMail Template dialog box shown in Figure 5.79. You can use Word to create custom templates.

Figure 5.78

Use this dialog box to
edit existing stationeries
and create new ones.

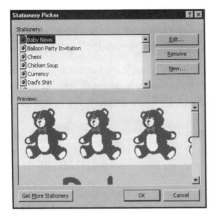

Figure 5.79

Use this dialog box to
choose any Word
template available to
your computer.

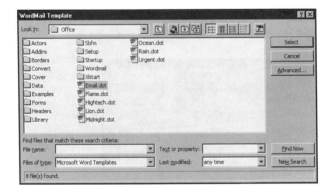

Signature

Open the **Use this Signature by default** drop-down list and select the signature you want to
attach to outgoing messages.

Choose **Signature Picker** to display the dialog box shown in Figure 5.80.

Spelling Options

Use the Spelling tab of the Options dialog box (shown in Figure 5.81) to set your preferences
for spell checking.

General Options

Use the check boxes in the General Options section to specify how you want spell checking to
function:

- **Always suggest replacements for misspelled words**
- **Always check spelling before sending**

- Ignore words in <u>U</u>PPERCASE
- Ignore words with <u>n</u>umbers
- Ignore <u>o</u>riginal message text in reply or forward

Figure 5.80

Use this dialog box to edit any existing signature or to create a new one.

Figure 5.81

The Spelling tab has three sections.

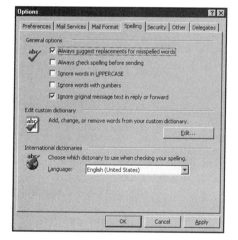

Edit Custom Dictionary

Choose **Edit** to open a Notepad window that contains words in your custom dictionary. You can add words to this dictionary, delete words from it, and edit existing words. The custom dictionary is shared by other Office applications.

International Dictionaries

Open the **Language** drop-down list to select the dictionary you want to use to check your spelling. The list includes those dictionaries you selected when you installed Outlook.

Security Options

Use the Security tab shown in Figure 5.82 to set your preferences for message security. This section assumes you already have a good understanding of the basics of e-mail security. (Chapter 16 of Que's *Using Microsoft Internet Explorer 4*, is a good source of information on this subject. For more comprehensive information, refer to *Internet Security Professional Reference*, published by New Riders.)

To use Outlook's security capabilities, you must first obtain a Digital ID. If you're using Corporate/Workgroup Outlook, have the Microsoft Exchange Server information service in your profile and have an Exchange Server account. You'll probably receive a Digital ID from your Exchange administrator. If you're using Internet Only Outlook, you'll probably obtain a Digital ID from a company such as VeriSign. In either case, choose **Get a Digital ID** in this dialog box to obtain a Digital ID. (Refer to **Get a Digital ID**, page 623, later in this chapter for information about this.)

Figure 5.82

The Security tab has three sections.

Secure E-mail

Use the Secure e-mail section to specify the security options you want to use for all outgoing messages. (The options in this section are available only if you have a Digital ID.)

On this tab, the following options are available:

- Check **Encrypt contents and attachments for outgoing messages** if you want this to be your default setting. After you choose this, you can still send individual messages unencrypted.

■ Check **Add digital signature to outgoing messages** if you want all your outgoing messages to be authenticated by a digital signature. After you choose this, you can still send individual messages without a digital signature.

■ Check **Send clear text signed message** (available only if **Add digital signature to outgoing messages** is checked) if you want people who don't have an e-mail application that supports S/MIME to be able to read your messages.

■ Open the **Default Security Setting** drop-down list to choose from a list of security settings (if you have created such a list).

■ Choose **Change Settings** to open the Change Security Settings dialog box. Use this dialog box to create new security settings.

Secure Content

Use the Secure Content section of the dialog box to specify the Internet Explorer security zone to use when you receive HTML messages or attachments. (Refer to Chapter 16 in Que's *Using Microsoft Internet Explorer 4* for detailed information about security zones.)

Open the **Zone** drop-down list and select your choice for a default zone.

Choose **Zone Settings** to display the dialog box shown in Figure 5.83.

Figure 5.83

Use this dialog box to change the security settings that affect the way scripts and other active content run.

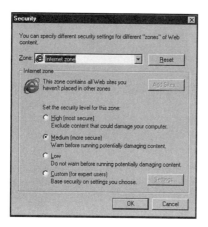

In this dialog box, you can set **High**, **Medium**, **Low**, or **Custom** security levels for the local intranet zone, the trusted sites zone, the Internet zone, and the restricted sites zone.

Choose **Attachment Security** to display the dialog box shown in Figure 5.84.

Figure 5.84

Use this dialog box to choose a security method for message attachments.

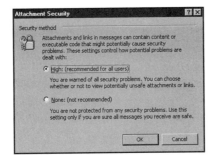

Digital IDs (Certificates)

Choose **Import/Export Digital ID** to display the dialog box shown in Figure 5.85.

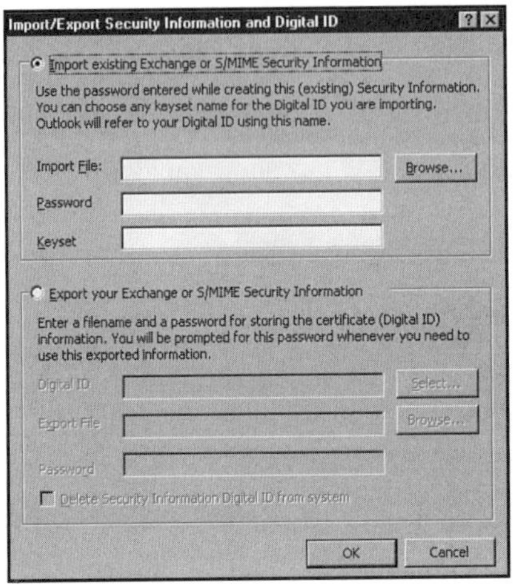

Figure 5.85

Use this dialog box to import or export a Digital ID.

Use this dialog box to make a copy of a Digital ID file either to keep as a backup, or when you want to copy your Digital ID to another computer.

Choose **Import Existing Exchange or S/MIME Security Information** to import a security file into your computer. Enter the full path name of the security file into the **Import File** box, the password associated with the file into the **Password** box, and a name for your Digital ID (typically your mailbox name) into the **Keyset** box.

Choose **Export your Exchange or S/MIME Security Information** to export your security information as a file. If you haven't previously exported your security information, the **Digital ID** box is initially empty. Choose **Select** to display the Select a Certificate dialog box that lists the Digital IDs available on your computer, and then select the Digital ID you want to export. Choose **OK** to close the dialog box and return to the previous dialog box that now displays the selected Digital ID. Enter a name for the Digital ID file into the **Export File** box, and enter a password into the **Password** box. Choose **OK** to save the file.

If you move your work from one computer to another, you can delete your security information from that computer before someone else inherits it. To do so, choose **Delete Security Infor-mation Digital ID from system**.

Get a Digital ID

The information in this section is about getting your personal Digital ID from a company that issues them. If you're working on a LAN, consult your LAN administrator for information about getting a Digital ID.

Establish a connection to your Internet server and then choose **Get a Digital ID** to open your Internet browser and access the Web page:

www.microsoft.com/ie/ie40/oe/certpage.htm

This Web page contains information about companies that supply Digital IDS (shown in Figure 5.86).

Figure 5.86

Use this Web page to select a Digital ID supplier and access that supplier's home page.

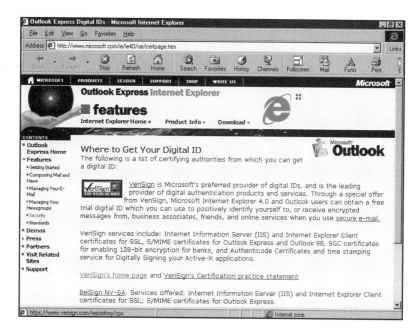

Choose a Digital ID supplier and access that supplier's home page for instructions about how to obtain a Digital ID. If you decide to get a Digital ID from VeriSign, as Microsoft suggests, you can obtain detailed information about obtaining, installing, and using a Digital ID in the Web page:

www.verisign.com/securemail/outlook98/Outlook.htm

Other Options

Use the Other tab of the Options dialog box (shown in Figure 5.87) to set your preferences for how you want Outlook to deal with items in the Deleted Items folder, how you want AutoArchive to work, and to customize the Preview pane.

Figure 5.87

The Other tab has three sections.

General

Check the **Empty the Deleted Items folder upon exiting** if that's what you want to do. If you leave this box unchecked, items remain in your Deleted items folder when you close Outlook.

Choose **Advanced Options** to display the dialog box shown in Figure 5.88.

Figure 5.88

This dialog box has two sections and several buttons.

General Settings

Open the **Startup in this folder** drop-down list and select the folder you want Outlook to display when it starts.

Check or uncheck the following boxes:

Startup folder options

Check Box	Purpose
Warn before permanently deleting items	Displays a warning message before you permanently delete items.
When selecting text, automatically select entire word	Selects an entire word and the space after it when you select text. (This is not available when you're using Microsoft Word as your mail format.)
Provide feedback with sound	Plays a sound when you perform certain actions.

Appearance Options

Choose **Font** to display a dialog box (similar to that displayed by other Office applications) in which you can choose the font used by the Date Navigator.

If you want notes to display the time and date when they were created, check **When viewing Notes, show time and date**.

Enter the appropriate number of hours in the **Task working hours per day** box.

Enter the appropriate number of hours in the **Task working hours per week** box.

Reminder Options

Choose **Reminder Options** to display the Reminder Options dialog box (shown in Figure 5.89).

Figure 5.89

Use this dialog box to choose whether Outlook should display a reminder and play a sound when a reminder becomes due.

If you want Outlook to display reminders, check the **Display the reminder** box.

If you want Outlook to play a sound, check the **Play reminder sound** box. After you do so, you see the name of the sound file that Outlook will play. To select another sound file, choose **Browse** to display the Reminder Sound File dialog box and navigate to find the sound file you want to use.

Add-In Manager

Choose **Add-In Manager** to display the Add-In Manager dialog box shown in Figure 5.90.

Figure 5.90

This dialog box contains a list of the Outlook Add-Ins currently installed.

The Add-Ins listed depend on choices you made when you installed Outlook and which Add-Ins you may have subsequently installed.

A check box adjacent to each Add-In name indicates whether that Add-In is activated or not. Make sure the Add-Ins you want to use are checked.

You can press the Down-arrow key on your keyboard to highlight each Add-In in turn. The dialog box displays text that shows the purpose of the highlighted Add-In.

You can install Add-Ins in the following three ways:

- Install standard Outlook Add-ins by opening the Windows Control Panel and choosing **Add/Remove Programs**. Select Outlook 98 from the list of installed software, and choose **Add/Remove**. Choose **Add New Components** and then follow the onscreen instructions.
- Install Add-Ins available on disk by choosing **Install**.
- Install certain third-party Add-Ins in the same way that you install other Windows applications.

Advanced Tasks

Choose Advanced Tasks to display the dialog box shown in Figure 5.91.

Figure 5.91

You can check or uncheck these three options in this dialog box:

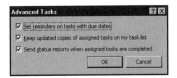

- **Set reminders on tasks with due dates**
- **Keep updated copies of assigned tasks on my task list**
- **Send status reports when assigned tasks are completed**

Custom Forms

Choose **Custom Forms** to display the dialog box shown in Figure 5.92. (This is not available in Internet Only Outlook.)

Figure 5.92
Use this dialog box to work with custom forms.

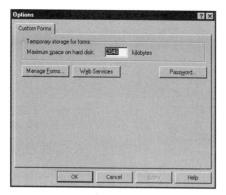

Use the **Maximum space on hard disk** box to assign a certain amount of temporary storage for forms.

Choose **Manage Forms** to display the dialog box shown in Figure 5.93.

Figure 5.93
Use this dialog box to work with existing forms.

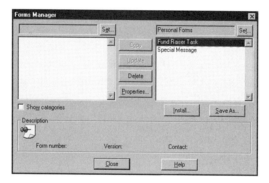

You can use this dialog box to

- Copy a form
- Update a form
- Delete a form
- View and modify the properties of a form
- Set up a form
- Save a form as a file

Choose **Web Services** to open the dialog box shown in Figure 5.94.

You can also use this dialog box to add a command to the Actions menu that provides a link to a Web page library of HTML forms.

Choose **Password** to display the dialog box shown in Figure 5.95.

Figure 5.94

Use this dialog box to set Outlook to open a form that it doesn't recognize in HTML format and to use your browser to display the form.

Figure 5.95

Use this dialog box to change your Windows NT network password.

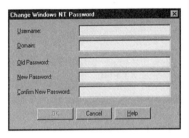

AutoArchive

Outlook's AutoArchive facility moves old items into an archive file and deletes items in your wastebasket. Use this section of the Other tab to customize autoarchiving.

By default, Outlook autoarchives items at the following ages:

AutoArchiving ages

Item Type	Age
Calendar	6 months
Deleted items	2 months
Journal	6 months
Sent items	2 months
Task	6 months

Contact, draft, inbox, and note items are, by default, not autoarchived.

To change the default AutoArchive properties for a type of Outlook item, right-click the name of the folder for that type of item in the folder list, choose **Properties** in the context menu, and choose the AutoArchive tab of the Properties dialog box.

Choose **AutoArchive** to display the AutoArchive dialog box shown in Figure 5.96.

Figure 5.96

Use this dialog box to set default autoarchiving conditions.

Check **AutoArchive every** to enable autoarchiving; uncheck it to disable autoarchiving. If you have autoarchiving enabled, you can choose the interval at which autoarchiving occurs. Autoarchiving occurs the first time you start Outlook after the prescribed number of days.

Check **Prompt before AutoArchive** if you want to be alerted before autoarchiving starts. Otherwise, autoarchiving starts without any warning.

Check **Delete expired items when AutoArchiving (e-mail folders only)** if you want e-mail items to be deleted instead of being saved in the archive file.

The **Default archive file** box displays the full path name of the file Outlook proposes to use for archiving. If you want to choose a different path, choose **Browse** and navigate to the folder that contains the file you want to use.

Preview Pane

Choose **Preview Pane** to display the dialog box shown in Figure 5.97.

Figure 5.97

Use this dialog box to customize the appearance and behavior of the preview pane.

Check **Mark messages as read in preview window** if you want Outlook to automatically mark messages as read when they have been displayed in the preview pane for a certain period. By default, that period is five seconds. To change that period, enter your preferred period in the **Wait** box.

Check **Mark item as read when selection changes** if you want Outlook to automatically mark a selected message as read when you select a different message.

If you don't check one or both of the preceding items, Outlook doesn't automatically mark items as read. In that case, you can open the **Edit** menu and choose **Mark as Read** to mark selected items as read.

Check <u>S</u>ingle key reading using spacebar if you want to be able to press the **Spacebar** to select one message after another.

Choose **Fon<u>t</u>** to open a dialog box (similar to that used in other Office applications) in which you can select the font to be used in the preview header that contains the From, To, Subject, and Cc fields.

Delegates Options

This tab (shown in Figure 5.98) is only available if you're using Corporate/Workgroup Outlook and you have the Microsoft Exchange Server information service in your profile.

Figure 5.98

Use the Delegates tab to allow other people to send messages on your behalf.

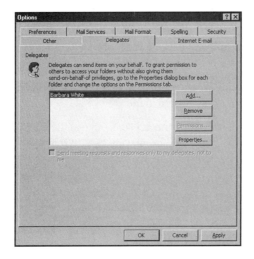

The Delegates box lists the names of people who can send items on your behalf. You can choose the following buttons to modify this list:

Delegates tab buttons

Button Name	Purpose
A<u>d</u>d	Displays the Add Users dialog box shown in Figure 5.99 in which you can choose a name listed in the Global Address List.
<u>R</u>emove	Remove the selected name from the list of delegates.
<u>P</u>ermissions	Displays the Delegate Permissions dialog box (shown in Figure 5.100) in which you can specify the folders to which you want to give the selected delegate access and the permission level for that delegate. This button is not available if you are using offline folders or a Personal Folders file.
Proper<u>t</u>ies	Displays the Properties dialog box (shown in Figure 5.101) in which you can view and modify a selected delegate's properties, providing you have appropriate permissions.

Figure 5.99

Use the Add Users dialog box to name delegates.

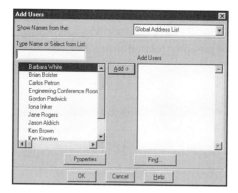

When you add a delegate, Outlook displays that person's permissions in the Delegate Permissions dialog box (shown in Figure 5.100). Use this dialog box to define the access permissions the delegate has for each of your folders.

Figure 5.100

Use the Permissions dialog box to modify a delegate's permissions.

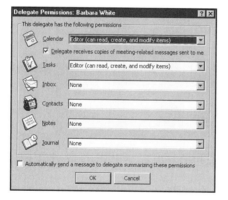

Figure 5.101

Use the Properties dialog box to examine and modify a delegate's properties.

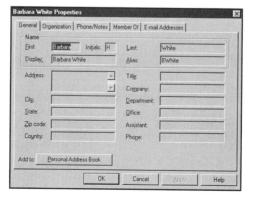

You can check the **Send meeting requests and responses only to my delegates, not to me** box. After you do so, meeting requests and responses sent to you are not added to your

Inbox folder and are not displayed in your Inbox Information viewer. This option is available when you give editor permission for your Calendar folder to a delegate, and then select **Delegate receives copies of meeting-related messages sent to me** in the Delegate Permissions dialog box.

Internet E-mail Options

This tab (shown in Figure 5.102) is only available if you're using Corporate/Workgroup Outlook and you have the Internet information service in your profile. Some of the items in this tab are available in Internet Only Outlook's Mail Delivery tab.

Figure 5.102

This tab has two sections.

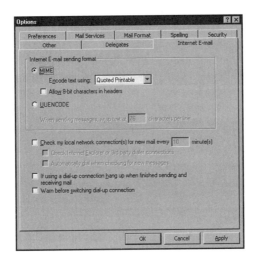

Internet E-mail Sending Format

Outlook uses the encoding formats that you select in this tab to send other than ASCII text, such as pictures and other binary files.

You can choose any of these encoding formats for e-mail messages that you send:

E-mail message formats

Format	Purpose
MIME	Encodes messages using the Multipurpose Internet Mail Extensions (MIME) format to send messages and attachments to people who use an e-mail application that supports MIME, as most Internet e-mail applications do
UUENCODE	Encodes messages using the UNIX-to-UNIX Encode (UUENCODE) format to send messages and attachments to people who use a text-based e-mail application on a UNIX system or any other e-mail application that doesn't support MIME

If you choose MIME, Outlook uses the Quoted Printable format to encode text. You can open the **En̲code text using** drop-down list and choose None or Base 64.

Also if you choose MIME, Outlook treats characters in headers in the same way as other message characters. You can check **Allo̲w 8-bit characters in headers** so that Outlook allows headers to contain foreign character sets, high ASCII, or double-byte character sets in the message header.

If you choose UUENCODE, Outlook automatically starts a new line in a message after a certain number of characters, 76 by default. You can change this number of characters in the **When sending messages, wr̲ap text at** box.

Unnamed Section

This section contains miscellaneous Internet options.

Check **C̲heck my local network connection(s) for new mail every** if you want Outlook to regularly check your Internet e-mail server for new messages and send messages from your Outbox. This capability operates only if you have an Internet connection by way of a local area network, not if you use a dial-up connection to an Internet service provider. When this box is checked, you can do the following:

- Specify how often Outlook checks for Internet e-mail
- Check **Check Internet E̲xplorer or 3rd party dialer connections** if you want to use a dialer application and settings other than dial-up networking to connect to your Internet service provider
- Check **Automatically d̲ial when checking for new messages** if that's what you want to do
- Check **If using a dial-up connection h̲ang up when finished sending and receiving mail**
- Check **Warn before s̲witching dial-up connection** if you have two or more dial-up connections and you want to be able to cancel a connection that isn't working

Fax

The Internet Only Outlook configuration uses Symantec Winfax Starter Edition to send and receive faxes. Use the Options dialog box Fax tab described in this section to setup default fax parameters.

In contrast, the Corporate/Workgroup Outlook configuration uses Microsoft Windows At Work Fax when running under Windows 95, or Microsoft Personal Fax for Windows when running under Windows NT. Use the Windows Control Panel to set up default fax parameters for these optional Windows components.

Use the Fax tab (shown in Figure 5.103) to set up fax parameters for Internet Only Outlook. This tab isn't available if you're using Corporate/Workgroup Outlook.

Figure 5.103
This tab has three sections.

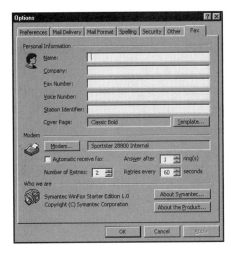

Personal Information

Enter personal information in the five text boxes. Outlook can use the information you enter here on a fax cover page.

The **Cover Page** box contains the name of the default cover page template. Choose **Template** to display the Cover Page Properties dialog box (shown in Figure 5.104).

Figure 5.104
This dialog box displays a preview of the default cover page.

Open the **Template** drop-down list to select a different cover page to be the default.

Modem

The **Modem** box contains the name of the currently selected modem, if any. Choose **Modem** to display the Modem Properties dialog box that lists modems installed on your computer.

Select the modem you want to use and choose **OK**. Outlook displays the first Modem Configuration Wizard window. Follow through the steps in this wizard to install the selected modem for use with WinFax. When you choose Finish in the final wizard window, Outlook displays the previous dialog box with the name of the selected modem in the **Modem** box.

Check **Automatic receive fax** if you want Outlook to receive faxes automatically. If you do, set the number of rings in the **Answer after** box.

In the **Number of Retries** box, set the number of times Outlook should attempt to send a fax. Set the interval between retries in the **Retries every** box.

Who We Are

Choose **About Symantec** to display information about Symantec. Choose **About the Product** to display information about WinFax.

Action

The Actions menu is where you choose what you want Outlook to do. The menu items available vary according to the Information viewer selected.

Actions ➥ New Mail Message

Choose **Actions**, **New Mail Message** to open the Message form in which you can create a mail message. (Refer to **Message Form**, page 667, later in this chapter for information about this form.)

Quick Choices   *NEW MAIL MESSAGE*

■ Alternatively, press **Ctrl+N** to open the Message form.

Available only when the Outlook Today, Inbox, or Deleted Items Information viewer is selected.

Actions ➥ New Fax Message

Choose **Actions**, **New Fax Message** to open the Fax form in which you can create a fax message. (Refer to **Fax Form**, page 665, later in this chapter for information about this form.) This is available only when you're using Internet Only Outlook. In Corporate/Workgroup Outlook, use the Message form to create a fax message.

Actions ➥ New Mail Message Using

Move the mouse pointer onto **Actions**, **New Mail Message Using** to display a menu:

New Mail Message options

Menu Item	Purpose
More Stationery	Displays the Select a Stationery dialog box (shown in Figure 5.105) in which you can select a background for your message. Backgrounds are only available when you're using HTML as your message format. After you've chosen stationery, the name of the stationery appears in this menu.
No Stationery	Removes your previous choice of stationery, but leaves the name of that stationery in this menu.
Microsoft **W**ord	Selects Microsoft Word as your message format.

Figure 5.105
Select the stationery
you want to use in this
dialog box.

Available only when the Outlook Today, Inbox, or Deleted Items Information viewer is selected.

Actio**n**s ➥ **F**lag for Follow Up

Choose **Actio**n**s**, **F**lag for Follow Up to open the Flag for Follow Up dialog box (shown in Figure 5.106).

Quick Choices   *FLAG FOR FOLLOW UP*

■ Alternatively, press **Ctrl+Shift+G** or choose the **Flag for Follow Up** button 🚩 in the Standard toolbar to display the Flag for Follow Up dialog box.

Figure 5.106

Use this dialog box to attach a follow-up (or other) flag to selected messages.

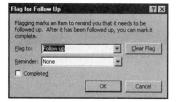

You can also choose a time in the future when you want to be reminded about the flagged message. After you've attended to the message, you can choose **Completed**. Choose **Clear Flag** in this dialog box to remove the flag.

Available only when the Inbox, Contacts, or Deleted Items Information viewer is selected.

Actions ➥ Junk E-mail

Move the pointer onto **Actions, Junk E-mail** to display a menu with the following choices:

Junk E-mail options	
Menu Item	**Purpose**
Add to Junk Senders List	Adds the name of the sender of the currently selected message to a list of junk e-mail senders.
Add to Adult Content Senders List	Adds the name of the sender of the currently selected message to a list of adult-content e-mail senders.

Actions, Junk E-mail is effective only after you have turned on Outlook's Junk E-mail capability. To do so, choose **Tools, Organize,** and then choose **Junk E-Mail**. Choose **Turn on** for Junk messages or for Adult Content messages, or both.

To remove, and to use another way to add, names from your lists of junk e-mail senders and adult-content senders, follow these steps:

1. Display the Inbox Information viewer.
2. Choose **Tools, Organize** to open the Ways to Organize Inbox pane.
3. Choose Junk E-mail.
4. Choose **Click here**.
5. Choose **Edit Junk Senders** or **Edit Adult Content Senders** to display a dialog box that contains the e-mail addresses already in the list.
6. Choose the **Add** button to add an e-mail address to the list, select an e-mail address and choose the **Delete** button to delete an e-mail address from the list, or select an e-mail address and choose the **Edit** button to edit an e-mail address.

This is available only when the Inbox or Deleted Items Information viewer is selected.

Actio̲ns ↦ F̲ind All

Move the pointer onto **Actio̲ns**, **F̲ind All** to display a menu with the following options:

Find All options	
Menu Item	**Purpose**
R̲elated Messages	Displays a list of messages that have the same conversation topic (subject) as the selected message
M̲essages from Sender	Displays a list of messages that have been sent by the same person as the selected message

This is available only when the Inbox or Deleted Items Information viewer is selected.

Actio̲ns ↦ R̲eply

Choose **Actio̲ns**, **R̲eply** to open the Message form in which you can create a reply to the selected message. (Refer to **Message Form**, page 667, later in this chapter for information about the Message form.)

Quick **Choices**   *REPLY*

■ Alternatively, press **Ctrl+R** to reply to the sender of the selected message.

The form opens with the original message displayed and with space above it for you to enter your reply. Outlook automatically addresses your reply to the person who sent the original message.

This is available only when the Inbox or Deleted Items Information viewer is selected.

In addition to writing a reply, you can add annotations to the original message. By default, Outlook includes the text of the original message with your reply, but not any attachments to the original message.

Actio̲ns ↦ Reply to A̲ll

Choose **Actio̲ns**, **Reply to A̲ll** to open the Message form in which you can create a reply to the selected message. (Refer to **Message Form**, page 667, later in this chapter for information about the Message form.)

Quick **Choices**   *REPLY TO ALL*

■ Alternatively, press **Ctrl+Shift+R** to reply to all who received the selected message.

The form opens with the original message displayed and with space above that for you to enter your reply. Outlook automatically addresses your reply to the person who sent the original message and to everyone who was sent a copy of the original message (those on the Cc list, but not those on the Bcc list).

This is available only when the Inbox or Deleted Items Information viewer is selected.

Actions ➥ Forward

Choose **Actions**, **Forward** to open the Message form in which you can forward the selected message to other people. (See **Message Form**, page 667, later in this chapter for information about the Message form.)

Quick Choices   *FORWARD*

■ Alternatively, press **Ctrl+F** to forward the selected message.

The form opens with the original message displayed and with space above that for you to enter comments about the message you're forwarding. By default, Outlook forwards the text of the original message and all attachments to the original message.

You can use the Actions, Forward command to forward messages from your Inbox folder, calendar items from your Calendar folder, contact items from your Contacts folder, task items from your Tasks folder, and journal items from your Journal folder.

This command is not available when the Outlook Today Information viewer is selected.

Actions ➥ New Appointment

Choose **Actions**, **New Appointment** to open the Appointment form ready for you to create a new appointment. (Refer to **Appointment Form**, page 646, later in this chapter for information about the Appointment form.)

This is available only when the Calendar Information viewer is selected.

Actions ➥ New All Day Event

Choose **Actions**, **New All Day Event** to open the Appointment form ready for you to create a new all day event. (Refer to **Appointment Form**, page 646, later in this chapter for information about the Appointment form.)

This is available only when the Calendar Information viewer is selected.

Actions ➥ New Meeting Request

Choose **Actions**, **New Meeting Request** to open the Meeting form ready for you to create a new meeting request. (Refer to **Meeting Form**, page 675, later in this chapter for information about the Meeting form.)

This is available only when the Calendar Information viewer is selected.

Actions ➥ New Online Meeting Request

Choose **Actions**, **New Online Meeting Request** to open the Meeting form ready for you to create a new online meeting request. (Refer to **Meeting Form**, page 675, for information about the Meeting form.)

This is available only when the Calendar Information viewer is selected.

Actions ➥ Plan a Meeting

Choose **Actions**, **Plan a Meeting** to open the Plan a Meeting form ready for you to plan a meeting. (Refer to **Plan a Meeting Dialog Box**, page 678, for information about the Plan a Meeting form.)

This is available only when the Calendar or Contact Information viewer is selected.

Actions ➥ New Recurring Appointment

Choose **Actions**, **New Recurring Appointment** to open the Appointment Recurrence form ready for you to create a new recurring appointment. (Refer to **Appointment Recurrence Dialog Box**, page 654, for information about the Appointment Recurrence form.)

This is available only when the Calendar Information viewer is selected.

Actions ➥ New Recurring Meeting

Choose **Actions**, **New Recurring Meeting** to open the Appointment Recurrence form ready for you to create a new recurring meeting. (Refer to **Appointment Recurrence Dialog Box**, page 654, for information about the Appointment Recurrence form.)

This is available only when the Calendar Information viewer is selected.

Actions ➥ Forward as a vCalendar

Choose **Actions**, **Forward as a vCalendar** to open the Message form with the selected calendar item already attached as a vCalendar (virtual calendar) file. (Refer to **Message Form**, page 667, for information about the Message form.) You can send the message to other people who can open the vCalendar file to place it in their Outlook calendars.

This is available only when the Calendar Information viewer is selected.

Actions ➥ New Contact

Choose **Actions**, **New Contact** to open the Contact form ready for you to create a new contact. (Refer to **Contact Form**, page 657, for information about the Contact form.)

This is available only when the Contacts Information viewer is selected.

Actions ➥ New Contact from Same Company

Choose **Actions**, **New Contact from Same Company** to open the Contact form with the company name, address, business phone, and business fax information copied from the previously selected contact item. You can enter personal information about another person. (Refer to **Contact Form**, page 657, for information about the Contact form.)

This is available only when the Contacts Information viewer is selected.

Actions ➥ New Message to Contact

Choose **Actions**, **New Message to Contact** to open the Message form ready for you to create a message to the selected contact. Alternatively, choose the **New Message to Contact** button on the Standard toolbar. (Refer to **Message Form**, page 667, for information about the Message form.)

This is available only when the Contacts Information viewer is selected.

Actions ➥ New Letter to Contact

Choose **Actions**, **New Letter to Contact** to open Word's Letter Wizard. Follow the steps in the wizard to write and address a letter to the selected contact. (Refer to **Letter Wizard**, page 217, in Chapter 2, "Word," for information about Word's Letter Wizard.)

This is available only when the Contacts Information viewer is selected.

Actions ➥ New Meeting with Contact

Choose **Actions**, **New Meeting with Contact** to open the Meeting form ready for you to create a message requesting a meeting. (Refer to **Meeting Form**, page 675, later in this chapter for information about the Meeting form.)

This is available only when the Contacts Information viewer is selected.

Actions ➥ New Task for Contact

Choose **Actions**, **New Task for Contact** to open the Task form ready for you to create a new task. (Refer to **Task Form**, page 679, for information about the Task form.) When you choose Actions, Assign Task in the form, Outlook automatically provides the e-mail address of the selected contact.

This is available only when the Contacts Information viewer is selected.

Actions ➥ Call Contact

Move the pointer onto **Actions**, **New Contact**, to display a menu with the following items on the following table.

New Contact menu	
Menu Item	**Purpose**
Business: (followed by the phone number)	Place a call
Business Fax: (followed by the fax number)	Send a fax
Redial	Redial the phone number
Speed Dial	Call a number on your speed dial list
New Call	Call a different number

Quick Choices   **AUTODIALER**

■ Alternatively, choose the **AutoDialer** button 🔘 on the Standard toolbar to display the New Call dialog box in which you can start a call.

This is available only when the Contacts Information viewer is selected.

Actions ➥ Call Using NetMeeting

Choose **Actions**, **Call Using NetMeeting** to start a NetMeeting with the selected contact. The contact item must contain the name of the directory server on which the contact's name can be found (the **Directory Server** box is in the Contact form's Details tab).

This is available only when the Contacts Information viewer is selected.

Actions ➥ Forward as vCard

Choose **Actions**, **Forward as vCard** to open the Message form with the selected contact item already attached as a vCard (virtual card) file. (Refer to **Message Form**, page 667, for information about the Message form.) You can send this message to people who can open the vCard file to add the contact item to their Contacts folders.

This is available only when the Contacts Information viewer is selected.

Actions ➥ Forward

Choose **Actions**, **Forward** to open the Message form with selected contact items already attached. (Refer to **Message Form**, page 667, for information about the Message form.)

This is available only when you're using Corporate/Workgroup Outlook and have selected the Contacts Information viewer.

Actions ➥ New Task

Choose **Actions**, **New Task** to open the Task form ready for you to create a new task. (Refer to **Task Form**, page 679, for information about the Task form.)

This is available only when the Tasks Information viewer is selected.

Actions ➥ New Task Request

Choose **Actions**, **New Task Request** to open the Task form ready for you to create a new task and send a task request to someone. (Refer to **Task Form**, page 679, for information about the Task form.)

This is available only when the Tasks Information viewer is selected.

Actions ➥ New TeamStatus Report

Choose **Actions**, **New TeamStatus Report** to display a report listing Project tasks in the Outlook database.

This is available only when the Tasks Information viewer is selected.

Actions ➥ Save Task Order

Choose **Actions**, **Save Task Order** to save tasks in the order they are listed in the task list.

This is available only when the Tasks Information viewer is selected.

Actions ➥ New Memo

Choose **Actions**, **New Memo** to open the Memo form ready for you to create a new memo.

Outlook saves the new memo in the selected task's Notes field.

This is available only when you're using Corporate/Workgroup Outlook and the Tasks Information viewer is selected.

Actions ➥ New Journal Entry

Choose **Actions**, **New Journal Entry** to open the Journal Entry form ready for you to create a new journal entry. (Refer to **Journal Entry Form**, page 665, for information about the Journal Entry form.)

This is available only when the Journal Information viewer is selected.

Help

You can use the Help menu to look up information about using Outlook.

Help ➥ Microsoft Outlook Help

Choose **Help**, **Microsoft Outlook Help** to display the Office Assistant.

(Refer to **Word's Help - Microsoft Word Help**, page 240, for information about using the Office Assistant.)

Help ➡ Microsoft Mail Help Topics

This menu item is available only if you're using Corporate/Workgroup Outlook and you have the Microsoft Mail information service in your profile. It provides access to information about sending and receiving e-mail using Microsoft Mail.

Choose **Help**, **Microsoft Mail Help Topics** to display the Microsoft Mail dialog box in which you can choose the Contents, Index, and Find tabs. (Refer to **Word's Help - Contents and Index**, page 242, for information about using this dialog box.)

Help ➡ Contents and Index

Choose **Help**, **Contents and Index** to display the Microsoft Outlook dialog box in which you can find general information about using Outlook. This dialog box contains three tabs: Contents, Index, and Find. (Refer to **Word's Help - Contents and Index**, page 242, for information using this dialog box.)

Help ➡ What's This?

Choose **Help**, **What's This?** to add a question mark to the mouse pointer. (Refer to **Word's Help - What's This?**," page 246, for information about using this pointer.)

Help ➡ Microsoft on the Web

Move the mouse pointer onto **Help**, **Microsoft on the Web** to display a menu that lists sources of information about Outlook in particular and Office in general. (Refer to **Word's Help - Microsoft on the Web**, page 246, for detailed information.)

Help ➡ Microsoft Outlook Forms Help

This Help item is available only if you're using Corporate/Workgroup Outlook and have included Microsoft Forms Help in your Outlook installation. This item contains detailed information about creating custom forms and writing Visual Basic Scripting Edition code to customize Outlook. To install this help item:

1. Select any standard Information viewer except Outlook Today.

2. Move the mouse pointer into **Tools**, **Forms** and then choose **Design a Form**.

3. In the Design Form dialog box, select any form and then choose **Open**.

4. Select a numbered tab such as [P.2].

5. Choose the View Code button (the rightmost button in the Design toolbar).

6. In the Script Editor window, choose **Help**. Choose **Microsoft Outlook Object Library Help**.

7. Follow the onscreen instructions to install Outlook Forms Help.

When you next choose **Help** in the Outlook menu bar, you see Microsoft Outlook Forms Help in the list of menu items.

Choose **Word's Help – Microsoft Outlook Forms Help** to display the Outlook Customization and Forms dialog box in which you can choose the Contents, Index, and Find tabs. (Refer to **Word's Help – Contents and Index**, page 242, for information about using this dialog box.)

Help ↪ About Microsoft Outlook

Choose **Help, About Microsoft Outlook** to find detailed information about the version of Outlook running on your computer, such as that shown in Figure 5.107.

Figure 5.107

This is an example of the About Microsoft Outlook information box.

Outlook displays an information box that contains the following:

- The name of the application, such as Microsoft Outlook 98
- The build number, such as 8.5.5104.6
- How Outlook is installed on your computer, **Corporate or Workgroup**, **Internet Mail Only**, or **No E-mail Usage**
- Copyright information and credits
- Information about the person to whom the product is licensed, including the Product ID number

This information box contains two buttons: **System Info** and **Tech Support**.

Appointment Form

Use the Appointment form, shown in Figure 5.108, to enter information about a new appointment or edit information about an existing appointment.

To create a new appointment, open the Calendar Information viewer, open the **Actions** menu, and choose **New Appointment**.

Figure 5.108

The Appointment form has three tabs. This is an example of the Appointment tab.

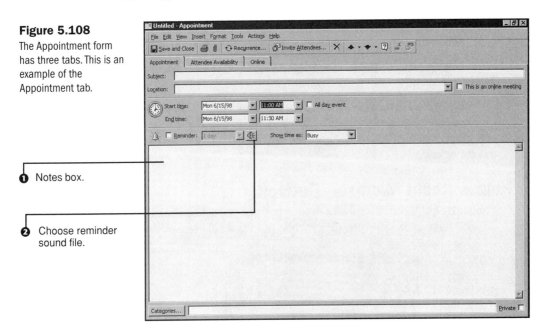

❶ Notes box.

❷ Choose reminder sound file.

Quick **Choices**   *NEW APPOINTMENT*

■ Alternatively, open the File menu, move the mouse pointer onto New, and choose **Appointment** from the drop-down list; or choose **Calendar** on the Outlook Bar and press **Ctrl+N**; or choose **Calendar** on the Outlook Bar and then choose the **New Appointment** button on the Standard toolbar.

To view or edit the details of an existing appointment, open the Calendar Information viewer and double-click the appointment.

Appointment Tab

Enter information into the various boxes as follows.

Subject

Enter a brief description of the subject of the appointment. Use as few words as possible because the text you enter here is subsequently displayed in your calendar in which there is quite limited space.

Location

Enter a brief description of the appointment's location. If you have previously created appointment items, you can open the Location drop-down list and choose a location from that list.

This is an online meeting

Leave this box unchecked for a face-to-face meeting. Check the box for an online meeting.

Start time

Open the date drop-down list and select a date. Alternatively, enter a date using any standard Windows format.

Open the time drop-down list and select a time. Alternatively, enter the time using any standard Windows format.

Here and elsewhere in Outlook, you can use descriptive dates and times. For example, you can enter a date as tomorrow, next Wednesday, second day of next month, two months from now, and so on. You can enter times by using descriptive terms such as noon, midnight, three o'clock pm, and so on.

End time

Open the date drop-down list and select a date. Alternatively, enter a date using any standard Windows format.

Open the time drop-down list and select a time. Alternatively, enter the time using any standard Windows format.

All day event

Leave this box unchecked if the appointment has specific start and end times. Check the box if the appointment is something that happens on a day, but with no specific start and end times. After you check this box, the start time and end time boxes are hidden.

Reminder

Check this box if you want reminder; uncheck it if you don't want a reminder. If you check the box, Outlook automatically provides the default reminder time. You can open the Reminder drop-down list to select a different reminder time. You can also enter a reminder time into the Reminder box.

Choose the button at the right of the reminder time to display the Reminder Sound dialog box (shown in Figure 5.109).

If the meeting is an online meeting and you have chosen to have NetMeeting start automatically, the reminder time you choose is the time ahead of the scheduled start of the online meeting that NetMeeting starts.

Figure 5.109

Use the Reminder Sound dialog box to select the sound file you want Outlook to play as a reminder.

Show time as

Open the drop-down list and choose among Free, Tentative, Busy, and Out of Office. The choice you make here determines the color in which appointments are outlined on your calendar.

Notes

The large, unnamed box that occupies most of the lower part of the form is known as the Notes box. You can use this box to enter any notes relevant to the appointment. Any attachments you add to the item are shown as icons in the Notes box.

Categories

Choose the **Categories** button to display the Categories dialog box (refer to Figure 5.31). Check the categories you want to assign to the appointment and choose **OK**. (Refer to **Edit Categories**, page 567, earlier in this chapter, for information about categories.)

Private

This box has an effect only if you share your calendar with other people. If you leave the box unchecked, people with whom you share your calendar can see all the information about the appointment. If you check the box, people with whom you share your calendar can only see that you have an appointment; they can't see any information about the appointment.

Attendee Availability Tab

This tab is used only when you use this form for planning a meeting. (Refer to **Plan a Meeting Dialog Box**, page 678, for information about it.)

Online Tab

Use this tab only if you're using the Appointment form for an online meeting (see Figure 5.110).

Figure 5.110

Use this form for information about an online meeting.

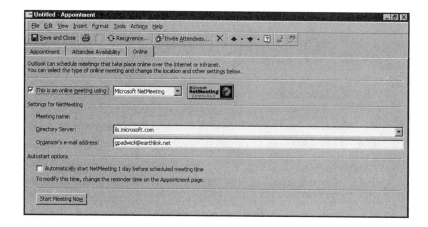

This is an online meeting using

Open the drop-down list and select the type of online meeting.

You can install Microsoft NetMeeting at the time you install Outlook. If you didn't do so, you can install it by choosing the **Microsoft NetMeeting Download** button.

If you have installed an online meeting application from another source, you should see that listed in the drop-down list.

Settings for NetMeeting

Open the **Directory Server** drop-down list and select the name of your NetMeeting server. Alternatively, enter the name of your NetMeeting server.

In the **Organizer's e-mail address** box, enter the e-mail address of the meeting organizer.

Autostart Options

Check the **Automatically start NetMeeting** box if you want NetMeeting to start automatically. The time ahead of the scheduled meeting time is the Reminder time you set in the Appointment tab. To change this time, open the Appointment tab and change the Reminder time.

Choose **Start Meeting Now** when you want to start the meeting manually.

Menu Bar

Many of the menu items are the same as those available when the Calendar Information viewer is displayed. Only those items that are specific to the forms are described here.

File Menu

The File menu contains some of the menu items that are available when an Information viewer is displayed, and some menu items that are specific to forms.

File ⮕ *Save*

Choose **File**, **Save** to save the current appointment as an Outlook item, leaving the current Appointment form displayed.

Quick **Choices**   *SAVE THE CURRENT ITEM*

■ Press **Ctrl+S** to save the current item.

File ⮕ *Save As*

Choose **File**, **Save As** to open the Save As dialog box (similar to that available in other Office applications). You can save the current appointment as a file, or Outlook template, or save it in Exchange Client message format or vCalendar format. (See **Word's File ⮕ Save As...**, page 29, for more information about using the **Save As** command.) **Save As** works identically in all Office applications.

File ⮕ *Save Attachments*

Choose **File**, **Save Attachments** to open the Save Attachments dialog box (similar to the Save As dialog box used in other Office applications). Outlook saves attachments in the format in which those attachments were created. For example, if an attachment is an Excel workbook, Outlook saves that attachment as an Excel (XLS) file.

File ⮕ *Properties*

Choose **File**, **Properties** to display the Properties dialog box. This dialog box has only a General tab. You can use this dialog box to examine the current item's properties or to change certain properties.

File ⮕ *Close*

Choose **File**, **Close** to close the current appointment item without saving it. If you haven't previously saved the form, Outlook displays a message box that asks you to confirm that you want to close the item.

Quick **Choices**   *CLOSE*

■ Press **Alt+F4** to close the item without saving it.

View Menu

The View menu contains menu items you can use to display one item after another in the Appointment form. These items are available only if you are using the form to display information about existing items, not if you are creating a new item.

View ⮕ *Previous*

Move the pointer to **View**, **Previous** to display a menu with the following:

Previous menu items

Menu Item	Purpose
Item	Display information about the previous calendar item. If there is no previous item, the current item is displayed in the Information viewer using the currently selected view.
Unread Item	This has no relevant meaning for Calendar items. When you choose this, Outlook opens the Calendar Information viewer with the current Calendar item selected.
First Item in Folder	Displays information about the first item in the Calendar folder.

View – Next

Move the pointer onto View, Next to display a menu with the following:

Next menu options

Menu Item	Purpose
Item	Display information about the next calendar item. If there is no next item, the current item is displayed in the Information viewer using the currently selected view.
Unread Item	This has no relevant meaning for Calendar items. When you choose this, Outlook opens the Calendar Information viewer with the current Calendar item selected.
Last Item in Folder	Displays information about the last item in the Calendar folder.

View – Calendar

Choose View, Calendar to open the Calendar Information viewer with the current item selected.

Insert Menu

The Insert menu contains menu items you can use to insert objects into the Calendar item.

Insert – File

Choose Insert, File to display the Insert File dialog box (shown in Figure 5.111).

Navigate to find the folder that contains the file you want to insert, select that file, and then choose OK. An icon representing the file is displayed in the Appointment Form's Notes box. Double-click the file's icon to open it using the application associated with it.

Insert – Item

Choose Insert, Item to display the Insert Item dialog box (shown in Figure 5.112).

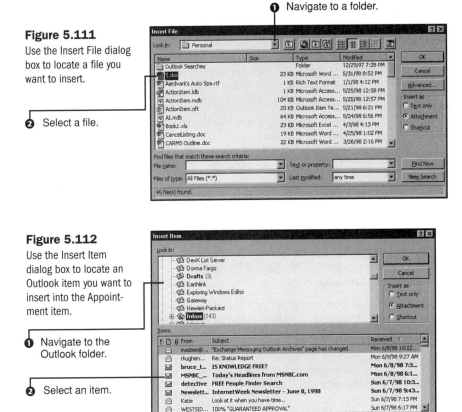

Figure 5.111

Use the Insert File dialog box to locate a file you want to insert.

➊ Select a file.

❶ Navigate to a folder.

Figure 5.112

Use the Insert Item dialog box to locate an Outlook item you want to insert into the Appointment item.

➊ Navigate to the Outlook folder.

➋ Select an item.

Navigate to find the Outlook folder that contains the item you want to insert, select that item, and then choose **OK**. An icon representing the item is displayed in the Appointment Form's Notes box. Double-click the item's icon to open it in the appropriate Outlook form. For example, if the inserted item is a message, Outlook displays it in the Message form.

Insert ‑ Object

Choose **Insert, Object** to display the Insert Object dialog box (shown in Figure 5.113).

This dialog is used in the same way as the Insert Object dialog box in Word. (Refer to **Word's Insert ‑ Object**, page 158, for detailed information.) The inserted object appears as an icon in the Calendar form's Notes box.

Double-click the object's icon to open it using the application associated with it.

Format Menu

Use Format menu items to format text in the Calendar form's Notes box.

Figure 5.113
Use the Insert Object
dialog box to create a
new object or to create
an object from a file.

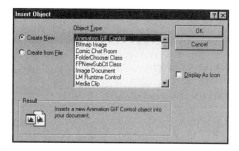

Format ⇥ Font

Select text in the Calendar form's Notes box and then choose **Format**, **Font...** to open the
Font dialog box, which is the same as that used in other Office applications.

Format ⇥ Paragraph

Select one or more paragraphs in the Calendar form's Notes box and then choose **Format**,
Paragraph to open the dialog box shown in Figure 5.114.

Figure 5.114
Use this dialog box
to format selected
paragraphs in the
Calendar form's
Notes box.

Tools Menu

Only the Spelling command is significant when you're using the Calendar form.

Tools ⇥ Spelling

Use this command to check the spelling of all the text in the Notes box or to check the spelling
of selected text in the Notes box. Spell checking works the same way it does in Word. (See
Word's Tools ⇥ Spelling and Grammar..., page 188.

Quick Choices   *SPELLING*

- Press **F7** to check spelling.

Choose **Tools**, **Spelling...** to initiate a spelling check.

Actions Menu

Some of the Actions menu items are covered in detail elsewhere in this book.

Actio<u>n</u>s ▪ *<u>N</u>ew Appointment*

Choose **Actions**, **New Appointment** to open a new Appointment form with all fields empty.

Quick **Choices**   *NEW APPOINTMENT*

■ Alternatively, choose **Ctrl+N** to open a new Appointment form.

Actio<u>n</u>s ▪ *New Recurring <u>A</u>ppointment*

(Refer to **Appointment Recurrence Dialog Box**, page 654, later in this chapter for information on this subject.)

Quick **Choices**   *RECURRENCE*

■ Press **Ctrl+G** to open the Appointment Recurrence dialog box.

Actio<u>n</u>s ▪ *For<u>w</u>ard*

(Refer to **Actions ▪ Forward**, page 639, for information about this.)

Quick **Choices**   *DELETING ITEMS*

■ Press **Ctrl+F** to forward an appointment.

Saving an Appointment

After you've completed creating an appointment, choose <u>S</u>ave and Close in the Standard toolbar to save the appointment and close the Appointment form.

Appointment Recurrence Dialog Box

Use the Appointment Recurrence dialog box (shown in Figure 5.115) to enter information about a new recurring appointment, or edit information an existing recurring appointment.

Figure 5.115

This is an example of an Appointment Recurrence dialog box that defines a weekly appointment.

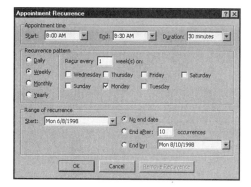

To create a new recurring appointment, open the Calendar Information viewer, open the **Actions** menu, and choose **New Recurring Appointment**.

To view or edit recurrence information about an existing recurring appointment, double-click the appointment in the Calendar Information viewer, and then choose **Actions**, **Recurrence**.

You can also convert a one-time appointment into a recurring appointment by displaying the appointment in an Appointment form, and then choosing **Actions**, **Recurrence**.

Appointment Time Section

Use the Appointment time section at the top of the dialog box to enter or edit the appointment time. If you enter the **Start** time and **End** time, Outlook automatically calculates and displays the **Duration**. If you enter the **Start** time and the **Duration**, Outlook automatically calculates and displays the **End** time.

Recurrence Pattern Section

You can create **Weekly** recurrence patterns (refer to Figure 5.115). You can also create **Daily** recurrence patterns (shown in Figure 5.116), **Monthly** recurrence patterns (shown in Figure 5.117), and **Yearly** recurrence patterns (shown in Figure 5.118).

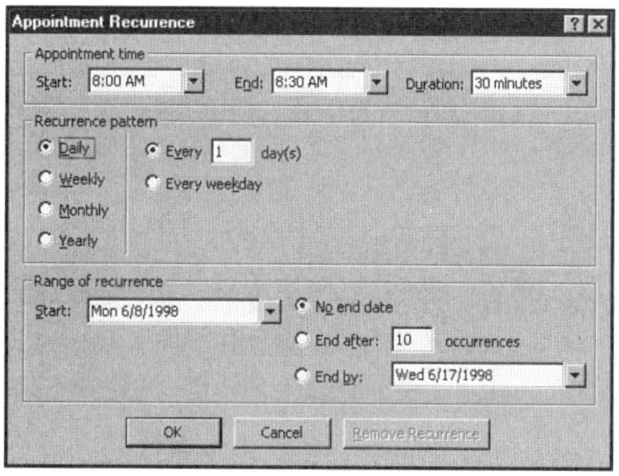

Figure 5.116

This is an example of a Daily recurrence pattern.

Figure 5.117

This is an example of a Monthly recurrence pattern.

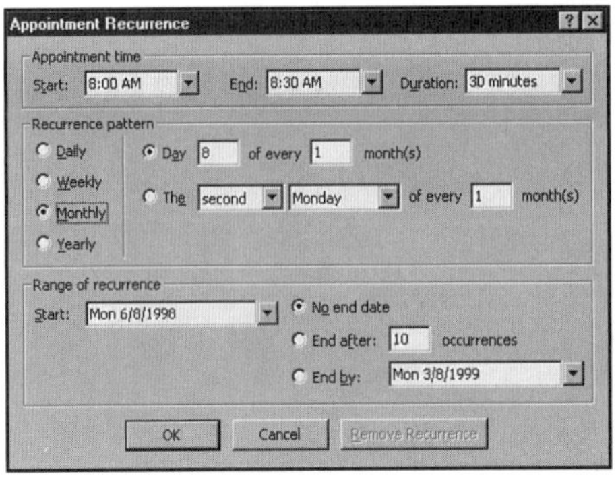

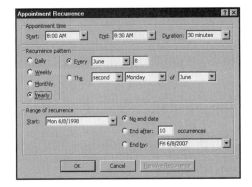

Figure 5.118

This is an example of a Yearly recurrence pattern.

Select which type of recurrence pattern you want and then select the details of the pattern.

Range of Recurrence Section

Define the range of the recurrence in the section at the bottom of the dialog box.

By default, Outlook starts the recurrence pattern on the date you create the recurring appointment. If you want to start at a different date, open the **Start** drop-down calendar and select a start date.

Also by default, Outlook sets no end date for the recurring appointment. You can choose to have the recurring appointment end after a specific number of occurrences, or by a certain date.

Saving the Recurrence Pattern

After you've finished defining the recurrence pattern, choose **OK** to close the Appointment Recurrence dialog box. When you do so, the Appointment form displays a summary of the recurrence pattern. Use this Appointment form to provide additional information about the recurring appointment.

Contact Form

Use the Contact form (shown in Figure 5.119) to enter information about a new contact, or to edit information about an existing contact.

⑤ Choose to display a list of phone number types.

Figure 5.119

This is an example of a Contact form.

② Choose to display how Outlook breaks down the name.

③ Choose to display how Outlook breaks down the address.

④ Choose to select Home, Business, or Other address.

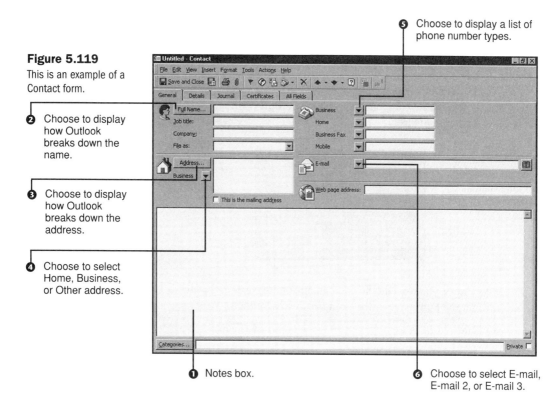

① Notes box.

⑥ Choose to select E-mail, E-mail 2, or E-mail 3.

A contact is either a person or an organization. To create a new contact, open the Contacts Information viewer and choose **Actions**, **New Contact**.

Quick Choices   CONTACT FORM

■ Open the **File** menu, move the mouse pointer onto **New**, and choose **Contact**; or choose **Contacts** on the Outlook Bar and press **Ctrl+N**; or choose **Contacts** on the Outlook bar and then choose the **New Contact** button on the standard toolbar.

To view or edit information about an existing contact, open the Contact Information viewer and double-click the contact. Outlook can use your contact information to automatically address letters, place telephone calls, send e-mail, send faxes, and access Web sites.

General Tab

The General tab contains the most-used information about a contact. Enter information into the various boxes as follows.

Full Name

Enter the full name of a person in this box. Usually, enter a first name, middle name or initial, and a last name. You can also enter a prefix such Mr, Ms, or Dr; and you can enter a suffix such as an abbreviated university degree.

When you enter a name, Outlook breaks down the name into its separate components. You can see these separate components by choosing **Full Name** to display the Check Full Name dialog box (shown in Figure 5.120).

Figure 5.120
The Check Full Name dialog box shows the components of a person's name.

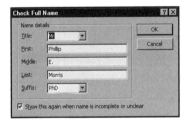

If necessary, you can edit the components of the name in this dialog box. You must enter text in either the Full Name or the Company boxes, or both.

Job Title

Enter the person's job title in this box. This information is optional.

Company

Enter the name of the organization with which the person is associated. This information is optional, unless you have left the **Full Name** box empty.

File as

Outlook automatically creates a **File as** name based on the information you have entered into the **Full Name** and **Company** boxes. Open the drop-down list and select from the list. Alternatively, you can enter whatever you like into this box—a nickname, for example. Outlook uses the text in the **File as** box to alphabetize the contact information it displays in the Address Cards and Detailed Address Cards views of the Contacts Information viewer.

Telephone and Fax Numbers

Outlook initially offers space for four telephone and fax numbers. You can, however, choose one of the down-arrow buttons at the left of the number boxes to display a list of 19 different numbers. Enter a number into any of the initially displayed boxes or choose a different box from the list and enter a number. Although you can only see four numbers at a time in the Contact form, Outlook saves and can use all the numbers you enter.

Always enter the area code with a telephone number, even if the number is within your local area code. If appropriate, you can also enter a country code.

Address

Enter the contact's address in the **Address** box. Enter the address in the same way that you enter a full name. If you like, choose **Address** to see how Outlook breaks down an address into its components.

Use state abbreviations, not full state names.

Outlook automatically provides the country name according to the location you specified in the Windows Control Panel Regional Settings dialog box. If the country name for a specific context is different from your own country name, enter the country name after the postal code.

By default, Outlook assumes the address you enter is a business address. To select Home, or Other, choose the down-pointing arrow button below **Address**. You can enter separate Business, Home, and Other addresses.

Also, by default, Outlook assumes the first address you enter is the contact's mailing address. To make another address the mailing address, choose that address and then choose **This is the mailing address**.

E-mail

Enter the contact's e-mail address in the **E-mail** box. If you already have the contact's e-mail address in an address book, choose the button at the right of the address book to open the Select Name dialog box, go to the address book that contains the information (it can't be your Outlook Address Book), choose the name, and choose **OK**. Outlook automatically places the contact's e-mail address in the **E-mail** box.

You can save three separate e-mail addresses for each person. Choose the down-pointing arrow button at the left of the e-mail box and choose E-mail, E-mail 2, or E-mail 3.

Web Page Address

If the person or organization has a Web page, enter the Web address (URL) in the **Web page address** box.

Notes

The Contact form uses notes the same way the Calendar form does. (See **Note Form**, page 677.)

Categories

The Contact form uses categories the same way the Calendar form does. (See **Note Form**, page 677.)

Private

This box has an effect only if you share your contacts with other people. If you leave this box unchecked, people with whom you share your contacts can see all the information about the contact. If you check this box, information about this contact is not available to other people.

Details Tab

The Details tab (shown in Figure 5.121) contains boxes in which you can provide additional information about a contact.

Figure 5.121

Enter information into the various boxes in this tab. All are optional.

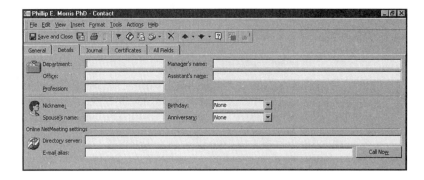

Journal Tab

The Journal tab (shown in Figure 5.122) displays all journal entries related to the currently selected contact. If you are in the process of creating a new contact, the box is empty.

Figure 5.122

The Journal tab shows journal entries relating to the selected contact.

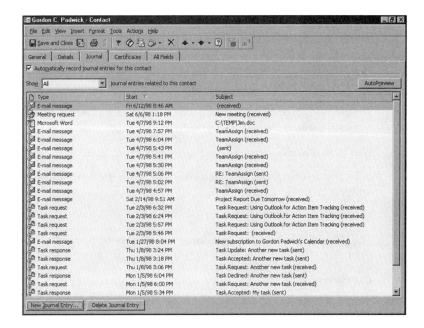

You can open the **Show** drop-down list to select a specific type of journal entry you want to see.

Choose **New Journal Entry** to create a new journal entry for the selected contact. To delete a journal entry, select that journal entry and choose **Delete Journal Entry**.

Certificates Tab

This tab contains a list of Certificates (Security IDs) you have available, as shown in Figure 5.123.

Figure 5.123

Choose the Security ID you want to use when sending e-mail to this contact.

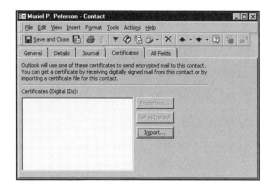

All Fields Tab

Outlook provides more than 100 fields for information about each contact, only a few of which are available in the other tabs. You can use this tab to enter information into any of these fields. You can also use this tab to create custom fields to suit your own needs.

When you first open the tab, it displays a list of user-defined fields. If you haven't created any fields, this list is empty.

Open the **Select from** drop-down list to see the names of various groups of fields as shown in Figure 5.124.

You can select any group of fields, to see the information already present in those fields, to edit that information, and to enter information into empty fields.

Some fields are read-only—you can't change the information in those fields. For example, the Created field contains the date and time a contact item was created; you can't change that.

To create a custom field, choose **New** to display the New Field dialog box (shown in Figure 5.125).

Menu Bar

The Contact form's menu bar is similar to Appointment form's menu bar. Most of the menu items are the same as, or very similar to, those in the Contact Information viewer's menu bar or the Appointment form's menu bar. Two exceptions occur in the Actions menu.

Figure 5.124

This is the All Fields tab with the Select from drop-down list open.

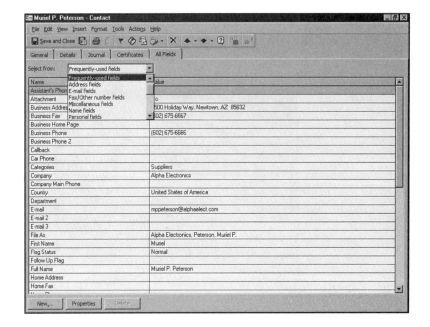

Figure 5.125

Use this dialog box to create a new field.

Actions Menu

The Actions menu contains two menu items that are particularly useful.

Display Map Address

You can use this menu item to display a map showing the geographic location of a contact. To do so, follow these steps:

1. Establish a connection to the Internet.
2. Double-click a contact in the Contacts Information viewer to display information about that contact in a Contact form.
3. In the form's menu bar, choose **Actions**, **Display Map of Address**. Your browser opens and finds the Microsoft Media Maps site. After a short delay, a map displaying the location of your contact is displayed, as shown in Figure 5.126.

Figure 5.126

This is an example of a map displayed by Media Maps.

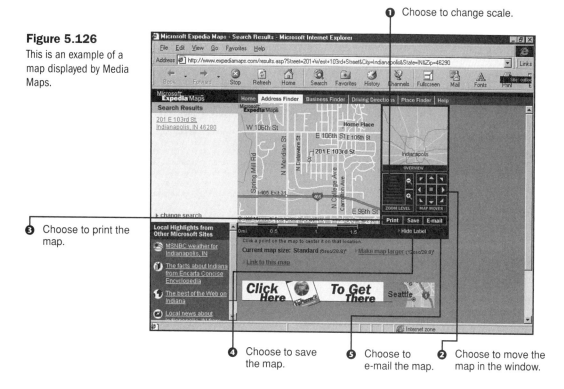

Choose to change scale.

Choose to print the map.

Choose to save the map.

Choose to e-mail the map.

Choose to move the map in the window.

You can use the various buttons on the display to change its magnification and to print the map.

Explore Web Page

You can use this menu item to access a contact's Web page.

1. Establish a connection to the Internet.

2. Double-click a contact in the Contacts Information viewer to display information about that contact in a Contact form.

3. In the form's menu bar, choose **Actions**, **Explore Web Page**. Your browser opens and finds the contact's Web page.

Quick Choices **EXPLORE WEB PAGE**

■ After completing the first two steps, press **Ctrl+Shift+X**.

Saving a Contact

Choose **Save and Close** in the Standard toolbar to save the contact item and close the Contact form.

Discussion Form

The Discussion form is shown in Figure 5.127.

Figure 5.127

Use the Discussion form to create a message to be posted in a public folder on the Exchange mail server.

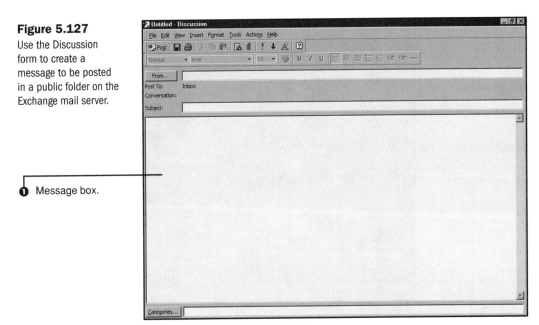

1 Message box.

To create a new item in a public folder, open the Mail Information viewer, open the **File** menu, and choose **Post in This Folder**.

Quick Choices **DISCUSSION FORM**

■ With the Inbox Information viewer displayed, press **Ctrl+Shift+S** to open the Discussion form.

To view or edit an existing item in a public folder, open the public folder in an Information viewer and double-click the item.

Enter the subject of the item in the **Subject** box. Enter text for the item in the unnamed message box. Choose **Categories**, and select one or more categories for the item.

Choose Post in the Standard toolbar to post the message in the public folder.

The menus in the menu bar, and the items in those menus, are similar to those for the Message form. The toolbar buttons are the same as those in the Message form.

Fax Form

Use the Fax form, available only if you're using Internet Only Outlook, to create a new fax message. If you're using Corporate/Workgroup Outlook, use the Message form to create a fax message.

In almost all respects the Fax form is identical to the Message form. The only difference is its name in the title bar. (Refer to **Message Form**, page 667.)

Journal Entry Form

The Journal Entry form is shown in Figure 5.128.

Figure 5.128

Use the Journal Entry form to create a Journal item or to edit an existing one.

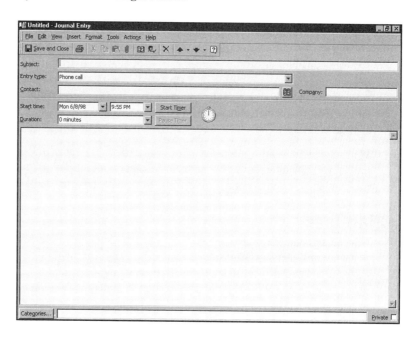

To create a new journal entry, open the Journal Information viewer, open the **Actions** menu, and choose **New Journal Entry**. Alternatively, open the **File** menu, move the mouse pointer onto **New**, and choose **Journal Entry**; or choose the **New Journal** button [icon] in the Standard toolbar.

Quick Choices *JOURNAL ENTRY FORM*

■ Open the **File** menu, move the mouse pointer onto **New**, and choose **Journal Entry**; or choose **Journal** on the Outlook Bar and press **Ctrl+N**; or choose Journal on the Outlook Bar and choose the **New Journal** button [icon] on the Standard toolbar.

To view or edit an existing journal entry, open the Journal Information viewer and double-click a journal entry.

Enter information into the various boxes as follows.

Subject

Enter a brief description of the subject of the journal entry. Use as few words as possible because the text you enter here is displayed in the Journal Information viewer in which space is limited.

Entry Type

Open the drop-down Entry type list and select one of the available types.

Contact

If the journal entry involves a contact, choose the unnamed icon at the right of the **Contact** box to open the Select Names dialog box. Open the drop-down **Show names from the** list, and select the address book or list that contains the name you want to use. Select that name, choose **Add->**, and then choose **OK**. The name you select appears in the Contact box on the Journal Entry form.

You can select several contacts from one or more address books or lists. Instead of selecting names, you can enter names. Separate one contact from the next with a semicolon. (For more information about choosing a contact name from a list, refer to "To," later in this chapter.)

Start Time

Outlook automatically enters the current date and time into the **Start time** boxes. If you want to enter a different date, choose the down-arrow button at the right of the date box to display a calendar and then select a date on the calendar. If you want to have a different time, choose the down-arrow button at the right of the time box to display a list of times and select one. Instead of selecting a date and time from lists, you can enter a date and time, using any of the standard Windows date and time formats.

Duration

By default, Outlook enters 0 minutes in the **Duration** box. If the journal item has a duration associated with it, choose the down-arrow button at the right of the **Duration** box and select a duration from the list. Alternatively, you can enter a duration.

If you're creating a journal entry while something is happening, such as a telephone call, choose **Start timer** when the happening starts. At the completion of the happening, choose **Pause timer**. Outlook automatically displays the duration of the event in minutes in the **Duration** box. After you've chosen **Pause timer**, you can press **Start timer** to continue recording time.

Notes

Use the unnamed Notes box in the same way you do in the Appointments form. (Refer to **Notes**, page 648, earlier in this chapter for information about this.)

Categories

Use the **Categories** box the same way you do in the Appointments form. (Refer to **Categories**, page 648, earlier in this chapter for information about this.)

Private

Use the **Private** box the same way you do in the Appointments form. (Refer to **Private**, page 648, for information about this.)

Menu Bar

The Journal Entry form's menu bar and the items in the menu are similar to those in the Appointments form.

Saving a Journal Entry

Choose **Save and Close** in the Standard toolbar to save the journal entry and close the Journal Entry form.

Message Form

Use the Message form (shown in Figure 5.129) to create a new message. Also use this form to continue working on a message saved in the Drafts folder and to edit a message in the Outbox folder.

The appearance of the Message form varies somewhat according to the message format you're using. The form shown in the preceding figure is the one you see when you're using HTML format. The selected format is shown in brackets at the right of the form name in the form's title bar. This section refers specifically to using the HTML message format. If you choose the Microsoft Word message format, you have all the facilities of Word 97 at your disposal; however, message recipients only see your formatting if they also have Word 97 available.

To create a new message, open the Inbox Information viewer, open the **Actions** menu, and choose **New Mail Message**.

Figure 5.129

Use the Message form to create an e-mail message.

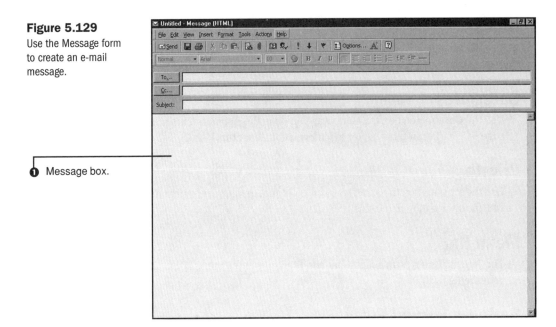

❶ Message box.

Quick Choices   MESSAGE FORM

■ Open the **File** menu, move the mouse pointer onto **New**, and choose **Journal Entry**; or choose **Journal** on the Outlook Bar, and then press **Ctrl+N**; or choose **Journal** on the Outlook bar and choose the **New Mail Message** button on the Standard toolbar.

To continue working on a message in the Drafts folder, open the Drafts Information viewer and double-click the message on which you want to work.

To edit a message in the Outbox folder, open the Outbox Information viewer and double-click the message you want to edit.

Enter information into the various boxes as follows.

To

The recommended way to address an e-mail message is to select the address from a list. That way you can be sure you get the name correct.

To address the message, follow these steps:

1. Choose **To...** to display the Select Names dialog box (shown in Figure 5.130).

Figure 5.130
The Select Names dialog box shows a list of names in one of your address books or lists.

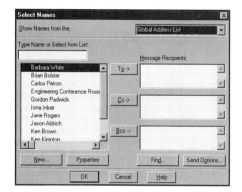

2. Open the Show names from the drop-down list to display a list of address books and lists, and select the address book or list that contains the name of the contact to whom you want to send the message.

3. Select one or more names and press **To->** to display those names in the **Message Recipients** list. Repeat this step as often as necessary to add more names to the list.

4. Choose **OK** to close the dialog box and return to the Message form that now has the selected contacts in the **To...** box.

If you enter contacts directly into the **To...** box (instead of selecting them from a list), you can verify the validity of those names by asking Outlook to check names. After you've entered a contact's e-mail address, choose the **Check Names** button in the Standard toolbar. If the e-mail address you entered is in an address book or list, Outlook underlines the address. If the address is not in an address book or list, Outlook displays a warning message.

Cc

Enter e-mail addresses for those people to whom you want to send carbon (courtesy) copies of the message. Use the same method that you used to select or enter names in the **To.**box.

When you're using the Select names dialog box, you can select names and press **To->** to copy names to the To section of the Message Recipients list. Select names and press **Cc->** to copy names to the Cc section of the recipients list. Select names and press **Bcc->** to copy those names to the Bcc section of the Message Recipients list.

Contacts in the Cc section receive a copy of your message and those who receive the message see their names in the message. Contacts in the Bcc section receive a copy of your message, but their names don't appear in the message that everyone else receives.

Subject

Enter a brief title for the message. Use as few words as possible because the text you type appears in Information viewers in which space is limited. The subject of a message is also known as the conversation. The conversation can be used to group messages so that people can see a thread of messages on the same subject.

Message

The unnamed Message box that occupies the lower part of the form is where you enter your message. It is the equivalent of the Notes box on other forms.

To create the message, place the insertion point in the Message box and start typing. In addition to text, the Message box can contain graphics and shortcuts to other objects.

Options

Unlike some other forms, the Message form doesn't contain a Categories button. To assign categories to a message (and to use other message options) choose **Options** in the standard toolbar to display the Message Options dialog box (shown in Figure 5.131).

Figure 5.131

Use this dialog box to assign categories to a message.

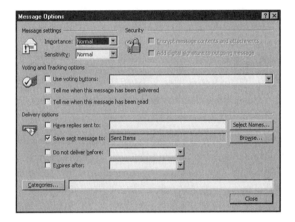

Choose **Categories** to assign one or more categories to a message. (Refer to "Categories," page 667, earlier in this book for information about assigning categories.)

You can also use the Message Options dialog box to include Importance, Sensitivity, Voting, Tracking, and Delivery options. (Refer to Que's *Using Microsoft Outlook 98* by Gordon Padwick, for information about these subjects.)

After you've specified message options, choose **Close** to return to the Message form.

Menu Bar

Seven of the menus have the same names as other forms and Information viewers and many of the menu items in these menus are the same as, or similar to, the items in those menus. The Message form has one additional menu: Format.

The following sections describe those menu items that have particular significance in the Message form.

View Menu

This menu contains menu items you can use to change what is displayed in the Message form.

View - Message Header

The default message header displays the To, Cc, and Subject boxes. After you choose **View**, **Message Header**, the message header contains only the To box.

Choose **View**, **Message Header** a second time to restore the other two fields.

View - From Field

Choose **View**, **From Field** to add the From field at the top of the message header. Then you can choose **From** to open the Choose Sender dialog box and choose the name of a sender from an address book or list. You do this if you are writing a message on behalf of someone else and want recipients to know this.

Choose **View**, **From Field** a second time to hide the From field.

View - Bcc Field

Choose **View**, **Bcc Field** to add the Bcc field to the message header immediately below the Cc field.

Choose **View**, **Bcc Field** a second time to hide the Bcc field.

View - Options

Choose **View**, **Options** to open the Message Options dialog box. (See **Options**, page 670, earlier in this chapter for information about the Options dialog box.)

In the Options dialog box, choose **Close** to close the dialog box.

Insert Menu

Use this menu to make insertions into a message.

Insert - File

Choose **Insert**, **File**, to insert a file into a message. (Refer to **Insert File**, page 651, earlier in this chapter for information about inserting a file.)

Quick **Choices**   *INSERT FILE*

■ Alternatively, choose the **Insert File** button 🔘 on the Standard toolbar.

Insert - Item

Choose **Insert**, **Item** to insert an Outlook item into a message. (Refer to **Insert Item**, page 651, earlier in this chapter for information about inserting an item.)

Insert ➤ Signature

Move the mouse pointer to **Insert**, **Signature**, and select from the list of signatures.

Quick Choices *INSERT SIGNATURE*

■ Alternatively, choose the **Insert Signature** button 🖃 on the Standard toolbar.

Format Menu

Use menu items in the Format menu to apply standard HTML formats to your message text. (To learn more about HTML, see Que's *Using HTML 4.0, Fourth Edition*.)

Format ➤ Style

Select one or more paragraphs of text, and move the mouse pointer to **Format**, **Style** to display a list of HTML formats. Select the format you want to apply to the selected text.

Format ➤ Font

Select a range of text, and choose **Format**, **Font** to display the Font dialog box. Select the font you want to apply to the text, and choose **OK**.

Format ➤ Paragraph

Select one or more paragraphs (or place the insertion point within a paragraph), and choose **Format**, **Paragraph** to display the Paragraph dialog box. Choose **Left**, **Center**, or **Right** alignment. You can also choose **Bullets** to add bullets to the selected paragraphs.

Format ➤ Background

With the insertion point within the Message box, move the mouse pointer to **Format**, **Background** to display a choice of **Picture** or **Color**.

Choose **Picture** to display the Background Picture dialog box. Use this dialog box to locate the picture file you want to use as a background. Choose **OK** to place the picture into the Message box.

Move the mouse pointer to **Color** to display a choice of colors. Select the color you want for the message background.

Format ➤ Language

Move the mouse pointer to **Format**, **Language** to display a list of languages (alphabets). Select the language you want to use.

Format ➤ Plain Text

Choose **Format**, **Plain Text** to change the message format from HTML to plain text. Do this when recipients do not have the capability to recognize HTML. Outlook displays a warning that all text formatting will be removed.

Format ▸ Rich Text (HTML)

Choose **Format, Rich Text (HTML)** to format the text as HTML-rich text which enables bolding and other types of text formatting. This is the Outlook default when you choose HTML as your message format.

Format ▸ Send Pictures from the Internet

Choose **Format, Send Pictures from the Internet** to format the message so that included JPEG and GIF pictures are sent with the message.

Tools Menu

The Spelling menu item is the same as that used in the Calendar form. (Refer to **Tools, Spelling,** page 188, for information about this.)

Tools ▸ Check Names

Move the insertion point into one of the recipient fields (To, Cc, or Bcc) and choose **Tools, Check Names**. Outlook uses your address books and lists to verify the names. (See **To,** page 668, for more information.)

Tools ▸ Address Book

Choose Tools, Address Book to open the Select Names dialog box. (Refer to **To,** page 668, for more information.)

Tools ▸ Forms

Move the mouse pointer onto **Tools, Forms** to display a menu you can use to work with forms. (Detailed treatment of this subject is beyond the scope of this book.)

Tools ▸ Fax Attributes

This menu item applies only when you're using Corporate/Workgroup Outlook. Choose **Tools, Fax Attributes** to display the Fax Message Attributes dialog box (shown in Figure 5.132). This dialog box doesn't appear if you haven't previously addressed the message to a fax address.

Figure 5.132
Use this dialog box to define how a fax is to be sent and which cover page, if any, to use.

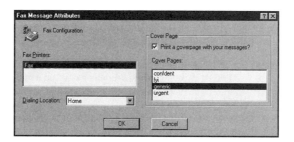

Sending a Message

After you've created a message, choose **Send** in the Standard toolbar to send the message. Outlook places the message in your Outbox folder. The next time Outlook connects to the appropriate mail server, the message is sent to the server, and Outlook keeps a copy of the message in the Sent Items folder.

Receiving a Message

You can see messages you've received listed in the Inbox Information viewer. By default, Outlook displays the message header and the first three lines of text for all unread messages. Only the header is shown for the message you've read.

Select any message to display that message in the Preview pane. You can scroll through the Preview pane to see the entire message.

Double-click any message to open that message in the Message form (not the same Message form that you use to create messages). If the message has attachments, those attachments are represented by icons. Double-click an icon to open the attachment in the application with which the attachment type is associated on your computer (normally the application in which it was created).

You can choose Reply, Reply to All, or Forward in the form's Standard toolbar to reply to the message or to forward it.

To save information about the message sender in your Contacts folder, right-click the sender's name at the top of the message. This opens a context menu that contains these significant menu items:

Saving message sender information options	
Menu Item	**Purpose**
Properties	Displays the sender's properties.
Add to Contacts	Creates a new Contact item that contains the sender's name and e-mail address. Outlook creates a new Contact item, even if a Contact item with information about the sender already exists.
Look up Contact	Displays the Contact item (if it is available) that contains information about the sender. Use this to see whether a Contact item exists before you create a new Contact item.
Add to Personal Address Book	Create a new entry in your Personal Address Book that contains the sender's name and e-mail address. Outlook creates a new entry, even if an entry for the sender already exists.

Replying to a Message

To reply to a message you've received, select that message in the Inbox Information viewer, and then choose **Reply** or **Reply to All** in the Standard toolbar.

- Choose **Reply** to send your reply only to the sender of the original message.
- Choose **Reply to All** to send your reply to the sender of the original message and to everyone on the sender's Cc list (not to people on the Bcc list).

Outlook opens the Message form with the original message displayed in the Message box. Use the space above the original message to write your reply. You can delete all or part of the original message. You can also annotate the original message. However, Outlook doesn't send attachments to the original message with your reply.

Choose **Send** in the Standard toolbar to send your reply.

Forwarding a Message

To forward a message you've received, select that message in the Inbox Information viewer, and then choose **Forward** in the Standard toolbar. Outlook opens the Message form with the original message displayed in the Message box. Use the space above the original message to add your comments. You can edit the original message and add annotations to it. Outlook includes attachments to the original message with the forwarded message.

Choose **Send** in the Standard toolbar to forward the message.

Meeting Form

Use the Meeting form (shown in Figure 5.133) to create invitations to a meeting and to send those invitations by e-mail. You can also use this form to reserve resources such as a conference room or projector.

Figure 5.133

This is an example of a Meeting form, which is quite similar to the Appointment form.

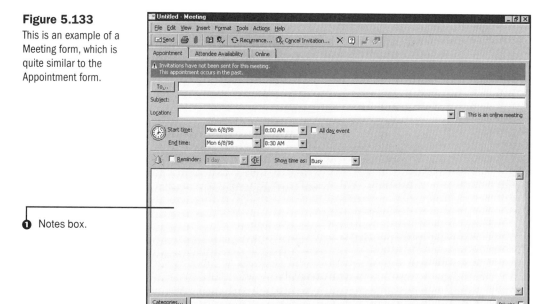

❶ Notes box.

To create a new meeting request, open the Calendar Information viewer, open the **Actions** menu, and choose **New Meeting Request**. Alternatively, open the **File** menu, move the mouse pointer onto **New**, and choose **Meeting Request**.

Quick `Choices`   *NEW MEETING REQUEST*

- Open the **File** menu, move the mouse pointer onto **New**, and choose **Meeting Request**; or choose **Calendar** on the Outlook Bar and press **Ctrl+Shift+Q**.

To view or edit the details of an existing meeting request, open the Calendar Information viewer and double-click the meeting.

Appointment Tab

The Appointment tab is quite similar to the Appointment form's Appointment tab. The significant differences are:

- It has an information bar immediately under the tabs.
- It has a **To...** box near the top.

When you first open the Meeting form to create a meeting request, the information bar contains the words "Invitations have not been sent for this meeting". In addition, the Information bar may contain the words "Conflicts with another appointment on your calendar" if the dates and times Outlook chooses by default conflict with something already on your schedule. The information bar contains other information after you've sent the invitation.

To

Choose **To...** to open the Select Attendees and Resources dialog box (shown in Figure 5.134).

Figure 5.134

Use this dialog box in much the same way you use the Select Names dialog box when you're creating an e-mail message.

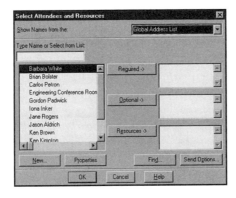

Open the Show names from the drop-down list, choose the address book or list that contains attendee names or required resources, and select names and resources. Unlike the Select Names dialog box, you can use this dialog box to add names and resources to **Required, Optional**, and **Resources** lists. After you've selected names and resources, choose OK to close the dialog box and return to the Meeting form. The names and resources you selected are now shown in the **To...** box. Also, any item you entered into the Resource list is shown in the **Location** box.

In many cases, resources are meeting rooms, so it's appropriate for the names of those resources to appear in the **Location** box. If a resource is not a location, delete it from the box.

Complete the remaining parts of the Appointment tab in the same way that you do in the Appointment form. (Refer to **Appointment Tab**, page 646, for detailed information.)

Sending an Invitation

Choose **Send** in the Standard toolbar to send the invitation. Outlook sends the invitation just as it sends any other e-mail.

Receiving an Invitation to a Meeting

Recipients see the meeting invitation as an e-mail message in their Inboxes. They can open the message to see its details in a meeting response form. This form has **Accept**, **Tentative**, and **Decline** buttons in its Standard toolbar. Recipients can enter a note in the form's message box and then choose one of the buttons to send a reply back to the person who sent the invitation.

Receiving a Response to an Invitation

The person who originally sent the invitation sees the response in the Inbox. The message header indicates the recipient's response. On opening the message, the original sender sees any comments the recipient sent with the response, and also a summary of how many of the people to whom the original message was sent have definitely accepted, tentatively accepted, or declined the invitation.

Note Form

Outlook's Note form is very simple. It is a yellow box with the current date and time at the bottom (shown in Figure 5.135). Use this form to make temporary notes about any subject.

Figure 5.135

This is an example of a Note form.

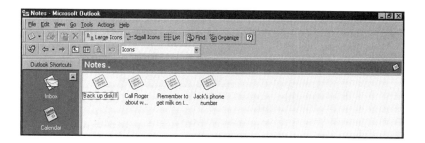

To create a new note, open the Notes Information viewer, open the **Actions** menu, and choose **New Note**.

Quick Choices NOTE

■ Open the **File** menu, move the mouse pointer onto **New**, and choose **Note**; or choose **Notes** on the Outlook bar and then press **Ctrl+N**; or choose **Notes** on the Outlook bar and then choose the **New Note** button on the Standard toolbar.

To view or edit an existing note, Open the Notes Information viewer and double-click the note. Enter or edit the text you want to include in the note. As you type, the text automatically wraps within the width of the note. If you enter more text than fits into the note, the text automatically scrolls.

You can change the size of the note as it appears on your screen by pointing onto one of its edges and dragging that edge. Alternatively, point onto the shaded region at the bottom-right corner and drag in any direction.

When you've finished entering or editing text, point to the Notes Information viewer outside the note and click to save the note and display it as an icon with the first few lines of the text. The date and time the note was created displays in the Information viewer.

Plan a Meeting Dialog Box

Use the Plan a Meeting Dialog Box (shown in Figure 5.136) to plan a meeting when the people you want to attend and resources you need are available.

Figure 5.136

This is an example of the Plan a Meeting dialog box.

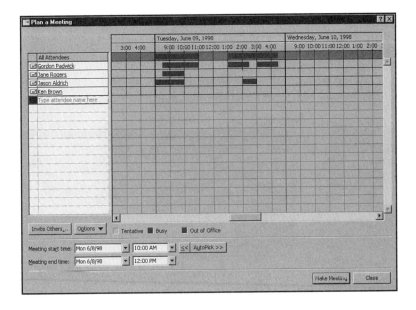

Using the Outlook's Plan a Meeting capability depends on sharing calendars with other people. To do this, you must either be using Exchange Server as your mail server or Net Folders to share calendars. You and other people must have made your calendars available for sharing.

To use the Plan a Meeting dialog box, open the Calendar Information viewer, open the **Actions** menu, and choose **Plan a Meeting.** (Alternatively, you can use the same capabilities by choosing the Meeting form's Attendee Availability tab.) When the dialog box (or tab) opens, you see only your own schedule.

Seeing Other People's Schedules

Choose **Invite Others…** to open the Select Attendees and Resources dialog box, which is similar to that shown previously in Figure 5.130. Select the names of attendees and resources; copy those names into the **Required, Optional,** and **Resources** lists; and then choose **OK.** The grid now shows time commitments for the attendees and resources you chose. The rows corresponding to any attendees or resources who haven't made their calendars available for sharing are blanked out.

Choosing the Meeting Time

At the bottom of the dialog box (or tab), enter a tentative **Meeting start time** and **Meeting end time.** These times are principally to establish the duration of the meeting.

Choose **AutoPick.** Outlook searches through the combined schedules to find the first time when all have an opening for the duration you specified. Alternatively, you can drag the green and brown vertical bars to manually set start and end times.

Making the Meeting

If you're using the Plan a Meeting dialog box, choose **Make Meeting** to open the Meeting form with the times of the meeting shown in the **Start time** and **End time** boxes.

If you're using the Meeting form's Plan a Meeting tab, choose the Appointment tab.

Task Form

Use the Task form (shown in Figure 5.137) to enter information about a new task or edit information about an existing task.

To create a new task, open the Task Information viewer, open the **Actions** menu, and choose **New Task**. Alternatively, open the **File** menu, move the mouse pointer onto **New**, and choose **Task**.

Quick Choices NEW TASK

- Open the **File** menu, move the mouse pointer onto **New**, and choose **Task**; or choose **Tasks** on the Outlook Bar and then press **Ctrl+N**; or choose **Tasks** on the Outlook bar and then choose the **New Task** button on the Standard toolbar.

Figure 5.137

The Task form has two tabs. This is an example of the Task tab.

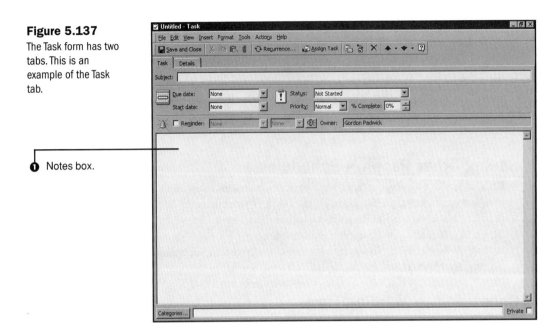

① Notes box.

To view or edit the details of an existing task, open the Action Information viewer and double-click the task.

Task Tab

Enter information into the various boxes as follows.

Subject

Enter a brief description of the subject of the task. Use as few works as possible because the text you enter here is displayed in the calendar's TaskPad in which there is quite limited space.

Due Date

By default, Outlook creates a new task with the **Due Date** shown as None. This is appropriate if the task is something that has to be done, but there's no specific date by which it should be completed. If you want to enter a due date, choose the down-arrow button at the right of the **Due Date** box and select a date from the calendar. Alternatively, you can enter a description of the due date, such as Next Week or Next Month.

After you've selected a due date, an information bar appears immediately under the tabs showing how many days from the current date the task is due.

Start Date

By default, Outlook creates a new task with the **Start Date** shown as None. This is appropriate if there is no specific date by which the task should be started. If you want to enter a start date, choose the down-arrow button at the right of the **Start Date** box and select a date from the calendar.

If you select a start date after the due date, Outlook changes the due date to be the same as the start date. If you leave the due date as None and then select a start date, Outlook automatically shows the due date the same as the start date.

Status

By default, Outlook shows the **Status** of a new task as Not Started. At the time you create a new task, or later, you can open the drop-down list and select Not Started, In Progress, Completed, Waiting on someone else, or Deferred.

Priority

By default, Outlook shows the **Priority** of a new task as Normal. At the time you create a new task, or later, you can open the drop-down list and choose Low, Normal, or High.

% Complete

By default, Outlook shows the % **Complete** of a new task as "0%". At the time you create the task or later, you can choose the arrow buttons at the right of the box to change the percentage value. Alternatively, you can enter a percentage value into the box (you don't have to enter the % sign).

Reminder

By default, Outlook displays the Task form with the **Reminder** box unchecked. Outlook automatically checks the box when you select a due date or start date and sets the reminder date to the same as the due date. In the case of a task that doesn't have a due date or start date, you can manually check the **Reminder** box. When the Reminder box is checked, you can choose the down-arrow button at the right of the box to select a date from the calendar.

By default, Outlook sets the reminder time to 8:00 a.m.. To change this time, display any Information viewer and choose **Tools**, **Options** to display the Options dialog box. In the Tasks section of the Preferences tab, change the default task reminder time.

To set Outlook to give you an audible warning at the time of a reminder, choose the button at the right of the reminder time. Outlook displays the Reminder Sound dialog box in which you can check a box that enables a sound to be played. Select the sound file to be played.

Owner

Each task item is initially owned by the person who creates it. When you create a task, you own it, and your name is displayed in the Owner box. The only way to change ownership of a task is to ask someone else to accept the task and for that person to take ownership of it.

Notes

The large, unnamed box that occupies most of the bottom part of the form is where you can enter text that provides information about the task. Any objects you insert into the task are displayed as icons in this box.

Categories

You should assign one or more categories to a task, just as you assign categories to other Outlook items. (Refer to **Categories**, page 667, earlier in this chapter for additional information about categories.)

You should consider creating a category for each of your projects. Then you can assign a project name as a category for each task so that you can easily group related tasks by project.

Private

By default, Outlook leaves the **Private** box unchecked. If you give other people permission to see your folders, they can see the details of all your tasks in which Private is left unchecked. If you check this box for certain tasks, other people can't see the information about those tasks.

Details Tab

The Details tab (shown in Figure 5.138) contains boxes in which you can provide additional information about a task. These boxes are particularly useful if you need to keep information about a task that you can use when billing a client.

Figure 5.138
Use the Details tab for additional information about a task.

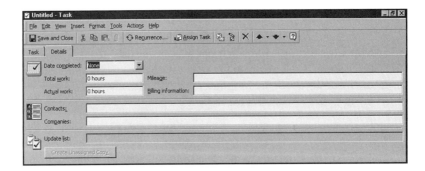

Date Completed

By default, Outlook sets this field to None. When the task is completed, choose the down-arrow button at the right of the box and select the appropriate date from a calendar. When you select a date, Outlook automatically sets the **Status** box in the Tasks tab to Completed, and sets the % Complete box to 100%.

Total Work

By default, Outlook initially sets the **Total work** box to 0 hours. Change this value to your estimate of the number of hours you expect the task to take.

Actual Work

By default, Outlook initially sets the **Actual work** box to 0 hours. As work progresses, you can update the value in this box to keep track of the number of hours spent on the task.

If the number of hours you enter into the Total work or Actual work boxes is an exact multiple of the number of hours in a workday, Outlook changes the values you enter to an equivalent number of days. Similarly, if the number of hours you enter is an exact multiple of the number of hours in a workweek, Outlook changes the values you enter to an equivalent number of weeks.

By default, Outlook assumes 8 hours in a workday and 40 hours in a workweek. To change these values, display any information viewer, choose **Tools**, **Options** to display the Options dialog box. In the Other tab, choose **Advanced Options**. Change the values in the Appearance Options section to change the default number of hours in a workday and in a workweek.

Mileage

Use the **Mileage** box to keep track of any mileage that should be charged to the task.

Billing Information

Use the **Billing Information** box to record billing information associated with the task.

Contacts

Use the **Contacts:** box to record the names of people relevant to the task.

Companies

Use the **Companies** box to record the names of companies and organizations relevant to the task.

Update List

The **Update list** box is initially empty and remains empty for your personal tasks.

When you assign a task to another person, you can ask to be updated whenever that person updates the task item. Assuming that person accepts the task, that person's Task form shows your name in the **Update list** box.

Create Unassigned Copy

The **Create Unassigned Copy** button is initially disabled and remains disabled for your personal tasks.

After you assign a task to someone else, and that person accepts the task (keeping a copy of the task in your own Tasks folder), Outlook enables this button. Choose this button to send an unassigned copy to another person for that person's information.

Menu Bar

The menu bar contains the same menus as most other forms. Most of the menu items are the same as, or similar to, menu items in other forms. One exception is the Actions menu.

Actions Menu

The following paragraphs explain some of the menu items in the Task form's Actions menu.

Actions → Send Status Report

If someone has assigned a task to you and you have accepted it, choose **Actions, Send Status Report** to send a status report to the person who created the task.

Actions → Mark Complete

Choose **Actions, Mark Complete** to mark the task as completed.

Actions → Recurrence

All tasks are initially created as on-time tasks. Choose **Actions, Recurrence** to convert a one-time task to a recurring task. Outlook displays the Task Recurrence dialog box that, apart from its title, is the same as the Appointment Recurrence dialog box. (Refer to **Appointment Recurrence Dialog Box**, page 654, earlier in this chapter for detailed information.)

Actions → Assign Task

Choose **Actions, Assign Task** to assign an existing task to someone else. (Refer to **Task Request Form**, page 684, later in this chapter for information.)

Saving the Task

Choose the **Save and Close** button in the Standard toolbar to save the task and close the form.

Task Request Form

Use the Task Request form (shown in Figure 5.139) to create a task and assign it to someone else.

To create a new task to be assigned to someone else, open the Tasks Information viewer, open the **Actions** menu, and choose **New Task Request**. Alternatively, open the **File** menu, move the mouse pointer to **New**, and choose **Task Request**.

To view or edit the details of an existing task request (before you have assigned it to someone else), open the Tasks Information viewer and double-click the task.

Task Tab

The Task tab is almost the same as the Task form's Task tab. One exception is that it contains a **To...** box near the top. Use this box similarly to how you use the same box in a Message form to select the person to whom you want to assign the task. (Refer to **To**, page 668, earlier in this chapter for information.)

Figure 5.139

The Task Request form is similar to the Task form.

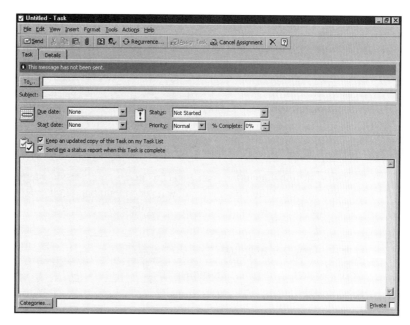

The complete functionality of assigning tasks is available when you assign a task to only one other person. If you assign a task to two or more people, you are not able to receive status reports from them.

The Task Request form, unlike the Task form, contains two check boxes, both of which are checked by default:

Task Request form options

Check Box Name	Purpose
Keep an updated copy of this task on my task list	Uncheck this box if you don't want to keep a copy of the assigned task in your task list.
Send me a status report when this task is complete	Uncheck this box if you don't want to be notified automatically when the person to whom you assigned the task marks it as complete.

Details Tab

This tab is identical to the Task form's Details tab.

Sending a Task Request

Choose **Send** in the Standard toolbar to send a task request. Outlook sends the task as an e-mail message to the person to whom you want to assign the task. That person sees a message in the Inbox. On opening the message, the person can choose **Accept** or **Decline** to send a message back to you. After choosing **Accept**, the person inherits ownership of the task. Ownership remains with you if the person chooses **Decline**.

Print Preview

With any Information viewer open, you can choose **File**, **Preview** to display a preview of a page to be printed. The Print Preview window has no menu bar, but it does have a toolbar. The following table describes the buttons on the toolbar.

Preview toolbar buttons	
Button Name	**Purpose**
Page Up	Display the preceding page.
Page Down	Display the next page.
Actual Size	Display the page at the actual size it will be printed. Click anywhere in the Page Preview window to return to the original magnification.
One Page	Display one page at a time.
Multiple Pages	Display multiple pages.
Page Setup Page Setup...	Display the Page Setup dialog box.
Close Preview Close	Close the Page Preview window.

Index